The Real Story

Recent Titles in
Genreflecting Advisory Series

Diana T. Herald, Series Editor

The Real Story

A Guide to Nonfiction Reading Interests

Sarah Statz Cords

Edited by Robert Burgin

Genreflecting Advisory Series

Diana T. Herald, Series Editor

LIBRARIES

U N L I M I T E D

A Member of the Greenwood Publishing Group

Westport, Connecticut • London

Library of Congress Cataloging-in-Publication Data

Cords, Sarah Statz, 1974-
    The real story : a guide to nonfiction reading interests / by Sarah Statz Cords ; edited by Robert Burgi
        p. cm. — (Genreflecting advisory series)
    Includes bibliographical references and index.
    ISBN 1-59158-283-0 (alk. paper)
    1. Readers' advisory services—United States. 2. Public libraries—Reference services—United
States. 3. Books and reading—United States. 4. Reading interests—United States. I. Burgin,
Robert. II. Title. III. Series.
    Z711.55.C67 2006
    025.5'40973—dc22   2006003712

British Library Cataloguing in Publication Data is available.

Library of Congress Catalog Card Number: 2006003712
ISBN: 1–59158–283–0

First published in 2006

Libraries Unlimited, 88 Post Road West, Westport, CT 06881
A Member of the Greenwood Publishing Group, Inc.
www.lu.com

Printed in the United States of America

The paper used in this book complies with the
Permanent Paper Standard issued by the National
Information Standards Organization (Z39.48–1984).

10 9 8 7 6 5 4 3 2 1

Copyright Acknowledgment

Quotation from Norman Macclean. *A River Runs Through It, and Other Stories.* University of Chicago Press, 1976. Used by permission.

*For dad, who loves the stories, and for mom,
who always wants to know if they're true.*

Contents

Part 1: Nonfiction Genres

Part 2: Nonfiction Subject Interests

Part 3: Life Stories

Part 4: Stylistic Genres

Foreword

The renaissance in readers' advisory has been one of the most exciting trends in librarianship in the last twenty-five years. The founding of the Adult Reading Round Table in 1984 and the publication of *Readers' Advisory Service in the Public Library* in 1989 set off an explosion of interest in fiction readers and their needs.

The spread of this excitement into the realm of nonfiction has been a more recent phenomenon, but one that has generated equal enthusiasm among librarians who work with nonfiction readers. Librarians have learned that people read nonfiction for pleasure, that nonfiction has genres and subgenres, that some nonfiction reads like fiction; that there are nonfiction-fiction "read-alikes"; and that the readers' advisory interview ("Tell me about a book you have really enjoyed") applies to nonfiction as well as fiction.

Until now, however, readers' advisory for nonfiction has lacked a comprehensive guide to nonfiction titles and genres. There has been no equivalent for nonfiction to the many tools that fiction advisors have had access to: tools as diverse as general guidebooks like Saricks and Brown and *Genreflecting,* more specific guidebooks like *Make Mine a Mystery* and *Hooked on Horror,* online databases like Novelist and "What Do I Read Next?", and lists like FICTION_L and DorothyL.

This book is a first and very impressive step toward filling that gap. It clearly defines both the genres and subgenres of nonfiction, explains the appeal factors that draw readers to these categories, identifies titles that readers can start with in order to get a feel for each genre, and suggests fiction titles that might also interest readers of the various nonfiction genres.

Readers' advisory is about making connections, and this book is particularly good at providing the kinds of connections that will enable librarians to better serve their users. We now know, for example, that readers who liked Sebastian Junger's *The Perfect Storm* may also like Douglas Campbell's *The Sea's Bitter Harvest,* about the sinking of four commercial fishing vessels, or Todd Lewan's *The Last Run,* another book that provides details of rescue attempts at sea. We now have suggestions for fans of Jon Krakauer's *Into Thin Air,* titles that include Anatoli Boukreev's *The Climb* (a different telling of the same events that Krakauer relates) and Jochen Hemmleb's *Ghosts of Everest* (about the 1924 expedition of Mallory and Irvine).

Readers' advisory is also about making distinctions, about understanding how books in a single genre differ enough to place them in separate subgenres, and again, this book provides guidance in breaking down large genres into more specific areas of interest. Just as fiction readers' advisors are aware that a mystery may be a cozy or a police procedural or hard boiled, now nonfiction readers' advisors will learn that true crime may mean a book about violent killers (like Truman Capote's *In Cold Blood*) or a book about a member of the Mafia (like Peter Maas's *Underboss: Sammy the Bull Gravano's Story of Life in the Mafia*) or a police procedural (like Ann Rule's *Green River, Running Red*). Just as fiction readers' advisors know that science fiction can be broken down into subgenres that range from alien civilizations to cyberpunk to utopias, now nonfiction readers' advisors will know that travel can be as diverse as books that focus on discovering exotic locations (Gretel Ehrlich's *This Cold Heaven: Seven Seasons in Greenland*), those that focus on discovering one's self (Pete McCarthy's *McCarthy's Bar: A Journey of Discovery in the West of Ireland*), and those that focus on living in—not just traveling to—another country (Peter Mayle's *A Year in Provence*).

In short, until now, readers' advisors have lacked an adequate map to the rich and varied world of nonfiction. This book provides such a map, one that fills in much of the unknown territory that once marked the world of nonfiction and provides readers' advisors with an extremely useful tool that will enable them to provide better service to those who read nonfiction for pleasure.

Robert Burgin

Acknowledgments

I am indebted, as always, to my entire family, the members of which happen to be both my favorite requesters of books, as well as my most trusted source of book recommendations.

I am extremely grateful to past and present book and library colleagues. These include Richard Schwartz, who taught me the value of the circulation department; Pat McDermott and Lisa Bitney, in whose employ and bookstore I spent many happy hours; Kori Wex, reference librarian extraordinaire and my preferred source for all Elvis Presley and Princess Diana biography recommendations; and Jane Jorgenson, my readers' advisory buddy at Madison Public Library, who always knows the answers to my (and patrons') mystery and romance genre questions. I also need to acknowledge my indebtedness to my former professor, Wayne Wiegand, whose library school classes I was lucky enough to attend, which were always illuminating and suffused with an obvious love for books, in all their physical and cultural glory.

All of the dedicated professionals with whom I worked at Libraries Unlimited have my heartfelt thanks, particularly Barbara Ittner, for her unstinting dedication to this title, and her generous assistance and participation in its creation; as well as Emma Bailey and Sharon DeJohn, who did a remarkable job editing and producing it. Robert Burgin also deserves my profuse thanks for his contributions to this work, as well as for his inspiring dedication to nonfiction and nonfiction readers.

In a field of already numerous debts of gratitude, the largest is owed to my husband, Kevin Cords, who listened to every single nonfiction fun fact I had to share, even when he was just trying to watch some TV. I always knew he was a nice guy, but I had no idea how nice. Thanks, Kevin.

Introduction

Once, for instance, my father asked me a series of questions that suddenly made me wonder whether I understood even my father whom I felt closer to than any man I have ever known. "You like to tell true stories, don't you?" he asked, and I answered, "Yes, I like to tell stories that are true."

Then he asked, "After you have finished your true stories sometime, why don't you make up a story and the people to go with it?

Only then will you understand what happened and why . . . ."

—Norman Maclean, *A River Runs Through It*

One day not long ago I was spending a little quality time in the children's nonfiction section of the library where I work, shelving, tidying, and generally just enjoying the experience of being in the stacks. Suddenly I heard an adult on the other side of the shelves ask someone, "Well, what are you interested in this week?" There was a lengthy pause, during which I shelved two books on dinosaurs, and then a child's voice answered, decisively, "Monkeys." That answer made me happy for the rest of the day.

So often when patrons or friends approach me with the question for which they believe librarians were made ("Can you recommend a good book?") , I assume that they are looking for a good *fiction* book. We librarians and "book people" can hardly be blamed for this perception; with the exception of the generally accepted golden age of nonfiction readers' advisory from 1920 to 1940 (Crowley 2004, 13–17), the development of a body of theory regarding and best practices of readers' advisory has focused almost exclusively on fiction. In 1987 Joyce Saricks and Nancy Brown codified that inclination in their definition of the service in *Readers' Advisory Service in the Public Library*, and they did so again in their 1997 second edition, stating that "readers' advisory service, as discussed in this book, is a patron-oriented library service for adult fiction readers" (Saricks and Brown 1997, 1).

Nor can those two pioneers in the field be faulted for their original definitions (especially since they changed it to include all "adult leisure readers" in their 2005 third edition). After all, don't nonfiction books usually come complete with informative subtitles, as well as with numerous subject headings, assigned by fellow information science professionals, to aid in their discovery? If children, or adults for that matter, want to find books about monkeys, or holidays, or history, isn't that what the catalog and the various classification schemes, including the venerable Dewey Decimal and Library of Congress systems, are designed for?

Why a Nonfiction Reader's Guide Is Needed: The Rise of the Real

In a November 2004 article, "The Rise of the Real," pop culture commentator and essayist Chuck Klosterman announced: "It has come to my attention that there is a burgeoning generation of Americans who are suddenly and deeply engrossed with the consumption of nonfiction. I like to refer to these people as the Suddenly and Deeply Engrossed with Nonfiction Generation" (Klosterman 2004, 194). The tone is tongue-in-cheek, but the sentiment is not: Realism is currently dominating all forms of the media. Reality television programs top the ratings (*Survivor, The Apprentice, Dancing with the Stars*), while many of the most critically acclaimed films being made are either based at least in part on true stories (*Seabiscuit, The Aviator*) or outright documentaries (*Murderball, The Yes Men*). Klosterman backs up his assertions with numbers: "From 1992 to 2002, the number of Americans who read literature dropped 7 percent. Yet this trend hasn't affected nonfiction: Since 2000, sales for adult nonfiction have increased 32 percent. Memoir is now the dominant genus of publishing" (Klosterman 2004, 194). Whether or not you ascribe to the belief that more nonfiction being published leads to more sales, or increasing sales lead to more titles being published, the increase in numbers of titles published is a fact: In the decade from 1993 to 2004, the number of biographies published more than doubled, from 3,554 to 7,241. In 1993, 6,507 works of history were published; by 2004 the number was 9,662 (Bookwire U.S. Book Production Web site 2005).

The "rise of the real" in all areas of the media is also drawing the attention of those who make their living trying to match readers to books. In his extremely helpful chapter in the collection *The Readers' Advisor's Companion*, "Readers' Advisory and Nonfiction," Robert Burgin first addressed the amount of nonfiction being read using the anecdotal evidence he garnered when searching Amazon.com's 100 best-selling titles. He accessed the list at the end of 2000 and decided, from the number of titles included on it, titles such as Jacques Barzun's *From Dawn to Decadence: 500 Years of Western Cultural Life, 1500 to the Present* and Sebastian Junger's *The Perfect Storm*, that "large numbers of people read nonfiction for pleasure" (Shearer and Burgin 2001, 214). Nearly five years later, and casting about myself for some vague idea of just how much nonfiction was being read, I decided to replicate his search. Would Dan Brown and John Grisham hold sway and my theory about the enduring popularity of nonfiction be thoroughly discredited? I needn't have worried; with the exception of *Harry Potter and the Half-Blood Prince* in the number one spot, seven of the top ten sellers were nonfiction titles. Nor were all of the seven self-help or other purely "informational" titles: number two was Thomas Friedman's *The World Is Flat: A Brief History of the Twenty-First Century*, number three was Malcolm Gladwell's *Blink: The Power of Thinking without Thinking*, number eight was the same author's *The Tipping Point: How Little Things Can Make a Big Difference*, and number nine was Jane Fonda's biography *My Life So Far* (Amazon.com 1995–2005).

If the presence of two titles by Malcolm Gladwell on Amazon.com's list is any indication, I am persuaded that readers do not choose nonfiction based on subject alone; Gladwell's two most popular books are cataloged under the Dewey subjects "social psychology" and "causality". Have you ever in your readers' advisory career answered the query of a reader looking for a book about "causality"? Although there can be no doubt that readers can and do gravitate toward books in broad subject areas in which they are interested (science, history, biography), as well as more specific areas (gardening, "foodie" books, etc.), librarians must recognize that there will always be books within subjects that most patrons, happy to browse in their habitual subject areas, would never see but might enjoy nonetheless. Robert Sullivan's superlative *Rats: Observations on the History and Habitat of the City's Most Unwanted Inhabitants*, with its Dewey number 599.35 and placement within the animal books, will never be found by the reader who typically enjoys micro-histories, or even by the reader who loves Henry David Thoreau's *Walden*. However, with its many digressions into New York City history, as well as allusions to *Walden* and the natural world, Sullivan's book is a logical read-alike for either of those readers.

Even when a book is assigned multiple subject headings, no matter how accurate those classifications are, there will always be some degree of disconnect between their accuracy and usability. Robert Kurson's popular *Shadow Divers: The True Adventure of Two Americans Who Risked Everything to Solve One of the Last Mysteries of World War II* has the Dewey subject headings "shipwrecks—New Jersey" and "World War, 1939–1945—Naval Operations—Submarine," while the very similar adventure story *Deep Descent: Adventure and Death Diving the* Andrea Doria, by Kevin McMurray, which even shares a couple of main characters with Kurson's narrative, is cataloged as "shipwrecks—Atlantic Coast" and "scuba diving accidents—Atlantic Coast." Despite appropriate cataloging, even a highly proficient search on related works for one title would not find the other. After four years of working with it, I consider myself fairly experienced in the use of my home library catalog, but when trying to find read-alikes for nonfiction books I've enjoyed, I didn't have much luck when relying on subject headings alone; one particularly eye-opening experience occurred when I considered the subject headings for Carolly Erickson's *The Girl from Botany Bay* and Siân Rees's *The Floating Brothel: The Extraordinary True Story of an Eighteenth-Century Ship and Its Cargo of Female Convicts*, both of which are titles that describe the transfer of female British convicts to Australia aboard ships in the eighteenth century, but neither of which shows any relation to the other in the catalog, as the former is listed under "women prisoners" and the latter under "penal colonies."

The difficulty of relying on subject headings is also apparent in very different levels of specificity and generality within headings. Joseph Wambaugh's true crime story *Fire Lover* doesn't appear under "arson," but rather "arson—California—case studies." Haven Kimmel's memoir *A Girl Named Zippy: Growing Up Small in Mooreland, Indiana* is classified under "girls—Indiana—Mooreland—biography," and is, unsurprisingly, the only book available in my library catalog with that heading. Likewise, Annie Dillard's environmental classic and Pulitzer Prize winner, the reflective *Pilgrim at Tinker Creek*, is buried in the nearly 150 other titles that share the classification "nature" (assuming the user knows how to search for "nature" as a subject keyword). Incidentally, errors of omission and just plain errors often impact the effective use of library catalogs; nowhere in the record display for Dillard's seminal work does the information that it did win a Pulitzer Prize appear. In my local library catalog, many of the volumes in Crown Publisher's *Journeys* series are cataloged as such, but Chuck Palahniuk's volume, *Fugitives and Refugees: A Walk in Portland, Oregon*, is not included among them, simply because the "Crown Journeys Series" heading was not linked to it.

Before catalogers become too defensive, I must state that I don't think cataloging is the problem (and, if it is, online booksellers and databases exhibit the same weaknesses, in even greater degree; readers searching Amazon.com for books similar to Kimmel's *A Girl Named*

Zippy are offered the related subject headings "biography," "women," and "childhood memoir," which take the user to literally thousands of titles, even when multiple options are combined). Obviously, books have to go somewhere, and just as there is always ambiguity in fiction genre assignments (when does a novel become "romance," or "adventure"?) so there will be in nonfiction subject assignments. The question is then, if subject headings alone cannot be depended on to pair readers with nonfiction books they might enjoy, what other knowledge and classification skills must librarians and other book industry professionals apply to suggest appropriate titles for each reader?

In addition to subject headings, genre groupings may be particularly useful for organizing and familiarizing ourselves with popular titles. Diana Tixier Herald refers to genre fiction as "books that have content that allows them to be easily categorized as belonging to a specific genre" (Herald 2000, xv) and goes on to state that settings and plot are two of the most easily identifiable criteria for determining a book's placement in a certain genre. Although she was referring to fiction categories that have been firmly established in the literature and in practice (romance, science fiction, mysteries), there seems little reason not to refer to at least some nonfiction forms as "genres." Although some nonfiction genres are already widely recognized (true crime, true adventure, travel) and used as reader interest categories by publishers (when purchasing books, look on the back cover for the suggested classifications or shelf locations such as "Adventure," "Business," "Memoir," "Personal Recovery," etc.), as yet there have been few attempts to define them and provide literature guides for them. This is a misfortune for nonfiction (and all) readers, as many head predictably to their favorite genre and subject areas (such as history and biography) in bookstores, and probably would do so in libraries, given half the chance. It is no longer enough to classify our nonfiction books by their one main subject and exile them to their lonely spine-out locations in the intimidating "nonfiction stacks." We must at least begin to think in terms of what truly makes "Environmental" books environmental books, or "Investigative" books investigative, and start offering them to readers in more manageable groupings.

A second part of the task of determining which nonfiction books readers might enjoy is determining and applying "appeal factors." As defined by Saricks and Brown, and as used in many subsequent genre readers' guides, appeal factors are those elements "which, singly and in combination, seem to address the ways in which books affect readers" (Saricks and Brown 1997, 38). These elements have become such an accepted tool of readers' advisory work that Nancy Pearl even used variations of them to organize both of her literary fiction guidebooks, *Now Read This* and *Now Read This II*, in the forms of setting, story, characters, and language (Pearl 1999, xii–xiii). Factors more typically associated with "mood" preferences, such as whether a book is a quick or epic read, gentle or more blunt, humorous or reflective, also come into play when recommending nonfiction titles, just as they do for fiction selections. A reader who likes Augusten Burrough's often shocking memoir *Running with Scissors*, or Mary Karr's brutally honest *The Liar's Club*, will not necessarily be drawn to titles such as Sterling North's more nostalgic *Rascal: A Memoir of a Better Era*, or Nicholas Sparks's more gentle *Three Weeks with My Brother*, even though all of these titles are memoirs (genre) about family relationships (subject).

Although the use of appeal factors is becoming a standard part of readers' advisory practice for fiction, the practice has yet to make inroads into the world of nonfiction readers' advisory. Currently no reference works or Internet sites are devoted solely to nonfiction books, leading to a situation in which, as Saricks describes in her introduction to the collection *Non-*

fiction Readers' Advisory, "reference librarians new to readers' advisory in general may be more troubled by the lack of precise answers, as well as the paucity of useful resources to turn to for assistance" (Burgin 2004, xii). The majority of booklists available on many public library Web sites, although useful in their own way and thoughtfully compiled, focus primarily on the reading of nonfiction for informational or directional purposes only ("Alzheimer's Disease Resources," or "Energy in the 21st Century," Madison Public Library Web site 2005). On the rare occasions when nonfiction choices are offered alongside fiction recommendations, they are often linked by subject alone, with little description of the author's writing style, use of characterization or other narrative techniques, or the overall mood of the work.

That said, I must add that classification of nonfiction works along either genre or appeal-factor lines alone would constitute as much of a difficulty as their current classification solely along purely subject-oriented lines. Just as readers of nonfiction do not always seek to fulfill informational or prescriptive needs alone, neither are they often attracted exclusively to an author's style or character development, at least not to the exclusion of caring about the subject. Readers know nonfiction works are based on true events, which is a realization that may affect their enjoyment of an otherwise well-told story. Alice Sebold's books are a perfect example; her beautiful prose style is apparent in both her fiction title *The Lovely Bones* and her nonfiction memoir *Lucky*, and although both contain violence, the realization that the violence in her memoir actually happened to her when she was eighteen may prove overwhelming for a fan of *The Lovely Bones*. Therefore, it seems only logical to assume that the information professional seeking to provide comprehensive readers' advisory service must approach the process of recommending nonfiction titles based on knowledge of a book's subject matter, genre categorization, and the source of its primary appeal and stylistic factors.

So, why is a nonfiction reader's guide necessary? It is my hope that this guide will provide, at the very least, a descriptive overview of some of the most popular and enduring nonfiction works available, as well as placing them within a framework consisting of reading interests related to subject matter, genre, appeal, and mood. By no means do I profess to think that this guide can be called "comprehensive" or be considered the final word on the subject; there is simply too much quality nonfiction out there (as well as more being published every day) to promise that. It is simply a tool designed to help readers consider new ways to find nonfiction books that will appeal to them, as well as to provide new ways to group and publicize nonfiction genres and subgenres for those who work with books and readers. Because many nonfiction readers also enjoy reading fiction, it is also meant to be used in conjunction with the many helpful fiction literature guides already available, such as Nancy Pearl's *Now Read This* and *Now Read This II* or Diana Tixier Herald's and Wayne Wiegand's sixth edition of *Genreflecting*, not to mention the many Web sites and blogs that exist to provide up-to-the-minute reviews and commentary on new fiction and nonfiction titles.

I also hope to demonstrate how skills and techniques that have been developed for and used in the course of providing fiction readers' assistance can also be used for nonfiction (or preferably, dual fiction and nonfiction) services. If Catherine Ross's preliminary interviews with readers are any indication, there is a need for both such services; she reports that "some readers said that they never read nonfiction (too boring, too much like school or like their work-related reading) and some said that they read only nonfiction (fiction wasn't real enough). But a great many readers read both" (2004, 107). Providing booklists, creating displays, and choosing titles for book discussions need not be practices that revolve solely around fiction, and this guide seeks both to provide a framework for grouping nonfiction titles by genre and to provide substantive annotations that can help book professionals select and work with books in subject matters that they normally wouldn't read themselves.

In the end, however, the most compelling reason for this guide (and many other readers' guides like it) is provided by Robert Burgin, who wrote that "the central problem of the readers' advisory transaction—finding 'more like that'—is complex, and we need all the help that we can get" (Shearer and Burgin 2001, 226).

Definition of Nonfiction, and How It Differs from Fiction

For starters, nonfiction is the only literary genre, or collection, defined by what it is *not* (fiction). It is *not* an "invented story" (as defined by Merriam-Webster), but rather, as David Carr put it, it "differs from fiction in its presentation of documented experience as a written record, without fabrication" (Carr 2004, 51). Popular techniques of making nonfiction conform to a narrative flow (using "creative transitions," a la John Berendt in *Midnight in the Garden of Good and Evil*, or using novelistic writing techniques to ascribe thoughts and feelings to real characters as Truman Capote did in *In Cold Blood*) have led to discussions about what constitutes actual fact and true nonfiction, but for the most part that scholarly discussion is beyond the scope of this work. Because readers don't seem to care unduly about those issues, as evidenced by the continued best-selling nature of at least the just-mentioned works, not to mention the recent surge in popularity of memoirs that consist largely of "remembered" or "re-created" details and feelings rather than documented ones, such matters won't be debated here. What does follow is a more practical consideration of how nonfiction differs from fiction within the confines of the readers' advisory encounter.

The first major difference between fiction and nonfiction books is most easily perceived when visiting a bookstore immediately after stopping at the library. Walk into the fiction stacks in the bookstore and the library (for the most part). and you will find diverse sections designed to appeal to different readers: not only fiction but also romance, science fiction, fantasy, Westerns, and horror, among others. In that same bookstore, across the aisle, you'll be offered adventure, travel, business, biography, and many other categories of nonfiction; in the library you'll find undifferentiated (except by numbers or letters that must be coaxed from the catalog first) and endless rows of nonfiction books, shelved according to the one subject a cataloger had to pick as the title's only access point. Some librarians have gone so far as to suggest the arrangement of their nonfiction collections by "reader interest categories—natural language categories that correspond to user needs and interests—rather than by Dewey Decimal, Library of Congress, or another alphanumeric classification scheme" (Baker and Wallace 2002, 286). I don't know if I have the energy to face that task (the books still have to be physically placed in *one* shelf location, after all), but Baker and Wallace describe examples of situations wherein libraries increased their circulation of nonfiction 30 percent by doing just that. Although these points may someday be rendered moot by e-books and other ways of offering book collections (audio book downloads for IPods being another example) that don't depend on physical shelf location, locating books in ways besides searching or asking for them by title or author will most likely present readers with a challenge for many years to come. The fact remains that fiction readers who are comfortable within certain genres and, to a lesser extent, with certain authors and types of titles (and how to find them regardless of format), have someplace to go, whereas nonfiction readers with genre interests not frequently addressed by subject headings (relationships, memoirs) do not.

A second major difference between nonfiction and fiction is the number of books by the same author that can be offered to readers. Fans of LaVyrle Spencer, Robert Parker, Robert Jordan, Stephen King, or Anne Tyler have numerous titles from which to choose. Within many genres (Parker is a fine example of this as well), recurring characters and storylines can also mean an easier readers' advisory experience for the librarian, who can often meet the reader's need simply by providing the next title in the series. With a few notable exceptions (Isaac Asimov, Stephen Ambrose, and David Halberstam among them), nonfiction writers just don't write as many books per author as many fiction writers do. Likewise, although children's nonfiction series are plentiful, there are few series for adults to depend on, other than a few biographical and travel series, to round out a reader's "to read" list. The obvious exception to that rule is readers who exhaust, or at least try to, all the works on a certain subject or person. Civil War buffs will never have any shortage of classic or new titles to choose from, just as readers of James Dean and Princess Diana biographies face bookshelves full of titles on the subjects of their obsession. For fans of nonfiction books in general, however, particularly those based on investigative research and narratives based on an author's unique task or experience, there is usually a quicker conclusion to the task of reading everything one author has written. When I finished all of William Langewiesche's five books (and they're short books, too), that was it . . . or at least until he writes another one, and no one knows when that will be. I am left only with the recourse of finding related works based on subject headings, which, in the case of his books *Inside the Sky: A Meditation on Flight* and *Sahara Unveiled: A Journey across the Desert*, I can assure you I probably wouldn't be too interested in pursuing further. Reader loyalty, just as exists for many fiction authors, is there for numerous nonfiction authors as well (David Sedaris, Malcolm Gladwell, and Dava Sobel to name a few), despite the usually shorter lists of available titles.

A third difference between nonfiction and fiction has already been discussed in this introduction, and that is the lack of resources devoted either solely to nonfiction, or more substantively to any of its more popular genres, such as memoirs or biographies. Works of literary criticism do exist for many of those, but although they are often comprehensively researched and informative, they are not often written for any audience other than a scholarly one. Practical resources developed for librarians, by librarians, outside of random booklists that vary widely in quality, simply don't exist for nonfiction books. That point is supported by anecdotal evidence, for example, the absence of any works about nonfiction in the most recent "Recommended Readers' Advisory Tools" article in the Summer 2004 issue of *Reference & User Services Quarterly*, as well as the exclusive or nearly exclusive focus on fiction of many book- and reading-related Web sites such as overbooked.org and bookbitch.com. In researching and writing this guide, it even proved difficult to find such basic information as nonfiction genre definitions and histories in the usual popular or scholarly sources (either in print or online); when no other information could be found, definitions and overviews from Wikipedia (an online and international encyclopedia written collaboratively by its own readers) have been offered to provide, at the very least, a brief foray into the subjects at hand.

It should also be noted that nonfiction does not always lend itself to a quick read; comprehensive works of biography and history, in particular, commonly are longer than 300 and 400 pages, with each page densely written at that. These somewhat intimidating books might discourage librarians who believe they must read every page of every book they recommend from starting them and using and arranging them in thematic and seasonal book displays and booklists. In addition to often being lengthy or demanding, there is quite simply a LOT of nonfiction published: according to statistics published by R. R. Bowker, in 2003 17,021 fiction titles were published, which seems scary enough, until the nonfiction numbers are totaled for biography, history, general works, science, and travel books alone (leaving out a myriad of other nonfiction categories such as business and law), yielding 33,347 titles in that same year (Bookwire U.S. Book Production Web site 2005). We are also fighting the perception, held by readers and many of our colleagues, that nonfiction is to be used for information-finding purposes only, and in view of the massive amounts of fiction published every year, to neglect reviewing or even flipping through nonfiction books that we assume will appeal only to readers interested in a certain subject. There is a fundamental disconnect between our assumption that nonfiction is only for "serious" or information-seeking readers and Ross's finding that "while readers value the prolonged experience of uninterrupted reading when they are immersed in the world of the book, they also value books such as letters, memoirs, cookbooks, and encyclopedias that can be dipped into and read a bit at a time, as magazines are read" (Ross 2004, 109). In a world where competition for people's leisure time is increasingly stiff and multi-tasking has become a mainstay of even our downtime, we must realize that, although many works of nonfiction are lengthy, the experience of reading them need not be limited to reading them from cover to cover (either as librarians or as typical readers).

I am hampered in making my next suggestion by a lack of available research, but it is my feeling that, to a certain extent, we have trained our patrons to use our classification schemes too well. Nonfiction readers, like readers of other genres, most likely know their area of preferred subjects (science, travel, true crime, etc.) and, as often described in the research, may be reluctant to disturb the librarian who appears to be busy at the reference desk, especially with a question they might assume to be less important (e.g., recreational reading queries) than those of other patrons requiring more technical assistance. If another of Ross's suggested findings holds true, namely, that nonfiction readers like to "know about things and they read to find out" (Ross 2004, 113), it may also be safe to assume that they are readers who will take steps to learn to use the catalogs on their own. If this is true, then suggestions like those made by Keddy Ann Outlaw become even more important: "Post a few short reading lists on a bulletin board near the fiction or popular nonfiction. . . . Highlight oldies but goodies by creating a display of bestsellers from another date ten, twenty, or thirty years ago" (2005, 9). It is vital that we do not neglect nonfiction when following such suggestions, if only to entice nonfiction readers with new and enjoyable serendipitous browsing experiences that might introduce them to other types of nonfiction and fiction titles.

The general consensus seems to be that recreational nonfiction readers are currently being neglected, not only for reasons already mentioned but also, according to Vicki Novak, in part because "our libraries are not structured to provide this service. Libraries that offer a separate readers' advisory desk often place it in the fiction room and even call it the 'Fiction Desk'. . . . Another reason for our lack of service is that the readers' advisory tools available just do not cover nonfiction with any depth" (Novak 2004, 215–16). Before considering the scope and structure of this book, I'd like to offer a perfect example of what can happen when readers are not neglected and are presented with reading choices that complement the selections they've already made. Chris Anderson reported on a phenomenon he referred to as the "long tail," as observed in sales at Amazon.com, in the October 2004 issue of *Wired* magazine. The crux of Anderson's article is the best-selling success story of Joe Simpson's nonfiction book *Touching the Void*, sales of which were fueled by the popularity of Jon Krakauer's personal narrative of disaster on Mount Everest, *Into Thin Air*, published ten years after Simpson's book. When Amazon.com shoppers purchased *Into Thin Air* and also found and purchased *Touching the Void* from the same source, the site's algorithm-fueled database took over and started recommending the decade-old title alongside the newer one. Anderson describes the importance of the long tail, which consists of those items that are considered too obscure to be offered anywhere but in online markets, especially considering that "the average Barnes & Noble carries 130,000 titles. Yet more than half of Amazon's book sales come from *outside* its top 130,000 titles . . . in other words, the potential book market may be twice as big as it appears to be, if only we can get over the economics of scarcity" (Anderson 2004, 174). Sure, we're only human, and our brains are not relational databases directly linked to real-time sales. But if Anderson is right, and the time of long-tail merchandising has come, there is no reason librarians can't step up and take advantage of it. We've already started the job for fiction and strive to provide the same type of recommendation service that Amazon does, offering readers displays, lists, and programs that suggest, based on our reading, expertise, and interaction with other professionals and patrons, formulations such as "if you liked *The Da Vinci Code*, you'll love . . . " It's time to do the very same for nonfiction as well, in addition to linking fiction and nonfiction together.

Where to Begin? The Selection Process

This guide provides a representative sampling of the best, most popular, and most current nonfiction titles available to readers, along with a healthy dose of nonfiction classics and benchmark titles. Following the lead of Nancy Pearl, who began her work on literary fiction by "including novels selected by the American Library Association's Notable Books Council" (Pearl 1999, xiv), the first titles to be selected and annotated for this book were those that appeared on the ALA Notable Nonfiction lists from 1993 through 2005. Although not every single title listed there is annotated in this collection (some are offered in the "Now try" listings instead), the vast majority of them are, and they appear throughout the book in a variety of categories. Other awards lists that contributed numerous titles were the Pulitzer Prizes (in the biography, history, and general nonfiction categories), the American Booksellers Association's Book Sense Award winners, the National Book Critics Circle awards (in both biography and nonfiction), and the National Book Awards. A more subject-specific award, the John Burroughs Medal for outstanding nature writing, was also considered when making selections for the environmental chapter.

In addition to these notable books and award winners, a selection of best sellers culled from *Publishers Weekly* best-seller lists and other popular (but not necessarily award-winning) nonfiction books and authors was included, such as Mitch Albom's *Tuesdays with Morrie* and Ruth Reichl's *Tender at the Bone: Growing Up at the Table*. A listing was also compiled of all nonfiction titles reviewed in a year-and-a-half's worth of weekly issues of *Publishers Weekly* (from December 2004 back through July 2003) to provide a representative sampling of recent offerings from a variety of publishers and authors. A conscious effort was made to include books published by both large publishers (typically the more established and traditional players in the industry, such as Knopf and HarperCollins), as well as newer or more independent players such as the Minneapolis-based Milkweed Editions or Vermont's Destiny Books.

The majority of the books chosen for annotation were published within the last fifteen years (1990 through 2005), a span of years that provided a wealth of titles that are largely still quite current and readable. That time frame was not used as a strict guideline, however, and when "classic," well-known, or just plain enjoyable titles were found that were published before 1990, they were included. Although many of these older titles can be found throughout the entire book, many of the titles with the most staying power appear in the environmental chapter; Henry David Thoreau's *Walden* was first published in 1854, while Mary Austin's *Land of Little Rain* has a copyright date of 1903, and Edward Abbey produced *Desert Solitaire* in 1968.

Last but not least, although I hope my own personal favorite authors and titles from a decade of reading and loving nonfiction are not immediately recognizable by the adulatory tone of their annotations, there are a few of those here as well. I also included a healthy dose of titles that I found while checking in stacks of returned books at the circulation desk, which had the double bonus of being joyously and serendipitously discovered, as well as having the burden of proof of their "circulation-worthiness" met. I also feel compelled to add that this collection is a first attempt at organizing and annotating enjoyable, popular, and noteworthy nonfiction titles, which will hopefully undergo expansion and revision in future editions. With that hope in mind, I welcome any and all title suggestions, which can be submitted to me through the publisher at http://www.genreflecting.com or http://www.lu.com, or by e-mail at theend@merr.com.

What Is *Not* Included

A number of colleagues have asked me how on earth I could pretend to be writing a guide that could even come close to covering all the areas of nonfiction. The short answer is, I'm not. Not only can each chapter here be best defined as a sampling, rather than an exhaustive compendium, there are categories that are not directly in this edition. Readers may find not only a handful of "Political" and "Religion" titles throughout other chapters (e.g., Woodward and Bernstein's *All the President's Men* is annotated in the "Investigative Writing" chapter, as are "spirituality" books like Kathleen Norris's *The Cloister Walk* and Cheryl Reed's *Unveiled: The Hidden Lives of Nuns*), but also titles that are most typically thought of as political writing (candidate biographies, or commentator's collections such as Bill O'Reilly's *Who's Looking Out for You?*) or inspirational (*The Prayer of Jabez* or any of the Chicken Soup for the Soul Books). Although many such titles currently appear on best-seller lists, I have by and large followed the maxim "not to discuss religion or politics," for several reasons. One reason is the obviously sensitive nature of such topics, particularly in an era when states are described as "red" or "blue" ones, according to their voting records. Another is the ability of our current system of cataloging by subject to successfully yield such titles to those readers seeking them: Readers looking for informational books on Islam or Judaism, or reference sources such as Bible concordances, should be able to find them quite easily through a subject or title search; those readers looking for ideological works by their favorite politicians likewise should be able to easily find them using an author search. Third, the staying power of popular works on politicians is less than stellar; any bookstore worker can tell you that biographies about, or treatises written by, John Kerry were dead wood on November 3, 2004. A brief list of popular political pundits and their defining works, as well as a list of popular "Spirituality" writers, are appended at the end of the book. Future editions may address these areas in more detail.

Although poetry and works of classic literature are often included in public library nonfiction collections, no attempt has been made to organize them here due to their imaginative nature. Poetry in particular may be said to be based in truth (especially if one believes that truth is beauty, and beauty truth), but it is not usually requested or recommended as "nonfiction." I do believe that much poetry appeals across genre lines; Robert Frost's and Wendell Berry's poetry, for example, may appeal to readers of environmental works, with their strong use of natural world imagery, and I heartily encourage readers' advisors to work poetry selections into their repertoire.

I have also not included reference, how-to, or largely informational works, such as self-help books, gardening manuals, or cookbooks. Although many readers can and do dip into such works for recreational purposes (Bridget Jones's addiction to self-help books in Helen Fielding's novels is the most hilarious proof of that fact), the sheer enormity of the task of reading, selecting, and annotating them in the absence of guidelines such as those provided by "Notable Books" lists (which also do not typically include such works) or major awards was too daunting to consider adding to an already daunting task. That is not to say that we should not strive to provide advisory services for such works, or to become familiar with titles currently being published. I am only suggesting that a compilation of such titles is a task for another time, and another book.

There are dishearteningly few works in translation, although some are included (*Machete Season*, *The Bookseller of Kabul*, and Anne Frank's *Diary of a Young Girl* among them), and it is our hope that publishing companies will continue to increase their offerings of translated works, and that readers will find and read more of them, so that future editions of this work or other nonfiction reading guides may have more titles from which to choose. By and large all of the books annotated are works of "popular" nonfiction, although many great academic and research works exist in all of the subjects covered, and university presses are beginning to offer more accessible and affordable books (the University of Nebraska's *American Lives* series, edited by memoirist Tobias Wolff, is a great example of this trend). That said, readers and readers' advisors alike will still find a few academic works sprinkled throughout the title suggestions here, from publishers such as the Harvard University Press and the Columbia University Press.

Although it may seem as though the only titles listed herein are those consisting of narrative nonfiction, or those works of nonfiction that, as Tom Wolfe opined, can be read like novels, that is not the case. A work like Lynne Truss's popular *Eats, Shoots, and Leaves* does not tell a story as much as provide a series of related chapters explaining different points of grammar. Many essay collections are also included here, and they cannot be said in any way to constitute a true narrative. The majority of titles in the "Making Sense . . ." chapter also do not conform to a narrative structure but are more synthesizing and scholarly works.

As alluded to previously, no judgments were made regarding whether books consisted of only "true" or "real" nonfiction, as opposed to "creative nonfiction," which is defined at Wikipedia (2005) as "a genre of literature, also known as literary nonfiction and narrative journalism, which uses literary skills in the writing of nonfiction. A work of creative nonfiction, if well written, contains accurate and well-researched information and also holds the interest of the reader."

Those professionals interested in that debate are encouraged to read Lee Gutkind's introduction to the collection of pieces from the journal he founded, *Creative Nonfiction*, and to learn there that while Gutkind does not wish to be considered the "nonfiction police," he does offer technique guidelines for writers in the form, including the admonitions to "strive for truth," "recognize the important distinction between recollected conversation and fabricated dialogue," and "don't round corners—or compress situations or characters—*unnecessarily*" (2005, xxx–xxxi). Whenever possible, I have tried to provide clues in the annotations regarding the author's adherence to exacting journalistic methods, or lack thereof.

How to Use This Book

Organization of the Chapters

This book is divided into eleven different nonfiction "genres." Some chapters, such as those listing true adventure and travel, will reflect familiar nonfiction genre categorizations. Other chapters, such as those labeled "Science and Math," "History," and "Biography," will reflect recognizable classification schemes, but differ in that they are typically thought of in terms of their subject matter, rather than in terms of their genre characteristics (and are called "Nonfiction Subject Interests"). Still others, such as the final chapters, "Investigative Writing," and "Making Sense . . . ," reflect groupings designed to more closely examine what it is about their authors' and titles' writing styles and story conventions that makes them similar enough to each other to convincingly refer to them as "genres." Each chapter is further divided into categories, or subgenres, reflecting some of the more popular subdivisions within vast subject and genre areas. All eleven chapters open with a short definition and history of the genre (when available), as well as an explanation of the overall appeal of the genre and its subcategories. Shorter explanations also accompany each subgenre, in order to help both librarians and readers get a feeling for how each is differentiated from the others by subject matter, appeal factors, and stylistic conventions. Whenever possible an effort has been made to cite scholarly sources when referring to category descriptions and histories, although, as previously noted, at times the frustrating lack of research materials on nonfiction reading interests compelled us to turn to Wikipedia and other more popular sources for discussion points and historical precedents.

Although all of the categories are referred to as "genres," they are organized and presented in terms of their larger attractions. As the most familiar and accepted genre categories, the chapters on true adventure, travel, true crime, and environmental writing are given first; genres that are typically thought of in terms of their subject matter—science and math, and history—are presented next. The middle grouping, "Life Stories," reflects the character-driven features of the three genres represented therein: biography, memoirs and autobiography, and relationships. Rounding out the manual are two genres that are more cohesive in their stylistic conventions and styles than they are in their coverage of certain subjects. Investigative writing authors do just that: investigate their stories, whether they're about body farms or inner city life, and use interviews, research, and often an extremely straightforward prose style to tell their stories. Books in the "Making Sense . . ." classification are also stylistically related; authors in that genre tend to refer to vast numbers of other books and popular culture sources to provide a more synthesizing and literary, rather than story-driven, account of their topic.

The Annotations and "Now Try" Recommendations

Each title listing is accompanied by an annotation, the content of which is designed to be brief enough to be read quickly but substantive enough to provide users of this guide with sufficient information so that reading each book personally might not be necessary to provide good related recommendations (which, it is hoped, will be helpful for those readers and professionals who find it hard to read works outside of their own personal genre or subject interests). Each title and annotation also includes subject headings that were designed to reflect both the Dewey Decimal and the Library of Congress classification systems, as well as to provide clues about a book's appeal and stylistic concerns (e.g., "Classics," "Humor," "Fast Reads," "Gentle Reads"). A book's status as a notable title or an award winner is also noted in the subject headings listings. The bibliographic citation following each title reflects that title's original publication information. The most recent publication data are given in parentheses following the original data. We have also included each book's number of pages and ISBN, which correspond to the most recent bibliographic data provided.

In addition to the annotations, each title is followed by "Now try" suggestions, including both fiction and nonfiction titles, which were selected on the basis of both their subject and appeal similarities and were compiled from a variety of sources, including library catalog "related work" subject links, Amazon.com's algorithm-fueled "Customers who bought this title also purchased . . . " recommendations, librarian- and academic-created read-alike and subject booklists, and personal experience or the recommendations of colleagues and friends. Each of these methods of tracking down titles designed to provide similar reading experiences offers both pros and cons, but it is hoped that in combining them a somewhat objective list of suggestions has been created.

More than 550 titles have been annotated for this manual, and each "Now try" suggestion includes, typically, two to five more titles that might appeal to readers. Both the annotations and the "Now try" suggestion sections are rather longer than most you'll find in genre fiction readers' guides. This was done by design, both to provide substantial information about a large variety of nonfiction genre titles in one place (sure, a lot of information can be found on Amazon.com, but searching for the requisite titles and then skimming through both professional and reader reviews, few of which provide whole book summaries, can take a lot of time, regardless of your Internet connection speed) and in recognition of the complexity of combining nonfiction books' subject matters, genre conventions, and appeal factors in order to make connections to other nonfiction (and fiction) titles that may share any or all of those characteristics.

"Consider Starting With . . . " and Fiction Read-Alikes Sections

At the end of each chapter additional reading suggestions are provided, beginning with a short list of "Consider Starting With . . . " recommendations. These titles were chosen for their status as recognized hits within each genre, as well as for their level of accessibility. Readers, librarians, and book professionals pressed for time (and who isn't, nowadays?) are strongly encouraged to read (or even skim) those selections to both get a "feel" for each genre and familiarize themselves with some of the most enduringly popular titles in each category. They are also what I would consider each chapter's "greatest hits"; even if some of them are not the most famous books ever published, they represent in some way the best of what each section has to offer. Steven Mishler's *A Measure of Endurance* made no best-seller lists and won no awards, but it remains one of the best books ever written, in my opinion, to make personal the struggle for restitution in the face of corporate negligence, and exemplifies the best of what the genre investigative writing has to offer.

Next is a list of "Fiction Read-Alikes." The authors and titles listed here were selected not only to further illustrate the overall appeal of each nonfiction genre (e.g., the read-alike authors listed in both the "Memoirs and Autobiography" and "Biography" chapters primarily appeal to their readers through the development of their characters, much as the nonfiction authors in those chapters form their narratives around the real people who are the subjects of their stories), but also to make inroads into bridging the gap between fiction and nonfiction advisory services. The great majority of author and title information listed in these sections was compiled from Gale Thomson's extremely helpful Literature Resource Center database.

Suggestions for Use

There will doubtless be some controversy about the omission of such genre/format headings as "Humor" or "Essays." However, in keeping with Bookslut.com editor Jessa Crispin's insightful caveat regarding graphic novels (and publishers' and reviewers' tendency to lump all of them together in stores and reviews), we have viewed such categories as a "medium, not a genre." Such "medium" designations are provided as subject headings within each title's annotations (including "Classics," "Essays," "Gentle Reads," "Humor," and "Quick Reads," to name a few) and can all be found in the subject index. Readers can also use the indexes to locate their favorite authors and titles by name.

In addition to using the guide to find both nonfiction and fiction read-alike suggestions and story synopses of popular nonfiction titles, readers are encouraged to browse through chapters, to start gaining familiarity with popular authors in all nonfiction genres. Before I started this project, I was not a person who read many science books, and I would have been totally lost had a reader asked for more books like those by Carl Sagan or Brian Greene. After reading a number of science books to research this manual, however, I am happy to report that even though I still may not understand a lot of what either of those authors have written, I can at least recognize that Sagan fans might be looking for more language-driven and speculative works on cosmology, while Greene fans are most likely looking for books on physics, and rather rigorously detailed and straightforward ones at that. Just as fiction readers' advisors are enjoined never to turn a patron away with the dismissive, "I've never read in that genre, I couldn't possibly help you," so should nonfiction readers' advisors strive to gain an understanding of the subjects and appeals of a variety of nonfiction books.

Full Disclosure: Why I Love Nonfiction

Like many of the readers in Ross's study cited earlier, I am not an exclusively nonfiction reader. I began my reading life as a fan of fiction and fantasy (encouraged by a father who loved King Arthur stories), found Agatha Christie, J. D. Salinger, and Anne Tyler in high school and college, and continued on quite happily into my professional career reading novels by Jim Crace, Minette Walters, and numerous other fiction authors. Although nonfiction staples like Sterling North's *Rascal*, Truman Capote's *In Cold Blood*, and Studs Terkel's oral histories were always on my menu, I didn't really begin my love affair with nonfiction until I began working at the public library. Surrounded by books, I gorged myself on contemporary fiction and found myself unsatisfied by the vast majority of it, although many also became favorites (Matt Ruff's *Set This House in Order*, Liza Ward's *Outside Valentine*, Zadie Smith's *White Teeth*, Julian Gough's *Juno and Juliet*, Dennis LeHane's *Shutter Island*, and George Hagen's *The Laments* among them). Then one day I chanced across Matthew Hart's nonfiction *Diamond: Journey to the Heart of an Obsession*, and my whole world changed in the course of the night it took me to read it (my world was already changing in other ways; I'd recently gotten engaged and opted out of receiving a diamond ring, which was one of the reasons I'd picked up the book in the first place). As I waded deeper into the nonfiction collection, I discovered ever more titles in subject areas I never would have thought to search the catalog for, and found myself drawn into nearly every book I picked up, regardless of whether it was about Joe Namath, Walden Pond, disasters at sea, or even, as the child I overheard requested, monkeys. The major problem in compiling this collection was not a lack of enjoyable reading material, but an overabundance of it, and my personal desire to keep reading instead of starting writing; as Barbara Tuchman once confessed she discovered about her own historical research, "one must stop *before* one has finished; otherwise, one will never stop and never finish" (Tuchman 1981, 20). As stated previously, I have no illusions that this will constitute a comprehensive work; it is intended primarily as a starting point for readers and a very brief selection of nonfiction titles across genre, reading interest, and stylistic lines.

I love nonfiction. I hope that in picking up this guide you will discover how very much "stories that are true" have to offer, and come to love them and recommend them to others, as well. In light of that desire, then, it may seem odd that the quote that stands at the head of this introduction is from a work of fiction (although I myself tend to think of it as memoir, since Maclean based it on his own life and family), one that expresses the great appeal of fictional stories at that; namely, that fiction authors can usually end their stories after telling the reader what happens, and why. Nonfiction authors have no such luxury. They can study, and they can speculate; they can even produce beautiful prose and impose some sort of narrative closure, but in the end, their readers may never really know what happened, or how, or why. The more we want to figure out, or understand, or be inspired or entertained by true stories, the less we have a choice in the matter: We must keep reading.

References

Amazon.com. © 1995–2005. www.amazon.com (accessed April 17, 2005).

Anderson, Chris. 2004. "The Long Tail." *Wired* (October): 171–77.

Baker, Sharon L., and Karen L. Wallace. 2002. *The Responsive Public Library: How to Develop and Market a Winning Collection.* Englewood, Colo.: Libraries Unlimited.

Bookwire U.S. Book Production Web site. © 2005. www.bookwire.com/bookwire/decadebookproduction.html (accessed July 21, 2005).

Burgin, Robert, ed. 2004. *Nonfiction Readers' Advisory.* Westport, Conn.: Libraries Unlimited.

Carr, David. 2004. "Many Kinds of Crafted Truths: An Introduction to Nonfiction." In *Nonfiction Readers' Advisory,* ed. Robert Burgin, 47–65. Westport, Conn.: Libraries Unlimited.

Crowley, Bill. 2004. "A History of Readers' Advisory Service in the Public Library." In *Nonfiction Readers' Advisory,* ed. Robert Burgin, 3–29. Westport, Conn.: Libraries Unlimited.

Gutkind, Lee, ed. 2005. *In Fact: The Best of Creative Nonfiction.* New York: Norton.

Herald, Diana Tixier. 2000. *Genreflecting: A Guide to Reading Interests in Genre Fiction.* 5th ed. Westport, Conn.: Libraries Unlimited.

Klosterman, Chuck. 2004. "The Rise of the Real." *Esquire* 142, no. 6 (December): 194–95; 236.

Maclean, Norman. 1976. *A River Runs Through It, and Other Stories.* Chicago: University of Chicago Press.

Madison Public Library Web site. 2005. madisonpubliclibrary.org/booklists/ (accessed April 20, 2005).

Novak, Vicki. 2004. "The Story's the Thing: Narrative Nonfiction for Recreational Reading." In *Nonfiction Readers' Advisory,* ed. Robert Burgin, 213–28. Westport, Conn.: Libraries Unlimited.

Outlaw, Keddy Ann. 2005. "Self-Service Readers Advisory." *Public Libraries* 44, no. 1 (January/February): 9–11.

Pearl, Nancy. 1999. *Now Read This: A Guide to Mainstream Fiction, 1978–1998.* Englewood, Colo.: Libraries Unlimited.

"Recommended Readers' Advisory Tools." 2004. *Reference & User Services Quarterly* 43, no. 4 (Summer): 294–305.

Ross, Catherine. 2004. "Reading Nonfiction for Pleasure: What Motivates Readers?" In *Nonfiction Readers' Advisory*, ed. Robert Burgin, 105–20. Westport, Conn.: Libraries Unlimited

Saricks, Joyce, and Nancy Brown. 1997 (1987). *Readers' Advisory Service in the Public Library.* Chicago: American Library Association.

Shearer, Kenneth D., and Robert Burgin. 2001. *The Readers' Advisor's Companion.* Englewood, Colo.: Libraries Unlimited.

Tuchman, Barbara. 1981. *Practicing History: Selected Essays.* New York: Knopf.

Wikipedia. 2005. http://en.wikipedia.org/wiki/Creative_nonfiction (accessed April 21, 2005).

Part 1

Nonfiction Genres

True Adventure

Travel

True Crime

Environmental Writing

Chapter 1

True Adventure

Definition of True Adventure

In trawling the Internet and various literature databases, the closest I could get to an in-depth description of nonfiction true adventure writing was a sentence referring to both fiction and nonfiction: "sometimes called 'men's books,' most of these are novels of survival, adventure, intrigue and espionage, war, militias, and other thrilling, suspenseful topics" (Waterboro Library Web site 2005). Three of the most well-known titles annotated in this chapter clearly fit that definition: Jon Krakauer's *Into Thin Air* tells a story of mountain climbing danger and survival; Sebastian Junger's *The Perfect Storm* is a suspenseful read about the many dangers of the sea; and Mark Bowden tells an intense story of a horrific military experience in *Black Hawk Down*. All three are textbook examples of what is meant by "True Adventure."

True adventure stories have been with us for, literally, thousands of years. Epic poems such as Homer's *Iliad* and *The Odyssey* have been found to be based at least partly on true historical events, while others, like *The Epic of Gilgamesh* and *Beowulf*, often include a mainstay of contemporary adventure stories: their main characters' depiction as larger-than-life heroes. Librarians willing to apply fiction definitions of adventure to nonfiction stories can also refer to Diana Tixier Herald's statement that "the heroic exploits of larger-than-life protagonists and the ultimate triumph of the goods guys over the bad are the driving forces in this type. Strong plots, heavy with action, are powerful lures to readers" (2000, 154). That certainly holds true for the character-driven (or horse-driven) narrative *Seabiscuit*, as well as for a title like Frank Abagnale's *Catch Me If You Can*, which, even if it doesn't center on the ultimate triumph of the "good guys," certainly does provide a larger-than-life protagonist.

Early examples of travel narratives, including those by Marco Polo (produced in the thirteenth century!), provide more historical evidence for the development of the true adventure genre. Later centuries would find readers be enthralled by works combining tales of exploration, travel, and adventure, such as those by Henry Stanley, who told the story of his search throughout Africa for the explorer and missionary David Livingstone in 1871 in *How I Found Livingstone*. The founding of the National Geographic Society in 1888 also reflects the popularity of all stories exotic and exciting, and the continuing popularity of the *National Geographic* magazine (not to mention its subsidiaries, *National Geographic Adventure* and *National Geographic Traveler*) indicates that interest in this genre remains high. A definition found in the introduction to *Dead Reckoning: Tales of the Great Explorers, 1800–1900*, edited by Helen Whybrow, suggests that the nineteenth century was the glory age of the adventurous exploration tale, but that "in the dwindling of geographic conquests left to make, our celebration of individual achievement has grown, and modern adventure writing is more personal and psychological than in the past" (2003, 17). In the past or not, popular historical and exploration titles such as Caroline Alexander's *The Endurance: Shackleton's Legendary Antarctic Expedition* remain hugely popular works, as do works examining the psychological effects of adventure and danger, such as David Roberts's *The Mountain of My Fear*.

There is seldom one area of the library nonfiction stacks that corresponds directly to adventure narratives; readers will find many of the suggested titles in the sports sections, particularly those that tell mountain climbing survival stories, which are all classified as books about mountain climbing. Likewise, books about poker and gambling heists will be found in the cards and games section; exploration and survival titles are often classified according to their settings; the placement of war and espionage stories correspond to their events or time periods. The nature of the challenges or obstacles in these narratives, in addition to dictating their locations on the shelves, is also important to consider when making recommendations: Is the reader interested in natural disasters and how bystanders withstood them, or more interested in adventurers who actively place themselves in dangerous situations as a way to challenge themselves? Setting and location can also play a part; some readers may be interested only in survival and exploration stories set in arctic climates, while others may only want stories about maritime disasters.

Appeal of the Genre

We may lack resources to provide a cohesive true adventure genre history, but that shouldn't stop us from asking questions: What has contributed to the long tradition of the great popularity of adventure narratives, both fictional and based in fact? Why do publishers (and often, bookstores) offer an interest category on the back of their books entitled simply "Adventure," and why are these books usually so popular among male readers? The answer may lie in the genre's appeal. Adventure books are often page-turners; readers respond to them in physical ways (flipping pages quickly, reading on the edges of their seats, quickened breathing, etc.) and often report that they "can't put them down." It seems safe to assume, therefore, that the primary appeal of adventure is story. Those titles listed in this chapter are primarily driven by story and also read extremely quickly (although not quickly enough for some readers). This may also explain the attraction of the genre to male readers; studies of young readers often indicate that if boys read at all, they tend to gravitate to adventure and thriller stories (not to mention comic books and graphic novels) that they can read quickly.

This habit may stay with them through adulthood. True adventure titles also tend to be skewed toward subjects that are popular among men (sports stories, James Bond-esque espionage and spy stories, and military history and war adventure).

Although the appeal of adventure can often be traced directly to its authors' mastery of storytelling and pacing, its stories of exploration, sports triumphs, survival, and intrigue do leave the door open for a secondary appeal to burst through—primarily in the form of the hero. Heroes, those legendary beings who overcome incredible odds both for their own goals and in the service of others, are represented in all their glory here. From Ernest Shackleton to climber Joe Simpson to the horse Seabiscuit, heroes often face what seem like insurmountable obstacles and overcome them by drawing on their inner stores of determination and perseverance, providing inspiring as well as exciting character portraits. Although he was referring to fictional adventure stories, John Cawelti may have provided insight into the popularity of nonfiction adventure tales when he said, "the appeal of this form is obvious. It presents a character, with whom the audience identifies, passing through the most frightening perils to achieve some triumph" (1976, 40).

True adventure titles allow us to have thrilling adventures and read about larger-than-life characters without putting ourselves in any danger. In this respect, they are quite similar to many titles in the travel genre, which allow us to vicariously experience adventure and travels in unfamiliar terrain without putting ourselves at risk. Likewise, there may also be some cross-genre appeal from true adventure to true crime, as true crime narratives are often character-driven tales to which we respond due to our curiosity about the most repellant of antiheroes.

Organization of the Chapter

The most recognizable true adventure titles (Krakauer's *Into Thin Air* and Kurson's *Shadow Divers*) can be found at the beginning of the chapter, in the "Survival and Disaster Stories" section. These are immediately followed by more subject-oriented groupings such as "Sports Adventures," "Cons and Card Games," "War Stories," and "Espionage and Intrigue." Rounding out the chapter's categories is the "Historical and Exploration Adventure" section, which includes popular and enduring narratives about exploring the unknown, such as the story of Shackleton's journey to Antarctica, but in which the focus is less on the page-turning suspense of the story than on evoking the spirit of expeditions and travels into the unknown, and overcoming hardships through strength and endurance rather than fast action. In these accounts, the authors also typically include more historical details than are found in other true adventure titles.

Survival and Disaster Stories

Survival and disaster stories constitute one of the most enduring and popular subgenres of adventure. Whether the disasters are natural (*The Perfect Storm*) or the result of daring and dangerous sporting choices (*Between a Rock and a Hard Place*), the vicarious thrills readers derive from these narratives can be likened to those that Michael Gannon speculates disaster fiction readers feel: "it's scary, it's horrendous, it's exciting . . . and it's not happening to me" (2004, 31).

Many of the titles listed below are classics well-known to librarians, as well as dependable best sellers. Books like Jon Krakauer's *Into Thin Air* and Piers Paul Read's *Alive* exhibit all the best features of story-driven writing. The stories are thrilling, told with brisk language and often in short chapters, and give the reader the best reason of all to keep reading the book until it's done—will the heroes, even if they're not all that likable, survive? These are the books that readers read, as Sven Birkerts describes, "with anxious intakes of breath and eyes zigzagging down the page" (1999, 118). Although these titles are distinguished by their use of story, librarians should not discount their characters as part of their appeal. Whether heroes whose inner strength and willingness to do whatever it takes to survive inspires readers, or antiheroes whose account of a disaster is compromised due to physical and environmental strain, they are very seldom dull.

Many of these titles are also noteworthy for their frequent adaptations into blockbuster films (*The Perfect Storm* and *Alive*) and their appearance on multiple booklists that promise "nonfiction books that read like fiction," and may be offered to entice adventure and other fiction readers into more areas of nonfiction reading.

Junger, Sebastian.

The Perfect Storm: A True Story of Men Against the Sea. New York: Norton, 1997 (New York: HarperTorch, 2000). 301pp. ISBN 006101351X.

Junger's investigative work, based on research and personal interviews, details the "perfect storm": the October 1991 confluence of several storm fronts into a powerful nor'easter at Gloucester, Massachusetts, in which the crew of the swordfishing vessel *Andrea Gail* was killed. Junger also intersperses the story of the *Andrea Gail* with that of other people and vessels threatened by the storm, and the courageous efforts of the Coast Guard to rescue them. Although there is some character exposition of the crew and their families and friends, Junger's real skill lies in building the suspense of the *Andrea Gail*'s fateful last voyage to the tragic climax of its demise.

Subjects: ALA Notable Books • Classics • Death and Dying • Investigative Stories • Maritime Disasters • Massachusetts • Oceans • Professions • Quick Reads • Weather

Now try: Douglas A. Campbell tells a similarly heartbreaking story in *The Sea's Bitter Harvest: Thirteen Deadly Days on the North Atlantic*, in which he narrates the 1999 sinking of four commercial fishing vessels. Todd Lewan's *The Last Run: A True Story of Rescue and Redemption on the Alaska Seas* also highlights the dramatic details of rescue attempts at sea, while R. A. Scotti's *Sudden Sea: The Great Hurricane of 1938* might appeal more to readers who are drawn to people's attempts to withstand the awful power of violent storms. Erik Larson's classic and best-selling title *Isaac's Storm: A Man, a Time, and the Deadliest Hurricane in History* may also appeal to these readers.

Krakauer, Jon.

Into Thin Air: A Personal Account of the Mt. Everest Disaster. New York: Villard, 1997 (New York: Anchor Books, 1999). 332pp. ISBN 0385494785.

In May 1996 two rival expedition companies promised to take their charges to the top of Mt. Everest, the peak in the Himalayas that was first scaled in May 1953. Although equipped with the most modern equipment and led by experienced guides, nine of the climbers, some from each group, died when they were caught in a sudden and vicious storm at the peak. Journalist Jon Krakauer, an experienced climber in his own right, was a member of one of the teams; he was along to write an article about it for *Outside* magazine. In addition to providing the details of the climb and the various problems inherent in high-altitude climbing (altitude sickness and nausea, headaches, and increased difficulty breathing without oxygen), Krakauer also paints a vivid picture of the differing and sometimes conflicting personalities of both the leaders of the expeditions and their many clients. He himself barely made it back to base camp alive, and one of the most harrowing sequences in the book is when he admits that, due to confusion brought on by altitude sickness, he reported seeing Andy Harris, one of his fellow climbers, much closer to camp and survival than later evidence would support.

> **Subjects:** Accidents • ALA Notable Books • Classics • Climbing and Hiking • Death and Dying • Friendships • Investigative Stories • Mountains • Quick Reads • Sports • Survival Stories • Weather

> **Now try:** The very same events are detailed by Anatoli Boukreev in his account of the tragic expedition in *The Climb*, which might prove to be interesting for its vastly different viewpoint for the reader who is fascinated by the story. Other titles by Krakauer may appeal to those readers who enjoy his firsthand accounts and unique prose style: *Eiger Dreams: Ventures Among Men and Mountains* is another sensational climbing story, and *Into the Wild* tells the story of driven individualist Christopher McCandless, the type of character Krakauer excels at exploring. In addition, patrons drawn to narratives about climbing Everest in particular will not be disappointed; one of the best available, and also mentioned by Krakauer in this book, is *Everest: The West Ridge*, by Thomas Hornbein; while the recent *Ghosts of Everest: The Search for Mallory and Irvine* by Jochen Hemmleb et al. describes the mysterious 1924 expedition of the title characters. Maria Coffey's *Fragile Edge: A Personal Portrait of Loss on Everest* might also prove interesting to readers who wonder how mountain climbers' tragic deaths affect those they leave behind.

Kurson, Robert.

Shadow Divers: The True Adventure of Two Americans Who Risked Everything to Solve One of the Last Mysteries of World War II. New York: Random House, 2004. 375pp. ISBN 0375508589.

Talk about a book that has everything: This extreme history adventure combines the thrilling world of deep-sea diving with a history mystery dating from World War II. In 1991 Bill Nagle and John Chatterton found a U-boat shipwrecked off the coast of New Jersey, and risking diving deeper than 200 feet (divers start to feel the adverse effects of the water pressure at sixty-six feet), they brought back artifacts from the wreck to try to identify it through extensive research. One of the artifacts, a knife inscribed with the name "Horenburg," provided their best clue, but even after finding it their research task was far from complete.

> **Subjects:** Classics • Diving • Exploration • Friendships • Germany • Maritime Disasters • Quick Reads • World War II

Now try: Two of the most compelling characters mentioned in Kurson's work are father and son Chris and Chrissy Rouse, the story of whose tragic deaths while diving on the U-boat is told in fellow diver Bernie Chowdhury's *The Last Dive: A Father and Son's Fatal Descent into the Ocean's Depths*. Kevin McMurray's *Deep Descent: Adventure and Death Diving the* Andrea Doria also provides a thrilling diving narrative centered on the 1956 shipwreck that has often been referred to as the "Mt. Everest of diving," and provides some overlap of characters in the form of divers Bill Nagle and John Chatterton. For those more interested in the World War II naval history aspect of Kurson's adventure, Andrew Williams's compelling *The Battle of the Atlantic: Hitler's Grey Wolves of the Sea and the Allies' Desperate Struggle to Defeat Them* might be a closely related and enjoyable read; other titles from the "Immersion History" subgenre of the history section, in which authors investigate historical mysteries or journeys, might also be viable suggestions.

Maclean, Norman.

Young Men and Fire. Chicago and London: University of Chicago Press, 1992. 301pp. ISBN 0226500624.

Known for his lyrical work of autobiographical fiction, *A River Runs Through It*, Maclean brings his unparalleled and redemptive use of language and character description to the tale of the fifteen firejumpers who battled the August 5, 1949, Mann Gulch forest fire, to which twelve of them lost their lives. Maclean worked for the Forest Service in Montana as a young man and uses his extensive knowledge of the area and the firejumpers' jobs to re-create the fire and the men's battle against it, as well as his own journey to revisit the sites of the fire and their deaths.

Subjects: Accidents • ALA Notable Books • Death and Dying • Fires • Investigative Stories • Montana • Professions

Now try: Maclean's son, John N. Maclean, has also produced two venerable works on wildfires and the fighters who combat them: *Fire on the Mountain: The True Story of the South Canyon Fire* and *Fire and Ashes: On the Front Lines of American Wildfire*. Although broader than wildfires in subject, Edward Goodman's thrilling *Fire: The 100 Most Devastating Fires Through the Ages and the Heroes Who Fought Them* might also prove to be a good companion read to Maclean's narrative. Jim Dwyer's and Kevin Flynn's *102 Minutes: The Untold Story of the Fight to Survive Inside the Twin Towers* also provides a compelling look at the tragedy of September 11, 2001 from the viewpoints of many of the day's survivors and rescue workers.

Ralston, Aron.

Between a Rock and a Hard Place. New York: Atria Books, 2004. 354pp. ISBN 0743492811.

While hiking by himself in the canyonlands of Utah, Ralston became pinned underneath a boulder in Blue John Canyon. Although only his arm was caught, Ralston was trapped in the canyon for days before he eventually made the decision to amputate his own arm in order to escape. The chapters tell the story of his ordeal, both mental and physical, while trapped, but are interspersed with other stories from his childhood and young adulthood, most of which divulge his history of and love for hiking and climbing. The book also includes several shocking photographs that the author was able to take himself, both before the amputation and after, while he was

1

hiking out of the canyon to safety. In addition, Ralston employs an epi-logue to tell the story of his recovery and eventual return to the sport he still loves.

> **Subjects:** Accidents • Climbing and Hiking • Memoirs • Sports • Survival Stories • Utah

> **Now try:** Joe Simpson's *Touching the Void: The True Story of One Man's Miraculous Survival* tells a similar story of overcoming astronomical odds to survive his own fall into a crevasse and being left for dead by his climbing partner, focusing on the emotional struggle within the author, and will also be familiar to viewers of public television, where a movie based on the book first aired in 2004. Another story of a climber's battle to survive being trapped and the eventual amputation of both his legs is Warren Macdonald's *A Test of Will: One Man's Extraordinary Story of Survival.* Both of these narratives also in-clude details of the story as told by the climber's sole companions, which adds a layer of complexity and nuance to the already vivid tales.

Read, Piers Paul.

Alive: The Story of the Andes Survivors. Philadelphia: Lippincott, 1974 (New York: HarperCollins, 2005). 352pp. ISBN 0060778660.

Journalist Read tells the true story of the Uruguayan rugby team that set out from Montevideo to Santiago, Chile, in October 1972, but crashed in the Andes Mountains en route. Read interviewed the survivors to compile the narrative of the harrowing and almost unbelievable seventy days spent in the harsh climate of the mountains, with very little protection from the elements or food, which followed the horrific plane crash that immediately killed nearly half of the passengers. Only sixteen of the youths survived, including Roberto Canessa and Nando Parrado, who eventually made their way down from the mountain and made contact with their rescuers. The fast-paced story is not free from disturbing details: During their ordeal, re-lationships among the few survivors were often strained, physical discom-forts were many, and they eventually had to resort to cannibalizing their deceased fellow passengers to survive.

> **Subjects:** Accidents • Cannibalism • Chile • Classics • Death and Dying • Flying • Friendships • Mountains • Survival Stories • Uruguay

> **Now try:** An edited collection of both fiction and nonfiction survival stories entitled *Survive: Stories of Castaways and Cannibals* may provide readers with more details on the subject than they need. Another superlative survival narrative centering on both physical difficulties and emotional relationships is *All Brave Sailors*, by J. Revell Carr, which tells the story of seven survi-vors of a British ship that was sunk by a German submarine in World War II. Peter Maas's story of a submarine rescue is told in *The Terrible Hours*.

Roberts, David.

The Mountain of My Fear. New York: Vanguard Press, 1968. 157pp. No ISBN.

Although less horrific than *Into Thin Air*, Roberts's account of his ascent, with three other climbers, of the previously untouched western face of Alaska's Mt. Huntington provides another look at the tenacious hold that mountain climbing exerts on its practitioners. Although this narrative also details a tragedy, it is not the focus, and if anything, this is more a pure and exhilarating adventure story.

> **Subjects:** Accidents • Alaska • Climbing and Hiking • Friendships • Memoirs • Mountains • Quick Reads • Sports • Survival Stories

> **Now try:** For readers interested in climbing narratives who might be willing to try a sampler approach, you may want to suggest *Epic: Stories of Survival from the World's Highest Peaks*, edited by Clint Willis and containing stories told by David Roberts and Jon Krakauer, among many others. George Willig's unforgettable story of how he planned to and did climb one of the World Trade Center towers, *Going It Alone*, although involving a completely different type of climbing, also captures the high-flying spirit of adventurers who are driven to climb things because they're there.

Sports Adventures

Stories of mental and physical endurance need not always involve surviving accidents or disasters, but can also display the mettle of the athlete, the underdog, and above all, the competitor. Although these sports narratives provide quickly paced, edge-of-the-seat reads, they are also appealing on the basis of their unique and often sympathetic characters. Unlike the characters in survival stories, whose personalities, foibles, and not always heroic motives are more fully explored, sports stories tend to expose only those aspects of their protagonists that contribute to their inspiring and heroic triumphs.

As shown by Laura Hillenbrand's award-winning and runaway (no pun intended) best seller *Seabiscuit*, publishers and information professionals should never minimize the appeal of a story that transcends its subject matter (and publishers, at least, are trying not to, as evidenced by the numerous horse-racing books rushed into print after the somewhat shocking success of Hillenbrand's book) due to the strength of its characters. The book also perfectly illustrates both an opportunity and a challenge for the intrepid readers' advisor; it's easy to find books on horse racing, but finding books that capture the essence of the triumph of the underdog is not so easy, proving once again that the truly proficient nonfiction advisor must go beyond offering titles with related subjects to offer read-alikes that address more intangible aspects of a book's appeal.

Coffey, Wayne.

The Boys of Winter: The Untold Story of a Coach, a Dream, and the 1980 U.S. Olympic Hockey Team. New York: Crown, 2005. 288pp. ISBN 0786274484.

My older brother still swears the 1980 victory of the American hockey team over the Russian team in the Lake Placid winter Olympics was one of the greatest moments of his life; that's a big feat for a game that wasn't even technically the gold medal game. Coffey outlines the pivotal game period by period and examines a number of the coaches and players from both sides who made this event a legend. The play-by-play narration of the game also makes for thrilling and evocative reading.

> **Subjects:** Friendships • Hockey • Olympics • Quick Reads • Soviet Union • Sports • Underdogs

Now try: Even more character portraits of the 1980 team can be found in John Powers's and Arthur Kaminsky's *One Goal: A Chronicle of the 1980 U.S. Olympic Hockey Team*. Jeff Pearlman's jubilant story, with equally jubilant subtitle, about a great year in baseball is recounted in *The Bad Guys Won! A Season of Brawling, Boozing, Bimbo-chasing, and Championship Baseball with Straw, Doc, Mookie, Nails, The Kid, and the Rest of the 1986 Mets, the Rowdiest Team Ever to Put on a New York Uniform—and Maybe the Best*. Baseball fans might also enjoy Michael Sokolove's poignant *The Ticket Out: Darryl Strawberry and the Boys of Crenshaw*, while football fans might find much to sustain them in Mark Krieger's favorably-reviewed biography of Joe Namath and his underdog New York Jets, simply titled *Namath*.

Feinstein, John.

A Season on the Brink: A Year with Bob Knight and the Indiana Hoosiers. New York: Macmillan, 1986 (Simon & Schuster, 1987). 337pp. ISBN 0671688774.

One of the best-selling sports books of all time, Feinstein's story takes as its main character the volatile coach Bobby Knight, and tells the inside story of the 1985–1986 season of the Indiana University Hoosiers. Love him or hate him, very few sports fans don't have an opinion one way or the other about Coach Knight, and Feinstein uses telling details and evocative storytelling to bring the season to life.

Subjects: Basketball • Classics • Indiana • Investigative Stories • Knight, Bobby • Sports

Now try: Tom Stanton's *Hank Aaron and the Home Run That Changed America* also tells a story based on a strong character and a volatile period in baseball history (the early 1970s), while Adrian Wojnarowski's *The Miracle of Saint Anthony: A Season with Coach Bob Hurley and Basketball's Most Improbable Dynasty* returns to the subject of basketball.

Hill, Lynn, with Greg Child.

Climbing Free: My Life in the Vertical World. New York: Norton, 2003. 270pp. ISBN 0393049817.

Hill opens her rock-climbing memoir with a shocking story of her seventy-two-foot free fall off a cliff in France, and she doesn't slow her pace much throughout the rest of her story. She does frequently detour from her action tales by relating stories from her childhood and relationships, but the overall thrust of the story is her drive to become one of the world's best climbers, complete with thrilling details of the physical challenges of the sport. The book also contains nearly enough fantastic color photographs to be considered an illustrated book.

Subjects: Climbing and Hiking • Family Relationships • Memoirs • Sports • Women Athletes

Now try: Hill's work is a compelling blend of biography and athletic adventure; readers who enjoy it might also be drawn to Lance Armstrong's *It's Not about the Bike: My Journey Back to Life*, which combines stories of his bicycling prowess with the details of his struggle with testicular cancer. Those readers more interested in the climbing aspect of Hill's narrative might also enjoy Heidi Howkins's *K2: One Woman's Quest for the Summit*, or the collection *The Greatest Climbing Stories Ever Told: Incredible Tales of Risk and Adventure*, edited by Bill Gutman. And, although the central event of Ruth Anne Kocour's climbing memoir, *Facing the Extreme: One Woman's Story of True Courage, Death-Defying Survival, and Her Quest for the Summit*, is a disaster, the book also speaks to the experience of being a female mountain climber.

Hillenbrand, Laura.

Seabiscuit: An American Legend. New York: Random House, 2001. 399pp. ISBN 0375502912.

Hillenbrand smoothly combines the histories of an ebullient owner, a solitary trainer, a tenacious jockey, and a little knobby-kneed racehorse to narrate how Seabiscuit became the long shot the nation needed to cheer for in the midst of the Great Depression. Although all of the characters are extensively described, the pull of the story is such that the reader will feel compelled to try to read it in one sitting.

Subjects: ALA Notable Books • American History • Animals • Book Sense Award Winners • Classics • Gambling • Great Depression • Horses • Sports • Underdogs

Now try: Those readers interested primarily in the horse racing aspects of the story might also enjoy *Native Dancer: The Grey Ghost, Hero of a Golden Age,* by John Eisenberg, about the most famous racer of the 1950s. Those most intrigued by the "beating the odds" style of winning employed by Seabiscuit might also enjoy Bill Crawford's *All American: The Rise and Fall of Jim Thorpe*, the inspiring but often heartbreaking story of the country's first hugely successful Native American athlete.

Patterson, Kevin.

The Water in Between: A Journey at Sea. New York: Nan A. Talese, 1999 (New York: Anchor Books, 2001). 289pp. ISBN 0385498845.

Trying to outrun his broken heart, Patterson took to sea with a newly found friend to sail to Tahiti, and in the process found more sailing danger and fellow travelers seeking the comforting anonymity of the ocean than he was really prepared for. Although the majority of the narrative focuses on his reactions to the process of sailing and traveling, as well as many references to the various books he spends his time reading and reflecting upon, the latter third of the book has a decidedly adventurous tone. (Patterson sails alone and in dangerous weather from the Hawaiian Islands to Victoria, British Columbia.)

Subjects: Friendships • Memoirs • Oceans • Pacific Islands • Sailing • Travel

Now try: Although set in the 1930s, Patrick Leigh Fermor's *Between the Woods and the Water: On Foot to Constantinople from the Hook of Holland* also relates a traveler's appreciation for both the social and solitary aspects of adventuring. Patterson also reflects on the works of many other travel writers (including Redmond O'Hanlon, Bruce Chatwin, and Eric Newby) in his text, and readers may be interested in tracking down some of those authors' popular works (many of which are annotated in the travel chapter).

Remnick, David.

King of the World: Muhammad Ali and the Rise of an American Hero. New York: Random House, 1998 (New York: Vintage Book, 1999). 326pp. ISBN 0375702296.

Based on the author's 1989 interviews with Muhammad Ali, the majority of this narrative is taken up with thrilling reenactments of Ali's defining victories. Remnick also investigates the creation of Ali's transformation from Cassius Clay to heavyweight champion Muhammad Ali, and describes his political and cultural impact, especially when compared with other famous fighters of the time (such as Floyd Patterson and Sonny Liston). The writing is immediate and personal and contributes to the brisk readability of the story.

> **Subjects:** ALA Notable Books • Ali, Muhammad • American History • Biographies • Boxing • Investigative Stories • Race Relations • Society • Sports

> **Now try:** Strange as it may seem to find a straightforward biography in the adventure section, Bill Zehme's zippy biography, *The Way You Wear Your Hat: Frank Sinatra and the Lost Art of Livin'*, similarly captures the air of excitement around its title character and may appeal to fans of Remnick's book, as well as to adventure readers who like punchy writing. Nick Tosches's *The Devil and Sonny Liston* might provide another perspective on the era in question and the clashing personalities within the boxing world.

Cons and Card Games

If survival stories sometimes yield characters with questionable motives and personality quirks, heist and con narratives offer characters that are often downright bad to the bone. Luckily for the reader, the characters in most of the titles below are so deliciously bad that they're good; no one can deny that Frank Abagnale, the famous con artist featured in the book and movie *Catch Me If You Can*, is a criminal, but he's an extremely titillating and likable criminal (or at least he is for his readers, if not for those law enforcement officials charged with apprehending him). In addition to their level of suspense, pacing, and fascinating characters, these books also often supply elements of humor and irony that are not readily apparent in other adventure titles. Their seamy undercurrents are emphasized by the fact that, for large chunks of each of these narratives, the "bad guys" (the con artists and card cheaters, to name just a few) win out over the good guys. They also constitute a handy collection of read-alikes for those titles listed in the "Murder's Not the Only Crime" section of the true crime chapter, which also reflect aspects of adventure storytelling, without the violence or graphic descriptions that characterize many other true crime works.

Abagnale, Frank W., with Stan Redding.

Catch Me If You Can: The Amazing True Story of the Youngest and Most Daring Con Man in the History of Fun and Profit! New York: Grosset & Dunlap, 1980 (New York: Broadway Books, 2002). 293pp. ISBN 0767905385.

Frank Abagnale left home at the age of sixteen, and after spending a week at gainful employment, promptly turned to writing bad checks, impersonating an airline pilot, a doctor, and a professor, among others. Abagnale's a believer in the maxim that the devil's in the details, and he provides them, right down to the skinny on how he falsified numerous documents, degrees, and ID cards. Less than five years after leaving home, Abagnale had amassed a personal fortune of more than $2 million, but he was eventually caught in France and jailed in Sweden.

Subjects: Con Artists • Memoirs • Professions • Quick Reads

Now try: Bill Mason's *Confessions of a Master Jewel Thief*, written with Lee Gruenfeld, is also enjoyable reading, and although it is not as quick a read, Mason's ability to live a "normal" life while simultaneously pulling off huge jewel thefts is always intriguing. Readers might also find David W. Maurer's *The Big Con: The Story of the Confidence Man*, first published in 1940, an entertaining look at some of the most lucrative scams of that era; likewise, Gary Mayer's sports memoir *Bookie: My Life in Disorganized Crime* might appeal to readers drawn to stories about less-than-legal activities.

McManus, James.

Positively Fifth Street: Murderers, Cheetahs, and Binion's World Series of Poker.
New York: Farrar, Straus & Giroux, 2003 (New York: Picador, 2004). 436pp. ISBN 0312422520.

What started as a $4,000 advance from *Harper's* magazine to write an article about women poker players eventually became McManus's stake as he won his way into a spot at the final table of the World Series of Poker. Although most of the book is told in the first person and details that accomplishment, it also makes journalistic forays into the connected stories of the murder trial of Sandy Murphy and Rick Tabish, charged in the death of Ted Bunion, the grandson of the contest's founder. Although not as fast-paced as many other adventure titles, the stomach-cramping anxiety the author displays when losing vast quantities of money will prove as exhilarating as actually gambling for the reader.

Subjects: Gambling • Homicide • Las Vegas • Marriage • Memoirs • Poker • True Crime

Now try: Andy Bellin's first-person narrative and huge best seller *Poker Nation: A High-Stakes, Low-Life Adventure into the Heart of a Gambling Country* would be a great recommendation for readers who don't want their poker stories to include any digressions from the game itself. An earlier book on the subject, Andres Martinez's *24/7: Living It Up and Doubling Down in the New Las Vegas*, is a very similar narrative to McManus's (right down to Martinez using his advance money as his blackjack and slots betting stake) and includes stories about Las Vegas that are less salacious than Ted Bunion's murder, but no less descriptive of the strange and heady atmosphere of the city. Readers who find the murder trial the most compelling part of McManus's narrative might also be interested in some titles in the true crime chapter, such as Kent Walker's *Son of a Grifter: The Twisted Tale of Sante and Kenny Kimes, the Most Notorious Con Artists in America*, or John Douglas's *The Cases That Haunt Us: From Jack the Ripper to JonBenet Ramsey, the FBI's Legendary Mindhunter Sheds Light on the Mysteries That Won't Go Away*.

Mezrich, Ben.

Bringing Down the House: The Inside Story of Six MIT Students Who Took Vegas for Millions. New York: Free Press, 2002 (2003). 257pp. ISBN 0743249992.

From 1994 to 1998, MIT student Kevin Lewis spent the majority of his time, when he wasn't attending classes, flying to Las Vegas and trying to "take" the casinos through a complicated blackjack card-counting scheme. Originally recruited into a group of students who took turns working the casinos by his friends and an ex-MIT professor, Lewis soon found himself the subject of massive surveillance, as well as a participant in several frightening back-room interrogations. Most of the action is related in flashbacks that are supported by Mezrich's interviews with Lewis and his associates, although there are brief interludes during which he himself attempts to board a plane while concealing the massive amount of cash needed to place bets, as well as carrying out other counting and betting maneuvers that the students did. The writing can be a bit overwrought at times but does serve to add to the feeling of slightly seedy exhilaration.

> **Subjects:** Con Artists • Friendships • Gambling • Investigative Stories • Las Vegas • Mathematics • True Crime

> **Now try:** Ben Mezrich's follow-up title, *Ugly Americans: The True Story of the Ivy League Cowboys Who Raided the Asian Market for Millions*, tells a similar tale of smart young things seeking to beat the system, this time the Asian financial markets. Nick Leeson's autobiography about corruption in those same markets, *Rogue Trader: How I Brought Down Barings Bank and Shook the Financial World* tells that story with more personal immediacy and a decadently enjoyable, conceited air.

Sinclair, David.

The Land That Never Was: Sir Gregor MacGregor and the Most Audacious Fraud in History. Cambridge, Mass.: Da Capo Press, 2003. 358pp. ISBN 0306813092.

The front cover copy of this truly audacious story tells it all: "a group of Scottish immigrants looking for a new life set sail for this tropical Eden. . . . The only catch was that it didn't exist." In brisk and suspenseful prose Sinclair tells the story of Sir MacGregor, who convinced numerous investors to buy land in the nonexistent South American country Poyais, which he supposedly governed. Once the colonists arrived where Poyais was supposed to be and were faced with blank wilderness and the hardships of life on the Mosquito Coast, they had no choice but to await rescue, which eventually came in the form of a British ship and crew. In this erudite combination of history and adventure, Sinclair provides a fascinating story of the most famous con of 1823.

> **Subjects:** Con Artists • Exploration • Nineteenth Century • Scotland • South America

> **Now try:** Jan Bondeson's *The Great Pretenders: The True Stories behind Famous Historical Mysteries*, which tells the stories behind multiple cases of disputed identity and impostors looking for fame, might appeal to readers who enjoy reading about the skills of impostors.

Zuckoff, Mitchell.

Ponzi's Scheme: The True Story of a Financial Legend. New York: Random House, 2005. 390pp. ISBN 1400060397.

Part biography, part true crime story, this is a tale of the roaring 1920s and one of its slickest characters, Charles Ponzi. Ponzi used his elaborate (and, he always maintained, legal) scheme, in which he used money from new investors to provide returns to earlier investors (also known as "robbing Peter to pay Paul"), to bilk numerous investors of their savings. Brought down only by newspaper reporters intent on exposing his scheme as fraud, Ponzi died a pauper, but his legend lives on.

Subjects: 1920s • American History • Biographies • Business • Con Artists • Finance • Great Depression • True Crime

Now try: Part heartrending biography, part history, part sports scandal, Eliot Asinof's *Eight Men Out: The Black Sox and the 1919 World Series* is a similarly eye-opening look at cons that are run out of a desire for financial security more than for a passing thrill. Fans of Ponzi's biography might also enjoy many of the titles found in the "Murder's Not the Only Crime" subgenre of the true crime chapter.

War Stories

War is a terrible and complex subject that is often dealt with under the auspices of history writing. However, as is recognized in the definition of adventure fiction, it is also a popular subject for true adventure narratives. In addition to their skill at telling suspenseful stories, which often include elements of their characters' will and ability to survive (*Black Hawk Down*, *We Die Alone*), these adventure authors also recognize that the characterization of the heroes of the following titles contributes to their books' appeal. Joyce Saricks's expanded definition of military adventure states, "Usually there is a group of men, although one emerges as the leader (not necessarily because of rank) when the difficult situation arises" (2001, 25). Readers are also often inspired by the bravery and camaraderie exhibited among military colleagues under especially difficult situations and in surroundings that are often unfamiliar to them.

Michael Gannon raises another important point when discussing the appeal of fictional military thrillers: "Although the main allure of this subgenre has to do with its battle sequences and the character of the hero—a common man thrown into uncommon circumstances—setting can also play an important role" (2004, 49). Much like history readers, readers of "War Stories" and military adventure can often be quite subject-oriented; fans of Hampton Sides's *Ghost Soldiers* may be more interested in other works about World War II than they are in Mark Bowden's *Black Hawk Down;* although both books are impressively researched works and tell similar stories of survival against the odds, they are about vastly different conflicts. Readers and readers' advisors should also consider the fact that many of the following titles sometimes contain subtle (as well as more overt) references to political beliefs and value systems, with which the reader may not agree.

Bowden, Mark.

Black Hawk Down: A Story of Modern War. New York: Atlantic Monthly Press, 1999 (New York: New American Library, 2002). 486pp. ISBN 0451205146.

Extensively researched and journalistically written, Bowden retells in the third person the disastrous 1993 mission in Somalia to arrest two of the political movement Habr Gidr's leaders. Eventually two massive Army helicopters, known as Black Hawks, were shot down, and eighteen Army Rangers lost their lives in the fight that followed. The story is told from the points of view of various members of the Ranger and Delta Task Force assigned to the mission, and it is a dense but still fast-moving story that the author obtained through numerous interviews, with both the participants of the lethal skirmish and their family members and Somali civilians who were in Mogadishu on that day.

Subjects: Africa • ALA Notable Books • American History • Classics • Friendships • Investigative Stories • Military • Somalia • War Stories

Now try: Harold G. Moore's and Joseph L. Galloway's tale from told both sides of a brutal battle in the Vietnam War, *We Were Soldiers Once . . . and Young*, has a similar gritty and suspenseful tone to Bowden's work, and both were eventually made into successful motion pictures.

Cain, Kenneth, Heidi Postlewait, and Andrew Thomson.

Emergency Sex and Other Desperate Measures: A True Story from Hell on Earth. New York: Hyperion, 2004. 308pp. ISBN 1401352014.

The subtitle of this trinity of interwoven narratives should more properly read "hells on earth," because in their different missions as UN peacekeepers, Cain, Postlewait, and Thomson describe a variety of ever more volatile global locations, from Cambodia and Haiti to Somalia and Rwanda. Each of the authors brings his or her own unique voice (the narrative is literally divided among the three of them, reporting from their various locations) and back story to the increasingly dangerous jobs, and the immediacy of their interactions with both the native populations they are trying to help and the difficult situations in which they are placed makes this a surprisingly suspenseful and fascinating story.

Subjects: Africa • Friendships • Haiti • Memoirs • United Nations • War Stories

Now try: Although some reviewers have reviled what they refer to as the authors' infantile focus on sex and drug stories within their disparate missions, their almost absurd honesty about their experiences in the midst of chaos might serve as an approachable stepping-stone to more compelling investigative works such as *We Wish to Inform You That Tomorrow We Will Be Killed with Our Families* or Tracy Kidder's *Mountains Beyond Mountains: The Quest of Dr. Paul Farmer*. Michael Kelly's ALA Notable Book *Martyr's Day: Chronicle of a Small War* may also appeal to these readers, as Kelly narrates his experiences during the first Persian Gulf War in a highly personal and immediate manner.

Clancy, Tom, with General Chuck Horner.

Every Man a Tiger. New York: Putnam, 1999 (New York: Berkley Books, 2000). 564pp. ISBN 0425172929.

Although better known for his military and adventure fiction, Clancy has also collaborated with a number of military personnel to produce books such as this one, which is an insider's view of Desert Shield and Desert Storm, as told by retired General Chuck Horner, commander of the U.S. and allied air forces in the conflicts. The general's story is told in the present tense, and displays all of Clancy's proficiency with technical description, as well as historical analysis regarding other conflicts, most notably the Vietnam War.

> **Subjects:** Biographies • Horner, Chuck • Military • Persian Gulf War • War Stories
>
> **Now try:** Clancy now has a series of nonfiction works in his "commander" series; two others that readers who enjoy this book might like are *Shadow Warriors: Inside the Special Forces* and *Into the Storm: A Study in Command.* Of course, readers who enjoy the technical and strategic detail of these volumes will most likely also be drawn to Clancy's numerous works of military fiction.

Howarth, David.

We Die Alone: A World War II Epic of Escape and Endurance. New York: Macmillan, 1955 (New York: Lyons Press, 1999). 231pp. ISBN 1558219730.

In 1943 a group of twelve Norwegians set sail from the Shetland Islands, bound for Norway with the objective of teaching their fellow Norwegians how to engage in sabotage against Germany. Although the group arrived safely in Norway, they were betrayed to the Germans by a shopkeeper there, and the majority were killed in battle as they tried to make their way back to their small oceangoing craft. Jan Baalsrud, the sole survivor of the fight, escaped and fled into the mountains, where he was concealed from the enemy by a succession of defiant local villagers. The narrative is chronological but includes flashbacks to provide character development for Baalsrud. Although the book is fifty years old and is more slowly paced than much modern writing, there are several harrowing episodes that will keep readers turning pages.

> **Subjects:** Community Life • Norway • Survival Stories • War Stories • World War II
>
> **Now try:** Slavomir Rawicz's *The Long Walk: The True Story of a Trek to Freedom* tells the author's story of escaping from a Soviet labor camp in 1941, during the course of which he and his fellow escapees traveled thousands of miles, through Siberia, Mongolia, and the Gobi Desert, to finally reach India. Ben Macintyre's tale of wartime survival and village relationships, *The Englishman's Daughter: A True Story of Love and Betrayal in World War I,* tells the story of a band of British soldiers who were trapped behind German lines and hidden by the residents of a small French village. One of the soldiers fell in love with and fathered the child of one of the village's most beautiful residents, only to eventually be betrayed to and executed by the Germans.

Mason, Robert.

Chickenhawk. New York: Penguin Books, 1984. 476pp. ISBN 0140072187.

Mason's memoir of his career as a helicopter pilot in the Vietnam War, from 1965 to 1966, is as unflinchingly honest and adrenaline-driven an account of his 1000 plus combat missions as the reader is likely to find. The author's language is straightforward and often quite technical in its description of the helicopters and the missions, but the parts of the narrative that describe his post-war interactions with his wife and son, as well as with other civilians, is no less compelling when told in the same undecorated prose.

Subjects: American History • Classics • Epic Reads • Family Relationships • Flying • Memoirs • Mental Health • Military • Vietnam War • War Stories

Now try: Mason's sequel, *Chickenhawk: Back in the World*, continues the story and is a must-read for anyone who is struck by this book. Much of Tim O'Brien's fiction, particularly books such as *The Things They Carried* or *In the Lake of the Woods*, employs prose of the same honest type, with the same backdrop of the Vietnam War. Also, although *Library Journal* pointed out in its review that some of the details are so fantastic they inspire disbelief, readers interested in the aerial side of the Vietnam War might also find themselves drawn to Dennis Marviscin's adrenalin-charged account (as written by Jerold Greenfield) of his ordeal, *Maverick: The Personal War of a Vietnam Cobra Pilot*.

Sides, Hampton.

Ghost Soldiers: The Forgotten Epic Story of World War II's Most Dramatic Mission. New York: Doubleday, 2001 (New York: Anchor Books, 2002). 344pp. ISBN 038549565X.

Sides relates the little-told story of the hundreds of American and British POWs who were held in a Japanese prison in the Philippines under appalling conditions, as well as the story of the army Rangers and Filipino forces, led by officer Henry Mucci, who marched steadfastly into what they believed might be a significant Japanese force, to save them. Reminiscent of Mark Bowden's writing in his extreme attention to detail, Sides doesn't flinch from recounting the most horrible of the survivors' stories, or from saluting the heroism of their struggle or that of the men who rescued them.

Subjects: American History • Investigative Stories • Military • Philippines • Prisons • War Stories • World War II

Now try: Tales of extreme acts of heroism in war are readily available, although more so for World War II than any other conflict; readers may want to consider any of the following titles for related reading on World War II: *In Harm's Way: The Sinking of the USS* Indianapolis *and the Extraordinary Story of Its Survivors* by Doug Stanton; James Bradley's *Flags of Our Fathers: Heroes of Iwo Jima* or *Flyboys: A True Story of Courage*; Stephen Ambrose's *D-Day, June 6, 1944: The Climactic Battle of World War II;* Alex Kershaw's *The Bedford Boys: One American Town's Ultimate D-Day Sacrifice;* Bill Sloan's *Given Up for Dead: America's Heroic Stand at Wake Island;* or Ron Steinman's *The Soldiers' Story: Vietnam in Their Own Words*.

Intrigue and Espionage

If the continuing marketability of James Bond films is any indication, readers who feared that the end of the Cold War would mean the end of intrigue and espionage fiction worried in vain. The same is true for nonfiction. It's true that many of the

books annotated in this subgenre date from Cold War events or earlier, but readers looking for more current tales about interrogation and CIA techniques need only visit the "Secret Histories" section in the history chapter for further recommendations. When one says "intrigue," however, images of the Communist flag and KGB spies may still predominate in readers' minds.

These titles continue to appeal to readers, based primarily on the pace of the author's writing and on the suspense created by the storytelling, as well as the added bonus of the typical "top secret" tone of surreptitiousness. However, the roles of the hero and the antihero (defined by *Merriam-Webster's Collegiate Dictionary* (11th ed.) as the protagonist who is conspicuously lacking in heroic qualities) are also strong here; if you don't like the dictionary definition, think of these books as focusing on characters that readers love to root *against*. Even in heroic tales like Hélène Deschamps's autobiography *Spyglass*, there is no shortage of enemies.

Like travel books, these stories often take place at least partially in foreign and exotic locales, which sometimes offer a third appeal factor of setting to their readers. As Gannon has pointed out about espionage novels, these true intrigue stories also offer readers the chance to "visit exotic places, be privy to secrets, jump from one narrow escape to another, and still feel secure that it was all for the good of society" (2004, 1).

Deschamps, Hélène.

Spyglass: An Autobiography. New York: Henry Holt, 1995. 308pp. ISBN 0805035362.

> The thrilling first-person narrative of a woman who volunteered to serve the French Resistance after watching the Germans march into Paris in 1940, this personal story is a female action narrative that blends history and action to provide a story of underground information gathering in the World War II era. Deschamps also candidly relates the details of her relationships with many other members of both the Resistance and the American OSS (precursor to the CIA), particularly her friendship with agent Jacqueline Bouquier, who was killed in the course of their activities.

> > **Subjects:** Espionage • France • Friendships • Love Affairs • Memoirs • Women's Contributions • World War II

> > **Now try:** Richard Skinner's novel *The Red Dancer: The Life and Times of Mata Hari*, is a fictionalized account of another bold young woman, Margaretha Zelle, who would become better known to history as the female spy Mata Hari; her story is also told in the nonfiction account *Mata Hari: The True Story*, by Russell Warren Howe. Although she spent most of her career working for the KGB, readers drawn to tales about women involved in espionage may find the biography *Clever Girl: Elizabeth Bentley, the Spy Who Ushered in the McCarthy Era*, written by Lauren Kessler, a worthwhile read.

Earley, Pete.

Family of Spies: Inside the John Walker Spy Ring. New York: Bantam Books, 1988. 385pp. ISBN 0553052837.

> In short, action- and suspense-filled chapters, Earley details the exploits of one of the most successful spy rings in history: that of John Anthony Walker Jr. and his son, brother, and best friend. Walker initiated his activities by simply walking into the Soviet Embassy in Washington, D.C., and offering to sell the Soviets naval se-

crets (which he was privy to as an officer); he has always maintained that he was motivated solely by his desire for money for himself and his family. A reporter with *The Washington Post*, Earley based his narrative on his hundreds of interviews with the entire family and extensive research, all of which he weaves into his quickly paced story.

> **Subjects:** Cold War • Espionage • Family Relationships • Investigative Stories • Soviet Union • Walker, John

> **Now try:** Although not as action-oriented, Verne Newton's *The Cambridge Spies: The Untold Story of Maclean, Philby, and Burgess in America* tells the story of another infamous group of spies, who were recruited by the Soviet Union while they attended Cambridge, all of whom eventually betrayed many American and British secrets to their communist bosses. Other famous spy stories (primarily fictional ones) are explored in Frederick Hitz's *The Great Game: The Myth and Reality of Espionage* (annotated in the "Making Sense . . ." chapter). John Banville's novel *The Untouchable* might also appeal to readers who enjoy a good work of espionage; it is based on the exploits of Cambridge spy Anthony Blunt.

Lindsey, Robert.

The Falcon and the Snowman: A True Story of Friendship and Espionage.
New York: Simon & Schuster, 1979 (Guilford, Conn.: Lyons Press, 2002). 359pp. ISBN 1585745022.

Why would two affluent and well-educated young men who had everything, including a strong friendship with each other, turn to a life of espionage and collusion with the Soviet Union? That's the central question author Lindsey seeks to answer in his story of the lives and activities of Christopher Boyce (the Falcon) and Andrew Daulton Lee (the Snowman). Boyce used his position as an employee of an aerospace government contractor to obtain spy satellite information, apparently because he didn't believe the government was living up to his ideals; he passed that information to Lee, who was often the courier who handed the information to his Russian contacts for more capitalistic reasons. Lindsey's narrative is quickly paced but factual in tone and conveys the excitement and illicit nature of such activities.

> **Subjects:** Best Fact Crime Edgar Award Winners • Biographies • Cold War • Espionage • Friendships • Investigative Stories • Quick Reads • Soviet Union

> **Now try:** Peter Maas's slim and action-packed narrative of the activities of convicted spy Aldrich Ames, *Killer Spy: The Inside Story of the FBI's Pursuit and Capture of Aldrich Ames, America's Deadliest Spy*, is as immediate as Lindsey's account of Boyce's and Lee's espionage activities but is even more horrific in its implications: Ames was responsible for the execution of several KGB officers who were colluding with CIA operatives. Likewise, Ronald Kessler's story about Glenn Michael Souther, *The Spy in the Russian Club*, relates the chilling details of Souther's career as an American in the employ of the KGB. Readers who are drawn to these suspenseful true crime accounts might also enjoy the novels of Len Deighton, Ian Fleming, or John Le Carré, listed in the "Fiction Read-Alikes" section of this chapter.

O'Donnell, Patrick K.

Operatives, Spies, and Saboteurs: The Unknown Story of the Men and Women of WWII's OSS. New York: Free Press, 2004. 384pp. ISBN 074323572X.

Although closer in writing style to an oral history than to true adventure, Patrick K. O'Donnell's collection of firsthand stories from the American OSS (the precursor to the CIA) operatives during World War II is also an exciting and action-packed compilation of intrigue stories. There is no shortage of fascinating character portraits here, either; from convicted criminals recruited to burgle foreign embassies to operatives who used their sex appeal to gather information, O'Donnell allows a variety of history's nearly forgotten espionage agents to tell their stories.

Subjects: Biographies • Espionage • Oral Histories • World War II

Now try: Although his narrative focuses more on courtroom drama than on actual spy activities, Michael Dobbs's *Saboteurs: The Nazi Raid on America* does relate many chilling details of the Nazi plan to land multiple saboteurs on the East Coast (via U-boats), with the goal of wreaking havoc on American munitions plants; had it not been for two of the saboteurs deciding to turn themselves in and report on their colleagues, the plan might have gone off without a hitch. Former head of Soviet intelligence operations in the United States and handler of Julius Rosenberg, Alexander Feklisov has provided an unprecedented look behind the scenes of Cold War espionage, mixed with a healthy dose of history, in his memoir, *The Man Behind the Rosenbergs.*

Historical and Exploration Adventure

Rounding out this chapter is another familiar and popular subgenre for adventure readers, which lists, as Helen Whybrow did in her collection of exploration and journey narratives, both "explorations of those sent out by governments or institutions on a quest for worldly knowledge," and "engrossing travelogues that embody the personal quest at its finest" (2003, 19–20). I tend to think of the following stories as true ones that provide not only an edge-of-the-seat reading experience but also setting and details framed in different historical times. While Caroline Alexander's *The* Endurance: *Shackleton's Legendary Antarctic Expedition* is every bit as thrilling as Krakauer's more current *Into Thin Air*, there's no escaping the fact that it offers much more in the way of historical detail and writing technique and is subsequently a meatier (and lengthier) reading experience. The experience of reading these historical and slightly more sedate adventure stories might also differ from that of reading other, more suspenseful, adventure titles, in that readers generally know the final outcome of many of these tales.

In their use of historical details, background, and framing, these books correspond to titles suggested in the "Immersion History" subgenre of the history chapter; in addition to sharing the same author, Mark Honigsbaum's *Valverde's Gold* (below) and *The Fever Trail* (in the history chapter) both combine the author's present-day experiences while researching history with their telling of the real historical story. Likewise, many of these stories describe journeys, which makes them suitable read-alikes for many titles from the travel chapter; Nicholas Clapp's *The Road to Ubar* (below) and Tahir Shah's *In Search of King Solomon's Mines* (in the travel chapter) differ only in the authors' stated destinations.

Alexander, Caroline.

The Endurance: Shackleton's Legendary Antarctic Expedition. New York: Knopf, 1998. 211pp. ISBN 0375404031.

Alexander's gripping narrative tells the story of Ernest Shackleton's famous expedition to the Antarctic in 1914. Twenty months after their ship, the *Endurance*, became trapped in and then destroyed by ice, Shackleton and his fellow adventurers and crew members were rescued by the tug *Yelcho*; the majority of Alexander's story relates their attempts to save themselves by taking to the ocean in smaller boats taken from the *Endurance*, and their ingenuity in keeping themselves alive and sane during the entire ordeal.

> **Subjects:** Arctic Regions • Exploration • Illustrated Books • Maritime Disasters • Shackleton, Ernest • Survival Stories

> **Now try:** The historical details in Alexander's gripping books are surpassed only by her vivid descriptions of the actions of people caught in dire straights; readers who enjoy this title might also be drawn to her more recent title, *The Bounty: The True Story of the Mutiny on the Bounty*. Readers interested in survival stories at the poles but who would like a bit shorter work might enjoy Valerian Albanov's 200-page *In the Land of White Death: An Epic Story of Survival in the Siberian Arctic*, a firsthand account of his experience as a Russian navigator whose ship, the *Saint Anna*, became trapped in Arctic ice while on an expedition in 1912. A more recent tale of being "trapped on the ice" is told by Jerri Nielsen (with Maryanne Vollers) in her best-selling memoir *Ice Bound: A Doctor's Incredible Battle for Survival at the South Pole*, an account of her self-treatment for aggressive breast cancer, undertaken at the South Pole because she could not be evacuated for treatment during the winter months' brutal weather.

Bergreen, Laurence.

Over the Edge of the World: Magellan's Terrifying Circumnavigation of the Globe. New York: William Morrow, 2003. 458pp. ISBN 0066211735.

Bergreen fleshes out the wild story of the dangerous and daring journey of Ferdinand Magellan and his shipmates when, in 1519, they set out to try to find an ocean route to the Spice Islands. The author also places the perilous journey in historical and interpersonal contexts, describing the political climate and figures of the time, as well as Magellan's own complex nature, all of which contributed to the adventures and eventual success (but at a terrible price) of his mission and the naming of the Strait of Magellan at the southern tip of South America.

> **Subjects:** Biographies • Epic Reads • Exploration • Magellan, Ferdinand • Sixteenth Century • South America

> **Now try:** Although it is about a much less famous explorer, Ken McGoogan's *Ancient Mariner: The Arctic Adventures of Samuel Hearne, the Sailor Who Inspired Coleridge's Masterpiece* is less about the poem than it is about the lengthy travels of Samuel Hearne, and it is rich with historical detail.

Erickson, Carolly.

The Girl from Botany Bay. Hoboken, N.J.: John Wiley, 2005. 234pp. ISBN 0471271403.

Erickson tells the story of hardscrabble and indomitable Mary Broad, who was convicted of highway robbery in England in 1786, and her subsequent voyage along with other convicts to a new colony in Australia. Once there, Mary married another convict (in a move to gain more prestige and escape enforced prostitution) and eventually joined him and seven others in a successful escape attempt (sailing over 3,600 miles of open ocean); the author vividly describes the hardships of all Mary's ocean voyages. Eventually the convict was caught and returned to England, where her incredible life continued and the famous author James Boswell became her patron. This is a fast-paced biography of a fascinating woman.

> **Subjects:** Australia • Biographies • Eighteenth Century • Exploration • Marriage • Prisons • Quick Reads • Women Travelers

> **Now try:** Siân Rees's superlative debut, *The Floating Brothel: The Extraordinary True Story of an Eighteenth-Century Ship and Its Cargo of Female Convicts,* is similar to Erickson's work in both subject matter and a slight tone of admiration for the wealth of hardships women in the eighteenth century could endure. Erickson is also a prolific producer of biographies of historic female figures, and many of them are written with the same gripping narrative style: *Josephine: A Life of the Empress* and *Bloody Mary* are about women who were higher in social status than Mary Broad but were nevertheless strong and adventurous individuals in societies that didn't afford them many opportunities.

Fleming, Fergus.

Barrow's Boys: The Original Extreme Adventurers. New York: Atlantic Monthly Press, 1998. 489pp. ISBN 0871138042.

Great Britain's boom in naval exploration was largely supported in the early nineteenth century by John Barrow, the Second Secretary of the British Admiralty. Detailing the many expeditions he supported, to locations as varied as the Arctic, Antarctica, and Africa, this rather leisurely paced narrative might appeal to those readers who like a liberal dose of historical research with their tales of adventure.

> **Subjects:** Africa • ALA Notable Books • Arctic Regions • Barrow, John • England • Epic Reads • Exploration • Nineteenth Century

> **Now try:** Fleming's subsequent title about exploration, *Ninety Degrees North: The Quest for the North Pole*, is also an impressively researched chronicle of North Pole explorers, including the most famous ones: Robert Peary, Frederick Cook, Gregoriy Sedov, Roald Amundsen, Lincoln Ellsworth, and Robert Evelyn Byrd. Nathaniel Philbrick's ALA Notable Book *Sea of Glory: America's Voyage of Discovery* is also an impressively researched history of the 1838 U.S. Exploring Expedition, also paced more slowly than many adventure titles.

Honigsbaum, Mark.

Valverde's Gold: In Search of the Last Great Inca Treasure. New York: Farrar, Straus & Giroux, 2004. 348pp. ISBN 0374191700.

Honigsbaum combines the historical tale of the Spanish abduction of the Inca king Atahualpa in 1533, and the raising by his subjects of the gold to ransom him, with the tale of two British explorers who actually found the trove in 1887 but died before they could return to it. Although the details of their historical stories include elements of adventure, the last chapter, following Honigsbaum's own excursion into Ecuador to try to find the treasure, is the most exciting.

> **Subjects:** Ecuador • Exploration • Incas • Investigative Stories • Nineteenth Century • Travel

> **Now try:** Catherine Scott-Clark and Adrian Levy also offer a more slowly paced "history mystery" involving lost treasure in *The Amber Room: The Fate of the World's Greatest Lost Treasure*. Honigsbaum's earlier work, *The Fever Trail: In Search of the Cure for Malaria*, also provides a dose of adventure along with its history as the author embarked on his own journey to find quinine, the only treatment for the disease.

Kinder, Gary.

Ship of Gold in the Deep Blue Sea. New York: Atlantic Monthly Press, 1998 (New York: Vintage Books, 1999). 536pp. ISBN 0375703373.

Impressively researched but nevertheless written with novelistic suspense and character development, Kinder's book relates, in alternating chapters, the tragic and prolonged sinking of the steamer ship the *Central American* and the gargantuan efforts undertaken by an undersea salvage team, led by an engineer named Tommy Thompson, to find and excavate the wreck in the 1980s. When the *Central American* sank in a hurricane off the coast of South Carolina in 1857, it took nearly 500 passengers and crew, as well as millions of dollars in California gold rush gold, along with it; the immediate and tragic details of its sinking alone (not to mention the incredible determination of Thompson and his crew) make this narrative a true page-turner.

> **Subjects:** ALA Notable Books • American History • Diving • Epic Reads • Exploration • Maritime Disasters • Nineteenth Century • Survival Stories

> **Now try:** Those readers fascinated by the science of diving technology might enjoy looking through the illustrated book *The History of Shipwrecks* by Angus Konstam, which details how divers find wrecks and excavate them and includes a few of the most famous sinking stories.

Taylor, Stephen.

Caliban's Shore: The Wreck of the Grosvenor *and the Strange Fate of Her Survivors.* New York: Norton, 2004. 288pp. ISBN 0393050858.

Although slightly more slowly paced (and heavier in historical detail) than most adventure nonfiction, this story of the shipwreck of the *Grosvenor* and the subsequent journey of her thirteen survivors holds it own among survival narratives. In 1782 the ship ran aground on the South African coast, killing most of its English passengers en route from India to England, and stranding the remaining thirteen far away from any European settlements. The survivors could not agree who would lead them or how they would make their way to safety, and they were often approached by the tribal natives, whom they viewed as "savages," with unfortunate results. Some eventually made it to safety, even if it was a kind different than they had originally anticipated: years later, their descendants were found living among the Pondo and other tribes with whom they interacted.

> **Subjects:** Africa • Anthropology • Eighteenth Century • England • Maritime Disasters • Survival Stories

> **Now try:** Less than forty years later, in 1815, the American vessel *Commerce* also sank off the coast of Africa, and the survivors were first confronted by native peoples and then driven across the Sahara in search of safety; Dean King relates that story masterfully in his *Skeletons on the Zahara: A True Story of Survival*. David Roberts's fascinating tale of four Russians who survived for more than six years on a tiny Arctic island, on which they were shipwrecked in 1743, is told in *Four against the Arctic: Shipwrecked for Six Years at the Top of the World;* it might appeal to readers who enjoy historical survival stories.

Consider Starting With . . .

These are some of the tried and true titles that most fans of adventure stories, as well as readers new to the genre, are likely to enjoy:

> Abagnale, Frank, with Stan Redding. *Catch Me If You Can: The Amazing True Story of the Youngest and Most Daring Con Man in the History of Fun and Profit!*

> Hillenbrand, Laura. *Seabiscuit: An American Legend.*

> Howarth, David. *We Die Alone: A World War II Epic of Escape and Endurance.*

> Krakauer, Jon. *Into Thin Air: A Personal Account of the Mt. Everest Disaster.*

> Lindsey, Robert. *The Falcon and the Snowman: A True Story of Friendship and Espionage.*

> Read, Piers Paul. *Alive: The Story of the Andes Survivors.*

> Taylor, Stephen. *Caliban's Shore: The Wreck of the* Grosvenor *and the Strange Fate of Her Survivors.*

Fiction Read-Alikes

- **Brown, Dale.** Himself a former Air Force pilot, Brown is known for his military adventures, many of which feature Major General Patrick McLanahan and are often quite heavy on technical details. *Flight of the Old Dog* and *Silver Tower* are his first two books; *Plan of Attack* and *Air Battle Force* are two of his most recent.

- **Clancy, Tom.** Ever since the runaway success of Clancy's first adventure and suspense novel, *The Hunt for Red October* (which was initially rejected by all major publishers and eventually published by the Naval Institute Press), he has really needed no introduction or description as an adventure novelist. His "techno-thrillers" also lean heavily on military subjects, although many of his stories also involve espionage; his most popular recurring character, Jack Ryan, a former Marine, works for the CIA. He has lent his name to several series, including Net Force, Op-Center, and Power Plays, and his most recent novels include *Red Rabbit* and *The Bear and the Dragon*.

- **Cornwell, Bernard.** Combining historical fiction with adventure, Cornwell is best known for his novels set in the early 1800s and featuring recurring character and British officer Richard Sharpe. As many war stories are, Cornwell's can be somewhat graphic, and there is less emphasis on dialogue than on nonstop action in his books. The first in the Sharpe series was *Sharpe's Eagle: Richard Sharpe and the Talavera Campaign* (1981); two of the most recent are *Sharpe's Havoc* and *Sharpe's Escape*. He has recently also started two new series, one of which is set in the American Civil War and starts with *Rebel* (the <u>Starbuck chronicles</u>); the other focuses on King Arthur (the <u>Warlord series</u>) and begins with *The Winter King*.

- **Cussler, Clive.** Not only does Cussler write exploration and underwater adventure tales featuring his most popular character, Dirk Pitt, he also lives the lifestyle; he has funded and led many expeditions to study shipwrecks and lost aircraft. His first Dirk Pitt novel was *The Mediterranean Caper;* the most recent are *Black Wind* (2004) and *Trojan Odyssey* (2003). Previously an advertising copywriter, he is known for his short and catchy prose style more than for his dialogue or character development.

- **DeMille, Nelson.** DeMille's books include a variety of settings and characters, but all are fast-paced stories that tell military-based suspense stories (*Word of Honor* and *The General's Daughter*), or more straightforward mystery narratives (*Plum Island*) and governmental conspiracy stories (*Night Fall*).

- **Flynn, Vince.** In his novels, such as *Executive Power* and *The Third Option,* Flynn tells politically and technically charged espionage stories, many of which feature CIA operative Mitch Rapp. All of the reader reviewers at Amazon.com attest to the page-turning appeal of Flynn's fast-paced stories.

- **Follett, Ken.** Critics often note that Follett's primary skill is combining historical stories and detail with action-filled situations and often well-developed character relationships. *The Third Twin*, a thriller that examines the nature versus nurture debate, features a female protagonist; a more recent title, *Jackdaws*, also features strong female characters but in the more stereotypical adventure setting of World War II.

- **Forester, C. S.** An entire generation has recently rediscovered the seafaring adventures of Forester's famous British naval officer Horatio Hornblower, thanks to the popularity of the A&E Network's recent miniseries of the same name. Set in the same time period of the Napoleonic War as Bernard Cornwell's Richard Sharpe books, Forester's stories offer both naval and battle action; the series opens with, in order, *Beat to Quarters*, *Ship of the Line*, and *Flying Colours*.

- **Furst, Alan.** Quite possibly the most familiar book at the circulation desk (it's checked in and out constantly) is Furst's recent *Dark Voyage*, a literary and historical thriller set during World War II. Furst is also the author of such adventure classics as *Dark Star* (set in the 1930s Soviet Union) and *Red Gold*, set in Nazi-occupied Paris in 1940 and featuring a depressed protagonist who eventually finds the strength to organize resistance.

- **Griffin, W. E. B.** Griffin is a hugely prolific author and offers numerous military adventure series, such as his Brotherhood of War series (which began with *The Lieutenants* in 1983; two of the most recent volumes in the series are *Retreat, Hell* [2004] and *Under Fire* [2002]). He has also written a series called Badge of Honor, based on the officers of the Philadelphia Police Department; that series started with *Men in Blue* (1988), *Special Operations* (1989), and *The Victim* (1991).

- **Higgins, Jack.** Higgins (real name Harry Patterson) has written more than sixty thriller and adventure novels; he is best known for those set in World War II that mix biographical fact with fiction, such as his best seller *The Eagle Has Landed*, which follows a group of Nazi paratroopers who landed in Britain in 1943 to kidnap Winston Churchill. His latest works are *Dark Justice* (2004), *Bad Company* (2003), and *Midnight Runner* (2002).

- **Le Carré, John.** Le Carré infuses his espionage thrillers with a literary sensibility and a slightly more reflective pace and focus on his characters than many adventure writers; those readers being introduced to his works may want to start with some of his classics, such as *The Spy Who Came in from the Cold*; *Tinker, Tailor, Soldier, Spy*; *The Russia House*; or *The Tailor of Panama*.

- **Ludlum, Robert.** Matt Damon has introduced Ludlum's suspenseful spy stories to a whole new audience; readers may want to start with his classic *The Bourne Identity* (followed by *The Bourne Supremacy* and *The Bourne Ultimatum*) or move on to his other and less well-known (but still thrilling) Covert-One series, which began with *The Hades Factor* (2000) and *The Cassandra Compact* (2001), and all of which are coauthored with other writers.

- **Smith, Wilbur.** Wilbur is known for what his fans describe as "swashbuckling adventure novels," many of which are set in Africa. His first series, about European colonialism in Zimbabwe, comprises the three novels *A Falcon Flies*, *Men of Men*, and *The Angels Weep*; another popular series of his is set in ancient Egypt and is composed of the novels *River God*, *The Seventh Scroll*, and *Warlock*.

Further Reading

"**Adventure Travel.**" *Bookmarks* (May/June 2005): 10–13.

> *Bookmarks* regularly features "What One Book: Expert Recommendations on a Selected Topic," and the annotated list of adventure travel titles includes both recent and older titles, as well as a variety of locations and writing styles.

The Best American Sports Writing (series). Boston: Houghton Mifflin, 1991–present.

> Compiled by numerous guest editors, from David Halberstam (1991) to George Plimpton (1997) to Dick Schaap (2000) to Buzz Bissinger (2003; he's best known as the author of *Friday Night Lights*), this series provides more information about the personal characteristics of the athletes than details about their sports; as such, it provides an interesting starting place for those librarians looking for typically triumphant or underdog sports stories and the magazines from which they came. As usual, most of the authors included have at least one book-length work of sports journalism to their name.

***The Best of* Outside: *The First 20 Years*. New York: Villard, 1997. 420pp. ISBN 0375500642.**

Some of the most famous books in the genre originally started as articles in *Outside* magazine, and this anthology offers a veritable who's who of adventure writers, from Tim Cahill and Jon Krakauer to Sebastian Junger and Jim Harrison. Thirty-one stories are included. ranging in subject from bullfighting to meeting up with grizzly bears, and all share masterful and quickly paced narrative writing.

The Greatest [   ] Stories Ever Told. Guilford, Conn.: Lyons Press.

An imprint of the Globe Pequot Press, the Lyons Press has an impressive series of outdoor, sporting, and adventure anthologies with titles that all follow the pattern above. Adventure readers may enjoy the books on their own merit; librarians might like to peruse them to familiarize themselves with some of the most popular stories and authors in the genre. Titles include but are not limited to *Hunting*, *Adventure*, *Boxing*, *Climbing*, *Cowboy*, *Disaster*, *Gambling*, *Hunting*, *Sailing*, and *War*.

Whybrow, Helen, ed.

***Dead Reckoning: Tales of the Great Explorers, 1800–1900*. New York: Norton, 2003 (2005). 566pp. ISBN 0393326535.**

The librarian or other book professional seeking a brief and enjoyable overview of exploration adventure tales need look no further than this collection, which contains excerpts from thirty-two widely acknowledged classics of the genre. Authors excerpted include Richard Henry Dana, Meriwether Lewis, John Muir, Francis Parkman, Henry Morton Stanley, and Henry David Thoreau, among others. Each piece is introduced with a short paragraph about the author's adventure and his style of telling it.

References

Birkerts, Sven. 1999. "Read at Your Own Risk." *Esquire* 132, no. 3 (September): 118–19.

Cawelti, John G. 1976. *Adventure, Mystery, and Romance: Formula Stories as Art and Popular Culture*. Chicago: University of Chicago Press.

Gannon, Michael B. 2004. *Blood, Bedlam, Bullets, and Badguys: A Reader's Guide to Adventure/Suspense Fiction*. Westport, Conn.: Libraries Unlimited.

Herald, Diana Tixier. 2000. *Genreflecting: A Guide to Reading Interests in Genre Fiction*. 5th ed. Englewood, Colo.: Libraries Unlimited.

Saricks, Joyce. 2001. *The Reader's Advisory Guide to Genre Fiction*. Chicago: American Library Association.

Waterboro Library Web site. 2005. www.waterborolibrary.org/bklista.htm#adv (accessed April 21, 2005).

Whybrow, Helen, ed. 2003. *Dead Reckoning: Great Adventure Writing from the Golden Age of Exploration, 1800–1900*. New York: Norton.

Chapter 2

Travel

Definition of Travel Writing

Travel writing is often said to have originated in the fifth century B.C.E. with the writer Herodotus (ca. 480 to ca. 425 B.C.E.), who is also sometimes referred to as the father of history (he wrote the *History of the Persian Wars*). In his excellent collection of travel writing and authors, *The Norton Book of Travel*, Paul Fussell describes Herodotus's travels from ancient "Greece and her islands; to North Africa, Sicily, and Southern Italy; to the Black Sea and the area known now as Turkey; and the Persian Empire, embracing Syria, Palestine, Babylon, and Egypt" (1987, 27). History's first travel writer was evidently an intrepid one as well, and this genre was off to a strong start. Later narrators of journeys and describers of new exotic landscapes include Marco Polo (*Travels*, ca. 1299); James Boswell, of biography-writing fame (*The Journal of a Tour to Corsica*, 1768); Charles Darwin (*The Voyage of the* Beagle, 1845); and Jack Kerouac (*On the Road*, 1957). Many of these writers and others throughout the heyday of travel and exploration in the nineteenth century focused on both the geographical descriptions and adventurous aspects of their travel; hallmarks that abated slightly in the twentieth- and twenty-first centuries as our geographical and cultural world, thanks to technology, has shrunk. Travel books highlighting new and exotic locales, the journey itself, and adventurous episodes do still exist, and still constitute a large part of many popular travel writers' current catalogs.

In addition to books describing the exotic and the travails of travelers, recent travelogues and travel narratives have been, in the words of Jan Morris (one of the genre's acknowledged masters), "writing as subjectively as though they were writing fiction"; the authors of such works "are frequently novelists too, and often fact and imagination are blended in their work" (Morris 1997, 37). This trend toward memoir-like styling and "re-created" dialogue and memories with a more straightforward setting and descriptive tales may have contributed to such books' frequent appearance on lists of nonfiction books that have been chosen to appeal to fiction readers. Travel writers' widespread and expected use of exaggeration, drama, and hyperbole, and their selective use and organization of facts (a charge that has often been leveled against Bruce Chatwin, for one) add to their narrative appeal and the quickness of their pacing, and advisors should consider these factors when recommending them to readers of forms of nonfiction that are more stringently researched and documented, such as history and science.

Appeal of the Genre

Many travel books obviously rely heavily on the appeal of setting and their authors' skill in describing unfamiliar or exotic locations. The more descriptive and reflective among them are quite similar to their counterparts in the environment chapter (Peter Matthiessen, for example, has written both classic travel and nature titles). However, as Casey Blanton stated in *Travel Writing: The Self and the World*, modern travel writing is also a body of literature in which "the reverberations between observer and observed, between self and world, allow the writer to celebrate the local while contemplating the universal" (1997, 5). Furthermore, both Fussell and Blanton agree that travel narratives bear little or no relation to their cousins, the travel guidebooks, which have a tendency to become quickly outdated and do not typically include any of the autobiographical or interpersonal asides that constitute a large part of the appeal of true travel literature. In addition to setting, then, these two historians of the genre seem to be suggesting that another large component of travel books is their emphasis on character details, both those of the traveler and of the place's local residents with whom he or she comes into contact.

Many of the more adventurous travel titles (such as Tom Hart Dyke's and Paul Winder's *The Cloud Garden*, in the "Armchair Travel: Adventures" subgenre) also offer quickly paced and compelling stories to their readers, particularly when authors describe their "fish out of water" experiences in unfamiliar landscapes and when traveling on less than reliable modes of transportation. In this way they may also appeal to readers of true adventure books.

Organization of the Chapter

In keeping with the assumption that setting and vicarious experiences provide much of the recreational value of travel genre reading, the first subgenre described is "Armchair Travel," which is further subdivided into "Foreign Places and Exotic Locales" and works that focus on unique and often exciting travel experiences, in "Armchair Travel: Adventures." Two other easily recognizable and popular subgenres follow: "Journey Narratives" and "The Expatriate Life" (which, with the one-two punch of Peter Mayle's *A Year in Provence* and Frances Mayes's *Under the Tuscan Sun*, has been one of the most popular of the travel subgenres of late). Titles in the last two categories, "Travel Humor" and "Literary Travel," are less cohesive as a group of travelogues that make use of locations or the act of traveling as their main narrative framework. They are, rather, similar to each other in their authors' use of humorous and reflective tones and language, respectively.

Armchair Travel

Foreign Places and Exotic Locales

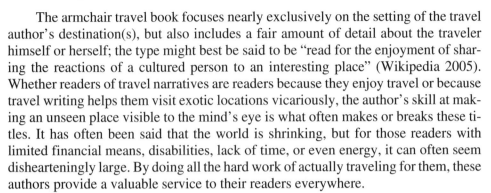

The armchair travel book focuses nearly exclusively on the setting of the travel author's destination(s), but also includes a fair amount of detail about the traveler himself or herself; the type might best be said to be "read for the enjoyment of sharing the reactions of a cultured person to an interesting place" (Wikipedia 2005). Whether readers of travel narratives are readers because they enjoy travel or because travel writing helps them visit exotic locations vicariously, the author's skill at making an unseen place visible to the mind's eye is what often makes or breaks these titles. It has often been said that the world is shrinking, but for those readers with limited financial means, disabilities, lack of time, or even energy, it can often seem dishearteningly large. By doing all the hard work of actually traveling for them, these authors provide a valuable service to their readers everywhere.

Many readers will pick up travel books because they have an interest in a certain location (either because they plan to travel there, because they are from there, or any other of a myriad of possible reasons), and the readers' advisor should not be afraid to use subject interest to generate suggestions, as long as the titles actually fall into the "armchair" category. Many more readers will follow authors that they enjoy to the setting of their choosing. Frank Conroy, a popular memoirist, takes the reader to Nantucket, while fans of Graham Greene, a classic author in this category, are invited to see and sense the African terrain, which he did.

Ehrlich, Gretel.

This Cold Heaven: Seven Seasons in Greenland. New York: Pantheon Books, 2001 (New York: Vintage Books, 2003). 377pp. ISBN 0679758526.

In 1993, spurred onward by a desire to travel above the treeline, Ehrlich took a plane to the world's largest island, Greenland. As her inspiration she carried the writings of Knud Rasmussen, a Danish-Inuit ethnographer who made seven expeditions to Greenland from 1902 to 1933 and exhaustively documented the people and landscape he encountered on each trip. Eventually Ehrlich made seven trips in succeeding seasons, and she describes both the island's geography and the residents who served as her hosts and guides, interspersed with her re-created versions of Rasmussen's adventures and discoveries.

Subjects: Arctic Regions • Exploration • Greenland • Landscape • Women Travelers

Now try: The heart of Ehrlich's writing is her ability to describe landscape; readers who enjoy this book might also be tempted by Ehrlich's environmental works, such as *The Solace of Open Spaces,* or her most recent book, *The Future of Ice: A Journey into Cold.*

Greene, Graham.

Journey Without Maps. Garden City, N.Y.: Doubleday, 1936 (New York: Penguin, 1992). 249pp. ISBN 0140185798.

Greene recounts his journey through Sierra Leone and Liberia in the early 1930s, from his impressions of the bureaucratic hoops through which he was forced to jump to his reflections on the landscape and the inhabitants of the countries he visited. Although some readers might find the work either outdated or simplistic in its observations about the countries' residents, others might be equally drawn to his somewhat mystical and always highly lyrical writing style. The narrative is not chronological or particularly well-organized, but rather proceeds from one sensory-rich episode to another, which Greene combines to create the somewhat disjointed record of his travels and impressions.

> **Subjects:** Africa • Classics • Liberia • Memoirs • Sierra Leone

> **Now try:** Edward Hoagland's tale of his journeys through Africa, *African Calliope: A Journey to the Sudan,* shares the same combination of disbelief at the harshness of desert life with wonder at the spirit and individuality of the people he met, as well as the naturalist's eye for the details of landscape. Although his fiction is not as widely read as it used to be, readers of Greene's nonfiction travel writings may also want to branch out into his fiction titles, many of which are set in exotic locales, such as *The Power and the Glory* (Mexico) and *The Heart of the Matter* (West Africa). Julia Llewellyn Smith's re-enactment of Greene's journeys in *Travels Without My Aunt: In the Footsteps of Graham Greene,* might also appeal to these readers.

McCarthy, Pete.

McCarthy's Bar: A Journey of Discovery in the West of Ireland. New York: St. Martin's Press, 2000 (2001). 338pp. ISBN 0312272103.

Following a set of travel rules that dictate never passing a bar that has your name on it, McCarthy narrates his serendipitous travels through Ireland in search of his heritage and a sense of connectedness to his mother's native country. Mostly self-deprecating, particularly about his English upbringing, and always humorous, particularly when describing the parts of Ireland and its residents he most particularly loves, McCarthy provides an enjoyable narration of a journey through his own history as much as through Ireland.

> **Subjects:** Essays • Humor • Ireland • Memoirs

> **Now try:** McCarthy's next book, *McCarthy's Ireland*, also sold well internationally, and readers who liked his first volume should be amused by his further travel adventures in the Emerald Isle. Joe Queenan's similarly humorous travel collections, *Red Lobster, White Trash & the Blue Lagoon: Joe Queenan's America*, or *Queenan Country: A Reluctant Anglophile's Pilgrimage to the Mother Country,* may also be enjoyed by McCarthy's target audience.

Stevenson, Andrew.

Kiwi Tracks: A New Zealand Journey. Melbourne, Australia: Lonely Planet Publications, 1999. 222pp. ISBN 0864427875.

Stevenson's tone is light and his use of prose simply elegant, making this short volume an extremely illuminating read about New Zealand. In chapters that are less organized and more serendipitous reflections of his unstructured journey around the island, he reflects on the landscape, as well as on the indigenous Maori and the nonindigenous residents of the country, and provides plenty of dialogue (both inner and with his fellow travelers and others whom he meets) to keep the narrative moving quickly along.

> **Subjects:** Humor • Landscape • New Zealand • Quick Reads

> **Now try:** All of the Lonely Planet <u>Journeys series</u> titles currently available are light and fascinating reads; a few of the most recent titles are Stevenson's *Summer Light: A Walk Across Norway*, Sean Condon's *My 'Dam Life: Three Years in Holland*, Zoe Bran's *Lonely Planet Enduring Cuba*, and Thornton McCamish's *Lonely Planet Supercargo: A Journey Among Ports.*

Trillin, Calvin.

Feeding a Yen: Savoring Local Specialties, From Kansas City to Cuzco. New York: Random House, 2003 (2004). 197pp. ISBN 0375759964.

Trillin has a proud history of masterfully combining two popular nonfiction genres, "foodie" books and travel narratives, and this most recent book, in which he describes local cuisines as characters in their own right, is a fine example of his skill. In short and witty chapters that read as quickly as the popular light prose verses he writes for *The Nation* magazine, Trillin describes some of his favorite foods: barbecue in Kansas City, bagels in New York City. The list of locations is deeply personal, the narrative told in the first person, and the specialty of each place lovingly lauded for its place on the author's "Register of Frustration and Deprivation" (the list of foods he often craves but that are only perfectly available in their hometown).

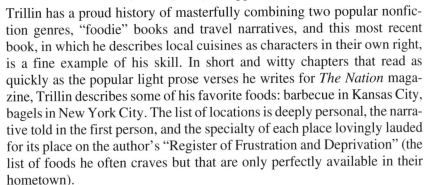

> **Subjects:** Essays • Food • Humor • New York City • Quick Reads • World Travel

> **Now try:** Readers who love travel and food might also be tempted by Trillin's other tales of traveling mainly to eat: *American Fried: Adventures of a Happy Eater, Alice, Let's Eat: Further Adventures of a Happy Eater, Third Helpings*, and *Travels with Alice*. Other "foodie" authors such as Ruth Reichl and M. F. K. Fisher might also appeal to Trillin's readers, as might Anthony Bourdain's slightly more profane and adventurous worldwide tour in search of culinary adventure, *A Cook's Tour: Global Adventures in Extreme Cuisines*. If candy can be said to constitute a cuisine, then Steve Almond's travelogue of various cities known for their regional candies, *Candyfreak: A Journey Through the Chocolate Underbelly of America*, will provide a scrumptious read as well.

Adventures

In addition to journey narratives, "extreme travel adventure" stories have long been a mainstay of this subgenre. These books, with their emphasis on storytelling in conjunction with locale, offer more reading bang for their buck; much as readers of regular adventure stories often read while sitting on the edges of their seats, so too do readers of travel adventure. These are not books that go into great detail describing the beauty of a writer's surroundings or dwell on how or why the author got into whatever adventurous jam he or she is in; for the most part, as in David Yeadon's collection *The Back of Beyond*, the story starts with the author already in some sort of exciting and little-visited situation or place.

Not surprisingly, readers who enjoy these titles might also want to consider titles from the true adventure chapter, whether they select nonfiction titles from the body of the chapter or fiction suggestions from the end of the chapter. These readers are in it for the excitement, the story, and the exotic locales.

Birkett, Dea.

Serpent in Paradise. New York: Anchor Books, 1997 (1998). 296pp. ISBN 0385488718.

Feeling the need for a change in her life, Birkett undertook a lengthy journey to the most exotic locale she could think of: Pitcairn Island, where the mutineer Christian Fletcher (of mutiny on the *Bounty* fame) eventually landed with his followers, and where their few descendants still live. Birkett was accepted by the community, a rather fractious one at the best of times, and spent much of her time on the island being alternately warmly included or coolly ignored. A somewhat unstable narrator, Birkett's tone never lacks feeling of adventure when describing the surreal isolation of the island and its ever-dwindling number of inhabitants.

Subjects: Adventure • Community Life • Friendships • Islands • Love and Dating • Memoirs • Pitcairn Island • Women Travelers

Now try: Any reader who is fascinated by Birkett's modern experiences on Pitcairn Island might not mind learning more about it; *Fragile Paradise: The Discovery of Fletcher Christian,* Bounty *Mutineer* was written by Glynn Christian, a descendant of the title character, while Caroline Alexander's *The* Bounty*: The True Story of the Mutiny on the* Bounty provides the back story of the original mutiny.

Bissell, Tom.

Chasing the Sea: Lost Among the Ghosts of Empire in Central Asia. New York: Pantheon Books, 2003 (New York: Vintage Books, 2004). 388pp. ISBN 037572754X.

Bissell first traveled to Uzbekistan as a Peace Corps volunteer; his second trip was the result of his convincing a magazine that there was a story to be written about the slow shrinking of the Aral Sea, and that he was the writer to do it. While he does an admirable job of describing the environmental impact of the steady disappearance of the sea on the country, as well as recounting Uzbekistan's complex political and ethnic history, the true appeal of his narrative lies in his portrayal of his friendship with his young translator, Rustam, as well as with the many other individuals he encounters.

Subjects: Adventure • Conservation • Friendships • Humor • Memoirs • Uzbekistan

Now try: Stanley Stewart's suitably wild and personal journey from Turkey to Mongolia, as recounted in *In the Empire of Genghis Khan: An Amazing Odyssey Through the Lands of the Most Feared Conquerors in History*, also outlines a rather epic quest undertaken by a lone traveler through an area seldom visited by more conventional tourists. Redmond O'Hanlon's journey to the Congo with his friend Lary Shaffer is similarly character-driven and darkly humorous, and is titled *No Mercy: A Journey to the Heart of the Congo*. Dave Eggers's fiction *You Shall Know Our Velocity!* is the story of one young man's decidedly unplanned but never dull journey through various

Eastern European countries, and is also somewhat surreal in its description of the protagonist's travels.

Clapp, Nicholas.

The Road to Ubar: Finding the Atlantis of the Sands. Boston: Houghton Mifflin, 1998. 342pp. ISBN 039587596X.

Documentary filmmaker Clapp and his wife, prompted by their experiences while filming the story of the return to the wild of several Arabian oryxes, undertook the scholarly and archaeological task of proving that the mythical city of Ubar did exist, as well as setting out to find it. Clapp details their studies and their exotic journeys with an admirable mix of historical background and the present-day excitement of locating and excavating the fabled city on the Arabian peninsula, as well as relating the tragic tale of its fantastic but true demise when it tumbled into a sinkhole opened by geological tremors.

Subjects: Adventure • ALA Notable Books • Arabia • Archaeology • Exploration

Now try: Tahir Shah's extremely enjoyable *In Search of King Solomon's Mines* provides an adventurous travel narrative that is similar to Clapp's journey of discovery. Readers who are not averse to this slightly slower form of adventure reading might also enjoy a title that pops up in science nonfiction: Oliver Morton's *Mapping Mars: Science, Imagination, and the Birth of a World*, which is to Clapp's work due to its focus on exploring and mapping a previously misunderstood landscape.

Dyke, Tom Hart, and Paul Winder.

The Cloud Garden: A True Story of Adventure, Survival, and Extreme Horticulture. Guilford, Conn.: Lyons Press, 2004. 323pp. ISBN 1592284302.

Told in alternating sections by the two authors and cotravelers, this book would nicely complement any of the exploration titles in the adventure chapter. During their combined quest to cross the dangerous Darién Gap between Panama and Colombia (Dyke went for adventure; Winder in search of rare orchids), they were kidnapped by political guerrillas and held captive for nine months. The reader may not know whether they should be cringing at the authors' oblivious flaunting of caution (travel guides routinely refer to the area as one of the most violent in the world) or laughing about such exploits as the pair return to their captors to ask for directions after being released and wandering lost in the jungle.

Subjects: Adventure • Central America • Colombia • Friendships • Horticulture • Kidnapping • Panama • Quick Reads

Now try: Ewan McGregor's and Charley Boorman's combined tale of camaraderie and motorcycle travel, *Long Way Round*, is written in the same alternating style, and although the authors are never kidnapped, they do drive through some rather dodgy parts of the world. The travelogue *Lost in Mongolia: Rafting the World's Last Unchallenged River* follows the exploits of three men setting out to conquer the Yenisey River (in Mongolia and Siberia). *On the Wing: To the Edge of the Earth with the Peregrine Falcon* also follows two men as they follow the migratory pattern of a peregrine falcon.

Winder's obsessive search for rare orchids is reminiscent of Susan Orlean's story about orchid enthusiast John Laroche, *The Orchid Thief* (annotated in the investigative writing chapter).

Elliot, Jason.

An Unexpected Light: Travels in Afghanistan. New York: Picador, 1999 (2001). 473pp. ISBN 0312288468.

Elliot combines descriptive travel writing with historical background and personal adventure; his first visit to Afghanistan consisted of smuggling himself in and traveling with the mujaheddin fighting the Soviet occupation forces. He eventually made several more visits to the country and experienced many different political regimes, including the arrival of the Taleban. In addition to the political and military climate, Elliot also describes the hospitality of the Afghani people and the landscape, in dramatic and sometimes poetic language.

Subjects: Adventure • Afghanistan • ALA Notable Books • Epic Reads • Investigative Stories • Politics

Now try: Elaine Sciolino's similar book about Iran, *Persian Mirrors: The Elusive Face of Iran*, was also an ALA Notable Book, and although more dryly journalistic in tone, it provides a similar holistic picture of the country, its people, and their history since the Islamic Revolution. Elinor Burkett's politically charged travel memoir, *So Many Enemies, So Little Time: An American Woman in All the Wrong Places*, provides a journalistic recounting of her experience as a Fulbright professor in Kyrgyzstan, as well as she and her husband's risky forays into Afghanistan, Iran, Uzbekistan, and Vietnam; Christiane Bird's *A Thousand Sighs, A Thousand Revolts: Journeys in Kurdistan* is less geographically defined (much like Kurdistan itself) but also portrays its characters with journalistic attention to details.

Morris, Jan.

Coronation Everest: Eyewitness Dispatches from the Historic Hillary Climb. Short Hills, N.J.: Burford Books, 1958 (2000). 150pp. ISBN 1580800475.

So named because it celebrates the simultaneous coronation of Queen Elizabeth II and the first ascent of Everest in 1953, Morris's short work consists of his journalistic dispatches from Everest itself, where he filed his stories via runner back to Katmandu. It therefore combines elements of both the naïve pleasure Morris found in the adventure and his already mature travel writing, culminating in his interview with Hillary and Tenzing directly after they returned from the summit. Librarians should note that the book was written in the 1950s and contains terms that are no longer in use today, a point that the author addresses in his preface.

Subjects: Adventure • Classics • Climbing and Hiking • Mountains • Mt. Everest • Quick Reads

Now try: Although slightly more mystical in tone, Ian Baker's *The Heart of the World: A Journey to the Last Secret Place*, a story about Baker's experiences exploring the previously unexplored Tsangpo Gorge, might also appeal to readers of Morris's book. Readers who enjoy Morris's travel dispatches from Everest might also find a lot to enjoy in more adventurous tales of mountain climbing such as Heidi Howkins's *K2: One Woman's Quest for the Summit* or Jon Krakauer's tale of disaster on Everest, *Into Thin Air* (annotated in the true adventure chapter).

Nichols, Peter.

Sea Change: Alone Across the Atlantic in a Wooden Boat. New York: Viking, 1997 (New York: Penguin, 1998). 238pp. ISBN 0140264132.

Nichols and his wife initially sailed their engineless yacht, the *Toad*, to Europe together. Upon the breakup of their marriage, however, Nichols returned across the Atlantic to America alone. Describing his return journey, he reflects on his history and his family and marriage, but most of his time and narrative are spent dealing with a leak the boat springs in the approximate middle of the ocean. Written in diary-entry form, Nichols's prose is dryly humorous, even when considering his sinking options, and suspenseful to the very end.

> **Subjects:** Adventure • Exploration • Humor • Marriage • Memoirs • Sailing • Solitude • Travel

> **Now try:** Nichols's novel, *Voyage to the North Star*, is also a sailing adventure, although it's set in 1932, and it might appeal to readers who enjoy his nonfiction. Readers who enjoy his dual battle with the ocean and his own thoughts about the breakup of his marriage might also be drawn to Jonathan Raban's extremely similar and soul-searching adventure narrative, *Passage to Juneau: A Sea and Its Meanings*.

Yeadon, David.

The Back of Beyond: Travels to the Wild Places of the Earth. New York: HarperCollins, 1991 (New York: HarperPerennial, 1992). 449pp. ISBN 0060922745.

The journeying parts of Yeadon's trips are excluded; each chapter offers an immediate and discrete narrative of different portions of the world that the author considers "the back of beyond." From Haiti and Costa Rica to the Outer Hebrides of Scotland to Nepal and Inner Mongolia, Yeadon provides elaborate word pictures of the landscapes and locals he visits, as well as his own sketches. There is also plenty of dialogue in Yeadon's chapters, which yields more quickly paced stories than many description-heavy travel books.

> **Subjects:** Adventure • Illustrated Books • Landscape • Memoirs • World Travel

> **Now try:** Tim Cahill's collection of adventure essays set in varying locales, *Jaguars Ripped My Flesh*, also provides a vicarious thrill for the armchair traveler, and each tale drops the reader into a new locale with no transitional journeying details. A slightly older book in the same vein is Eric Newby's compilation of essays describing varied destinations more than the journey, *A Traveller's Life*, which also includes episodes from his childhood (outings with his nurse, etc.) as destinations. Those readers who are particularly interested in the details of the destinations (rather than the journeys) might also enjoy illustrated books such as Eric Hansen's and Hugh Swift's *The Traveler: An American Odyssey in the Himalayas*.

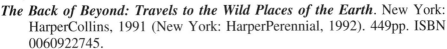

Journey Narratives

Travel writers have long since branched out from writing more straightforward narratives describing the setting of their final destinations to providing the often interesting and humorous details of their actual travel process. Journey narratives, in addition to providing the how of travel, often also provide the why; many of the titles annotated for this subgenre include healthy doses of autobiographical and explanatory information from their authors, who frequently write in the first person and with a more personal style similar to that found in memoirs. In addition to offering the mainstream travel writing appeal of setting and location, these stories have the appeal of character, primarily that of the author or his or her closest and most influential traveling companions, and often include elements of the travelers' reactions to transforming events or revelations of their own personal growth (as such, they may appeal to readers of memoirs). They also prove that getting there can be more than half the fun.

Journey narratives also provide many of the small but telling mechanical details of travel movement; Ken McAlpine spends a large portion of time at the beginning of *Off Season* explaining his rationale for traveling by car, as well as joining a friend who needs help fixing up his boat, which has seen better days. Likewise, V. S. Naipaul and Eric Newby spend time explaining the vagaries of river travel and its various conveyances, and one could almost argue that Paul Theroux's fascination with both the rail car and its system of tracks constitutes a separate character. Writers of journey narratives are also quite susceptible to running into unforeseen snags and obstacles, but rather than overcoming or powering through these difficulties, they often use such enforced pauses as times for offbeat exploration and reflection.

Chatwin, Bruce.

The Songlines. New York: Viking, 1987 (New York: Vintage, 1998). 293pp. ISBN 0099769913.

Chatwin details the story of his journey across Australia in the paths along which the Aboriginal peoples "sing up the country," along with his friend Arkady, a thirty-three-year-old Russian citizen of Australia. Part mystic tale, part philosophical musing, part travelogue, Chatwin's ethereal language in this book makes his descriptions of the Aboriginals' beliefs and totems all the more concrete for the reader.

Subjects: Anthropology • Australia • Classics • Culture Clash • Friendships • Spirituality

Now try: Robert Kaplan's *Mediterranean Winter: The Pleasures of History and Landscape in Tunisia, Sicily, Dalmatia, and Greece* is another reflective travelogue that combines Kaplan's journey with musings on the history of his destinations, and offers use of language as another strong appeal factor. Chatwin is something of a cultural icon in the field of travel writing; rabid fans of his narratives might also try Nicholas's Shakespeare's recent *Bruce Chatwin: A Biography*.

Conroy, Frank.

Time and Tide: A Walk through Nantucket. New York: Crown Publishers, 2004. 141pp. ISBN 1400046599.

A short walk through both the author's memory of his earliest experiences on Nantucket, as well as the geography of the island and the community's attitudes toward neighborly conduct and "native" and "summer" people, this book packs a lot into a narrative that can be read in one sitting. Conroy's prose is simple and evocative and never delves into sentimentality, although his love for the island is always apparent.

> **Subjects:** Crown <u>Journeys Series</u> • Essays • Massachusetts • Nantucket • Quick Reads • Walking

> **Now try:** Other volumes in this series of slim but meaty travelogues by well-known authors include Tim Cahill's *Lost in My Own Backyard: A Walk in Yellowstone National Park*, Roy Blount's *Feet on the Street: Rambles around New Orleans*, and Chuck Palahniuk's *Fugitives and Refugees: A Walk in Portland, Oregon*.

Matthiessen, Peter.

The Cloud Forest: A Chronicle of the South American Wilderness. New York: Viking Press, 1961 (New York: Penguin Books, 1996). 280pp. ISBN 0140255079.

Matthiessen's story is the quintessential journey narrative; with no set destination or travel itinerary, he relates his experiences traveling through Central and South America in diary form, providing evocative and detailed descriptions of the landscapes and peoples he encounters.

> **Subjects:** Central America • Classics • Conservation • Landscape • South America

> **Now try:** Matthiessen's novel *At Play in the Fields of the Lord* is also set in South America and explores themes of civilization and primitivism. Readers might also enjoy the author's more environmental works, such as *The Snow Leopard*. Readers might also enjoy works by David Quammen (*Monster of God*, *The Song of the Dodo*), another writer who combines adventure, animal, and nature writing.

McAlpine, Ken.

Off Season: Discovering America on Winter's Shore. New York: Three Rivers Press, 2004. 290pp. ISBN 1400049733.

Choosing to travel during the "off season," from Labor Day through the winter, McAlpine is treated to the sights of the coast road from Key West to Maine that few tourists will ever see. Along with describing his stops along the way, McAlpine also has a knack for portraying the characters he finds and their multiple quirks. Paced languidly and written with a focus on his own reactions to his method of travel, this is a uniquely voiced travel narrative.

> **Subjects:** Atlantic Coast • Essays • Seasons • Solitude

> **Now try:** John Steinbeck's classic *Travels with Charley* is another languidly paced book that captures the spirit of a certain type of traveler's desire to see more than regular tourists do as well as a montage of heart-warming characters. Jenny Diski's travelogue memoir, *Stranger on a Train: Daydreaming and Smoking around America with Interruptions* might also appeal to fans of McAlpine's measured pace.

Naipaul, V. S.

An Area of Darkness. New York: Macmillan, 1964 (New York: Vintage Books, 2000). 290pp. ISBN 0375708359.

Naipaul's novelistic treatment of his yearlong journey to India, where his family originated (before they went to Trinidad as indentured laborers) combines both lyrical descriptions of its landscape and frustrated observations on the peculiarities of its bureaucracy and class system. The narrative feels much more contemporary in its empathetic recounting of India's poverty and history than its 1960s copyright date might lead the reader to believe.

Subjects: India • Landscape • Memoirs • Politics • Poverty

Now try: India figures prominently in the work of many fine novelists; Naipaul himself has written many novels set there (*A Bend in the River*, *A House for Mr. Biswas*), as has Anita Desai. Other nonfiction works about the country and its culture, such as Suketu Mehta's *Maximum City: Bombay Lost and Found*, or Ved Mehta's eleven-volume (they're each very short, no worries) Continents of Exile series of Indian memoirs, may also appeal to fans of this travel classic.

Paterniti, Michael.

Driving Mr. Albert: A Trip Across America with Einstein's Brain. New York: Dial Press, 2000 (New York: Dell, 2001). 211pp. ISBN 038533303X.

When Paterniti offered to drive former pathologist Thomas Harvey and the brain of Albert Einstein, which Harvey obtained when he performed the autopsy on the famous physicist, across the country to deliver the brain to Einstein's granddaughter, he thought it would be more of a caper, a lark, a true road trip, rather than a journey that would set him to examining his own life and relationships, as well as acquiring a deeper appreciation for Einstein himself and the universality of even his most esoteric physics theories.

Subjects: Einstein, Albert • Investigative Stories • Memoirs • Physics

Now try: Carolyn Abraham's superlative *Possessing Genius: The Bizarre Odyssey of Einstein's Brain*, published in 2002, is a more factual history of the removal and safekeeping of Albert Einstein's brain by pathologist Thomas Harvey, and includes a reference to Paterniti's and Harvey's road trip as described in *Driving Mr. Albert*. A slightly different but no less interesting road trip through Yemen (on a quest to retrieve travel diaries he lost there ten years previously) is the subject of Eric Hansen's *Motoring with Mohammed: Journeys to Yemen and the Red Sea*.

Shah, Tahir.

In Search of King Solomon's Mines. New York: Arcade Publishing, 2003. 240pp. ISBN 1559706414.

Shah's journeys throughout Ethiopia by any means available were inspired by his finding of a treasure map in a tourist shop in Jerusalem that makes reference to the gold mines of King Solomon. The physical journey, during which Shah met numerous characters and visited sites as disparate as Ethiopia's only licensed gold mine and a monastery on a mountaintop, provide enough landscape detail to create a serviceable travel narrative, but the author also discusses the myths and history surrounding both Solomon and the Queen of Sheba, as well as their treasure.

Subjects: Africa • Archaeology • Ethiopia • Humor

Now try: Mark Honigsbaum's mix of scholarship and personal travel narrative in both *Valverde's Gold: In Search of the Last Great Inca Treasure* and *The Fever Trail: In Search of the Cure for Malaria* might make them enjoyable read-alikes for Shah's title. Readers who enjoy a combination of travel, adventure, and history might also consider adventure author Fergus Fleming's meaty titles, including *The Sword and the Cross: Two Men and an Empire of Sand,* and *Ninety Degrees North: The Quest for the North Pole.*

Theroux, Paul.

The Old Patagonian Express: By Train through the Americas. Boston: Houghton Mifflin, 1979 (1997). 404pp. ISBN 039552105X.

Theroux proves the saying that getting there is truly the best part of the journey, as he narrates his travel by rail from Massachusetts to Patagonia, South America (literally to the "end of the line"; he ends his narrative with his thoughts right before he gets to Esquel, the last stop). Theroux's talent for locale description is obvious, but better yet are his often surreal conversations with his fellow travelers: Does milk cause mucus production, and thus explain why children who drink milk always have runny noses? Is Spanish a better language than English because it has more words? In addition to his chats with travelers, Theroux also shares his interactions with transportation workers, and even, in Buenos Aires, with Jorge Luis Borges.

Subjects: Central America • Classics • Rail Travel • South America

Now try: Theroux has written many other travel books that the reader might enjoy, particularly his earlier work about train travel, *The Great Railway Bazaar.* Bruce Chatwin's seminal work *In Patagonia* also shares a location with Theroux's title and might be offered as a related read, although it is more about the landscape and history of the region than the actual process of traveling.

Watkins, Nan.

East Toward Dawn: A Woman's Solo Journey around the World. New York: Seal Press, 2002. 232pp. ISBN 1580050646.

Watkins set out alone to journey "east toward the dawn" from her home in North Carolina, and accomplished both a physically and a spiritually refreshing journey through locations including Kathmandu Valley, New Delhi, Munich, and Hawaii. She does a masterful job of combining her current travels (undertaken after her sixtieth birthday) with flashbacks from trips she took as a young girl, and includes many personal reflections, particularly regarding the death of her twenty-two-year-old son and the end of her marriage, along the way.

Subjects: Family Relationships • Germany • Hawaii • India • Memoirs • Women Travelers • World Travel

Now try: Two uniquely feminine viewpoints on travel can be found in two very different books: Susan Orleans's collection of travel essays, *My Kind of Place: Travel Stories from a Woman Who's Been Everywhere,* will delight solitary women travelers everywhere; while Barbara Hodgson's *No Place*

for a Lady: Tales of Adventurous Women Travelers will inspire them to indulge in longer and farther treks. Freya Stark, a legend among female travel authors, might also appeal to fans of Watkin's feisty narrative with *The Valley of the Assassins* or *Baghdad Sketches* (or, for the big picture of Stark's life, librarians may wish to offer *Passionate Nomad: The Life of Freya Stark*, by Jane Geniesse). The collection *Expat: Women's True Tales of Life Abroad*, edited by Christina Henry de Tessan, might also appeal to these readers.

Wren, Christopher S.

Walking to Vermont: From Times Square into the Green Mountains—A Homeward Adventure. New York: Simon & Schuster, 2004. 273pp. ISBN 0743251520.

When Wren retired from *The New York Times*, he set out to walk from his office at Times Square to his retirement home in Vermont. Although his journey was rich with false starts (after being rejected by an ATM at 180th Street in New York City, he had to take the subway back downtown to resolve the problem) and wrong turns, he did meet a variety of kind people along the way, and visited a number of historical sites, including some that were most pertinent to his own history and reminiscing, such as his former school. Wren did eventually make it to Vermont, weary from carrying everything on his sixty-five-year-old back, but fulfilled by the experience.

Subjects: Climbing and Hiking • Memoirs • New York City • Retirement • Vermont • Walking

Now try: Nathaniel Stone's *On the Water: Discovering America in a Rowboat*, describes a similarly personal odyssey; namely, the author's attempt to circumnavigate the eastern half of the United States using the Hudson and Mississippi Rivers, as well as the Atlantic Ocean. He, much like Wren, met a number of people whose kindness to strangers (strangers on strange journeys, no less) is truly inspirational. Peter Jenkins's *A Walk across America* also relates the author's experiences of getting to know a landscape by walking over it.

The Expatriate Life

Strictly speaking, many of the following titles are less travel narratives than they are memoirs of lives (or portions of lives) that happen to be lived in other countries. These stories offer more in-depth considerations of environment and landscape, and the authors often live in their chosen locations long enough to describe the turning of the seasons and the vagaries of community life that are typically seen in environmental stories. Many of these stories are also awash in evocative language, used to create sensual depictions of any given region's climate, vegetation, culture, and food and drink. Other "Foodie Memoirs" may appeal to readers of this subgenre, and advisors might consider recommending authors like Ruth Reichl (her *Tender at the Bone* is annotated in chapter 8, "Memoirs and Autobiography") in addition to offering other travel titles.

These are usually quite gentle reads as well. Authors in this category, including Peter Mayle and Frances Mayes, tend to inspire strong loyalty within their fan base, and the astute advisor may want to make sure all other books by the favored author have been offered and read before offering different writers or subgenres.

De Blasi, Marlena.

A Thousand Days in Tuscany: A Bittersweet Adventure. Chapel Hill, N.C.: Algonquin Books of Chapel Hill, 2004. 325pp. ISBN 1565123921.

The appeal of De Blasi's travel and food memoir is definitely the language and pace she uses to describe her life in Tuscany. The book is strangely onomatopaeic; her prose can only be described in terms of the languid pacing and sun-drenched language she uses to describe her home and community in Tuscany. There is no real story to follow, but she does provide short vignettes about her experiences and neighbors, and each chapter is followed by recipes.

Subjects: Community Life • Food • Gentle Reads • Homes • Italy • Memoirs • Women Travelers

Now try: The author's previous book, *A Thousand Days in Venice*, is as similar to this book as its title suggests. Readers who enjoy this brand of travel and foodie writing might also find Ruth Reichl's memoir *Tender at the Bone* enjoyable; she also uses food stories and recipes to evoke a sense of place.

Macdonald, Sarah.

Holy Cow: An Indian Adventure. New York: Broadway Books, 2002. 291pp. ISBN 0767915747.

Macdonald, a native Australian, originally flounced through India on a backpacking trip in her twenties, and was skeptical about a local soothsayer's prediction that she would return to the country. In her thirties, however, that's exactly what Macdonald did, following her boyfriend (and eventual husband) back to India when he got a job there with the Australian Broadcasting Company. Macdonald describes her fish out of water existence with stories regarding her illnesses caused by the country's extreme pollution (including the loss of most of her hair!), her extreme discomfort with having, but eventual dependence on, her household staff, who helped her with simple daily tasks such as shopping and cooking, and her spiritual discoveries in Hinduism. Lighthearted but honest, this is an enjoyable culture shock story that ends happily.

Subjects: Culture Clash • Friendships • India • Marriage • Women Travelers

Now try: Rita Golden Gelman's (yes, she's also author of the children's classic, *More Spaghetti, I Say!*) travels started when she ended her marriage; she details the most unique among them in her *Tales of a Female Nomad: Living at Large in the World*. Macdonald also brings a definite "Chick Lit" sensibility to her writing; readers who are drawn to the romantic aspects of her adventure might also enjoy some classics of the romance genre, such as Melissa Bank's *The Girls' Guide to Hunting and Fishing* or Helen Fielding's *Bridget Jones's Diary* or *Olivia Joules and the Overactive Imagination*.

Mayes, Frances.

Under the Tuscan Sun: At Home in Italy. San Francisco: Chronicle Books, 1996 (New York: Broadway Books, 1997). 280pp. ISBN 0767900383.

Mayes tells a tale of purchasing a home in Tuscany and the process of her acclimatization to all things Italian, in a book that is less a story than a series of highly evocative vignettes of Italian community and cultural life. Although the book will appeal to readers of travel narratives, the author's desire to turn a Tuscan house, Bramasole, into her home, should also appeal to readers of environmental writing who are interested in stories of how people connect to the places in which they live. The book also includes a chapter of recipes for those readers who will want to experience a taste of Tuscany in their own homes.

Subjects: Classics • Community Life • Food • Gentle Reads • Homes • Italy • Memoirs • Women Travelers

Now try: Both *A Year in Provence* by Peter Mayle, and *C'est la Vie: An American Conquers the City of Light, Begins a New Life, and Becomes—Zut Alors!—Almost French*, by Suzy Gershman, offer much the same type of stories, but set in France. Although the majority of locations in *The Lawrence Durrell Travel Reader* (edited by Clint Willis) are islands such as Cyprus, Corfu, and Sicily, it concludes in Provence, and Durrell's adopting of various locales as semi-permanent homes (rather than as travel destinations) is similar to Mayes and Mayle.

Mayle, Peter.

A Year in Provence. New York: Knopf, 1989 (New York: Vintage Books, 1991). 207pp. ISBN 0679731148.

Organized by months, Mayle's diary of his year in Provence, France, provides for the reader exactly what it promises. The author's intention here is emphatically not to provide narrative flow, but rather to evoke a sense of living in, rather than just visiting, another culture. This is accomplished through clear and pleasant writing and the provision of an interconnected series of vignettes about fixing up their temporary home, eating French food, and interacting with both their neighbors and the local bureaucrats.

Subjects: Classics • Community Life • Food • France • Gentle Reads • Homes • Memoirs • Seasons

Now try: Patrick Moon's recent *Virgile's Vineyard: A Year in the Languedoc Wine Country* is also the story of a man's year in southern France and his life at his uncle's vineyard. *Under the Tuscan Sun* by Frances Mayes also offers the narrative of a new resident in Italy, as opposed to a travel narrative. Last but not least, Lawrence Durrell's travel classics *Prospero's Cell* and *Reflections on a Marine Venus* also describe the author's long-term living experiences on Greek islands, also in diary form.

Stewart, Chris.

Driving Over Lemons: An Optimist in Andalucía. New York: Pantheon Books, 1999 (New York: Vintage Books, 2001). 249pp. ISBN 0375709150.

Chris Stewart (the original drummer for the band Genesis) tells an engaging story of getting to know a new country and neighbors in this travelogue about southern Spain. From the moment he and his wife Ana moved into their new home, El Valero, they were of course beset by new (old) home problems, farm chores such as harvesting figs and feeding pigs, and the challenges of getting to know their nearest neighbor, Domingo.

Subjects: Community Life • Friendships • Gentle Reads • Homes • Rural Life • Spain

Now try: Stewart is also the author of the sequel to *Driving Over Lemons, Parrot in the Pepper Tree*; readers fascinated with Spain might also want to try Derek Lambert's

Spanish Lessons: Beginning a New Life in Spain. David Yeadon's *Seasons in Basilicata: A Year in a Southern Italian Hill Village* is similar in both structure and tone, although it is slightly slower paced, while Ann Vanderhoof's *An Embarrassment of Mangoes: A Caribbean Interlude* is more adventurous.

Travel Humor

  2

Sometimes there's just not much explaining to be done: These books are funny. Not only are they funny as far as the travel genre is concerned, but they may also be winners as far as nearly all of nonfiction is concerned. Although the source of the stories' humor is still the journey (as well as the characters sharing the journey, in some cases), all of these authors' proficiency with quick and witty writing and distinctive turns of phrase will truly leave their readers wanting more. Much of the humor in these titles is derived from the awkwardness of the situations in which travelers often find themselves, confused and at the mercy of strangers (some of whom don't even speak the same language!) in unfamiliar landscapes. In locations where author and subjects do speak the same language (Englishman Tony Hawks is at his finest traveling through Ireland and conversing with any number of unique individuals there), humorous dialogue can also be a mainstay of this subgenre and is responsible for some of its most sparkling moments. With their emphasis on witty writing and often self-deprecating humor, these titles might also appeal to fans of the "Humorous Memoir" subgenre of the "Memoirs and Autobiography" chapter.

Bryson, Bill.

A Walk in the Woods: Rediscovering America on the Appalachian Trail. New York: Broadway Books, 1998 (1999). 284pp. ISBN 0767902521.

Back in the United States after living abroad for many years, travel writer Bryson decided to walk the length of the Appalachian Trail. Bryson's strongest talent is his use of dry humor, and some of the best moments in this journey travelogue are those when he was most sick of his somewhat ill-suited traveling companion, Stephen Katz. In addition to spats with his friend and asides on the natives and other hikers, Bryson mixes a good bit of science and history into his travel story, making this a fast but still educational read.

Subjects: Appalachian Trail • Classics • Climbing and Hiking • Friendships • Humor • Mountains • Quick Reads • Walking

Now try: Bryson is the author of many other hugely popular and similarly dryly humorous travelogues, among them *Notes from a Small Island* and *In a Sunburned Country*. Tony Horwitz's adventurous account of his journey to relive the eighteenth-century explorations of Captain James Cook, *Blue Latitudes: Boldly Going Where Captain Cook Has Gone Before*, is a nautical version of Bryson's lighthearted but completely serious attempt to complete a set and historical itinerary.

Cahill, Tim.

Hold the Enlightenment. New York: Villard, 2002 (New York: Vintage Departures, 2003). 297pp. ISBN 0375713298.

Cahill's unique and sometimes curmudgeonly, but always honest, voice comes across strongly in this collection of travel essays. The author also manages to combine the stories of some of his most thrilling exploits (looking for the Caspian tiger in the mountains of Turkey, exploring toxic waste dumps in the United States) with humor and self-effacing admissions of his own failings as an adventurer (not the least of which is his extreme attractiveness to bugs, due to his propensity to sweat). The stories vary greatly in length as well as in locale and tone, but all are quickly paced and include more dialogue than is typically present in travel narratives.

Subjects: Adventure • Essays • Humor • Spirituality • World Travel

Now try: Tim Cahill is a big name in travel writing, and his other, more adventurous stories, such as *Road Trip, Pass the Butterworms: Remote Journeys Oddly Rendered,* and *Pecked to Death by Ducks,* will most likely become must-reads for his fans. His self-deprecating humor is similar to that of Bill Bryson, another popular travel writer who offers librarians numerous titles to recommend to the avid travel reader.

Hawks, Tony.

Round Ireland with a Fridge. New York: Thomas Dunne Books, 1998 (2001). 247pp. ISBN 0312274920.

Based on a "totally purposeless idea, but a very fine one," Hawks's whimsical hitchhiking journey around the circumference of Ireland was undertaken to win a bet with a friend. The rub? Hawks had to make the journey with a small refrigerator in tow. This story of his journey, adoption of his quest by a radio personality in Ireland, and the many fine Irish citizens he met, including the King of Tory Island, is a completely amusing and quick read, and the suspense of learning whether or not Hawks will win his bet adds to its page-turning character.

Subjects: Community Life • Humor • Ireland • Quick Reads • Walking

Now try: In *Join Me!* Danny Wallace, another young and amusing Brit whom the reader may suspect doesn't have quite enough to do, puts a small ad in the paper advertising for individuals to "Join Me!" and send a photo to his address; the only problem was that he had to then decide what his applicants were joining him for! Hawks's subsequent bet and travel narrative, *Tennis with the Moldovans,* although a victim of terrible cover art, relates his quest to beat all of the members of the Moldovan soccer team at tennis. John Pollack's *Cork Boat* is not based on a bet, but is an enjoyably light account of the author's dream of building a sailable boat entirely out of wine corks, including the often amusing details of collecting the necessary corks.

Lansky, Doug.

Up the Amazon without a Paddle: 60 Offbeat Adventures Around the World. Minnetonka, Minn.: Meadowbrook Press, 1999. 277pp. ISBN 0881663344.

National Public Radio commentator and travel writer Lansky provides a thoroughly enjoyable and quickly readable series of sixty travel stories related solely by the author's ability to display his laconic wit and somewhat absurdist humor. The experiences vary widely by geography and experience, making the character of Lansky himself the primary draw: from describing himself as a snack for the various native animals when he was on a canoe in an African river to bypassing Bangkok sex shows because he found them icky, he remains a personable tour guide for the reader throughout.

Subjects: Adventure • Essays • Humor • Quick Reads • World Travel

Now try: *Not So Funny When It Happened*, an anthology of short and humorous travel pieces, is edited by well-known travel writer Tim Cahill, and provides interesting travel experiences from a variety of travel and other writers (Bill Bryson and Anne Lamott are just two examples). Edited by Rosemary Caperton, Anne Mathews, and Lucie Ocenas, *The Unsavvy Traveler: Women's Comic Tales* is also a light and humorous read consisting of short and immediately arresting chapters; *Women in the Wild*, edited by Lucy McCauley (and part of the <u>Travelers' Tales</u> series) is less humorous but more adventurous and contains rich descriptions of the landscape.

Moore, Tim.

Frost on My Moustache: The Arctic Exploits of a Lord and a Loafer. New York: St. Martin's Press, 1999 (2001). 280pp. ISBN 0312270151.

Looking for a way to travel and also get a story out of it, British journalist Moore chanced upon the idea of re-creating the Artic journey of Lord Dufferin, a Victorian explorer who eventually served as both Governor-General of Canada and Viceroy of India, as related in his travelogue *Letters from High Latitudes*. What Moore eventually realized is that Dufferin, although a very nice bloke, was more the adventurous type; Moore found more to identify with in the person of Dufferin's valet Wilson, who is emphatically described as more of a wet blanket. Moore's reactions to his journey north with Dufferin's descendants and his Icelandic wife are humorously cantankerous in tone and heavier on character, rather than landscape, descriptions.

Subjects: Arctic Regions • Exploration • Humor

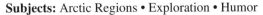

Now try: Although Moore's sense of humor is a large part of the appeal of this title, readers may also be drawn to its sense of exploration. For these readers, consider offering some of the classics of Arctic travel narratives, including Valerian Albanov's 200-page *In the Land of White Death: An Epic Story of Survival in the Siberian Arctic* and Fergus Fleming's *Ninety Degrees North: The Quest for the North Pole*. Moore has also produced other titles focusing on his travel experiences; they include *French Revolutions: Cycling the Tour de France* and my nominee for best title ever, *Travels with My Donkey: One Man and His Ass on a Pilgrimage to Santiago*.

O'Hanlon, Redmond.

Into the Heart of Borneo. New York: Random House, 1985 (New York: Vintage Books, 1987). 191pp. ISBN 0394755405.

Part journey narrative, part humorous and mishap-laden story of multiple and mismatched traveling companions, O'Hanlon's classic of travel writing takes the reader along on his journey to the heart of Borneo in all its heat and jungle glory, accompanied by his Oxford friend James Fenton, as

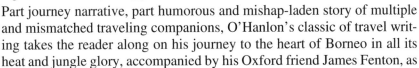

well as several guides. O'Hanlon uses his understated humor to describe both his interactions with the native residents of Borneo and the beauty of the rain forest landscape.

Subjects: Borneo • Exploration • Friendships • Humor • Islands

Now try: Peter Fleming's (brother to Ian Fleming) *Brazilian Adventure* might also appeal to O'Hanlon fans, as might Tony Horwitz's *One for the Road* or William Laurance's *Stinging Trees and Wait-a-Whiles* (the latter two both set in Australia). Although set in vastly different locales, all combine the sense of "in over my head but enjoying it anyway" style of simultaneously humorous and adventurous travel writing for which O'Hanlon is (justly) famous.

Troost, J. Maarten.

The Sex Lives of Cannibals: Adrift in the Equatorial Pacific. New York: Broadway Books, 2004. 272pp. ISBN 0767915305.

In which the author moves, with his girlfriend Sylvia, to the small island Tarawa in the Kiribati Islands group, and many hilarious misadventures ensue. If that sentence annoys you, or you think it might annoy your reader, this is not the book for you; hilariously tongue-in-cheek, Troost opens each chapter with just such a description. Although overwhelmingly lighthearted in tone and refreshingly open-minded toward island lifestyles, not all of Troost's writing is frivolous; he does consider the effects of colonialism and nuclear testing on the islands and their environmental future.

Subjects: Community Life • Environment • Humor • Pacific Islands • Pollution • Quick Reads

Now try: Paul Collins's enjoyable recounting of the year he and his wife spent living in the Welsh town of Hay-on-Wye, famous for having 1,500 residents and 40 antiquarian bookstores, *Sixpence House*, may appeal to readers who find Troost's self-effacing humor refreshing.

Literary Travel

This last subgenre is distinguished from the rest not by its authors' laudable command of language and prose styling, but rather by how they apply their skills not to landscape or character description, but to more existential concerns of being and belonging. If that sentence isn't warning enough that these are very different travel works, I can say it more plainly: These are reflective stories, not written to describe a place or tell the story of a journey, but rather to provoke thoughts about the nature of our regular places in the world, as well as our world's many unique geographies, cultures, and peoples.

In addition to reflecting on the many differences they find between themselves and residents of "elsewhere," these authors usually manage to bring their thoughts and writings around to those characteristics and experiences that they believe to be illustrative of the universal. In commenting on the adaptation of Western influences into Eastern culture in *Video Night in Kathmandu*, Pico Iyer questions what it is that truly defines those influences as Western. Ian Frazier, in researching and describing the historical sites he visits in *Great Plains*, wonders what the future will bring for the region's inhabitants and tourists. In short, these narratives explore what it means to be social and cultural, if not geographical, citizens of the world. As such, they may appeal to fans of titles found in the "Of Our Surroundings" subgenre of the "Making Sense . . ." chapter, which also focus on how we interact with our homelands or our residential geographies.

Allende, Isabel.

My Invented Country: A Nostalgic Journey through Chile. Translated by Margaret Sayers Peden. New York: HarperCollins, 2003 (New York: Perennial, 2004). 199pp. ISBN 0060545674.

Allende brings her novelistic and lyrical fiction writing skills to this memoir of her life in Chile, including details on its culture, politics, and history. The niece of Salvador Allende, whose government was overthrown in a 1973 coup that was planned by the CIA, Allende brings a personal immediacy to the story of her homeland's often violent past and governance. The family members and friends she describes are as fully realized as most compelling characters in fiction, and also add to the appeal of this travelogue that is a journey as much through time and memory as through place.

Subjects: Chile • Family Relationships • Memoirs • South America • Women Travelers

Now try: John Gimlette's *At the Tomb of the Inflatable Pig: Travels Through Paraguay*, although longer and less linguistically artistic, is a union of Gimlette's personal history with that of his adoptive South American country, which has also seen its share of dictators and discord. Likewise, Mary Lee Settle's *Spanish Recognitions: The Roads to the Present* offers both her present-day travel observations about her trip through Spain with no itinerary (undertaken when she was in her eighties) and her vast store of knowledge about how the country's geography and inhabitants have formed its history and society.

Frazier, Ian.

Great Plains. New York: Farrar, Straus & Giroux, 1989 (New York: Penguin Books, 1990). 292pp. ISBN 0140131701.

Equal parts history lesson and travel narrative, Frazier's stories of his multiple drives across the Great Plains states (Montana and North Dakota south through Texas) are rich with character portraits of fellow travelers and hitchhikers that he met, as well as with historical narratives regarding westward expansion by the post–Civil War pioneers and their clashes with the American Indian residents of the region. The author lived in Montana for several years and brings to his observations an appealing sense of belonging to the region he's writing about.

Subjects: American Indians • Great Plains • History • Montana

Now try: Although more historical, Tony Horwitz's *Confederates in the Attic: Dispatches from the Unfinished Civil War* is also a travel narrative of sorts, in that the author travels to various historical sites and gets to know many historical battle re-enactors, describing them with admirable objectivity.

Iyer, Pico.

Sun After Dark: Flights into the Foreign. New York: Knopf, 2004. 223pp. ISBN 0375415068.

A compilation of stories about some of Iyer's most thought-provoking travels over the years, this slim volume contains characters and locations as varied as Leonard Cohen in an Asian meditation camp and a businessman on Easter Island. Although Iyer's use of language is fluid and skillful and his descriptions of many disparate landscapes powerful, the true appeal of this narrative is the character portraits he provides in each story.

Subjects: Culture Clash • Essays • Philosophy • World Travel

Now try: All of Iyer's collections of travel writings are beautifully written and seek to make deeper connections between locations than mere geographic similarities; *Video Night in Kathmandu: And Other Reports from the Not-So-Far East,* his first book, examines the mixture of Western pop culture and Eastern traditional culture; subsequent titles, such as *Falling off the Map: Some Lonely Places of the World* and *The Global Soul: Jet Lag, Shopping Malls, and the Search for Home* illustrate Iyer's journeys made not only to travel, but also to unravel the reasons for traveling. In a similar vein, Alain de Botton's philosophical treatise on the compulsion to travel, *The Art of Travel,* makes for reflective reading.

Newby, Eric.

Slowly Down the Ganges. New York: Scribner, 1966 (New York: Penguin Books, 1986). 298pp. ISBN 0140095721.

Don't let the copyright date fool you: Newby's skillful writing and respectful consideration of the Ganges River and its role in the lives of India's people feels as contemporary as if it had just been published. Traveling the length of the river with his wife, Newby focuses less on the adventure of their trip than on the tactile sense of traversing it at a slow and deliberate pace; conversely, the chapters are relatively short and packed with beautiful descriptions of both the landscape and their encounters with their guides and other travelers and residents of the country.

Subjects: India • Landscape • Rivers

Now try: Although journalist Edward Gargan's writing style is less polished than Newby's, his *The River's Tale: A Year on the Mekong* also considers the importance of a major river in the history of its landscape and in the current lives of its human residents. Although told over the course of a longer period of time, Eric W. Morse's quietly and naturally profound *Freshwater Saga: Memoirs of a Lifetime of Wilderness Canoeing in Canada* is also a tale of personally fulfilling travel in the traveler's favorite environment.

Pham, Andrew X.

Catfish and Mandala: A Two-Wheeled Voyage Through the Landscape and Memory of Vietnam. New York: Farrar, Straus & Giroux, 1999 (New York: Picador, 2000). 344pp. ISBN 0312267177.

Pham's no-holds-barred honesty makes this travelogue successful as both the story of his bicycle journey through Vietnam, the land of his birth, and an immigrant experience memoir. In alternating chapters he contrasts his journey as a "Viet-kieu" (foreign Vietnamese) bicycling solo through Vietnam with childhood memories of growing up Vietnamese American in a family that struggled to overcome culture shock and tragedies such as the suicide of his sister.

> **Subjects:** Culture Clash • Family Relationships • Immigration • Memoirs • Vietnam • Vietnam War

> **Now try:** Although Pham's book is classified as a travelogue, it includes extended personal stories of his family's experiences as refugees. Many other titles from the "Immigrant Experience" subgenre of the "Memoirs and Autobiography" chapter, such as Lydia Minatoya's *Talking to High Monks in the Snow* and Marie Arana's *American Chica: Two Worlds, One Childhood*, might be complementary reads for Pham's readers.

Quindlen, Anna.

Imagined London: A Tour of the World's Greatest Fictional City. Washington, D.C.: National Geographic, 2004, 162pp. ISBN 0792265610.

Quindlen first physically traveled to London when she was in her forties, but by her own admission, she had traveled there in spirit many times through works of literature, since her very earliest childhood. In a somewhat surreal but thoroughly enjoyable (particularly for Anglophiles or bibliophiles, and doubly so for those readers who are both!) narrative, she combines her current wanderings throughout the city with numerous literary allusions, all in a subtly fluid prose style.

> **Subjects:** Books and Learning • England • Literary Lives • London • National Geographic <u>Directions Series</u> • Women Travelers

> **Now try:** Susan Allen Toth's *My Love Affair with England: A Traveler's Memoir* shares the location and enthusiasm of Quindlen's book about London. *Crete* by Barry Unsworth is much the same, although more historical in its allusions. The books in the National Geographic <u>Directions series</u> are all short, quick reads that are personal to their authors (examples of series titles are *Oaxaca Journal*, by Oliver Sacks; *Sicilian Odyssey* by Francine Prose; and Louise Erdrich's *Books and Islands in Ojibwe Country*). Last but not least, readers might also enjoy being referred to any of the authors Quindlen discusses in her text, including John Galsworthy (*The Forsyte Saga*), Jane Austen (*Pride and Prejudice*), and Charles Dickens, among many others.

Raban, Jonathan.

Passage to Juneau: A Sea and Its Meanings. New York: Pantheon Books, 1999 (New York: Vintage Departures, 2000). 435pp. ISBN 0679776141.

Raban's description of his travels through his own reflections takes almost as much space in this narrative as do the stories regarding his physical travels through the "Inside Passage" from Puget Sound to Alaska. His writing is extremely evocative ("meringue-like gobbets of fog were caught in shady, northward facing hollows") and extremely leisurely in pace; pages can go by during which he hardly moves, except for broad traverses across historical legends and his inner thoughts, especially regarding his own interpersonal relationships.

> **Subjects:** ALA Notable Books • Alaska • Exploration • Family Relationships • Memoirs • Sailing

Now try: Peter Nichols's *Sea Change: Alone Across the Atlantic in a Wooden Boat* is a similarly reflective journey undertaken by a man seeking to understand himself and the failure of his marriage, although it is more quickly paced than Raban's narrative. Raban's award-winning work of reflective history, *Bad Land: An American Romance*, might also appeal to readers who enjoy his more lugubrious pace.

Steinbach, Alice.

Educating Alice: Adventures of a Curious Woman. New York: Random House, 2004 (New York: Random House Trade Paperbacks, 2005). 289pp. ISBN 0812973607.

A former feature reporter for the Baltimore *Sun*, Steinbach decided to combine her love of travel and learning by attending courses at various cultural institutions, from the Ritz Escoffier École de Gastronomie Française in Paris to the annual meeting of the British Jane Austen Society, as well as by exploring little known corners of Havana and Prague. Peppered with a variety of characters and locations, this is a truly great sampler of both travel and new experiences, told in a distinctive and highly personal way.

Subjects: Education • Europe • Food • Memoirs • Women Travelers

Now try: Steinbach's previous work, *Without Reservations: The Travels of an Independent Woman,* takes the author through Paris, Oxford, and Milan, as well as through a variety of experiences and into friendships with fellow travelers. *Appetite for Life: The Biography of Julia Child*, by Noël Riley Fitch, also follows the adventures of a fascinating woman who always wanted to keep learning.

Stuever, Hank.

Off Ramp: Adventures and Heartache in the American Elsewhere. New York: Henry Holt, 2004. 297pp. ISBN 0805075739.

A staff writer for *The Washington Post,* Stuever has written a travel book about the United States that is less about the states themselves than about different states of mind. Linked less by geography than by style, Stuever expounds upon his fascination with the feel of locations and the often strange characters that inhabit them, from the woman who stalks the traveling cast of the musical *Jesus Christ Superstar* to what he describes as the "Krazy n' Kool" vibe of most decidedly not famous American places.

Subjects: Essays • Investigative Stories • Memoirs • Pop Culture

Now try: Another group of chapters about experiences in the worldwide "elsewhere" that are fairly disparate in geography and tone is Geoff Dyer's existential *Yoga for People Who Can't Be Bothered to Do It*. Mark Singer's *Somewhere in America: Under the Radar with Chicken Warriors, Left-Wing Patriots, Angry Nudists, and Others* is an extremely similar collection of journalistic essays.

Thubron, Colin.

In Siberia. New York: HarperCollins, 1999 (2001). 285pp. ISBN 006095373X.

Part travelogue, part history, in this book Thubron weaves a hauntingly evocative tale of his travels through Siberia. Opening with a description of the city in the Ural Mountains where Czar Nicholas II and his family were executed and interspersed with the historical details of their deaths, Thubron then travels east and describes the inhabitants and places of Siberia's five million square miles. Along the way he speaks with current residents, who offer both unstinting hospitality and calmly horrific stories of their history in the region's Gulag, or prison camps, as well as current economic and environmental problems, and their feelings about their future.

Subjects: ALA Notable Books • Arctic Regions • Prison • Russia • Soviet Union

Now try: Thubron is also the author of the similar title *Among the Russians*, as well as an Asian travelogue, *Behind the Wall: A Journey through Asia*. Readers who want to learn more about the history of Russia, which Thubron often alludes to, may find David Remnick's *Lenin's Tomb: The Last Days of the Soviet Empire* an informative read; those not averse to larger books of history might find Anne Applebaum's *Gulag: A History* a darkly fascinating complementary read.

Winchester, Simon.

The River at the Center of the World: A Journey up the Yangtze and Back in Chinese Time. New York: Henry Holt, 1996 (2004). 414pp. ISBN 0312423373.

Winchester brings his geological experience along for the ride in this travel narrative of a journey on the seldom-traveled (by Westerners, at least) Yangtze River. With his traveling companion, Li Xiaodi (whom he refers to as Lily), he travels the river from east to west, describing the attributes of the land around them and telling stories about China's history. His prose is leisurely and often winds around his topics as inexorably as the river itself winds itself through China, and is more reflective in tone than much travel writing.

Subjects: ALA Notable Books • China • Culture Clash • Epic Reads • Rivers

Now try: Although it also pops up in the environmental chapter, *River: One Man's Journey Down the Colorado, Source to Sea*, written by Colin Fletcher, is another river-based narrative that combines a bit more adventure with a similarly reflective tone. David Haward Bain's *The Old Iron Road: An Epic of Rails, Roads, and the Urge to Go West* combines the author's scholarly interest in the American West and railroad history with his family's journey across the country.

Consider Starting With . . .

Here are some popular travel titles, likely to appeal to readers of this genre.

Ehrlich, Gretel. *This Cold Heaven: Seven Seasons in Greenland.*

Hawks, Tony. *Round Ireland with a Fridge.*

Iyer, Pico. *Sun after Dark: Flights into the Foreign.*

Mayes, Frances. *Under the Tuscan Sun: At Home in Italy.*

Theroux, Paul. *The Old Patagonian Express: By Train through the Americas.*

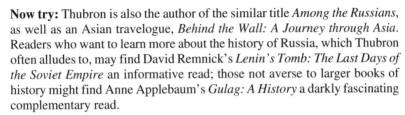

Troost, J. Maarten. *The Sex Lives of Cannibals: Adrift in the Equatorial Pacific.*

Fiction Read-Alikes

- **Buffett, Jimmy.** Reading Buffett's wonderfully escapist travel fiction is like vicariously living his famous song "Margaritaville." In his novels, such as *Tales from Margaritaville* (inspired by readings of Bruce Chatwin and Joseph Campbell), *Where Is Joe Merchant? A Novel Tale*, and *A Salty Piece of Land*, he provides an ever-sunny account of life in equatorial locations and atmosphere.

- **Durrell, Lawrence.** In addition to being a talented poet and well-respected nonfiction travel writer, Durrell also produced the critically acclaimed <u>Alexandria</u> quartet of novels: *Justine, Balthazar, Mountolive*, and *Clea*, extended prose poems that combine historical, personal, and landscape details in the telling of their stories.

- **Greene, Graham.** His fiction classics may hold more timeless appeal than his nonfiction travelogue; *Travels with My Aunt* is a thoroughly enjoyable romp around the world, undertaken by a rather stuffy former bank manager, his free-spirited aunt, and her lover, Wordsworth.

- **Kerouac, Jack.** Kerouac's frenetic prose (Truman Capote referred to it as typing, not writing) and bohemian ideals are not for all readers, but those who find themselves drawn to travel literature for its stories of journeys rather than destinations might find much to like in his stream-of-consciousness road novels *On the Road, Big Sur*, and *The Dharma Bums*.

- **Mahfouz, Naguib.** Mahfouz, winner of the 1988 Nobel Prize for Literature, does not technically write travel narratives, but the setting of many of his works in his native Egypt, and his ability to describe the landscape and its residents completely and skillfully, gives his novels an air of realism that makes them feel like narrative nonfiction. His <u>Cairo</u> trilogy, consisting of the books *Palace Walk, Palace of Desire*, and *Sugar Street*, relates the story of a Muslim family in British-occupied Egypt in the early twentieth century; *Midaq Alley* further details the lives of poverty lived by many residents of Cairo.

- **Mayle, Peter.** In addition to his works of narrative nonfiction, Mayle has also authored several popular works of fiction set in France, including *Hotel Pastis: A Novel of Provence* and *Anything Considered*.

- **Theroux, Paul.** Although well known for his nonfiction travel narratives, Theroux is also a prolific writer of fiction stories set in far-flung and exotic locations; *Saint Jack* (set in Singapore), *The Mosquito Coast* (set in Honduras), and *Hotel Honolulu* (set in Hawaii) are three of his most famous and well-received titles.

Further Reading

<u>The Best American Travel Writing</u> **(series)**. Boston: Houghton Mifflin, 2000–present. 2004 editor: Pico Iyer. Previous editors: Ian Frazier, Frances Mayes, Paul Theroux, Bill Bryson.

Blanton, Casey.

Travel Writing: The Self and the World. New York: Twayne (Studies in Literary Themes and Genres series), 1997. 148pp. ISBN 0805709673.

Blanton's slim volume discussing travel writing as a genre includes a timeline of major events and authors; a comprehensive introductory essay on the history, types, and appeal of travel writings; and several chapters examining the works of influential writers in the field (including James Boswell, Mary Kingsley, Graham Greene, Peter Matthiessen, V. S. Naipaul, Bruce Chatwin, Paul Theroux, and Roland Barthes), as well as a list of suggested representational readings. Although it is heavily historical in content, librarians might find the timeline and introductory essay particularly helpful in drawing a larger picture of the genre.

Holland, Patrick, and Graham Huggan.

Tourists with Typewriters: Critical Reflections on Contemporary Travel Writing. Ann Arbor, Mich.: University of Michigan Press, 1998 (2000). 261pp. ISBN 0472087061.

Holland's and Huggan's book is a bit too interested in developing a body of literary criticism (complete with lit crit terms like "narratives of disappearance" and "postmodern metanarratives") about travel writing to be a true pleasure read, but it does offer insights into the appeal of much modern travel writing, as well as brief but interesting references to the genre's history and best- known authors.

References

Blanton, Casey. 1997. *Travel Writing: The Self and the World.* (Studies in Literary Themes and Genres series). New York: Twayne.

Fussell, Paul. 1987. *The Norton Book of Travel.* New York: Norton.

Morris, Jan. 1997. "Travel Lit's Novel Pursuit." *The Nation* 265, no. 10 (October 6): 37–38.

"Travel Literature" Web site. 2005. http://en.wikipedia.org/wiki/Travel_Literature (accessed July 20, 2005).

Chapter 3

True Crime

Definition of True Crime

True crime, as a genre, gets very little respect. Its titles rarely win the big literary awards, nor are they often named as Notable Books by either the American Library Association or the *New York Times Book Review*. The number of titles published annually doesn't show up in the Bowker statistics available at bookwire.com, and its authors aren't often listed among those whose works librarians or other book purveyors and reviewers are encouraged to provide to readers who may want to augment their fiction reading with nonfiction reading.

This may in large part be due to the often disturbing subject matter of the titles included in the genre, compounded by the fact that unlike the violence described in mystery and horror titles, the violence described in true crime narratives is real, and actually happened to the unfortunate victims of the crimes involved. It's true, it's not a genre to read casually or recommend lightly, but it's not one to be avoided, either. Although the stories contained in these titles are often closer in subject matter to horror fiction than to mystery, they also contain some of the most suspenseful narratives outside of true adventure and character portraits that are rivaled only by those in biography and memoir titles, although the characters in this genre tend to be of the most unsavory type.

The genre developed during the Victorian era (latter half of the nineteenth century), when crime fiction authors such as Wilkie Collins and Charles Dickens used elements and story lines from actual crimes in their novels. Sadly, there has been no shortage of true crime events on which to report, and the advent of the twentieth century brought such salacious cases as Lizzie Borden supposedly taking an axe and giving her mother and father "forty whacks," as well as the kidnapping of the Lindbergh baby and the exploits of murderers Richard Loeb and Nathan Leopold. Newspaper journalists took the lead in reporting most of those stories, which resulted in serialized and highly sensationalistic accounts of both the crimes and the investigations of them. Newspaper accounts were supplemented by the publication of

increasing numbers of true crime books, and the Mystery Writers of America trade association began awarding titles the "Best Fact Crime" Edgar® awards in 1948. Eventually Truman
Capote produced the watershed work combining nonfiction reporting techniques with fictionalized near-novel writing; with *In Cold Blood*, first published in 1965, Capote introduced
a story that had as much to do with the inner world of the criminal as it did with the events of
the crime, and the popularity of such psychological and narrative-driven true crime works
continues to this day.

Appeal of the Genre

Some of the most distinguishing characteristics of this genre can be discerned from a
how-to article written by one of its finest authors, Susan Kelly, who recommends that true
crime writers over-research their topics, interview as many of the case participants as they
can, and pick a case that has been solved or about which they have a theory, as publishers prefer to see a story with a beginning, a middle, and an end (Kelly 1996, 21–22). Characters and
suspenseful stories make these books the thrilling reads that they often are. These books also
unabashedly provide a forum for our (at times) morbid human curiosity; our propensity to
stare at the site of traffic accidents and our desire to understand the deeper motives and causes
of criminal psychology and behavior are just two examples of our fascination with the darker
side of human nature (also evidenced by the enduring popularity of the horror fiction genre).
The authors of the *The Mystery Readers' Advisory: The Librarian's Clues to Murder and
Mayhem* speculate that some readers might be drawn to true crime books because they "are
fascinated by the extremes of human behavior, illustrating that the world's real murderers are
more twisted and fiendish than any villain or predator dreamed up for the pages of a novel"
(Charles, Morrison, and Clark 2002, 45). That sentiment holds true particularly for those perpetrators who are considered (for lack of a better term) "criminal celebrities," individuals
who are not famous for good reasons, but rather for the shocking and truly unforgettable nature of their crimes, such as Charles Manson, Jeffrey Dahmer, Bonnie and Clyde, and unfortunately many others. For ease of identification, books telling these individuals' stories
include the term "Celebrity Criminals" among their subject headings.

In addition to the more stereotypical crime narratives, which focus on the details of the
crime and the criminals (and which offer a vicarious scare more akin to that obtained from
horror novels), new types of true crime stories are appearing all the time, including in-depth
investigations of police work such as Miles Corwin's *Homicide Special* or true crime/history
hybrids like Erik Larson's hugely popular *Devil in the White City*. Fans of these more investigative true crime stories may also be amenable to branching out into closely related genres of
fiction, such as mystery and thriller stories and authors like James Patterson and Ian Rankin.

The true crime publishing juggernaut shows no signs of slowing or ceasing production
any time soon. As pointed out by Stephen Michaud, whose own book about Ted Bundy is one
of the classics in the canon, "The subject matter has evergreen appeal; there's a murder on
page three of *Genesis*" (2005, 10).

Organization of the Chapter

The first books that readers think of when they hear the label "True Crime" are those that tell the stories of how crimes were committed and explore the psyches of the individuals who committed them. Accordingly, we have the "Committing Crimes" subgenre, further subdivided into "True Horror: Violent Crimes and Criminals," "Murder Where You Live: Family and Lover Crimes," "Wise Guys: Mafia Crimes," "Murder's Not the Only Crime," "Horrific Historical Crimes," and "Street and Prison Life." Although some of the titles annotated include more detail than many readers (particularly those who haven't read widely in the true crime genre) will want to dwell upon, most of them are listed in the "True Horror," "Murder Where You Live," and "Horrific Historical Crimes" sections; while less graphic titles are offered in the remaining sections. The flip side of the genre, which we've titled "Investigating Crimes," is further divided into "Police Procedurals," "Unsolved Mysteries," and "Courtroom Dramas." Many of the titles resemble more stereotypical mystery titles and contain less horrific detail; for example, even when Ann Rule is describing the crimes of the Green River Killer (*Green River, Running Red*), she spends less time re-creating the killer's actions and inner thoughts than she does describing how law enforcement officials used the clues he left to apprehend him.

Committing Crimes

True Horror: Violent Crimes and Criminals

If librarians and other readers' advisors know only one true crime title, it's usually Truman Capote's novelistic *In Cold Blood*, which became a huge best seller when it was first published in the 1960s and has continued to sell well ever since. Although Capote used more fictional narrative techniques than are usually found in nonfiction, such as describing the thought processes and feelings of the murderers in his story, his book is still seen as a benchmark in the field. Along with Capote's book, the other titles in this psychologically thrilling subgenre often appeal to the majority of true crime readers, who usually "want to know why these people turned into such monsters" (Charles, Morrison, and Clark 2002, 45).

In addition to their character appeal, these scary stories also feature large amounts of suspense and often quickly paced storytelling. They are also typically told in a journalistic style (although Jack Olsen's *I: The Creation of a Serial Killer* is told at least partially from the killer's point of view) and are based on extensive research and interviews. They tend to be more objective than titles in the "Unsolved Mysteries," subgenre, in which the authors provide more speculation on how crimes were actually committed.

Capote, Truman.

In Cold Blood: A True Account of a Multiple Murder and Its Consequences. New York: Random House, 1965 (2002). 343pp. ISBN 0375507906.

Every bit as chilling now as when it was written, Capote's classic novelistic account of the horrific murder of the entire Clutter family in Kansas in 1959 features as its two main characters the murderers: Richard Hickok and Perry Smith. Often cited for its blurring of the line between fiction and nonfiction, Capote's re-creation of the murders and his speculation about the killers' actual thought processes while committing the crime and afterwards were based on numerous interviews and research that he conducted shortly after the crime.

> **Subjects:** Best Fact Crime Edgar Award Winners • Classics • Community Life • Family Relationships • Homicides
>
> **Now try:** Liza Ward's superlative work of fiction, *Outside Valentine*, is based on the true story of the murders committed by the young couple Caril Ann Fugate and Charles Starkweather in 1958 and is similar in both setting (rural Nebraska) and time period (1950s) to Capote's seminal work of true crime reporting. Ward also tells the story from a variety of points of view and describes her characters' mental states, much as Capote did. Screenwriters J. Dwight Dobkins and Robert J. Hendricks provide a similar reading experience in their 1973 title about one of the Great Depression's most infamous murder cases, *Winnie Ruth Judd: The Trunk Murders*, while John Berendt's near-novel *Midnight in the Garden of Good and Evil* (about a murder in Savannah, Georgia) might also appeal to fans of Capote's novelistic style.

Carlo, Philip.

The Night Stalker: The Life and Crimes of Richard Ramirez. New York: Kensington Books, 1996 (1997). 559pp. ISBN 0786003790.

Carlo uses a journalistic reporting style to relate the crime details, capture, and trial of the "Night Stalker," a ruthless rapist and murderer who went on a crime spree in Los Angeles, as well as detailing the childhood of Richard Ramirez, the man convicted of the crimes and sentenced to nineteen death sentences. Carlo also details the satanic nature of Ramirez's motivation and the rather chilling effect he had on several women, who fell in love with him during his trial and continue to visit him in prison.

> **Subjects:** Homicides • Law Enforcement • Rape • Serial Crimes
>
> **Now try:** David Abrahamsen details the methods and crimes of David Berkowitz, the "Son of Sam," who killed several women in New York City over the course of a full year, from 1976 to 1977, in *Confessions of Son of Sam* (ironically, Abrahamsen in the psychiatrist who declared Berkowitz mentally fit to stand trial).

Cummins, Jeanine.

A Rip in Heaven: A Memoir of Murder and Its Aftermath. New York: New American Library, 2004. 302pp. ISBN 0451210530.

The only thing more horrific than the crime at the center of this narrative is the subsequent story of police suspicion and erroneous belief that one of the victims was actually the prime suspect. In 1991, teenagers Tom Cummins and his two cousins, Robin and Julie Kerry, snuck out of the Kerry home, where Cummins was visiting, to hang out on the abandoned "Old Chain of Rocks" bridge between Illinois and

Missouri, a popular spot for local high school students. There they were overpowered by four young men, who beat the trio, raped the girls, and then threw all three off the bridge to what they assumed would be their deaths. Only Cummins survived; when he finally made his way to the authorities, they refused to believe that he could have survived such a fall and immediately began treating him as their main suspect. Cummins was eventually exonerated, and the real criminals were apprehended and convicted. The author tells the entire harrowing story with honesty and provides an afterword questioning the efficacy of capital punishment, which in her opinion only serves to make the convicted killers the undeserving victims of compassion.

Subjects: Capital Punishment • Family Relationships • Friendships • Homicides • Law Enforcement • Rape

Now try: In my humble opinion, only Alice Sebold's gut-wrenching account of her rape, as told in *Lucky: A Memoir*, even comes close to packing the same emotional wallop as Cummins's narrative, and it is told with the same intense stylistic skill. Burl Barer's tale of another violent and heartbreaking crime perpetrated on a family, *Murder in the Family*, is also poignantly told.

Jones, Richard Glyn.

The Mammoth Book of Women Who Kill. New York: Carroll & Graf Publishers, 2002. 547pp. ISBN 0786709537.

The writing is sensationalistic, and there is no denying that anyone who has an interest in the actions and the psyches of female killers will find much to titillate in this volume. From historical murderesses such as Agrippina (in ancient Rome) and Lizzie Borden to more recent cases such as those of Myra Hindley and Aileen Wuornos (although most stories seem to take place from the end of the nineteenth century through the 1930s), very few details are spared in these thumbnail sketches of the women and their crimes.

Subjects: Biographies • Celebrity Criminals • Essays • Homicides • Quick Reads

Now try: Carroll & Graf offer several such quick-reading and salacious volumes of true crime stories, including *The Mammoth Book of Illustrated Crime*, *The Mammoth Book of Murder and Science*, *The Mammoth Book of Unsolved Crimes,* and *The Mammoth Book of True Crime*.

Mailer, Norman.

The Executioner's Song. Boston: Little, Brown, 1979 (New York: Vintage International, 1998). 1,056pp. ISBN 0375700811.

In this famous blending of fiction and nonfiction, one of the earliest examples of "creative nonfiction," Mailer tells the story of Gary Gilmore, who killed two men in one night in Utah and was executed by firing squad just a few months later. The story unfolds through the varying perspectives of the family members and the lover with whom Gilmore lived his last few months, not only providing chronological and narrative details, but also ascribing feelings and attitudes to the principal characters. Mailer based those attributions on extensive research and interviews, but the writing of this account is novelistic (some say sensationalistic) and can be read surprisingly quickly in light of how long it is. The narrative is also fascinating for its attention to the story behind the story; namely, the details of Gilmore's execution (which he openly lobbied for) and the many reporters and interviewers, including Larry Schiller, who spoke with the principal characters before and after Gilmore's death.

> **Subjects:** Capital Punishment • Classics • Epic Reads • Homicides • Investigative Stories • Mormonism • Utah

> **Now try:** If your reader enjoys *The Executioner's Song*, most definitely suggest Mikal Gilmore's excellent *Shot in the Heart* as a companion read. Readers who enjoy Mailer's novelistic writing approach might also enjoy Truman Capote's literary nonfiction classic, *In Cold Blood*. Mailer also applies his narrative skills to his and Larry Schiller's exploration of the man who shot John F. Kennedy, Lee Harvey Oswald, in *Oswald's Tale: An American Mystery*.

McGuire, Christine, and Carla Norton.

Perfect Victim. New York: William Morrow, 1988 (New York: Dell, 1989). 370pp. ISBN 0440204429.

An entirely disturbing recitation of the facts in the "Girl in the Box" case, in which twenty-year-old Colleen Stan was abducted by a seemingly normal young married couple named Cameron and Janice Hooker, then held by the pair as a sexual and labor slave for nearly seven years. Although Cameron Hooker originally kept their captive locked in a box in the family's basement and only allowed her out long enough to indulge in his sadomasochistic fantasies, her imprisonment eventually became more mental than physical, with Cameron brainwashing Stan into believing that her slavery to him was real and legitimate. Chapters relating the bizarre details of Stan's enslavement alternate with those in which the sequence of Hooker's trial is described. The struggles of Stan's attorney, the author, to understand the mentality of her client provide a logical counterpoint to an otherwise unbelievably strange story.

> **Subjects:** Kidnapping • Law and Lawyers • Marriage • Mental Health • Sexuality

> **Now try:** Another entry in the St. Martin's True Crime Library, John Glatt's *Cries in the Desert*, also tells a sordid and detailed tale of a disturbed couple and their sadistic proclivities. Corey Mitchell's *Dead and Buried: A Shocking Account of Rape, Torture, and Murder on the California Coast* is another scary and detailed read that is not for the faint of heart.

Morrison, Helen, and Harold Goldberg.

My Life among the Serial Killers: Inside the Minds of the World's Most Notorious Murderers. New York: William Morrow, 2004 (New York: Avon, 2005). 289pp. ISBN 0060524081.

Forensic psychiatrist and author Morrison shares the stories of her many interviews with some of the most infamous twentieth-century serial killers; John Wayne Gacy, Ed Gein, and Green River Killer Gary Ridgway all make appearances here, in addition to equally frightening but lesser known murderers. Although Morrison strives to keep her tone medical and scientific and maintains that any details provided are not intended to titillate, her very choice of subjects entails a certain amount of darkly horrifying but fascinating detail (Gein's dancing in a suit of female skin he made himself is a particularly vivid image), and her conclusion that serial murderers are largely created by genetics rather than environmental factors makes this a thoroughly disturbing read.

> **Subjects:** Celebrity Criminals • Homicides • Psychology • Serial Crimes

> **Now try:** There are a multitude of true crime books about serial killers. *Lethal Intent*, by Sue Russell, tells the story of Aileen Wuornos, the female serial killer whose story was the basis for the movie *Monster*. Other works on infamous serial killers include Terry Sullivan's *Killer Clown: The John Wayne Gacy Murders*, Donald A. Davis's *The Jeffrey Dahmer Story: An American Nightmare*, and Harold Schechter's *Deviant: The Shocking True Story of Ed Gein, the Original Psycho*; librarians and readers alike are warned that very few details are spared in these accounts.

Olsen, Jack.

I: The Creation of a Serial Killer. New York: St. Martin's Press, 2002. 365pp. ISBN 0312241984.

Author Olsen has produced many solid works of true crime reporting, and his latest tells the story of serial rapist and murderer Keith Hunter Jesperson, who was convicted of killing eight women during the 1990s. Although Olsen bases much of his narrative on interviews, he also tells part of the story from Jesperson's point of view, and the horrible details of the crimes and the chilling use of the killer's vocabulary and voice may be a bit much for some readers.

> **Subjects:** Homicides • Psychology • Rape • Serial Crimes

> **Now try:** Olsen is a prolific and popular true crime author, and readers who can handle his unstinting attention to detail might consider others of his books, such as *The Man with Candy: The Story of the Houston Mass Murders*, *Doc*, or *Cold Kill*. Diane Fanning is similar to Olsen in her detail-laden writing; readers might also consider her *Through the Window: The Terrifying True Story of Cross-Country Killer Tommy Lynn Sells* or *Into the Water*.

Rule, Ann.

The Stranger Beside Me. New York: Norton, 1980 (New York: Signet, 2001). 548pp. ISBN 0451203267.

In this story, first published in 1980, Rule varies slightly from her usual crime/investigation pattern to tell the unique story of her friendship with Ted Bundy, the serial killer who was eventually convicted and executed, whom she first met while they both worked at a crisis hotline service. Although the circumstances of the victims' disappearances and deaths are provided, Rules focuses primarily on seeking to understand Ted Bundy's childhood, relationships, and personality, as well as his terrifying ability to maintain what she (and many others) took to be a completely normal life, even in the midst of committing numerous brutal crimes.

Subjects: Classics • Friendships • Homicides • Psychology • Rape • Serial Crimes

Now try: Rule is one of the genre's best-known and biggest-selling writers, and no discussion of true crime would be complete without mentioning her. A former police-woman, her works (including the recent *Kiss Me, Kill Me, Heart Full of Lies*, and *Last Dance, Last Chance*) often include quickly paced accounts of horrific murders combined with detailed investigative descriptions of the police work undertaken to solve those crimes. Stephen G. Michaud's and Hugh Aynesworth's comprehensive investigation and detailed descriptions of Bundy's crimes appear in *The Only Living Witness: A True Account of Homicidal Insanity*, written after the pair spent many hours interviewing Bundy before his execution. Although the story is not as personal to the author in Ted Schwarz's *The Hillside Strangler*, the fantastic nature of Ken Bianchi's crimes, which few people who knew him could believe he actually committed, is similar in scope to that of Ted Bundy's crimes. Both killers were often perceived as totally normal, which creates most of the horror of their crimes.

Schechter, Harold.

Deranged: The Shocking True Story of America's Most Fiendish Killer. New York: Pocket Books, 1990. 306pp. ISBN 0671678752.

Well-known genre author Schechter is not afraid to use a truly horrifying level of detail in his storytelling, and this book about killer and cannibal Albert Fish (supposedly the real-life inspiration for the fictional character Hannibal Lecter) is no exception. Fish was a kidnapper and murderer who abducted young children, killed them, and ate parts of their bodies; law enforcement officials and the participants in his trial were shocked to hear of his many torturous and sexual dysfunctions. Schechter is a professor of American culture at Queens College, and although he is a skillful storyteller, this narrative is not recommended for anyone other than the truly dedicated true crime reader; it is part of a series of books described by its publisher as designed to combine "true crime and horror to create a uniquely unsettling reading experience."

Subjects: 1920s • Cannibalism • Celebrity Criminals • Homicides • Serial Crimes

Now try: Schechter is also the author of *Deviant*, about Ed Gein, and *Fiend: The Shocking True Story of America's Youngest Serial Killer*. Another horrific story is told in Donald A. Davis's *The Jeffrey Dahmer Story: An American Nightmare*. That book is also part of the St. Martin's True Crime Library; true crime readers may consider the many titles in that series for further reading.

Murder Where You Live: Family and Lover Crimes

The crimes detailed in this subgenre's stories are not only violent and often beyond comprehension, but are distinguished by another horrifying attribute: They are crimes committed against family members, significant others, or friends. For that reason, although their primary appeals center on the crime story, they also offer strong character development (particularly in the case of Mikal Gilmore's hauntingly beautiful memoir, *Shot in the Heart*) and the exposition of interpersonal relationships (Lois Duncan's *Who Killed My Daughter?* is heartbreaking but also provides a compelling vision of the love between a mother and her daughter). These titles offer the same "inside look" into the minds and psyches of the killers and criminals they profile, but include even more tragic overtones due to their focus on crimes perpetrated on family members or close friends or lovers.

Several classics of the genre, including Joe McGinniss's *Fatal Vision* and Ann Rule's *Bitter Harvest,* are included here; these are titles librarians should be familiar with. McGinniss's book is often cited as an example of "immersion journalism" (see chapter 10, "Investigative Writing"), while Ann Rule is a hugely popular and sympathetic author of numerous books about true crime.

Duncan, Lois.

Who Killed My Daughter? New York: Delacorte Press, 1992 (New York: Dell, 1994). 354pp. ISBN 0440213428.

Children's author Lois Duncan, known for her fiction thrillers, is charged here with telling a more intimately horrible story, that of the murder of her teenaged daughter, Kaitlyn Arquette, in 1989. The immediate suspect, although he strove to remain close to the Duncan family, was Arquette's boyfriend Dung Nguyen, whom it was later discovered was involved with insurance fraud and Vietnamese gangs. Duncan also describes her many encounters with crime-solving psychics in her quest to discover who shot her daughter, and includes transcripts of many of her sessions with them in the text of the narrative.

Subjects: Culture Clash • Family Relationships—Mothers and Daughters • Homicides • Love and Dating • Parapsychology

Now try: Dominick Dunne's collection of crime stories, *Justice: Crimes, Trials, and Punishments*, includes many stories about crimes committed by and against many of the famous Hollywood characters he has spent a lifetime observing, but the most haunting story is that of the murder of his own daughter at the hands of her ex-boyfriend. George Lardner Jr. also provides the point of view of a victim's parent in his first-person investigation of the facts behind his daughter's murder by her boyfriend in *The Stalking of Kristin: A Father Investigates the Murder of His Daughter*. Although supernatural means were not necessary to discover that teenagers Marlene Olive and Chuck Riley were the killers of Marlene's parents, many of the details of the crime were only made available to prosecutors when they put Riley under hypnosis, and author Richard Levine weaves those confessions into the narrative of *Bad Blood: A Family Murder in Marin County*.

Gilmore, Mikal.

Shot in the Heart. New York: Doubleday, 1994 (New York: Anchor Books, 1995). 403pp. ISBN 0385478003.

Gilmore, brother of convicted and executed murderer Gary Gilmore, provides a violent and sad family history of his parents and two other brothers, beginning with his mother Bessie's childhood in a large family with an abusive father and the often violent history of her Mormon faith and background. In the course of trying to understand the dynamics of his family and the cause of his brother's crimes, Gilmore also examines the brothers' relationships with each other and with their father, whose own past included violence, fraudulent crimes, and several previous marriages and children. Although few details of the murders for which Gary Gilmore was convicted are given, this story is nonetheless rooted in violence and shares much of the suspenseful foreshadowing of typical true crime narratives.

Subjects: ALA Notable Books • Con Artists • Dysfunctional Families • Family Relationships • Homicides • Memoirs • Mormonism • National Book Critics Circle Award Winners • Utah

Now try: Gary Gilmore was also the subject of Norman Mailer's famous *The Executioner's Song*, and whether readers start with that narrative or this one, these tales, when read together, provide a chilling picture of the causes and effects of familial violence. Jack Olsen's *Salt of the Earth: A Mother, a Daughter, a Murder* is also a testament to a strong woman and mother's ability to withstand criminal tragedy. Timothy Tyson's memoir *Blood Done Sign My Name* also examines the effect of a murder on the author's childhood and on broader community relationships.

McGinniss, Joe.

Fatal Vision. New York: Putnam, 1983 (New York: New American Library, 1989). 684pp. ISBN 0451165667.

McGinniss lived with the protagonist of his true crime story, Jeffrey MacDonald, while the latter was awaiting trial for the murder of his pregnant wife and two young daughters. The result is an exhaustively researched and described story of the crime, the investigation, and the trial. It includes many short chapters that are transcribed directly from interviews with MacDonald, describing his personal history with his wife and family.

Subjects: Family Relationships • Homicides • Investigative Stories • Marriage

Now try: Sadly, there is no shortage of true crime narratives that outline crimes committed within families. Three of the strongest examples of this subgenre are Jon Krakauer's *Under the Banner of Heaven;* Jerry Bledsoe's *Bitter Blood: A True Story of Southern Family Pride, Madness, and Multiple Murder;* and Richard Levine's *Bad Blood: A Family Murder in Marin County.* Another book that relies heavily on its author's involvement with the story is Michael Finkel's *True Story: Murder, Memoir, Mea Culpa.*

Provost, Gary.

Without Mercy: The True Story of the First Woman in South Florida to Be Sentenced to the Electric Chair. New York: Simon & Schuster, 1990. 252pp. ISBN 0671669966.

Provost tells the story of Dee Casteel, who received the death penalty for conspiring with the man she loved (who emphatically did not love her) to hire killers to murder his male lover, Art Valencia. Eventually they killed again, when they perceived that Valencia's mother was a security risk. In this frightening story of alcoholism and unhealthy interpersonal relationships, the author often intersperses the details of the crimes with imaginative re-creations of the conspirators' and victims' inner thoughts.

Subjects: Alcoholism • Capital Punishment • Drug Addiction • Friendships • Homicides • Love Affairs

Now try: Another horrific story of interpersonal relationships leading to family murders is told in Gary C. King's *Angels of Death: A True Story of Murder and Innocence Lost*, which is a title in the St. Martin's <u>True Crime Library</u> series. This series includes a variety of authors and subjects, the latter told with similar breakneck pacing and enough details to shock even the most dedicated of true crime readers.

Rule, Ann.

Bitter Harvest: A Woman's Fury, a Mother's Sacrifice. New York: Simon & Schuster, 1997 (New York: Pocket Star Book, 1999). 482pp. ISBN 0671868691.

Rule provides a sturdy chronicle of a horrific crime without dwelling on the more graphic details or lingering on psychological or investigative speculation. Half of this narrative follows the family relationships of Debora Green and Mike Farrar and their three children, as well as the horrible night in October 1995 when their house burned down and two of their children perished in the fire. The second half of the book follows the trial of Dr. Green, who was accused not only of arson but also of leaving her children to die, as well as the theory that she had tried to poison her husband on several occasions before the fire.

Subjects: Arson • Dysfunctional Families • Family Relationships • Homicides • Law and Lawyers • Marriage

Now try: Rule's *Everything She Ever Wanted* follows the criminal exploits of Patricia Vann Radcliffe Taylor Allinson, a Southern woman whose family's devotion to her overstepped all normal bounds of family interaction. Joe McGinniss's epic *Fatal Vision* also describes the story of family murders, in which the father, Jeffrey MacDonald, was accused of murdering his pregnant wife and their two young daughters, and also includes many details of the trial and the author's interviews with the suspect.

Walker, Kent.

Son of a Grifter: The Twisted Tale of Sante and Kenny Kimes, the Most Notorious Con Artists in America. New York: William Morrow, 2001. 405pp. ISBN 0060188650.

Walker relates stories of his childhood, intertwined with accounts of the criminal activities of his mother and his brother. Less reflective than Mikal Gilmore's familial account but compellingly and simply told, Walker's tale is also illustrative of the ties that can bind in families that engage in criminal activities together.

Subjects: Celebrity Criminals • Con Artists • Dysfunctional Families • Family Relationships • Memoirs • Serial Crimes

Now try: Jonathan Coleman's *At Mother's Request: A True Story of Money, Murder and Betrayal* takes as its subject the murder of an elderly gentleman for his money, perpetrated by his grandson and ordered by his grandson's mother (his own daughter).

Wise Guys: Mafia Crime

Thanks to the HBO series *The Sopranos*, we're in the midst of another surge in popularity of all stories that have to do with mafia and organized crime (a surge also occurred after the publication of and subsequent movies based on Mario Puzo's *The Godfather*). Because these stories have traditionally been popular fiction and nonfiction narratives, their basic plot lines and characters should be somewhat familiar to librarians and readers. The following titles are characterized by a somewhat brash tone, as well as action-packed narratives and a complicated network of characters, most of whom are either related, owe each other something, or are out to kill each other. In their own strange way they tell stories of teamwork and camaraderie not unlike that found in many police and investigation procedurals; unfortunately, however, their teamwork is undertaken in the service of their criminal activities and master plans.

Although many of the most popular works detailing mob crimes refer to the Italian mafia (as does the *Sopranos* series), they certainly don't have a lock on the book market; many of the stories below feature more international and every bit as dangerous syndicates, such as the Asian and Russian mafias.

Brasco, Donnie.

The Way of the Wise Guy. Philadelphia: Running Press, 2004. 224pp. ISBN 0762418397.

Told in punchy, extremely short chapters, this tough-talking memoir of Donnie Brasco's (a.k.a. Joseph D. Pistone) undercover experiences with the Mafia serves as a primer for understanding "wise guys." Sometimes uncomfortably explicit, the stories describing the quintessential qualities (they're not nice, most of them have women on the side but are good family men) of mob wise guys read as quickly as watching an episode of HBO's *The Sopranos*.

Subjects: Law Enforcement • Memoirs • Organized Crime • Quick Reads

Now try: Pistone's first book, *Donnie Brasco*, was a *New York Times* best seller and the basis for the popular movie of the same name, starring Johnny Depp and Al Pacino. Those readers more interested in the viewpoint of a woman previously married to a wise guy might enjoy Andrea Giovino's crime and family memoir, *Divorced from the Mob: My Journey from Organized Crime to Independent Woman.*

Friedman, Robert I.

Red Mafiya: How the Russian Mob Has Invaded America. Boston: Little, Brown, 2000 (2002). 266pp. ISBN 0425186873.

Journalist Friedman visited numerous establishments run by the Russian mafia in America and interviewed a number of the organization's top power brokers. He has produced a dark and disturbing portrait of the growing influence the "Mafiya" is having on American crime. The book is dense with information and names, but Friedman still tells a compelling tale of the rise of corrupt capitalism in Russia and its effect on crime syndicates in this country.

Subjects: Investigative Stories • Organized Crime • Russia

Now try: The Italian and Russian mafias are not the only ones readers of this subgenre might want to read about; other books on the subject with international twists include *Born to Kill: America's Most Notorious Vietnamese Gang, and the Changing Face of Organized Crime,* by T. J. English, and Dick Lehr's Edgar Award–winning *Black Mass: The True Story of an Unholy Alliance Between the FBI and the Irish Mob.*

Kobler, John.

Capone: The Life and World of Al Capone. New York: Putnam, 1971 (Cambridge, Mass.: Da Capo Press, 2003). 409pp. ISBN 0306812851.

This quick-moving biography of Chicago mob boss extraordinaire Al Capone is rich in period detail and written with a dramatic flair. From Capone's childhood in New York City to his earliest criminal activities and eventual crime syndicate control of the entire city of Chicago, Kobler combines research and primary source quotes to paint a vivid picture of the man, without dwelling unnecessarily on the sometimes gory details of the criminal activities that he supervised.

> **Subjects:** American History • Biographies • Capone, Al • Celebrity Criminals • Chicago • Gangsters • Organized Crime

3

> **Now try:** William Roemer's *Accardo: The Genuine Godfather*, tells the story of former Capone bodyguard Tony Accardo, who participated in the St. Valentine's Day massacre and eventually became a high-ranking member of the Chicago mafia in his own right. Readers interested in a broader history of mafia activity might consider Thomas Reppetto's *American Mafia: A History of Its Rise to Power*, while the insider's view of mob activities in the Windy City, found in Robert Cooley's mob-attorney-turned-informant memoir, *When Corruption Was King: How I Helped the Mob Rule Chicago, Then Brought the Outfit Down*, provides a more contemporary overview of crime syndicate activity.

Maas, Peter.

Underboss: Sammy the Bull Gravano's Story of Life in the Mafia. New York: HarperCollins, 1997 (New York: HarperPerennial, 1999). 308pp. ISBN 0060930969.

Based on the author's interviews with Gravano, this narrative provides an inside look at the wise guy lifestyle. From Gravano's youth to his activities as part of the Gambino organized crime family to his testimony against his former mob bosses, Mass skillfully presents Gravano's own words to form a suspenseful and personal story.

> **Subjects:** Biographies • Law Enforcement • Organized Crime • Prisons

> **Now try:** Henry Hill's first-person narrative (as told to Gus Russo) in *Gangsters and Goodfellas: The Mob, Witness Protection, and Life on the Run* is not as eloquent as Maas's story, but it packs a definite descriptive punch with Hill's lively narration of the travails of a former wise guy trying to adjust to life in the slow lane. Michael Walsh's skillful fictionalization of the real-life "Irish Godfather," Owen Madden, in his novel *And All the Saints*, provides a stylized mafia story that might also appeal to readers of this genre.

Murder's Not the Only Crime

This subgenre contains books that offer suspenseful and thrilling stories, as well as in-depth examinations of the criminal psyche, but veer closer to the suspense/thriller in tone and exposition and tend to contain much less violence (although fatalities may still be involved, as in Joseph Wambaugh's *Fire Lover*). Similar to the "Cons and Card Games" true adventure subgenre, they may even be darkly humorous. Greed and money, rather than hatred or bloodlust, are the general motivating forces here.

From an armored vehicle theft gone wrong (*Heist!*) to a thrilling portrait of recent crimes in the art world (*The Irish Game*), these titles offer thrills with many fewer chills, and even elements of dark humor.

Diamant, Jeff.

Heist! The $17 Million Loomis Fargo Theft. Winston-Salem, N.C.: John F. Blair, 2002. 241pp. ISBN 0895872528.

When David Ghantt, Kelly Campbell, and Steve Chambers combined forces in 1997 to rob one of the armored cars that Ghantt drove for the Loomis Fargo company, their heist resembled nothing so much as a Keystone Kops routine. From the very beginning, although the robbers thought they were being clever, they made multiple mistakes, culminating with two of them immediately spending a large portion of their ill-gotten cash on a new and expensive house. No one was harmed in the robbery, and Diamant tells a briskly paced story, making this a good read for patrons who don't necessarily want their true crime too violent.

Subjects: Law Enforcement • Love Affairs • Quick Reads • Robberies

Now try: Mark Bowden's *Finders Keepers: The Story of a Man Who Found $1 Million*, also centers on an average man, Joey Coyle, who found two bags of cash, couldn't resist their lure, and was eventually caught after blowing the cash everywhere around town. Scott Smith's novel *A Simple Plan* is built around a murder, and the characters, in their inability to think themselves out of getting caught, are quite similar to the real-life characters in Diamant's story.

Hart, Matthew.

The Irish Game: A True Story of Crime and Art. New York: Walker & Company, 2004. 220pp. ISBN 0802714269.

Hart is a master at creating unified stories out of many disparate events and facts (see also *Diamond*, in the "Investigative Writing" chapter), and this book, with its combination of both artistic and robbery methods, is no different. Although superficially centered on the burglary of eighteen valuable paintings from Ireland's Russborough House in 1986, Hart the journalistic narrative includes the history of the paintings, their owners, and the criminal life of the master burglar himself, Martin Cahill. Although there's a lot of information here, the book is short and quickly paced enough to nearly be read in one sitting.

Subjects: Art and Artists • Ireland • Quick Reads • Robberies

Now try: Robert Noah's novel, *The Man Who Stole the Mona Lisa*, inspired by the true theft of the masterpiece in 1911, might also appeal to readers enthralled by Hart's tale of art theft; likewise, Arturo Perez-Reverte's fantastic art world thriller/novel *The Flanders Panel,* made art conspiracies cool long before Dan Brown. Crime in the art world is also a popular subject for nonfiction works such as Christopher Mason's *The Art of the Steal* and Edward Dolnick's *The Rescue Artist: A True Story of Art, Thieves, and the Hunt for a Missing Masterpiece.*

Marcus, Richard.

American Roulette: How I Turned the Odds Upside Down—My Wild Twenty-Five-Year Ride Ripping Off the World's Casinos. New York: Thomas Dunne Books, 2003. 370pp. ISBN 0312291396.

Neither ego nor exotic locations are lacking in Marcus's first-person account of his many years spent making a living by cheating the casinos. His style is brisk in the tradition of quickly paced adventure writing, and readers should be aware that his language and jargon are definitely on the raw side of honest. Describing his many partners and numerous scams, Marcus takes great pride in his livelihood and provides a spirited account of his less than legal activities.

Subjects: Autobiographies • Con Artists • Gambling • Las Vegas • Memoirs • Robberies

Now try: There are blurbs on this book from both Michael Konik and Bill Mason; readers may want to try their similarly themed titles, *Telling Lies and Getting Paid: Gambling Stories* and *Confessions of a Master Jewel Thief* (respectively).

Wambaugh, Joseph.

Fire Lover: A True Story. New York: William Morrow, 2002 (New York: Avon, 2003). 396pp. ISBN 0060095288.

Wambaugh tells the story of arson investigator John Orr, who was eventually convicted of being the arsonist responsible for numerous and extremely damaging residential and commercial property files, the worst of which resulted in four deaths. In addition to providing insight into the mechanics of fires and arson investigation, the author also examines Orr's employment and psychiatric history. Nearly half of the narrative is consumed by the detailed and comprehensive account of Orr's trial.

Subjects: Arson • Best Fact Crime Edgar Award Winners • Investigative Stories • Law and Lawyers • Law Enforcement • Serial Crimes

Now try: Arson turns up in a surprising number of crime fiction and thrillers; some of the most recent are Sean Doolittle's *Burn*, Peter Robinson's *Playing with Fire*, and Patricia MacDonald's *Suspicious Origin*.

Horrific Historical Crimes

Our current era has no monopoly on human cruelty and crimes; some of the most enduring criminal legends and stories occurred a century or more ago. Historical crime narratives, although they often contain factual and detailed accounts of murders or other atrocities, also offer the appeal of more rigorous historical research and writing, and because they are being written and marketed to an audience that, for the most part, wasn't even alive when the crimes in question were being committed, they necessarily focus on "celebrity criminals" and some of the most mysterious and complex cases ever investigated. They also typically include elements of "whodunit?" reporting and speculative interpretation; Patricia Cornwell's *Portrait of a Killer* purports to offer the first-ever hard evidence of the true identity of Jack the

Ripper, while *Crime of the Century: The Lindbergh Kidnapping Hoax* questions the guilt of the man convicted for the crime.

Ahlgren, Gregory, and Stephen Monier.

Crime of the Century: The Lindbergh Kidnapping Hoax. Boston: Branden Books, 1993. 286pp. ISBN 0828319715.

The authors present the bare facts of the infamous kidnapping of Charles Lindbergh's infant son, the media and investigative frenzy that followed the report of the kidnapping, and the finding of the baby's body and the elevation of the case to murder. They also relate the details of the trial of Bruno Richard Hauptmann, who was eventually convicted of the crime. In addition to their factual retelling of the crime, the authors speculate that Hauptmann was in fact innocent, that the entire investigation was slapdash from the start, and that Charles Lindbergh himself might have had something to do with the crime.

Subjects: American History • Celebrity Criminals • Homicides • Investigative Stories • Kidnapping • Law and Lawyers • Lindbergh, Charles

Now try: There's no doubt this is one of the more fantastic theories being offered about the Lindbergh kidnapping; those readers who'd like a bit more straightforward account of the case might consider Jim Fisher's *The Ghosts of Hopewell: Setting the Record Straight in the Lindbergh Case*, which agrees with the conviction of Hauptmann. Readers who want to read more about Bruno Hauptmann but may not be ready for theories regarding Lindbergh's possible involvement might be better served by journalist Anthony Scaduto's investigation into the case, *Scapegoat: The Lonesome Death of Bruno Richard Hauptmann.*

Cornwell, Patricia.

Portrait of a Killer: Jack the Ripper, Case Closed. New York: Putnam, 2002 (New York: Berkley Books, 2003). 383pp. ISBN 0425192733.

Cornwell, best known for her Kay Scarpetta mysteries, boldly runs down the case for proving that Walter Richard Sickert, an artist and one-time apprentice to James Whistler, was actually the infamous Jack the Ripper. Cornwell tells both the stories of the victims and of the life of Sickert (who died in 1942) in chronological order, forcefully intermingling the details of her personal historical research and the many clues that, in her opinion, add up to his guilt. Cornwell is not squeamish about sharing the details of the murders, but the reader should be aware that the narrative here focuses on the present-day research and findings of the author more than on the story of the crimes.

Subjects: Art and Artists • Celebrity Criminals • Homicides • Investigative Stories • Jack the Ripper • Serial Crimes

Now try: Readers interested in more speculative tales about the true identity of Jack the Ripper might enjoy the *The Mammoth Book of Jack the Ripper*, edited by Maxim Jakubowski and Nathan Braund. It includes both a brief synopsis of the crimes and sixteen different theories, by different authors, about who the killer may have been. Compiled from the journals of an observer of the crimes, Rick Geary's *Jack the Ripper: A Journal of the Whitechapel Murders* is a straightforward narration of the atrocities, in graphic novel form. Although it describes a different crime, David Kent's *Forty Whacks: New Evidence in the Life and Legend of Lizzie Borden* is less dismissive of former theories about the truth behind the case, but also considers alternatives to Borden's guilt and discusses the inaccuracies about her in most reported histories. Rick Geary has also produced a graphic novel about that crime, *The Borden Tragedy*.

Larson, Erik.

The Devil in the White City: Murder, Magic, and Madness at the Fair That Changed America. New York: Crown Publishers, 2002 (New York: Vintage Books, 2004). 447pp. ISBN 0375725601.

Had you asked me whether this book had "best seller" written all over it, I would have thoroughly pooh-poohed the notion. It's a good thing I'm not an acquisitions editor, because this story, a historical mixture of the terrible murders committed by Henry H. Holmes during the 1893 Chicago World's Fair and an architectural and bureaucratic discussion of the direction of the fair itself, led by Daniel Hudson Burnham, almost defies classification. Larson entwines the stories of the two men (who never met) and uses court transcripts and other research to present some "imagined" episodes, primarily those that re-create the murders, in this baffling but never dull mix of true crime and urban construction.

3

> **Subjects:** American History • Best Fact Crime Edgar Award Winners • Biographies • Chicago • History • Homicides • Serial Crimes

> **Now try:** Simon Worrall's short but compelling twin study of the forging of an Emily Dickinson poem by convicted murderer and master forger of historical documents Mark Hofmann (*The Poet and Murderer*) is not as gory as Larson's but combines historical and literary detail with a crime narrative. Simon Winchester's popular book *The Professor and the Madman: A Tale of Murder, Insanity, and the Making of* the Oxford English Dictionary contrasts the stories of a London murder, perpetrated by an insane American, and the life and work of the studious creator of the *Oxford English Dictionary*. *The Affair of the Poisons* by Anne Somerset also includes some "imagined" murderous details and mixes history with true crime.

Milner, E. R.

The Lives and Times of Bonnie & Clyde. Carbondale: Southern Illinois University Press, 1996. 187pp. ISBN 0809319772.

A concise and crisply moving account of the early lives, relationship, and crime spree of notorious criminals Bonnie Parker and Clyde Barrow, this book is a marvel of reporting and exposition. Before their deaths at the hands of law enforcement officials in 1934, the pair and various members of their gang stole cars, committed robberies, and killed numerous people across a wide swath of the American Midwest, from Missouri to Texas.

> **Subjects:** American History • Biographies • Celebrity Criminals • Gangsters • Great Depression • Law Enforcement • Robberies • Serial Crimes

> **Now try:** *The Family Story of Bonnie and Clyde*, written by Phillip Steele and Clyde's sister Marie Barrow Scoma, provides a bit of the biographical and psychological background that readers of Milner's concise crime spree narrative might feel is missing in that book. Those readers not averse to trying a fictional account of the love and career of Bonnie and Clyde might also

find Bill Brooks's short but unflinching novel *Bonnie and Clyde: A Love Story* a good fictional read-alike. Two decades after Bonnie and Clyde went on their rampage, Charles Starkweather and Caril Ann Fugate began theirs; in 1958 they killed Fugate's entire family and eventually killed several more people in one of the country's worst cases of mass murder ever. Their story is told in *Starkweather: The Story of a Mass Murderer*, by William Allen (another work that considers the time period and media coverage of the event is Ninette Beaver's *Caril*) and is portrayed in fiction by Liza Ward's excellent novel *Outside Valentine*.

Wise, Sarah.

The Italian Boy: A Tale of Murder and Body Snatching in 1830s London. New York: Metropolitan Books, 2004. 375pp. ISBN 0805075372.

Although classified as a work of history, Wise's narrative outlining the murder of an Italian immigrant boy by three unsavory characters planning to sell his fresh cadaver (at a high price) to a London medical school is too downright creepy not to include it in true crime. Wise sets a convincing scene of 1830s London so the reader can easily imagine the actual circumstances of the crime, and he devotes a healthy portion of the story to relating the investigation of the crime and the trial of the perpetrators, so that readers of both suspenseful true crime and police procedurals will find much to keep them enthralled here.

Subjects: England • History • Homicides • Law Enforcement • London • Medicine • Nineteenth Century

Now try: Two recent books relating the story of the murder of the Earl of Sandwich's mistress, Martha Ray, in London in 1779, also provide a wealth of historical context and detail combined with the crime narrative; they are John Brewer's *A Sentimental Murder: Love and Madness in the Eighteenth Century* and Martin Levy's *Love and Madness: The Murder of Martha Ray, Mistress of the Fourth Earl of Sandwich*. Readers enthralled by tales of murders in Victorian times may also consider the books in Anne Perry's popular mystery fiction series, most of which are set in that time period (*The Cater Street Hangman* is the first in her Charlotte series, and *The Face of a Stranger* is the first in her Monk series).

Street and Prison Life

With the exception of crimes that take place in exotic locales or regional crime spree stories, setting doesn't typically play a prominent role in true crime stories. This category is the exception that proves the rule; these narratives of life on the streets and "on the inside" describe the simultaneous mind-numbing routine and possibility for volatility and sudden violence of both street and prison life.

Many of the titles listed below are told from the point of view of the inmates; however, readers who enjoy these books might also be profitably directed to more investigative works such as Ted Conover's *Newjack: Guarding Sing Sing* (annotated in chapter 10, "Investigative Writing") or Ralph Blumenthal's biography of pioneering warden Lewis Lawes, *Miracle at Sing Sing* (annotated in chapter 7, "Biography"), which share the same setting and subject matter.

Babyak, Jolene.

Breaking the Rock: The Great Escape from Alcatraz. Berkeley, Calif.: Ariel Vamp Press, 2001. 275pp. ISBN 0961875232.

Babyak is the daughter of Alcatraz's warden at the time of the famous prisoner escape from "the Rock" on June 11, 1962. Although she was living on the island at the time; she didn't start researching and writing this account until 1978; nonetheless, she provides a methodical but quickly paced rundown of the convicts involved, the details of their escape plan, the enactment of that plan, and the aftermath and speculation regarding three of the convicts, who were never seen again and were presumed drowned.

Subjects: Adventure • Investigative Stories • Prisons

Now try: A far bloodier escape incident took place in 1946, when six inmates planned to escape from Alcatraz and ended up in a prison shootout instead; Ernest Lageson tells that story in *Battle at Alcatraz: A Desperate Attempt to Escape the Rock.*

Lerner, Jimmy A.

You Got Nothing Coming: Notes from a Prison Fish. New York: Broadway Books, 2002 (2003). 397pp. ISBN 0767909194.

Convicted of manslaughter in Las Vegas, Jimmy A. Lerner was sent to serve his time in a Nevada state prison; he tells the story of his years there in this graphic and honest memoir. Lerner's reporting on his fellow inmates and re-creation of their dialogue makes this a quick read, and although come critics found the idea of reading a convicted felon's prison narrative distasteful, readers may find themselves drawn in by his writing skill and charisma, as well as by his narrative prowess in relating the details of the crime for which he was convicted.

Subjects: Homicides • Memoirs • Prisons • Quick Reads

Now try: Pete Earley's brutal stories of life in one of the harshest prisons in the nation can be found in his *The Hot House: Life Inside Leavenworth Prison,* which spares no details and is the result of two years of intensive research and interviews with inmates; readers interested in prison life might also try Robert Ellis Gordon's *The Fun House Mirror: Reflections on Prison.* Although told by an investigative reporter, Joseph Hallinan's *Going up the River: Travels in a Prison Nation* might provide a complementary read about prison overcrowding and incarceration as an ever-growing industry.

Prejean, Helen.

Dead Man Walking. New York: Random House, 1993 (New York: Vintage Books, 2004). 276pp. ISBN 0679751319.

Becoming famous when it was made into a motion picture of the same name, Sister Helen Prejean's narrative follows the development of her relationship with Pat Sonnier, who was convicted and executed in 1982 for murder and rape. Along with his brother Eddie, Sonnier killed couple David LeBlanc and Loretta Bourque, and although the author spares no details of the crime (most of which are related by Sonnier himself), fully half of the narrative takes place after Sonnier's execution and details Prejean's fight to expose the use of the death penalty as barbaric and ineffectual. The character portraits of the criminals that Prejean provides are an interesting lot to have chosen; in their honesty and lack of remorse, none of them is a particularly sympathetic victim, which makes the author's sincerity all the more thought-provoking.

Subjects: ALA Notable Books • Capital Punishment • Classics • Homicides • Nuns • Prisons

Now try: Prejean is quoted on the back of Eliza Steelwater's more historical work on executions in America, *The Hangman's Knot: Lynching, Legal Execution, and America's Struggle with the Death Penalty*; although Steelwater's book is less personal, she also pulls no punches in her description of executions. Joe Loya's *The Man Who Outgrew His Prison Cell: Confessions of a Bank Robber*, also provides an immediate and visceral narrative of both prison life and the genesis of one man's lifelong struggle with criminal activity.

Sikes, Gini.

8 Ball Chicks: A Year in the Violent World of Girl Gangsters. New York: Anchor Books, 1997 (1998). 276pp. ISBN 0385474326.

Author Sikes spent a year moving among the girl gangs of various cities (Los Angeles, San Antonio, Milwaukee) and found a world fully as violent as that of their male counterparts. Sikes's writing is crisp and provides admirable character portraits in the midst of describing violent situations; she also provides a bit of commentary on how these young women have "slipped through the cracks" and fallen into gangs while looking for a group identity and purpose.

Subjects: Friendships • Gangs • Serial Crimes • Urban Life

Now try: Sanyika Shakur tells the male side of the story in his *Monster: The Autobiography of an L.A. Gang Member*; Joseph Rodriguez's *East Side Stories: Gang Life in East L.A.* combines essays and photographs to powerful effect.

Wynn, Jennifer.

Inside Rikers: Stories from the World's Largest Penal Colony. New York: St. Martin's Press, 2001 (New York: St. Martin's Griffin, 2002). 223pp. ISBN 0312291582.

Wynn, the director of the Prison Visiting Project at the Correctional Association of New York, provides a great number of well-drawn character portraits of Rikers inmates whom she's met and visited over the years. Each chapter is named for an individual and tells that person's story ("Angel," "Frank," etc.). Wynn's prose is both cleanly descriptive and coolly appraising of the inmates' crimes and their struggles toward rehabilitation and plunges into recidivism, and she also weaves into her accounts much thought-provoking statistical information regarding poverty and other causes of crime.

Subjects: Alcoholism • Drug Addiction • Investigative Stories • Poverty • Prisons

Now try: There's a complimentary blurb from Ted Conover on the back cover of Wynn's books; readers might also find his story of life as a prison guard, *Newjack: Guarding Sing Sing*, a strong read-alike in this category. A similar story from the female point of view is told in Andi Rierden's *The Farm: Life Inside a Women's Prison*.

Investigating Crimes

Police Procedurals

In *Make Mine a Mystery: A Reader's Guide to Mystery and Detective Fiction*, Gary Warren Niebuhr notes that publicly funded police forces have only been in existence for about 200 years. He further credits Ed McBain with the creation of the "contemporary police procedural" in the 1950s (Niebuhr 2003, 141). It seems like a rather recent history, especially considering how old (timeless, really) crime is, but just because it's a short history doesn't mean it isn't populated with quality works of fiction and nonfiction.

The following titles are less sensational than many others in the true crime genre, but they compensate for that in the clarity of their writing and the insiders' point of view, the investigators' point of view, that they reveal. They appeal to readers who want "the facts" or the logistics of how crimes are solved. These readers aren't so concerned with "why" the crime was committed, but with "how" it was committed, and "how" the criminal is brought to justice. These stories also depict the interactions of a team working together toward a solution, so dialogue and interpersonal relationships come into play.

These authors tend to display very succinct and extensively researched journalistic writing (Miles Corwin, in *Homicide Special*), and readers who enjoy these books might also be tempted by many titles in the "Investigative Writing" chapter. Readers should be aware that not all true crime police procedurals are flattering to their investigative protagonists; Lawrence Schiller's *Perfect Murder, Perfect Town*, for instance, raises several questions about the effectiveness of the law enforcement investigation of JonBenét Ramsey's death.

Botz, Corinne May.

The Nutshell Studies of Unexplained Death. New York: Monacelli Press, 2004. 223pp. ISBN 1580931456.

Frances Glessner Lee provided the funding for a professor of legal medicine at Harvard in 1931, but she is better known for her construction of eighteen tiny but exceptionally detailed "nutshell studies of unexplained death," which look like extremely macabre dollhouses. The dioramas were actually used in the training of police officers, who attended Lee's weeklong seminars to learn about homicide investigation methods. Although there is a biographical essay of Lee's life, the majority of the book consists of eerie photographs of the tiny scenes, line drawings and descriptions of their most valuable clues, and solutions for just a few of them; all of the solutions could not be revealed because the models are still used for training.

Subjects: Biographies • Homicides • Illustrated Books • Law Enforcement

Now try: The more modern face of forensic examination is revealed in Emily Craig's *Teasing Secrets from the Dead*, annotated in the "Investigative Writing" chapter; fiction titles by Kathy Reichs and Patricia Cornwell, both authors who feature criminologists as their main characters, might also appeal to readers who find Botz's work here fascinating.

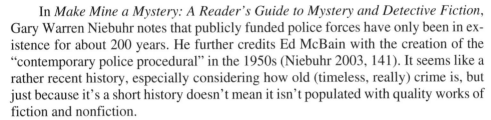

Burrough, Bryan.

Public Enemies: America's Greatest Crime Wave and the Birth of the FBI, 1933–1934. New York: Penguin Press, 2004. 592pp. ISBN 1594200211.

Although closer in length and style to a work of history, Burrough's narrative so clearly and evocatively details the various crime gangs' activities in the 1930s (indeed, the book is organized in geographic order, following the locations and dates of each gang's thefts and murders) that true crime fans might find more of interest here than students of history. Burrough's chapters are long and the writing, although lively, is dense with details and takes some time to read. Although Hoover's FBI agents and their struggles to conquer crime are described, the true main characters of the story are the criminals: John Dillinger, Pretty Boy Floyd, and the infamous Ma Barker are just a few examples.

> **Subjects:** American History • Celebrity Criminals • Epic Reads • Gangsters • Great Depression • Law Enforcement • Organizations • Organized Crime

> **Now try:** Richard Powers's *Broken: The Troubled Past and Uncertain Fate of the FBI* considers the more recent history and travails of that agency. Those readers more interested in the criminals than in the law enforcement officers trying to apprehend them might also enjoy Dary Matera's *John Dillinger: The Life and Death of America's First Celebrity Criminal.*

Corwin, Miles.

Homicide Special: A Year with the LAPD's Elite Detective Unit. New York: Henry Holt, 2003 (2004). 389pp. ISBN 0805076948.

A true nonfiction police procedural, Corwin's story outlining his year spent observing Homicide Special, the unit responsible for dealing with the toughest cases in Los Angeles, is actually the story of six disparate cases in one. He provides details of both the crimes the unit is assigned and of the homicide detectives' methods and working styles in this quickly paced and impressively investigated and written account. An epilogue describing the outcomes of most of the six cases investigated is also provided.

> **Subjects:** Homicides • Investigative Stories • Law Enforcement • Work Relationships

> **Now try:** Corwin is also the author of *The Killing Season: A Summer Inside An LAPD Homicide Division*; readers who enjoy his inside looks at police work might also be tempted by Edward Conlon's memoir *Blue Blood*, although it provides more personal details than either of Corwin's books. Although the authors of *The Mormon Murders: A True Story of Greed, Forgery, Deceit, and Death*, Steven Naifeh and Gregory White Smith, did not travel with the Salt Lake City police force, their narrative is an example of superlative police work, from their description of the crime scene investigation to their crediting of the forensic document examiners with breaking the case. Those readers less interested in the details of crimes than in the lives and experiences of cops might also enjoy Bernard Kerik's *The Lost Son.*

Gourevitch, Philip.

A Cold Case. New York: Farrar, Straus & Giroux, 2001 (New York: Picador USA, 2002). 183pp. ISBN 0312420021.

Short, meaty, beautifully written, this is Gourevitch's impossible-to-stop-reading narrative of New York investigator Andy Rosenzweig's thirty-year pursuit of petty criminal and murderer Frank Koehler, who shot two men in a continuation of a bar disagreement in 1970. Using research and interviews, the author takes the reader back in time to Rosenzweig's early days as a New York city cop, describes Koehler's family background and crime, and eventually culminates with Rosenzweig's renewed efforts as his retirement neared to track down the elusive Koehler, who was found living in California under the assumed name Frank O'Grady.

> **Subjects:** Homicides • Investigative Stories • Law Enforcement • Quick Reads

> **Now try:** A. M. Rosenthal's short but journalistically detailed *Thirty-Eight Witnesses: The Kitty Genovese Case*, was first published in 1964, but the chilling nature of the case (Genovese was stabbed, raped, and murdered near her home in Queens, New York, while thirty-eight nearby residents failed to intervene or call the police) sticks in the cultural psyche, much like Koehler's case stuck with Rosenzweig.

Rule, Ann.

Green River, Running Red: The Real Story of the Green River Killer, America's Deadliest Serial Killer. New York: Free Press, 2004. 436pp. ISBN 0743238516.

Rule alternates between telling the stories of the multiple victims of the Green River (Washington state) Killer, the eventual capture and sentencing of the suspect who eluded law enforcement agencies for years, and her own creepily personal side of the story (the murderer was familiar with her work and attended many of her readings). A former policewoman, Rule does an admirable job of providing brief portraits of each crime (and there are a lot of them; the Green River Killer was responsible for forty-eight murders) without describing too many horrific details, and is actually at her best when profiling the investigators and their police procedures.

> **Subjects:** Homicides • Law Enforcement • Rape • Serial Crimes • Washington

> **Now try:** Sheriff David Reichert provides the same story from the law enforcement and investigative point of view in his highly personal and detailed account of the hunt for Gary Ridgway in *Chasing the Devil: My Twenty-Year Quest to Capture the Green River Killer*. Rule is, of course, a prolific true crime writer, and several of her investigative works examine the crimes of brutal serial killers: *The Want-Ad Killer* (Harvey Louis Carignan), *The Lust Killer* (Jerry Brudos), and *The I-5 Killer* (Randall Woodfield).

Unsolved Mysteries

Whodunits are the mystery novels of the true crime genre, particularly because many of them end with some sort of theory or suggested guilty party, even if no convictions were ever brought; this may be because, as Susan Kelly has said, publishers (and readers) like to get some sort of closure at the end of their stories. Although they are often speculative and revisit former, and still unsolved, crime stories, they are not really historical in their use of frame details, nor are they usually as graphic in their descriptions of the crimes as the titles in the previous two categories (the lone exception being Susan Kelly's *The Boston Stranglers*, although she also does not linger over the physical evidence of the murders). For that reason, these may constitute a safe group of titles to recommend to readers who are less interested in "true crime books" than they are in interesting stories that present a problem to be solved.

Douglas, John, and Mark Olshaker.

The Cases That Haunt Us: From Jack the Ripper to JonBenét Ramsey, the FBI's Legendary Mindhunter Sheds Light on the Mysteries That Won't Go Away. New York: Scribner, 2000 (New York: Pocket Books, 2001). 487pp. ISBN 0671017063.

A virtual primer on some of the most infamous murder cases throughout history, this narrative admirably provides the facts of each case, as well as an interpretation of each crime's investigations, suspects, and outcomes, without ever veering into the sensational. Although some true crime readers may find the book, written by criminologist Douglas and writer Olshaker, too analytical and without the typically satisfying conclusion of convictions or theories, others may prefer its emphasis on the police investigations and historical context surrounding the still-unsolved cases of Jack the Ripper, Lizzie Borden, the Lindbergh kidnapping, the Zodiac crimes, the 1947 "Black Dahlia" murder, and JonBenét Ramsey.

> **Subjects:** Celebrity Criminals • Homicides • Law Enforcement • Serial Crimes

> **Now try:** Douglas and Olshaker previously collaborated on *Mindhunter: Inside the FBI's Elite Serial Crime Unit* and *The Anatomy of Motive: The FBI's Legendary Mindhunter Explores the Key to Understanding and Catching Violent Criminals,* which both provide an insider's view of the extent to which FBI investigators have to understand the psyches of the criminals they're hunting.

Kelly, Susan.

The Boston Stranglers. Secaucus, N.J.: Carol Publishing, 1995 (New York: Kensington Publishing, 2002). 511pp. ISBN 0786014660.

Boston in the early 1960s was the site of multiple murders of female victims by strangulation, and the perpetrator who confessed to being the "Boston Strangler" was Albert DeSalvo, a man with a checkered past and prior misdemeanor convictions. Kelly not only sets about proving that DeSalvo could not be the killer, but offers different murder scenarios to describe the multiple suspects who took advantage of the rampant fear in the Boston area to commit crimes of their own.

> **Subjects:** 1960s • Homicides • Law Enforcement • Massachusetts • Rape • Serial Crimes

> **Now try:** The last victim of the Boston Strangler (whoever it was) was Mary Sullivan, and no one was ever charged with the crime; her nephew, Casey Sherman, has recently written a new history about her murder and the case, *A Rose for Mary: The Hunt for the Real Boston Strangler.* Mystery writer Barbara D'Amato's *The Doctor, the Murder, the Mystery: The True Story of the Dr. John Branion Murder Case* examines a case in which a man was convicted of the murder of his wife, and outlines the author's research, from which she concludes that Dr. Branion could not have committed the crime for which he was convicted.

Schiller, Lawrence.

Perfect Murder, Perfect Town: JonBenét and the City of Boulder. New York: HarperCollins, 1999 (New York: HarperPaperbacks, 1999). 814pp. ISBN 0061096962.

Schiller's extensively researched and explicitly detailed book provides a more richly nuanced alternative to the national scandal newspapers from which most people learned about the murder of JonBenét Ramsey, who was reported missing in the early morning hours of December 26, 1996. Police investigators later found Ramsey's dead body in the wine cellar of her own home, leading to her parents becoming the prime suspects in her murder. Compiled from 25,000 pages of interviews conducted with 194 individuals, Schiller's narrative provides many different sides of the story, and, with admirable restraint, declines to posit his own theory about what really happened to Ramsey, preferring instead to let readers draw their own conclusions from the interviews, police reports, and numerous newspaper articles detailed.

Subjects: Classics • Colorado • Community Life • Epic Reads • Family Relationships • Homicides • Investigative Stories • Law Enforcement

Now try: Hal Higdon's story of the kidnapping and murder of Bobby Franks by Richard Loeb and Nathan Leopold is told in a similarly straightforward "just the facts" style in *Leopold and Loeb: The Crime of the Century*. Although that crime was solved, unlike the murder of JonBenét Ramsey, the sense of extreme injustice that flavors all works revolving around the death of a child (Franks was fourteen) is also present in Higdon's work. Mark Arax's personal account of the murder of his father, a bar owner who knew more than was healthy about an upcoming drug deal in Fresno, also considers the significance of place in many murder cases; it's titled *In My Father's Name: A Family, a Town, a Murder*. John Berendt's classic *Midnight in the Garden of Good and Evil* also explores a murder case in the complex and character-rich setting of Savannah, Georgia, where Jim Williams was tried for the murder of his sometime lover, Danny Hamsford.

Courtroom Dramas

The crimes have been committed, the police have done their investigating, so it seems only logical that the next subgenre of true crime would be "Courtroom Dramas." As anyone knows who has ever been involved with any kind of court case, even the simplest ones can often be lengthy and complicated affairs. While not all of these titles are long, many of them are heavily detailed and feature courtroom personnel such as lawyers as the main characters (*Helter Skelter* being one of the classic examples).

If the current proliferation of detective and legal dramas on television is any indication, people really enjoy stories about the machinations of the legal system. The primary appeal of these titles, as for most of those in the true crime genre, remains story and character, although the suspense of waiting for a verdict and the characters of lawyers and judges, instead of the suspense of impending violence and the characterization of victims and perpetrators, sets these titles apart.

Batt, Marissa N.

"Ready for the People": My Most Chilling Cases as a Prosecutor. New York: Arcade Publishing, 2004. 237pp. ISBN 1559707054.

Although she has spent twenty-five years as a Los Angeles deputy district attorney, Batt also displays impressive writing skills as she relates the stories of three of her most challenging cases with great storytelling verve and empathy. From the crime spree perpetrated by three young men that culminated in the rape and beating of two women they knew and their elderly friend, to a hate crime against a homosexual victim, to an overzealous neighborhood patrol group's beating of a young man selling marijuana, Batt tells compelling stories from commission of the crime through conviction.

> **Subjects:** Hate Crimes • Homicides • Law and Lawyers • Quick Reads • Rape

> **Now try:** Although he is not a prosecutor himself, investigative journalist Gary Delsohn provides an insider's view of the Sacramento criminal justice system in *The Prosecutors: A Year in the Life of a District Attorney's Office.* Although the O. J. Simpson case is receding ever further into history, former prosecutor Jeffrey Toobin's book about the trial, *The Run of His Life: The People Versus O. J. Simpson,* remains one of the best works on both the Simpson trial, as well as on criminal justice in general.

Bugliosi, Vincent, with Curt Gentry.

Helter Skelter. New York: Norton, 1974 (1994). 687pp. ISBN 0393322238.

Written by the prosecutor who tried and obtained convictions against Charles Manson and his accomplices, this famous work of true crime storytelling also includes sixty-four pages of photographs that make the shocking story all the more real. Bugliosi leaves no detail behind as he describes the crimes, the victims (who included film director Roman Polanski's pregnant wife, actress Sharon Tate), Charles Manson and his followers (who lived commune-style and referred to themselves as "the Family"), the police investigation, and the trial.

> **Subjects:** Best Fact Crime Edgar Award Winners • Celebrity Criminals • Classics • Homicides • Law and Lawyers • Manson, Charles • Serial Crimes

> **Now try:** Bugliosi is a masterful storyteller of complex crimes and courtroom dramas; two of his other titles, *The Sea Will Tell* and *Til Death Do Us Part: A True Murder Mystery,* are also compelling reads, even without the perverse attraction of Charles Manson and his oddly enthralled Family members.

Oney, Steve.

And the Dead Shall Rise: The Murder of Mary Phagan and the Lynching of Leo Frank. New York: Pantheon Books, 2003. 742pp. ISBN 0679421475.

This heavily detailed and historically contextual narrative tells the story of the murder in 1913 (in an Atlanta, Georgia, pencil factory) of thirteen-year-old Phagan; the charging of Leo Frank (a northern and Jewish supervisor at the plant) with the murder; the courtroom battle, which ended in Frank's conviction; and Frank's abduction and lynching in 1915, after his death sentence was commuted. Oney relies heavily on newspaper accounts and primary sources to tell the lengthy but gripping story.

> **Subjects:** Epic Reads • Hate Crimes • Homicides • Investigative Stories • Law and Lawyers

Now try: Joyce King's investigative *Hate Crime: The Story of a Dragging in Jasper, Texas*, is much shorter than Oney's book and is set in a much more recent time period (1998), but it is similar in its emphasis on placing a horrible crime in the context of its surroundings (as is Mamie Till-Mobley's *Death of Innocence: The Story of the Hate Crime That Changed America*, which examines the 1955 murder of Emmett Till and was written by his mother).

Consider Starting With . . .

The following list provides a sampling of the titles most popular with readers who enjoy true crime.

Capote, Truman. *In Cold Blood: A True Account of a Multiple Murder and Its Consequences.*

Gilmore, Mikal. *Shot in the Heart.*

Larson, Erik. *The Devil in the White City: Murder, Magic, and Madness at the Fair That Changed America.*

Maas, Peter. *Underboss: Sammy the Bull Gravano's Story of Life in the Mafia.*

Rule, Ann. *Green River, Running Red: The Real Story of the Green River Killer, America's Deadliest Serial Killer.*

Schiller, Lawrence. *Perfect Murder, Perfect Town: JonBenét and the City of Boulder.*

Fiction Read-Alikes

- **Block, Lawrence.** Block is a hugely prolific mystery and crime writer. His series of novels about New York City police detective Matthew Scudder might appeal to true crime readers most interested in police procedurals; that series started with *Sins of the Fathers* and *In the Midst of Death*. He also has something to offer to readers who like a bit of heist nonfiction; his series of books about book dealer/cat burglar Bernie Rhodenbarr includes *Burglars Can't Be Choosers* and *The Burglar in the Closet*.

- **Carr, Caleb.** Fans of books about famous crimes and criminals in history might enjoy Carr's historical (set at the turn of the twentieth century) novels focusing on serial crimes and psychological profiling, including *The Alienist* and *The Angel of Darkness*.

- **Chandler, Raymond.** Written by one of the masters of hard-boiled detective fiction, Chandler's books featuring Philip Marlowe (personified by Humphrey Bogart in the film version of *The Big Sleep*) are spare and gritty crime novels set in urban locations. Readers who enjoy cops with a dark side of their own might also like his novels *Farewell, My Lovely* and *The Long Goodbye*.

- **Child, Lee.** Many reviewers classify Child's works firmly in the "guilty pleasure" category, but his thrillers all include a strong ex-military policeman character in the form of Jack Reacher, and they certainly mimic the gritty detail and search for justice that seem present in many true crime narratives; 1997's *Killing Floor* was his first novel, and *The Enemy* and *One Shot* are his most recent ones.

- **Clark, Mary Higgins.** Clark's best-selling formula of suspenseful writing and the exploration of the darkness underlying seemingly normal situations is exhibited in many of her popular novels, such as *Loves Music, Loves to Dance* (about a murderer who works through newspaper personal ads), *Moonlight Becomes You* (about murderous dealings in a nursing home), and her first novel, *Where Are the Children?* (about kidnapping).

- **Connelly, Michael.** Thriller writer Connelly is best known for his crime novels featuring LAPD detective Hieronymous "Harry" Bosch, which include *The Black Echo*, *The Black Ice*, and *Angels Flight*, although his non-Bosch books, such as *The Poet* and *Blood Work* (which was made into a movie starring Clint Eastwood), have also been enthusiastically received by his fans.

- **Cornwell, Patricia.** Cornwell's popular series of mystery novels revolving around her recurring character, medical examiner Kay Scarpetta, are based on research Cornwell performed in a Virginia medical examiner's office. Her <u>Scarpetta</u> series began with *Postmortem* and *Body of Evidence*; recent titles include *Blow Fly* and *Trace*.

- **Goines, Donald.** Goines lived the hard and gritty lifestyle of a heroin addict, and it shows in his unflinching narratives, many of which feature recently incarcerated drug dealers and extremely bitter and cynical protagonists who exploit weaknesses for profit (in *Black Gangster* his main character establishes a civil rights organization that is a front for illegal activities). *Whoreson* and *Dopefiend*, about a pimp and a drug addict, respectively, were both written while Goines was serving time in prison.

- **Kellerman, Faye.** Kellerman's thrillers offer deeper psychological portraits of her criminals than do many other titles in this genre; however, readers and librarians are warned that she can also be quite graphic in her description of crimes and crime scenes. She also brings romantic elements to her stories, most vividly on display in her books about Rina Lazarus and Peter Decker, *The Ritual Bath*, *Milk and Honey*, and *Day of Atonement*.

- **King, Stephen.** The unrivaled king of the horror genre very rarely stints on gory details in his downright scary novels; true crime readers might explore some of his more suspenseful titles, such as *Rage*, *Misery*, *Dolores Claiborne*, and the prison story *The Green Mile*.

- **Leonard, Elmore.** Leonard's unique books, often populated by down-on-their luck protagonists looking to get rich quick through scams and heists, are experiencing a resurgence in popularity due to recent film adaptations of his work. Some of his biggest titles are *The Big Bounce*, *Get Shorty*, *Out of Sight*, and *Be Cool* (the sequel to *Get Shorty*).

- **McBain, Ed.** McBain's massively successful <u>87th Precinct</u> novels started appearing in 1956 with *Cop Hater*, and the author has slacked off in neither quantity nor quality of police procedural novels since then, most recently producing

Money, Money, Money, Fat Ollie's Book, and *The Frumious Bandersnatch*.

- **Patterson, James.** Patterson writes thrillers that contain a healthy amount of violent imagery, which is often in plentiful supply in true crime narratives. His <u>Alex Cross</u> series began with *Along Came a Spider*, a narrative focused on a serial killer, and *Kiss the Girls*, which tells the story of the abduction of investigator Cross's niece.

- **Sandford, John.** Sandford's <u>Prey</u> series, in which there are now sixteen titles, feature recurring character Minneapolis cop Lucas Davenport and are action-filled and just plain scary. The series started with *Rules of Prey* and *Shadow Prey*, and the most recent volumes are *Naked Prey*, *Hidden Prey*, and *Broken Prey*.

 3

- **Westlake, Donald.** Under his pseudonym Richard Stark, Westlake produced caper and heist novels such as *The Hunter, The Man with the Getaway Face*, and *Butcher's Moon*, which blended humor and crime writing. Writing as Westlake, he is best known for his series featuring burglar John Dortmunder, in titles including *The Hot Rock, Bank Shot*, and *Drowned Hopes*.

Further Reading

Court TV's Crime Library. www.crimelibrary.com/.

Those librarians or readers looking for short descriptions of a variety of murderers and other criminals can always refer to this informative site, which offers biographies and stories about criminals in the categories "serial killers," "notorious murder cases," "gangsters and outlaws," and "the criminal mind."

Huff, Steve.

The Dark Side (blog and true crime book review site). www.planethuff. com/darkside/archives/cat_true_crime_books.html

Huff posts frequently updated true crime and investigation articles, as well as comprehensive reviews of new true crime books.

MacNee, Marie J.

The Crime Encyclopedia: The World's Most Notorious Outlaws, Mobsters, and Crooks. Detroit: UXL, 1999. 495pp. ISBN 0787631639.

A well-written book in its own right, MacNee's reference work about the wide world of crime can serve as a broad introduction and useful resource for readers looking for stories and books about mobsters, racketeers, robbers, computer criminals, spies, gunslingers, terrorists, bootleggers, and swindlers. Informative articles include both numerous pictures and suggested resources for further reading. *The Encyclopedia of Serial Killers*, written by Michael Newton and published by Facts on File in 2000, might also prove useful for research purposes.

Munro, Vicky.

> **An Introduction to the True Crime Press.** www.crimeculture.com/Contents/
> True%20Crime.html.
>
> Crimeculture.com is dedicated to providing information to those educators who
> teach the subjects of crime fiction, film, and graphic art, and in addition to a history
> of the true crime genre, it provides many other valuable links and suggestions for
> further reading.

Schechter, Harold.

> ***The Serial Killer Files: The Who, What, Where, How, and Why of the World's Most***
> ***Terrifying Murderers.*** New York: Ballantine Books, 2004. 421pp. ISBN
> 0345465660.
>
> Many reference sources listing serial killers are available, but Schechter is also a
> prolific true crime author and provides a succinct rundown of the some of the most
> horrific crimes ever perpetrated. In addition to numerous murderers' names that
> readers may want to follow up, he also provides a bibliography and list of Internet
> resources.

Willis, Clint, ed.

> ***Mob: Stories of Death and Betrayal from Organized Crime.*** New York: Thunder's
> Mouth Press, 2001. 331pp. ISBN 156025324X.
>
> Willis provides thirteen stories that can, if browsed, provide a list of starter ideas
> for mafia and organized crime stories and authors that may appeal to readers in this
> genre. From stories about such notorious criminals as Sammy "the Bull" Gravano
> (written by author Peter Maas) to Joseph Pistone's undercover life as Donnie Bras-
> co to author Nicholas Pileggi's account of mob activity in Las Vegas as described
> in *Casino*, these short pieces combine the flavor and appeal of true crime writing
> with the emphasis on classics and must-reads of a reference work. As a bonus, Wil-
> lis also includes excerpts from fiction writers on the subject, such as William
> Kennedy and Mario Puzo.

References

Charles, John, Joanna Morrison, and Candace Clark. 2002. *The Mystery Readers' Advisory: The Librarian's Clues to Murder and Mayhem.* Chicago: American Library
Association.

Kelly, Susan. 1996. "Writing True Crime." *Writer* 109, no. 10 (October): 21–22.

Michaud, Steven. 2005. "Best True Crime Books." *Bookmarks* (March/April): 10–11.

Niebuhr, Gary Warren. 2003. *Make Mine a Mystery: A Reader's Guide to Mystery and
Detective Fiction.* Westport, Conn.: Libraries Unlimited.

Chapter 4

Environmental Writing

Definition of Environmental Writing

Nature writing, which is often described as having "emerged in response to the industrial revolution of the late eighteenth century" (Scheese 1996, 6) and is often thought of as being best exemplified by Henry David Thoreau's treatise *Walden*, published in 1854, has been defined many ways. One anthology posits that the genre has been "limited to landscape descriptions, accounts of animal behavior, or treatises on 'environmental issues' " (Finch and Elder 2002, 21). Another collection is introduced with the assertion that "the literature of nature has three dimensions to it: natural history information, personal responses to nature, and philosophical interpretation of nature" (Lyon 2001, 20).

Although both definitions are serviceable as far as they go, each has limitations. The first definition, which emphasizes the amount of landscape description in a story, does address such landmark titles as Mary Austin's *Land of Little Rain* or John Muir's *My First Summer in the Sierra*. Although it also accounts for works with a strong, environmentally activist point of view, such as Edward Abbey's *Desert Solitaire* or Rachel Carson's *Silent Spring*; it does not leave any room for works of a more interpersonal and reflective nature, such as Annie Dillard's Pulitzer Prize–winning *Pilgrim at Tinker Creek*. The second definition, while it does address "personal" and "philosophical" approaches to nature, does not leave much room for the inclusion of such animal story titles as Joy Adamson's *Born Free* or Dian Fossey's *Gorillas in the Mist*. Neither definition makes room for the sizable subgenre of agricultural or "back to the land" titles, exemplified by such titles as *Here and Nowhere Else*, Jane Brox's searingly honest memoir of her return to her family's farm and land.

Finally, the vast majority of reference books and anthologies referring to nature writing do just that: refer to it as "nature writing." Why then, have we chosen "Environmental Writing" as the title for this chapter? This label has been chosen in the hope that we can broaden the genre to include not only landscape descriptions, animal studies, and ecological treatises, but also works exploring how we interact with those landscapes and animals, as well as what it means to feel a "sense of place," either by birthright or through life experience.

Appeal of the Genre

Why readers enjoy environmental nonfiction should be readily apparent from a short free association exercise: What are the first thoughts that come to your mind when you encounter some of the biggest names in the genre, namely Henry David Thoreau, John Muir, or Aldo Leopold? By any chance, did you answer Walden, the Sierra Mountains (half credit for the Sierra Club), and Sand County? Did you, in short, respond to the names of the authors with names of places? If so, you have correctly discovered that readers are often drawn to natural and environmental writing works primarily by the places and settings they describe.

Setting is far and away the greatest attraction of many of these titles. In our fast-paced lives, not many of us get a lot of chances to touch nature directly, let alone immerse ourselves in it, either by withdrawing to a cabin in the woods like Thoreau or by going on glorious summer-long adventures into the Sierra Mountains like John Muir. Those readers seeking evocative descriptions of the natural world, from the biting cold of Alaska and the arctic region to the desert heat of Death Valley, will most certainly find them here. Language is often another appeal of these works, and other readers who delight in lyrical sentences pondering how both humans and animals coexist with the natural world will also be richly rewarded by many of those titles.

Readers who don't normally browse the Dewey 500s or the Library of Congress S or QH sections need not be intimidated by the subject matter. Many of the titles involving animals also include elements of great adventure and companionship, not to mention character portraits fully as complex as those of their human counterparts in modern novels. Likewise, many of the stories of building or finding one's home prominently feature details of friendships and family relationships; nature writing may be best known for propagating the stereotype of the lone woodsman or woodswoman, but as shown below, many nature writers are also astute at exploring the terrain of human relationships. Readers who enjoy more personal environmental titles such as Jane Brox's memoir *Here and Nowhere Else* and Anne LaBastille's Woodswoman series might also find titles to enjoy in the "Memoirs and Autobiography" and "Relationships" chapters. Some genre crossover is also evident between science and environmental titles; fans of Annie Dillard's *Pilgrim at Tinker Creek* may find a similarly smooth prose stylist in science writer Diane Ackerman, whose *A Natural History of the Senses* explores the environment of our bodies and senses, while fans of Rachel Carson's *Silent Spring* will find another of her titles, *The Sea Around Us*, annotated in the science chapter.

Organization of the Chapter

The first two subgenres listed, "Natural Places" and "Reflective Environmental Stories," contain many of the subject area's most famous titles and authors, and best exemplify the use of setting details and reflective/philosophical language and pacing that are the hallmark of environmental writing. The next two, "Back to the Land" and "Political," also contain immediately recognizable names but rely more heavily on the skill and charm of their narrators (as well as their use of language) than on the inclusion of landscape descriptions, while the last category, "Animal Stories," includes not only well-written works but also more character- and story-driven narratives about animals and the humans who either live with or observe them.

Natural Places

As befits a chapter in which the settings are the key draw of the works listed, this category describing specific places and containing many classics of the genre must be listed first. The mantra for this segment is the same as that for real estate: location, location, location. All other considerations are a distant second; instead, the setting itself is often the main and only character. In their pursuit of capturing the essence of the place, however, these authors do range further in scope than the reader might expect. History, science, philosophy, and travel, for instance, are just a few of the subjects that can also be found in the following titles.

Austin, Mary.

The Land of Little Rain. Boston: Houghton Mifflin, 1903 (New York: Modern Library, 2003). 109pp. ISBN 0812968522.

The only clue that this small but substantial ode to desert living is more than a hundred years old is the copyright date. In short, disparate chapters, Austin paints a detailed picture of her California desert, from its "blunt and burned" hills to its coyote and rabbit inhabitants.

Subjects: American West • California • Deserts • Landscape • Quick Reads • Rural Life • Solitude

Now try: Although slightly more political in tone, Janisse Ray's *Pinhook: Finding Wholeness in a Fragmented Land* is similar in its brevity of prose style and loving descriptions of Georgia's Pinhook Swamp region. Readers who enjoy Austin's lean prose may also enjoy John Steinbeck's novella *The Red Pony*, which in addition to telling a powerful story about a boy and his pony, includes similar evocative descriptions of the Salinas Valley in California, where it is set.

De Villiers, Marq, and Sheila Hirtle.

Sable Island: The Strange Origins and Curious History of a Dune Adrift in the Atlantic. New York: Walker & Company, 2004. 276pp. ISBN 0802714323.

In depicting a tiny, (mostly) uninhabited island in the North Atlantic, the authors leave very few stones unturned in describing the natural surroundings, historical events, and scientific principles of climate and maritime environment that led to Sable Island's reputation as the "Graveyard of the Atlantic." The island is less than 100 miles long and surrounded by deadly and ever-shifting sandbars, and hundreds of hapless mariners were sunk along its shores before the advent of modern navigational technology; today it is less deadly but no less interesting. Among its current inhabitants are wild horses, the descendants of animals most likely marooned there by English explorers in the 1700s, as well as harbor seals, numerous birds, and the human staffers of the island's weather station.

Subjects: Animals • Horses • Investigative Stories • Islands • Landscape

Now try: Readers who like this sort of "deep geography" (and history, and science) might also enjoy William Least Heat Moon's similar work, *PrairyErth*. Also, more adventurous readers might enjoy a work such as

Sebastian Junger's *A Perfect Storm,* in which Sable Island and the deadly Atlantic Ocean feature tragically.

Ehrlich, Gretel.

The Solace of Open Spaces. New York: Viking, 1985. 131pp. ISBN 0670806781.

Ehrlich does for Wyoming what Mary Austin does for her California desert: describes it in such understated and sensuous detail that you feel you have lived there, as opposed to simply having been there. Ehrlich, however, includes more personal and introspective details about her home, family, and neighbors than do many other nature writers, making this slim volume evocative not only of place, but also of interpersonal relationships.

Subjects: American West • Friendships • Landscape • Memoirs • Rural Life • Wyoming

Now try: Ehrlich's favorably reviewed travelogue, *This Cold Heaven: Seven Seasons in Greenland,* is also a meticulously researched chronicle of life on an island that is 95 percent ice; it was one of Amazon.com's 2001 books of the year.

Leopold, Aldo.

A Sand County Almanac: And Sketches Here and There. New York: Oxford University Press, 1949 (1987). 228pp. ISBN 0195053052.

First published nearly a century after *Walden,* Leopold's signature book tells a similar story of living on and in communion with the land, but it includes several more politically charged essays regarding the ever-growing need for conservation. Organized by month, the segment of the book that details the Leopold family's life on their sandy farm in Wisconsin includes tales of both labor and wildlife observations; the setting is described in simple prose. The essays tackle such topics as the ecology of Wisconsin marshlands, ecological invaders in the form of weeds from Europe growing on the plains of Oregon, and the effects of the tourist industry on natural landscapes.

Subjects: Animals • Classics • Conservation • John Burroughs Medal Winners • Landscape • Seasons • Wisconsin

Now try: Marcia Bonta's *Appalachian Spring* provides a similar month-by-month diary of springtime in the mountains of central Pennsylvania, albeit with fewer farm and family details and more observations of the native wildlife.

Lopez, Barry.

Arctic Dreams: Imagination and Desire in a Northern Landscape. New York: Scribner, 1986 (New York: Vintage Books, 2001). 464pp. ISBN 0375727485.

Combining elements of travel and adventure, landscape description, and spiritual reflection, Lopez describes his journeys in the arctic region in an aggregate work that is greater than the sum of its parts. No facet of the arctic landscape is left unexplored, from details of the shifting nature of the true magnetic north pole, to the habits and habitat of the musk oxen (one of the few animals to have survived the last ice age in North America), to the history of arctic exploration.

Subjects: Animals • Arctic Regions • Landscape • National Book Award Winners • Travel

Now try: Although it is much shorter and covers less geographical territory, Ellen Melloy's *Raven's Exile: A Season on the Green River* is similar to Lopez's book in that Melloy considers all aspects of the landscape and history around her as she and her husband (a river ranger) spend a season living on and around Wyoming's Green River.

Muir, John.

My First Summer in the Sierra. Boston: Houghton Mifflin, 1911 (San Francisco: Sierra Club Books, 1990). 188pp. ISBN 0871567482.

Muir's journal of his summer 1869 trip into the Sierra Mountains combines elements of travel writing with overwhelming attention to the details of landscape. Muir, who founded the Sierra Club, is often mentioned in current nature writing and is best known for his assertion that we should strive to make as little negative impact on nature as possible.

Subjects: California • Classics • Landscape • Memoir • Mountains • Nineteenth Century

Now try: *River: One Man's Journey Down the Colorado, Source to Sea*, by Colin Fletcher, also tells the story, in diary form, of a naturalist's journey in one of his favorite environments, combining the adventure of travel writing with the setting description of nature writing (Eric W. Morse's *Freshwater Saga: Memoirs of a Lifetime of Wilderness Canoeing in Canada* also evokes the importance of landscape to travel). Pulitzer prize–winning author and naturalist Edwin Way Teale's four-book American Seasons series (*North with the Spring, Journey into Summer, Autumn across America,* and *Wandering through Winter*) relates his 76,000 miles of travel across the United States, and might also appeal to readers who enjoy Muir.

Shelton, Richard.

Going Back to Bisbee. Tucson: University of Arizona Press, 1992 (2001). 377pp. ISBN 0816516650.

During the course of a drive from his current home in Tucson to his hometown of Bisbee, Arizona, Shelton describes the Southwest desert landscape and his own movements through it in languid and descriptive chapters. He endows the flora and fauna he observes on his drive with almost human characteristics, and is also capable of sympathetically describing his friends who stayed in Bisbee and are trying to maintain their small-town lifestyle in the absence of the town's economic mainstay, copper mining.

Subjects: ALA Notable Books • Arizona • Community Life • Landscape • Travel

Now try: Readers who enjoy the journey in Bisbee's reflective work might also like several titles in the travel chapter, such as Gretel Ehrlich's *This Cold Heaven: Seven Seasons in Greenland* or Frank Conroy's *Time and Tide: A Walk through Nantucket.*

Reflective Environmental Stories

Readers who enjoy works by writers like Annie Dillard often cite their need to carry such books around with them and read them in small, digestible bits over longer periods of time. The titles in this segment speak to that need: less adventure than reflection, they often combine the appeal of setting with a masterful use of language to provoke deep thought, and urge their readers to ponder the nature of our interactions with the natural world. There are no page-turning stories here, but rather word pictures designed to arouse feelings and thought.

Dillard, Annie.

Pilgrim at Tinker Creek. New York: Harper Magazine's Press, 1974 (New York: HarperPerennial, 1998). 288pp. ISBN 0060953020.

While describing her home in the Roanoke Valley of Virginia, Dillard offers more contemplation than story; she describes herself as an explorer in her neighborhood, and uses that fresh perspective to explore historical and scientific aspects of her environment. Narrated in the first person and rich in sensory detail, the book is immediately accessible and is widely cited in many other environmental books.

Subjects: Classics • Landscape • Memoirs • Philosophy • Pulitzer Prize Winners • Virginia

Now try: In her focus on natural processes, Dillard's writing also closely resembles many of the titles in the "Micro-Science" subgenre of science and math writing. Readers might also enjoy any one of Dillard's many other autobiographical and thought-provoking works, such as *An American Childhood* or *For the Time Being.* For those readers who may not be averse to perusing essays that combine a tone of reflection and naturalistic observations, celebrated natural history author Edward Hoagland's collection *Red Wolves and Black Bears: Nineteen Essays* might also appeal to readers who enjoy Dillard's mix of environmental and autobiographical stories, while May Sarton's *Journal of a Solitude* may particularly appeal to those readers interested in memoirs about living peacefully and alone. Sue Hubbell's science/memoir blend in *Waiting for Aphrodite: Journeys into the Time before Bones* may also appeal to Dillard fans.

Eiseley, Loren.

The Immense Journey. New York: Random House, 1957 (New York: Vintage Books, 1973). 210pp. ISBN 0394701577.

Although Eiseley was trained as an anthropologist, his collection of essays about natural history, evolution, and our place within our surroundings is much less a scholarly work than it is borderline poetry. He often mixes his personal experiences, such as his anthropological excursions, with his more reflective speculations on human history and our interconnectedness with flowers, the earth, and other animals.

Subjects: Anthropology • Classics • Essays • Evolution • Philosophy

Now try: Eiseley was a well-respected and influential natural history writer; he won the John Burroughs Medal for *The Firmament of Time*, another collection of essays that focused on the history of science, particularly in evolutionary theory; Rachel Carson was also an admirer of his writings, and her own poetic volumes, *The Sea Around Us* or *The Sense of Wonder,* might provide enjoyable related and similar reads.

Hay, John.

In the Company of Light. Boston: Beacon Press, 1998. 172pp. ISBN 0807085383.

Hay's fluid sentences evoke less a definite sense of one place (in this book, Maine) than a sense of the universality of all places. Although he describes the actual goldenrod that he sees near his home, he also refers to it as "one of the great continental symbols of America"; in describing the scream of a blue jay, he wonders if it makes such a noise because its habit of spreading seeds helped the regrowth of trees in the aftermath of the last ice age.

> **Subjects:** Animals • Essays • Landscape • Maine • Philosophy

> **Now try:** *Dwellings: A Spiritual History of the Living World*, by Linda Hogan, includes even more philosophical and spiritual ruminations on the importance of living in balance with the environment.

Heat Moon, William Least.

PrairyErth (A Deep Map). Boston: Houghton Mifflin, 1991. 624pp. ISBN 0395486025.

Much like Abbey's *Desert Solitaire*, this "deep geography" of the 774 square miles of Chase County, Kansas, is not a narrative page-turner, but rather an extended and lyrical description of the land itself, as well as its communities, history, and natural properties. Heat Moon uses both research and personal interviews to describe each quadrant of the county, and between the chapters provides selections from the "Commonplace Book," quotes from other historical and naturalistic writers that illustrate his points and have the added benefit of providing a ready-made bibliography of similar readings for the alert librarian.

> **Subjects:** American History • Classics • Community Life • Kansas • Landscape • Rural Life

> **Now try:** Gary Ferguson's 2004 history of the Rocky Mountains, *The Great Divide*, provides a similar "deep" look at a more stereotypically majestic setting.

Nollman, Jim.

Why We Garden: Cultivating a Sense of Place. New York: Henry Holt, 1994. 312pp. ISBN 080502719X.

Although this text, like many other in this genre, is organized according to the months of the year, it's less a chronicle of each season's happenings in the garden than a series of thoughts on what it means to garden and to take the long-term view necessary when planting things that will take months or even years to fully mature. In addition to his own planting and nurturing experiences, the author draws on many other literary and natural texts to connect the act of gardening with other human experiences.

> **Subjects:** Gardening • Memoirs • Philosophy • Seasons

> **Now try:** Michael Pollan, author of the recent and extremely popular book *The Botany of Desire*, also wrote a beautifully considered treatise on gardening, *Second Nature*, detailing lessons he learned after buying a Connecticut farm.

Olson, Sigurd.

The Singing Wilderness. New York: Knopf, 1956 (Minneapolis: University of Minnesota Press, 1997). 244pp. ISBN 0816629927.

Although his name is not as recognizable as Thoreau's or Audubon's, Sigurd Olson wrote numerous best-selling books on nature and served as president of the National Parks Association. This volume details the natural wonders of the Quetico Provincial Park in Ontario and the Superior National Forest of Minnesota. Olson writes about all of the seasons in turn, paying close attention to the animals in their natural habitats (the song of the landscape is that of the loons) and using his first-person narration to invite the reader along on his northwoods travels.

> **Subjects:** Animals • Canada • Classics • Landscape • Minnesota

> **Now try:** Ann Zwinger is a well-known naturalist and writer in her own right, and although her *The Mysterious Lands: A Naturalist Explores the Four Great Deserts of the Southwest* describes a much different landscape than Olson's, she offers the same attention to detail and smooth writing.

Powning, Beth.

Home: Chronicle of a North Country Life. New York: Stewart, Tabori & Chang, 1996. 143pp. ISBN 1556704607.

In prose that borders on poetry, Powning offers a series of sensory images that represent her family's life on a farm in New Brunswick, Canada. The book's emphasis is less on relating the details of rural living than on speculating about the nature of home and how it relates to where one actually physically lives. Although the book acknowledges the seasons in their order and the differing challenges and joys of each one, the reflections of the author take precedence over the description of both nature and events.

> **Subjects:** Canada • Homes • Illustrated Books • Landscape • Quick Reads • Rural Life • Seasons

> **Now try:** Another beautifully illustrated book is Hannah Hinchman's *Little Things in a Big Country: An Artist & Her Dog on the Rocky Mountain Front*, which also pays homage to her surroundings and her interactions with both the land and its other residents. Readers who enjoy this short book might also enjoy slightly longer and more naturalistic works such as *Walden* (Powning quotes Thoreau in the beginning of one of her chapters) or titles from the "Back to the Land" subgenre, below.

Ray, Janisse.

Ecology of a Cracker Childhood. Minneapolis, Minn., Milkweed Editions, 1999. 285pp. ISBN 1571312471.

Ray grew up at the edge of a junkyard in Baxley, Georgia. She combines the story of her childhood and family relationships with her observations on the environmental health of Georgia, as well as a history and discussion of the state's disappearing native longleaf pine forests. In Ray's capable hands Georgia's flora and fauna become characters as fully realized as any of her family members.

> **Subjects:** American South • Conservation • Family Relationships • Georgia • Landscape • Memoirs

> **Now try:** Native Kentuckian Jo Anna Holt Watson also roots her memoir in the land and rural lifestyle in which she grew up, in *A Taste of the Sweet Apple: A Memoir.* Al-

though such a recommendation oversteps the bounds of environmental writing, readers who enjoy Ray's honest portrayal of her sometimes troubled family life may also enjoy Mary Karr's *The Liar's Club: A Memoir*, or Kim Barnes's *In the Wilderness: Coming of Age in an Unknown Country*, set in Idaho. Those readers more interested in Ray's descriptions of her connection to her native Georgia countryside might consider Norman Maclean's flawless *A River Runs Through It and Other Stories*, in which he describes not only his and his brother's love for the wild Montana of their youth, but also the troubles his brother finally succumbed to.

Sanders, Scott Russell.

Writing from the Center. Bloomington: Indiana University Press, 1995. 196pp. ISBN 0253329418.

Born in Ohio and currently working as a professor of English at Indiana University, Sanders uses much of his nonfiction to explore the experience of being a Midwesterner. This book is no exception, and it addresses questions such as why many Midwestern writers write about their "home ground" but very few live there; how regional differences are disappearing and what that means for society; and why it is so easy to see and become burdened by many inessential things when we should be focusing on what Sanders considers the authentic. In many ways the book veers slightly from being a treatise on living in harmony with the earth, but the earthy language and setting are a large part of its appeal and place it firmly in this category.

Subjects: Essays • Landscape • Midwest • Philosophy

Now try: Ben Logan's gentle but never dull memoir, *The Land Remembers: The Story of a Farm and Its People*, is a perfect example of a poignant story of childhood in the rural Midwest (Wisconsin), told by an author who has lived most of his life elsewhere, and it is also a fast and enjoyable read in its own right.

Thoreau, Henry David.

Walden. Boston: Ticknor & Fields, 1854 (Boston: Beacon Press, 1997). 312pp. ISBN 0807014184.

Even those who have never read *Walden* are familiar with Thoreau's assertion that the "mass of men lead lives of quiet desperation." In 1845, at the age of twenty-eight, Thoreau took an axe into the woods in Concord, Massachusetts, and endeavored to live a completely sustainable life there. The book is not quickly paced, but Thoreau's polished prose style has led many reviewers to refer to him as a "poet-naturalist."

Subjects: American History • Classics • Landscape • Massachusetts • Rural Life • Solitude

Now try: A more modern look at living apart from technology is Eric Brende's *Better Off: Flipping the Switch on Technology*, which chronicles his and his wife's year in Maine without electricity or running water; a similar story is told in Daniel Hays's *On Whale Island: Notes from a Place I Never Meant to Leave*, which describes he and his family living on their own island for a year. David M. Carroll's *Self-Portrait with Turtles* is a memoir of communion with wilderness through the observation of turtles, complete with hand-drawn illustrations and sojourns into both solitude and urban experiences, in a tone that closely matches the reflective one of *Walden* (although, at 181 pages, it's considerably shorter).

Back to the Land

Many taxonomies of nature writing include at least one heading regarding "farm" or "agricultural" writing; many of those listed in books like the resources found at the end of this chapter are well-written and enjoyable stories, but fewer are being written as it becomes more challenging for a largely urban population to even contemplate returning to farming as a way of making a living. Not all individuals included in this subgenre have chosen to live on a farm in order to live more closely in harmony with the land; Anne Bastille wanted to test her ability to live self-sufficiently, while Kathleen Norris returned to her native birthplace but continued to make her living through her writing. Although location and setting play a part in these stories, these books also explore the characters, primarily of the authors, in their quest to feel connected to the world in which they live.

Brox, Jane.

Here and Nowhere Else: Late Seasons of a Farm and Its Family. Boston: Beacon Press, 1995. 143pp. ISBN 0807062006.

The Dewey classification "Homes and Haunts" is eerily appropriate for this small but dense book about the author's connection to her family and their small farm in the Merrimack Valley of Massachusetts. Opening with a description of the farm house in all its jerry-rigged wonder and continuing through the working relationship between her father and brother, then chronicling her own return to the farm, the book provides an immediate and sensory introduction to family farming in the late twentieth century.

> **Subjects:** Agriculture • Family Relationships • Homes • Massachusetts • Memoirs • Rural Life

> **Now try:** Although heavier on history and slightly lighter on family relationships, Brox's *Five Thousand Days Like This One* provides the reader with a more complete picture of the Merrimack Valley in Massachusetts, where she grew up. Susan Brind Morrow's *Wolves and Honey: A Hidden History of the Natural World*, although somewhat inaccurately titled—it's not so much a history of the natural world as it is a personal memoir of her youth in rural upstate New York—is similar in both language and theme.

LaBastille, Anne.

Woodswoman: A Young Ecologist's Life in the Log Cabin She Built Herself in the Adirondack Wilderness. New York: Dutton, 1976. 277pp. ISBN 0525237151.

LaBastille combines the very best of Thoreau's instinct for solitude with a more modern need for grounded community. Combining the very best attributes of Thoreau's desire to live more naturally with more modern writers' struggles to explain what "home" means to them, LaBastille's tale of building her own cabin near Black Bear lake in the Adirondacks makes for both active and reflective reading.

Nature and friendships combined to make LaBastille's cabin her home for nearly a decade.

> **Subjects:** Friendships • Landscape • Love and Dating • Memoirs • New York • Solitude

> **Now try:** LaBastille wrote several sequels (*Woodswoman II* and *III*) in which she describes her continuing quest to balance solitude with companionship. Kate Whouley's *Cottage for Sale—Must Be Moved: A Woman Moves a House to Make a Home* also features a strong woman protagonist who manages to make the story of buying a $3,000 cottage and attaching it to her three-room house engaging. There are also several stories of families setting out to live the "simpler life" in more pastoral settings; two of the most recent are *Arctic Homestead* by Norma Cobb and *The Final Frontiersman: Heimo Korth and His Family, Alone in Alaska's Arctic Wilderness* by James Campbell. One of the most famous is Richard Proenneke's and Sam Keith's *One Man's Wilderness: An Alaskan Odyssey*, based on Proenneke's experiences building his own cabin in Alaska.

Norris, Kathleen.

Dakota: A Spiritual Geography. New York: Ticknor & Fields, 1993. 224pp. ISBN 0395633206.

Norris produced this memoir after returning to her native Lemmon, South Dakota, and living there for twenty years with her husband. The chapters outline life in a prairie town, complete with local farming and gossipy details, and are interspersed with short "weather reports," in order by months, which use descriptive language to evoke feelings for climate and setting. The book works as a whole, but the chapters could also be enjoyed as stand-alone essays.

> **Subjects:** Community Life • Great Plains • Landscape • Memoirs • South Dakota • Spirituality

> **Now try:** Deborah Tall's *From Where We Stand: Recovering a Sense of Place* describes her journey to find her own home landscape and her adoption of the Finger Lakes region of upstate New York as her own.

White, E. B.

One Man's Meat. New York: Harper, 1942 (Gardiner, Maine: Tilbury House, 1997). 279pp. ISBN 0884481921.

These essays originally appeared in *Harper's Magazine* and *The New Yorker*, and in them White shares the details of his life after moving from New York City to his Maine farm. Collected into a book, they provide a look at farm life in the late 1930s, and although they mostly contain mundane details of animal husbandry, land management, and domestic work, White's singular talent with language enables him to give the pieces a sense of universality and of deeper truths revealed. The last entries in the collection are dated 1941 and provide a sense of American life at the beginning of U.S. involvement in World War II.

> **Subjects:** Agriculture • Classics • Community Life • Essays • Maine • Rural Life

Now try: Henry Beston's less contemplative *Northern Farm: A Chronicle of Maine* is so similar in time and place to White's book that it reads almost like a sequel (it was first published in 1948), while Noel Perrin's *First Person Rural: Essays of a Sometime Farmer*, published four decades later, matches White's humorously self-deprecating tone. A more contemporary example of the same "city resident moves to the country" theme can be found in Max Alexander's *Man Bites Log: The Unlikely Adventures of a City Guy in the Woods*.

Political

There is a strong tradition of activism and proscriptive writing in the nature writing canon, and many works of environmental and nature writing, particularly those with a strong emphasis on conservationism, are often referred to as "green literature." Far from being merely descriptive, many of the genre's best-known writers have, in one work or another, issued calls for preservation, conservation, and more deeply considered environmental actions and policy. Although many of the writers listed below have advocated political action, much of their writing is also recognizable for its insistence that our culture, even more than our politics, has a great (but not always good) effect on our wild and native spaces. Readers with a strong interest in conservation and preserving the environment will enjoy these books, and any reader who is drawn to passionate writing will find much to inspire here.

Abbey, Edward.

Desert Solitaire: A Season in the Wilderness. New York: McGraw-Hill, 1968 (New York: Ballantine, 1998). 337pp. ISBN 0345326490.

Abbey spent summers from 1957 through 1960 working as a park ranger in the Arches National Monument in Moab, Utah. The emphasis here is not on chronology or story but rather on Abbey's descriptions of living in the park. Chapters vary from physical descriptions of the landscape, to character sketches of his colleagues and their environmental attitudes, to a travel narrative of his journey down the Colorado River with a friend. He uses a straightforward writing style to decry the advent of "industrial tourism," road-building in the park, and his frustration with the encroachment of the human world upon natural habitats.

> **Subjects:** American West • Classics • Conservation • Landscape • Memoirs • Solitude • Utah

> **Now try:** Rick Bass is a bit less caustic than Abbey, but his 1996 title *The Book of Yaak* is no less an impassioned cry for conservation, particularly in his beloved Yaak Valley in Montana. Colin Woodard's *The Lobster Coast: Rebels, Rusticators, and the Struggle for a Forgotten Frontier* provides an in-depth look at Maine's Monhegan Island and its historical struggle to combine its old world community involvement with new world economic realities.

Berry, Wendell.

The Long-Legged House. New York: Harcourt Brace, 1969 (Washington, D.C.: Shoemaker & Hoard, 2004). 213pp. ISBN 1593760132.

Berry's first work of nonfiction is a collection of essays that vary from poetic and naturalistic descriptions of his Kentucky hill country to forcefully political statements of his opposition to the Vietnam War. Although the book is forty years old, the overall theme of the essays is the author's surprisingly contemporary assertion that the answers to all questions, natural or political, must be based on ideals of both civil rights and conservation.

> **Subjects:** Agriculture • Conservation • Essays • Human Rights • Kentucky • Landscape • Politics • Rural Life
>
> **Now try:** Berry's better-known book of essays, *The Unsettling of America: Culture and Agriculture*, is very similar to this title in subject matter but is less accessible than its predecessor. Although Paul Gruchow's *Grass Roots: The Universe of Home* is more memoir (growing up in Rosewood Township, Minnesota) than essay, much of his book also argues persuasively for the importance of preserving and perpetuating rural culture and conservation.

Carson, Rachel.

Silent Spring. Boston: Houghton Mifflin, 1962 (2002). 378pp. ISBN 061825305X.

At one point in her career Carson was the editor of all the U.S. Fish and Wildlife Service's publications, and the writing skills necessary for that position are evidenced in this book, one of the defining works of the twentieth century's environmental movement. Although a scientist, Carson devoted much of the book to decrying the post–World War II attitude that environmental concerns should be secondary to scientific advances, particularly those that result in excessive pesticide use and pollution. In a terse but lyrical writing style, she explains synthetic pesticide development and use, effects on animals and birds and their habitats, and the variety of ways in which chemicals find their way into our food and water sources and our bodies. This book is often referred to as the start of the American environmental movement, and the fact that Carson was dying from breast cancer while she wrote it makes it all the more poignant.

> **Subjects:** Birds • Chemistry • Classics • Conservation • Health Issues • Investigative Stories • Pollution • Women Scientists
>
> **Now try:** Carson's John Burroughs Medal and National Book Award–winning book *The Sea Around Us*, published in 1951, is a lyrically stirring description of the age-old ocean, a story of its creation and our connection to it. For all her skill with language, Carson was also a distinguished scientist, and readers who enjoy her writing may also enjoy titles in the "Science and Math" chapter. Although not as beautifully styled, Charles Little's ALA Notable title *The Dying of the Trees: The Pandemic in America's Forests* is an alarming treatise on the state of the planet's forests and what effects their demise could have on our climate; the recent *The Empty Ocean: Plundering the World's Marine Life* by Richard Ellis is also a frank discussion of industrial fishing that is designed to make readers more carefully consider their seafood consumption habits.

McKibben, Bill.

The End of Nature. **New York: Random House, 1989 (New York: Anchor Books, 1999). 232pp. ISBN 0385416040.**

Although written more than a decade ago, many of the warnings offered by McKibben in his exploration of the environmental challenges facing our earth are still valid today. In addition to sounding the alarm, McKibben also describes the science behind many of the harmful processes that humans have adopted; from the details of burning carbon fuels to the overall heating of the earth, he makes a strong case for both how and why many of our economic and personal choices are becoming ever more self-destructive.

> **Subjects:** Conservation • Investigative Stories • Pollution • Sociology

> **Now try:** Jonathan Schell's *The Fate of the Earth* also sounded a warning about the state of our environment. McKibben's book boasts blurbs from Edward Hoagland, another popular environmental writer, and James Gleick, a science writer, whose *Faster: The Acceleration of Just About Everything* provides another look at our society at the end of the twentieth century.

McPhee, John.

Coming into the Country. New York: Farrar, Straus & Giroux, 1977 (New York: Noonday Press, 1991). 438pp. ISBN 0374522871.

McPhee does for Alaska what Abbey does for Utah: He links his physical descriptions of the landscape to his own experiences within it and uses that connection to lend weight to his case for the need for conservation efforts. The book, split into three sections, consists of the story of his journey with colleagues down the Salmon River; the historical controversy surrounding the choice of Juneau as the state's capital; and the particular appeal and difficulties for the people living in the "Upper Yukon," the bush region in the very north of the state, most of which lies beyond the Arctic Circle. The third part of the book in particular gives the reader a feel for the region's residents and their combined pride and insularity; as McPhee says, the natives, both Indian and white, refer to their home simply as "the country," and any stranger appearing in it is said to be "coming into the country."

> **Subjects:** Alaska • Classics • Community Life • Conservation • Landscape • Memoirs

> **Now try:** In his most recent book, *No Man's River*, Farley Mowat describes living and working with a fur trapper and among Eskimos in the 1940s and 1950s. Both his personal involvement in the story and its arctic setting are similar to McPhee's narrative.

Williams, Terry Tempest.

Refuge: An Unnatural History of Family and Place. New York: Pantheon Books, 1991 (New York: Vintage Books, 2001). 314pp. ISBN 0679740244.

Williams frames her thoughts on people and their environment with twin tragedies: the steady rise of Utah's Salt Lake in the early 1980s, which consumed her beloved Bear River Migratory Bird Refuge, and her mother's death from cancer in her mid-fifties. Each chapter is headed by the lake's level at the time of writing, varying from 4,203 to 4,211 feet, the effects of which slowly drowned the Bird Refuge, and combines those losses with a personal and honest account of witnessing her mother's pain and struggle with a disease that Williams links to living downwind from an open-air nuclear testing facility in the 1950s. Although the characters are fully realized, both alone and in terms of their relationships to their family, Williams's skillful use of language and setting are the book's primary strengths.

> **Subjects:** Birds • Cancer • Conservation • Family Relationships—Mothers and Daughters • Health Issues • Memoirs • Radiation • Utah

> **Now try:** Jack Turner includes a trip with Terry Tempest Williams in his 1996 book of essays, *The Abstract Wild*, and although his text is less personal than *Refuge*, he

also uses philosophical language to underscore the vast need to appreciate and conserve wild spaces.

Wilson, Edward O.

The Future of Life. New York: Knopf, 2002. 229pp. ISBN 0679450785.

Although Wilson opens his book with an essay celebrating the diversity and tenacity of earth's life forms (including the bacteria that inhabit Antarctica's barren soil), the succeeding chapters disabuse the reader of the notion that the earth and its inhabitants are indestructible. Exploring various issues from overpopulation to deforestation, Wilson offers possible solutions and the optimistic assertion that the problems can be solved.

Subjects: ALA Notable Books • Animals • Biology • Conservation • Essays

Now try: David Quammen's *The Song of the Dodo: Island Biogeography in an Age of Extinctions* (another ALA Notable Book) also deals seriously but optimistically with the subjects of conservation and extinction. Those readers interested in learning more about ecological debates, issues, and possible solutions may also enjoy Chip Ward's *Hope's Horizon: Three Visions for Healing the American Land*, which reads like a Who's Who in recent environmental activism. Librarians can feel particularly proud when recommending Ward's work; he's also the assistant director of the Salt Lake City Public Library System.

Animal Stories

Animal stories have long been a mainstay of nature literature. These stories often take place in the animals' home environments (as is the case in Dian Fossey's *Gorillas in the Mist*), and some trouble is typically taken to describe those environments, placing these stories firmly and logically within the environmental and natural history genre. However, they vary widely in their levels and descriptions of human and animal interaction. In such works as Peter Matthiessen's *Tigers in the Snow* or Lynn Schooler's *The Blue Bear,* the animals are observed from afar and afforded the space necessary to retain their "wildness." In more personal and character-driven stories like Jane Goodall's *In the Shadow of Man* and Joy Adamson's *Born Free*, much of the story's appeal revolves around the relationships and, most often, friendships, between humans and animals. These authors also tend to draw parallels between human and animal environments and societies, as well as to make many and impassioned pleas for greater conservation efforts and tolerance of animal habits and habitats.

Adamson, Joy.

Born Free: A Lioness of Two Worlds. New York: Pantheon Books, 1960 (2000). 220pp. ISBN 0375714383.

A first-person account of the friendship between Joy and George Adamson and the lioness named Elsa, whom they adopted and came to love deeply. In 1956 Adamson's husband George was the Senior Game Warden in Africa, and in that capacity he was required to kill Elsa's mother, a lioness that had attacked several people in the area, and adopt her three cubs. Two were eventually sent to a zoo, but the Adamsons kept Elsa and undertook her training, not only allowing her free access to their house and grounds, but also attempting to fill the parental role of training her to hunt and survive in the wild. The book is nearly fifty years old, and the language can seem dated at times, but the chronological narrative of the family's and Elsa's three-year friendship is timeless.

Subjects: Africa • Animals • Classics • Conservation • Friendships • Lions • Memoirs

Now try: Adamson followed this book with two more about Elsa and her adult life in the wild: *Living Free* and *Forever Free*. Vince Smith's 2003 memoir *A Chimp in the Family* details his family's adoption of a chimpanzee that was originally rejected by her own mother.

Fossey, Dian.

Gorillas in the Mist. Boston: Houghton Mifflin, 1983 (2000). 326pp. ISBN 061808360X.

The result of thirteen years of observing mountain gorillas in Rwanda, *Gorillas in the Mist* is one of the finest examples of animal "ethologies," which detail species' specific and genetically encoded behavior. Although the characters described are almost exclusively the gorilla families and individuals that Fossey observed, their personalities are vividly drawn. Chapters are not ordered chronologically but rather by subject; family relationships, characteristics of individual gorillas, the effects of poachers, etc. Travel or adventure readers might also be drawn to this book's exotic locale and the nature of Fossey's achievement as a woman living among and studying animals in this secluded and often dangerous (politically and naturally) geographic area.

Subjects: Animals • Classics • Conservation • Gorillas • Memoirs • Rwanda • Women Scientists

Now try: *Woman in the Mists*, by Farley Mowat, offers more personal details of Fossey's incredible life and tragic death. Although it was published twenty years earlier (1964), George Schaller's *The Year of the Gorilla* might be enjoyable background reading (Fossey refers to Schaller often) for readers interested in animal studies. Readers who enjoy the travel or adventure aspects of this book might also enjoy the exploits of two men following peregrine falcons on their worldwide journeys, detailed in Alan Tennant's *On the Wing: To the Edge of the Earth with the Peregrine Falcon.*

Goodall, Jane.

In the Shadow of Man. Boston: Houghton Mifflin, 1971 (2000). 297pp. ISBN 0618056769.

Narrated in the first person and with great honesty and humor, Goodall's account of her journey to Tanzania to observe chimpanzees in the wild spares no details of the animal's interpersonal relationships and societal quirks. In addition to the personable and quickly paced text, the many photographs (contributed by Goodall's husband Hugo van Lawick) are fabulous and add much to the reading experience.

Subjects: Africa • Animals • Chimpanzees • Classics • Conservation • Memoirs • Women Scientists

Now try: Readers who want to learn more about Goodall's chimpanzee studies in particular should read the sequel, *Through a Window*, while readers more interested in Goodall herself might enjoy her two-volume autobiography in letters, *Africa in My*

Blood and *Beyond Innocence. Gorillas in the Mist* by Dian Fossey (annotated above) would also be a great companion read for Goodall's seminal work. For those readers interested in branching out from mammal to bird observation, Bernd Heinrich's *The Geese of Beaver Bog* is a personal look at a flock of Canada Geese that spend their summers near his home.

Heinrich, Bernd.

Mind of the Raven: Investigations and Adventures with Wolf-Birds. New York: Cliff Street Books, 1999. 380pp. ISBN 0060174471.

Heinrich's brand of animal observation often seems to involve forging intimate relationships with animals he is observing (see *The Geese of Beaver Bog*, above), and this story is no exception. Heinrich adopted four ravens and building an aviary for them near his Maine home, and he enlightens the reader on every aspect of raven physiology and behavior, including the details of their "mutes" (droppings), hunting and feeding proclivities, and personalities. In addition to the four ravens he cared for and observed, Heinrich and his colleagues also studied ravens in the wild, in groups, and in their relationships with wolves, with such painstaking attention to detail that the book reads more like a sociological study of bird behavior than a simple physical description of ravens.

Subjects: Animals • Biology • Birds • John Burroughs Medal Winners • Maine

Now try: Although more detached in tone, Durward Allen's *Wolves of Minong: Their Vital Role in a Wild Community* provides extensive details about the wolf community on Michigan's Isle Royale as well as many interesting black-and-white photographs.

Longgood, William.

The Queen Must Die: And Other Affairs of Bees and Men. New York: Norton, 1985. 234pp. ISBN 0393018962.

In short, engaging, and sometimes humorous chapters, Longgood shares the specifics of bee physiology, social structure, and personalities. In addition to describing the bees and his own beekeeping activities, he delves into their history and appearance in studies and literature to draw parallels between their societies and ours.

Subjects: Animals • Bees • Biology • Investigative Stories • Philosophy • Sociology

Now try: Oddly enough, the year 2005 saw a burst of publishing on the subject of bees; two of the most recent are Stephen Buchmann's *Letters from the Hive: An Intimate History of Bees, Honey, and Humankind* and Holley Bishop's *Robbing the Bees: A Biography of Honey, the Sweet Liquid Gold That Seduced the World.* Another short and enjoyable look at a particular insect is Sharman Apt Russell's *An Obsession with Butterflies: Our Long Love Affair with a Singular Insect.* Both Robert Sullivan's *Rats* (in the history chapter) and Richard Schweid's *The Cockroach Papers* (in the science and math chapter) also combine a light tone with impeccable research and detail to provide an inside look into animal and insect societies.

Matthiessen, Peter.

Tigers in the Snow. Photographs by Maurice Hornocker. New York: North Point Press, 2000. 185pp. ISBN 0865475768.

This beautifully photographed story provides the particulars behind the Siberian Tiger Project, which began in 1989 with the mandate of studying the reclusive tiger in its habitat. Due to the tiger's secretive nature, direct observation is extremely difficult, and most of the observations were gathered with the assistance of transmitters and radiotelemetry. The descriptive language and landscape details ensure that this book will appeal to readers of both nature and travel writing, while the first-person narrative is quite gripping and often provides as many insights into the process of studying animals as it does into the tigers themselves.

Subjects: Animals • Conservation • Illustrated Books • Tigers

Now try: Matthiessen is perhaps best known for his earlier work, *The Snow Leopard*, published in 1978, in which he describes his and George Schaller's journey to the Himalayas in search of the reclusive animal. Incidentally, George Schaller can tell a good story of his own; his provocative *The Last Panda* details his journey to China to observe and help preserve the habitat of the giant panda (and is also an ALA Notable Book). Matthiessen is also recognized as a classic travel author, and readers might enjoy his *The Cloud Forest*, which is annotated in the travel chapter.

Mowat, Farley.

Never Cry Wolf. Boston: Little, Brown, 1963 (Boston: Back Bay Books, 2001). 246pp. ISBN 0316881791.

Suitable for fans of both humor and adventure writing, Mowat's classic work detailing his experiences as a field biologist in Canada, studying the behavior of and relationships among the caribou and wolves of Manitoba, is quickly paced and driven mainly by a compelling narrative. Often frustrated by bureaucracy, and with a well-developed sense of humor regarding his own shortcomings as a suitably studious scientist, Mowat uses his distinctive voice to argue for the necessity of understanding native species and cultures.

Subjects: Animals • Canada • Classics • Conservation • Humor • Wolves

Now try: *Ghost Grizzlies: Does the Great Bear Still Haunt Colorado?* by David Petersen is also a highly enjoyable and informal account of grizzly bear sightings and management in Colorado's San Juan Mountains, employing the same tone of hope for conservation in the midst of sometimes difficult bureaucratic procedures. Although not as quickly paced or as cynically humorous, *Beluga Days: Tracking a White Whale's Truths* by Nancy Lord is another adventurous look at an often misunderstood Arctic animal.

Nelson, Richard.

Heart and Blood: Living with Deer in America. New York: Knopf, 1997. 389pp. ISBN 0679405224.

Nelson is less an observer of the American deer than a storyteller of deer history, lore, and hunting customs. Although the story is personal in that Nelson is himself a tracker and hunter of deer, he also interviewed other hunters, conservation experts, and Native Americans in order to present a comprehensive picture of the current relationship of deer to humans and the ecosystem.

Subjects: Animals • Community Life • Conservation • Deer • Hunters and Hunting

Now try: Robert Sullivan's *A Whale Hunt: How a Native-American Village Did What No One Thought It Could* also provides insight on how animals and human communities coexist, as well as exploring the controversy surrounding tribal rights and hunting. If your reader isn't averse to trying a different animal and a different continent, Martin Meredith's opus about the African elephant, *Elephant Destiny: Biography of an Endangered Species in Africa* is similarly comprehensive in its consideration of both the history and future of the elephant, while Stephen Alter's *Elephas Maximus: A Portrait of the Indian Elephant* is a more literary treatment of the same subject.

Quammen, David.

Monster of God: The Man-Eating Predator in the Jungles of History and the Mind. New York: Norton, 2003. 515pp. ISBN 0393051404.

Quammen examines the biology and history of the large animals that view humans simply as meat, and what it means and has meant to humans to be forced to think of themselves as being in a position on the food chain other than at the top. In chapters on the various predators, including lions in India, crocodiles in Australia, brown bears in the Carpathian Mountains, and Siberian tigers in Russia, Quammen describes the animals and their landscapes, as well as considering their historical place in such literary and mythic works as *The Epic of Gilgamesh* and the Bible. The author, who also writes for *Outside* magazine, uses highly descriptive language to describe both the animals and their habitats, and the story's many exotic locations might also appeal to readers who enjoy travel stories.

Subjects: ALA Notable Books • Animals • Biology • Landscape

Now try: Nigel Marven and Jasper James, the creators of the *Walking with Dinosaurs* television program, provide an enjoyable prehistoric "look" (the monsters themselves are computer-generated) at prehistoric sea monsters in their illustrated book, *Chased by Sea Monsters: Prehistoric Predators of the Deep.*

Schooler, Lynn.

The Blue Bear: A True Story of Friendship, Tragedy, and Survival in the Alaskan Wilderness. New York: Ecco, 2002. 272pp. ISBN 0066210852.

Although the author's search for the seldom-seen blue (or glacier) bear provides the structure for the story, his friendship with renowned Japanese wildlife photographer Michio Hoshino and their travels together in search of the bear, humpback whales, and other natural wonders in Alaska is the real heart of the tale. Although complex character portraits, some punctuated by tragedy, are in abundance here, Schooler's obvious love of and respect for animals and the Alaskan landscape place this book firmly among its setting-centric counterparts.

Subjects: Alaska • Animals • Bears • Friendships • Memoirs

Now try: This is a truly unique book, and Schooler is as adept at describing the Alaskan landscape as he is at exploring his own interpersonal relationships. Readers who enjoy the natural story may enjoy Hoshino's pictorial

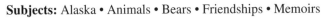

works on grizzly bears and other northern animals, including *Grizzly* and *Moose*, or the beautifully photographed *Tigers in the Snow* by Peter Matthiessen. Fans of this book may also enjoy many of the titles suggested in the "Relationships" chapter, particularly those listed under the "With a Little Help from My Friends" subgenre.

Consider Starting With . . .

Here are some of the most enduring and popular titles in environmental writing.

Austin, Mary. *The Land of Little Rain.*

Carson, Rachel. *Silent Spring.*

Dillard, Annie. *Pilgrim at Tinker Creek.*

Mowat, Farley. *Never Cry Wolf.*

Thoreau, Henry David. *Walden.*

Fiction Read-Alikes

- **Berry, Wendell.** Berry's <u>Port William</u> series of fiction titles, such as *Nathan Coulter, Jayber Crow*, and *Hannah Coulter,* are all set in the fictional community of Port William, Kentucky, and all feature strong connections between the characters and that setting.

- **Cather, Willa.** Most of Cather's works evoke a strong sense of the plains states in which they are set, but *My Ántonia* in particular describes the haunting beauty of the Nebraska prairie, as well as her immigrant title character's love of it.

- **Erdrich, Louise.** Many of Erdrich's novels, including *Love Medicine, The Beet Queen, The Bingo Palace*, and *The Last Report on the Miracles at Little No Horse,* are set on and around fictional Native American reservations in North Dakota.

- **Guterson, David.** Although Guterson's novels, such as *Snow Falling on Cedars* and *Our Lady of the Forest,* are primarily character-driven, they are also highly evocative of the Pacific Northwest region in which they are set.

- **Harrison, Jim.** *The Road Home*, chosen as a 1998 *Publishers Weekly* best book, is set in Nebraska and considers the interactions of its characters with nature.

- **Haruf, Kent.** Both *Plainsong* and *The Tie That Binds* are beautifully written novels set in Colorado; the former takes place in the 1990s, and the latter is set at the beginning of the twentieth century.

- **Kelton, Elmer.** Many Westerns would be strong read-alike possibilities for environmental books, but in particular *The Time It Never Rained*, a story of a Western rancher's struggle to keep his ranch and land viable during a drought, is a classic of the setting-centered Western genre.

- **Kingsolver, Barbara.** Much of the appeal of Kingsolver's first novel, *The Bean Trees*, is her description of Arizona and her characters' involvement in their adopted community in Tucson.

- **Michener, James.** Although many of his titles more closely resemble historical epics than setting-based novels, the appeal of Michener's location-titled books, such as *Hawaii, Mexico*, and *Texas,* is at least partly the setting.

- **Proulx, Annie.** Proulx won the Pulitzer Prize in 1994 for *The Shipping News*, set in Newfoundland and filled with achingly lyrical descriptions of that setting. *Close Range* and *That Old Ace in the Hole*, set in Wyoming and Texas, respectively, might also appeal to readers who like distinct settings described in their novels.

- **Stegner, Wallace.** The most famous of Stegner's works place his characters and stories firmly within the mythology of the "American West," particularly his Pulitzer Prize–winning *Angle of Repose* and *The Big Rock Candy Mountain.*

- **Steinbeck, John.** Most of Steinbeck's stories are firmly rooted in and around Monterey and the Salinas Valley of California. For readers who are ready to try some more adventurous classics, *To a God Unknown* explores its main character's connection to his farmland, while the epic *East of Eden* combines the characters' family history with the true history of the Salinas Valley, which Steinbeck researched for many years.

- **Watson, Larry.** *Montana 1948*, set in the title state, won Watson the Milkweed National Fiction Prize, but the author also offers different settings: Vermont and Minnesota in *Laura*, and Wisconsin in his latest, *Orchard: A Novel.*

Further Reading

Bergon, Frank.

The Wilderness Reader. Reno, Nevada: University of Nevada Press, 1994 (1980). 372pp. ISBN 0874172500.

Less an overview of nature writing than a selection of the very best environmental pieces addressing the specifics of wilderness and the struggle to both preserve and commune with it. Authors included range from John Burroughs to Rachel Carson to Aldo Leopold, and the entire reader serves as a short introduction to many important writers whose longer works are referred to in this chapter (for example, reading just the excerpt from Rachel Carson's *The Edge of the Sea* provides a feeling for the author's use of language and style that is very apparent in *Silent Spring*, annotated above).

Finch, Robert, and John Elder, eds.

Nature Writing: The Tradition in English. 2d ed. New York: Norton, 2002. 1152pp. ISBN 0393049663.

A typical "Norton anthology" that provides a variety of short readings from both widely acknowledged and relatively unknown nature and environmental writers. It also includes a helpful introduction describing the genesis of the term "nature writing" and current trends and influences in the field, as well as the introduction to the first edition (published in 1990), which provides a historical overview of the genre.

Lyon, Thomas J.

This Incomparable Land: A Guide to American Nature Writing. Minneapolis, Minn.: Milkweed Editions, 2001. 277pp. ISBN 1571312560.

Although the first chapters of this book are interesting and provide history and context for the broader picture of American environmental writing (the sixth chapter, on the twentieth century, in particular quickly introduces the reader to the importance and style of authors such as John McPhee, Edward Abbey, and Wendell Berry, to name just a few), the real gem here is the extensive and annotated bibliography of both classic and current nature writing titles, which comprises half the text.

Stewart, Frank.

A Natural History of Nature Writing. Washington, D.C.: Island Press, 1995. 279pp. ISBN 1559632798.

An immensely readable "story behind the stories" of many of the naturalists listed in the first section of the chapter. In addition to providing background information on the nature writing genre in America, Stewart places many of the writers and their experiences in the greater context of American history and society.

References

Finch, Robert, and John Elder, eds. 2002. *Nature Writing: The Tradition in English.* 2d ed. New York: Norton.

Lyon, Thomas J. 2001. *This Incomparable Land: A Guide to American Nature Writing.* Minneapolis, Minn.: Milkweed Editions.

Scheese, Don. 1996. *Nature Writing: The Pastoral Impulse in America.* (Studies in Literary Themes and Genres). New York: Twayne.

Part 2

Nonfiction Subject Interests

Science and Math

History

Chapter 5

Science and Math

Definition of Science and Math Writing

Scientists and observers of nature have been writing science treatises since ancient times. The Greek philosopher Aristotle produced many works of what was then referred to as "natural philosophy," including his massive *Physics*, in which he recorded his natural and cosmological observations of the world around him. In view of current debates centering on whether evolution or creationism should be taught, it is interesting to note that the field of natural philosophy and observation is considered to have logically followed the search by religious thinkers for greater understanding of their surroundings and theology (*History of Science* 2005).

The advent of the "Scientific Revolution" at the dawn of the seventeenth century (although some date its beginning to as early as 1543, with the publication of Nicolaus Copernicus's *De revolutionibus* [*On the Revolutions of the Heavenly Spheres*]) ushered in an age of science writing that was less philosophical and more focused on the recording of systematic observation and scientific experimentation. Many figures from this time (Copernicus, Johannes Kepler, Isaac Newton, and Galileo Galilei among them) not only produced their own major treatises and advanced their respective fields, but also serve today as the subjects for a great many books and biographies being produced for nonscientific readers. The Scientific Revolution lasted until 1687, when Newton published his *Principia Mathematica*, a work about the laws of motion, which was based at least in part on the new mathematics of calculus he had developed.

As can be deduced from the frequent news of scientific advances and breakthroughs that are reported so quickly as to have become rather humdrum to those of us living in the twenty-first century, the growth of scientific inquiry and writings from the eighteenth through the twentieth centuries was exponential and included such noteworthy events as Antoine Lavoisier's discovery of oxygen in 1783 (chemistry), the publication of Charles

Lyell's *Principles of Geology* in 1827 (geology), Charles Darwin's introduction of evolutionary theory in *On the Origin of Species* in 1859, the birth of the theory and field of quantum mechanics first advanced at the turn of the century by Max Planck (and numerous others), Albert Einstein's development and publication of his theory of relativity in 1915, James Watson's and Francis Crick's explanation of the basic structure of DNA in 1953, and space travel and the moon landing of 1969. A sentence like that omits the vast majority of 300 years' worth of scientific theories and discoveries, but you get the idea of the varied and fascinating facts, theories, and stories that the subject area encompasses.

Although many fields of inquiry are considered to be sciences in their own right, including economics and the social sciences such as psychology and sociology, for the most part books on these topics are not included here. A reader who identifies an area of interest as "science," pure and simple, is not usually seeking books on economics or sociology, as fascinating or scientifically rigorous as those particular titles might be. More often science readers gravitate toward the colloquially recognized "natural science" titles, or those that take as their subject such branches of knowledge as physics, chemistry, geology, or biology, to name just a few (and which are most aptly represented by authors such as Richard Feynman in *Six Easy Pieces*, or Michio Kaku in *Hyperspace*).

Science and math titles may not top most librarians' preferred reading lists. They don't constitute a stereotypical genre so much by adhering to formats and conventions as by sharing a common subject. They do, however, represent a very specific reading interest area that their readers are extremely familiar with and that we should embrace as yet another possible area for growth in our readers' advisory services. It is also an area of great diversity—from reflective and philosophical treatises and fun fact books to lively biographies and highly technical reads. This chapter includes many books and authors I had heard of but never read; as I made my way through the majority of these titles, I found myself wishing, not that I didn't have to read them, but that I'd read them much earlier.

Appeal of the Genre

In his discussion of types of nonfiction in the recent essay collection *Nonfiction Readers' Advisory*, David Carr lists several important scientists' names (Ernst Mayr, Edward O. Wilson, James D. Watson, and Stephen Pinker) and their books and explains their appeal thus: "These are the Big Minds, asking and answering some of the Big Questions of our time, for the awed child at Mr. Wizard's elbow who lives inside us all" (2004, 58).

Due to the demands of their professions, scientists and mathematicians (and typically science and math readers as well) are detail-oriented individuals with a well-developed appreciation for the beauty of order and logical systems. They are often curious about how and why things work, as well as about how other scientists worked out, through theory or experimentation, the mysteries of how things work. This curiosity, the need to figure out, solve, or understand, motivates the science reader, and good science writing rises to the challenge.

Contrary to their stereotypes as "nonliterary" types, they enjoy narratives in which the authors not only know their numerous facts, but can also arrange them in elegant ways, using succinct and well-crafted prose. Brian Greene's best-selling book (and basis for a popular PBS program by the same name) *The Elegant Universe* is a good example of a perfect book for this type of reader: It is heavily detailed and scientifically accurate, but also accessible to the general reader and beautifully written in its own right.

Many science and math books also offer glimpses into the lives of those historical figures who made discoveries or breakthroughs in their respective fields, and therefore offer character appeal as well. In addition to those titles listed under "Scientists," below, readers' advisors might also want to consider offering these readers titles from the "Problem Solvers and Experimenters" subgenre of the biography chapter. Fans of "Literary Science" titles might also be offered titles from the "Environmental Writing" chapter due to their authors' often thoughtful and lyrical writing styles (Rachel Carson, who is not read by nearly enough people, is an example of an author who may appeal to readers of many nonfiction genres). It is also important to remember that many authors in this chapter are well-known because they appeal to the nontypical science readers; Carl Sagan, for example, is famous for making such varied subjects as astronomy, biology, and physics more accessible to lay readers.

Edmund Blair Bolles, the editor of the wonderfully comprehensive and informative science writing collection *Galileo's Commandment*, really said it all when he summed up the appeal of these titles: "Science writing can be great writing in precisely the same sense that other genres are great: it has something important to say; it says it by presenting readers with unique imaginations; and readers in turn are inspired to think in ways that, by themselves, they never could" (1999, xv).

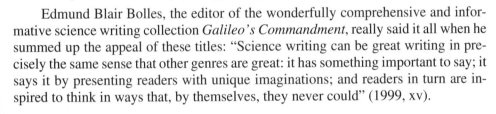

Organization of the Chapter

"Deep Science" titles lead off the chapter, followed closely by "Investigative Science" and "Adventures in Science"; all three categories offer the very best of puzzles and complex stories for readers to assuage their curiosity or provoke their understanding. Of those three subgenres, the titles suggested in "Adventures in Science" typically offer the quickest pacing and reading experience for the reader who enjoys works of popular science.

"Micro-science" and "History of Science" appear next, offering some of the most readable titles in the chapter, particularly for those readers or librarians looking to get their science stories with a healthy dose of historical and personal information rather than a wealth of complex and specialized detail. A subgenre relating the stories of "Scientists and Science Enthusiasts" relies heavily on the character appeal of its titles, while the last subgenre, "Literary Science," offers works by authors whose command and use of evocative and lyrical language is the source of their popularity.

Deep Science

This subgenre, more than any other discussed in this guide, may be the one most likely to send public and other librarians, the majority of whom come from liberal arts backgrounds, screaming and running from the stacks in fear. These are the stories that aren't afraid to throw mathematical notations and problems in with their text, or to use phrases like "space-time continuum" "quantum mechanics," "fractals," "tessalation," or "superstrings," and to go on about the beauty of their properties and structure, and

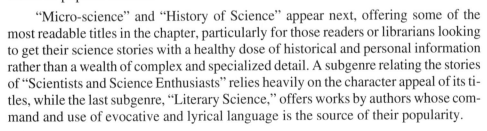

the development of theories surrounding them, at some length. The good news is that the authors of these works, in addition to being highly respected theorists and scientists in their chosen fields, are also spectacular and vivid storytellers. I may not understand everything that Brian Greene posits in his best-selling *The Elegant Universe*, but that doesn't stop me from enjoying how he posits it.

These titles tackle the big issues, often in physics and astronomy, and the payoff is increased understanding from a broad perspective—often that of a scientific or mathematical genius. They appeal to readers because of their in-depth explanations of complicated scientific principles, but also owe much of their popularity to their authors' straightforward and lyrical writing styles, as well as their ability to make their highly detailed, complex, and often lengthy stories accessible.

Derbyshire, John.

Prime Obsession: Bernhard Riemann and the Greatest Unsolved Problem in Mathematics. Washington, D.C.: Joseph Henry Press, 2003 (New York: Plume, 2004). 422pp. ISBN 0452285259.

Nineteenth-century mathematician Riemann is known for his Riemann Hypothesis, which has remained unsolved for 150 years. In addition to providing context for the hypothesis and a brief discussion of the great characters in mathematics history, Derbyshire also orders his book in an impressively scientific manner; odd-numbered chapters cover the math, complete with equations, and even-numbered chapters provide history and character details.

> **Subjects:** Biographies • History of Science • Mathematics • Nineteenth Century

> **Now try:** The Joseph Henry Press does a lovely job of producing quick-reading books that illuminate scientific problems, discoveries, and concepts through the prism of the scientists most often associated with them, as is evident in their other titles, such as David Lindley's *Degrees Kelvin: A Tale of Genius, Invention, and Tragedy* and *Einstein Defiant: Genius Versus Genius in the Quantum Revolution.*

Feynman, Richard P.

Six Easy Pieces: Essentials of Physics Explained by Its Most Brilliant Teacher. Reading, Mass.: Addison-Wesley, 1995. 146pp. ISBN 0201409550.

Nobel Prize winner Feynman is one of the most famous theorists in twentieth-century physics and was asked to provide a series of lectures on the essential tenets of physics while he was a professor at the California Institute of Technology in 1961. Those lectures were eventually published as this book; originally devised to get incoming students excited about and interested in physics, they evolved over time to remind experts in the field of the importance of distilling complicated processes to their most basic components. Through the use of analogies, diagrams, and commonsense language, Feynman illuminates such topics as atomic motion, quantum physics, and the connection of physics to other sciences such as chemistry and astronomy.

> **Subjects:** Classics • Education • Essays • Physics

> **Now try:** With just enough math to lift it out of the realm of the casual nonscience reader, John Gribbin's *In Search of Schrödinger's Cat: Quantum Physics and Reality* might prove to be a valuable source for those readers looking to expand on what they read in Feynman's work. For those readers more interested in Feynman himself, you

may want to suggest science writer James Gleick's biography, *Genius: The Life and Science of Richard Feynman*, or the physicist's autobiography, *"Surely You're Joking, Mr. Feynman!": Adventures of a Curious Character*.

Gleick, James.

Chaos: Making a New Science. New York: Viking, 1987 (New York: Penguin, 1988). 352pp. ISBN 0140092501.

A former science writer for *The New York Times*, Gleick is noteworthy for his ability to write a technically solid and still briskly paced story about various hard-core science subjects, and this book is no exception. Although he ostensibly tells the story behind the birth of chaos theory (the seemingly random patterns that characterize many natural phenomena) as a subject area, he also includes numerous character portraits of the scientists at the forefront of the field.

> **Subjects:** Chaos Theory • Mathematics • Physics

> **Now try:** Gleick is also the author of *Faster: The Acceleration of Just About Everything*. Robert Laughlin's *A Different Universe: Reinventing Physics from the Bottom Down* might also provide more scientific detail for the dedicated science reader, and fewer character profiles.

Greene, Brian.

The Elegant Universe: Superstrings, Hidden Dimensions, and the Quest for the Ultimate Theory. New York: Norton, 1999 (2003). 448pp. ISBN 0393058581.

Greene eloquently describes the search for a single theory that will describe all physical phenomena and illuminates the current opinion that "superstring" theory may do just that. Developed chronologically from conflicts regarding the nature of light in the nineteenth century through today's study of relativity and quantum mechanics, the story takes precedence over the actual science and is written (by the author's admission) for the reader with no science or math training.

> **Subjects:** ALA Notable Books • Classics • History of Science • Physics

> **Now try:** Greene has produced a new book to try to answer the question, "What is reality?" as it applies to space and time, *The Fabric of the Cosmos: Space, Time, and the Texture of Reality*. Both *Origins: Fourteen Billion Years of Cosmic Evolution* (Tyson and Goldsmith) and Alan Guth's *The Inflationary Universe* tackle heavy science topics with an admirably simplified technique.

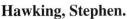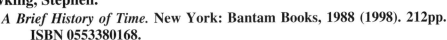

Hawking, Stephen.

A Brief History of Time. **New York: Bantam Books, 1988 (1998). 212pp. ISBN 0553380168.**

When first published, this work, which made Hawking a cultural icon, sold millions of copies (approximately 1 in 750 people worldwide bought it). A treatise on the nature of science and time, the work veers closer to history than math; there are no equations here but rather a chronological discussion of theories regarding gravity, the universe, and infinity, from Aristotle to Copernicus to Newton to Einstein. In the end Hawking posits that the most advanced current theories will eventually lead to principles so simple to understand that everyone will be "able to take part in the discussion of the question of why it is that we and the universe exist."

Subjects: Classics • Einstein, Albert • History of Science • Physics • Time

Now try: Hawking produced another popular work in 2002 that was light on math and long on the rather metaphysical search for a simpler understanding of the universe, *The Theory of Everything: The Origin and Fate of the Universe.*

Kaku, Michio.

Hyperspace: A Scientific Odyssey Through Parallel Universes, Time Warps, and the Tenth Dimension. New York: Oxford University Press, 1994 (New York: Anchor Books, 1995). 359pp. ISBN 0385477058.

Those readers fairly comfortable with basic precepts of quantum physics will get the most out of Kaku's signature work, in which he suggests the existence of ten real dimensions (as opposed to the three we typically think of ourselves as living in). Much of the text is straightforward and doesn't rely too heavily on understanding higher level mathematics, but the latter half of the book does introduce more complicated and speculative aspects of astrophysics, such as wormholes and time travel.

Subjects: Classics • Cosmology • Epic Reads • Mathematics • Physics

Now try: Paul Halpern's *The Great Beyond: Higher Dimensions, Parallel Universes, and the Extraordinary Search for a Theory of Everything* also focuses on making the theories of many past and present scientists more accessible through analogy and well-organized writing and devotes a chapter to the development of hyperspace theories. Leon Lederman's and Christopher Hill's *Symmetry and the Beautiful Universe* might also appeal to Kaku's readers.

Penrose, Roger.

The Emperor's New Mind: Concerning Computers, Minds, and the Laws of Physics. New York: Oxford University Press, 1989 (1999). 602pp. ISBN 0192861980.

Penrose, a physicist and mathematician, and co-winner of the 1988 Wolf Prize (which he shared with Stephen Hawking), combines an explanation of relativity and quantum physics with his belief that computers will never be able to effectively achieve what we think of as human "consciousness." Penrose has a lot of ground to cover, and he does so through snappy pacing combined with an impressive use of detail.

Subjects: Classics • Computers • Neuroscience • Philosophy • Physics

Now try: Reviewers at Amazon.com note that Penrose's book is often considered controversial: "some love it, some hate it." Steven Pinker's *How the Mind Works* and Daniel C. Dennett's *Consciousness Explained* provide less rigorous scientific detail than does Penrose's book, but readers might find their related subject matters complementary reading.

Investigative Science

Stories of scientific discoveries can be very exciting, but what is often forgotten is that the process of getting to those discoveries can be a tedious and lengthy one of repeated experimentation and observation. The following titles describe the long slogs of science; the tedium of formulating theories, setting up experiments, and repeating and observing them until they yield results.

Many of the experiments, discoveries, and theoretical formulations described in the following titles are not carried out in stereotypical laboratory environments, but instead involve animal and human participants, which means that many of these stories have a dimension of character development as well, both for the experimenters and the subjects (as exhibited in *Next of Kin* and *Born That Way*). Because they often include descriptions of difficulties that can arise in experimental situations, they also provide an inside look at the daily struggles of scientists seeking to understand their experiments' results. For that reason they may also appeal to readers of "Investigative Writing," which is often also succinct and descriptive.

Fouts, Roger, with Stephen Tukel Mills.

Next of Kin: What Chimpanzees Have Taught Me About Who We Are. New York: William Morrow, 1997. 420pp. ISBN 068814862X.

Fouts, an experimental psychologist, began working with chimpanzees at the University of Nevada in 1967. More specifically, he was asked to teach a chimpanzee named Washoe how to communicate using American Sign Language. In this highly personal first-person narrative, he describes that process and many other observational studies to which he contributed, providing insight into chimpanzee behavior but also into scientific methodology. He also details his and others' struggles to provide a natural habitat for animals being studied.

 5

> **Subjects:** ALA Notable Books • Animals • Biology • Chimpanzees • Experiments • Gentle Reads • Memoirs

> **Now try:** Jane Goodall wrote the foreword for this book, and readers who enjoy the interaction between animals and their human observers might also like her seminal work, *In the Shadow of Man*. Likewise, Dian Fossey's classic study *Gorillas in the Mist* might also appeal to fans of Fouts's work.

McPhee, John.

Annals of the Former World. New York: Farrar, Straus & Giroux, 1998 (2000). 696pp. ISBN 0374518734.

This massive tome is actually four books, and the individual titles might be more recognizable than the whole: *Basin and Range*, *In Suspect Terrain*, *Rising from the Plains*, and *Assembling California*. Taken together, they represent McPhee's many years of traveling with and observing geologists, U.S. Geological Survey employees, and plate tectonics scientists. In addition to describing the physical characteristics of the earth and its landscapes, McPhee provides detailed character portraits of the scientists he followed, from David Love, who was born in the Rocky Mountains he studies, to Anita Harris, a native Brooklynite who is skeptical about plate tectonic theory and studied geology primarily to ensure she'd never have to live in New York City.

> **Subjects:** Classics • Epic Reads • Geology • Investigative Stories • Pulitzer Prize Winners

Now try: Those readers who are both interested in geology and enjoy McPhee's character sketches might also enjoy Simon Winchester's character-driven (the main character being William Smith, maker of the world's first geological map in 1815) history, *The Map That Changed the World*. McPhee is also the author of *Coming into the Country*, annotated in the "Environmental Writing" chapter, which describes the state of Alaska in great geological, social, and political detail.

Rhodes, Richard.

The Making of the Atomic Bomb. New York: Simon & Schuster, 1986 (1988). 886pp. ISBN 0684813785.

Rhodes details the history of the development of the atomic bomb, telling the stories of the scientists involved as well as describing the scientific principles behind nuclear chain reactions and atomic weaponry. Although many readers might see this as primarily a work of history, the details of the scientific processes that led to the development of the bomb (and the result of its detonations in Japan) are rigorously set forth, as are the discoveries made by the physicists and other scientists. In that capacity the book also doubles as a "Who's Who" of modern physics.

Subjects: Atomic Bomb • Epic Reads • History of Science • Physics • Pulitzer Prize Winners • Radiation • Weapons

Now try: Peter Goodchild's similarly epic biography *Edward Teller: The Real Dr. Strangelove* may appeal to readers interested in the history and development of the atomic bomb. Readers may also want to consider complementing their reading of Rhodes's scientific history of the atomic bomb with John Hersey's *Hiroshima*, a much shorter and more politically charged dissertation on the effects of the bombs in the cities on which they were dropped. If patrons want to consider a graphic novel that combines the history of this subject with narrative storytelling, they might also try *Fallout: J. Robert Oppenheimer, Leo Szilard, and the Political Science of the Atomic Bomb*, by Jim Ottaviani and numerous other author-artists.

Sacks, Oliver.

The Man Who Mistook His Wife for a Hat: and Other Clinical Tales. New York: Harper & Row, 1970 (New York: Simon & Schuster, 1998). 243pp. ISBN 0684853949.

In a series of unrelated vignettes, Sacks recounts some of the more fascinating and perplexing clinical tales from his own medical and psychological practice and experiences. They range from the bizarre (the man who literally couldn't differentiate between common items and tried to place his wife on his head as his hat) to the strangely comforting (the elderly woman who heard Irish songs from her childhood loudly and incessantly replayed in her head) to the increasingly common (Tourette's Syndrome and its victims' shouted profanities and nervous tics). The stories are comprehensively detailed and the individuals described adequately, but Sacks's tone is indeed clinical and focuses less on story and character development than on clarity in reporting.

Subjects: Classics • Essays • Medicine • Mental Health • Neuroscience

Now try: Fans of Oliver Sacks tend to be very devoted; therefore, suggest his other medical science titles such as *Awakenings* (on which the popular movie starring Robin Williams was based) or the similarly rich in case studies *An Anthropologist on Mars: Seven Paradoxical Tales*. Atul Gawande's more lyrically written medicine memoir, *Complications: A Surgeon's Notes on an Imperfect Science,* may also appeal to readers interested in strange medical cases and their treatments.

Tompkins, Peter, and Christopher Bird.

The Secret Life of Plants. New York: Harper & Row, 1973 (New York: Perennial, 2002). 402pp. ISBN 0060915870.

Although not written by scientists, this book gives an impressive and comprehensive tour of the history of and breakthroughs in the study of plants. It opens with a description of the work of Clive Backster, America's foremost lie-detector examiner, who attached a galvanometer (which causes the polygraph needle to chart the emotional surges of the suspect) to plants to prove that they did have feelings. In straightforward prose and five sections the authors describe the studiers of plant structure, environmental factors in plant growth (such as talking to them), and how plants are connected to the greater human sphere.

Subjects: Biology • Experiments • Investigative Stories • Plants

Now try: Although more journalistically written and on a completely different subject (physics), science writer Tom Siegfried's intentionally non-science-reader-friendly text *Strange Matters: Undiscovered Ideas at the Frontiers of Space and Time* also describes some of the stranger theories at the heart of our studies of matter and the very planes of our existence. In Michael Pollan's *The Botany of Desire*, the author looks at the natural world from the viewpoints of four disparate and hugely influential plants.

Weiner, Jonathan.

The Beak of the Finch: A Story of Evolution in Our Time. New York: Knopf, 1994 (New York: Vintage Books, 1995). 332pp. ISBN 067973337X.

Weiner describes the work of biologists Peter and Rosemary Grant, who visit the island of Daphne Major in the Galapagos Islands on a yearly basis to observe and study "Darwin's finches," the birds Darwin first observed on his voyage on the *Beagle*, during which many of his ideas concerning evolution were formed. Weiner uses the Grants' work to clarify finer points of natural selection and evolution and discuss related topics such as global warming and creationism. Weiner paints a comprehensive portrait of the Grants, but the true characters of the story are the finches and their defining physical characteristics.

Subjects: ALA Notable Books • Biology • Birds • Darwin, Charles • Evolution • Investigative Stories • Pulitzer Prize Winners

Now try: Weiner's *Time, Love, Memory* follows the work of another famous biologist, Seymour Benzer, and he used similar investigative techniques (observing Benzer's work personally for five years) to provide an unbelievable level of scientific detail and insight. Readers particularly interested in learning more about the development of evolutionary theory might also try Edward Larson's *Evolution: The Remarkable History of a Scientific Theory.*

Wohlforth, Charles.

The Whale and the Supercomputer: On the Northern Front of Climate Change. New York: North Point Press, 2004. 322pp. ISBN 0865476594.

Wohlforth offers a personal and investigative look at both Eskimo culture and whale hunting, combined with a description of the newest supercomputers attempting to use mathematical models to predict climate change. He does a creditable job of contrasting the long-term and naturally developed ability of the native Iñupiat to observe and adapt to the climate changes in their environment with that of the scientists, who use a more focused approach and travel to Alaska to measure and sample transects of the arctic snow.

Subjects: Anthropology • Arctic Regions • Community Life • Computers • Investigative Stories • Weather

Now try: Jim Nollman's travel/nature book *The Beluga Café: My Strange Adventure with Art, Music, and Whales in the Far North* provides a similar setting and journey narrative feel to Wohlforth's book. Readers who enjoy this book might also enjoy many of the titles found in the political section of the "Environmental Writing" chapter (Robert Sullivan's *A Whale Hunt: How a Native-American Village Did What No One Thought It Could* or Bill McKibben's *The End of Nature* might be good places to start); Wohlforth considers the use of fossil fuels and the future of conservation at many points in his narrative.

Wright, William.

Born That Way: Genes, Behavior, Personality. New York: Knopf, 1998 (New York: Routledge, 1999). 303pp. ISBN 0415924944.

When University of Minnesota researchers spent seventeen years studying more than 100 pairs of twins who had been separated at birth and reared apart, they didn't really expect to find so many startling similarities within each pair that they would change the entire course of the nature versus nurture debate. Wright details that study and others linking biology and behavior, in briskly paced chapters and accessible language.

Subjects: Biology • Experiments • Genetics

Now try: Those readers interested in learning more about the ongoing debate regarding nature versus nurture might also try Matt Ridley's *Nature Via Nurture: Genes, Experience, and What Makes Us Human*. In addition to these more straightforward titles, books describing new genetic theories and discoveries abound; one of the most provocative currently available is Bryan Sykes's *Adam's Curse: A Future Without Men*, in which the author ruminates on human sexual reproduction and the weakness of the male Y chromosome, concluding with the possibility that males may become extinct within 5,000 generations (or 125,000 years). Not exactly, as the author himself concedes, "the day after tomorrow," but possibly a vision of the future nonetheless.

Investigating the Applied Sciences

Science is not exclusively the province of those who theorize and spend a lifetime engaging in pure research; in applied science, practitioners quite literally take knowledge gained through scientific research and observation and apply it to practical and technological problems. For those readers with an interest in the more day-to-day applications of science, such as learning how roads are engineered, buildings are built, and software applications are created, the following titles are custom-made to provide satisfying and informative (and fun) reading experiences.

Eberhart, Mark.

Why Things Break: Understanding the World by the Way It Comes Apart. New York: Harmony Books, 2003. 256pp. ISBN 1400048834.

Who knew a book about the chemistry of materials, written by a professor at the Colorado School of Mines, could be so enjoyable? Eberhart uses many everyday and more unique examples, such as the sinking of the *Titanic*, to illustrate his points regarding the theories of how atoms interact and allow materials and products to bend and withstand pressure.

> **Subjects:** Chemistry • Engineering • Experiments • Quick Reads

> **Now try:** Deborah Cadbury's informational but intensely readable history, *Dreams of Iron and Steel: Seven Wonders of the Nineteenth Century, from the Building of the London Sewers to the Panama Canal,* is less about materials science than about structural wonders, but it also makes effective use of examples to illustrate material properties and architectural feats.

Fisher, Len.

How to Dunk a Doughnut: The Science of Everyday Life. New York: Arcade Publishing, 2003. 255pp. ISBN 1559706805.

5

By his own admission, Fisher uses the "science of the familiar" to introduce readers who may feel intimidated by science to some basic precepts such as capillary rise (what draws the coffee through channels in your doughnut) and the kinetic energy that leads to a perfect boiled egg. The book also contains helpful diagrams and photographs to help the reader imagine the theories in action, and the author's tone is quite humorous, for example, when he explains that he offered to give a talk on the physics of sex to a school science club, and the audience at that meeting was "rather larger than most."

> **Subjects:** Biology • Essays • Experiments • Humor

> **Now try:** Fisher's subsequent title, *Weighing the Soul: Scientific Discovery from the Brilliant to the Bizarre*, provides another introduction to some of the weirder stories in science for readers who don't usually browse the Dewey 500s. K.C. Cole's *The Universe and the Teacup: The Mathematics of Science and Beauty* seeks to demystify mathematics by offering more personal and recognizable human stories to demonstrate the utility of math in everyday life. Another biological treatise with a light tongue-in-cheek tone is Olivia Judson's *Dr. Tatiana's Sex Advice to All Creation.*

Petroski, Henry.

Pushing the Limits: New Adventures in Engineering. New York: Knopf, 2004. 288pp. ISBN 1400040515.

Form follows function even in Petroski's writing, which is as ordered and elegant as the bridges he describes in this two-part observation on engineering triumphs and failures. Those readers who might think engineering dull may be pleasantly surprised by the photographs and explanations behind some of the world's most famous bridges. Petroski's stories include not only technological detail but also the political histories involved in getting the structures built, and also travelogue-like detail regarding some of their settings.

Subjects: Engineering • Essays • Technology • Transportation

Now try: Petroski has written many other books that strive to make engineering principles interesting and accessible to nonengineer readers; two of the best known are *The Pencil: A History of Design and Circumstance* and *The Evolution of Useful Things*. On a related subject, Donald A. Norman considers our relationship to everyday objects (less than the process of buying them) in his detailed but rarely dull *Emotional Design: Why We Love (Or Hate) Everyday Things*. William Langewiesche's *Inside the Sky: A Meditation on Flight* also provides a technical overview (this time, of flight) tinged with the author's inspiring love for and personal history with his subject.

Wolke, Robert L.

What Einstein Told His Cook: Kitchen Science Explained. New York: Norton, 2002. 350pp. ISBN 0393011836.

Wolke's wonderfully informative and thoroughly delightful tour of the chemistry behind cooking is written in a question-and-answer format, with just enough science to be helpful and not enough to be intimidating to the lay reader. It also includes multiple recipes and is written in an informal tone by the author, who is also a professor emeritus of chemistry at the University of Pittsburgh and a syndicated food columnist for the *Washington Post*.

Subjects: Chemistry • Food • Investigative Stories

Now try: Wolke has his own Einstein-centered cottage industry; he's also the author of *What Einstein Didn't Know: Scientific Answers to Everyday Questions* and *What Einstein Told His Barber*. Readers more interested in the food side of Wolke's work might consider *How to Read a French Fry*, by Russ Parsons, or Mark Bittman's *How to Cook Everything*, or even some of the titles from the "Foodie Memoirs" subgenre in the "Memoirs and Autobiography" chapter.

Provocative Science

Good scientific writing often tells stories that prove the maxim that truth is stranger than fiction. The titles in this "Provocative Science" subgenre of investigative science offer theories that may not be proven or accepted, even within the author's respective fields, but that doesn't mean they're not true. Like many history narratives, these books offer facts and evidence but may differ in the way their authors interpret the available data. These works are the quintessential examples of investigative science writing, which "can give us essential information to calm or alarm" (Carr 2004, 58).

Because they often describe topics that can be quite strange or scary to us (bioterrorism, the spread of viruses, the threat of overpopulation, etc.), we tend to read these stories while sitting on the edge of our seats (as we do many true adventure titles, for example). In addition to being descriptive, many of these books also happen to be page-turners, which may appeal both to readers of more adventurous nonfiction titles and to readers of suspense and thriller fiction titles.

Dawkins, Richard.

The Selfish Gene. New York: Oxford University Press, 1976 (1999). 352pp. ISBN 0192860925.

Dawkins speculates in this best-selling popular science title that all human activity, sexual or otherwise, is driven by our genes' "selfish" need to preserve themselves, combined with their surprisingly subtle drive toward altruism meant primarily to help themselves while superficially helping others. Densely written, Dawkins's book might be a tough sell for readers who don't usually enjoy science reading, but it does provide an introduction to both the advances in the biological sciences over the last quarter-century and some of the more controversial theories that have sprung up around genetic studies, including the idea of "memes," which are units of culture spread by imitation and "natural selection" within society.

Subjects: Biology • Classics • Evolution • Genetics • Sociology

Now try: Susan Blackmore's *The Meme Machine* builds on ideas Dawkins originally proposed. Niles Eldredge's *Why We Do It: Rethinking Sex and the Selfish Gene*, published in 2004, provides a readable response to Dawkins's landmark work and is a surprisingly moderate consideration of the interplay between genetic determinism and sociobiological factors in our human decision to pursue sexual relationships. Michael Shermer's *The Science of Good and Evil: Why People Cheat, Gossip, Care, Share, and Follow the Golden Rule* is a similarly provocatively titled but densely challenging work that seeks to explain human moral (or immoral) behavior through evolutionary psychology.

 5

Ehrlich, Paul, and Anne Ehrlich.

One with Nineveh: Politics, Consumption, and the Human Future. Washington, D.C.: Island Press, 2004. 447pp. ISBN 1559638796.

Paul and Anne Ehrlich (the authors of the inflammatory *The Population Bomb*, first published in 1968) warn that the collapse of our current society is coming and will be as final and irrevocable as the ecological collapse of the ancient city of Nineveh in Mesopotamia. Addressing such varied factors as overpopulation, overconsumption, and technological advances designed more to ease short-term needs than address long-term environmental concerns, the authors cite ecological, economic, and sociological sources and studies to examine and offer solutions to what they term our "human predicament."

Subjects: ALA Notable Books • Environment • Politics • Sociology • Technology

Now try: Readers interested in the subject may also wish to try Joel E. Cohen's more speculative *How Many People Can the Earth Support?* or the collection *Beyond Malthus: Nineteen Dimensions of the Population Challenge*. Readers who enjoy Ehrlich's sweeping suppositions might also enjoy Jared Diamond's similarly lengthy and global study, *Collapse: How Societies Choose to Fail or Succeed.*

Kelleher, Colm A.

Brain Trust: The Hidden Connection Between Mad Cow and Misdiagnosed Alzheimer's Disease. New York: Paraview Pocket Books, 2004. 312pp. ISBN 0743499352.

Kelleher, a biochemist, speculates that the nearly 9,000 percent jump in deaths caused by Alzheimer's disease over the past two decades may be at least partly attributable to the undetected presence of the infectious agent that causes mad cow disease in our food supply. As if that weren't scary enough, he also provides a history of the disease, in its many forms across animal species, and his further theory that materials from infected animals may have been brought to the North American continent by an overzealous research scientist, and that incidents of the disease are covered up by government bureaucrats both here and abroad. In short and concise chapters, Kelleher's crisp scientific writing is all the more frightening in its understatement.

> **Subjects:** Animals • Biology • Experiments • Food • Health Issues • Medicine • Quick Reads

> **Now try:** Although more investigative and less scientific, Eric Schlosser's now-classic *Fast Food Nation: The Dark Side of the All-American Meal* might also appeal to readers who won't mind being scared of food by the time they're done reading. Michael Carroll's similarly shocking *Lab 257: The Disturbing Story of the Government's Secret Plum Island Germ Laboratory*, about the U.S. government's biological experiments during World War II, may also appeal to readers drawn to more speculative science, as might Nelson DeMille's novel, the thriller *Plum Island*. Also consider offering Debbie Bookchin's and Jim Schumacher's *The Virus and the Vaccine* (annotated in the history chapter).

Pringle, Peter.

Food, Inc. Mendel to Monsanto—The Promises and Perils of the Biotech Harvest. New York: Simon & Schuster, 2003 (2005). 256pp. ISBN 074326763X.

Journalist Pringle tries to demystify the definition, creation, and distribution of genetically modified foods, describing historical developments as old as Gregor Mendel's genetics experiments with pea plants, as well as agribusiness companies like Monsanto's most recent innovations and patenting techniques. This is an admirably well-rounded portrait of an issue that will become ever more pertinent in the coming years.

> **Subjects:** Agriculture • ALA Notable Books • Business • Food • Genetics • Investigative Stories

> **Now try:** Eric Schlosser's *Fast Food Nation* is much more alarmist in tone but similar in subject (possible perils in our food sources) and similarly investigated and journalistically written. Richard Manning's *Against the Grain: How Agriculture Has Hijacked Civilization* might also appeal to readers who are interested in the current state of agribusiness.

Adventures in Science

Science news stories are typically exciting because they herald new discoveries, or because they describe human leaps in understanding that are often precursors to improved medical or other technological advances. For science readers who are already comfortable in the genre, and who read primarily to learn new things or to further their knowledge in a specific subject, these stories might be good opening recommendations to determine their reading needs. Although all of them are enjoyable in their own right, advisors should be aware that most habitual science readers will have very particular and subject-oriented areas of interest (chemistry, biology, physics, etc.) and that some exploratory questions regarding readers' previous science title choices may be in order to determine their interests.

Whether celebrating more historical breakthroughs like the moon landing (*Man on the Moon*) or recent technological developments in undersea exploration techniques (*Return to Titanic*), these books are often highly descriptive, but the stories move at a fairly fast pace and are often somewhat suspenseful. Because they tell tales of exciting discoveries, they also appeal to readers who just plain like a good story (*Journey Beyond Selene* and *The Doctor's Plague*, for example, are short and compelling stories that may particularly appeal to readers who don't typically browse the science shelves).

Alvarez, Walter.

T. rex and the Crater of Doom. Princeton, N.J.: University of Princeton Press, 1997 (New York: Vintage Books, 1998). 185pp. ISBN 0375702105.

In this book that reads more like an adventure or science fiction story, Alvarez and his research associates provide evidence for the "impact theory," which posits that a comet or asteroid hit the earth 65 million years ago, and its impact resulted in sufficient climatic and terrain changes to cause the extinction of the dinosaurs. The discovery in question is that of the Chicxulub Crater, on Mexico's Yucatán Peninsula, which was found exactly where proponents of impact theory thought it should be. Engaging and quickly paced, this is truly a dinosaur book for adults.

Subjects: Adventure • ALA Notable Books • Ancient History • Dinosaurs • Gentle Reads • Geography • Quick Reads

Now try: Those adult readers still interested in dinosaurs (like the vast majority of young nonfiction readers!) might also enjoy John Noble Wilford's systematic overview of the discovery and study of dinosaur remains in *The Riddle of the Dinosaurs*. Readers interested in the extinction of other prehistoric animals, like saber-tooth tigers, might also enjoy Michael Benton's *When Life Nearly Died: The Greatest Mass Extinction of All Time*, which is also controversial for its suggestion that big events account for more biographical and geological phenomena than gradual change. Last but definitely not least (in size of beast and speculation), Peter D. Ward's *Gorgon: Paleontology, Obsession, and the Greatest Catastrophe in Earth's History* describes the Gorgon, an animal that preceded the dinosaurs and was also wiped out in an environmental cataclysm similar to the one that annihilated the dinosaurs.

Ballard, Robert D., with Michael S. Sweeney.

Return to **Titanic:** *A New Look at the World's Most Famous Lost Ship.* Washington, D.C.: National Geographic, 2004. 192pp. ISBN 0792272889.

Ballard originally discovered the *Titanic* in 1985, and in this beautifully photographed book he tells the story of his return to the ship, in addition to describing the scientific advances that continue to make deep sea diving and exploration safer and more efficient.

Subjects: Adventure • Diving • Illustrated Books • Maritime Disasters • Technology • *Titanic*

Now try: Taking as his subject the depths of space, rather than the depths of the ocean, Michael Benson's beautifully illustrated *Beyond: Visions of the Interplanetary Probes* includes both spectacular pictures of the wonders of our solar system and essays regarding the science behind the technology that took the pictures. Readers interested in the science of diving might also enjoy the illustrated *The History of Shipwrecks*, by Angus Konstam.

Chaikin, Andrew.

A Man on the Moon: The Voyages of the Apollo Astronauts. New York: Viking, 1994 (New York: Penguin Books, 1998). 670pp. ISBN 0140272011.

This is a fascinating and extremely personal narrative describing the characteristics and journeys of all of the Apollo moon flight astronauts, as well as their Mercury and Gemini space flight predecessors. Chaikin was eventually able to interview all of the surviving astronauts, and the intimate nature of the stories shared by these typically very private pilots makes this volume read much faster than its 600+ pages would indicate. From tragedy to triumph, Chaikin provides a compelling history of the scientific and personal challenges encountered and surmounted in the American quest to put men on the moon.

Subjects: Adventure • ALA Notable Books • Biographies • Classics • Exploration • Space • Work Relationships

Now try: Tom Wolfe's creative nonfiction classic *The Right Stuff* relates the stories of the first astronauts in his quickly paced narrative account of the space race between the United States and Russia. John Noble Wilford, the *New York Times* reporter who wrote the lead story of the first human steps on the moon, also wrote a book about the landmark event, *We Reach the Moon*, which provides a historical portrait of the feeling of the times (it was first published in 1969). Former astronaut Eugene Cernan's account (with Don Davis) of his experiences as the pilot of *Gemini 9* and commander of *Apollo 17*, *The Last Man on the Moon*, opens with the horrific *Apollo 1* fire and doesn't pull any other punches in a dramatic first-person narrative.

Henig, Robin Marantz.

Pandora's Baby: How the First Test Tube Babies Sparked the Reproductive Revolution. Boston: Houghton Mifflin, 2004. 326pp. ISBN 0618224157.

Journalist Henig relates the suspenseful tale of the earliest days of IVF (in vitro fertilization) technology and, in particular, the story of Doris and John Del-Zio, who might have become the parents of the first test tube baby in 1973, had their fertilized egg been transplanted into Doris rather than destroyed by a supervising physician who hadn't been informed of its development. In alternating chapters, Henig tells both the Del-Zios' story and that of the development of fertility technology and the cultural debates it fostered.

Subjects: ALA Notable Books • Biology • Genetics • Investigative Stories • Medicine • Pregnancy • Technology

Now try: David Plotz's investigative *The Genius Factory: The Curious History of the Nobel Prize Sperm Bank* is quite similar to Henig's book in subject and tone. Jonathan

Weiner's *His Brother's Keeper: A Story from the Edge of Medicine*, may also appeal to readers interested in recent advances in medical technology, as it follows the story of two brothers, one diagnosed with ALS (Lou Gehrig's Disease) and the other a genetics engineer dedicated to understanding and conquering the disease. Those readers not averse to trying a fiction thriller might also consider Kevin Guilfoyle's *Cast of Shadows*, in which a fertility doctor seeks to clone his daughter's killer (so that he can discover who it was) from evidence left at the scene.

Kluger, Jeffrey.

Journey Beyond Selēnē: Remarkable Expeditions Past Our Moon and to the Ends of the Solar System. New York: Simon & Schuster, 1999 (2001). 314pp. ISBN 0684865599.

Kluger sings the praises of the unrecognized adventurers of space exploration: the scientists and engineers employed by NASA's Jet Propulsion Laboratory (JPL) in Pasadena, California. The book opens with the fantastic tale of the first pictures taken of Jupiter's moons by the spacecraft *Voyager I* in 1979, which proved there was warmth (and therefore the possibility of life) on several of them, and proceeds at breakneck speed through various other lab projects and breakthroughs and the people who made them possible. As regards both character and story the book reads as compellingly as any novel.

> **Subjects:** ALA Notable Books • Astronomy • Exploration • Space • Work Relationships

> **Now try:** Mark Wolverton's similarly novelistic account of the *Pioneer 10* and *11* spacecrafts, *The Depths of Space: The Story of the Pioneer Planetary Probes*, continues the story of interstellar exploration and travel. The beautifully illustrated *NASA and the Exploration of Space: With Works from the NASA Art Collection*, by Roger Launius, might also be a nice complementary read (with pictures!) to Kluger's work.

Preston, Richard.

The Hot Zone: A Terrifying True Story. New York: Random House, 1994 (New York: Anchor Books, 1995). 422pp. ISBN 0385495226.

Using horrific and descriptive details and suspenseful foreshadowing, Preston describes the processes that many filoviruses (such as Ebola) follow when replicating themselves inside monkey and human hosts, causing cell death, organ deterioration, and frequently death. In addition to drawing frightening parallels to the spread of HIV in humans, Preston lucidly relates a 1989 outbreak of Ebola in research monkeys at a research lab near Washington, D.C., and their subsequent eradication by the military unit responsible for studying infectious agents. Although that strain of the virus proved lethal in monkeys but never caused illness in several humans who were contaminated, Preston ends with the chilling suggestion that any day could bring a fresh outbreak of any mutated virus from anywhere in the world.

> **Subjects:** Adventure • Biology • Classics • Experiments • Health Issues • Medicine • Quick Reads

Now try: Those readers who wouldn't mind a bit of espionage with their science might also try Ken Alibek's tell-all about his years as a Soviet bioweapons expert (written with Stephen Handelman), *Biohazard: The Chilling True Story of the Largest Covert Biological Weapons Program in the World—Told from Inside by the Man Who Ran It*. Titles from the "Natural Disasters and Disease Epidemics" sub-subgenre in the history chapter might be worth recommending to these readers as well. Robin Cook's novels of medical suspense, especially *Outbreak*, or Michael Crichton's *The Andromeda Strain*, might also appeal to this audience.

Watson, James D.

The Double Helix: A Personal Account of the Discovery of the Structure of DNA.
New York: Atheneum, 1968 (New York: Touchstone, 2001). 226pp. ISBN 074321630X.

Told chronologically and in the first person, this story of the discovery of the double helix of DNA is aptly named in that it is an extremely personal story. The complicated procedures that led to the theory (X-ray photography, crystallography, chemistry based model-building) are referred to but are less explained than used as the backdrop for the disparate and unique cast of scientists pursuing the discovery. Watson's working relationship with his partner, Francis Crick, is engagingly described, as are their many clashes with their English colleagues, Maurice Wilkins and Rosalind Franklin, and their rivalry with their American counterpart, Linus Pauling, in their pursuit of the true structure of DNA. The book was heavily criticized when first published, primarily for its harsh depiction of Rosalind Franklin, and although readers might find Watson's personality distracting, the work remains an important example of informal and gripping science writing.

Subjects: Adventure • Biographies • Biology • Chemistry • Classics • Friendships • Genetics • Memoirs • Quick Reads • Work Relationships

Now try: Readers tend to either love or hate Watson's sometimes conceited tone and frank admissions, but those who find him amusing might also enjoy his later memoir, *Genes, Girls, and Gamow: After the Double Helix*. Readers who are interested in Watson but don't want to hear any more directly from him might be pointed instead to Victor McElheny's unauthorized biography, *Watson and DNA: Making a Scientific Revolution*. Brenda Maddox's *Los Angeles Times* Book Prize–winning biography, *Rosalind Franklin: The Dark Lady of DNA*, can and should be offered as the well-researched but still intimate antidote to Watson's narrative and many slights to that great scientist, who died from ovarian cancer at the age of thirty-seven.

Micro-Science

Although "Micro-Science" is not yet an accepted literary term, perhaps this will start the trend. Like their very popular counterparts in the history chapter ("Micro-Histories"), micro-science titles offer a wealth of historical and contextual detail in books whose subject matter is very narrowly defined, and the skill of their authors in weaving those details into broader historical narratives and scientific or philosophical themes can often make or break them as suitable for pleasure reading.

Like all science titles, these books also fulfill many nonfiction readers' desire to learn something through their reading. In addition to details about the physical and molecular structures of objects and phenomena (apparent in David Bodanis's *Electric Universe*) or, in the case of diseases, the pathology of their symptoms (displayed in Andrew Solomon's detailed journal of clinical depression, *The Noonday Demon*), many of these stories include historical asides or settings as well (Richard Schweid's *The Cockroach Papers*, or Dava Sobel's best-selling *Longitude*). Therefore they may appeal to readers of Micro-Histories, and vice versa.

Bodanis, David.

Electric Universe: The Shocking True Story of Electricity. New York: Crown Publishers, 2005. 308pp. ISBN 1400045509.

Bodanis tells the story of huge discoveries and innovations made in the past two centuries about the elusive existence and properties of electricity, through the life stories of the discoverers and scientists. In quick and personal chapters, he relates stories such as Alexander Graham Bell's desire to woo his deaf student Mabel by studying how sounds are made and produced; Joseph Henry's invention of the telegraph to keep his rural students amused in New York State in the 1830s (and Samuel Morse's patenting of the idea); and Otto Loewi's discovery of how neurotransmitters transmit signals in our brains. The personal stories are so prominent here that Bodanis even includes an epilogue to tell what eventually happened to the researchers he describes.

Subjects: Biographies • Experiments • Inventions • Quick Reads • Technology

Now try: Less science than history, Jill Jonnes's *Empires of Light: Edison, Tesla, Westinghouse, and the Race to Electrify the World* might provide a nicely complementary and contextual read to Bodanis's book. One of the more controversial historical uses of electric current is described in Richard Moran's similarly character-driven history of the electric chair, *Executioner's Current: Thomas Edison, George Westinghouse, and the Invention of the Electric Chair.*

Pollan, Michael.

The Botany of Desire: A Plant's-Eye View of the World. New York: Random House, 2001 (2002). 271pp. ISBN 0375760393.

Science writer and gardening enthusiast Pollan examines history through the case studies of four plants: the apple, tulips, marijuana, and the potato. The result is a personable work of history and investigative journalism, in which Pollan relates the fruits of his research about such historical characters as Johnny Appleseed, as well as more current stories about his personal experiments growing cannabis and recent statistics about America's drug war.

Subjects: Biology • Classics • Gardening • Horticulture • Plants

Now try: Amy Stewart's *The Earth Moved: On the Remarkable Achievements of Earthworms* is also a scientific and personal gardener's ode to a seldom respected pillar of the ecosystem, the lowly earthworm, who helps clean up pollution and creates more fertile earth. Readers who agree with Pollan's idea that plants are complex organisms that affect and are affected by their environment might also be talked into reading Peter Tompkins's and

Christopher Bird's *The Secret Lives of Plants*, which examines several scientific studies of plants and their sensory abilities.

Ridley, Matt.

Genome: The Autobiography of a Species in 23 Chapters. New York: HarperCollins, 1999 (New York: Perennial, 2000). 344pp. ISBN 0060932902.

Ridley set out to match human traits with each of our twenty-three base pairs of chromosomes, and the result is an "autobiography" of select genes from each of the pairs, exploring both the history of genetic discoveries and the consequences of recognizing that the human genome "is a record of our history written in the code for a working machine." From fate to intelligence, instinct to stress, Ridley considers the biological underpinnings of many processes that contribute to our sense of self, in deceptively simple and almost poetic prose.

Subjects: ALA Notable Books • Biology • Classics • Genetics • Psychology

Now try: Readers fascinated by Ridley's pairing of chromosomes with our most human traits might also enjoy Gary Marcus's recent title on nature, nurture, and genetics, *The Birth of the Mind: How a Tiny Number of Genes Creates the Complexities of Human Thought.* Jennifer Ackerman's essay collection *Chance in the House of Fate: A Natural History of Heredity* is similar to Ridley's book in its use of artful prose to explain scientific tenets. Jonathan Margolis's provocatively titled but impressively rigorous *O: The Intimate History of the Orgasm* might also appeal to Ridley's readers.

Schweid, Richard.

The Cockroach Papers: A Compendium of History and Lore. New York: Four Walls Eight Window, 1999. 193pp. ISBN 1568581378.

Although few readers will admit or believe they would want to know this much about cockroaches, Schweid's in-depth look at their history, physiology, mating rituals, habitats, and interactions with humans is fascinating. Schweid combines his crisp scientific prose with extensive investigative work on his subject; he not only met and interviewed experts in the field, but even traveled to Nicaragua at one point to do so, managing to keep his sense of humor despite his choice of topic.

Subjects: Cockroaches • Humor • Insects • Quick Reads

Now try: Although not as humorous, Schweid's *Consider the Eel* offers the same exhaustive discussion about the title animal. Robert Sullivan's superlative *Rats: Observations on the History and Habitat of the City's Most Unwanted Inhabitants* (annotated in the history chapter under "Micro-Histories") also provides a wealth of fascinating information about another animal commonly thought of as icky. Pamela Nagami's fascinating *Bitten: True Medical Stories of Bites and Stings* provides a closer look at the biology and pathology of animal and insect bites and stings.

Seife, Charles.

Zero: The Biography of a Dangerous Idea. New York: Viking, 2000. 248pp. ISBN 067088457X.

Starting with the Egyptian, Babylonian, and Greek number systems, Seife illustrates the birth of the concept of the number zero and continues on to detail its troubled history, from its rejection by Western philosophers, who espoused the idea that there is no void, to its appearance in Eastern philosophy and modern mathematics. Although Seife has obviously striven to ground the work in understandable equations and historical detail, there is still some mathematical description that readers who don't typically enjoy science or math may find hard to conquer.

Subjects: Ancient History • History of Science • Mathematics • Philosophy

Now try: Robert Kaplan's *The Nothing That Is: A Natural History of Zero*, was published around the same time as Seife's book and is a more heavily historic alternative for readers. Readers fascinated by the concept of books written entirely to explain "nothing" might also enjoy the less numeric and more accessible and all-encompassing *The Hole in the Universe: How Scientists Peered over the Edge of Emptiness and Found Everything,* by K. C. Cole.

Sherman, Joe.

Gasp! The Swift and Terrible Beauty of Air. Washington, D.C.: Shoemaker & Hoard, 2004. 414pp. ISBN 1593760256.

Sherman combines history and science in this exhaustive and nearly poetic look at air and, more specifically, how we breathe it in. Each chapter is subdivided into readable segments covering such phenomena as our first breath, the physiology of how we breathe, the components of the atmosphere, mythology surrounding air, and the impediments (including smoke, smog, and ozone) to our search for "fresh air."

Subjects: Biology • History of Science • Investigative Stories • Pollution

Now try: Related in both subject and use of language, Jan DeBlieu's *Wind: How the Flow of Air Has Shaped Life, Myth, and the Land* evokes the same sense of wonder at a natural phenomenon we often take for granted. Scott Huler's micro-history *Defining the Wind: The Beaufort Scale, and How a 19th-Century Admiral Turned Science into Poetry* might also appeal to readers interested in histories of science. Joe Sherman is also the author of an organizational history of the Saturn car company, *In the Rings of Saturn*, that garnered surprisingly good reviews for its readability.

Solomon, Andrew.

The Noonday Demon: An Atlas of Depression. New York: Scribner, 2001 (2003). 571pp. ISBN 0684854678.

In addition to detailing his own struggle with depression, Solomon takes the reader on a wider tour of the disease, discussing symptoms, treatments, and its overall effect on the lives of its many sufferers. Although the language is much more metaphorical than that found in most science writing ("depression is the flaw in love"), there is so much medical and pharmaceutical detail here (in addition to multiple interviews and research) that it really does read like a treatise on the disease.

Subjects: ALA Notable Books • Epic Reads • Medicine • Memoirs • Mental Health • National Book Award Winners

Now try: Kay Redfield Jamison's *The Unquiet Mind: A Memoir of Moods and Madness* relates the author's struggle with both her manic depression and her resistance to treating her disease with lithium; James Frey's searing portrait of drug addiction in *A Million Little Pieces* also examines mental and physical health issues in a highly personal manner.

History of Science

History of science titles pack double the subject matter into their narratives; they may appeal both to readers of more straightforward science books, as well as to readers of history who enjoy the genre due to its more leisurely pace; its authors' frequent use of chronological organization; and often immense amounts of research, typically condensed into readable and enjoyable stories.

Many history of science books tackle broad scientific subject areas (Bill Bryson's *A Short History of Nearly Everything*, for example) in addition to historical research and exposition. Because they are genreblenders (or, more accurately, reading interest-blenders) they may not appeal as strongly to readers of "Deep Science." However, due to their broader and less complex narratives, they may also appeal to readers who typically wouldn't touch a science or math book with a ten-foot pole. As an added bonus, they're often written by authors with familiar and popular names; Stephen Jay Gould, Timothy Ferris, and Carl Sagan are all represented here, and may appeal to readers who think they "should" know something about science topics and want to learn from writers recognized to be experts in their fields.

Bryson, Bill.

A Short History of Nearly Everything. New York: Broadway Books, 2003 (2004). 544pp. ISBN 076790818X.

Best known for his travel narratives, Bryson compiled this book of science history and factoids to answer his "quiet, unwanted urge" to find out more about both scientific matters and those figures who discovered or studied them. The author does a commendable job marrying research and reading (librarians should pay attention to his bibliography) with interviews with scientists to explain just a little bit about such broad-ranging topics as the cosmos, earth science, physics, and biological organisms.

Subjects: Epic Reads • Essays • History of Science

Now try: Those readers interested in another briskly paced book on the "history of everything" might also try James C. Davis's *The Human Story: Our History, from the Stone Age to Today*, which is annotated in the history chapter. Bryson is much better known as a hugely popular travel writer, and those readers who enjoy his often self-deprecating humor and descriptive narrative skills might also want to branch out into some of his travel titles, such as *A Walk in the Woods: Rediscovering America on the Appalachian Trail* or *In a Sunburned Country*. Those readers interested in a complementary read not about where science has been but about where it may be going might try John Horgan's *The End of Science* (annotated in the "Making Sense . . . " chapter).

Emsley, John.

The 13th Element: The Sordid Tale of Murder, Fire, and Phosphorous. New York: Wiley, 2000 (2002). 352pp. ISBN 047144149X.

Emsley weaves a fascinating narrative about the most unlikely of subjects: the thirteenth element, phosphorous, from its discovery as the accidental by-product of an experiment in which seventeenth century alchemist Hennig Brandt boiled and reduced his own urine into a paste that contained it, through the history of its more contemporary uses in bombs and as poison.

Subjects: Biographies • Chemistry • History of Science

Now try: Eileen Welsome's historically contextual and suspenseful *The Plutonium Files: America's Secret Experiments in the Cold War* is superficially about the government's unpardonable decision to secretly inject hospital patients with plutonium to judge its effect on the body, but it also tells the history of the discovery and development of another famously unstable element.

Ferris, Timothy.

Coming of Age in the Milky Way. New York: Morrow, 1988 (New York: Perennial, 2003). 510pp. ISBN 0060535954.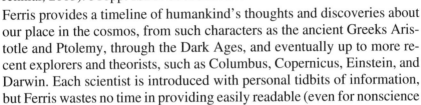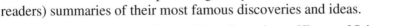

Ferris provides a timeline of humankind's thoughts and discoveries about our place in the cosmos, from such characters as the ancient Greeks Aristotle and Ptolemy, through the Dark Ages, and eventually up to more recent explorers and theorists, such as Columbus, Copernicus, Einstein, and Darwin. Each scientist is introduced with personal tidbits of information, but Ferris wastes no time in providing easily readable (even for nonscience readers) summaries of their most famous discoveries and ideas.

Subjects: Astronomy • Biographies • Cosmology • History of Science

Now try: Although still more informal in style, David Grinspoon's work of popular science (he even uses a smiley emoticon in his introduction), *Lonely Planets: The Natural Philosophy of Alien Life,* considers our history of belief in extraterrestrial life forms and our scientific search to find them, and provides a nice sequel of sorts to Ferris's consideration of our existence in the solar system by providing more information about our planetary neighbors.   **5**

Gee, Henry.

Jacob's Ladder: The History of the Human Genome. New York: Norton, 2004. 272pp. ISBN 0393050831.

Science writer Gee makes the importance of human genome sequencing both more understandable and approachable in his brisk but almost reflectively written history of the human race's understanding of our origins and composition, from Pliny and Aristotle to Darwin and William Bateson (the latter being the scientist who actually coined the term "genetics"). In addition to narrating the history of genetic study, Gee also proposes that the study of genes and the genome, by creating new possibilities for genetic modification and creation, will challenge our current ideas of what it really means to be human.

Subjects: Biology • Genetics • History of Science • Investigative Stories

Now try: Carl Zimmer's extremely readable history of science, *Soul Made Flesh: The Discovery of the Brain—and How It Changed the World,* does for the brain what Gee's book does for the genome.

Gould, Stephen Jay.

Time's Arrow, Time's Cycle: Myth and Metaphor in the Discovery of Geological Time. Cambridge, Mass.: Harvard University Press, 1987 (New York: Penguin, 1988). 222pp. ISBN 0140228195.

Paleontologist and evolutionary theorist Gould reflects on the meaning of "deep time" as we currently know it (an Earth hundreds of millions of years old) versus the view that time is only 6,000 years old (an idea propagated only a short hundred years ago). Gould bases his reflections on three very different scientists and their works: Thomas Burnet's seventeenth-century theory of the earth, James Huttons's eighteenth-century work of nearly the same title, and Charles Lyell's early nineteenth-century *Principles of Geology.*

>**Subjects:** Geology • History of Science • Time

>**Now try:** Although more straightforward in prose style and historical detail, Martin Gorst's *Measuring Eternity: The Search for the Beginning of Time* also provides the long view of our changing conception of the idea of "time"; likewise, Clive Trotman's brisk *The Feathered Onion: Creation of Life in the Universe* is written in a conversational style that might also appeal to readers who don't tackle much science reading. Alan Cutler's biography of Nicolau Steno, a Danish scientist skilled in both anatomy and geology, *The Seashell on the Mountaintop*, might also appeal to science readers. Gould is of course a best-selling science writer, and readers may also want to consider his more recent works, *The Structure of Evolutionary Theory* or *I Have Landed: The End of a Beginning in Natural History.*

Larson, Edward J.

>*Evolution: The Remarkable History of a Scientific Theory.* New York: Modern Library, 2004. 337pp. ISBN 0679642889.

>Not many scientific theories have been as widely discussed or as controversial as evolution. Author Larson takes the reader on a whirlwind historical tour of the development of the theory and its basic tenets, and concludes with a lively consideration of the arguments, both scientific and not, that have arisen around it right up through the dawn of the twenty-first century. Particularly interesting and not often discussed in scientific writing, Larson's discussion of the eugenics movement and "Social Darwinism" might particularly appeal to readers who prefer sociological or historical topics to scientific ones.

>>**Subjects:** Darwin, Charles • Evolution • History of Science • <u>Modern Library Chronicles Series</u>

>>**Now try:** Larson is also the author of the Pulitzer Prize–winning *Summer of the Gods: The Scopes Trial and America's Continuing Debate Over Science and Religion,* which might also appeal to history readers. Although a history of physics and the search for an answer to everything, Dan Falk's history of science title, *Universe on a T-Shirt: The Quest for the Theory of Everything,* provides a more historical overview of physics theory than a scientific one, and also sports a lovely (and annotated) history of science bibliography. David Berlinski's *Infinite Ascent: A Short History of Mathematics,* another entry in the <u>Modern Library Chronicles series</u>, might also appeal to those readers who like the format of Larson's book.

Morris, Richard.

>*The Last Sorcerers: The Path from Alchemy to the Periodic Table.* Washington, D.C.: Joseph Henry Press, 2003. 282pp. ISBN 0309089050.

>A veritable "Who's Who" of history's most famous chemists, this story unfolds chronologically from ancient Greece to present-day studies of new elements. Although the stories themselves are fascinating (particularly the story of Hennig Brandt endeavoring earnestly to make gold from urine), the character portraits of

influential scientists and their discoveries make this an accessible read for even the most unscientific of readers.

> **Subjects:** Biographies • Chemistry • History of Science

> **Now try:** Paul Strathern's *Mendeleyev's Dream: The Quest for the Elements* also presents an intensely readable and character-driven history of chemistry. It begins and ends with the story of Dmitri Mendeleyev, who strove to find a way to order the elements and claimed to have received a final vision outlining that order in a dream.

Sagan, Carl.

Cosmos. New York: Random House, 1980 (2002). 365pp. ISBN 0375508325.

Written in conjunction with the popular television series of the same name, Sagan's epic tale of the science of astronomy and the physical characteristics of space and all its occupants reads like an introductory history of planetary science. In accessible language he explains the dimensions of the cosmos, basic tenets of evolutionary theory, the birth of astronomy and Johannes Kepler's theory of planetary motion, more recent studies of other planets in our star system, the life expectancies of stars, and our continuing duty to become more aware of both our terrestrial and our galactic responsibilities.

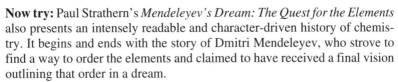

5

> **Subjects:** Astronomy • Classics • Cosmology • History of Science

> **Now try:** Timothy Ferris's excellent *The Whole Shebang: A State of the Universe(s) Report* is an updated and slightly more reflective look at the cosmos as well as recent theories and advances in quantum physics and string theory. Michio Kaku's *Parallel Worlds: A Journey through Creation, Higher Dimensions, and the Future of the Cosmos* provides a similar but even more all-encompassing view of cosmology.

Sobel, Dava.

Longitude: The True Story of a Lone Genius Who Solved the Greatest Scientific Problem of His Time. New York: Walker, 1995 (New York: Penguin, 1996). 184pp. ISBN 0140258795.

Although ostensibly about the marine chronometer, a device used to keep perfect time while at sea, which then enables sailors to keep track of their longitudinal positions, Sobel first defines longitude and details the difficulties of measuring it, and then tells the personal story of John Harrison, the chronometer's inventor. In addition to the scientific story, Sobel includes the story of Harrison's struggle to battle the entrenched scientific establishment of England in the mid-1700s to have his device recognized for the brilliant mechanical solution that it was.

> **Subjects:** ALA Notable Books • Biographies • Classics • Exploration • Gentle Reads • History of Science • Inventions • Quick Reads • Technology

> **Now try:** James Gleick's immensely readable treatise on our concept of time and his theory that "society is in overdrive" is presented in quickly-paced chapters in *Faster: The Acceleration of Just about Everything*. Alan Gurney's *Compass: A Story of Exploration and Innovation* is also the story of a tool that is often taken for granted but that revolutionized travel, as well

as a historical overview of its users and innovators. Sobel is also the author of the best-selling biography *Galileo's Daughter: A Memoir of Science, Faith, and Love*, which details the close relationship between the great scientist and his illegitimate daughter Sister Maria Celeste, whose letters to him provided support during his trial by the Inquisition.

History of Medicine

Closely related to "History of Science" titles are those that deal exclusively with the history of medicine. Noteworthy for their extreme popularity and the high quality of the writing in them, the following titles may appeal not only to science and math readers, but also to those individuals who typically read works of history on diseases and epidemics (including but not limited to the titles listed in the "History's Darkest Hours: Natural Disasters and Disease Epidemics" section of the history chapter).

Glasser, Ronald.

The Light in the Skull: An Odyssey of Medical Discovery. Boston: Faber & Faber, 1997. 209pp. ISBN 057119916X.

Medical doctor Glasser recounts the history behind numerous medical discoveries. He weaves a fascinating story around such topics as cancer, genetics, and the immune system, and includes vivid portrayals of researchers and doctors who made breakthroughs in their respective fields (as well as how they were often ridiculed for their supposedly radical ideas and theories).

> **Subjects:** Biographies • Experiments • Genetics • Health Issues • Medicine

> **Now try:** Those readers who won't be averse to taking a step back and learning about cellular biology might try Lewis Thomas's essay collection, *The Lives of a Cell: Notes of a Biology Watcher*; readers wanting to stick with pure medical history might try Edward S. Golub's *The Limits of Medicine: How Science Shapes Our Hope for the Cure*.

Lax, Eric.

The Mold in Dr. Florey's Coat: The Story of the Penicillin Miracle. New York: Henry Holt, 2004. 307pp. ISBN 0805067906.

This is an interesting history of the work in the penicillin/antibiotics revolution, looking closely at Howard Florey and Alexander Fleming, and the accidental discovery of the mold that killed bacteria. It also includes character and historical details, including the scientists drenching their coats in spores to keep studying them in the uncertain times of World War II (and scientists "whose ingenuity was inversely proportional to their financial backing").

> **Subjects:** Biographies • Experiments • Health Issues • Medicine • World War II

> **Now try:** David Oshinsky's *Polio: An American Story*, or Stephen Bown's *Scurvy: How a Surgeon, a Mariner, and a Gentleman Solved the Greatest Medical Mystery of the Age of Sail*, might appeal to these readers.

Nuland, Sherwin B.

The Doctor's Plague: Germs, Childbed Fever, and the Strange Story of Ignác Semmelweis. New York: Norton, 2003 (2004). 205pp. ISBN 039332625X.

In 1847, one in six new mothers in Vienna's hospital died from puerperal (childbed) fever. Nuland's text illuminates the development of contagion theory, detailing different theoretical causes of childbed fever and the pathology of the disease. In addition to the compelling story, Nuland draws detailed and empathetic portraits of the doctors involved, including Ignác Semmelweis, who eventually discovered the true cause of the "epidemic."

Subjects: Biographies • <u>Great Discoveries Series</u> • Health Issues • History of Science • Medicine • Nineteenth Century • Pregnancy • Quick Reads

Now try: Those readers interested in the doctors and scientists behind many other medical miracles might turn to J. M. Fenster's *Mavericks, Miracles, and Medicine: The Pioneers Who Risked Their Lives to Bring Medicine into the Modern Age* (which actually opens with Semmelweis shouting "WASH YOUR HANDS!" in the maternity ward in his Vienna hospital).

Scientists and Science Enthusiasts

"Scientists and Science Enthusiasts" literally describes these stories as character-driven narratives in which the human practitioners of scientific study and experimentation are the main focus. In addition to providing the factual and descriptive information that science readers demand, the authors of these titles also create character portraits that rival those found in any of the more typically personal genres such as biography or memoirs.

Readers who enjoy these books may also be referred to the "Problem Solvers and Experimenters" subgenre of the biography chapter, in which numerous titles about historical and more contemporary scientists are listed.

Brockman, John, ed.

Curious Minds: How a Child Becomes a Scientist. New York: Pantheon Books, 2004. 236pp. ISBN 0375422919.

The editor offers twenty-seven essays written by famous scientists (examples include experts in fields ranging from physics and computer science to evolutionary psychology, from Steven Pinker and Freeman Dyson to Richard Dawkins) to answer the question of what led them to pursue a life in science. Each essay is introduced with a short description of the scientist's work, and the essays themselves, ranging from about five to fifteen pages in length, are extremely personable and enlightening.

Subjects: Biographies • Essays • Gentle Reads • Professions • Quick Reads

Now try: Steve Olson's *Count Down: Six Kids Vie for Glory at the World's Toughest Math Competition* is a fast read that explores the annual Mathematical Olympiad and the reasons for students' varying math abilities. Readers more interested in the more personal and creative side of great scientists might also enjoy Melyvn Bragg's favorably reviewed *On Giants' Shoulders: Great Scientists and Their Discoveries from Archimedes to DNA.*

Kidder, Tracy.

Mountains Beyond Mountains: The Quest of Dr. Paul Farmer, a Man Who Would Cure the World. New York: Random House, 2003 (2004). 322pp. ISBN 0812973011.

Although the name of Dr. Paul Farmer is not well-known enough to immediately present itself as belonging to one of the "Great Minds" of science, his pioneering medical work treating infectious diseases, and particularly tuberculosis, has made him famous in medical circles. More interesting than his scientific breakthroughs, however, is the story Kidder masterfully tells in narrative form of his work among some of the world's poorest citizens, in Haiti and elsewhere. Cofounder of the charitable organization Partners in Health, Farmer is portrayed as a completely unique and almost unbelievably dedicated character.

Subjects: ALA Notable Books • Biographies • Haiti • Human Rights • Investigative Stories • Medicine

Now try: Dominique Lapierre's *The City of Joy* provides fewer medical details than Kidder's narrative but presents a similar view of the crushing poverty still rampant in Calcutta. Edwidge Danticat's novel *Behind the Mountains* is also set in Haiti and might complement Kidder's story about Paul Farmer and his experiences among the people of that country.

O'Neill, Dan.

The Last Giant of Beringia: The Mystery of the Bering Land Bridge. Boulder, Colo.: Westview Press, 2004. 231pp. ISBN 0813341973.

Alaska resident O'Neill offers an enjoyable, extended character portrait of Dave Hopkins, the geologist widely credited with discovering and proving the existence of the Bering Land Bridge, which connected Asia to North America during the last glacial age and now lies, shallowly submerged, beneath the Bering Sea. In addition to the personal details of Hopkins' youth and career, other scientists' contributions, and the journey to acceptance of the Beringia theory are succinctly and lucidly described.

Subjects: Ancient History • Arctic Regions • Geology • Landscape

Now try: There's a blurb from author David J. Meltzer on the back of O'Neill's book, and his *Search for the First Americans*, discussing various theories of the peopling of the Americas, might also appeal to readers who enjoy this title. A semiautobiographical description of archaeological study, Peter Storck's *Journey to the Ice Age: Discovering an Ancient World,* might also appeal to fans of O'Neill's works.

Overbye, Dennis.

Einstein in Love: A Scientific Romance. New York: Viking, 2000 (New York: Penguin Books, 2001). 416pp. ISBN 0141002212.

Drawing on newly available letters and personal papers of Albert Einstein, Overbye has constructed a biography that focuses on Einstein's early years (roughly, his studies and discoveries from the age of seventeen into his late thirties) and his often complex relationships with women, particularly his first wife, Mileva Maric, as well as a history and description of some of this most famous scientist's theories and writings. Dense but accessible, Overbye's writing is a model of clarity and exposition.

Subjects: Biographies • Einstein, Albert • Family Relationships • Love Affairs • Physics

Now try: Those readers who are sufficiently interested in Einstein's personal life to enjoy Overbye's partial biography might also be drawn to Einstein's personal beliefs and opinions as divulged in *Ideas and Opinions*, a collection of his speeches and essays. *Einstein's Cosmos: How Albert Einstein's Vision Transformed Our Understanding of Space and Time*, by Michio Kaku (and a title in the <u>Great Discoveries series</u> from Atlas Books) also provides details about Einstein's personal life, but links those details to his theoretical and scientific breakthroughs and the impact his ideas are still having on modern physicists. Sylvia Nasar's rigorous biography of mathematician and game theorist John Nash, *A Beautiful Mind* (annotated in the biography chapter), might also appeal to readers of these character-driven science books.

Silverstein, Ken.

The Radioactive Boy Scout: The True Story of a Boy and His Backyard Nuclear Reactor. New York: Random House, 2004. 209pp. ISBN 037550351X.

Originally a feature article in *Harper's* magazine, Silverstein's lightning-paced narrative tells the story of teenager David Hahn, who, using radioactive materials he scrounged from various sources and a 1960s book entitled *The Golden Book of Chemistry Experiments*, built a crude nuclear breeder reactor in a shed in his backyard in Michigan. Silverstein does not re-create dialogue, but rather relies on interviews with Hahn, his friends, family members, and teachers to illustrate both the scientific and interpersonal aspects of the story.

Subjects: Biographies • Chemistry • Experiments • Family Relationships • Investigative Stories • Quick Reads • Radiation

Now try: Jon Katz's similar fast-paced and short *Geeks: How Two Lost Boys Rode the Internet Out of Idaho* is a similar narrative, about two young men consumed and propelled forward by their obsession, and, fittingly enough, a large part of the story is told through their e-mails to the author. Although a bit more challenging in science, length, and era, Tim Birkhead's *A Brand-New Bird: How Two Amateur Scientists Created the First Genetically Engineered Animal* also illustrates the results that can be achieved with less scientific training and more personal interest and passion. Mark Haddon's novel *The Curious Incident of the Dog in the Night-time* features a similar main character, a fifteen-year-old protagonist who's skilled at math, borderline autistic, and never dull.

Literary Science

Some people accuse scientists and engineers of being "too logical," or of being unable to successfully communicate their thoughts and feelings to others. The titles in this subgenre seem designed specifically to put those allegations to rest; although they discuss biological phenomena and other scientific tenets, they do so using lyrical language (*An Alchemy of Mind*) and often poetic explanations (*The Tao of Physics*).

These books do not offer new scientific theories or narratives of scientific experimentation or discoveries, and as such, they may constitute a subgenre that will not appeal to your more hard-core science readers, who may view them as too philosophical and not scientifically objective. Intending to provoke thought rather than to prove theorems, the authors in this subgenre put science and science issues into the broader contexts of life, humanity, and spirituality. Compared to titles in other science subgenres, these books provide a more relaxing and lyrical read when readers are looking for something just a little more reflective or more leisurely paced than usual.

Ackerman, Diane.

An Alchemy of Mind: The Marvel and Mystery of the Brain. New York: Scribner, 2004. 300pp. ISBN 0743246721.

Closer to poetry than prose, Ackerman's work describes the human brain using phrases such as "that mouse-gray parliament of cells," and conducts a tour of the brain's evolution, physical characteristics, and intangibles such as memory and the multiple facets of the self. Ackerman is a well-respected writer in her field and uses ample research to support her descriptions, but this title's short chapters and evocative language will appeal to readers who are more philosophically than scientifically inclined.

Subjects: Biology • Evolution • Neuroscience

Now try: Ackerman's *A Natural History of the Senses* uses similar sensual language to describe each of the five senses, and the book was also a national best seller. Readers interested in the processes of the human brain and psyche who might prefer less romanticized language should try V. S. Ramachandran's recent *A Brief Tour of Human Consciousness: From Impostor Poodles to Purple Numbers.* Ackerman's writing has also been compared to that of the poet Mary Oliver; readers may be interested in trying volumes of her poetry such as *American Primitive* or *Blue Pastures.*

Capra, Fritjof.

The Tao of Physics: An Exploration of the Parallels Between Modern Physics and Eastern Mysticism. New York and Boston: Shambhala, 1975 (2000). 366pp. ISBN 1570625190.

As far as subtitles go, this one more succinctly describes the book than any annotation could. Capra does indeed detail the interconnectedness of Eastern philosophy (from Hinduism and Buddhism to Chinese Thought and Zen) with the "new" physics (by which he means the atomic view of physics). One example of such a connection is the author's opinion that many advances in physics have been made in flashes of understanding that are similar to those that occur in many mystical experiences.

Subjects: Classics • Epic Reads • Philosophy • Physics • Religion

Now try: Capra is often described as a science writer for right-brained people; he's also written two other popular books, *The Turning Point: Science, Society, and the Rising Culture* and *The Web of Life: A New Scientific Understanding of Living Systems*, in which he applies his broad philosophical constructs to biology. Leonard Shlain's *Art and Physics: Parallel Visions in Space, Time, and Light* shares a similar subtitle and the theory that great advances in both art and science are often temporally connected. *Trialogues at the Edge of the West*, by Ralph Abraham, Terence McKenna, and Rupert Sheldrake, might also appeal to those readers who like a bit of philosophy with their science (as might another title written by that trio along with Jean Houston, *Chaos, Creativity, and Cosmic Consciousness*).

Carson, Rachel.

The Sea Around Us. New York: Oxford University Press, 1951 (1989). 250pp. ISBN 0195069978.

The subject designations (used to aid in retail display) for Carson's book say it all: "Science/Environmental Studies." Carson's *Silent Spring* appears in the "Environmental Writing," but her crisp scientific writing, combined with her evocative imagery, are even more impressively on display here. Carson's descriptions move from the surface of the sea to its depths and examine every aspect of their depths and creation, from the "long snowfall" of sediments drifting to the ocean floor to an explanation of the tides and the ocean's effect on climate.

> **Subjects:** Classics • John Burroughs Medal Winners • National Book Award Winners • Oceans • Weather • Women Scientists

> **Now try:** Carson was undoubtedly a science writer with impeccable credentials, but her writing is also infused with an appreciation for natural history and landscape that is normally found in classics of environmental writing; fans of this work may also want to try Aldo Leopold's *A Sand County Almanac: And Sketches Here and There*, Annie Dillard's *Pilgrim at Tinker Creek*, John McPhee's *Coming into the Country*, or even Sue Hubbell's *Waiting for Aphrodite: Journeys into the Time before Bones*. Readers fascinated by the ocean setting might also be drawn to William Langewiesche's vaguely unsettling *The Outlaw Sea: A World of Freedom, Chaos, and Crime*.

5

González-Crussi, F.

On Being Born: And Other Difficulties. New York: Overlook Press, 2004. 217pp. ISBN 1585674494.

Medical doctor González-Crussi has crafted a thoroughly enjoyable and completely unclinical treatise on the scientific and practical processes of intercourse, conception, life inside the womb, birthing, and fertility drugs and breakthroughs. The medical details are unsparingly but lyrically provided, and along the way the author considers more philosophical and seemingly simple matters (why, for example, does it take two to create one?) and cites many other scientific and literary works.

> **Subjects:** Biology • Essays • Philosophy • Pregnancy • Quick Reads

> **Now try:** Pathologist González-Crussi is not prolific, but both of his previous books of essays have been well-received by critics. They represent the other end of life's spectrum, as their subject matter is death and mortality: *Notes of an Anatomist* and *The Day of the Dead: And Other Mortal Reflections*. Henry Gee's *Jacob's Ladder: The History of the Human Genome* would be a lovely and complementary companion read, backtracking from the mechanics of reproduction to the mechanics of the human genome.

Nuland, Sherwin B.

How We Die: Reflections on Life's Final Chapter. New York: Knopf, 1994 (New York: Vintage Books). 278pp. ISBN 0679742441.

Surgeon and professor Nuland dispenses with what he calls the myth of "death with dignity" by straightforwardly describing exactly how the body dies from a number of causes: heart disease, old age, Alzheimer's, AIDS, cancer, accidents, and murder. The details are too clinical to be horrific, and Nuland admirably achieves his goal of making death less frightening with knowledge of its processes. All of the chapters were reviewed by experts in each medical field, and the result is truly unprecedented in its honesty, including Nuland's memories of the death of his mother and brother from cancer.

> **Subjects:** ALA Notable Books • Cancer • Death and Dying • Medicine • Memoirs • National Book Award Winners

> **Now try:** Nuland followed this work with *How We Live,* in which every chapter outlines the workings of a different part of the body. F. González-Crussi provides a nice philosophical counterpoint to both of Nuland's earthy dissertations on bodily functions in *On Being Born: And Other Difficulties.*

Ulin, David L.

The Myth of Solid Ground: Earthquakes, Prediction, and the Fault Line Between Reason and Faith. New York: Viking, 2004. 290pp. ISBN 0670033235.

Although there is scientific detail in the author's discussion of how earthquakes occur, are predicted, and affect geography, an equal amount of space is devoted to the psychology of living with and accepting their occurrence. Ulin provides an inside look at the science of earthquake prediction through the use of research and interviews, but he uses more philosophical language to explore their meaning rather than emphasising specific earthquake events and descriptions.

> **Subjects:** Geology • Natural Disasters • Philosophy

> **Now try:** Those interested in the history of earthquake measurement science might also consider Jake Page's and Charles Officer's *The Big One,* which describes the huge 1811 earthquake in Missouri and the subsequent development of quake prediction methods. Readers interested in the effects of geological and natural environments on humans (and vice versa) might also enjoy Sueellen Campbell's slightly more political and reflective *Even Mountains Vanish: Searching for Solace in an Age of Extinction.*

Consider Starting With . . .

The titles listed below are some of the most accessible and popular in the science genre.

Ackerman, Diane. *An Alchemy of Mind: The Marvel and Mystery of the Brain.*

Greene, Brian. *The Elegant Universe: Superstrings, Hidden Dimensions, and the Quest for the Ultimate Theory.*

Schweid, Richard. *The Cockroach Papers: A Compendium of History and Lore.*

Silverstein, Ken. *The Radioactive Boy Scout: The True Story of a Boy and His Backyard Nuclear Reactor.*

Watson, James D. *The Double Helix: A Personal Account of the Discovery of the Structure of DNA.*

Wright, William. *Born That Way: Genes, Behavior, Personality.*

Fiction Read-Alikes

- **Anderson, Poul.** Anderson was a hugely prolific writer, widely recognized for his works of "hard" science fiction with their plots firmly grounded in plausible science. He started publishing in the 1950s, but one of his most famous works, *Tau Zero*, appeared in 1970. Later works include such titles as *Starfarers* and *Genesis*, set in the near future, which were also well received by readers and critics alike.

- **Asimov, Isaac.** As stunningly prolific Asimov was at producing nonfiction, he also produced numerous works of science fiction. He was famous for devising the "Three Laws of Robotics"; readers approaching his work for the first time might consider starting with *I, Robot*, or *Foundation* and *Foundation and Empire*, the first volumes in his extremely popular <u>Foundation</u> series, which were written from the "future history" perspective, set in a distant future society.

5

- **Bear, Greg.** Bear is one of the most award-winning writers in science fiction. One of his earlier works, *Eon*, describes the orbit of a hollowed-out asteroid around the earth and the subsequent discovery that it is in reality a spaceship; it was followed by the sequel *Eternity*. He also writes stories with a more biological bent: *Blood Music* explores the fusion of technology and biology to create new life, and *Queen of Angels* centers on an extreme vision of psychotherapy and its effects on society; his more recent *Darwin's Radio* is a thriller about dormant viruses awakening in human DNA and threatening the future of the human race.

- **Benford, Gregory.** In addition to being a writer, Benford is also an astrophysicist, and he brings his copious scientific knowledge to his storytelling. Although stories of his own creation are popular, among them *The Stars in Shroud*, *Timescape*, *Against Infinity*, and *Beyond Infinity*, he is also the author of *Foundation's Fear*, a continuation of Isaac Asimov's <u>Foundation</u> series (the next two books in the continuation series were written by David Brin and Greg Bear, respectively).

- **Crace, Jim.** Crace examines the effects of technological advances on a prehistoric society in his novel *The Gift of Stones*, allying himself even closer to scientific writing with his detailed description of the physical decomposition of the murdered couple at the center of *Being Dead,* his National Book Critics Circle Award–winning novel.. Both novels, while not overtly scientific in subject, exhibit all the clarity and theoretical curiosity often found in the best science nonfiction.

- **Crichton, Michael.** Crichton is generally credited for helping to create the "technothriller" genre, with his first hugely popular title *The Andromeda Strain*, the story of a deadly virus brought back to Earth from space. Other Crichton titles that might appeal to science buffs include *The Terminal Man*, *Jurassic Park*, *Prey*, and *State of Fear*.

- **Dick, Philip K.** Dick's preoccupation with alternate universes mirrors that of many physicists with the properties of our universe; two of his most popular novels on that subject are *The Man in the High Castle* and *Flow My Tears, the Policeman Said*. He was also interested in what he termed "simulacra," or the relationships of mechanical beings to human ones; *Do Androids Dream of Electric Sheep?* dealt with that idea.

- **Gibson, William.** Gibson singlehandedly created and defined the "cyberpunk" subgenre of science fiction with titles such as *Neuromancer* (and its sequels *Count Zero* and *Mona Lisa Overdrive*), which combined cynical characters dripping with noir sensibilities and interdependence on computers and technology. His 2003 novel, *Pattern Recognition*, was also favorably reviewed; it is set in a present that strongly resembles our own consumption-driven times.

- **Lethem, Jonathan.** Many of Lethem's genre-bending novels owe at least part of their story line to scientific precepts: *Gun, with Occasional Music*, is a futuristic mystery novel in which genetically modified animals talk and interact with humans; *Amnesia Moon* is a road novel in which the protagonists discover setting-specific psychoses in an America that has survived the apocalypse; and his main character in *Motherless Brooklyn* suffers from the difficult to treat Tourette's syndrome.

- **Lightman, Alan.** Lightman began his career as a writer of science nonfiction but diverged into scientific and historical fiction in 1993 with *Einstein's Dreams*, in which the physics master dreams his ideas about time. Lightman's subsequent novels, *Good Benito* and *The Diagnosis*, also offer main characters heavily influenced and affected by science and technology.

- **Robinson, Kim Stanley.** Science readers interested in the cosmos may be particularly intrigued by Robinson's famous trilogy, *Red Mars*, *Green Mars*, and *Blue Mars*, set in the twenty-first century (!),about the colonization of Mars. His 1998 novel *Antarctica*, which he wrote after winning a National Science Foundation grant to research it, is set in the near future among scientists posted to the region.

- **Vonnegut, Kurt.** Although most of his works are described as "bitterly anti-technology," they nonetheless raise important questions about the effects of technological advances on human lifestyles, and they do so with Vonnegut's trademark dark humor. Some of his most germane works for this category are classics such as *Player Piano*, *The Sirens of Titan*, *Cat's Cradle*, and *Slaughterhouse-Five*, which reworks Vonnegut's personal memories of digging corpses out of the rubble after the firebombing of Dresden during World War II into a story including war, time travel, and the famous character Billy Pilgrim.

Further Reading

The Best American Science Writing (series). New York: Ecco Press, 2000–present.
Edited by such notable science writers as Dava Sobel (2004), Oliver Sacks (2003), and Timothy Ferris (2001), this annual collection can provide many ideas for the librarian seeking to become familiar with science writers, including Atul Gawande,

Michael Pollan, and William Langewiesche (most of whom have at least one book to their credit), as well as with science and general interest magazines like *Discover*, *Science*, *Wired*, and *The Atlantic Monthly*.

Bolles, Edmund Blair, ed.

Galileo's Commandment: 2,500 Years of Great Science Writing. New York: W. H. Freeman, 1997 (1999). 485pp. ISBN 0716736934.

Bolles's compilation of the best examples of science writing is wide-ranging in both time and subjects covered; starting with Herodotus's piece regarding the natural history of the Nile River (dating from 444 B.C.E.) and including pieces from a wide variety of scientific names (including Galileo, Darwin, Newton, Oppenheimer, Asimov, and Feynman, to name just a few), it is a monument of historical and literary compilation. Beautifully organized and indexed, the book also includes a brief introductory essay on the appeal of science writing.

References

Bolles, Edmund Blair. 1999. *Galileo's Commandment: 2,500 Years of Great Science Writing.* New York: W. H. Freeman.

Carr, David. 2004. "Many Kinds of Crafted Truths: An Introduction to Nonfiction." In *Nonfiction Readers' Advisory,* ed. Robert Burgin, 47–65. Westport, Conn.: Libraries Unlimited.

History of Science. 2005. Wikipedia. http://en.wikipedia.org/wiki/History_of_science (accessed July 18, 2005).

Chapter 6

History

Definition of History

Providing a single chapter of history title annotations is like trying to provide one for biographies; intimidating, and heavily dependent on a belief in the maxim that all you can do is start somewhere. *Merriam-Webster's Collegiate Dictionary* (11th edition) offers a myriad of definitions for "history," all of which provide a sense of why so many readers are drawn to the subject: it is, variously, "a chronological record of significant effects" (Jacques Barzun's *From Dawn to Decadence: 500 Years of Western Cultural Life, 1500 to the Present*), "a branch of knowledge that records and explains past events" (Barbara Tuchman's dense and heavily researched *A Distant Mirror: The Calamitous 14th Century*); and "a treatise presenting systematically related natural phenomena" (John Barry's *The Great Influenza: The Epic Story of the Deadliest Plague in History*). Even those multiple definitions, as broad as they are, do not address the tightly focused stories of how single objects or ideas evolve over vast periods of time ("micro-histories" such as Mark Kurlansky's *Cod: A Biography of the Fish That Changed the World* or Alice Turner's *The History of Hell*) or historical biographies, including Robert Caro's massive *Master of the Senate*, about Lyndon B. Johnson, or Peter Ackroyd's comprehensive *The Life of Thomas More*.

The subgenre historical biography is interesting for another reason, as the two broad reading interest categories of history and biography are often discussed together in literary and library literature, and numerous titles exist that link the genres, such as Stephen Oates's *Biography as History*. If biographies are the stories of lives, histories are often (not always) stories best told through lives. Barbara Tuchman, a prolific historian and author, knew this when she told the story of the fourteenth century through the lens of the experiences of her main character, the French knight Enguerrand de Coucy VII. Stephen Ambrose and Joseph Ellis, two more fabulously popular history authors, also realize this connection between history and biography (or, if you prefer, story and character), and utilized it to write works about World War II told from the points of view of the infantry (*Band of Brothers*) and works about the American Revolution through the life stories of its principal writers (*Founding Brothers*), respectively.

The writing of "history" has been with us for some time. Widely acknowledged as the "Father of History," the Greek Herodotus produced one of the very first works to treat historical events as subjects of research and study (as opposed to incorporating them into narrative and mythological chronicles and epics): *The Histories of Herodotus*, which was an account of the Persian invasion of Greece in the fifth century B.C.E. In addition to researching events, Herodotus also offered his opinion of how or where events took place when research could provide him with no clear answers. That tendency would lead many subsequent scholars and historians to refer to him as the "Father of Lies," although recent evidence suggests that the majority of his accounts were actually quite accurate. The work of another prominent Greek historian, Thucydides, whose *History of the Peloponnesian War*, about the battles between Sparta and Athens, also in the fifth century B.C.E., is likewise considered a timeless classic in the historical canon, and Thucydides is often considered the more rigorous researcher of the two for his refusal to include hearsay and rumors in his historical accounts.

Ever since the floodgates were opened by Herodotus and Thucydides, a multitude of writers and historians have stepped up in every era and location to record the events of our shared human histories. Although writing styles and methodologies continue to wax and wane in popularity, as well as to evolve into new formats and genreblending categories that combine travel adventures with historical study, or character portraits with historical exposition, readers continue to be very loyal to the genre and consistently make it one of the most popular sections for browsing and circulation (or purchase).

Appeal of the Genre

In her discussion of the appeal of historical fiction, Joyce Saricks recognizes the combined appeals of story and characterization to its readers, but adds a third appeal: the frame of the story, or, as she puts it, the "wealth of accurate historical detail relating to setting (geography, customs, beliefs, culture, society, habits) as well as to characters and events" (2001, 82). Although period details and descriptions are used in fiction to make a story believable or more evocative of a specific era, the use of detail (particularly the small, telling details that make true history "come alive") in historical nonfiction can also be a part of what draws readers to certain authors and titles and not to others.

The question of what is appealing about historical fiction, as opposed to historical nonfiction, does not hinge only on whether or not it includes good characters or stories. Subject matter, perhaps more than for any other nonfiction genre, may play the largest part in what makes readers choose certain works of history over others. Fans of historical writing are often driven to books by their need to know about history, or by their curiosity regarding real and defining historical events. Unlike historical fiction genre readers, whom Herald speculates may prefer "a somewhat romanticized, sanitized view of the past" (2000, 1) nonfiction history readers want the facts as discovered or researched by (often) well-known writers with solid credentials.

Although the use of details, facts, eyewitness statements, and other types of historical information can be a large factor in determining what makes certain works of history enjoyable or engaging reads, it could arguably be said that even more than seeking facts, historical nonfiction readers are searching for truth: the truth of what really happened, the truth of how things and events developed and evolved, and the truth of what certain people whom we'll never be able to meet were really like. Facts and research, both anecdotal and more scholarly, are used by historians and authors to corroborate their interpretations of historical events and happenings. The continuing debate about what constitutes purely true nonfiction in general, and history writing in particular, encroaches on this chapter. Tuchman distills the essence of the debate as it pertains to history; in a series of essays describing her historical research and writing, she acknowledged, "we can never be certain that we have recaptured it as it really was. But the least we can do is stay within the evidence" (1981, 18). Although Tuchman is a particularly zealous and well-regarded historical researcher, many writers of history strive to corral that evidence into a story that coincides with their theories about events, their causes, and the personalities of the people living through the events. Even if historians and scholars are able to agree on the evidence or the facts (and even that doesn't really happen all that often), the creation of history itself (through the writing of it) always depends to a certain extent on each author's interpretation of evidence and events. Historical writing, much like current affairs reporting or any storytelling dependent on subjective opinions and viewpoints, will continue to depend in large part on differing theories about causes and effects of events, not to mention personal and communal motivations involved with those events. As historian Bernard Bailyn put it, a bit more formally, "when you go beyond factual re-establishment into the interpretation of large subjects, there is no definitive history" (Bailyn and Lathem 1994, 68).

As previously noted, many history readers often enjoy historical (and other) titles from the biography genre, particularly if they are reading history to gain a feel for the personalities of history or enjoy historians/writers who produce titles in both categories (such as Joseph Ellis and Stephen Ambrose). Many history books also offer strong and distinctive linear storytelling (particularly titles in the "History's Darkest Hours" subgenre), and so might appeal to readers of true adventure books. In their zeal to track down historical facts and truths, history writers also often produce stories that feel similar in mood and format to many titles found in the "Investigative Writing" chapter; John Micklethwait and Adrian Wooldridge, authors of *The Company: A Short History of a Revolutionary Idea*, are both journalists, and their book might appeal (and vice versa) to fans of Bob Ortega's incendiary and investigative *In Sam We Trust: The Untold Story of Sam Walton and How Wal-Mart Is Devouring America*.

Organization of the Chapter

In making title selections for this chapter, we strove to provide a variety of titles that would include the primary and often intertwined appeals of a history book's story and character, as well as a number of descriptive and popular titles that would provide the frame, or visual and other sensory details, of history, which truly indicate the author's dedication to historical research and methods. Because subgenres defined by their organization were included ("Historical Biographies," "Immersion History," "New Perspectives," and "Epic History"), an author's ability to use language and writing style to weave those details into a greater narrative whole were also taken into account when choosing titles to annotate.

One of the most recognizable subgenres of history, and the one that opens the chapter, is "Defining Times" books, which offer chronological retellings of significant or particularly interesting time periods and eras. Closely related to those titles are the enduringly popular titles that deal with particularly bleak or contentious moments or events in history; those books are gathered in the story-driven "History's Darkest Hours" subgenre, which is further subdivided into stories about human cruelties and natural disasters and disease epidemics. In keeping with this organization by subject matter, the next subgenre explores the "Settings of History," which are books that readers look for based primarily on a geographic area of interest (e.g., those interested in Irish history might enjoy Thomas Cahill's *How the Irish Saved Civilization*). Although setting and location serve as the subject heading for these titles, keep in mind that many of them also include vivid characterizations of people and events.

The subgenre "Micro-Histories" and its further sub-subgenre "Ideas of History" signal a shift in emphasis from subject to authors' writing styles and abilities to frame the broad scope of history by telling the stories of specific things and ideas. Micro-histories, which tell vast stories from the point of view of single or seemingly insignificant objects, reflect their authors' dedication to framing the stories of history in a slightly different way than by offering pure chronologies or subject studies. Mark Kurlansky's *Salt* or Robert Sullivan's *Rats* are not books that readers might find based on their subject matter, but rather through their classification as accessible and story-driven pieces of genre writing. Likewise, authors of "New Perspectives" history books, which follow the micro-histories, are not as interested in telling a story based on their subjects as they are in enlightening their readers with new or previously underexplored theories and interpretations. Part of the appeal of both these subgenres (as well as that of the "Immersion History" titles, which follow the "New Perspectives" ones) is definitely the skill of their authors in using language and exposition to tell stories from a different angle.

The "Epic History" subgenre marks a return to what many readers think of when they ask to be ushered to the history books section. Epic in length, often epic in subject matter, and exhibiting a high level of research integrity and attention to detail, these are the books for the hard-core readers of history who want to know everything there is to know about a subject. The last subgenre, "Caught in History's Web" (further divided into the stories of individuals and groups) closely mirrors the "Historical Biography" subgenre found in the biography chapter, with one important difference: Even though the biographies found here are still character-driven stories, they offer much more in the way of historical detail and context than their counterparts in the biography chapter. Although Thomas More was a fascinating individual, we tend to remember him more for his interactions with Henry VIII and the volatile period of the Reformation in English history rather than for himself; likewise, although all of the individuals described in Stephen Ambrose's *Band of Brothers* are highly unique characters, Ambrose is telling their story because of the historical event (World War II) in which they took part.

Defining Times

Dates and eras are an integral part of the study of history (e.g., what year did the American Civil War start?) and are also important in the writing of it. One of the easiest and most recognizable ways of organizing historical stories is by chronology, which is an organizational principle all of the following narratives share; John Dower examines the cultural, political, and social milieu of Japan, but only in the period following World War II (*Embracing Defeat*), while John Wills explores an entire globe's worth of history, but only as it occurred in one year (*1688*).

There is often an intense amount of description in these titles, including details about the settings, people, and things that historians spend their time researching and that readers enjoy, as they clearly evoke the historical setting. As a result, although they often focus on fascinating stories and can be highly informative and enjoyable reads, they cannot really be considered quickly paced page-turners.

Danziger, Danny, and John Gillingham.

1215: The Year of the Magna Carta. New York: Simon & Schuster, 2004. 312pp. ISBN 0743257731.

Not entirely about the year 1215 (globally, at least) or the nitty gritty details of the Magna Carta, this small book provides a very entertaining look behind the scenes of rural, city, and castle life, while also providing other contextual details for the time (and only for England) about topics such as schooling, religion, and other cultural tenets. The book includes many historical dates and obviously well-researched details, but the tone is light, is decidedly nonscholarly in its liveliness and lack of footnotes or endnotes, and contributes to the speed with which readers will be able to consume this short book.

> **Subjects:** England • Government • Magna Carta • Quick Reads • Thirteenth Century

> **Now try:** These authors also wrote the best seller *The Year 1000.* James Chace's *1912: Wilson, Roosevelt, Taft & Debs—The Election That Changed the Country* also puts a very human face (or four) on the hotly contested election that reflected the era's culture and politics.

Dower, John W.

Embracing Defeat: Japan in the Wake of World War II. New York: Norton, 1999 (2000). 676pp. ISBN 0393320278.

Dower's incredibly readable narrative takes as its subject the often neglected period after World War II (from August 1945 to April 1952) during which Japan struggled to rebuild its infrastructure and its society under American occupation. In lengthy but quick-reading chapters, Dower examines Japan's capitulation; the repatriation of its millions of soldiers stranded abroad; the psychology of a nation suffering from widespread *kyodatsu* (a combination of exhaustion and despair); the Japanese people's attitudes toward Emperor Hirohito and General MacArthur; and above all the daily struggles against starvation, depression, and the many societal problems that arose under occupation. Dower includes many references to music, literature, and art from the period, as well as numerous photographs.

> **Subjects:** ALA Notable Books • Japan • Mental Health • National Book Award Winners • Pulitzer Prize Winners • Sociology • World War II

> **Now try:** Alex Kerr's rather pessimistic view of Japan's current cultural and economic milieu, *Dogs and Demons: Tales from the Dark Side of Japan,* paints a picture of a nation besieged by economic and political problems. Herbert P. Bix's massive biography of Japan's emperor for the majority of the latter twentieth century, *Hirohito and the Making of Modern Japan,* may

also appeal to fans of Dower's book. John Hersey's classic *Hiroshima* (annotated in the "Investigative Writing" chapter) provides more information about Japan's defeat.

Remnick, David.

Lenin's Tomb: The Last Days of the Soviet Empire. New York: Random House, 1993 (New York: Vintage Books, 1994). 588pp. ISBN 0679751254.

While working as a reporter for *The Washington Post*, Remnick spent several years during the late 1980s and early 1990s living in Moscow and watching the dissolution of the Soviet Empire. A well-written union of investigative journalism and historical storytelling, each of Remnick's chapters is formed around central characters in the twentieth-century history of the Soviet Union, combined with his immediate experiences of living under gradually weakening but still intimidating Soviet-style repression.

Subjects: ALA Notable Books • Cold War • Communism • Epic Reads • Investigative Stories • National Book Critics Circle Award Winners • Pulitzer Prize Winners • Soviet Union

Now try: Remnick produced a follow-up to his Pulitzer Prize winner in *Resurrection*, which examines the atmosphere of Russian government and social order in the 1990s. Readers interested in other works exploring Russia's most recent history might also try David Satter's *Darkness at Dawn: The Rise of the Russian Criminal State.*

Tuchman, Barbara.

A Distant Mirror: The Calamitous 14th Century. New York: Knopf, 1978 (New York: Ballantine, 1987). 677pp. ISBN 0345349571.

By detailing every aspect of the life of the unremarkable French knight Enguerrand de Coucy VII, Tuchman unceremoniously drops the reader directly into the fourteenth century. No facet of life in the 1300s is left unexplored, from politics to religion, family life to personal hygiene. Tuchman is a tireless historian and chronicler, and just a few of the events covered are a plague epidemic in 1348 and the papal schism of 1378. Although the level of detail sometimes creates a rather lugubrious pace, it is still a masterwork of historical context.

Subjects: Biographies • Classics • Epic Reads • Family Relationships • Fourteenth Century • France

Now try: Tuchman is beloved by her fans for producing multiple and massive, but still readable, works of history; in *The Guns of August* she examines the events leading up to World War I, she describes four very different military conflicts in *The March of Folly: From Troy to Vietnam;* and in *Bible and Sword: England and Palestine from the Bronze Age to Balfour,* she describes the intertwined history of England and Palestine. William Manchester produces similarly sweeping epics, and fans of Tuchman's medieval story might also enjoy his *A World Lit Only by Fire: The Medieval Mind and the Renaissance.*

Wills, John W., Jr.

1688: A Global History. New York: Norton, 2001 (2002). 330pp. ISBN 0393322785.

A history book for true history lovers, Professor Wills's worldwide excursion through the year 1688 is composed in dense but very readable prose. He opens his narrative with a definition of the period as the "Baroque" age and illustrates it with his discussion of the post-Renaissance explosion of knowledge and ever faster rate of change as personified by Sister Juana Inés de la Cruz and her contemporaries in Mexico. From explorers to businesses (such as the Dutch East India Company) and emperors to religious leaders, Wills manages to make the year 1688 seem the most interesting and significant ever experienced.

Subjects: Biographies • Books and Learning • Government • Religion • Seventeenth Century • World Leaders

Now try: Mark Kurlansky's 2005 ALA Notable Book *1968* is not as global in scope but still offers the title year as the main character. Those readers amenable to crossing over into science reading might also consider John Rigden's short but highly informative *Einstein 1905: The Standard of Greatness*, in which the author examines the one year in which Einstein wrote five (still) influential physics papers.

History's Darkest Hours

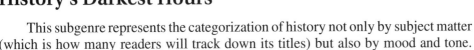

This subgenre represents the categorization of history not only by subject matter (which is how many readers will track down its titles) but also by mood and tone. These stories of history's darkest and often most tragic hours, which have been caused variously by natural occurrences and plagues, but also by the cruelty that human beings can and do inflict on each other, are both darkly compelling and subtly prescriptive in their oft-repeated admonition that those who don't know the lessons of history will be doomed to repeat them.

Therefore, although many of the following stories are very appealing in the suspenseful nature of their narratives, and fascinating in their exposition of both aggressors and victims, they can also be repellant to many readers (in much the same way that true crime books, although fascinating to their fans, are given a wide berth by many other recreational readers). These are important stories, well told, but they will not be for everyone.

Human Cruelties

Applebaum, Anne.

Gulag: A History. New York: Doubleday, 2003 (New York: Anchor Books, 2004). 677pp. ISBN 1400034094.

Part traditional chronological history and part topical oral history, Applebaum's epic story of the birth, development, and decline of the vast network of labor camps in the Soviet Union from 1917 through the 1980s is as story-driven and personal as a novel. The book consists of three parts; the origins of the gulag, various aspects of life in the prison camps (from arrest to work duty to guard personalities and the often horrific means employed by prisoners to survive), and the rise and decline of the camps as sources of industrial labor. The author cites extensive sources and personal accounts so skillfully that the book doesn't feel nearly as long as its nearly 700 scholarly pages might look to the reader.

Subjects: Atrocities • Cold War • Communism • Epic Reads • Human Rights • Prisons • Pulitzer Prize Winners • Soviet Union

Now try: If Applebaum's work can be said to describe the facilities of Stalin's gulag system, Donald Rayfield's *Stalin and His Hangmen: The Tyrant and Those Who Killed for Him* describes his most trusted and lethal personnel: the staff of assassins he employed to intimidate and murder those who defied him. Readers interested in personal narratives of life in the gulag prison system might also consider Aleksandr Solzhenitsyn's seminal, three-volume *The Gulag Archipelago, 1918–1956.* There's also a blurb on the back of Applebaum's *Gulag: A History* from author Richard Pipes; readers may also consider that author's *A Concise History of the Russian Revolution* for more contextual detail to complement Applebaum's history.

Chang, Iris.

The Rape of Nanking: The Forgotten Holocaust of World War II. New York: Basic Books, 1997 (New York: Penguin Books, 1998). 290pp. ISBN 0140277447.

Interested in the topic because of her Chinese parents' stories of the 1937 invasion of Nanking by the Japanese Imperial army, Chang uses primary sources, oral histories, and previously classified documents to piece together the graphic and horrifying sequence of events that led to the fall of that city. Not for the squeamish, this well-researched account tells the story of not only the hundreds of thousands of victims in the city, but also the multiple individuals who endeavored to create a safe zone in the center of Nanking as a refuge.

Subjects: Atrocities • China • Classics • Human Rights • Japan • Military • World War II

Now try: John Hersey's classic *Hiroshima*, annotated in the "Investigative Writing" chapter, might also appeal to Chang's readers. Readers who can face another work describing the horror of the fall of Nanking might also find John Rabe's diary of his time spent in the city as head of the German firm Siemens (much of which he spent trying to organize a refuge for the city's residents), *The Good Man of Nanking: The Diaries of John Rabe,* a complementary read. Although Iris Chang committed suicide in 2004 at the young age of thirty-six, she also wrote *The Chinese in America: A Narrative History*, and a biography of Chinese scientist Tsien Hsue-shen, *Thread of the Silkworm*.

Frantz, Douglas, and Catherine Collins.

Death on the Black Sea: The Untold Story of the Struma *and World War II's Holocaust at Sea.* New York: HarperCollins, 2003 (New York: Ecco, 2004). 353pp. ISBN 0060936851.

The 1942 sinking of the ship *Struma* and the death of all of her passengers (but one) in the Black Sea is not often taught in history classes, but Frantz and Collins have brought the story out of obscurity with their detailed narrative and character-rich portrayal of the tragedy. Loaded with Romanian Jewish passengers en route to safety in Palestine, the old and unseaworthy ship was delayed by officials at Istanbul and helplessly drifted in the Black Sea until it eventually sank. The authors also include the story of diver Greg Buxton's (whose grandparents perished aboard the ship) attempts to dive to the wreck in 2000. Although the book describes several complicated facets of history, including the effect of the holocaust in Romania and the intricacies of British and Turkish foreign policy, the writing is clear and the story and characters portrayed with great immediacy.

Subjects: Atrocities • Holocaust • Jews and Judaism • Maritime Disasters • Romania • Turkey • World War II

Now try: This compelling narrative paints a harrowing picture of the reach of the Nazi party during World War II; other histories of the genocide that took place outside Germany include Bob Moore's *Victims and Survivors: The Nazi Persecution of the Jews in the Netherlands, 1940–1945*, Gunnar Paulsson's *Secret City: The Hidden Jews of Warsaw, 1940–1945*, Peter Duffy's *The Bielski Brothers: The True Story of Three Men Who Defied the Nazis, Saved 1200 Jews, and Built a Village in the Forest* (set in Belarus), and Ronald W. Zweig's *The Gold Train: The Destruction of the Jews and the Looting of Hungary*.

Gourevitch, Philip.

We Wish to Inform You That Tomorrow We Will Be Killed with Our Families: Stories from Rwanda. New York: Farrar, Straus & Giroux, 1998 (New York: Picador, 2004). 355pp. ISBN 0312243359.

Although the mid-1990s are rapidly fading into history, they are a historical time period that is still quite immediate and affecting. In language and prose style so hauntingly beautiful that it only serves to increase the horror of the Rwandan genocide, Gourevitch describes the 1994 massacre wherein 800,000 Tutsis were killed in 100 days by the ruling Hutus. The author visited Rwanda years after the slaughter took place, and from that vantage point, he tries to place it in historical and political context, while also describing many of the individuals involved and their variously murderous and merciful acts (such as Paul Rusesabagina, who attempted to shelter Tutsis at the hotel he managed).

> **Subjects:** Africa • Atrocities • Classics • Human Rights • Investigative Stories • National Book Critics Circle Award Winners • Rwanda

6

> **Now try:** The superlative *Machete Season: The Killers in Rwanda Speak*, by French journalist Jean Hatzfeld, is a compilation of the author's interviews with ten Rwandan men convicted of killing their neighbors, and provides an important and chilling inner look at the genocide. Journalist Bill Berkeley investigates continent-wide instances of genocide and atrocities in Africa in *The Graves Are Not Yet Full: Race, Tribe, and Power in the Heart of Africa*; Samantha Baker investigates genocide in the Balkans, and America's response (or lack thereof) to it, in her Pulitzer Prize– and National Book Critics Circle–winning book *"A Problem from Hell": America and the Age of Genocide*.

Hochschild, Adam.

King Leopold's Ghost: A Story of Greed, Terror, and Heroism in Colonial Africa. Boston: Houghton Mifflin, 1998 (1999). 366pp. ISBN 0618001905.

Hochschild illuminates a seldom discussed or researched subject—King Leopold of Belgium's exploitative colonization of the Congo region from 1885 through 1920—providing a richly textured and character-driven history of the earliest explorations of Africa, throughout the colonial period and to the country's eventual proclaimed independence. The story is well documented and factual enough to appeal to the most hard-core of history readers (the four main causes of the millions of deaths in the region during Leopold's relentless driving of the native population to produce rubber are explored in depth), but Hochschild's main talent is making many of the main characters, such as the Belgian Edmund Dene Morel, the man who eventually raised the alarm regarding state-sponsored violence in the region, human in both their foibles and achievements.

> **Subjects:** Africa • ALA Notable Books • Atrocities • Belgium • Business • Colonialism • Congo • Human Rights

> **Now try:** A more comprehensive but still tragic history of the Congo is told in journalist Robert Edgerton's *The Troubled Heart of Africa: A History of the Congo*. Redmond O'Hanlon documented the natural wonders and atmosphere of oppressive uncertainty of the region in his travel narrative *No Mercy: A Journey into the Heart of the Congo*, and the dedicated advisor might also suggest Joseph Conrad's classic work of fiction, *The Heart of Darkness*, to particularly motivated readers.

Preston, Diana.

Lusitania: *An Epic Tragedy*. New York: Walker, 2002 (New York: Berkeley Books, 2003). 532pp. ISBN 0425189988.

Although Preston provides extensive detail about the actual submarine attack on the *Lusitania* and its sinking in 1915, she does so only after describing the greater context of World War I, foreign relations between European countries, the development of German naval technology, and the *Lusitania*'s interior and passengers. Starting 200 pages into the narrative, the story of the ship's sinking and the more than 1,200 victims is related in horrific detail. Preston also explores the tragedy's impact on U.S. entrance into the war, as well as different viewpoints regarding the legitimacy of the ship as a wartime target.

> **Subjects:** ALA Notable Books • Europe • Maritime Disasters • Submarines • World War I

> **Now try:** Although the vessel in David W. Shaw's *The Sea Shall Embrace Them: The Tragic Story of the Steamship* Arctic sank in 1854 in a collision with another ship, not under enemy fire, Shaw tells a similarly taut and tragic tale. Doug Stanton's *In Harm's Way: The Sinking of the USS* Indianapolis *and the Extraordinary Story of Its Survivors* is also a wartime narrative about a maritime disaster and might appeal to fans of Preston's work; likewise, many other titles in the "War Stories" and "Survival Stories" segments of the adventure chapter might appeal to readers who wouldn't mind an even quicker read than Preston's history.

Spiegelman, Art.

Maus: A Survivor's Tale (Volume 1: My Father Bleeds History, and Volume 2: And There My Troubles Began). New York: Pantheon Books, 1973 and 1986 (1997). 296pp. ISBN 0679406417.

Artist Spiegelman uses a memoir form of recording conversations with his father to provide a tragic and personal history of life in Poland during World War II, followed by the story of their struggle to survive imprisonment in Auschwitz and their eventual liberation and emigration to America. In Spiegelman's metaphorical depictions, his father and other Jewish family members are drawn as mice, while their Nazi tormentors appear as cats. The story of Spiegelman's difficult relationship with his father adds another level of complexity to an already all-consuming narrative. This may be a graphic novel, but the impact of its horrific subject matter is anything but childlike or cartoonish.

Subjects: Atrocities • Classics • Family Relationships—Fathers and Sons • Graphic Novels • Holocaust • Jews and Judaism • Memoirs • Pulitzer Prize Winners • World War II

Now try: Anne Frank's direct and horrific *Anne Frank: The Diary of a Young Girl* (annotated in the "Memoirs and Autobiography" chapter) is also a deeply personal story of the Holocaust. Aharon Appelfeld's memoir *The Story of a Life* provides a similarly personal look at the tragic consequences of the Holocaust, while Irene Eber's *The Choice: Poland, 1939 to 1945* is another well-written exposition of wartime life in Poland, from a feminine perspective. Those readers particularly drawn to the format of this history might also consider *Persepolis*, another fascinating personal memoir, about the author Marjane Satrapi's girlhood life in Iran before and during the Islamic Revolution.

Natural Disasters and Disease Epidemics

Barry, John M.

The Great Influenza: The Epic Story of the Deadliest Plague in History. New York: Viking, 2004 (New York: Penguin Books, 2005). 546pp. ISBN 0143034480.

Barry treats the 1918 worldwide influenza epidemic as a fascinating character in its own right in this epic story of the disease and its unstoppable destructive force. In ten chapters describing such various aspects of the pandemic as its biological characteristics, the world setting onto which it burst in the wake of World War I, and the many scientists and medical personnel who battled its spread, the author provides a comprehensive history of the disease that killed more people worldwide (nearly 100 million people) in twenty-four weeks than AIDS has claimed in the past twenty-four years.

Subjects: Biology • Epic Reads • Health Issues • Medicine • World War I

Now try: David Oshinsky's comprehensive *Polio: An American Story* tells the story of both the pathology of the disease and the journey of multiple scientists to discover the cure. *The Great Mortality: An Intimate History of the Black Death*, by John Kelly, might appeal to these readers, as might James Mohr's *Plague and Fire: Battling Black Death and the 1900 Burning of Honolulu's Chinatown*, which examines a medical emergency and the official health officers' method for containment, which led to further tragedy. Barry is also the author of a natural disaster title, *Rising Tide: The Great Mississippi Flood of 1927 and How It Changed America*.

Hayden, Deborah.

Pox: Genius, Madness, and the Mysteries of Syphilis. New York: Basic Books, 2003 (2004). 379pp. ISBN 0465028829.

Hayden combines a lot of medical history with a bit of revisionist history; in addition to referring to generally accepted sufferers of the disease, such as Gustave Flaubert, she also speculates that it might have afflicted Abraham and Mary Todd Lincoln, as well as Adolf Hitler. Although the author is a successful direct marketer by trade, not a science writer, she has compiled an impressive amount of detail about the causes, symptoms, and treatment of syphilis from a wide variety of sources, and her writing is extremely accessible to the nonscience reader.

Subjects: Biology • Health Issues • Medicine • Mental Health • Revisionist Histories

Now try: F. González-Crussi and Pamela Nagami collaborated on a disturbing medical anthology, *The Woman with a Worm in Her Head: And Other True Stories of Infectious Disease*. Readers fascinated by Hayden's history of syphilis might also want to check out Malcolm Gladwell's huge best seller, *The Tipping Point*, which includes a chapter on the current epidemic-like spread of syphilis in certain cities and neighborhoods.

Larson, Erik.

Isaac's Storm: A Man, a Time, and the Deadliest Hurricane in History. New York: Crown Publishers, 1999 (New York: Vintage Books, 2000). 323pp. ISBN 0375708278.

Larson's history of the 1900 hurricane that came ashore at Galveston, Texas, and was responsible for the deaths of more than 10,000 people is a highly personal one. Through his research of primary sources such as eyewitness accounts, he builds a person-by-person re-creation of the storm and its effects, and his masterful use of suspense makes this a history book that reads like an adventure story. The "Isaac" in question is Isaac Cline, a weatherman who claimed later to have reacted to the storm in a much more timely manner than he really did. Larson also tells his story, intertwining it with the story of the storm itself, with great aplomb.

Subjects: Adventure • American History • Biographies • Disasters • Quick Reads • Texas • Weather

Now try: Sebastian Junger's *The Perfect Storm: A True Story of Men Against the Sea* (annotated in the true adventure chapter) is also a testament to nature's awesome and sometimes destructive power, as is R. A. Scotti's *Sudden Sea: The Great Hurricane of 1938*.

Von Drehle, David.

Triangle: The Fire That Changed America. New York: Atlantic Monthly Press, 2003 (New York: Grove Press, 2003). 340pp. ISBN 080214151X.

Part labor history, part disaster and survival story, Von Drehle's detailed but compelling and suspenseful narrative discusses the Triangle Shirtwaist Factory fire of 1911. The author paints an evocative picture of the shock of the city's residents at the magnitude of the fire and the number of deaths it caused, primarily of young, immigrant female workers. He also examines the context of the city's labor history and the effect the disaster had on work safety reform efforts.

Subjects: Accidents • ALA Notable Books • American History • Business • Fires • Labor History • New York City

Now try: Character-driven tragedies are heartbreaking reads but offer history in one of its most approachable and poignant forms. Readers who enjoy Von Drehle's studious and encompassing history might also enjoy Elizabeth Sharpe's *The Shadow of the Dam: The Aftermath of the Mill River Flood of 1874* or Jay Bonasinga's novelistic *The Sinking of the* Eastland. Likewise, Adrian Tinniswood provides a view of history through the lens of tragedy in his readable *By Permission of Heaven: The True Story of the Great Fire of London*.

The Settings of History

Historical stories can be told in the context of their time periods, but they can also be told using a framework based on setting and a location's effect on its residents. As with the previous subgenre, the appeal in these titles is derived largely from their authors' skillful combination of many telling details to create the bigger picture of their overarching stories.

Although many historical narratives based on a place's geography and people can be quite long, a recent trend in publishing toward the creation of smaller and more tightly focused works for the nonscholarly history reader has resulted in a plethora of titles that nevertheless offer an amazing array of details and context, but take as their entire subject a much smaller location or event (James McPherson's *Hallowed Ground*, a title in the <u>Crown Journeys series</u>, is a fine example). As a result, readers' advisors should be aware that, in addition to being popular with more hard-core readers of history, many of these titles might also appeal to readers of travel or environmental nonfiction, which are also usually shorter than most history books and also focus on people and their environment.

Cahill, Thomas.

How the Irish Saved Civilization: The Untold Story of Ireland's Heroic Role from the Fall of Rome to the Rise of Medieval Europe. New York: Nan A. Talese, 1995 (New York: Anchor Books, 1996). 246pp. ISBN 0385418493.

Cahill tells the adventurous history of Ireland, a nation that he admits in his introduction is not usually the first country that comes to mind when the word "civilized" or "civilizing" is applied to countries. Nonetheless, he argues that in the course of the Dark Ages (from the fall of Rome through the Vikings' conquest of Ireland and eventual eviction from the island in the early eleventh century), matriarchal Celtic societies were revolutionary in their methods of worship, St. Patrick provided an earthy theology, and Irish monks were at the forefront of copying and preserving numerous texts that were written before the fall of the Roman Empire. The book also includes numerous informative sidebars that provide supplemental information but which, in their placement outside the text, make the rest of the book a quicker read.

6

Subjects: Books and Learning • Classics • Europe • Ireland • Religion • Western Civilization

Now try: Although it's more of a travel narrative in organization (the author offers his history in the context of his own walks up Mount Brandon), Chet Raymo's *Climbing Brandon: Science and Faith on Ireland's Holy Mountain* also describes the unique brand of Irish Christianity and its rare attention to its earthly surroundings as well as its otherworldly devotions. Cahill's Irish title is part of his own <u>Hinges of History</u> series, in which he examines pivotal moments and their settings in world history; other volumes in the series include *Sailing the Wine-Dark Sea: Why the Greeks Matter*, *Desire of the Everlasting Hills: The World Before and After Jesus*, and *The Gifts of the Jews: How a Tribe of Desert Nomads Changed the Way Everyone Thinks and Feels*.

McPherson, James M.

Hallowed Ground: A Walk at Gettysburg. New York: Crown Publishers, 2003. 141pp.
ISBN 0609610236.

Although part of the <u>Crown Journeys series</u>, and described on the back as a book of
travel essays, McPherson's short but meaty treatise re-creating the horrific (for
both sides) Battle of Gettysburg reads more like a travelogue through history, describing the battlefield itself through the lens of the historic battle staged there and
only secondarily relating the geographical details of the area.

> **Subjects:** American History • Civil War • <u>Crown Journeys Series</u> • Pennsylvania •
> Quick Reads • Travel

> **Now try:** Readers who enjoy McPherson's setting-rooted narrative might also enjoy
> "Armchair Travel" and "Literary Travel" titles. McPherson is also the author of the
> more comprehensive Civil War history *Battle Cry of Freedom*, which is still one of
> the top Civil War sellers at Amazon.com (along with Charles Frazier's *Cold Moun-*
> *tain*, a favorably reviewed and extremely popular Civil War novel). This is a perenni-
> ally popular subject, so you may wish to visit the "Civil War Bookshelf" Internet site
> at http://www.cw-book-news.com/.

Messer, Sarah.

*Red House: Being a Mostly Accurate Account of New England's Oldest Continuously
Lived-in House.* New York: Viking, 2004. 390pp. ISBN 0670033154.

Both Messer's family members and the famous Red House in which they spent
their childhood are the compellingly drawn main characters in this history of a
place as told through its inhabitants. Messer smoothly blends alternating chapters
regarding the house's history, starting with its construction in 1647, with the personal histories of the Hatch family, who lived in it for eight generations, until it was
purchased and occupied by her own family. The narrative is quietly philosophical
in tone and decidedly measured in pace.

> **Subjects:** American History • Atlantic Coast • Family Relationships • Homes •
> Memoirs

> **Now try:** Kate Whouley's good-natured chronicle of her quest to tack a $3,000 cot-
> tage onto her three-room house, *Cottage for Sale—Must Be Moved: A Woman Moves*
> *a House to Make a Home* evokes many of the same cozy feelings that Messer's chron-
> icle does; Lawrence LaRose tells the same story with less history and more relation-
> ship details in *Gutted: Down to the Studs in My House, My Marriage, My Entire Life.*
> Diane Roberts's history of a place focuses less on a dwelling and more on a state; her
> combined memoir and local history of Florida is inclusively entitled *Dream State:*
> *Eight Generations of Swamp Lawyers, Conquistadors, Confederate Daughters, Ba-*
> *nana Republicans, and Other Florida Wildlife.*

Morris, Jan.

Hong Kong. New York: Random House, 1988 (New York: Vintage Books, 1997).
320pp. ISBN 0679776486.

Morris's comprehensive study of Hong Kong society and its journey from British
empire to Chinese control is based on forty years of her own observations of the
country and its atmosphere. Densely detailed and rich with historical context, Morris's work is less a travel narrative than a travel epic; it alternates chronologically

ordered chapters (the colony in the 1840s, 1880s, 1920s, etc.) with thematic chapters/essays regarding the people of the area and their history of trade and commercial activities.

Subjects: China • Colonialism • England • History • Hong Kong • Society

Now try: Morris is more famous for her travel writing; an even more personal recounting of her experiences in ten Canadian cities illuminates a large country that very few travelers find inspiring enough to devote much time to; *O Canada: Travels in an Unknown Country* provides fewer historical details than *Hong Kong* but even more heartfelt description. Morris is also the author of the classic *Coronation Everest*, which is annotated in the travel chapter.

Rosenberg, Tina.

The Haunted Land: Facing Europe's Ghosts After Communism. New York: Random House, 1995 (New York: Vintage Books, 1996). 437pp. ISBN 0679744991.

Rosenberg's investigations of citizens in three countries trying to reorder their social and political lives after the fall of communism provide history through the prism of individual and highly varied experiences. In her conversations with former revolutionaries and their largely disillusioned children in Czechoslovakia, Poland, and Germany, she combines investigative storytelling with narrative and personal history. The communist histories of all three regions are complicated, which makes Rosenberg's writing necessarily dense, but readers who don't mind a slower but more nuanced read will enjoy this book.

Subjects: Cold War • Communism • Europe • Human Rights • Investigative Stories • National Book Award Winners • Pulitzer Prize Winners • Sociology

Now try: Slavenka Drakulic's *How We Survived Communism & Even Laughed* tells the story of life in Socialist Eastern Europe in darkly humorous essays (her recent *They Would Never Hurt a Fly: War Criminals on the Hague* also examines current social problems and the ongoing quest for postwar justice in the region).

Shorris, Earl.

The Life and Times of Mexico. New York: Norton, 2004. 780pp. ISBN 039305926X.

 6

Although this is an impressive labor of love and faultless in research and documentation, Shorris truly makes this history of Mexico come alive with his mastery of language and his skillful evocation of a more slowly paced old world mood and style. Although this is a meaty brick of a book, each chapter is clearly labeled and subdivided into more digestible and quickly read portions. The author uses scholarly, popular, and oral histories to show both the cultural and physical history of the land and its people, and makes tangible what he refers to as Mexico's fascination with the past rather than the future.

Subjects: Epic Reads • Mexico • Oral Histories • Sociology

Now try: Shorris also offers lyrical prose in novels: His epic *Under the Fifth Sun: A Novel of Pancho Villa,* and his shorter and more recent *In the Yucatan*

are both deeply rooted in Mexican history and culture. Although James Michener's epic novel *Mexico* didn't receive very positive reviews, readers of Shorris's leisurely paced history may find it enjoyable. Mexican author Carlos Fuentes has also produced a shorter and more modern history of Mexico (*A New Time for Mexico*) that may appeal to fans of Shorris's book, or might be offered to those seeking a shorter read; adventurous readers may also want to check out his novellas and other works of fiction.

Micro-Histories

"Micro-histories" are another nonfiction subgenre that every librarian seems to know about but very few define in the library literature. A short definition appears at Wikipedia: "microhistory is the study of the past on a very small scale" (*Microhistory* 2005), which seems logical, given the moniker. In providing the "behind the scenes" stories of specific places or things (one vase, as in *The Portland Vase*, or one animal, as in Robert Sullivan's *Rats*), micro-history authors provide not only great stories, but also a new perspective from which to view the big picture of history. The history of the bubonic plague (carried by rats) and the danger of world travel spreading non-native species and diseases look much different when told from the rats' point of view. Micro-histories provide a new prism through which to view the grand sweep of history; ironically, they do so by using a very specific subject matter or topical focus.

Some of the best examples of the genre, Mark Kurlansky's *Cod* and *Salt*, and Jack Turner's *Spice*, support Nancy Pearl's description of these titles as "one-word wonders" (Montagne and Pearl 2005), but their titles and subjects alone are not all what makes these often slim volumes noteworthy. Micro-histories are story-driven narratives that give their readers the chance to take in a lot of historical information and provide an excellent way for readers to get a "feel" for historical lives, places, and events. Because they are often short and their stories related in the more informal style that is used in works of "popular" history, they are also extremely quick reads and may be appealing to curious readers who don't have the time to devote to reading a longer or more scholarly work of history. This is not to say that they are slapdash; many of them are impressively researched, written, and organized to provide their readers with accessible surveys of entire historical eras or broad geographic coverage. They may also appeal to readers of micro-science books (and vice versa), namely, those books on tightly focused science subjects that are written for a more popular audience, such as Charles Seife's *Zero: The Biography of a Dangerous Idea* and Joe Sherman's *Gasp! The Swift and Terrible Beauty of Air*.

Brooks, Robin.

The Portland Vase: The Extraordinary Odyssey of a Mysterious Roman Treasure. New York: HarperCollins, 2004. 250pp. ISBN 0060510994.

This surprisingly exciting story of an unremarkable but beautiful ancient Roman vase, opening with its destruction at the hands of one William Mulcahy while it was being exhibited in the British Museum in 1845, tells about its provenance while considering the many historical mysteries surrounding it. Art historians are still squabbling about what the white-glass relief carvings covering its cobalt blue glass surface depict, there is still some debate about how and when the vase was first created, and no one has yet satisfactorily explained what prompted Mulcahy to so mercilessly smash it without any overt provocation.

Subjects: Ancient History • Archaeology • Art and Artists • Nineteenth Century

Now try: David Suzuki's *Tree: A Life Story* also has a particularly narrow focus, in this case on a single tree's life in the Pacific Northwest. Thatcher Freund's *Objects of Desire: The Lives of Antiques and Those Who Pursue Them* follows the lives of several historical objects and makes their acquisition and sale an exciting read. Sarah Messer's *Red House* is a similar telling of history as it is revealed by the story of a particular thing, in her case, the oldest continuously lived-in house in New England.

Handley, Susannah.

Nylon: The Story of a Fashion Revolution. Baltimore: Johns Hopkins University Press, 1999. 192pp. ISBN 0801863252.

Beautifully illustrated with numerous historical advertisements and color photographs, this history of nylon provides exactly that: the literal story of the chemical creation of nylon and multiple other synthetic fibers, beginning in the 1700s with French chemist Antoine Lavoisier and eventually culminating in DuPont and other corporations' mastery and marketing of the product. Although some description of the production process is included, the book focuses on the cultural and social impact of the material and is organized as a series of discrete chapters regarding different incarnations of the substance.

Subjects: Chemistry • Illustrated Books • Inventions • Pop Culture • Technology

Now try: Although *Nylon* includes many scientific facts regarding the creation of the synthetic fiber, it also examines the place of nylon as a beauty product used by women. The illustrated book *Decades of Beauty: The Changing Image of Women, 1890s to 1990s*, by Kate Mulvey and Melissa Richards, may also appeal to those readers interested in fashion history, as might Robert Friedel's *Zipper: An Exploration in Novelty*. David Owens also provides a microtechnology story in his *Copies in Seconds: How a Lone Inventor and an Unknown Company Created the Biggest Communication Breakthrough Since Gutenberg—Chester Carlson and the Birth of the Xerox Machine*.

Huler, Scott.

Defining the Wind: How a 19th Century Admiral Turned Science into Poetry. New York: Crown Publishers, 2004. 290pp. ISBN 1400048842.

While working as a copyeditor, Scott Huler stumbled across the 110-word Beaufort Scale, which describes wind speeds, was fascinated by it, and immediately set about researching the man for whom it was named and its creation. Huler alternates between vignettes from the life of Admiral Francis Beaufort and the process of performing his historical research.

Subjects: Biographies • Books and Learning • Beaufort, Francis • Nineteenth Century • Quick Reads • Weather

Now try: Witold Rybczynski's brief and similar tale about both the evolution of a simple tool and his experiences researching it, *One Good Turn: A Natural History of the Screwdriver and the Screw*, might also appeal to readers who enjoy a splash of science and research awareness with their micro-histories. *The Map That Changed the World: William Smith and the Birth of Modern Geology* by Simon Winchester also examines one person's impact on an entire field of study.

Kelly, Jack.

Gunpowder: Alchemy, Bombs, and Pyrotechnics: The History of the Explosive That Changed the World. New York: Basic Books, 2004. 261pp. ISBN 0465037186.

Although Kelly's subject matter is explosive by definition, his clear and precise writing style and exposition of the history of gunpowder is much more controlled than the actual substance. His story begins in China with exploding bamboo and proceeds in an orderly and crisp fashion through gunpowder's development in the eleventh century, King Edward III and his military applications of the weapon in the fourteenth century, the role of the explosive in Guy Fawkes's plan to blow up King James I in 1605, and onward through the American Civil War and present-day uses.

Subjects: China • Inventions • Technology • Weapons • Western Civilization

Now try: Those interested in less passionate and personal histories and more technologically focused tales might enjoy Andrea Sutcliffe's *Steam: The Untold Story of America's First Great Invention*. Edwin Tunis's illustrated *Weapons: A Pictorial History* may also interest readers who are less interested in the history of war than in the history of war's weapons. Martin Booth's informative micro-history *Cannabis: A History* is, like Kelly's book, rather more demanding than many other titles in the subgenre, but it is also crisply written (as is his companion title, *Opium: A History*).

Kurlansky, Mark.

Salt: A World History. New York: Walker, 2002 (New York: Penguin Books, 2003). 484pp. ISBN 0142001619.

Kurlansky explores world history through the lens of different societies' production and use of salt. His consideration of the topic is surprisingly scholarly, and although eminently readable, the book can't be read in a hurry. Chapters include stories from ancient Egypt, Jewish society, Celtic Britain, and many other times and places right up through the end of the twentieth century.

Subjects: Classics • Economics • Epic Reads • Food • Salt • Sociology

Now try: Micro-histories are probably the easiest and most diverse group of read-alikes available to nonfiction readers. They are so numerous that for every object you can name there has most likely been a book written about it that is titled after it. A few of the best recent examples are Barbara Freese's *Coal*; *Spice: The History of a Temptation*, by Jack Turner; *Vanilla*, by Patricia Rain, or Kurlansky's well-received *Cod: A Biography of the Fish That Changed the World*. Readers who can face another work about salt might also want to consider Pierre Laszlo's *Salt: Grain of Life*, which is a more sensuously written treatise about the grain of life and literary, cultural, and historical allusions to it.

Solnit, Rebecca.

Wanderlust: A History of Walking. New York: Viking, 2000 (New York: Penguin Books, 2001). 326pp. ISBN 0140286012.

Solnit offers a comprehensive history of the act of walking, as well as a literary history of the famous writers and philosophers, such as Thoreau and Kierkegaard, who have commented on it. Her narrative includes chapters on walking and thinking, pilgrimages, labyrinths, garden paths, the literature of walking, strolling in cities, and the dangers of walking after dark, as well as walking-related quotes along the bottom edge of each page. The text is dense and somewhat scholarly but very satisfying nonetheless.

> **Subjects:** Literary Lives • Philosophy • Rural Life • Urban Life • Walking
>
> **Now try:** Another very human activity is described in Tom Lutz's *Crying: The Natural and Cultural History of Tears.* Many works are quoted in it, from Wordsworth to Thoreau to Muir's *Thousand Miles to the Gulf*, and readers might also consider other books about walking, including Phillip Lopate's *Waterfront: A Journey around Manhattan* or *A Walk across America* by Peter Jenkins.

Sullivan, Robert.

Rats: Observations on the History and Habitat of the City's Most Unwanted Inhabitants. New York: Bloomsbury, 2004. 242pp. ISBN 1582343853.

Although Sullivan makes many allusions to Henry David Thoreau in this cultural history of rats and their environments, his version of retreating to the wild is staking out Edens Alley in New York City and observing the comings and goings of *Rattus norvegicus*, the common brown rat. Although his observations are set in the present day, he incorporates many obscure and fascinating short stories about New York City history, as well as entertaining interviews with other rat observers and extermination specialists. Sullivan's prose reads effortlessly, and the book, although comprehensive and well documented, could very nearly be read in one sitting.

6

> **Subjects:** American History • Biology • New York City • Quick Reads • Rats • Thoreau, Henry David • Urban Life
>
> **Now try:** Jeffrey Lockwood's *Locust: The Devastating Rise and Mysterious Disappearance of the Insect That Shaped the American Frontier* is very similar in tone and organization, although not quite as novelistic. Christopher Wren's travel narrative *Walking to Vermont: From Times Square into the Green Mountains—A Homeward Adventure* also combines history and personal experience, and makes similarly frequent allusions to Thoreau's *Walden.*

Yergin, Daniel.

The Prize: The Epic Quest for Oil, Money & Power. New York: Simon & Schuster, 1991 (New York: Free Press, 2003). 885pp. ISBN 0671799320.

Although Yergin's book has been rendered somewhat outdated by events in the Gulf War and Operation Iraqi Freedom, his sweeping history of the development of the oil industry before it was even demanded for automobiles is a valuable source of context for how we currently use and obtain the substance. Yergin is equally adept at developing the stories of both the individual discoverers and industrialists of the industry (such as John D. Rockefeller) and the corporations that would eventually both control and be controlled by the substance that, before the 1860s, was being used almost exclusively in patent medicines.

Subjects: Business • Epic Reads • Investigative Stories • Nineteenth Century • Oil • Pulitzer Prize Winners

Now try: Yergin's historical work is similar in writing style to many of the titles annotated in the "Investigative Writing" chapter. Oil is currently a big topic globally, and a number of recent titles reflect the mineral's place in our society: Paul Roberts's *The End of Oil: On the Edge of a Perilous New World*, Matthew Yeoman's *Oil: Anatomy of an Industry*, and Michael Economides's *The Color of Oil: The History, the Money, and the Politics of the World's Biggest Business* have all been published within the last five years. Librarians and readers are advised that books on this subject can lack subtlety, depending on their orientation; although Yergin's book is relatively objective, Roberts and Yeoman both display a bit of environmental activism, and Economides's story is more business-oriented.

Ideas of History

In addition to historical narratives organized chronologically or geographically, stories tracing the genesis and development of the "big ideas" in history constitute a large part of historical publishing. The story of the ideas of heaven and hell, for example, cannot be limited to one particular place or time because, for the most part, they have been present in many places and many times (see Alice Turner's *The History of Hell* or Jeffrey Burton Russell's *A History of Heaven*).

Because "big ideas" often come from one person, these stories also include colorful character profiles. Ross King examines one such colorful person in his best-selling *Brunelleschi's Dome*, while Pauline Maier examines the idea of a group of writers in *American Scripture: Making the Declaration of Independence*. Because these stories deal less with concrete things than with ideas and concepts, they tend to be more reflective and depend more heavily for their popularity on the writing skills of their authors.

King, Ross.

Brunelleschi's Dome: How a Renaissance Genius Reinvented Architecture. New York: Walker & Company, 2000 (New York: Penguin Books, 2001). 194pp. ISBN 0142000159.

This story of historical achievement is accurately titled; the author is sparse on personal details about the title character but long on the architectural traits of his dome on the Santa Maria del Fiore Cathedral in Florence, Italy. The dome design was the winner of a contest sponsored by the city's powerful Medici family in 1418, and although historical context is woven into the narrative, the main character of the book remains the dome, in all of its structural glory.

Subjects: Architecture • Biographies • Book Sense Award Winners • Fifteenth Century • Italy • Renaissance • Technology • Western Civilization

Now try: King is also the author of the ALA Notable Book *Michelangelo and the Pope's Ceiling*, which is similar in its rather leisurely pacing but also seeks to impart a sense of the era through its examination of the personalities and conflicts of the title characters. Readers interested in the time period dominated by the Medici might also appreciate Sarah Dunant's superb novel *The Birth of Venus*, which follows an individualistic young woman's life and struggle to experience all the artistic and cultural wonders the age had to offer.

Maier, Pauline.

American Scripture: Making the Declaration of Independence. New York: Knopf, 1997 (1998). 304pp. ISBN 0679779086.

Opening her narrative with the timely and interesting in its own right story of the current drive to preserve the physical Declaration of Independence and other historical documents, Maier nicely foreshadows her eventual conclusion that the American tendency to perfectly preserve and deify both the document and its creators may actually do it and them a disservice. By providing a biography of the Declaration and the historical context in which it was written, as well as many illuminating facts about its author's and signers' working styles, Maier has produced a work that may take some time to read but won't be easily forgotten.

> **Subjects:** ALA Notable Books • American History • Declaration of Independence • Eighteenth Century • Epic Reads • Government • Philosophy

> **Now try:** Readers interested in the documents of history might want to check out Thurston Clarke's *Ask Not: The Inauguration of John F. Kennedy and the Speech That Changed America*, or Garry Wills's even more scholarly *Lincoln at Gettysburg: The Words That Remade America* (Wills is also the author of *Inventing America: Jefferson's Declaration of Independence*). Maier's book is a weighty read (both in density of text and philosophical ideas), and readers who enjoy its speculation on the meanings of revolutionary history might also try Jack Rakove's Pulitzer Prize–winning *Original Meanings: Politics and Ideas in the Making of the Constitution*.

Micklethwait, John, and Adrian Wooldridge.

The Company: A Short History of a Revolutionary Idea. New York: Modern Library, 2003. 227pp. ISBN 0679642498.

Although the authors' discussion of the development and history of the structure and impact of societal groupings and companies, from prehistoric times to the present, can be disingenuously complimentary at times (the authors both work as editors at *The Economist*), they also provide a comprehensive look at the development of an institution. Their language is succinct and their coverage global, and since it clocks in at less than 200 pages (not counting the notes), this book offers readers a quick and accessible introduction to the subject.

> **Subjects:** Business • Economics • Modern Library Chronicles Series • Organizations • Quick Reads

> **Now try:** Nobody provides a more honest portrayal of corporations and their inner workings than *Fortune* magazine columnist Stanley Bing, in both his nonfiction titles, like *Crazy Bosses*, and his fiction titles, *Lloyd What Happened* and *You Look Nice Today*. Those readers interested in more straightforward company histories than those that are listed in the "Investigative Writing" chapter might consider Herbert Lottman's comprehensive but

readable *The Michelin Men Driving an Empire* or Richard Bak's *Henry and Edsel: The Creation of the Ford Empire*.

Ottaviani, Jim, et al.

Fallout: J. Robert Oppenheimer, Leo Szilard, and the Political Science of the Atomic Bomb. Ann Arbor, Mich.: G.T. Labs, 2001. 239pp. ISBN 0966010639.

Ottaviani and ten other artists and authors tell the story of the political and scientific birth of the atomic bomb. Each chapter is illustrated by a different artist, and these shifting perspectives contribute effectively to the unsettling history described in the text. The artists introduce each main character (Edward Teller, Leo Szilard, Einstein, etc.) in turn, as well as describing briefly exactly how the bomb was developed and tested. Librarians and readers should be aware that although much of the text contains direct quotes from primary sources, Ottaviani states in his preface that some details were fabricated "in service of the story."

Subjects: Atomic Bomb • Graphic Novels • Oppenheimer, J. Robert • Physics • Politics • Radiation • Weapons • World War II

Now try: Ottaviani is a reference librarian, so librarians can feel extra good about recommending his other graphic novels detailing the lives of scientists, including *Two Fisted Science: Stories about Scientists*, *Dignifying Science: Stories about Women Scientists*, and *Suspended in Language: Niels Bohr's Life, Discoveries, and the Century He Shaped*. Other "History of Science" titles might appeal to these readers as well. A graphic novel that strays even farther from pure nonfiction but does illustrate history is Jason Lutes's *Berlin: City of Stones*, which tells the story of the waning days of Germany's Weimar Republic, from September 1928 to May 1929; Osamu Tezuka's historical fiction graphic novel series <u>Adolf</u> might also be a valid option for nonfiction readers looking for graphic novel options.

Perrottet, Tony.

The Naked Olympics: The True Story of the Ancient Games. New York: Random House, 2004. 214pp. ISBN 081296991X.

Perrottet describes the historical details of the original Greek Olympic games in muscular and fast-moving prose, using such historical documents as a *Handbook for a Sports Coach*, a third-century training manual, and numerous illustrations from drinking vessels and other primary sources to flesh out his account of the original games, training regimes, customs, and spectator involvement. The details can be quite earthy (such as his description of the thriving prostitution that grew up around the festivities), and the author's skill in weaving them into a comprehensive narrative is admirable.

Subjects: Ancient History • Greece • Humor • Olympics • Sports • Western Civilization

Now try: Readers interested in the history of sporting and entertainment events might also enjoy Richard Cohen's vibrant history of swordplay, *By the Sword: A History of Gladiators, Musketeers, Samurai, Swashbucklers, and Olympic Champions*, or the illustrated *Tournaments: Jousts, Chivalry, and Pageants in the Middle Ages*, by Richard Barber and Juliet Barker. Perrottet is also the author of the slightly tongue-in-cheek travelogue *Pagan Holiday: On the Trail of Ancient Roman Tourists*.

Turner, Alice K.

The History of Hell. New York: Harcourt Brace, 1993 (1995). 275pp. ISBN
0156001373.

Turner's seemingly effortless prose makes this history of the idea of hell in
different eras and cultures all the more unsettling; she examines the theories of prominent theologians and philosophers, as well as artists and authors, from ancient times to the early twentieth century, to produce a
chronological history of hell as both place and psychological concept.

> **Subjects:** Hell • Illustrated Books • Philosophy • Religion

> **Now try:** Readers who enjoy Turner's history might also be drawn to many
> of the classical texts she mentions as related reading, such as Homer's *Odys-
> sey*, John Milton's *Paradise Lost*, Thomas Mann's *Doktor Faustus*, or
> Salman Rushdie's *The Satanic Verses*. Fans of Turner's lively and erudite
> work might also enjoy Karen Armstrong's *A History of God: The
> 4,000-Year Quest of Judaism, Christianity and Islam* or Jeffrey Burton Rus-
> sell's *A History of Heaven: The Singing Silence*, which is more scholarly to
> read and lacks the glorious illustrations of Turner's volume but still provides
> a similar history of the human view of heaven through art and culture.

New Perspectives

History may be based on evidence and facts, but it's also a dynamic field of
study, populated by interested and dedicated scholars seeking to uncover previously
unexplored perspectives, minority voices, or buried stories. The stories in this
subgenre are appealing due to their unique take on subjects that typically have a large
and established body of scholarship and set ideas and opinions in the general popu-
lace. They tell "the other side of the story" or sometimes (at least, according to their
authors) "the real story," and in doing so, may just change how history is generally
perceived. So, for example, although the story of the settling of the American West
had been told in many Eurocentric texts, not to mention popular works of fiction, Dee
Brown found a new way to view that history by researching the perspective of the
Native Americans who were displaced by the pioneers' settlements (*Bury My Heart
at Wounded Knee*). Likewise, it is widely assumed that the atomic bomb was used
during World War II to minimize future combat deaths, but Gar Alperovitz, focusing
his research on primary documents, seeks to re-create different motives for the use of
the weapon (*The Decision to Use the Atomic Bomb and the Architecture of an American Myth*). Many of these stories are written from the perspective of marginalized or
minority populations.

Brown, Dee.

Bury My Heart at Wounded Knee: An Indian History of the American West.
New York: Henry Holt, 1970 (2001). 487pp. ISBN 0805066691.

Historian Brown re-creates the horrific history of the American Indian in
the latter half of the nineteenth century, as politicians and westward-mov-
ing pioneers followed the ideal of Manifest Destiny and satisfied their need
for the land and resources where Native Americans had lived for generations. Told using multiple primary sources such as tribal autobiographies,

council records, and firsthand recollections, Brown presents the era from the points of view of many members of the Dakota, Sioux, Cheyenne, and other tribes as they struggled to honor treaties while still defending their lives and homes.

> **Subjects:** American History • American Indians • American West • Atrocities • Classics • Epic Reads • Government • Human Rights • Nineteenth Century

> **Now try:** N. Scott Momaday's history of the migration of the Kiowa Indians from Montana to Oklahoma, *The Way to Rainy Mountain*, is a highly stylized and lyrical recounting of another view of Native American history, personal to the author because it is the story of his ancestors. Vicki Rozema's edited collection *Voices from the Trail of Tears* is also a powerful oral history that examines the effects of the Indian Removal Act of 1830, and James Wilson's *The Earth Shall Weep: A History of Native America* offers the bigger picture of Native American history. Readers interested in graphic novels might also try Jack Jackson's illustrated *Comanche Moon*, in which he tells the story of Cynthia Ann Parker, who was abducted by a Comanche tribe and eventually had a son who became one of their most famous chiefs. The works of critically acclaimed novelist Sherman Alexie, who currently lives in his native Spokane Indian Reservation in Washington, might also appeal to Dee's readers; two of his best known are *The Lone Ranger and Tonto Fistfight in Heaven* and *Reservation Blues*.

Diamond, Jared.

Guns, Germs, and Steel: The Fates of Human Societies. New York: Norton, 1997 (2003). 494pp. ISBN 0393317552.

Diamond's personable but still scholarly text sets forth no smaller a goal than to describe the concurrent development of human societies over the course of the last 13,000 years. The crux of his historical and geographical theory is that different societies developed differently due to their environments and consequently different means of food production, and he supports this theory by citing many sources, statistics, and long-term comparisons relating to peoples on different continents. The book is written in the first person, and although it offers a whirlwind tour of thousands of years, its vast sources and geographies dictate a slower pace of reading.

> **Subjects:** Ancient History • Anthropology • Classics • Epic Reads • Geography • History of Science • Pulitzer Prize Winners • Sociology

> **Now try:** Jared's most recent book, *Collapse* (annotated in the "Making Sense . . ." chapter), is another broad epic concerning why certain societies failed throughout history, and will definitely appeal to those readers who enjoyed this work. Richard Manning's revisionist history of agriculture, *Against the Grain: How Agriculture Has Hijacked Civilization* briefly mentions Diamond's work and raises controversial questions about the long-term effects of animal and crop domestication. Orlando Patterson's National Book Award–winning *Freedom: Freedom in the Making of Western Culture*, also constructs a vast historical and geographical discussion of the roots of our concept of freedom in our human reaction to slavery, and is similar to Diamond's work in its broad consideration of a single theory. Barbara Ehrenreich's ALA Notable Book *Blood Rites: Origins and History of the Passions of War* provides a long-term and scholarly study of the roots and causes of violence that avoids easy stereotypes and seeks to provide a more universal understanding of the ritualistic nature of violence.

Fussell, Paul.

***The Boys' Crusade: The American Infantry in Northwestern Europe, 1944–
1945.*** New York: Modern Library, 2003. 184pp. ISBN 0679640886.

Fussell, a veteran of World War II, has no room in this spare history to ro-
manticize the experiences of thousands of teenaged American boys who
fought in the European ground war, and he doesn't try. Immediately
chronicling the many hatreds of the infantry soldier (primarily, anyone
who marched in behind the infantry) and their first wartime experience,
which was usually violently throwing up on the cross-Atlantic journey,
Fussell pulls no punches in providing an immediate and evocative, as well
as historically detailed, account of some of the war's worst battles.

> **Subjects:** American History • Europe • Military • <u>Modern Library Chroni-
> cles Series</u> • Quick Reads • War Stories • World War II

> **Now try:** The <u>Modern Library Chronicles Series</u> features numerous short
> works of history, written by popular historians and covering a variety of top-
> ics such as the pre–World War I empire of Germany, the Reformation, and
> the age of Napoleon. Fussell, who wrote literary criticism during the first
> part of his career, went on to write *The Great War and Modern Memory*,
> about the cultural aftermath of World War I, which was a best seller and won
> the 1976 National Book Award and the National Book Critics Circle Award.

George, Nelson.

***Post-Soul Nation: The Explosive, Contradictory, Triumphant, and Tragic
1980s as Experienced by African Americans (Previously Known as
Blacks and Before That Negroes).*** New York: Viking, 2004. 242pp. ISBN
0670032751.

George plots out the 1980s as experienced by African Americans literally,
listing events in strict date order and opening on January 25, 1979, with the
American Mavericks film festival in New York City, at which one black
film was shown, and ending December 20, 1988, with the U.S. military invasion of Panama, explained to the public by the chairman of the Joint
Chiefs of Staff, Colin Powell. Each date's historical event is crisply detailed and related through the lens of the African American experience of
history.

6

> **Subjects:** 1980s • African Americans • American History • Politics • Pop
> Culture • Race Relations • Sociology

> **Now try:** Gil Troy's *Morning in America: How Ronald Reagan Invented the
> 1980s* is also organized by date and provides another perspective on the de-
> cade. Another perspective on history, this one from a female point of view, is
> offered in Betsy Israel's *Bachelor Girl: The Secret History of Single Women
> in the Twentieth Century*. Those searching for similar books about specific
> eras and cultural conditions in the twentieth century may want to search un-
> der the Library of Congress heading "United States—Social Conditions,"
> along with the date; also, the <u>Politics and Society in Twentieth Century
> America</u> series, issued by the Princeton University Press, provides a number
> of readable books on specific eras and people in American history.

Nicholas, Lynn H.

The Rape of Europa: The Fate of Europe's Treasures in the Third Reich and the Second World War. New York: Knopf, 1994 (New York: Vintage Books, 1995). 498pp. ISBN 0679756868.

Nicholas's ambitious work follows the paths of some of the world's most famous works of art, as they were moved about Europe and among government agencies and personal collectors before and during World War II like so many chess pieces. They were often used for fundraising by the Nazis and sometimes taken as war loot by both the Axis and the Allied forces, and Nicholas provides the history behind many works of art that have since surfaced, as well as speculation regarding pieces that have never been found.

Subjects: Art and Artists • Epic Reads • Europe • Investigative Stories • National Book Critics Circle Award Winners • Robberies • World War II

Now try: Greg Campell's *Blood Diamonds: Tracing the Deadly Path of the World's Most Precious Stones* examines the similar use of diamonds to finance wars throughout history, while Matthew Hart's *The Irish Game: A True Story of Crime and Art* examines more mercenary thefts in the art world. Steve Berry's novel *The Amber Room* also takes as its subject the theft of art during World War II, as does Catherine Scott-Clark's and Adrian Levy's nonfiction *The Amber Room: The Fate of the World's Greatest Lost Treasure.*

Rowland, Wade.

Galileo's Mistake: A New Look at the Epic Confrontation between Galileo and the Church. New York, Arcade Publishing, 2003. 298pp. ISBN 1559706848.

Rowland argues that the traditional belief that Galileo's confrontation with the Roman Catholic Church arose solely from his acceptance of the Copernican theory that the earth traveled around the sun is misleading, and that the source of the conflict actually was a broader philosophical breach between science and religion. The author intersperses chapters describing his research in modern Rome with vignettes of Galileo's experiences there, before and during the Inquisition, and posits that Galileo's questioners were less interested in forcing obedience from him than in trying to forge a new atmosphere in which to combine scientific and religious thought.

Subjects: Astronomy • Galilei, Galileo • Religion • Revisionist Histories • Seventeenth Century

Now try: *Founding Myths: Stories That Hide Our Patriotic Past*, by Ray Raphael, also describes and seeks to reveal the facts behind our most enduring American stories about the Revolutionary era. Another great source for books of history that seek to correct what they view as errors of omission or outright untruths is Disinformation Press, purveyor of such titles as *Everything You Know Is Wrong*, by Russell Kick (the Web site at www.akpress.org is searchable by publisher). Another handy way to search for related titles is to search within the Dewey subject heading of "History—Errors, Inventions, etc."

Tye, Larry.

Rising from the Rails: Pullman Porters and the Making of the Black Middle Class. New York: Henry Holt, 2004. 314pp. ISBN 0805070753.

Tye masterfully combines the business history of the George Pullman sleeper railroad car with the labor history of the primarily African American workers the company hired to work as attendants (the famous Pullman porters), providing a completely fresh perspective on the history of race relations in America. Although the company ceased operations in the 1960s, Tye managed to find and interview several men who had worked as porters, as well as the family members of many others. Tye also provides a sense of the pride and ability of the porters; originally hired starting in the late 1860s because they were viewed as properly deferential, many of them used their earnings to provide better lives and education for their children.

> **Subjects:** African Americans • American History • Business • Gentle Reads • Race Relations • Sociology • Transportation
>
> **Now try:** Interestingly enough, basketball star Kareem Abdul-Jabbar (along with Anthony Walton) has produced a work of military history focusing on the experiences of African Americans serving during World War II: *Brothers in Arms: The Epic Story of the 761st Tank Battalion, WWII's Forgotten Heroes* (despite the presence of errors in the manuscript, it still garnered overwhelmingly favorable reviews from Amazon.com readers); another choice in that subject is Yvonne Latty's and Ron Tarver's *We Were There: Voices of African American Veterans, from World War II to the War in Iraq.* Those readers more interested in the economic history of Tye's narrative might also find David Shipler's informative *The Working Poor: Invisible in America* or Alice Kessler-Harris's *Out to Work: A History of Wage-Earning Women in the United States* to be a worthwhile read.

6

Secret Histories

The tremendous success of Dan Brown's novel *The Da Vinci Code* is attributable largely to his creation of a fast-paced and thrilling story, but also partly to the air of mystery it derives from purporting to be a "secret history" of both Da Vinci's painting of the Last Supper and the Roman Catholic Church. Secret histories are "a version of history that is at odds with commonly accepted historical events and which is claimed to have been deliberately suppressed or forgotten" (*Secret history* 2005). In addition to offering new or different information than had previously been accepted, these books might also take as their subjects events or organizations that have not previously been explored or studied with any degree of scrutiny, such as those that provide histories of secretive organizations and institutions. For the insatiably curious history reader, driven by the need for facts but also by a need to read a story that has an air of suspense or secrecy about it, these titles may serve admirably.

These books offer the surreptitious thrill of following their authors into previously unexplored territory, whether the authors are exposing questionable medical techniques (*The Virus and the Vaccine*) or military procedures (*Masters of Chaos*). For this reason they may also appeal to readers who enjoy any of the

"Exposé" titles in the "Investigative Writing" chapter. Although these titles are somewhat speculative or subjective, they are buttressed by the authors' research of primary documents and other materials.

Alperovitz, Gar.

The Decision to Use the Atomic Bomb and the Architecture of an American Myth. New York: Knopf, 1995 (New York: Vintage Books, 1996). 847pp. ISBN 067976285X.

Alperovitz's straightforward work sets out to examine the question of whether or not the use of atomic weapons against Japan during World War II was fully necessary, and he makes no bones about the fact that historians and readers must not be mere observers, but instead "judgments must be made at each step of the way concerning what is known (and still not known)." Using primary documents such as diaries, letters, and government reports, he seeks to lay bare not only the events surrounding the dropping of the bombs, but also the way that history itself was written and created after the event to foster the idea that the action taken was the only one available.

> **Subjects:** American History • Atomic Bomb • Epic Reads • Government • Japan • Politics • Secret Histories • Weapons • World War II

> **Now try:** Robert B. Stinnett's *Day of Deceit: The Truth About FDR and Pearl Harbor* reexamines the events at the beginning of World War II. Both of these histories were published by the Free Press (a division of Simon & Schuster); a quick look at the Free Press Web page reveals that the imprint publishes numerous works of history from less mainstream viewpoints. Edwin Black's lengthy and favorably reviewed *IBM and the Holocaust: The Strategic Alliance between Nazi Germany and America's Most Powerful Corporation* also makes public some disturbing allegations of collusion between American industry and Nazi genocide.

Bookchin, Debbie, and Jim Schumacher.

The Virus and the Vaccine: The True Story of a Cancer-Causing Monkey Virus, Contaminated Polio Vaccine, and the Millions of Americans Exposed. New York: St. Martin's Press, 2004. 380pp. ISBN 0312278721.

Although the subtitle of this book leaves little to the imagination, this is truly a frightening and briskly paced narrative regarding the monkey virus SV40 (Simian Virus 40) and its contaminating presence in polio vaccines that were produced from 1954 to 1963. The authors offer both a history of polio and Jonas Salk's creation of the inactivated virus vaccine, which was actually grown on the removed kidneys of rhesus monkeys (where it eventually came into contact with SV40). The discoveries of many other scientists, including Albert Sabin's live vaccine and Bernice Eddy's 1956 experiments, which first indicated that the vaccines might cause cancer in their human subjects, are also described. In addition to the history, the authors provide investigative details regarding the risk that vaccinations pose even today.

> **Subjects:** 1950s • American History • Health Issues • Investigative Stories • Medicine • Quick Reads • Secret Histories

> **Now try:** Richard Preston's *The Hot Zone* provides a medical narrative that is equal parts thrilling and horrifying; David Oshinsky's *Polio: An American Story* also describes a disease and the search for a vaccine but touches only superficially on Bookchin's and Schumacher's theories.

Robinson, Linda.

Masters of Chaos: The Secret History of the Special Forces. New York: Public Affairs, 2004. 388pp. ISBN 1586482491.

This rather deceptively titled book is less a comprehensive history of the U.S. military's Special Forces unit than an investigative look at the main missions and techniques used by the group during the last fifteen years. Special Forces units are known primarily for their ability to work with local militaries and to assimilate into their environment; fittingly, Robinson emulates that ability by using many personal interviews and much inside information to narrate recent missions and provide a synthesizing concluding chapter regarding the possible future tasks of the unit.

> **Subjects:** American History • Investigative Stories • Military • Secret Histories

> **Now try:** Readers interested in less publicized aspects of military history might also find Chris Mackey's *The Interrogators: Inside the Secret War against Al-Qaeda* worthwhile reading. And, although it is less a secret history than an investigative story, David Lipsky's recounting of his four-year stint observing one class from entrance to graduation in *Absolutely American: Four Years at West Point* may also appeal to military history readers.

Sora, Steven.

Secret Societies of America's Elite: From the Knights Templar to Skull & Bones. Rochester, Vermont: Destiny Books, 2003. 324pp. ISBN 0892819596.

Readers who enjoy the vicarious thrill of reading "secret" histories may enjoy this rather sensationalistic exposé of history's most famous secret and exclusive membership organizations. The book also draws several connections between famous figures in history and their connections to these secret organizations, and the emphasis of the writing is on quick pacing rather than scholarly detail.

6

> **Subjects:** American History • Organizations • Quick Reads • Secret Histories • Sociology

> **Now try:** Although many nonfiction readers might desire more rigorously researched and documented texts, many other readers will enjoy this author's fast pacing and surprising historical facts, and this publisher is noteworthy for listing several of its other similar secret and conspiracy-driven titles right on this back of this one. Particularly in light of the popularity of Dan Brown's *The Da Vinci Code*, readers who enjoy secret histories might also respond to Lynn Picknett's and Clive Prince's *The Templar Revelation: Secret Guardians of the True Identity of Christ*, which also speculates on the roles of John the Baptist and Mary Magdalene. Jasper Ridley's exhaustive *The Freemasons: A History of the World's Most Powerful Secret Society* might also appeal to readers interested in learning more about secretive organizations.

Immersion History

This subgenre offers a unique opportunity to the readers' advisor to make reading recommendations across nonfiction genres. The titles are quickly paced, primarily set in the present, and often told in the first person, and their appeal closely mirrors that of many of the titles listed in the adventure chapter. Their format differs slightly from that of many other historical narratives found in this chapter; their authors often juxtapose the story of their present-day research process with the story of the historical events or times they are researching. Although they may also appeal to readers who enjoy works of "Immersion Journalism" (annotated in chapter 10, "Investigative Writing"), they differ from those works because historical context and events play a prominent role in their stories. Their authors' dedication to both researching and experiencing the historical stories they're writing about truly sets these books apart. Mark Honigsbaum didn't just research the discovery and harvesting of the Cinchona plant as a cure for malaria, he got out there and traveled the actual "fever trail" through South America. Tony Horwitz not only interviewed Civil War reenactors, he participated in their reenactments and traveled through and stayed in their towns and homes.

Because the authors of many of these books combine the spirit of the researcher with the exploits of the traveler (*The Fever Trail* or *Bad Land*), they may also appeal to fans of the "Armchair Travel" subgenre of travel writing as well.

Honigsbaum, Mark.

The Fever Trail: In Search of the Cure for Malaria. New York: Farrar, Straus & Giroux, 2001 (New York: Picador, 2003). 315pp. ISBN 031242180X.

Honigsbaum makes the history of the search for the Cinchona plant (quinine), originally the only treatment for malaria, come alive by combining his research with his own travels into the South American jungle to track down the plant. In addition to his adventurous tone, he also has alternately lively and heartbreaking character sketches of the primary discoverers and harvesters of the plant, some of whom never received proper credit for their role in harvesting the plant's seeds. The book also includes a current treatise on the growing resistance of malaria to treatment and the continuing search for a vaccine or cure.

Subjects: Adventure • Exploration • Health Issues • Investigative Stories • Medicine • South America • Travel

Now try: Readers who enjoy Honigsbaum's history mysteries might also enjoy such recent and popular works as Robert Kurson's *Shadow Divers: The True Adventure of Two Americans Who Risked Everything to Solve One of the Last Mysteries of World War II*. An even more scholarly but no less fascinating example of a history mystery combined with the author's own travels and findings is Joann Fletcher's *The Search for Nefertiti: The True Story of an Amazing Discovery*. Those readers more interested in the medical history aspect of Honigsbaum's story might also enjoy works such as Jonathan B. Tucker's *Scourge: The Once and Future Threat of Smallpox* or David Oshinsky's *Polio: An American Story*.

Horwitz, Tony.

Confederates in the Attic: Dispatches from the Unfinished Civil War. New York: Pantheon Books, 1998 (New York: Vintage Books, 1999). 406pp. ISBN 067975833X.

Upon moving back to the United States from Australia, Horwitz rekindled his childhood love affair with Civil War history and decided to devote a year to traveling throughout the South, revisiting battle and other noteworthy sites and meeting and participating with a variety of enthusiasts and reenactors. Although the narrative is admirably light in tone, there are more serious moments, such as when the author visits a high school history class, where he ponders the still-present consequences of the bitterly divisive conflict.

> **Subjects:** Adventure • American History • American South • Civil War • Humor • Investigative Stories • Race Relations • Travel

> **Now try:** Ian Frazier's tales of his multiple drives through the Great Plains to examine their inhabitants and history is found in his best seller *Great Plains.* Readers who enjoy Horwitz's light but still serious journalistic story might also consider fiction from his spouse, reporter Geraldine Brooks, whose imaginative *March: A Novel* follows the Civil War experiences of Mr. March (the absent-at-war father and husband made famous in Louisa May Alcott's *Little Women*).

Raban, Jonathan.

Bad Land: An American Romance. New York: Pantheon Books, 1996 (New York: Vintage Departures, 1997). 364pp. ISBN 0679759069.

Somewhere between a history of the American West and an environmental book describing the landscape of Montana and the Dakotas lies Raban's work describing the struggles of the homesteaders who moved to those states in the early twentieth century, lured by the government promise of 320 free acres. Using language almost as surreal as the dry expanse of the landscape, Raban describes the current residents of the area, as well as exploring abandoned homesteads and their contents to ruminate on both the dreams and failures of the settlers.

> **Subjects:** ALA Notable Books • American History • American West • Landscape • Memoirs • National Book Critics Circle Award Winners • Travel

> **Now try:** Steve Fitch's illustrated *Gone: Photographs of Abandonment on the High Plains* provides a visual companion for Raban's book. Lowell Dingus also embarks on a journey of personal discovery through the American West in *Hell Creek, Montana: America's Key to the Prehistoric Past*, and even throws in a consideration of geologic time and dinosaur extinction while he's at it. Raban is a popular and favorably reviewed travel writer; other books he has written, which focus more on landscape and self-discovery, include *Passage to Juneau: A Sea and Its Meanings* and *Coasting: A Private Voyage.*

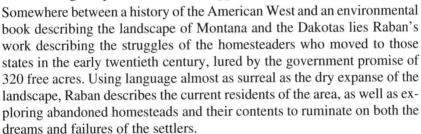

Vowell, Sarah.

Assassination Vacation. New York: Simon & Schuster, 2005. 258pp. ISBN 0743260031.

Vowell, an essayist and frequent contributor to National Public Radio, relates the details of her decidedly strange vacation visiting presidential assassination sites. In addition to her light and skillful writing, readers will find many particularly nuanced and interesting tidbits of presidential and U.S. history to enjoy in this history/travelogue genreblender.

Subjects: American History • Essays • Humor • Presidents • Travel

Now try: Another of Vowell's essay collections, *The Partly Cloudy Patriot*, examines her own conflicted relationship with American history (not to mention her family and friends). She is a master of making the borderline absurd humorous; her fans might also consider reading collections such as *Barrel Fever* and *Me Talk Pretty One Day,* by David Sedaris.

Epic History

We've explored history books that focus on places, things, and people; stories that are character portraits disguised as history; tales of horrible natural disasters and human atrocities; and secret, adventurous, and rare historical perspectives. This subgenre is characterized primarily by that feature that many readers think of as "history books": unapologetic and massive length. The following titles are all, quite honestly, meaty bricks of books.

That said, it must be further noted that these are big books for a good reason; they deal with huge and sweeping portions of history, not always just in terms of time periods but also in terms of broad and complex subject matter and world-changing events. They may not be quick reads, but each could serve as a comprehensive education in its specific subject areas; Rick Atkinson provides all the information any reader might ever need about the World War II battles fought in Africa (*An Army at Dawn*), while Jacques Barzun provides an arguably completely comprehensive look at the last 500 years of Western civilization (*From Dawn to Decadence*). Those readers who really want to know everything about everything that ever happened and don't mind taking some time to get it will love these books; otherwise, keep in mind that these titles often exceed 500 pages and may scare less-dedicated readers away from your desk (with the exception of Larry Gonick's *The Cartoon History of the United States*, which provides a big picture of sorts, but in a humorous and somewhat subjective manner).

Atkinson, Rick.

An Army at Dawn: The War in North Africa, 1942–1943. New York: Henry Holt, 2002 (2003). 681pp. ISBN 0805074481.

Definitely a solid entry in the military history canon, Atkinson describes both the history of the U.S. entry into World War II and the earliest battles on the African continent, as well as the military tactics and personalities of the commanding officers (Patton and Eisenhower among them). His writing is exceptionally detailed, and although he does provide much historical context and character detail, the strength of his narrative is definitely the intricate descriptions of the numerous battles fought and the tactics used to win them, making this a book most suitable for those readers with an interest in military history.

Subjects: Africa • American History • Epic Reads • Military • Pulitzer Prize Winners • World War II

Now try: Atkinson is planning two more books in his <u>Liberation Trilogy</u>: a history of the war in Italy, to be published in the fall of 2005, and a history of the war in Western Europe, to be published in 2008. This sort of massive military and political history might also appeal to fans of political history biography (such as titles about Patton and Eisenhower) as well as to readers of Tom Clancy's often highly technically detailed and lengthy novels.

Barzun, Jacques.

From Dawn to Decadence: 500 Years of Western Cultural Life, 1500 to the Present. New York: HarperCollins, 2000 (2001). 877pp. ISBN 0060928832.

Barzun's book is not one you pick up for a light read at the beach. He is a wonderful prose stylist, and his text is clear and educational, but his text is demanding in both its density and its subject matter. Not content to merely chronicle the events in history from 1500 to the present, Barzun also seeks to analyze the development of the overarching ideals of Western culture, and suggests that accepting and learning about our shared culture should encourage its participants to further its development. Barzun's book is organized chronologically but illustrates the distinct eras of the last 500 years using historical examples that are not often explored in popular works of history. Each chapter also features sidebars containing quotes from historical figures and suggestions for further reading on each subject being discussed.

Subjects: Classics • Epic Reads • Sociology • Western Civilization

Now try: Jacques Barzun is a well-known cultural critic, and although that title doesn't make him sound like much fun to read, his beautiful prose style might appeal to readers enough to lead them to some of his other works, including *The House of Intellect* and *A Jacques Barzun Reader: Selections from His Works.* Sebastian de Grazia's delightful consideration of our civilization's dependence on mechanization and progress, and the effects of that dependence on the portions of our lives spent at work and at play, *Of Time, Work, and Leisure,* is similar to Barzun's work in its epic story and lyrical prose style. This work also sports blurbs from John Lukacs and Gertrude Himmelfarb, both historians of note and prolific authors in their own right.

Branch, Taylor.

Pillar of Fire: America in the King Years, 1963–65. New York: Simon & Schuster, 1998 (1999). 746pp. ISBN 0684848090.

This huge and densely scholarly work examining the civil rights movement and its key leaders in the context of American society in the 1960s (including portrayals of Martin Luther King Jr., Malcolm X, Elijah Muhammad and the Nation of Islam, Lyndon Johnson, J. Edgar Hoover, and Diane Nash) provides a contextual history for the entire decade. Branch's prose is readable, but the text is challenging enough to be somewhat intimidating to the casual reader of history.

Subjects: 1960s • ALA Notable Books • American History • Civil Rights • Epic Reads • King, Martin Luther, Jr. • Politics • Race Relations

Now try: The first book in Branch's series, *Parting the Waters*, won the 1989 Pulitzer Prize. David Halberstam's *The Children* is similarly dense but follows the events of the civil rights movement through the stories of more ordinary (and less well known) but still passionate and important individuals who participated in it.

Davis, James C.

The Human Story: Our History, from the Stone Age to Today. New York: HarperCollins, 2004. 466pp. ISBN 0060516194.

History professor Davis has written an eminently readable account of our shared human history, starting with our very first appearance on the earth and our early migratory patterns that populated all its land area, and concluding with our calamitous twentieth-century progress, wars, and foreshadowing of our future. Each chapter is short and as perfectly formed as a discrete story; obviously, a 400-page book isn't long enough to consider human history in any real depth, but in providing so much beautifully written (and often quite subtly humorous) historical substance, the author includes much more than he omits.

> **Subjects:** Ancient History • Anthropology • Epic Reads • Evolution • Geography • Sociology

> **Now try:** Although Richard Fortey is considered more of a science writer, his broad and engaging epics, dating back millions of years, might also appeal to Davis's readers. His most recent title is *Earth: An Intimate History*, and in 1999 he published *Life: A Natural History of the First Four Billion Years of Life on Earth*.

Figes, Orlando.

A People's Tragedy: A History of the Russian Revolution. New York: Viking, 1996 (New York: Penguin Books, 1998). 923pp. ISBN 014024364X.

Weighing in at just under 1,000 pages, Figes's work is modestly subtitled "a" history of the Russian Revolution (in his estimation, covering the years from 1891 and famine outbreak to 1924 and the death of Lenin), but for readers with any interest in the subject, it could be argued that this impressively detailed but extremely readable account is "the" history of the era. Including numerous and informative photographs, and relating many of the details of the time through the main human players in the events (Tsar Nicholas, Lenin, and Trotsky are among the most extensively described, in personality and deed), this hefty book may scare the generalist reader but shouldn't.

> **Subjects:** ALA Notable Books • Communism • Epic Reads • Russia • Sociology • Soviet Union

> **Now try:** Readers who enjoy Figes's broad history of the Russian people might also enjoy the sweeping historic works of Robert Massie, whose biographical *Peter the Great: His Life and World, Nicholas and Alexandra,* and *The Romanovs: The Final Chapter* are readable stories from the royal (and losing) side of the Bolshevik Revolution.

Gonick, Larry.

The Cartoon History of the United States. New York: HarperPerennial, 1991. 392pp. ISBN 0062730983.

Gonick's lightning-fast review of the history of the United States, indeed presented as a cartoon, is a bit simplistic in its overview of extremely complicated issues in American history, but there's no denying that it's never dull and that Gonick manages to pack a lot of information into a graphic novel. Perhaps most impressively, the book has both an index and a bibliography, so those readers interested in augmenting their knowledge of history can't say the author didn't at least cite his sources.

> **Subjects:** American History • Graphic Novels • Humor • Quick Reads
>
> **Now try:** Gonick is his own cottage industry and has produced similar tongue-in-cheek and illustrated histories in a variety of subject areas: *The Cartoon History of the Universe* (volumes 1 through 3), *The Cartoon Guide to Chemistry*, *The Cartoon Guide to Physics*, and *The Cartoon Guide to Sex*.

Kennedy, David M.

Freedom from Fear: The American People in Depression and War, 1929–1945. New York: Oxford University Press, 1999 (2001). 936pp. ISBN 0195144031.

If you make it through all of Kennedy's nearly thousand pages, there's very little you won't know about the social, cultural, economic, and political milieu of America during the Great Depression and World War II. Extensively footnoted and told in terms of historical events rather than characterization, may be a dense, albeit informative, read.

> **Subjects:** American History • Epic Reads • Great Depression • Politics • Pulitzer Prize Winners • Sociology • World War II
>
> **Now try:** This is volume 9 in the <u>Oxford History of the United States</u> series, and although readers could grow old plowing through all of the volumes, they'll also surely gain an entire education in U.S. history through the series' other volumes, such as *Battle Cry of Freedom: The Civil War Era* and *Grand Expectations: The United States, 1945–1974*.

6

Schama, Simon.

A History of Britain: At the Edge of the World, 3500 B.C.–1603 A.D. New York: Hyperion, 2000. 416pp. ISBN 0786866756.

Schama's massive history of Britain continues in two additional volumes, *The Wars of the British, 1603–1776* and *The Fate of Empire: 1776–2000*, and can most likely satisfy the most devoted of Anglophile historians. Although the series is large, the writing is refreshingly brisk, and numerous color illustrations and photographs complement the text beautifully.

> **Subjects:** Ancient History • England • Epic Reads • Illustrated Books
>
> **Now try:** Any number of large national and regional histories exist, from Earl Shorris's *The Life and Times of Mexico* to John Reader's *Africa: A Biography of the Continent*.

Historical Biography: Caught in History's Web

The many similarities between biographical and historical writing are nowhere more apparent than in this subgenre, which includes stories about rather ordinary people who are caught up in their rather extraordinary times and circumstances. Although this historical subgenre, like the majority of the others, still depends heavily on the authors' ability to skillfully use details and researched facts in the telling of their stories, it also depends on extensive character development to further their narratives.

Trying to decide whether the characters in many of the following titles became famous because they lived in famous times, or whether the times were noteworthy for the noteworthy characters who lived in them, is a bit like arguing about whether the chicken or the egg came first. There is no doubt that Thomas More is famous because he was the infamous Henry VIII's advisor, but his hard-won position was also a by-product of his own personality and work (*The Life of Thomas More*). Likewise, the opportunity to explore the American West that was given to Meriwether Lewis and William Clark was remarkable, but they received that charge from Thomas Jefferson because of who they were and how they worked together (*Undaunted Courage*). For the most part, however, these are stories in which history remains the main character and exerts its influence on the individuals and groups whose stories are being told.

Individual Stories

Ackroyd, Peter.

The Life of Thomas More. New York: Nan A. Talese, 1998 (New York: Anchor Books, 1999). 447pp. ISBN 0385496931.

In short but densely detailed chapters, Ackroyd presents a comprehensive character portrait of Thomas More, one-time advisor to King Henry VIII (and punisher of heretics) and eventual Catholic saint and martyr, who was convicted of treason in 1534 for refusing to approve of his monarch's proposed Act of Succession, which was authored to establish the royal succession through the offspring of Anne Boleyn. Rich with historical detail, this is not a fast read, but Ackroyd is a skilled writer and storyteller who masterfully combines historical asides with details from More's personal life and makes use of such primary sources as More's letters and documents describing his appearances in court proceedings and trials.

Subjects: ALA Notable Books • Biographies • England • More, Thomas • Religion • Royalty • Sixteenth Century

Now try: Readers interested in either the main players or the era of the Reformation will be well-served by Diarmaid MacCulloch's daunting but well-received history of the event, *The Reformation: A History*. Readers interested in the London setting of More's biography might also be tempted to try Ackroyd's similarly exhaustive *London: The Biography*. Those readers who like Ackroyd's style but are daunted by the sheer weight of his tomes might want to try the first entry in his new series of brief biographies (published by Doubleday), *Chaucer: Ackroyd's Brief Lives*, and to watch for further volumes in the series.

Brady, Patricia.

Martha Washington: An American Life. New York: Viking, 2005. 276pp. ISBN 0670034304.

Brady does a creditable job of bringing America's first First Lady to life as an independent, spirited, and intelligent woman who was already a wealthy widow when she married George Washington. Although the lack of source materials must have been frustrating for the author (Martha burned all forty-one years' worth of correspondence between herself and her husband after his death) and her tone is very slightly hero-worshipful, this is still an interesting portrait of a heretofore little studied historical personage.

> **Subjects:** American History • Biographies • Eighteenth Century • Family Relationships • Government • Marriage

> **Now try:** Readers who enjoy histories and biographies from this period in American history might also consider better-known works such as Joseph Ellis's *His Excellency: George Washington* or David McCullough's *John Adams*. Those readers more interested in the stories of "minority voices" (women and minorities) might also consider titles like Cokie Roberts's *Founding Mothers* or Kay Mills's *This Little Light of Mine: The Life of Fannie Lou Hamer* (both annotated in the biography chapter).

Caro, Robert.

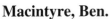

Master of the Senate. New York: Knopf, 2002 (New York: Random House, 2003). 1167pp. ISBN 0394720954.

Caro's master work is a surprisingly interesting and extremely personal, as well as historically illustrative, account of Lyndon Baines Johnson's mastery of the Senate and the passage of the first civil rights legislation. In addition to providing numerous biographical details, Caro also uses his compelling and narrative storytelling abilities to make the intricacies of governmental bureaucracy understandable.

> **Subjects:** ALA Notable Books • Biographies • Government • Johnson, Lyndon B. • National Book Award Winners • Politics • Pulitzer Prize Winners

6

> **Now try:** Robert Caro produces a lot of lengthy cultural and historical biographies; in addition to the first two volumes in his Johnson biography, *The Path to Power* and *Means of Ascent*, he has also written a dual biography of New York City and one of its most famous public servants, *The Power Broker: Robert Moses and the Fall of New York*. Stacy Schiff's *A Great Improvisation: Franklin, France, and the Birth of America* also provides a masterful combination of statesman biography and the larger context of Franklin's role in the American Revolution.

Macintyre, Ben.

The Man Who Would Be King: The First American in Afghanistan. New York: Farrar, Straus & Giroux, 2004. 351pp. ISBN 0374201781.

Macintyre alternates between telling the story of American adventurer Josiah Harlan and the turbulent nineteenth-century history of Afghanistan. Harlan, on whom Kipling's story "The Man Who Would Be King" is based, was a Pennsylvania Quaker who set off to explore the world after having his heart broken. Afghanistan has always been a nation with a rich historical and cultural heritage that has fascinated and lured outsiders to its challenging natural terrain and seemingly unceasing civil unrest, and the author blends both stories with skill and a wealth of historical detail.

> **Subjects:** Adventure • Afghanistan • Biographies • Exploration • Nineteenth Century

Now try: Rudyard Kipling's fiction classic *The Man Who Would Be King, and Other Stories* is based on the exploits of Harlan and may appeal to readers fascinated by the story. Jack Weatherford explores the cultural and historical impact of another well-known figure in *Genghis Khan and the Making of the Modern World*. Last but not least, you might also be able to steer fans of Macintyre's work toward historical adventure and exploration titles such as Laurence Bergreen's *Over the Edge of the World: Magellan's Terrifying Circumnavigation of the Globe* or Ken McGoogan's *Ancient Mariner: The Arctic Adventures of Samuel Hearne, the Sailor Who Inspired Coleridge's Masterpiece*.

McWhorter, Diane.

Carry Me Home: Birmingham, Alabama: The Climactic Battle of the Civil Rights Revolution. New York: Simon & Schuster, 2001 (2002). 719pp. ISBN 0743217721.

McWhorter combines both a memoir exploring her upbringing in a white Birmingham family and her father's possible Klan participation with an exceptionally researched and fact-packed history of the "Summer of Birmingham" in 1963, during which many key civil rights battles were fought and won. Both stories are compellingly told, but this epic history will take some time to read.

> **Subjects:** African Americans • Alabama • American History • American South • Civil Rights • Epic Reads • Memoirs • Pulitzer Prize Winners • Racism

> **Now try:** Edward P. Jones's debut novel and ALA Notable Book, *The Known World*, is similar in complexity to McWhorter's memoir of family ties and race relations, and is set in Virginia twenty years before the beginning of the Civil War. Kevin Boyle's National Book Award winner *Arc of Justice: A Saga of Race, Civil Rights, and Murder in the Jazz Age* tells a story that took place a few decades before McWhorter's, and might help set the contextual stage for readers.

Group Stories

Ambrose, Stephen.

Band of Brothers: E Company 506th Regiment 101st Airborne from Normandy to Hitler's Eagle's Nest. New York: Simon & Schuster, 1992 (2004). 333pp. ISBN 074322454X.

Ambrose's biography of a military company from training through one of the most triumphant moments in World War II history splits its coverage between the relationships between the members of the company and the military battles in which they were engaged. This is primarily a quickly paced oral history focusing on military action and camaraderie, rather than on in-depth character studies.

> **Subjects:** American History • Biographies • Classics • Friendships • Oral Histories • War Stories • World War II

> **Now try:** Ambrose is a hugely popular author, particularly on the subject of ordinary soldiers who fought on the front lines, and many fans of his work will enjoy his similar titles: *Citizen Soldiers: The U.S. Army from the Normandy Beaches to the Bulge to the Surrender of Germany* or *The Wild Blue: The Men and Boys Who Flew the B-24s Over Germany, 1944–45*. Readers who enjoy Ambrose's character-centric view of soldierly camaraderie during World War II might also enjoy Studs Terkel's *The Good War: An Oral History of World War II* or Tom Brokaw's successful series, including

The Greatest Generation and *The Greatest Generation Speaks: Letters and Reflections.* Those readers interested in World War II might also find *Ghost Soldiers: The Forgotten Epic Story of World War II's Most Dramatic Mission*, by Hampton Sides, to be a compellingly detailed and character-driven narrative about the rescue of American and British POWs from a Japanese camp in the Philippines.

Ambrose, Stephen E.

Undaunted Courage: Meriwether Lewis, Thomas Jefferson, and the Opening of the American West. New York: Simon & Schuster, 1996 (2003). 521pp. ISBN 0684826976.

Here Ambrose primarily tells the story of the famous Lewis and Clark expedition through the personal lenses of the three primary characters involved: Meriwether Lewis, complex, often consumed by melancholy, and a victim of his own incredibly high expectations; William Clark, his partner and possessor of many crucial skills that Lewis lacked, such as mapmaking and survival abilities; and Thomas Jefferson, whose desire to explore the new country he had helped to form was insatiable. Although there are some personal and biographical asides here, the book reads quickly primarily due to the adventurous tone of the fourth character, the expedition itself, and the exploration of the working relationships among the three men.

> **Subjects:** ALA Notable Books • American History • American West • Biographies • Clark, William • Jefferson, Thomas • Lewis, Meriwether • Nineteenth Century • Politics

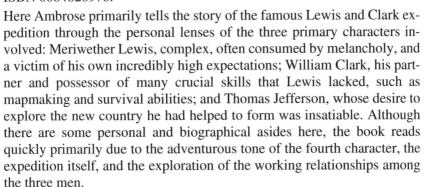

> **Now try:** In addition to being a prolific writer of books about World War II, Ambrose is also an avid chronicler of American westward expansion; he is the author of *Nothing Like It in the World: The Men Who Built the Transcontinental Railroad, 1863–1869*. Those readers more interested in the particulars of Thomas Jefferson's presidency might try Joseph Ellis's *American Sphinx: The Character of Thomas Jefferson*, while fans of the explorers might look into books like Landon Y. Jones's *William Clark and the Shaping of the West* or the explorers' own book, *The Journals of Lewis and Clark*, recently published in a new edition as a <u>National Geographic Adventure Classic</u> title.

Ball, Edward.

Slaves in the Family. New York: Farrar, Straus & Giroux, 1998 (New York: Ballantine Books, 2001). 505pp. ISBN 0345431057.

In the process of researching his own roots and his slave-owning ancestors, Ball created a vivid history of work and family life and relationships between slaves and their owners in South Carolina. In addition to providing this history, the author also undertook a search for descendants of the slaves his ancestors owned, and he provides many valuable revelations, gained through interviews, about their current lives and attitudes. Although exhaustively researched and written with admirable attention to character detail, this is a dense read.

Subjects: African Americans • American History • American South • Biographies • Family Relationships • National Book Award Winners • Racism • Slavery • South Carolina

Now try: Henry Wiencek's *The Hairstons: An American Family in Black and White*, which won the National Book Critics Circle Award, also details a Southern family's complicated family tree and the relationships between slave families and their owners. Likewise, Rhys Isaac's *Landon Carter's Uneasy Kingdom: Revolution and Rebellion on a Virginia Plantation* examines, through the use of the title character's daily diary, the complex relationships between plantation owners and their slaves, and combines very personal stories with broader historical research.

Ellis, Joseph J.

Founding Brothers: The Revolutionary Generation. New York: Knopf, 2000 (New York: Vintage Books, 2002). 288pp. ISBN 0375705244.

By his own admission, Ellis does not seek to tell a comprehensive history of the American Revolution; rather, he hopes to "write a modest-sized account of a massive historical subject," and if reviewers and the book-buying public are any indication, he succeeded (like his previous books, it was a popular best seller). In a roughly chronological series of character-driven vignettes, Ellis imaginatively fills in the personal and interpersonal details behind the characters' (Jefferson, Hamilton, Adams, Madison, etc.) struggle to create a path for the nation once independence had been gained.

Subjects: American History • American Revolution • Biographies • Classics • Eighteenth Century • Pulitzer Prize Winners

Now try: Ellis's best seller appealed to many readers of both biographies and histories because it explores his title characters' lives as representative of the time in which they lived. Readers who favor its biographical flair might enjoy biographies about the other movers and shakers of the Revolutionary era, such as Ellis's *His Excellency: George Washington*, Walter Isaacson's *Benjamin Franklin: An American Life*, or John K. Alexander's *Samuel Adams: America's Revolutionary Politician* (which is part of the American Profiles series from Rowman & Littlefield).

Hagedorn, Ann.

Beyond the River: The Untold Story of the Heroes of the Underground Railroad. New York: Simon & Schuster, 2002 (2004). 333pp. ISBN 0684870665.

Journalist Hagedorn provides a very personal and character-driven narrative of the Underground Railroad and the many volunteers who contributed to its success, as well as of the many slaves who used it to try to reach freedom in Canada. Most particularly she tells the meticulously researched story of Ohio abolitionist John Rankin, whose home in Ripley, directly across the river from slaveholding state Kentucky, served as a refuge for many fleeing slaves. The character portraits are compelling and the chapters quickly paced, but the mood of the writing is scholarly; this book may hold more appeal for readers used to more academic texts, but it is certainly accessible enough for more generalist readers.

Subjects: African Americans • ALA Notable Books • American History • Biographies • Kentucky • Ohio • Rankin, John • Slavery

Now try: The appeal of this historical work is largely the characterization of its central character, John Rankin; readers who enjoy it might also be drawn to Catherine

Clinton's recent biography of another hero of the underground railroad, *Harriet Tubman: The Road to Freedom*. George Hendrick's work of narrative history, *Fleeing for Freedom: Stories of the Underground Railroad, as Told by Levi Coffin and William Still*, provides a personal overview of the history of the railroad and those who traveled by and maintained it.

Hendrickson, Paul.

Sons of Mississippi: A Story of Race and Its Legacy. New York: Knopf, 2003 (New York: Vintage Books, 2004). 343pp. ISBN 0375704256.

The cohesive theme of Hendrickson's narrative centers on the photograph on the book cover: seven men, alternately laughing, glaring, or turning away from the camera's gaze, all white and all county sheriffs in 1960s Mississippi, prepare to make good on their threat to keep James Meredith from attending (and thereby integrating) the University of Mississippi. The lives of all the men pictured are described at length, as are the lives of their children, and James Meredith's children, in the author's attempt to provide a context for current issues of race relations. Personal and written with great focus, clarity, and objectivity, this is an extremely succinct historical read that starts with the very specific and manages to encompass a much larger general subject.

Subjects: American History • American South • Biographies • Civil Rights • Family Relationships • Integration • Law Enforcement • Mississippi • National Book Critics Circle Award Winners • Racism

Now try: Hendrickson is a master of using photographs to illustrate history; his *Bound for Glory: America in Color, 1939–43* provides an alternative picture of America during the Great Depression in Kodachrome color photographs. His less illustrated but still comprehensively researched *The Living and the Dead: Robert McNamara and Five Lives of a Lost War* is a character-driven history similar to *Sons of Mississippi*. For those readers interested in both photography and the battle for civil rights, librarians might want to offer the book that Hendrickson cites as the impetus for his story: *Powerful Days: The Civil Rights Photography of Charles Moore*, by Michael Schelling Durham and Charles Moore.

Koren, Yehuda, and Eilet Negev.

In Our Hearts We Were Giants: The Remarkable Story of the Lilliput Troupe—A Dwarf Family's Survival of the Holocaust. New York: Carroll & Graf Publishers, 2004. 305pp. ISBN 0786713658.

Koren and Negev tell the truly chilling story of the Ovitz family, seven of whose ten members were dwarves, and their ordeal in the Auschwitz prison camp in World War II. The family had worked before the war as a vaudeville act and, ironically, it was their genetic anomaly that kept them both together and alive, while also bringing them to the attention of Josef Mengele. This unique story, which begins with the family's life before the war and proceeds through the experiments they survived in the camp and their often trying lives afterward in Palestine, is told primarily through the lens of each member's experiences and perceptions.

Subjects: Atrocities • Biographies • Family Relationships • Holocaust • Jews and Judaism • Medicine

Now try: First-person accounts of Holocaust survival include Primo Levi's classic *Survival in Auschwitz*, Szpilman Wladyslaw's *The Pianist: The Extraordinary True Story of One Man's Survival in Warsaw, 1939–1945*, Victor Klemperer's two-part diary *I Will Bear Witness* (1933–1941 and 1942–1945), and Roma Ligocka's *The Girl in the Red Coat*. Readers may also be interested in fictional accounts of the atrocities such as Thomas Keneally's *Schindler's List*, Bernhard Schlink's *The Reader*, William Styron's *Sophie's Choice*, or Elie Wiesel's *Night*.

Tobin, James.

Ernie Pyle's War: America's Eyewitness to World War II. New York: Free Press, 1997 (Lawrence: University of Kansas Press, 1998). 312pp. ISBN 0700608974.

Although Tobin does a creditable job relating the biographical and personal details of the life of journalist Ernie Pyle, the second and nearly as important character is World War II and the U.S. military forces. The first two chapters cover the first forty years of Pyle's life, complete with details of his travel columns for the Scripps-Howard newspaper syndicate and his sometimes difficult marriage; after that the narrative turns almost exclusively to his reporting of the war while traveling with the soldiers fighting it, often at the front.

Subjects: American History • Journalism • Military • National Book Critics Circle Award Winners • Pyle, Ernie • World War II

Now try: Although Tobin's book includes a short appendix of Pyle's columns, readers who themselves remember Ernie Pyle may also enjoy two full collections of his travel and war columns, both edited by David Nichols: *Ernie's War: The Best of Ernie Pyle's World War II Dispatches* and *Ernie's America: The Best of Ernie Pyle's 1930s Travel Dispatches*.

Consider Starting With . . .

The titles listed below are some of the best and most popular and will likely appeal to readers who enjoy this genre.

Brown, Dee. *Bury My Heart at Wounded Knee: An Indian History of the American West.*

Cahill, Thomas. *How the Irish Saved Civilization: The Untold Story of Ireland's Heroic Role from the Fall of Rome to the Rise of Medieval Europe.*

Gourevitch, Philip. *We Wish to Inform You That Tomorrow We Will Be Killed with Our Families: Stories from Rwanda.*

Hendrickson, Paul. *Sons of Mississippi: A Story of Race and Its Legacy.*

Perrottet, Tony. *The Naked Olympics: The True Story of the Ancient Games.*

Sullivan, Robert. *Rats: Observations on the History and Habitat of the City's Most Unwanted Inhabitants.*

Von Drehle, David. *Triangle: The Fire That Changed America.*

Wills, John W., Jr. *1688: A Global History.*

Fiction Read-Alikes

- **Carey, Peter.** Both *Oscar and Lucinda* and *True History of the Kelly Gang* (which won the 2001 Booker Prize) are character-driven but also derive much appeal from their historical setting in late nineteenth-century Australia.

- **Dunnett, Dorothy.** Dunnett has created two massively popular and well-received historical fiction series. The <u>Lymond Saga</u> is a six-volume saga set in sixteenth-century Scotland; it begins with *The Game of Kings* and *Queens' Play*. The <u>House of Niccolo</u> series is set in the fifteenth century and covers a variety of settings (its first two volumes are *Niccolo Rising* and *The Spring of the Lamb*).

- **García Márquez, Gabriel.** García Márquez is not typically included on lists of historical fiction authors, primarily because the literary style he helped pioneer, "magical realism," is often described with more emphasis on its fantastic components than its realistic historic ones. However, in addition to *One Hundred Years of Solitude* (which is often viewed as his masterwork and follows the lives of numerous generations in one family in Colombia), he has also written novels rooted in historical events and facts, including *Chronicle of a Death Foretold* and *Love in the Time of Cholera*.

- **Harris, Robert.** Harris hasn't produced a lot of fiction, but the historical thrillers he has written have all been best sellers: *Fatherland* is an alternative history in which Hitler and the Nazis are victorious, set in the year 1964; *Enigma* is a World War II thriller about code-breaking; *Archangel* is set in Russia and follows the rise to power of Stalin's son; and *Pompeii* retells the events in the two days prior to the eruption of Mount Vesuvius in C.E. 79.

6

- **Jakes, John.** The author of the outstandingly popular *North and South* (which was eventually made into an epic miniseries) first hit the best-seller charts with his <u>American Bicentennial</u> series (also known as the <u>Kent Family Chronicles</u>). That series, which follows a family over the first hundred years of America's history, began with *The Bastard* and *The Rebels*. More recent titles from Jakes are *Charleston* (2002) and the two-part *Homeland* (1993) and *American Dreams* (1998).

- **O'Brian, Patrick.** O'Brian's <u>Aubrey-Maturin</u> books, much like C. S. Forester's maritime adventurers featuring Horatio Hornblower, are set during the Napoleonic Wars and feature the stories of two friends, Jack Aubrey and Stephen Maturin; *New York Times Book Review* reviewer Richard Snow has called O'Brian's books the "best historical novels ever written." The first volumes are *Master and Commander*, *Post Captain*, and *H.M.S. Surprise*; the series has been published steadily through the last couple of decades and continue through *Blue at the Mizzen* (1999) and *21: The Final Unfinished Voyage of Jack Aubrey* (which was published posthumously in 2004).

- **Pears, Iain.** Pears's meaty historical mysteries, including the popular *An Instance of the Fingerposts* (set in 1660s England), are rich in historical detail; fans of art history nonfiction like *The Amber Room: The Fate of the World's Greatest Lost Treasure* or *The Rape of Europa* and might also enjoy *The Dream of Scipio*.

- **Rutherford, Edward.** A lot of historical fiction tends to run into volumes of great length, and Rutherford's stories of places and people over the course of centuries are no exception. His novels published to date are *Sarum: The Novel of England, Russka: The Novel of Russia, London*, and *The Princes of Ireland: The Dublin Saga*.

- **Vidal, Gore.** Vidal's six books in his fictionalized series of American history are, in order: *Washington, D.C.; Burr; 1876; Lincoln; Empire;* and *Hollywood. Lincoln* in particular was a hugely popular fictionalized biography and had a first printing of 200,000 copies.

Further Reading

"America Unabridged." *American Heritage* (November/December 2004): 24–73.

The magazine asked twenty-one historians and writers to select the best books on different periods of American history and annotate their choices. The result is a ready-made, fifty-page bibliography of books on Americana, and a fascinating mix of both seminal and more unknown choices, on topics from the Revolution to the immigrant experience, sports, and women's history.

Bailyn, Bernard, and Edward Connery Lathem.

On the Teaching and Writing of History: Responses to a Series of Questions. Hanover, N.H.: University Press of New England, 1994. 97pp. ISBN 0874517206.

Surprisingly, this slim volume of questions and answers about the teaching and writing of history, asked of an historian I've never heard of, is one of the most interesting and concise texts I have seen on how historians gather their research (and what sorts of things they research), how they write their stories, and the importance of reading history in our schools and homes. It's really an illuminating little read for librarians wanting to know more about the craft of creating historical narratives.

Davis, Kenneth C.

Don't Know Much about History: Everything You Need to Know about American History But Never Learned. New York: Crown, 1990 (New York: HarperCollins, 2003). 678pp. ISBN 0060083816.

Davis's huge best seller first appeared in 1990 but has since been revised and expanded, and it can be quite a handy source for ideas for book displays. Written in a question-and-answer format, the book is accessible and covers all the bases of American history, from discovery to Revolution to the Cold War and the election of 2000. Some of the questions aren't ones that schoolchildren would ever be tested on ("Did Columbus's men bring syphilis back to Europe?") but they're still interesting and thought-provoking, and helpful reading suggestions are interspersed throughout the text under the heading "Must Read."

Lewis, Jon E., ed.

The Mammoth Book of Eyewitness History 2000: Eyewitness Accounts of Great Historical Moments from 2700 BC to AD 2000. New York: Carroll & Graf, 2000. 630pp. ISBN 078670747X.

The most valuable part of this compendium of eyewitness accounts of variously significant historical events is the chronology; any librarian wishing for a visual map of key moments in history (from political to religious and scientific to social) need look no further; it's not exhaustive but it might prove helpful when trying to place moments in history or jog ideas for a historical display.

Lorenzen, Michael.

World History Web Resources: An Annotated Guide. http://personal.cmich.edu/~loren1mg/world-history.html.

Central Michigan University head of reference services Lorenzen has created a highly useful and extremely comprehensive list of Internet resources for the study of world history. Librarians and other readers' advisors interested in browsing historical overview sites for booklist and annotation ideas might find his page an extremely useful jumping-off point.

O'Nan, Stewart, ed.

The Vietnam Reader: The Definitive Collection of American Fiction and Nonfiction on the War. New York: Anchor Books, 1998. 724pp. ISBN 0385491182.

Use this as a read-alike for any Vietnam War history, to lead librarians and readers to similar works in both fiction and nonfiction.

6

References

Bailyn, Bernard, and Edward Connery Lathem. 1994. *On the Teaching and Writing of History: Responses to a Series of Questions.* Hanover, N.H.: University Press of New England.

Herald, Diana Tixier. 2000. *Genreflecting: A Guide to Reading Interests in Genre Fiction.* 5th ed. Westport, Conn.: Libraries Unlimited.

Microhistory. 2005. Wikipedia. http://en.wikipedia.org/wiki/Microhistory (accessed July 25, 2005).

Montagne, Renee, and Nancy Pearl. 2005."Nancy Pearl Discusses Some Examples of Micro-Histories." *NPR Morning Edition* (radio; aired March 23).

Saricks, Joyce. 2001. *The Reader's Advisory Guide to Genre Fiction.* Chicago: American Library Association.

Secret History. 2005. http://en.wikipedia.org/wiki/Secret_history (accessed July 25, 2005).

Tuchman, Barbara. 1981. *Practicing History: Selected Essays.* New York: Knopf.

Part 3

Life Stories

Biography

Memoirs and Autobiography

Relationships

Chapter 7

Biography

Definition of Biography

Simply put, biography is a form of literature in which the stories of lives are recorded. The term itself comes from two Greek words: "bios," which means "life," and "graphein," which means "to write." As a reading interest it cuts across all subjects; any topic a reader can pursue typically has individuals associated with it, and the stories of their lives might appeal to even those readers who don't think of themselves as fans of "biography." Film buffs might be enticed into trying biographies of Marilyn Monroe or James Dean (and there are plenty to be had); sports adventure readers might enjoy reading Lance Armstrong's *It's Not about the Bike*; political or history junkies might profitably chance across Robert Caro's epic *Master of the Senate* about Lyndon B. Johnson or Edmund Morris's *Dutch* or *Theodore Rex*. The formats of biography are as varied as the subjects: Biographers can use a formal or more chatty tone; they can consult academic archives and sources or conduct personal interviews; they can focus on a seminal event in their subject's life and use it to illustrate the person's personality or legacy; they can choose to highlight one person's life or to consider multiple subjects and how they relate to each other. The possibilities, particularly when taking into account the number of noteworthy individuals and the numerous permutations of writing styles and formats that can be used to detail their exploits, are truly endless.

Biography is big. Bigger than big, really. Huge. It is a huge area of interest for many readers, it is a huge and profitable sector of publishing, and it is a venerable and just plain formidable body of work (more than 8,000 biographies were published in 2004 alone; Bookwire.com 2005). Luckily, many readers who want to read these "stories of lives" most often have a particular life in mind: Robert F. Kennedy, for example, or Dorothy Parker, or Elvis Presley. Not so luckily for us, readers' advisors also often hear: "I'm looking for something good to read, and I really enjoy biographies. Can you recommend any?" Or, "I just read that biography about Joe Namath. Can you recommend any other biographies like that one?"

Less often we get questions about the nature or historical development of biographical writing, but that doesn't mean we shouldn't know something about it. Two histories of biographies in particular provide both timelines of seminal biographical works, as well as considerations of their formats and popularity: Paul Kendall Murray's *The Art of Biography* and John A. Garraty's *The Nature of Biography*. Since both of those titles are listed in the "Further Reading" section of this chapter, and they tell the full history of biography far better than I ever could, with their assistance I provide here only the briefest of overviews of the genre.

Both authors take the genre back to the time of antiquity, with Garraty reaching back to ancient Egypt and the pharaohs, when it was the custom to "record the deeds of kings in the form of chronicles" (Garraty 1957, 32), and Kendall citing Plato's re-creation of the end of Socrates's life in both his *Apology* and his *Phaedo* (1985, 32–33). Both historians refer to the Roman biographer Plutarch and the importance of his volumes on the *Lives of the Noble Grecians and Romans*, written around the middle of the first century B.C.E., as well as to the gospels of the New Testament, with their four versions of the one life of Jesus of Nazareth, and to the many written records of the lives of saints in the early Christian church (1957, 54–55). Kendall pauses long enough between antiquity and the Renaissance to explore one of the first of many periodical swings into disfavor and unpopularity of the form; he notes that "the remainder of the Middle Ages [after the publication of Saint Augustine's *Confessions*] finds biography falling out of favor due to the due to the popularity of chivalric romance, allegory and satire" (1985, 49).

Biography as a format may be prone to falling out of style, but it is equally prone to exploding back into popularity. Kendall notes that epics such as Thomas More's (More is himself the subject of an award-winning biography by Peter Ackroyd) *History of Richard III*, published in 1513, as well as Vasari's famous *Lives of the Painters*, published in the same century, help to catapult the genre into popularity in an age when literacy was becoming ever more widespread, and the invention of the printing press loomed on the horizon. Garraty's history agrees, by and large, with Kendall's, and both writers examine the various periods of popularity and indifference. Readers in Elizabethan England, in the latter half of the sixteenth century, were uninterested in biographies, while the seventeenth century saw a resurgence of interest in life stories, particularly those of criminals (1985, 96).

In the latter eighteenth century, James Boswell published the comprehensive and extremely personal life story of his friend, famous literati and man about town, Samuel Johnson. Between them they have, as one literary scholar noted, "molded our ideas about biography and created the forms that embody its essential qualities" (Meyers 2002, 40). Librarians and fans of biography who have no idea who either Boswell or Johnson is and haven't read Boswell's *Life of Johnson* (I confess I didn't get through it) are indebted to them nonetheless; Boswell's tireless chronicling of the exacting minutiae of Johnson's life, including both his private and public life, his dress, his movements, his acquaintances, and even what he ate on a regular basis, was the first ever of its kind, and Johnson (a writer of biographies himself) would further insist that biographers not only capture the details of a life but also seek to make some kind of sense of it.

After the high point that was the publication of *Life of Johnson*, most of the nineteenth century saw a lull in the writing and publication of life stories, but that all changed with another seminal work, one that is discussed at length in every history of the biographical genre you're likely to pick up: Lytton Strachey's *Eminent Victorians*, published in 1917. Garraty describes that work as somewhat polite, but also points out that Strachey's work was literary, more than dryly historical, and was not only filled with wit and irony but also "broke away from documentation and the rigid bonds of fact" (1957, 122).

With the exception of a short backlash against the form during the 1940s, due to the increasingly lax or undocumented styles of many biographers writing during that time, the twentieth century seems to have seen a consistently high level of interest in these life stories. Another biography historian, Catherine Parke, speculates that in addition to recounting the details of lives and their significance in history, writing of biography in the twentieth century was heavily influenced by the development of the modern science of psychology: "[S]o profoundly did the founder of psychoanalysis influence twentieth-century notions of who we are, how we develop, our degrees of self-awareness, and the need for psychoanalytic insight to become conscious of these processes that, after Freud, no responsible biographer can justify knowing nothing about psychoanalytic interpretive methods" (1996, 26). The creation of *People* magazine in 1974 and the growth of "personality" journalism throughout the 1970s and 1980s was at the forefront of a celebrity-driven trend that continues today.

Biography is also is well-represented among lists of notable and readable non-fiction books; likewise, most of the major literary prizes, such as the Pulitzer Prize and the National Book Critics Circle Award, offer specific prizes in this category. The prestige and honors accorded many writers of biographies also contribute to their name recognition among readers; regardless of subject, many readers will flock to the newest titles by such venerated authors as Joseph Ellis, David McCullough, Stephen Greenblatt, and Ron Chernow.

Appeal of the Genre

So how can we account for the enduring appeal of biographies, especially after we have read a whirlwind tour of their development and learned that they have, at times, been extremely unpopular? Yet another historian makes a simple and eloquent case for their enduring nature: "Because biography makes history personal, readers understandably flock to it. People like to read about people" (Oates 1990, 7). And really, there you have it. The subject can be a famous person or a relative unknown, but the appeal of biography is its focus on people, or, in appeal characteristics lingo, character.

Just as people differ, biographies too vary widely in coverage, subject, style, form, and method of creation. Some biographers depend entirely on primary documents such as diaries or letters, produced by their subject or their subject's contemporaries; some seek to repackage other's primary source–based writings by examining more closely certain events or times in their subject's lives, which also provides an opportunity for readers less interested in huge chronological compilations: "the current vogue for looking at just a portion of a subject's life rather than a definitive examination gives readers a chance to step in—and then step back" (Mantell 2004, 19). These differing formats and approaches also contribute to the importance of story and setting as appeals for this genre; fans of David Reynolds's *Walt Whitman's America: A Cultural Biography* will also learn about America in the poet's time; Thurston Clarke's biography of JFK, *Ask Not*, offers a suspenseful day-by-day recounting of the creation of that president's most defining speech. Use of language and writing styles can also heavily influence a reader's enjoyment (or lack thereof) when reading biographies; they run the gamut from gossipy and chatty to downright academic and scholarly, from single-person studies to group or "buddy bios." When it comes to biographies, there truly is something for everyone. Readers who don't have the stamina or time for an 800-page work on President U. S. Grant might consider the much shorter entry, written by Josiah Bunting, in the American Presidents series from Times Books; likewise, those readers more interested in the story of Winston Churchill's and Franklin Roosevelt's friendship than the separate details of their lives will be amply served by *Franklin and Winston: An Intimate Portrait of an Epic Friendship*.

Literary theorist and critic Sven Birkerts accounts for the current popularity of biographies by speculating that in our complex and busy lives, fewer of us are feeling a sense of cultural identification and cohesion, and the act of reading about other people's lives and more clearly focused times helps compensate for that loss. As evidence for that theory, Birkerts points out that "there is no less important incentive for reading the lives of others, and this is to illuminate to ourselves the facets of our own experience" (1995, 24). If Birkerts is right, it may be safe to assume that as long as readers remain interested in figuring out themselves and those close to them, they will remain interested in reading biographies.

Readers of biographies might also enjoy the other "people stories" genres, memoir (which also includes autobiography) and relationships. Because these books often tell historical stories from a personal point of view, they might also appeal to readers who primarily read history books (and many of this chapter's most popular authors, such as the aforementioned Joseph Ellis and David McCullough, are also the authors of numerous works of history).

Organization of the Chapter

Now, you might ask, how can one expect to provide a comprehensive listing of suggested biographies? Further, how can anyone expect to keep current about any significant number of the new biographies that are published annually, not to mention the many serviceable biographies currently available? The answers are, of course, that we can't. However, I'm going to take my cue from Jacques Barzun on this one; just as he once said that objectivity may be hard to achieve but that does not excuse us from our responsibility to strive for it, I'd like to suggest that just because keeping our knowledge of available biographies current may be tough, it doesn't follow that we shouldn't attempt it.

What follows is merely a selection, and an extremely select one at that, of prize–winning, recent, noteworthy for their style, best-selling, or just plain fun biographies. Don't be afraid of them; after all, we're all just people here. The chapter opens with one of the most recognizable and enduring in popularity (think David McCullough and Joseph Ellis) categories, "American Presidents and World Leaders." Categories listing professional/subject area biographies of well-known or famous people follow: "Problem Solvers and Experimenters: Science Biography," "The Creative Life: Artists, Entertainers, Writers," and "Sports Biographies."

In addition to the life stories of famous people, many biographies of individuals who have lived groundbreaking lives or were experts in their chosen but less followed professions have also been written; their stories (including that of Lewis Lawes, the reform warden of the Sing Sing prison, and Frederick Law Olmsted, the designer of New York City's Central Park, to name just two) are compiled in the "Outstanding in Their Fields: Professional Biography" section. Another section, "Change-Makers and Activists," about historical figures who have struggled to make a positive difference in the world, follows.

The three final biography categories are more cohesive in their authors' writing and interpretative research styles than they are in subject matter. "Historical Biography" includes nearly as much historical detail and exposition as it does personal details, while in the "Better Together: 'Buddy' and Group Bios," the biographers have chosen to present their subjects' lives in the framework of their relationships to and effect on one another, rather than providing the biological timeline of only one individual. The last category, "Guilty Pleasures: Celebrities and Superstars" is a collection of biographies that are written more to be titillating and provide readers with all the gossip and "inside dirt" that they could possibly desire on their favorite celebrities; also included there is a list of well-known celebrity biographers who have written numerous works on a variety of subjects.

American Presidents and Other Political Leaders

From the first popular chronicle of George Washington's life, written by Mason Weems in 1799 (and reworked in 1806 to include the entirely fictional account of Washington's chopping down the cherry tree and refusing to lie about it), readers have been fascinated by the life stories of their elected officials and other political leaders. Although these heavily historical works also include many time period and cultural details, they are primarily character studies of the individuals we entrust with our governance, or of those people who were in the right place at the right time and had governing thrust upon them.

In addition to often being huge best sellers (Morris's *Theodore Rex* and Ellis's *American Sphinx*, about Thomas Jefferson, are the most popular of these "popular histories"), these titles are heavily represented on each awards list readers might choose to peruse for reading suggestions. They also tend to be seasonal; each year in November we get a rash of readers looking for works on John F. Kennedy (to correspond with the date of his assassination and the inevitable airing of PBS specials on the subject around the same time), while other titles will experience a surge of reader interest whenever their main subjects are in the news or are the subject of other newly published works.

7

Being a world or national leader is a big job, and stories written about leaders tend to be big stories. Although all of the titles below are well-written and designed to appeal to the nonscholarly reader, they also tend to be very detailed and long books. Readers' advisors should be aware that even the most devoted of biography readers may not be able to take on a number of these lengthy stories one right after the other, and may want to suggest shorter biographies or shorter titles from the history chapter when readers indicate they want something "just like that," only perhaps a little lighter.

Bix, Herbert P.

Hirohito and the Making of Modern Japan. New York: HarperCollins, 2000 (New York: Perennial, 2001). 814pp. ISBN 0060931302.

Somewhat revisionist in its assertion that Emperor Hirohito, whose reign lasted from 1926 to 1989, was less a passive participant in Japan's governance than an active determiner of social and wartime national policy, this biography is truly epic in scope and scholarly in its use of research, including many sources that had only recently become available. Although the personal aspect of Hirohito's life is covered, the story attempts to place the emperor within the historical context of several wars and a quickly changing world.

> **Subjects:** Emperor Hirohito • Epic Reads • Government • Japan • National Book Critics Circle Award Winners • Pulitzer Prize Winners • Royalty • World Leaders • World War II
>
> **Now try:** Readers who find Bix's exhaustive biography an informative read might enjoy biographies of other political and military figures of the time, such as William Manchester's *American Caesar: Douglas MacArthur, 1880–1964*, about the man who served as Military Governor in postwar Japan, or even books about other twentieth-century leaders who encouraged their own cults of personality, such as Adam Ulam's *Stalin: The Man and His Era*, or Ian Kershaw's two-volume biography of Adolf Hitler: *Hitler: 1889–1936, Hubris* and *Hitler: 1936–1945, Nemesis*.

Clarke, Thurston.

Ask Not: The Inauguration of JFK and the Speech That Changed America. New York: Henry Holt, 2004. 252pp. ISBN 0805072136.

Given on January 20, 1961, Kennedy's famous "ask not what your country can do for you" inaugural speech has long been a subject of debate among presidential scholars. Did the president himself write it? Was that soaring injunction actually the work of speechwriter Theodore Sorensen? Biographer Clarke addresses those questions and places the speech in the context of Kennedy's personality, working style, and political goals, complete with many very personal details regarding his relationships, religion, and oratory style.

> **Subjects:** 1960s • American History • Kennedy, John F. • Presidents • Quick Reads • Speeches • World Leaders
>
> **Now try:** Garry Wills's ALA Notable Book and Pulitzer Prize–winning *Lincoln at Gettysburg* places Lincoln's speech in similar biographical context, although it is more scholarly in tone and offers a more classical discussion of Lincoln's rhetoric and speechmaking abilities. Allen Guelzo's *Lincoln's Emancipation Proclamation: The End of Slavery in America* also considers the way in which one of history's most important documents was created, and compares its rather legalistic tone with Lincoln's other speeches and decrees. David Maraniss's short study of President Bill Clinton's four-minute speech denying his involvement with Monica Lewinsky also provides the personal context in *The Clinton Enigma: A Four and a Half Minute Speech Reveals the President's Entire Life*.

Dallek, Robert.

An Unfinished Life: John F. Kennedy, 1917–1963. Boston: Little, Brown, 2003. 838pp. ISBN 0316172383.

Hailed by critics as one of the defining biographies of JFK for current readers and scholars, this work provides a compelling narrative story of the president and his family as well as his political legacy, using the thorough research techniques of the scholar. The author is also frank about the more recently discussed extent of JFK's many and severe medical problems, as well as some of his less-attractive personal qualities. Overall, though, this is more pure biography than historical interpretation, and provides in one volume a comprehensive picture of Kennedy's life and times.

Subjects: 1960s • American History • Family Relationships • Kennedy, John F. • Presidents • World Leaders

Now try: Every year around the anniversary of the president's assassination, or concurrent with the airing of any PBS specials on the Kennedy family, there is invariably a sprinkling of requests for definitive biographical works about the Kennedy family. Readers who enjoy Dallek's book might also be referred to Evan Thomas's *Robert Kennedy: His Life* or Paul Fusco's excellent photographic study *RFK Funeral Train*, Richard J. Whalen's *The Founding Father: The Story of Joseph P. Kennedy*, Laurence Leamer's *The Kennedy Women: The Saga of an American Family*, or Doris Kearns Goodwin's massive *The Fitzgeralds and the Kennedys: An American Saga*.

Donald, David Herbert.

Lincoln. New York: Simon & Schuster, 1995 (New York: Touchstone, 1996). 714pp. ISBN 068482535X.

Well-respected historian and biographer offers the story of Abraham Lincoln with the stated desire to tell the narrative as much from the president's own viewpoint as possible. Free of the salacious details and speculations about Lincoln that current biographies often offer to differentiate themselves, Donald's narrative is based on Lincoln's personal papers and still offers enough personal detail to interest readers who are eager to learn more about his personality than just his experiences as the president during the Civil War.

Subjects: ALA Notable Books • American History • Civil War • Epic Reads • Lincoln, Abraham • Nineteenth Century • Presidents

Now try: Donald has won the Pulitzer Prize for biography twice: for *Charles Sumner and the Coming of the Civil War*, and more recently for *Look Homeward: A Life of Thomas Wolfe*. Although Donald covered most aspects of Lincoln's life to a heroic level of detail, those readers interested in reading even more about the events surrounding Lincoln's assassination and the man behind it might try Michael W. Kauffman's *American Brutus: John Wilkes Booth and the Lincoln Conspiracies*. Readers more interested in Lincoln's role in the Civil War might also consider James McPherson's Pulitzer Prize–winning *Battle Cry of Freedom: The Civil War Era*, or Gore Vidal's historical fiction title *Lincoln: A Novel*.

Ellis, Joseph J.

American Sphinx: The Character of Thomas Jefferson. New York: Knopf, 1997 (New York: Vintage Books, 1998). 440pp. ISBN 0679764410.

Told in a less straightforward historical and chronological style than most definitive biographies that take as their subject the American Founding Fathers, Ellis seeks rather to examine and illuminate the character and psychology of Thomas Jefferson. Ellis describes the author of the Declaration of Independence not only with biological details gleaned from historical research, but also in terms of the many conflicting theories about his life, work, and ambitions that are currently being studied by historians. The result is a good historical story that has a uniquely modern and nuanced feel.

Subjects: American History • Eighteenth Century • Jefferson, Thomas • National Book Award Winners • Presidents • Psychology

Now try: Those readers less interested in Jefferson's place in history than in his personal life might also want to try Andrew Burstein's surprisingly intimate biography *Jefferson's Secrets: Death and Desire at Monticello*. Readers more enthralled by Ellis's narrative writing style than by Thomas Jefferson might also want to consider his recent best-selling *His Excellency: George Washington* or his *Passionate Sage: The Character and Legacy of John Adams* (2001).

McCullough, David.

John Adams. New York: Simon & Schuster, 2001 (2002). 751pp. ISBN 0743223136.

McCullough takes as his subject the second president of the United States, John Adams, and develops the story of his life with lively and simple language and stories. Although his perspective is decidedly that of a historian who is fond of his subject, he does admit that Adams had a few personal faults; however, he focuses primarily on Adams's political genius and social prowess. McCullough also introduces other famous characters of the time, such as Thomas Jefferson, and spends much time developing narrative about these early politicians' friendships.

Subjects: Adams, John • ALA Notable Books • American History • Eighteenth Century • Epic Reads • Presidents • Pulitzer Prize Winners

Now try: Readers who might be interested in the more personal side of John Adams and the details of his marriage to his exceptionally helpful and well-suited partner Abigail might do well to track down a copy of *The Letters of John and Abigail Adams*, edited by Frank Shuffleton, or even Lynne Withey's *Dearest Friend: The Life of Abigail Adams*. McCullough also won the Pulitzer Prize for his biography of Harry S. Truman, titled simply *Truman*; that work is a similarly comprehensive and primarily upbeat profile of the president who was faced with some of the biggest challenges of the twentieth century.

Morris, Edmund.

Theodore Rex. New York: Random House, 2001 (New York: Modern Library, 2002). 772pp. ISBN 0812966007.

The sequel to the Pulitzer Prize–winning *The Rise of Theodore Roosevelt*, first published in 1979, and part two of a proposed trilogy, Morris's epic biography of Teddy Roosevelt is devoted entirely to his time as president, from 1901 to 1909. Although Morris is better known as the controversial biographer of Ronald Reagan (that biography, *Dutch*, received critical fire for Morris's controversial inclusion of an imaginary character/narrator), his historical re-creation of Roosevelt's time as the chief executive is much more conventional. His writing, however, is anything but academically dry, and he paints a vivid picture of both the period in the country's history and the personality of the chief executive.

Subjects: ALA Notable Books • American History • Epic Reads • Government • Presidents • Roosevelt, Theodore • World Leaders

Now try: Readers who enjoy more straightforward presidential biographies might be better served by David McCullough's *Truman* or Ron Chernow's ALA Notable Book *Alexander Hamilton*. Readers who want to read more about Theodore Roosevelt's unique charm and impact might also consider the group biography *The Three*

Roosevelts: Patrician Leaders Who Transformed America, by James MacGregor Burns and Susan Dunn.

Smith, Jean Edward.
Grant. New York: Simon & Schuster, 2001 (2002). 781pp. ISBN 0684849275.

As straightforward and unaffected as its simple one-word title, this rather sympathetic biography of Ulysses S. Grant focuses primarily on his military and political career, although the author does provide periodic asides regarding Grant's other (often unsuccessful) business ventures and his marriage and family life. In the introduction, the author explains his desire to provide a biography with more continuity than previous accounts of the eighteenth president, which often frame Grant as a successful military man but political failure, and he has done so with clear writing that reads surprisingly quickly.

Subjects: ALA Notable Books • American History • Civil War • Epic Reads • Government • Grant, Ulysses S. • Nineteenth Century • Presidents

Now try: Readers interested in Grant but who are daunted by the length of Smith's tome might consider Josiah Bunting's much shorter *Ulysses S. Grant*, which is part of the <u>American Presidents</u> series. Readers interested in both presidential lives and Grant's period in history might also enjoy Hans Trefousse's biography of the president who served before him, *Andrew Johnson: A Biography*. Smith is also the author of *New York Times* Notable Book *John Marshall: Definer of a Nation*, about fourth Supreme Court Chief Justice John Marshall, who was nominated by John Adams in 1801.

Taubman, William.
Khrushchev: The Man and His Era. New York: Norton, 2003 (2004). 871pp. ISBN 0393324842.

Taubman addresses both the personal details of Khrushchev's life and his roles as enabler to Stalin and reformer of his policies. The result is an extremely readable biography of a world leader who was by all accounts both personable and manic, intelligent but often viewed as an inferior thinker. Taubman's research was performed at both the previously off-limits Politburo Archive and many other archives throughout Russia, and includes many quotes from Khrushchev's own three-volume autobiography, as well as from personal interviews with his family members and Kremlin colleagues.

Subjects: ALA Notable Books • Epic Reads • Khrushchev, Nikita • National Book Critics Circle Award Winners • Pulitzer Prize Winners • Soviet Union • Stalin, Joseph • World Leaders

Now try: Taubman's Pulitzer Prize winner is so compelling that it may entice readers into reading further epic works of Russian/Soviet history; Orlando Figes's *A People's Tragedy: The Russian Revolution, 1891–1924* or Anne Applebaum's *Gulag: A History* might be two good further suggestions. *Lenin: A Biography*, by Richard Service, might also be offered to readers who don't want to stray as far from biographies.

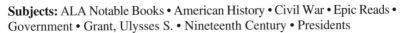

Problem Solvers and Experimenters: Science Biography

This subgenre is similar to the one we've chosen to call "Outstanding in Their Fields," which contains career- and work-centered biographies, but this subgenre is more specific in its focus on scientists and their discoveries. In addition to providing compelling characterizations and some little known facts about the individuals, authors of these science biographies also include impressive overviews of the details of scientific observation, experimentation, and breakthrough discoveries. This subgenre has also been delineated because the history of science is a huge and popular subject with many readers, and because so many quality and interesting biographies of great scientific figures are available. Do keep in mind that readers who enjoy books in this subcategory might also find many of the titles listed in the science chapter enjoyable and informational related reads.

Browne, Janet.

Charles Darwin: The Power of Place. New York: Knopf, 2002. 591pp. ISBN 0679429328.

Opening in 1858, Browne's narrative follows Darwin through the second half of his life, which was consumed more by authoring and defending his theories than by exploration and theorizing. The emphasis of this major academic work is on describing his written works and his interactions with colleagues, including lengthy discussions of his voluminous correspondence with many of the finest scientific minds of his era.

> **Subjects:** Darwin, Charles • Epic Reads • Evolution • Friendships • National Book Critics Circle Award Winners • Nineteenth Century • Work Relationships

> **Now try:** Browne's first volume, *Charles Darwin: Voyaging*, will of course complete the portrait of Darwin's travel experiences and era. A complementary read to Darwin's life story is Ross Slotten's scholarly and work-centered biography of Alfred Russel Wallace, *The Heretic in Darwin's Court*. After developing his theory of natural selection for twenty years, Darwin thought he would be alone in positing it; Wallace startled him into finally publishing by sending him a letter outlining the same theory, which he had developed separately from Darwin.

Connor, James A.

Kepler's Witch: An Astronomer's Discovery of Cosmic Order Amid Religious War, Political Intrigue, and the Heresy Trial of His Mother. San Francisco: HarperSanFrancisco, 2004. 402pp. ISBN 0060522550.

Although his name may not be as familiar to modern readers as that of Galileo, Johannes Kepler has nonetheless long been recognized as a pioneer of astronomy and the author of surprisingly elegant and accurate (for the early 1600s) planetary laws of motion. A dull life story cannot be blamed for this scientist's relative obscurity; Connor uses quickly paced prose and Kepler's own letters and other writings to illustrate a life lived against a backdrop of religious schism (Protestant versus Catholic), witchcraft trials (including that of his own mother), and difficult interpersonal and professional relationships. Heavy-duty science readers may be disappointed at the lack of exposition regarding Kepler's methods and discoveries, but readers more interested in social and familial details will find this a very enjoyable read.

Subjects: Astronomy • Family Relationships—Mothers and Sons • Health Issues • Kepler, Johannes • Politics • Seventeenth Century

Now try: Although it is more of a history mystery than a biography, Owen Gingerich's *The Book Nobody Read: Chasing the Revolutions of Nicolaus Copernicus,* in which the author tracks down physical copies of Copernicus's master work *On the Revolutions of the Heavenly Spheres*, also considers the life and era of another influential historical astronomer. Those readers with a deeper interest in astronomy might also consider the illustrated book *The Astronomers*, by Donald Goldsmith, which provides a history of astronomy's most influential thinkers and their theories.

Goldsmith, Barbara.

Obsessive Genius: The Inner World of Marie Curie. New York: Norton, 2005. 256pp. ISBN 0393051374.

Although Goldsmith's volume is one in a series published by Norton entitled <u>Great Discoveries,</u> hers is definitely a work of biography, outlining Marie Curie's fascinating life and scientific work, from her birth and childhood in Poland to her marriage to Pierre Curie and her discovery of radium (the couple's work served to enhance their relationship; their own daughter noted that "united by their intellectual passions, they had, in a wooden shack, the anti-natural existence for which they had both been made"), as well as their struggle with the fame the discovery would bring them. The work of their scientist daughter is also discussed in the latter third of the book.

Subjects: Chemistry • Curie, Marie • Family Relationships • <u>Great Discoveries Series</u> • Quick Reads • Radiation • Women Scientists • Women's Contributions

Now try: Norton's <u>Great Discoveries Series</u> offers numerous short and fascinating biographical and professional portraits of influential scientists, written by highly respected authors; other volumes in the series include Michio Kaku's *Einstein's Cosmos: How Albert Einstein's Vision Transformed Our Understanding of Space and Time*, Sherwin Nuland's *The Doctor's Plague: Germs, Childbed Fever, and the Strange Story of Ignác Semmelweis*, and Rebecca Goldstein's *Incompleteness: The Proof and Paradox of Kurt Godel*. Readers who like both biographies and books on science to be short might also enjoy Paul Strathern's *Curie and Radioactivity*, a ninety-nine-page entry in the Anchor Books <u>Big Idea</u> series. James Gleick's brief but comprehensive biography, *Isaac Newton*, also illuminates the life of a trailblazer in scientific thought and theory.

McElheny, Victor K.

Watson and DNA: Making a Scientific Revolution. Cambridge, Mass.: Perseus Publishing Group, 2003 (New York: Basic Books, 2004). 365pp. ISBN 0738208663.

Famous for discovering, along with Francis Crick, the helical structure of DNA, James Watson went on to cement his reputation as a sometimes volatile, often judgmental of his colleagues, but always brilliant scientist with his extremely personal account of the discovery, *The Double Helix* (1963). It seems only fitting, then, that McElheny has written this biography of him (which actually focuses more on his scientific and administrative work than on personal details) without his participation, and has depended instead on more than fifty interviews with other scientists who have worked with Watson over the course of his career. In the best spirit of its subject, however, this account of Watson's childhood, greatest discovery, and later involvement with the Cold Spring Harbor Laboratory and the Human Genome Project is lively and candid.

Subjects: Biology • Friendships • Genetics • Watson, James • Work Relationships

Now try: Again, although it is likely that any reader seeking out a biography of James Watson will have already read *The Double Helix*, a librarian can always suggest it, along with its sequel (of sorts), *Genes, Girls, and Gamow: After the Double Helix*. A less widely read book on the subject is that of Watson's codiscoverer of the double helix, *What Mad Pursuit: A Personal View of Scientific Discovery*, by Francis Crick. Eric Enno Tamm's *Beyond the Outer Shores: The Untold Odyssey of Ed Ricketts, the Pioneering Ecologist Who Inspired John Steinbeck and Joseph Campbell* is based on ecological science rather than biology, but also provides a look at how scientists and other individuals can inspire and influence each other.

Nasar, Sylvia.

A Beautiful Mind: The Life of Mathematical Genius and Nobel Laureate John Nash. New York: Simon & Schuster, 1998 (2001). 461pp. ISBN 0743224574.

Made into a hugely popular movie with the same title, Nasar's biography of John Nash is a comprehensive story of his life and relationships, focusing primarily on his mathematical triumphs in the fields of game theory and economics and his two-decade-long struggle with schizophrenia. The book is quickly paced and the chapters short, and as mentioned by more than one reviewer, it reads like a well-crafted novel.

Subjects: Classics • Family Relationships • Marriage • Mathematics • Mental Health • National Book Critics Circle Award Winners

Now try: Paul Hoffman's homage to another brilliant but decidedly eccentric mathematician (he published 1,475 mathematical papers in his career) is presented in the fascinating biography *The Man Who Loved Only Numbers: The Story of Paul Erdös and the Search for Mathematical Truth*. Flo Conway's and Jim Siegelman's biography, *Dark Hero of the Information Age: Norbert Wiener, the Father of Cybernetics*, tells the story of one of the pioneering figures of cybernetics, as well as his struggle with manic depression.

Rhodes, Richard.

John James Audubon: The Making of an American. New York: Knopf, 2004. 514pp. ISBN 0375414126.

Pulitzer Prize–winning author Rhodes provides a different look at one of the premier naturalists and wildlife artists of the nineteenth century, John James Audubon. For readers interested in this observer and illustrator of birds, this typically chronological but still fast-paced biography will provide many details not only about Audubon's personal life but also about the work involved in producing an ornithology that would meet both scientific standards as well as the entertainment requirements of pleasure readers. Several full-color plates of Audubon's bird illustrations are included.

Subjects: American History • Art and Artists • Audubon, John James • Birds • Marriage • Nineteenth Century • Professions

Now try: William Souder's *Under a Wild Sky: John James Audubon and the Making of the Birds of America*, also published in 2004, provides more of an alternative than a supplementary choice; it is less obviously a chronological biography and more an exposé of Audubon's master work and how, incidentally, the details of his life helped shape it. Another suggestion that is less scholarly and more illustrated is *Audubon's Elephant: America's Greatest Naturalist and the Making of the Birds of America*, by British naturalist Duff Hart-Davis.

The Creative Life: Artists, Entertainers, Writers

Biographies can't all be about world political leaders or scientific trailblazers. Readers are also often drawn to the life stories of artists, entertainers, and writers, many of whom truly dedicated the majority of their time and resources to creating their great and, in some cases, legendary, works and performances. How better to answer the needs of readers seeking creative expression and inspiration than to suggest the life stories of skillful entertainers or famous musicians or artists?

Lives lived creatively, or in the service of creating art or performances, are not always easy. Many artists and writers, in particular, have left ample proof for their biographers to interpret and organize around the theme of how their subjects "suffered for their art." More comprehensive and sympathetic than gossipy, many of the titles listed here refer to the trials and tribulations of their subjects' lives as part and parcel of their ability and drive to create art. There is, of course, a time and a place for more chatty and speculative works (see the "Guilty Pleasures" subgenre), but for the most part, the stories told here are full of complex characters and often quite challenging lives.

As with all other types of biographies, the formats represented here vary widely, from Valerie Boyd's straightforward and chronological exposition of Zora Neale Hurston's life, to Philip McFarland's exploration of that portion of Nathaniel Hawthorne's creative life that was spent living in Concord, Massachusetts.

Asimov, Janet Jeppson, ed.

It's Been a Good Life. Amherst, New York: Prometheus Books, 2002. 309pp. ISBN 1573929689.

Although Asimov himself produced a well-received three-volume autobiography, his wife's condensed version provides a personal and enjoyable story of the scientist and writer's life, including all the highlights of his childhood, youth, studies and teaching career in chemistry, and his most famous career as an unbelievably prolific science fiction and nonfiction writer. The book can very nearly be read in one sitting, and as one of Asimov's claims to fame is having authored a nonfiction book in every Dewey classification, it would behoove all librarians to be familiar with at least the broad details of his remarkable life.

Subjects: Asimov, Isaac • Chemistry • Family Relationships • Literary Lives

Now try: Although librarians again face the chicken and the egg problem with this book (that is, most readers who seek it out will most likely already be fans of Asimov's fiction), it may not hurt to recommend some seminal works from Asimov's huge catalog, several of which are listed in the "Fiction Read-Alikes" section of the science and math chapter. Asimov also produced a lot of adult nonfiction; some of his best-selling titles are *Asimov's Chronology of the World*, *Asimov's Chronology of Science and Discovery*, and *Isaac Asimov's Guide to Earth and Space*.

Boyd, Valerie.

Wrapped in Rainbows: The Life of Zora Neale Hurston. New York: Scribner, 2003 (2004). 527pp. ISBN 0743253299.

Boyd's subtly detailed text and short and briskly paced chapters make this biography of a little-studied literary great an immensely readable one. Hurston's family life was complex and her interpersonal relationships numerous and fascinating. After leaving her childhood home in the 1920s she attended Howard University and eventually made her way to Harlem, where she become friends with poet Langston Hughes and many other notable figures of the day. She spent a lifetime writing but died in 1960 without sufficient money for her funeral, and Boyd does a nice job of examining all her quirks as well as her talents in this sympathetic portrait.

Subjects: African Americans • ALA Notable Books • Family Relationships • Hurston, Zora Neale • Literary Lives • Love and Dating • New York City • Racism • Women's Contributions

Now try: Readers who are interested in learning more about Hurston need look no further than her own poetically simple autobiography, *Dust Tracks on a Road*. There are also blurbs on the jacket from other popular fiction authors, among them Edwidge Danticat and Alice Walker (about whom Evelyn C. White has also recently written a biography, *Alice Walker: A Life*). *Pieces from Life's Crazy Quilt*, by Marvin V. Arnett, is a superb autobiography of an African American woman's youth in Detroit in the 1930s and 1940s.

Brownlow, Kevin.

Mary Pickford Rediscovered: Rare Pictures of a Hollywood Legend. New York: Abrams, 1999. 256pp. ISBN 0810943743.

Brownlow combines his biography of Mary Pickford, "America's Sweetheart" during the early years of silent filmmaking and as keen a business mind as ever took on the film industry and its distributors, with numerous photographs and commentary on her role in Hollywood history. In addition to providing a long-overdue consideration of Pickford's personal and business life, Brownlow also provides synopses and other information about her films.

Subjects: Family Relationships • Illustrated Books • Marriage • Mass Media • Movie Stars • Pickford, Mary • Women's Contributions

Now try: Pickford was the cofounder, along with her husband, Douglas Fairbanks, and Charles Chaplin, of the United Artists film production company, which is still in operation today. Readers of her biography might enjoy related works such as Jeffrey Vance's *Chaplin: Genius of the Cinema*, or other books about strong-willed female actresses such as Greta Garbo (the subject of Mark Vieira's *Greta Garbo: A Cinematic Legacy*).

Cohodas, Nadine.

Queen: The Life and Music of Dinah Washington. New York: Pantheon Books, 2004. 559pp. ISBN 0375421483.

The author perfectly integrates the tumultuous personal life and great vocal talent of singer Dinah Washington with the turbulent political and social issues of the 1950s and 1960s. In an era when light skin was particularly prized within the African American community as a sign of beauty, Washington often felt stigmatized by her dark complexion. She also fell prey to a music industry in which vocalists and other musicians were often taken advantage of by recording companies and their managers. Married seven times and the mother of two children, Washington died of a prescription medication overdose (officially deemed an accident) in 1963.

> **Subjects:** 1950s • African Americans • Alcoholism • Drug Addiction • Family Relationships • Marriage • Music and Musicians • Racism • Washington, Dinah • Women's Contributions

> **Now try:** Cohodas is also the author of *Spinning Blues into Gold: The Chess Brothers and the Legendary Chess Records*, which was a *New York Times* Notable Book in 2000. Another soul singer who admits to being influenced by Washington, Etta James tells her own often troubling story (along with David Ritz) in her autobiography *Rage to Survive: The Etta James Story*. Peter Guralnick's *Dream Boogie: The Triumph of Sam Cooke*, examines the life of another influential African American musician, who died a violent death at age thirty-three. Matt Dobkin's history of a seminal song, *I Never Loved a Man the Way I Love You: Aretha Franklin, Respect, and the Making of a Soul Music Masterpiece*, is less a biography than a cultural history, but also relies on personal interviews with individuals present during the recording.

Gordon, Robert.

Can't Be Satisfied: The Life and Times of Muddy Waters. Boston: Little, Brown, 2002. 408pp. ISBN 0316328499.

In this succinct but complete biography of blues legend Muddy Waters, author Gordon also includes historical facts and admirable amounts of musical detail, such as the development of Waters's bottleneck style (literally sliding a bottle across guitar strings to produce a signature metallic sound). Exhaustively researched, much of the story is told in direct quotes from the blues master himself, culled from interviews, letters, and other sources.

> **Subjects:** African Americans • ALA Notable Books • American South • Music and Musicians • Racism • Waters, Muddy

> **Now try:** Readers who enjoy either the blues or biographies of musicians might also want to try Elijah Wald's *Escaping the Delta: Robert Johnson and the Invention of the Blues* or Chris Albertson's favorably reviewed *Bessie*, about blues legend Bessie Smith.

McCrum, Robert.

Wodehouse: A Life. New York: Norton, 2004. 530pp. ISBN 0393051595.

McCrum admirably matches the lightness of literary tone that Wodehouse was famous for in novels revolving around his brilliant comic characters Jeeves, Bertie Wooster, and Psmith (among others). Sadly, Wodehouse's

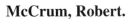

life was not as trouble-free as Bertie Wooster's; after his residence in Berlin under the Nazi government he was branded a Nazi sympathizer, and he spent much of his life as an expatriate from the very country whose "stiff upper lip" mentality his books so brilliantly portrayed. By interspersing multiple quotes and excerpts from Wodehouse's works, McCrum also provides a truly literary biography that will delight Wodehouse fans and serve as a good introduction to his works for readers new to his writings.

Subjects: England • Literary Lives • Wodehouse, P. G. • World War II

Now try: Although his writing was in a very different style, Douglas Adams was also a Brit and a cultural icon; Anglophile fans of Wodehouse and/or Adams might consider reading *Wish You Were Here: The Official Biography of Douglas Adams*. Those readers who enjoy a bit more literary criticism in their literary biography (again centering on a Brit, a female this time) should try Emily Auerbach's scholarly but immensely personable *Searching for Jane Austen*, in which the author provides the details of Austen's life and relationships and doesn't skimp on how those details are reflected in her novels.

McFarland, Philip.

Hawthorne in Concord. New York: Grove Press, 2004. 341pp. ISBN 0802117767.

McFarland combines the story of Nathaniel Hawthorne's life, marriage, and writing influences with a biographical sketch of the Concord, Massachusetts, area and the many influential thinkers and writers who were his neighbors while he lived there. The short chapters are succinctly written but contain a wealth of personal details about Hawthorne, as well as about his contemporaries, including Margaret Fuller, Henry Longfellow, and Henry David Thoreau, and the landscape in which they lived.

Subjects: American History • Friendships • Hawthorne, Nathaniel • Landscape • Literary Lives • Marriage • Massachusetts • Nineteenth Century

Now try: Of course, one of Hawthorne's associates literally wrote the book that first described the impact of landscape on a writer's life and work; *Walden*, by Henry David Thoreau, is annotated in the environmental chapter. Michael Reynolds considers the importance of place (specifically Paris, France) in the life, development, and art of another famous writer in *Hemingway: The Paris Years*. The illustrated *Henry James on Italy*, selected from James's text *Italian Hours*, might also prove enjoyable to readers with a combined interest in writers of Hawthorne's era and the importance of landscape to novelists.

Polito, Robert.

Savage Art: A Biography of Jim Thompson. New York: Knopf, 1995 (New York: Vintage Books, 1996). 543pp. ISBN 0679733523.

Polito uses extensive excerpts from Thompson's own mystery and noir fiction, as well as from interviews with friends and relatives, to create an eerily thrilling biography of the author that reads almost as deliciously as his own works. Although Thompson died in the depths of obscurity in 1977, the successful film *The Grifters* (based on Thompson's novel by the same name), released in 1990, jumpstarted interest in his life and writings, and Polito has contributed a quickly paced and admirably structured literary biography to Thompson's mythology.

Subjects: Literary Lives • National Book Critics Circle Award Winners • Thompson, Jim • True Crime

Now try: As is the case with most literary biographies, those readers who seek it out will most likely have already read Thompson's entire catalog, but a few titles of his that librarians may want to keep in mind as suggestions are *The Killer Inside Me*, *After Dark, My Sweet*, *Pop. 1280*, and his memoir, *Bad Boy*. Librarians might also consider offering other mystery noir titles, such as those by Raymond Chandler, to readers of this biography, or even asking readers how they would feel about any of the titles annotated in the true crime chapter (where Jim Thompson is listed as a fiction read-alike).

Reynolds, David S.

Walt Whitman's America: A Cultural Biography. New York: Knopf, 1995 (New York: Vintage Books, 1996). 671pp. ISBN 0679767096.

When one realizes that Reynolds has undertaken a biography of both a unique American poet and the cultural milieu in which he worked, the length of this mighty tome becomes much more understandable. Although it is organized chronologically, Reynolds devotes equal space to both the pertinent details of Whitman's birth, childhood, adulthood, relationships, and work and descriptions of both the locations and prevailing cultural attitudes in which he produced his poetry. This book will require a substantial investment of time on the reader's part, but it provides an entire education on its twin subjects of Whitman and America in the nineteenth century.

Subjects: ALA Notable Books • American History • Epic Reads • Literary Lives • Nineteenth Century • Poetry • Whitman, Walt

Now try: A librarian can have a lot of fun plugging the term "cultural biography" into the catalog: some titles that pop up in such a search include Peter Conn's *Pearl S. Buck: A Cultural Biography* (not a bad read-alike; it's about the only other female American novelist besides Toni Morrison to win the Nobel Prize, who also had an influence on her era) and Robert Gutman's *Mozart: A Cultural Biography*. Although most readers interested enough to seek out this biography will probably already have read Whitman's poetry, you could always suggest *Leaves of Grass* or *Walt Whitman: The Complete Poems*.

Secrest, Meryle.

Duveen: A Life in Art. New York: Knopf, 2004. 517pp. ISBN 0375410422.

This life story of Joseph Duveen (Lord Duveen of Millbank), the first such study of the art dealer extraordinaire who was famous in the early twentieth century, combines personal and professional details with equal skill and readable prose. Duveen was responsible for encouraging many previously unknown luminaries in the art world, as well as for assisting some of history's more famous collectors.

Subjects: Art and Artists • Business • Duveen, Joseph • Family Relationships

Now try: Further illumination of the art world can be found in Anthony Haden-Guest's tell-all *True Colors: The Real Life of the Art World*, set in the latter half of the twentieth century rather than the first half. Peggy Guggenheim, a famous art collector in her own right, also provides a history of modern art in her succinct *Confessions of an Art Addict*. Matthew Hart's *The Irish Game* illuminates the art world in terms of its most famous thefts.

Shakespeare, Nicholas.

Bruce Chatwin: A Biography. New York: Nan A. Talese, 1999 (New York: Anchor Books, 2001). 618pp. ISBN 0385498306.

Novelist Shakespeare relates a very complete tale of adventurer and travel writer Bruce Chatwin's life, based on his personal notebooks and letters, as well as on interviews with his wife Elizabeth and other family members. Chatwin, best known for *In Patagonia*, grew up in England, worked at Sotheby's, and became a traveler and writer; much of this biography illuminates his work methods, but it is also unstinting in detail regarding his personal life, friendships, and lifelong struggle to reconcile his homosexuality with the rest of his life.

> **Subjects:** ALA Notable Books • Chatwin, Bruce • Epic Reads • Family Relationships • Friendships • Homosexuality • Literary Lives • Sexuality • Travel

> **Now try:** Most readers will come to this book with knowledge of Chatwin and his writings (two of the best-known are *In Patagonia* and *The Songlines*), but it also makes frequent mention of other travel writers such as Colin Thubron and Paul Theroux, whom you may consider offering to readers as well.

Sisman, Adam.

Boswell's Presumptuous Task: The Making of the Life of Dr. Johnson. New York: Farrar, Straus & Giroux, 2000 (New York: Penguin, 2002). 351pp. ISBN 0142001759.

Sisman turns the tables on one of history's most famous biographers; best known for his massive *Life of Johnson* (about Samuel Johnson, one of Great Britain's most famous literary lights) James Boswell was a fascinating biographical subject in his own right. Sisman provides all the pertinent biographical details, the story of Boswell's and Johnson's friendship and the seven-year task of writing the biography, and how Boswell's work was received by his critics and edited by future generations.

> **Subjects:** Boswell, James • Classics • Eighteenth Century • England • Friendships • Johnson, Samuel • Literary Lives • National Book Critics Circle Award Winners

> **Now try:** Although it's a tough book for the modern reader to get through, Boswell's *Life of Samuel Johnson* (which is often cited as one of the most influential examples of the biographical literary form) should really be read by anyone who enjoys Sisman's biography of the biographer; born in 1709, Johnson was the quintessential literary man of his age and the source of many quotations still used today. Patricia Hampl's *I Could Tell You Stories: Sojourns in the Land of History* also provides the literary insider's view of the creation and lure of the memoir.

Solomon, Deborah.

Utopia Parkway: The Life and Work of Joseph Cornell. New York: Farrar, Straus & Giroux, 1997 (Boston: MFA Publications, 2004). 426pp. ISBN 0878466843.

Art critic and author Solomon has written a well-researched and sympathetic study of American artist Joseph Cornell, whose work in shadow boxes made him a fixture in the modern art scene from the 1940s through the 1960s. Although Solomon spends much of her time describing and considering Cornell's artwork, she also provides a deeper look into his home life in Queens, largely spent taking care of his brother, who suffered from cerebral palsy, and his aging mother.

> **Subjects:** 1960s • ALA Notable Books • Art and Artists • Cornell, Joseph • Family Relationships—Mothers and Sons • Love Affairs • New York City

> **Now try:** Cornell is often compared to nineteenth-century French artist Henri de Toulouse-Lautrec, who also had a formidable mother; a short book including a biography of him and a number of his famous works is Arnold Matthias's *Henri de Toulouse-Lautrec, 1864–1901: The Theatre of Life*, which is a volume in Taschen's <u>Basic Art</u> series (titles in the series include works on Marc Chagall, Vincent Van Gogh, and Edward Hopper). Cornell was a contemporary of numerous cultural icons such as Andy Warhol (Steven Watson's 2003 *Factory Made: Warhol and the Sixties* describes his most famous artistic period) and dated Susan Sontag (whose volume of essays regarding art and culture, *Against Interpretation*, also became a classic of the era). Jean Nathan's debut book *The Secret Life of the Lonely Doll: The Search for Dare Wright* sympathetically tells the life story of photographer, model, and author Dare Wright, whose children's book *The Lonely Doll* is a cult classic.

Wilson, Emily Herring.

No One Gardens Alone: A Life of Elizabeth Lawrence. Boston: Beacon Press, 2004. 334pp. ISBN 080708560X.

Herring has written a beautifully crafted biography of gardener extraordinaire and garden columnist and poet Elizabeth Lawrence. Although her name might not be very well known, this personal biography offers information regarding not only Lawrence's passion for gardening but also her heartfelt relationships with her friends, family, and her one true (but thwarted) love. Any reader who is interested in the story of an independent, successful, and personable woman will be well served by this one.

> **Subjects:** Family Relationships • Gardening • Gentle Reads • Lawrence, Elizabeth • Literary Lives • Love Affairs • Women's Contributions

> **Now try:** Readers interested in Lawrence's life will want to read her essays (if they haven't already); two rich collections are *Through the Garden Gate* and *A Garden of One's Own*. Garden columnist and author Elisabeth Sheldon's collection of gardening essays, *Time and the Gardener: Writings on a Lifelong Passion*, may also appeal to these readers. Carol Shields's Pulitzer Prize–winning *The Stone Diaries* also offers a complex main female character, who incidentally also writes a gardening newspaper column.

Sports Biographies

Biographies about famous athletes and driven competitors offer many of the same characteristics as true adventure stories: The athlete often appears as a larger-than-life hero, and these life stories often include some elements of the subject's most exciting competitions or hardest fought contests. Therefore readers of true adventure sports stories might find much to interest them here, and vice versa.

The best sports writing is typically very action-oriented and stylistically distinctive, which seems to be a trait that also appears in these sports biographies. Mark Kriegel's *Namath* is written in short and hard-hitting chapters, seemingly designed to mimic Namath's agile athleticism and legendary ability to play through the pain; Geoffrey Ward's *Unforgivable Blackness: The Rise and Fall of Jack Johnson* is richly nuanced and as uncompromising as the great fighter himself.

Armstrong, Lance, with Sally Jenkins.

It's Not about the Bike: My Journey Back to Life. New York: Putnam, 2000 (New York: Berkley Books, 2001). 289pp. ISBN 0425179613.

Part cancer memoir, part bicycle racing adventure story, in this book seven-time Tour de France champion Lance Armstrong tells the story of his battle with testicular cancer, which struck when he was twenty-five. Although he offers biographical and childhood details, he admits that introspection and reminiscence are not what typically drives athletes like himself to perform, and most of the narrative is devoted to his racing career and the medical details of his condition. Some of the story is outdated (he writes about his relationship with his first wife, from whom he is now divorced, in the present tense), but Armstrong continues to be an omnipresent athlete, and the quickly paced text will appeal to both his fans and fans of sports in general.

> **Subjects:** Athletes • Autobiographies • Bicycling • Cancer • Family Relationships • Health Issues • Quick Reads • Sports

> **Now try:** Armstrong followed his hugely successful first memoir with a second, *Every Second Counts*, in which he relates the challenges he faced after overcoming cancer, winning the Tour de France, and becoming a huge celebrity. Inspiring though both Armstrong's books are, Arthur Ashe's memoir *Days of Grace*, in which the tennis great speaks candidly about his struggles against racism and AIDS (a disease he contracted from a blood transfusion he received during a 1983 bypass operation) set the bar high for inspirational sports memoirs.

Kriegel, Mark.

Namath: A Biography. New York, Viking, 2004. 512pp. ISBN 0670033294.

Kriegel has written a larger than life story to match his larger than life subject: New York Jets quarterback "Broadway" Joe Namath. From his Hungarian and working-class roots, Namath went on to lead his team to Super Bowl victory, personify his era of flashy hustling, help top athletes obtain more control over their salaries, and persevere through various personal problems and severe physical pain to play the game he loved. In chapters that are rarely longer than five pages, Kriegel tells a life's story in breathless sports reporting form, without sugarcoating his subject.

> **Subjects:** 1970s • Alcoholism • Athletes • Family Relationships • Football • Love and Dating • Namath, Joe • Quick Reads • Sports

> **Now try:** Sportswriter Terry Pluto has written a biography of the entire 1964 Cleveland Browns team in the same punchy style, called *When All the World Was Browns Town: Cleveland's Browns and the Championship Season of '64*. Bill Zehme's *The Way You Wear Your Hat: Frank Sinatra and the Lost Art of Livin'*, Nick Tosches's *The Devil and Sonny Liston,* and James Dodson's *Ben Hogan: An American Life* all capture the larger-than-life auras of their title characters, who are similar to Namath in their cultural cachet. For readers who want a bit more weighty and investigative text,

David Halberstam's *Playing for Keeps: Michael Jordan and the World He Made* might also be a valid read-alike suggestion.

Stump, Al.

***Cobb: A Biography*.** Chapel Hill, N.C.: Algonquin Books of Chapel Hill, 1994. 436pp. ISBN 0945575645.

Eventually made into a movie of the same name, Stump's biography relates the life story of one of baseball's greatest players, who, according to many of the details found in Stump's account, also happened to be one of the least likable athletes around. The story behind the story is every bit as complex as Cobb himself; Stump was originally hired by Cobb to collaborate on his autobiography, and the result, *My Life in Baseball: The True Record* (1961) was widely regarded as a sanitized and inaccurate work. In addition to telling the details of Cobb's life and baseball exploits, in this volume Stump also tells the story of the contentious time he spent with Cobb during the earlier book project.

Subjects: Alcoholism • Athletes • Baseball • Classics • Cobb, Ty • Investigative Stories • Sports

Now try: Baseball fans are not a group of readers who suffer from a lack of available titles; consider offering Robert W. Creamer's *Babe: The Legend Comes to Life*, Leigh Montville's *Ted Williams: The Biography of an American Hero*, Jonathan Eig's *Luckiest Man: The Life and Death of Lou Gehrig*, or Richard Ben Cramer's *Joe DiMaggio: The Hero's Life*.

Ward, Geoffrey C.

***Unforgivable Blackness: The Rise and Fall of Jack Johnson*.** New York: Knopf, 2004. 492pp. ISBN 0375415327.

Jack Johnson, the first African American heavyweight boxing champion, was as well known for his interpersonal relationships and his flamboyant personality as for his prowess in the ring. Ward does a substantive job, detailing the champion's numerous bouts, his personal life, and the many challenges he faced as a black man in America at the turn of the twentieth century.

Subjects: African Americans • American History • Athletes • Boxing • Marriage • Racism • Sports

Now try: Jack Johnson set the historical biography precedent for another great champion, Muhammad Ali, and David Remnick's *King of the World: Muhammad Ali and the Rise of an American Hero* might also appeal to these readers. Other athletes who are famous not only for their skills and sportsmanship but also for their roles in helping to integrate sports events include Jackie Robinson and Arthur Ashe; readers might enjoy Sharon Robinson's *Stealing Home: An Intimate Family Portrait* or *Days of Grace*, Ashe's autobiography.

Outstanding in Their Fields:
Other Professional Biographies

We're all familiar with historical figures who are best known for their career and work accomplishments. Individualistic, confident, unique, and bold, some people quite simply seem born to lead the way in their chosen fields. The books in this section, like the majority of biographies, derive their appeal from character development, but also add elements of adventure, combined with the historical thrill of being "first": first to fly across the Atlantic alone (*Lindbergh*), first prison warden to protest the use of capital punishment (*Miracle at Sing Sing*), first American to master French cooking and make its preparation feasible for an entire nation of home cooks *(Appetite for Life)*; the list goes on and on. They may also appeal (and vice versa) to fans of the "All in a Day's Work: Profession Memoirs" subgenre of memoirs; often their character appeal is equaled by their author's use of "inside look" details about their work.

These stories also tend to be on the lengthy side but can often be read more quickly due to their authors' increased attention to the suspenseful storytelling of their subjects' adventurous exploits, as well as their characters' involvement in a variety of fields.

Berg, A. Scott.

Lindbergh. New York: Putnam, 1998 (New York: Berkley Books, 1999). 628pp. ISBN 0425170411.

As no-nonsense and straightforward as its stark one-word title implies, Berg's massive biography of flight pioneer, father of the tiny victim of the kidnapping "Crime of the Century," controversial World War II isolationist, and medical researcher Charles Lindbergh is impressive in its coverage of a complex and frenetic character. Although he was the first writer to have unrestricted access to Lindbergh's personal files, as well as to many of Lindbergh's family members and his wife, Berg never allows personal or relationship details to overshadow accounts of Lindbergh's work and drive, which seems ironically fitting due to the main character's lifelong desire for privacy.

Subjects: ALA Notable Books • American History • Aviation • Epic Reads • Family Relationships • Lindbergh, Charles • Professions • Pulitzer Prize Winners • World War II

Now try: Readers who enjoy this weighty biography might also enjoy the classic work of nonfiction by Lindbergh himself, *The Spirit of St. Louis*, for which he won the 1953 Pulitzer Prize (if they haven't already read it). Librarians might also be able to parlay readers' interest in pioneers of aviation to either Susan Butler's *East to the Dawn: The Life of Amelia Earhart* or Donald L. Barlett's *Howard Hughes: His Life & Madness*. A. Scott Berg is a prolific biographer of influential figures in American culture; readers who enjoy his huge biography of Lindbergh might enjoy his similarly comprehensive *Goldwyn: A Biography* or *Max Perkins: Editor of Genius*.

Blumenthal, Ralph.

Miracle at Sing Sing: How One Man Transformed the Lives of America's Most Dangerous Prisoners. New York: St. Martin's Press, 2004. 303pp. ISBN 0312308914.

Blumenthal narrates the story of Lewis Lawes, warden at New York's notorious Sing Sing Prison from 1920 to 1942, with much admiration and in quick, novelistic chapters. Warden, family man, voice for prison reform, and anti-capital punishment advocate, Lawes was indeed a unique prison administrator who strove to combine

discipline with kindness and had to reconcile the state's punitive requirements with his own methods and beliefs.

Subjects: American History • Capital Punishment • Great Depression •
Lawes, Lewis • New York • Prisons • Professions • Work Relationships

Now try: *Sing Sing: The View from Within* (1972), edited by Steven Schoen,
is an older book, but that doesn't take away its striking visual impact: Filled
with photographs taken by the inmates, it provides some context for
Blumenthal's stunning biography. Richard Moran's fascinating business
and cultural history of the first electric chair and the roles played by two
business leaders, Thomas Edison and George Westinghouse, is a similarly
compelling and character-driven narrative that provides a different perspective on the many different aspects of crime and punishment (although the author is not subtle about his position on capital punishment); it is titled
*Executioner's Current: Thomas Edison, George Westinghouse, and the In-
vention of the Electric Chair.*

Fitch, Noël Riley.

Appetite for Life: The Biography of Julia Child. New York: Doubleday, 1997
(1999). 569pp. ISBN 0385493835.

Even those readers who have never seen a Julia Child cooking show or
used her famous *Mastering the Art of French Cooking* cookbook will find
much in this full and action-packed biography. Child began her professional career working for the OSS (the precursor of the CIA) in India and
China, where she met her husband. After their marriage and relocation to
France she learned how to cook. Later, with two friends and coauthors, she
created her seminal cookbook, the publication of which helped her gain
entrance to the world of television. Although this biography appeared before Child's death, the author had access to all of her letters and diaries and
uses them with great alacrity to tell a fascinating life story.

Subjects: Espionage • Food • France • Love and Dating • Marriage • Professions • Women's Contributions • Work Relationships

Now try: A small compilation by Child of her own behind-the-scenes
kitchen tips and techniques is *Julia's Kitchen Wisdom: Essential Techniques
and Recipes from a Lifetime of Cooking*; it may be a fun companion read to
either Child's biography or any of her hugely popular cookbooks. Julia
Child was credited for the quote, "In the beginning there was Beard," referring to cooking authority James Beard, and personally recommended Robert
Clark's *New York Times* Notable Book *The Solace of Food: A Life of James
Beard* on one of her appearances on *Good Morning America*. Memoirs by
two other famous chefs may also appeal to fans of Fitch's book; librarians
might consider offering either Jacques Pepin's *The Apprentice: My Life in
the Kitchen* (Pepin starred with Child in several of her later PBS series) or
Anthony Bourdain's extremely earthy *Kitchen Confidential: Adventures in
the Culinary Underbelly*. Although it is not a biography, readers interested in
cooking and food writing might also consider a collection of M. F. K.
Fisher's food essays, *The Measure of Her Powers: An M. F. K. Fisher
Reader*, as in introduction to her numerous other works. Likewise, the
"Foodie Memoirs" subgenre of the "Memoirs and Autobiography" chapter
may appeal to Child fans.

Rybczynski, Witold.

A Clearing in the Distance: Frederick Law Olmsted and America in the Nineteenth Century. New York: Scribner, 1999 (New York: Simon & Schuster, 2000). 480pp. ISBN 0684865750.

Former architect Rybczynski gives equal space to both Olmsted's personal life and his many very public achievements in the form of the famous parks he designed. Strictly chronological and a well-researched account of Olmsted's life and work (small hand-drawn diagrams of many of his most famous parks are included), the story also features small asides, in italics, that strive to make the subject more personal to the reader by exploring his inner thoughts and daily routines. The designer of Central Park, cofounder of *The Nation* magazine, and writer of many books, Olmsted was a true Renaissance man, and his biography is one that many readers might not know to look for by name but shouldn't miss.

Subjects: ALA Notable Books • American History • Gardening • New York City • Nineteenth Century • Olmsted, Frederick Law • Professions • Work Relationships

Now try: The beautifully illustrated book *Central Park: An American Masterpiece*, by Sara Cedar Miller, might prove to be a sensual reading companion to Rybczynski's biography of its designer. Rybczynski has also written numerous titles on urban design and the form and function of architecture; two of his most popular are *Looking Around: A Journey through Architecture* and *City Life*.

Slack, Charles.

Hetty: The Genius and Madness of America's First Female Tycoon. New York: Echo, 2004. 258pp. ISBN 006054256X.

This wonderfully spare and straightforward biography of Hetty Green, more famously known as "The Witch of Wall Street," who inherited a small fortune and proceeded to turn it into a large one through a combination of financial savvy and rather miserly saving, takes little time to tell the compelling story of the ancestry, childhood, life, and legacy of the woman who was worth $100 million when she died (her fortune then translates to roughly $1.6 billion in today's dollars). Its quick pace is complemented by its succinct but well-crafted language.

Subjects: American History • Atlantic Coast • Business • Family Relationships • Finance • Green, Hetty • Quick Reads

Now try: Christopher M. Byron's business-focused biography of the most infamous business woman of the latter twentieth century, *Martha, Inc.: The Incredible Story of Martha Stewart Living Omnimedia* is a similarly fast-paced story of a driven and savvy business woman. Mark Arax's and Rick Wartzman's well-received *The King of California: J. G. Boswell and the Making of a Secret American Empire* also combines personal and business biography, to great effect. Charles Slack is a skilled business biographer; he also wrote the favorably reviewed *Noble Obsession: Charles Goodyear, Thomas Hancock, and the Race to Unlock the Greatest Industrial Secret of the Nineteenth Century*.

Change-Makers and Activists

Readers often choose biographies not only to learn more about the accomplishments of or historical era of fascinating people or to draw comparisons between themselves and people they admire, but also to be inspired or to feel as though they are witnesses to feats of great courage or perseverance. These stories of individuals who stood up for what they believed to be right are often thrilling reads, both because they appeal to readers' sense of right and wrong and because they often tell compelling stories of obstacles overcome and rhetorical (rather than physical) conflicts resolved. In their emphasis on both character and story they may also provide suitable read-alikes for fans of the survival stories in the true adventure chapter or of "Overcoming Adversity" titles in the memoirs chapter.

Chadha, Yogesh.

Gandhi: A Life. New York: John Wiley, 1997. 546pp. ISBN 0471243787.

Yadha makes extensive use of Gandhi's own numerous writings and an impressive amount of research and citations to tell the story of Gandhi's nonviolent struggle to gain liberation for India. He also includes enough personal details of the activist's life to satisfy even the most curious readers seeking to know the "real" Gandhi.

Subjects: England • Epic Reads • Gandhi, Mahatma • Government • India • Spirituality

Now try: Readers may also want to try Gandhi's autobiography or the story of another activist who is typically linked with his country (South Africa), Nelson Mandela's *Long Walk to Freedom*. Another idea might be to peruse the list of Nobel Peace Prize winners at http://nobelprize.org/peace/laureates/index.html for biographies of individuals thus recognized.

Elshtain, Jean Bethke.

Jane Addams and the Dream of American Democracy: A Life. New York: Basic Books, 2002. 329pp. ISBN 0465019129.

Jane Addams, Nobel Prize winner and champion of the rights of the poor and immigrants, is best remembered for founding Hull House in Chicago, which became a major center of social activism and cultural programs. The focus of Elshtain's story is definitely on the work Addams performed rather than on delving into details of her personal life, but this is nonetheless a readable and comprehensive look at one of the early twentieth century's most formidable women.

Subjects: Addams, Jane • American History • Chicago • Immigration • Poverty • Women's Contributions

Now try: Jane Addams's autobiographical *Twenty Years at Hull House* might also appeal to these readers, as might Gioia Diliberto's *A Useful Woman: The Early Life of Jane Addams*, which tells the story of Addams the woman rather than of Addams the activist. Another activist whose name may be vaguely familiar to readers but not the frequent subject of biographers is union organizer and activist Cesar Chavez; the illustrated *The Fight in the*

Fields: Cesar Chavez and the Farmworkers Movement, by Susan Ferriss and Ricardo Sandoval, also includes numerous guest essays.

Mills, Kay.

This Little Light of Mine: The Life of Fannie Lou Hamer. New York: Dutton, 1993 (New York: Plume, 2003). 390pp. ISBN 0452270529.

Journalist Mills has produced a comprehensive and page-turning biography of Fannie Lou Hamer, who was born into a sharecropping family of twenty children in 1917 and became one of the most recognizable figures in the drive for civil rights, improved economic conditions for African Americans in the South, and greater representation in government. Sterilized without her knowledge or consent in 1961, and the routine victim of threats to her employment and life when she tried to register to vote, Hamer experienced firsthand some of the most brutal discriminatory practices. In a story rich with historical detail, Mills has created an overwhelmingly personal and intimate character portrait of a woman who stood up to fight because, in her own words, "she was sick and tired of being sick and tired."

> **Subjects:** African Americans • ALA Notable Books • American History • American South • Civil Rights • Hamer, Fannie Lou • Quick Reads • Racism • Women's Contributions

> **Now try:** ALA Notable *Sojourner Truth: A Life, a Symbol*, by Nell Irvin Painter, is similar in both subject matter and tone, although it is more scholarly and less forcefully written, and details a subject about whom biographical details are harder to find because she was born while slavery was still in place, a century earlier. Although it is written in a much different, question-and-answer style, Mills's *From Pocahontas to Power Suits: Everything You Need to Know about Women's History in America* is also enjoyably educational; she has a real knack for making lively stories out of little-studied historical lives and facts.

Oates, Stephen B.

Let the Trumpet Sound: A Life of Martin Luther King, Jr. New York: Harper & Row, 1982 (New York: HarperPerennial, 1994). 560pp. ISBN 006092473X.

When it was first published in 1982, Oates's biography was the first major one about King to be published in eleven years, and it relies heavily on many new materials that had just been made available (the Martin Luther King Collection at Boston University, for example) as well as on many interviews the author conducted with people who knew the civil rights leader. Although the text includes scholarly references, the style of the story is definitely literary and includes inner thoughts and feelings ascribed by the author to the principal characters, which make it a faster read.

> **Subjects:** 1960s • African Americans • American History • Civil Rights • Classics • Epic Reads • King, Martin Luther Jr. • Race Relations • Racism

> **Now try:** Although much less comprehensive, Marshall Frady's biography of King in the <u>Penguin Lives</u> series, *Martin Luther King, Jr.*, is certainly a serviceable work and might be more appealing to readers looking for a shorter read on the civil rights leader. Readers who are fascinated by the life and times of the civil rights leader might also be interested in Taylor Branch's massive and critically hailed two-volume history of King and the civil rights movement, the Pulitzer Prize–winning *Parting the Waters*

and *Pillar of Fire: America in the King Years, 1963–65*. The illustrated biography *Gandhi*, by Peter Rühe, also provides a look at a practitioner of nonviolent resistance.

X, Malcolm, as told to Alex Haley.

The Autobiography of Malcolm X. New York: Grove Press, 1965 (New York: Ballantine Books, 1999). 466pp. ISBN 0345350685.

A national best seller and named one of *Time* magazine's ten most important nonfiction books of the century, this autobiography reflects the method of its creation (a story told by the principal character) in its quick pace and wealth of personal detail. Malcolm X unsparingly relates the details of his childhood, criminal activities, adoption of Islam and involvement with Elijah Muhammad and the Nation of Islam (as well as his break with that organization), and ideas regarding racial protest and Black Power. The last chapters also provide a careful recounting of the circumstances surrounding his assassination in 1965.

Subjects: 1960s • African Americans • American History • Autobiographies • Civil Rights • Islam • Race Relations • Malcolm X

Now try: Malcolm X died before the Black Panther Party was founded, but its strident voice protesting the treatment of African Americans in American society would also occupy an important place in history; the story of that party and its founder and leaders is told in member Bobby Seale's *Seize the Time: The Story of the Black Panther Party and Huey P. Newton*. Although this autobiography was told to Alex Haley (and therefore really authored by Malcolm X), interested readers might also want to check out Haley's hugely popular (and sometimes controversial) personal family history, his epic *Roots: The Saga of an American Family*.

Historical Biography

Historical biographies are the stories of people who remain noteworthy for both their achievements and their staying power across the ages. It is also important to note that in addition to the appeal of their main characters, "time and place achieve a symbolic importance in a biography, as they do in a novel. In these biographies, the setting is another character of sorts; it provides hurdles the protagonist must overcome" (Carlson 1999, 13). Although all biographies are the personal histories of individuals, these in particular manage to tell individual (and, in several cases, group) stories in the context of broader historical narratives.

Readers who are interested in the life stories of historical figures might also want to consider trying titles in the "Caught in History's Web" section of the history chapter. The primary difference between the two is the level of historical detail provided; obviously, the titles selected for each section reflect the subjectivity of our choices, but for the most part, the titles below focus on the people and only secondarily offer details of the historical times in which they lived.

Burge, James.

Heloise & Abelard: A New Biography. San Francisco: HarperSanFrancisco, 2004. 319pp. ISBN 0060736631.

Burge tells yet again the story of Heloise and Abelard, arguably the Middle Ages' most famous lovers. After meeting in 1115, the two became lovers, but Heloise's jealous uncle discovered their love and ordered that Abelard be brutally castrated. After that Abelard, already a famous philosopher, exiled himself to become an itinerant monk and suggested that Heloise become a nun; for the rest of their lives they only communicated in a series of letters, eight of which were preserved and made their story famous. Burge offers a dual biography based on the recent discovery of a hundred more letters; although the book is somewhat scholarly in tone, the inclusion of sentiments from the letters and the sheer tragedy of the story helps to make it more personal and character-driven.

> **Subjects:** Abelard and Heloise • Family Relationships • Love Affairs • Religion • Twelfth Century

> **Now try:** The actual text of the lovers' letters (most of which aren't included in Burge's biography, for lack of space) is offered in a Penguin Books edition entitled *The Letters of Abelard and Heloise*. Marion Meade, who also wrote a biography about Dorothy Parker, wrote a fictional account of this love story in her 1979 novel *Stealing Heaven*. Fiona Maddock's biography of another progressive twelfth-century woman, *Hildegard of Bingen: The Woman of Her Age*, might also be suggested as a biography from the same era. Although set much earlier (the late fourth century), Philip Freeman's *St. Patrick of Ireland: A Biography*, explores the life of another religious trailblazer.

De Grazia, Sebastian.

Machiavelli in Hell. Princeton, N.J.: Princeton University Press, 1989 (New York: Vintage Books, 1994). 497pp. ISBN 0679743421.

A lyrical piece of prose in its own right, De Grazia's biography of Niccolò Machiavelli effortlessly intertwines literary criticism (of Machiavelli's many books and plays, among them *The Prince*), historical context, and personal details about Machiavelli's childhood and career, in this scholarly but beautifully readable story. De Grazia includes many of his subject's letters and writing, much of which he himself translated, to give this book a feel of the true beauty that comes with authenticity and extensive knowledge of one's subject matter.

> **Subjects:** Government • Italy • Literary Lives • Machiavelli, Niccolò • Pulitzer Prize Winners • Renaissance

> **Now try:** Readers interested in this time period and style of writing might also enjoy Harriet Rubin's *Dante in Love: The World's Greatest Poem and How It Made History*, which details Dante's exile from Florence and how it shaped his life and work. Readers who care more for De Grazia's irreverent tone than his subject matter might also be tempted by his other slightly off-kilter works of history: *A Country with No Name: Tales from the Constitution* (about the Founding Fathers' adherence, or, more properly, their lack thereof, to the document they created) or *Of Time, Work, and Leisure* (about exactly what the title states).

Dunn, Jane.

Elizabeth & Mary: Cousins, Rivals, Queens. New York: Knopf, 2004 (New York: Vintage Books, 2005). 453pp. ISBN 0375708200.

This parallel examination of two very different queens who ruled neighboring nations in the 1500s will satisfy those readers who like history written with a bit of the flair of biography and biography tinged with a bit of history on many levels. Elizabeth, daughter of Henry VIII and longtime monarch of England, remained unmarried: her cousin, Mary, Queen of Scots, married three times in the hope of becoming ruler of all England. Dunn explores both the personalities of the two unique women as well as their relationship, as she tells the quickly paced story of their rivalry for the crown, to which they both had a legitimate claim.

Subjects: Biographies • Queen Elizabeth I • Europe • Family Relationships • Mary, Queen of Scots • Royalty • Sixteenth Century • Women's Contributions

Now try: David Starkey's biography of six of the most famous women in history, thanks to their husband's rather violent proclivities, *Six Wives: The Queens of Henry VIII,* might also appeal to Anglophile fans of history; it was also the subject of a multipart PBS documentary. Fiona Buckley's Elizabethan era mystery novels, including *The Robsart Mystery* and *To Shield the Queen*, feature a main character who is a confidant to the queen, and may also appeal to history readers.

Greenblatt, Stephen J.

Will in the World: How Shakespeare Became Shakespeare. New York: Norton, 2004. 430pp. ISBN 0393050572.

Greenblatt acknowledges early on in his narrative that very little quantifiable and verifiable information is available about the "real" Shakespeare; nevertheless he speculates about the bard's life and personality by using and quoting from the literature attributed to him as a true primary source. Greenblatt also provides a healthy dose of details about the daily lives of not only Shakespeare but all residents of sixteenth- and seventeenth-century England.

Subjects: Drama • England • Literary Lives • Shakespeare, William • Sixteenth Century

Now try: Of course, any of the plays or sonnets of Shakespeare might provide enjoyable further reading for fans of Greenblatt's work. Shakespeare's contemporary, Christopher Marlowe, is also the subject of a comprehensive work of biography by David Riggs, *The World of Christopher Marlowe.*

Herman, Eleanor.

Sex with Kings: 500 Years of Adultery, Power, Rivalry, and Revenge. New York: Morrow, 2004 (New York: HarperCollins, 2005). 320pp. ISBN 0060585447.

This history of Europe's monarchs and the societies over which they ruled is told from the perspectives of their mistresses and queens. The narrative here is not story-driven or chronological, but rather ordered thematically according to the personalities of the women portrayed. The many abilities of history's regal mistresses include those they employed in the bedroom, in the political intrigues of their courts, and of course in their friendships with their royal lovers. Herman does a good job of quickly placing the women she describes in their historical context and then moving on to their fascinating personal attributes and stories.

Subjects: Adultery • Europe • Government • Royalty • Sexuality • Women's Contributions

Now try: Readers who particularly enjoy stories about strong-willed women in history might also enjoy *The Affair of the Poisons*, by Anne Somerset, or Katie Hickman's more chronological study, *Courtesans: Money, Sex, and Fame in the Nineteenth Century*. Readers who aren't particularly fussy about the gender of the characters in their personality-driven history reading might also consider Ross King's recent ALA Notable Book *Michelangelo and the Pope's Ceiling*.

Nicholl, Charles.
Leonardo da Vinci: Flights of the Mind. New York: Viking Penguin, 2004. 622pp. ISBN 0670033456.

Epic in language, historical detail, and scope, this new biography of da Vinci, equally covering all portions of his life, spanning the years 1452 to 1519, might very well provide all the detail any reader could want about the scientist and artist whose name is on the tip of every fiction reader's tongue. Irreproachably researched and a serious work of scholarship, the book nonetheless achieves some lightness in tone when referring to some of da Vinci's more personal attributes.

Subjects: Art and Artists • da Vinci, Leonardo • Epic Reads • Fifteenth Century • Renaissance • Science

Now try: Readers who make it through Nicholl's impressively detailed biography might also want to peruse the illustrated *Leonardo da Vinci: The Complete Paintings*, edited by Pietro Marani. Da Vinci was an illegitimate child; the compelling life story of another illegitimate child is told in Dava Sobel's compelling biography of Maria Celeste Galilei, *Galileo's Daughter: A Historical Memoir of Science, Faith, and Love*, which is less exhaustive than Nicholl's work but provides a similarly rich portrait of life in the century after da Vinci's.

Stiles, T. J.
Jesse James: Last Rebel of the Civil War. New York: Knopf, 2002 (New York: Vintage Books, 2003). 510pp. ISBN 0375705589.

Stiles provides the usual life and times details about Jesse James but broadens the scope of his character study by speculating that his subject was more of a Confederate bushwhacker, still fighting to uphold the precepts of the South, than a free-wheeling Wild West outlaw. The author uses primary sources, quotes from witnesses to his many crimes, and many other historical details surrounding James's childhood experiences in 1850s and 1860s Missouri to back his speculations; this biography is considered a daring read largely due to the author's new speculations and is the most demanding read in this subgenre.

Subjects: ALA Notable Books • American History • American South • Civil War • Epic Reads • James, Jesse • Nineteenth Century • Revisionist Histories • True Crime

Now try: Stiles is also the editor of a series of illuminating and honest historical books based on primary documents, the <u>In Their Own Words</u> series from Berkley Publishing; those titles are (most recent first) *Founding Fathers*, *The Colonizers*, *Robber Barons and Radicals*, *Warriors and Pioneers*, and *Civil War Commanders*. Alice Kaplan's meaty biography of Nazi collaborator Robert Brasillach, another ALA Notable Book, looks at previously unexamined aspects of his life and politics in *The Collaborator: The Trial and Execution of Robert Brassilach*. Readers who find this rather revisionist history enlightening might also want to try some of the titles listed in the "New Perspectives" section of the history chapter; many of them feature slightly unorthodox theories about established historical events.

Winchester, Simon.

The Professor and the Madman: A Tale of Murder, Insanity, and the Making of the Oxford English Dictionary. New York: HarperCollins, 1998 (1999). 242pp. ISBN 0061030228.

Although technically a historical story about the creation of the *Oxford English Dictionary*, combined with true crime overtones in the account of a murder in 1850s London, Winchester's narrative includes enough biographical details of the three principal characters to make this book feel more like a group biography than a dry historical account of lexicography. The professor in question is James Murray, who led the group who created the dictionary and called for volunteers to submit word definitions, while the madman is the American Dr. W. C. Minor, a prodigious reader who was being held in a British asylum for shooting a man, and who contributed more than 10,000 definitions over the course of nearly two decades. Winchester's third character, the dictionary itself, is described with loving attention.

Subjects: England • Literary Lives • Nineteenth Century • Quick Reads • True Crime

Now try: As it is a sequel of sorts to this story, readers might also want to peruse Winchester's *The Meaning of Everything: The Story of the* Oxford English Dictionary, which provides even more detail on the huge and groundbreaking project. Erik Larson's *Devil in the White City: Murder, Magic, and Madness at the Fair That Changed America* contains more gory details than Winchester's book but is similar in its combination of true crime and historical narrative; the same goes for Simon Worrall's *The Poet and the Murderer: A True Crime Story of Literary Crime and the Art of Forgery.*

Better Together: "Buddy" and Group Bios

Referring to this subgenre as "Buddy Bios" may be controversial, since not all of the subjects of these titles could be considered "buddies" (but rather spouses, political helpmates, enemies, etc.), but let's face it, "Buddy Bios' is snappier than the heading "Group Bios." Quite simply, these books offer the character-driven stories of their multiple subjects, as well as the often compelling stories of their relationships and interactions with one another. As discussed in Suzanne Mantell's *Publishers*

Weekly article about the current surge in biography publishing, "Buddy Bios" are extremely popular with a wide variety of readers.

Chernow, Ron.

The House of Morgan: An American Banking Dynasty and the Rise of Modern Finance. New York: Atlantic Monthly Press, 1990 (New York: Grove Press, 2001). ISBN 0802138292.

Chernow brings the surprisingly readable style for which he is famous and critically lauded to this epic tale of four generations of the Morgan family, whose banking business shaped not only their lives but also American finance and the banking industry. The book is straightforwardly chronological and heavily researched and detailed, and his portrait of J. P. Morgan in particular is often referred to as the definitive personal and professional picture.

Subjects: American History • Business • Epic Reads • Family Relationships • Finance • Morgan, J. P. • National Book Award Winners

Now try: Chernow's ability to produce epic, well-received, and best-selling biographies of families and individuals is unprecedented; he is also the author of the vast (each weighs in at roughly 800 pages) personal and historical studies *The Warburgs: The Twentieth-Century Odyssey of a Remarkable Jewish Family* and *Titan: The Life of John D. Rockefeller, Sr.* (both of which were also ALA Notable Books).

Fleischner, Jennifer.

Mrs. Lincoln and Mrs. Keckly: The Remarkable Story of the Friendship between a First Lady and a Former Slave. New York: Broadway Books, 2003 (2004). 373pp. ISBN 0767902599.

Fleischner's book is a well-researched and clearly written biography of Mary Todd Lincoln and Elizabeth Keckly, although the subtitle is somewhat misleading in that it overstates the role of their relationship in the narrative as a whole. In the first half of the book the author provides straightforward biographical details about each of the principal characters, in alternating chapters, while the rest of the story does indeed follow the events of their acquaintance. Starting with their meeting when Mary retained Lizzy, who had previously purchased her own freedom from slavery, to be her dressmaker, the author details the growing closeness of their interactions with each other and Mary's growing dependence on Lizzy's solid advice and comfort during some of the most trying periods of her life as a president's wife and widow.

Subjects: American History • Buddy Bios • Family Relationships • Friendships • Keckly, Elizabeth • Lincoln, Mary Todd • Nineteenth Century • Slavery

Now try: Readers interested in both Lincolns and their interpersonal relationships might also want to consider David Herbert Donald's *"We Are Lincoln Men": Abraham Lincoln and His Friends*, or his *Lincoln at Home: Two Glimpses of Abraham Lincoln's Family Life,* as well as Doris Kearns Goodwin's *Team of Rivals: The Political Genius of Abraham Lincoln* (published in 2005).

Goodwin, Doris Kearns.

No Ordinary Time: Franklin and Eleanor Roosevelt: The Home Front in World War II. New York: Simon & Schuster, 1994 (1995). 759pp. ISBN 0684804484.

In telling the histories of the two principal characters, as well as detailing the dynamics of their relationships with each other and their various family members and friends, Goodwin strives to articulate how each affected the policies and politics of the country during the traumatic events of World War II. Although most of the narrative stays true to the subtitle and takes place from the start of the war through Franklin's death, the author also provides insights from the couple's childhoods and relationship to provide context for their achievements, which are presented in masterful prose and with a tone of reverence.

> **Subjects:** ALA Notable Books • American History • Buddy Bios • Family Relationships • Pulitzer Prize Winners • Roosevelt, Eleanor • Roosevelt, Franklin Delano • World War II

> **Now try:** Geoffrey C. Ward's National Book Critics Circle Award winner *A First-Class Temperament: The Emergence of Franklin Roosevelt*, as well as the ALA Notable Book and two-volume biography of Eleanor Roosevelt by Blanche Wiesen Cook (*Eleanor Roosevelt: 1884–1933* and *Eleanor Roosevelt: Volume 2, the Defining Years, 1933–1938*) will provide fans of Goodwin's double biography with even more details about the principal characters and their lives. Interestingly enough, David Oshinsky's medical history, *Polio: An American Story*, provides more details about Roosevelt's battle with polio and his spearheading of the fundraising campaign to fight it.

Meacham, Jon.

Franklin and Winston: An Intimate Portrait of an Epic Friendship. New York: Random House, 2003 (New York: Random House Trade Paperbacks, 2004). 490pp. ISBN 0812972821.

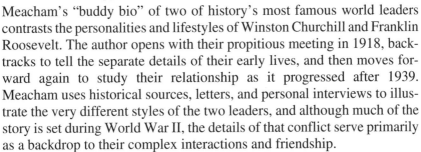

Meacham's "buddy bio" of two of history's most famous world leaders contrasts the personalities and lifestyles of Winston Churchill and Franklin Roosevelt. The author opens with their propitious meeting in 1918, backtracks to tell the separate details of their early lives, and then moves forward again to study their relationship as it progressed after 1939. Meacham uses historical sources, letters, and personal interviews to illustrate the very different styles of the two leaders, and although much of the story is set during World War II, the details of that conflict serve primarily as a backdrop to their complex interactions and friendship.

> **Subjects:** American History • Buddy Bios • Churchill, Winston • Friendships • Roosevelt, Franklin Delano • World Leaders • World War II

> **Now try:** Jack Matlock's recent *Reagan and Gorbachev: How the Cold War Ended* examines another international and political relationship and its impact on global history. Another important historical friendship is detailed in Mark Perry's *Grant and Twain: The Story of a Friendship That Changed America*. Although the four title characters were anything but friends, James Chace's group biography/history title *1912: Wilson, Roosevelt, Taft &*

Debs—The Election That Changed the Country also provides the human stories of four very different characters and their places in the history of early twentieth-century America. An earlier story of contention between political leaders is Thomas Fleming's *Duel: Alexander Hamilton, Aaron Burr, and the Future of America*. Although Paul Elie's *The Life You Save May Be Your Own* is not ostensibly about friendships, it does explore connections among four noteworthy literary figures—Dorothy Day, Walker Percy, Thomas Merton, and Flannery O'Connor—through the prism of their Catholicism.

Meyers, Jeffrey.

Inherited Risk: Errol and Sean Flynn in Hollywood and Vietnam. New York: Simon & Schuster, 2002. 368pp. ISBN 0743210905.

Meyers describes the biographical and adventurous parallels in the lives of father Errol and son Sean Flynn, the former a famous movie star and the latter a daring Vietnam War photographer who was last seen heading into Vietcong territory in 1970, at the age of twenty-nine. Both men had complicated relationships with their mothers and a similar need to seek out risks and adventure; before making his way to Hollywood, Errol lived the life of a gold prospector and diamond smuggler, while Sean spent much of his youth traveling and eventually studying to become a hunter and guide in Tanzania before he was sent to Vietnam. Although the biography is primarily devoted to Errol Flynn's life, the consideration of the two subjects together is what makes this a more complex biography.

Subjects: Buddy Bios • Family Relationships—Fathers and Sons • Flynn, Errol • Flynn, Sean • Mass Media • Movie Stars • Vietnam War

Now try: Another multiple-character biography that further examines the risks taken by Vietnam War correspondents is Richard Pyle's and Horst Faas's *Lost Over Laos: A True Story of Tragedy, Mystery, and Friendship*, which relates the details of the deaths of four combat journalists with whom the authors worked. Those readers more interested in the half of the story about Errol Flynn might also enjoy his frank and deliciously accurately titled autobiography, *My Wicked Wicked Ways: The Autobiography of Errol Flynn*. Those readers who enjoy Hollywood biographies might enjoy several others written by Meyers: *Gary Cooper: An American Hero* and *Bogart: A Life in Hollywood*, as well as several literary biographies of such luminaries as Edgar Allen Poe, F. Scott Fitzgerald, Somerset Maugham, and Ernest Hemingway.

Roberts, Cokie.

Founding Mothers: The Women Who Raised Our Nation. New York: William Morrow, 2004 (New York: Perennial, 2005). 359pp. ISBN 006009026X.

Roberts's collection of vignettes seeks to augment the collections of life stories of "the women who had the ears of the Founding Fathers." Each chapter details a different woman (Deborah Read Franklin and Abigail Smith Adams are two of the most prominent inclusions) and focuses on the details of her relationship with her corresponding husband or other more famous male relative rather than on chronological birth-to-death particulars. Although well researched, the book is informal in tone and includes among its appendixes recipes from the late eighteenth century.

Subjects: American History • Buddy Bios • Eighteenth Century • Essays • Family Relationships • Food • Marriage • Women's Contributions

Now try: Bonnie Angelo's *First Mothers: The Women Who Shaped the Presidents* is a much longer and meatier book than Roberts's but covers much the same subject and stylistic ground. In addition to its similar title and era, Joseph Ellis's *Founding Brothers: The Revolutionary Generation* might also provide a group biography reading experience that fans of Roberts's work would enjoy. Readers who find Roberts's focus on the feminine inspiring might also try her earlier *We Are Our Mothers' Daughters*, which poses the formidable question, "what is a woman's place?" and answers it with her own stories and those of women whom she has met over the years. Likewise, the personal insights into the lives of famous historical Americans gleaned from Dorie McCullough Lawson's (yes, she's the daughter of Pulitzer Prize winner David McCullough) collection *Posterity: Letters of Great Americans to Their Children*, might make that title a read-alike to Roberts's.

Schiff, Stacy.

Vera (Mrs. Vladimir Nabokov). New York: Random House, 1999 (New York: Modern Library, 2000). 456pp. ISBN 0375755349.

More a biography of the Nabokovs' fifty-two-year marriage than of Vera alone, Schiff's book tries to shine the spotlight on a woman who endeavored to present no public persona other than that of Mrs. Nabokov, the woman who existed to support and assist her author husband, who gained fame for his novel about a middle-aged man lusting after a prepubescent girl.

Subjects: ALA Notable Book • Buddy Bios • Literary Lives • Marriage • Nabokov, Vera • Nabokov, Vladimir • Pulitzer Prize Winners • Work Relationships

Now try: Readers drawn to Schiff's biography of Nabokov's wife might also consider Nabokov's, *Speak, Memory,* although it is much less linear than Schiff's work. Readers interested in literary figures' relationships might also consider Carole Seymour-Jones's *Painted Shadow: The Life of Vivienne Eliot, First Wife of T. S. Eliot, and the Long-Suppressed Truth about Her Influence on His Genius*, Hilary Spurling's *The Girl from the Fiction Department: A Portrait of Sonia Orwell*, Diane Wood Middlebrook's *Her Husband: Hughes and Plath, a Marriage*, or Julia Markus's *Dared and Done: The Marriage of Elizabeth Barrett and Robert Browning*.

Guilty Pleasures: Celebrities and Superstars

Not all biographies are prestigious prize winners or weighty tomes about an individual's place in history. Some of them, quite frankly, are just a lot of fun to read, and should be counted firmly among the ranks of those whopping good stories and fluffy novels that millions of readers annually carry to the beach with them. The appeal of these titles is first and foremost their subjects (cultural icons like Frank Sinatra, Princess Diana, Elvis Presley, and James Dean continue to make an appearance among biography titles, along with many, many others), but these titles also offer the closest thing to reading for the pleasure of escaping as any biographies will. Evocatively written, often focusing on the most salacious aspects of sometimes quite salacious characters, and not extensively footnoted, these books (and their authors, many of whom have multiple titles on their resume) simply provide a cracking good read, one that is often filled with all the "inside dirt" or gossip any celebrity-curious reader could desire. They offer a unique opportunity to offer readers who don't typically gravitate toward biographies to get their feet wet in the genre; I would not consider myself a reader of biographies per se, but I will admit I've read most things written about James Dean and Ewan McGregor, and heartily enjoyed myself while I did so.

Authors of celebrity and other biographies that constitute guilty pleasures who were not annotated for this selection include, but are not limited to, Jack Bass, Dominick Dunne, Marc Eliot, Joe Hyams, Chris Nickson, Donald Spoto, and Anthony Summers (just in case you're looking for some good starting places to collect guilty pleasure biography authors).

Foreman, Amanda.

Georgiana: Duchess of Devonshire. New York: Random House, 1998 (New York: Modern Library, 2001). 456pp. ISBN 0375753834.

A surprise best seller when it was first published (perhaps it was because Georgiana was a many-times-great aunt to the deceased Princess Diana), Foreman's extremely readable recounting of the life of Georgiana Spencer, who lived and romped through society in the eighteenth century, stands as an example of what the right biographer can do with the right subject. Chronologically ordered, the fascinating details of Georgiana's successful public and political life are matched by those of her often unhappy personal life, a major feature of which was her husband's long-time involvement with one of her best friends.

Subjects: Classics • Eighteenth Century • England • Family Relationships • Marriage • Spencer, Georgiana

Now try: Amanda Foreman also wrote the introduction for Nancy Mitford's biography of Louis XV's most famous mistress, *Madame de Pompadour.* Although more about a relationship than an individual, Benita Eisler's double biography of Frédéric Chopin and George Sand, *Chopin's Funeral,* is also noteworthy for its description of a forceful modern woman in the decidedly unmodern nineteenth century. If my guess is correct and some readers of *Georgiana* found it due to its connection to Princess Diana, librarians may wish to offer popular biographies of the Princess of Wales, such as Rosalind Coward's illustrated posthumous volume, *Diana: The Portrait,* Andrew Morton's *Diana: Her True Story, in Her Own Words*, or Sally Bedell Smith's *Diana in Search of Herself: Portrait of a Troubled Princess.*

Kelley, Kitty.

The Family: The Real Story of the Bush Family. New York: Doubleday, 2004. 736pp. ISBN 0385503245.

Kelley has often been derided for the rather intimate and unflattering nature of her celebrity biographies, and this one, her most recent, in its willingness to present rumor and the small talk of parties as fact, is quite similar to the rest of her titles. Kelley does indeed relate the history of the entire extended Bush clan, starting with Senator Prescott Bush and considering the family's role in American history and politics.

Subjects: Bush, George W. • Family Relationships • Government • Politics

Now try: Kelley is well known for her rather gossipy and "dishy" biographies of famous people, but that is what makes her a guilty pleasure and a famous name in her own right. Readers may also want to check out her previous works, including *The*

Royals, Jackie Oh!, Nancy Reagan: The Unauthorized Biography, or *His Way: An Unauthorized Biography of Frank Sinatra*.

Kolbert, Elizabeth.

The Prophet of Love and Other Tales of Power and Deceit. New York: Bloomsbury, 2004. 277pp. ISBN 1582344639.

These short but telling biographical sketches, or character profiles, feature a number of New York notables such as Hillary Clinton, Rudolph Giuliani, and Regis Philbin. Kolbert is a writer for *The New Yorker* magazine, and most of these pieces originally ran there; that does not, however, stop them from reading as quickly and as freshly as the very best gossipy tabloids.

Subjects: Essays • New York City • Politics • Quick Reads

Now try: Although much gentler and more quietly universal than Kolbert's personality pieces, *52 McGs: The Best Obituaries from Legendary* New York Times *Writer Robert McG. Thomas Jr.*, edited by Chris Calhoun, is a collection of obituaries of the less-than-famous but still noteworthy individuals whose lives Thomas memorialized through his obituary writing. Readers who enjoy the aura of New York City that pervades Kolbert's work might also like reading Calvin Trillin, who is better known for his food writing but has also written the essay collections *Too Soon to Tell* and *Uncivil Liberties*, as well as the very funny short novel *Tepper Isn't Going Out*.

Matera, Dary.

John Dillinger: The Life and Death of America's First Celebrity Criminal. New York: Carroll & Graf Publishers, 2004. 413pp. ISBN 0786713542.

Paced like an adventure story and written with the punchy detail of a true crime narrative, Matera's biography of the Depression's most famous bank robber, crime gang ringleader, and lover of "gun molls," John Dillinger, acknowledges as its source material the extensive research archives of former detective Joe Pinkston and historian Tom Smusyn. Although Matera does include standard biographical fare about Dillinger's childhood and other life experiences, the majority of the book relates the criminal activities of his gangs' thirteen-month crime spree (from May 1933 to July 1934) and the desperate efforts of law enforcement officials to catch him, and tells the stories of many of his criminal colleagues, love interests, and adversaries.

7

Subjects: American History • Celebrity Criminals • Dillinger, John • Gangsters • Great Depression • Quick Reads • True Crime

Now try: Fans of biographies of gangsters or "celebrity criminals" might also want to peruse many of the character-driven narratives annotated in the true crime chapter. Readers who enjoy Matera's fast-paced crime biography might also want to consider *My Life with Bonnie & Clyde*, written by Clyde's sister Blanche Caldwell Barrow and John Neal Phillips, or even the more broadly applicable collection *Gangsters and Outlaws of the 1930s: Landmarks of the Public Enemy Era*.

Zehme, Bill.

> ***The Way You Wear Your Hat: Frank Sinatra and the Lost Art of Livin'.*** New York: HarperCollins, 1997. 245pp. ISBN 006018289X.
>
> I was first exposed to this book by listening to it on tape, which I'm still convinced may be the best way to "read" it. Zehme, a journalist, provides a portrait of the snazzier aspects of Sinatra's personality (his loyalty to certain friends, his propensity to tip, or "duke," generously and often) in prose that's as clear and distinctive as the blue-eyed singer's song phrasings.
>
> > **Subjects:** 1950s • Music and Musicians • Quick Reads • Sinatra, Frank
> >
> > **Now try:** Those readers more interested in Frank Sinatra's connections to the mafia and less interested in his personal style might consider Anthony Summers's *Sinatra: The Life*. Nick Tosche's *The Devil and Sonny Liston* feels very similar; it's not an easy narrative to follow but it does make you feel you're right there in the action. Mark Kriegel's *Namath* is a jauntily written account of the life of a huge cultural icon, as is Joe Esposito and Elena Oumano's *Good Rockin' Tonight: Twenty Years on the Road and on the Town with Elvis.*

Consider Starting With . . .

> A small sampling of the most enduring and representative biographies is listed below.
>
> > Blumenthal, Ralph. *Miracle at Sing Sing: How One Man Transformed the Lives of America's Most Dangerous Prisoners.*
> >
> > Cohodas, Nadine. *Queen: The Life and Music of Dinah Washington.*
> >
> > Donald, David Herbert. *Lincoln.*
> >
> > Greenblatt, Stephen. *Will in the World.*
> >
> > Kriegel, Mark. *Namath: A Biography.*
> >
> > Meacham, Jon. *Franklin and Winston: An Intimate Portrait of an Epic Friendship.*
> >
> > Mills, Kay. *This Little Light of Mine: The Life of Fannie Lou Hamer.*
> >
> > Nasar, Sylvia. *A Beautiful Mind: The Life of Mathematical Genius and Nobel Laureate John Nash.*

Fiction Read-Alikes

> • **Ackroyd, Peter.** Ackroyd is an award-winning nonfiction biographer and has told the stories of such historical luminaries as Ezra Pound, T. S. Eliot, and Charles Dickens, but he is also an author of numerous works of literary fiction. His novel *The Last Testament of Oscar Wilde* purports to be that author's autobiography; *Chatterton* is based on the life of poet Thomas Chatterton; and his latest is *The Clerkenwell Tales*, which fleshes out the lives of the characters in Chaucer's *Canterbury Tales*.

- **Brooks, Geraldine.** Although Brooks won critical acclaim for her non-fiction *Nine Parts of Desire: The Hidden World of Islamic Women*, she has also produced two novels that provide biographical sketches of historical characters. *Year of Wonders* tells the story of a village afflicted by plague in seventeenth-century England, from the viewpoint of a housemaid who resides there, while her latest, *March: A Novel,* tells the story of Mr. March, the absent father in Louisa May Alcott's *Little Women*.

- **Chevalier, Tracy.** Chevalier once stated in an interview that she felt the character in her novel *Girl with a Pearl Earring* was "both universal and specific," which is a large part of the appeal of biographies. She is also the author of *Virgin Blue* and *Falling Angels*, which provides the details of the lives of two children in Victorian London.

- **Cunningham, Michael.** Cunningham's Pulitzer Prize–winning novel *The Hours* is actually three stories in one, exploring the lives of three women in different times and settings, one of whom is Virginia Woolf. Although I have not yet seen it, his 2005 novel, *Speciman Days*, is being hailed as a similar successor to the work, right down to the three characters whose stories are intertwined.

- **Doctorow, E. L.** Doctorow is known for using historical figures in his literary fiction titles; Julius and Ethel Rosenberg appear in *The Book of Daniel*, Emma Goldman and Harry Houdini in *Ragtime*, and Dutch Schultz in *Billy Bathgate*. Readers of history might enjoy him also; his novels are highly evocative of historical periods such as the Great Depression (*World's Fair*) and the latter part of the nineteenth century (*The Waterworks*).

- **Gregory, Philippa.** Gregory's historical novels, such as her recent *The Other Boleyn Girl,* imaginatively re-create the lives of historical figures (in this case, Anne Boleyn, her sister Mary, and their brother George). Other such novels include *The Queen's Fool* and *The Virgin's Lover* (about Queen Elizabeth).

- **Miller, Sue.** Miller's contemporary and character-driven stories, such as *The Good Mother*, *Family Pictures*, and *The World Below,* examine the complex emotions in love and family relationships, as well as the struggle for individuals to formulate their own identities.

- **Stone, Irving.** Stone has been called the "undisputed king of the literary genre he terms biographical novel" by reviewer Edwin McDowell of the *New York Times Book Review*. His works include *Lust for Life*, the fictionalized biography of Vincent van Gogh, as well as *The Agony and the Ecstasy* (about Michelangelo), *The Passions of the Mind* (about Sigmund Freud), and *The Origin* (about Charles Darwin).

- **Trevor, William.** Although Trevor does not fictionalize the lives of famous people, he does expend a tremendous amount of energy and tightly written prose exploring both the inner and social lives of his characters, particularly in novels such as *The Old Boys* and *Death in Summer*, as well as in his story collections, including *The Hill Bachelors* and *Nights at the Alexandra*.

- **Updike, John.** Over the course of three decades and four novels, Updike created and exposed the life of Harry "Rabbit" Angstrom, his most famous character, who was a high school sports star in the first title, *Rabbit, Run*, and passed through other stages in his life, including a work layoff and a failed marriage, before the eyes of Updike's readers in the sequels *Rabbit Redux*, *Rabbit Is Rich*, and *Rabbit at Rest*. The third book in the series, *Rabbit Is Rich*, won both the Pulitzer Prize and the National Book Award.

- **Vidal, Gore.** Vidal also appears as a fiction read-alike for history titles; his fictionalized biographies, including *Burr* and *Lincoln*, were huge best sellers.

Further Reading

Brian, Denis.

Fair Game: What Biographers Don't Tell You. Amherst: N.Y.: Prometheus Books, 1994. 373pp. ISBN 0879758996.

Through detailed profiles of the personalities and working styles of five famous biographers (Truman Capote, Kitty Kelley, Charles Higham, Bob Woodward, and Joe McGinniss), the author provides invaluable insight into different types of biography genres and why they are often so successful commercially, even when lambasted by book reviewers and often the subjects of the biographies themselves. The delicious irony inherent in delving into the lives of those writers who delve into the lives of their subjects makes this lively and important reading for librarians.

Parke, Catherine N.

Biography: Writing Lives. (Studies in Literary Themes and Genres series). New York: Twayne, 1996. 175pp. ISBN 0415938929.

Parke's slim but informative and readable study of biographies includes a short chronology, an introduction outlining the history of the genre and different methods of dividing biographies into taxonomies, as well as case studies of majority and minority biographies and a bibliography of selected biographies (although most of them are too old to appeal to many of our public library patrons).

Top North American Athletes of the Century. http://espn.go.com/sportscentury/athletes.html.

A valuable list of North American athletes in a wide variety of sports; this site can be particularly helpful for those individuals who don't closely follow sports news or history.

References

Birkerts, Sven. 1995. "Losing Ourselves in Biography." *Harper's Magazine* 290, no. 1738 (March): 24–26.

Bookwire.com. 2005. www.bookwire.com/bookwire/decadebookproduction.html (accessed April 21, 2005).

Carlson, Laurie Winn. 1999. "Snooping in the Past: Writing Historical Biographies." *The Writer* 112, no. 10 (October): 12–14.

Garraty, John A. 1957. *The Nature of Biography.* New York: Knopf.

Kendall, Paul Murray. 1985. *The Art of Biography.* New York: Norton.

Mantell, Suzanne. 2004. "This Is Your Life." *Publishers Weekly* 251, no. 22 (May 31).

Meyers, Jeffrey. 2002. "Johnson, Boswell & the Biographer's Quest." *The New Criteron* (November): 35–40.

Moore, Ellen, and Kira Stevens. 2004. *Good Books Lately: The One-Stop Resource for Book Groups and Other Greedy Readers.* New York: St. Martin's Griffin.

Oates, Stephen B. 1990. *Biography as History.* Waco, Tex.: Baylor University Press.

Parke, Catherine N. 1996. *Biography: Writing Lives.* (Studies in Literary Themes and Genres series). New York: Twayne.

7

Chapter 8

Memoirs and Autobiography

MEMOIRS

Definition of Memoirs

Memoirs are defined as narratives composed from personal experience. It's a straightforward and succinct definition, and it also answers the question of why memoir, perhaps more than any other nonfiction genre, has been the target of numerous accusations regarding the nature of its basis in fact or truth. Unlike history books, whose authors research primary and secondary documents to corroborate their version of events, or science books, in which theories and experiments are painstakingly described with as much accuracy as possible, memoirs are often based almost exclusively on personal experience, with "personal" denoting the experiences of, literally, one person.

At various times in their history memoirs have been considered either long-form personal (and often informal) essays or a category of autobiography. One of the most famous early examples of "memoirs" as autobiography was Ulysses S. Grant's popular *Personal Memoirs*. However, with fewer multivolume military or political "memoirs" being written or read, and a lack of publishing options for short-form literature of all types (short stories and essays among them), the book-length memoir has flourished as a published and recognized genre all its own. Such popular and best-selling authors as Augusten Burroughs, Ruth Reichl, David Sedaris, and Tobias Wolff have done much to advance the popularity and sales of these titles.

If we live in a golden age of creative and narrative nonfiction, then memoirs are the poster children of the movement. Perhaps because they are so pervasive, and so popular, they also tend to draw the most criticism for their authors' creative license, most often taken when re-creating scenes of dialogue or inner thoughts that were not recorded at the time and therefore cannot be verified. Very few memoir authors, unlike writers of "Investigative Stories," go around taperecording their lives or immediately commit their every thought to paper. They depend on memory, and memory can be a tricky thing. Many librarians, agreeing with the words of *Harper's* editor Virginia Heffernan, might well believe that "memoirs are straining the limits of what readers will accept as nonfiction" (quoted in Fitzgerald 2002, 16).

If the success of such representative titles as Anthony Bourdain's *Kitchen Confidential* and Tobias Wolff's *This Boy's Life* is any indication, many readers, librarians, and critics don't care a whole lot whether memoirs are the truth, the whole truth, and nothing but the truth. This lack of outrage may well be due to the particular appeal of memoir, which, as Charles Baxter has described it, may be that "every memoir argues that a personal memory is precious. No other artistic form makes that argument with the same specificity or urgency" (Baxter 1999, 151). Personal and remembered truths may be more subjective than "objectively" researched and completely factual ones, but apparently readers feel they are valid nonetheless.

Appeal of the Genre

Memoirs, like biographies, explore people's experiences and often all-too-human foibles and interactions with the world, in the immediate first-person voice; likewise, they tell stories, and often fascinating ones at that. These two factors are the secret of their widespread appeal. Unlike more straightforward works of history or biography, which often strive for some degree of objectivity, memoir authors tell a highly personal and often quickly paced story, and they tend to do so using stylized or unique or arresting prose. As Phillip Lopate described in the introduction to his collection of personal essays (a precursor to our current-day longer form memoirs), "so often the 'plot' of a personal essay, its drama, its suspense, consists in watching how far the essayist can drop past his or her psychic defenses toward deeper levels of honesty" (1995, xxv).

When memoirs are written by authors who also happen to describe their surroundings and environments, they can conceivably unite the entire range of appeals (character, story, language, setting) in a single work. They also offer an endless array of topics (coming-of-age, love, self-discovery, work experiences, etc.). No wonder they're fun to read; they have something for everyone. Readers who enjoy memoirs might also enjoy the "people stories" found in the biography and relationships chapters, as well as many of the more informal investigative writing titles in the "Immersion Journalism" and "Character Profiles" subgenres of that chapter. Their emphasis on the human reaction to experiences and change may also endear them to travel book readers, many of whom enjoy the personal asides and references of travel authors as they react to unfamiliar environments.

Organization of the Chapter

Perhaps the most familiar of all memoir forms is the "Coming-of-Age" theme, which is also used frequently in fiction, not to mention movies and television programs. This subgenre, which appears first, includes such titles as Jill Conway's *The Road to Coorain*, as well as Tobias Wolff's *This Boy's Life* (which, incidentally, was made into a critically acclaimed film starring Leonardo DiCaprio). Closely related to coming-of-age memoirs and included within that subgenre are "Self-Discovery" titles, which are similar in tone and mood but detail experiences other than those of a youth growing into adulthood. Another familiar category, "Overcoming Adversity" memoirs (also sometimes referred to as "Personal Recovery" titles), is listed next, and includes such often-requested titles as James Frey's excruciating *A Million Little Pieces*, Lucy Grealy's *Autobiography of a Face*, and Alice Sebold's brutal *Lucky*. Filled with painful, often shocking, details and stories, these books are not for the faint of heart, but do often leave their readers with an inspiring sense of the resiliency of human beings.

The next two subgenres, "The Immigrant Experience" and "Working Life Memoirs" (which includes the very popular "Foodie Memoirs"), also contain popular titles, grouped by their authors' experiences as immigrants and professionals, respectively. The final two categories, "Humorous Memoirs" and "Autobiography," are grouped according to their authors' writing styles and language skills, rather than by typical identity or experience exploration subjects.

Autobiographies in particular stand on their own more as a stylistic grouping and less as a true subgenre of memoirs. Although the distinctions between "Memoir" and "Autobiography" have always been somewhat indistinct, one of the easiest ways to differentiate between them is their scope. Although there are always exceptions to the rule, many memoir authors tend to tell stories of more specific experiences or eras in their lives, while many authors of autobiographies report their lives as a whole. "Autobiography" as a category is also noteworthy for its inclusion of authors who are not typically professional writers, but rather are famous or well-known individuals in their own right (exemplified by such titles as *My Life* by Bill Clinton or *If Chins Could Kill* by actor Bruce Campbell).

Coming-of-Age

"Coming-of-Age" is another of those literary terms that is bandied about quite frequently as a descriptor but is rarely defined or explored as a subject heading in its own right. For the most part, coming of age narratives reflect the growth of the author from childhood or adolescence into adulthood and often include descriptions of transforming experiences that aided in completing that transition. Or, as Patricia Hampl explains in her book about the craft of memoir, *I Could Tell You Stories*: "memoirs of childhood illustrate the fact that seeds planted in our youth have enormous impact on who we become as adults" (1999, 122).

Because they are often written many years after the experiences they cover happened, they are usually more leisurely in pace (which reflects the time spent by their authors to relive their memories) and depend less heavily on the appeal of story than many other and more immediately produced memoirs. However, what they lack in story appeal they more than make up for in character appeal, due to their focus on often highly private experiences, and language appeal, because their authors often tell the story from within some sort of reflective framework.

Arenas, Reinaldo.

> ***Before Night Falls.*** New York: Viking, 1993 (New York: Penguin Books, 2000). 317pp. ISBN 0140157654.
>
> > Arenas details his childhood and sexual coming-of-age as a gay male in short and highly descriptive chapters. His voice is forthright, and his portrait of Cuba during the Revolution is an important eyewitness account of a truly violent and volatile time; it concludes with his exile (achieved by admitting he was homosexual) to the United States during the Mariel boat lift in 1980.

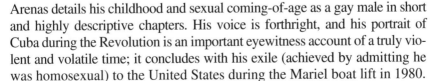

Subjects: ALA Notable Books • Classics • Coming-of-Age • Cuba • Homosexuality • Immigration • Love and Dating • Sexuality

Now try: Arenas was also an acclaimed novelist, and many of his novels are as relentlessly told as his memoir, including *Singing from the Well* and *Farewell to the Sea,* parts of which he wrote while in prison in Cuba. Peter Parker's biography of another famous author (Christopher Isherwood), *Isherwood: A Life Revealed,* uses diaries and letters to reconstruct the life of an author whose books often dealt with homosexual relationships and their place in society.

Barnes, Kim.

In the Wilderness: Coming of Age in Unknown Country. New York: Doubleday, 1996 (New York: Anchor Books, 1997). 257pp. ISBN 0385478216.

Barnes tells the story of her family's move from a relatively peaceful rural mining community to a more urban setting, where her parents became more entrenched in their newfound Pentecostal Christianity and eventually drove her to rebel during her high school years, when she became involved in a number of unhealthy relationships. Her writing is lyrical, which makes her story of being denied even the most harmless of worldly joys and experiences all the more unsettling.

Subjects: Coming-of-Age • Family Relationships • Religion • Rural Life

Now try: Both Dennis Covington's *Salvation on Sand Mountain: Snake-Handling and Redemption in Southern Appalachia* and Sheri Reynolds's novel *The Rapture of Canaan* examine extreme religiosity and its effect on family life and interpersonal relationships.

Benjamin, David.

The Life and Times of the Last Kid Picked. New York: Random House, 2002 (New York: Random House Trade Paperbacks, 2003). 271pp. ISBN 0812966589.

Raised in small-town Wisconsin, Benjamin relates the details of both his childhood in Tomah and his family's move to the south side of Madison, a city in the same state that was still small by city standards but immeasurably larger than his hometown. In addition to that culture shock, Benjamin also convincingly describes what life was like in the 1950s for kids from "broken" Catholic homes and offers numerous reminiscences about typically combative young boy friendships and the aura of complete separation between the worlds of "kid-dom" and adulthood. Readers who care about the level of truth in memoirs are warned that the author admits to changing many characters so that they wouldn't be recognizable to their real-life models, as well as to periodical exaggeration.

Subjects: 1950s • Coming of Age • Community Life • Friendships • Gentle Reads • Humor • Wisconsin

Now try: Jean Shepard's frank and hilarious collection of flashbacks to "kid-dom" in 1940s Indiana, *In God We Trust: All Others Pay Cash* (on which the popular movie *A Christmas Story* is based) is also a quick and humorous read about the wonders of BB guns and schoolyard dares. Although a bit more racy in subject and tone than Benjamin's story, Paul Feig's hilarious coming-of-age memoirs *Kick Me: Adventures in Adolescence* and *Superstud: Or How I Became a 24-Year-Old Virgin* provide another uniquely male viewpoint.

Brown, Chester.

I Never Liked You: A Comic Strip Narrative. Montreal: Drawn & Quarterly Publications, 1994 (2002). 185pp. ISBN 1896597149.

Brown relates the details of his childhood experiences with various neighborhood bullies, friends, and neighbor girls, with whom he had complicated adolescent relationships. Brown's extreme brevity, both in visuals and text, makes for a simultaneously quick but fulfilling graphic novel read.

> **Subjects:** Coming-of-Age • Family Relationships • Friendships • Graphic Novels • Love and Dating • Quick Reads

> **Now try:** Craig Thompson's *Blankets: An Illustrated Novel*, is fiction but is based on the author's own coming-of-age experiences in a fundamentalist Christian household; Adrian Tomine's collection of stories in the graphic novel *Summer Blonde* might also appeal to Brown's fans.

Conway, Jill Ker.

The Road from Coorain. New York: Vintage Books, 1989 (New York: Vintage Books, 1990). 238pp. ISBN 0679724362.

Conway, the first female president of Smith College, tells the story of her challenging childhood at Coorain, her family's farm in Australia, complete with her father's and brother's premature deaths and her mother's iron determination to both keep the farm and raise her family. In addition to descriptions of her relationship with her family, Conway also devotes a large portion of the narrative to her education, including her time at the University of Sydney.

> **Subjects:** Australia • Coming-of-Age • Education • Family Relationships • Rural Life

> **Now try:** Conway is a popular memoirist, and readers might want to try her other personal narratives, *True North: A Memoir* (the sequel to *The Road from Coorain*) and *A Woman's Education* (about her tenure as president of Smith College). Conway's writing style has also been compared to that of Annie Dillard; readers may wish to try that author's childhood memoir, *An American Childhood*. Another female memoirist with an international story to tell is Irish author Nuala O'Faolain; her *Are You Somebody: The Accidental Memoir of a Dublin Woman* received favorable reviews and was a big seller when it was first published. Books about other strong-willed female pioneers, such as Beryl Markham's *West with the Night* and Isak Dinesen's *Out of Africa*, may also appeal to this audience.

Frank, Anne.

Anne Frank: The Diary of a Young Girl (The Definitive Edition). Edited by Otto H. Frank and Mirjam Pressler. Garden City, N.Y.: Doubleday, 1952 (1995). 340pp. ISBN 038542695X.

A surprisingly honest and joyful account of an adolescent girl's thoughts and feelings in the midst of one of the worst periods in history, *The Diary of a Young Girl* was written by Frank over the course of more than two years, from June 12, 1942, to August 1, 1944. Primarily it describes her family's existence in an "Annex" to their father's business in Amsterdam, where they and another family and an elderly dentist hid from the Nazi authorities, but it is also a coming-of-age narrative about an impetuous and intelligent young girl who confided everything to her diary in the hope that it would be a "great source of comfort and support." The often routine and everyday details of the text are almost shocking when read with the realization that all who hid in the Annex, with the exception of Frank's father, eventually were discovered and lost their lives in concentration camps.

Subjects: Classics • Coming-of-Age • Diaries • Family Relationships • Friendships • Holocaust • Jews and Judaism • Sexuality • World War II

Now try: Carol Ann Lee's biography of Anne Frank's father, *The Hidden Life of Otto Frank*, is a well-researched and often surprising look at the complex life of a business-man caught in a bad historical moment; Lee previously wrote a biography of Anne, ti-tled *Roses from the Earth*. Although she never met Anne, Eva Schloss, herself a survivor of the Birkenau camp, became her posthumous stepsister when her mother married Otto Frank after the war; her memoir of camp life and the horrors of Nazi rule is titled *Eva's Story: A Survivor's Tale by the Step-Sister of Anne Frank*. Art Spiegelman's Pulitzer Prize–winning graphic novel *Maus* (annotated in the "His-tory's Darkest Hours" subgenre of the history chapter) might also make for tough but related reading to Anne Frank's story.

Hickam, Homer H., Jr.

Rocket Boys: A Memoir. New York: Delacorte Press, 1998 (New York: Delta, 2000). 368pp. ISBN 0385333218.

Hickam offers a book-length exploration of a turning point in one young boy's life, the story of his youthful infatuation with building rockets in the late 1950s and how that dream was encouraged by his mother, who viewed his scientific education and achievements as the best way for him to escape his coal-mining hometown, Coalwood, West Virginia. Hickam, who became an aerospace engineer with NASA, also details his often complex relationship with his mother, his brother, and particularly his father, a mine supervisor who both suffered the physical effects of coal dust and was also deeply proud of his labor in the mines and the community. Although the author notes that he took some liberties with the sequence of events and character details, readers will most likely forgive him in view of the poignant narrative he delivers.

Subjects: 1950s • Atlantic Coast • Coming-of-Age • Community Life • Education • Family Relationships • Physics • West Virginia

Now try: NASA scientist Hickam has made a second career out of memoir writing; he has also written books about the often provincial atmosphere of his hometown and his summer spent working with his coal mine supervisor father, *The Coalwood Way* and *Sky of Stone: A Memoir*. There's something of an underdog appeal about Hickam's boyhood struggles; it may seem like a leap, but fans of his work may also enjoy Laura Hillenbrand's *Seabiscuit: An American Legend* (*Rocket Boys* and *Seabiscuit* are two of my dad's favorite books even though their subjects vary widely), or even Tobias Wolff's memoir of growing up in the 1950s, *This Boy's Life: A Memoir*.

hooks, bell.

Bone Black: Memories of Girlhood. New York: Henry Holt, 1996. 183pp. ISBN 0805055126.

A highly stylized rendering of a young girl's memories of family, race, and education, hooks's slim volume says a lot in very few pages. As an African American female, hooks relates her memories of being considered a handful, a challenging child who wanted to think for herself, in a place and a time in which those traits were not encouraged. A rarity for a memoir because it alternates between first- and third-person narration (many chapters are entirely in the third person: "To her child mind old men were the only men of feeling"), the entire memoir still feels universal for its discussion of both gender and race expectations and experiences.

> **Subjects:** African Americans • Coming-of-Age • Quick Reads • Race Relations • Racism • Sexism

> **Now try:** hooks also wrote a memoir about her coming of age as a writer, *Wounds of Passion: A Writing Life.* Both Maya Angelou's autobiographies, starting with *I Know Why the Caged Bird Sings*, and Toni Morrison's works of fiction, particularly *The Bluest Eye* and *Song of Solomon,* may be related reads for this memoir. W. E. B. Du Bois's very readable classic *The Souls of Black Folk* might also appeal to fans of bell hooks.

Kimmel, Haven.

A Girl Named Zippy: Growing Up Small in Mooreland, Indiana. New York: Doubleday, 2001 (New York: Broadway Books, 2002). 282pp. ISBN 0767915054.

In language as unpretentious as the Midwest is generally assumed to be, Kimmel relates various stories of her youth in a small town (population 300) in the 1960s and 1970s. In short chapters, she weaves a tale of her status as the "Miracle Baby," who was born small and survived a serious infection at five months (but didn't speak for three years), as well as of her relationships with her family members and friends. Many readers will be able to read this book quickly, as its chapters are short and entertaining, and it is a gentle read.

8

> **Subjects:** 1960s • Coming-of-Age • Community Life • Family Relationships • Friendships • Gentle Reads • Indiana • Midwest

> **Now try:** Kimmel's first novel, *The Solace of Leaving Early*, is also set in a small town; her second, *Something Rising (Light and Swift),* is set in both small-town Indiana and New Orleans and features another strong main female character, who makes her living as a pool hustler. Fans of Kimmel's down-to-earth memoir may also enjoy Cynthia Kaplan's quick-reading collection of essays about her experiences growing up, from camp to romances to early professional life, *Why I'm Like This: True Stories.*

Klosterman, Chuck.

Fargo Rock City: A Heavy Metal Odyssey in Rural North Dakota. New York: Scribner, 2001 (2003). 272pp. ISBN 0743406567.

Raised in rural North Dakota, the author can pinpoint most of his formative teen experiences according to heavy metal music events, and he does so by relating big dates in headbanger history ("April 18, 1987: MTV premiers *Headbanger's Ball* at 11 P.M.") as well as events in his own music education ("In a CD review for my college newspaper, I call this record [Warrant's *Cherry Pie*] 'stellar.' It is three years before I am allowed to review another album."). Personable and extremely funny, Klosterman's memoir makes numerous pop culture references, and what's more, makes them enjoyable to read.

> **Subjects:** Coming-of-Age • Essays • Humor • Midwest • Music and Musicians • North Dakota • Pop Culture

> **Now try:** Klosterman is also the author of another pop culture manifesto/memoir, the catchingly titled *Sex, Drugs, and Cocoa Puffs: A Low Culture Manifesto.* Terry Pluto's memoir of his relationship with both his father and their shared love, the Cleveland Indians, makes for simultaneously humorous and poignant reading in *Our Tribe: A Baseball Memoir.* Nick Hornby's novel *High Fidelity*, about a thirty-something record store owner who loves music to nearly the exclusion of all else, may also appeal to Klosterman's readers.

McCarthy, Mary.

Memories of a Catholic Girlhood. New York: Harcourt Brace Jovanovich, 1957 (1998). 245pp. ISBN 0156586509.

McCarthy's exceptionally honest recollections of her childhood, spent variously with her parents, and, after their deaths, grandparents or aunts and uncles and in boarding schools, includes italicized interludes in which she discusses what may or may not be completely true in the preceding chapter of memories. Likewise, her extremely funny realizations about herself and how she came to know such adult phenomena as understanding when she was being laughed at, rather than with, or pretending to lose her faith to make waves in her convent school and then proceeding, through the charade, to really lose her faith, are all engagingly told with the flair of her exceptional talent as a fiction writer.

> **Subjects:** Classics • Coming-of-Age • Education • Family Relationships • Friendships • Literary Lives • Religion

> **Now try:** Virginia Woolf's extended essay about what women need to write fiction (money and a room of their own), *A Room of One's Own*, also examines the writer's life, but much of its appeal lies in its subtly humorous appeal for freedom for women similar to that enjoyed by men, and in Woolf's distinctive voice, which seems to be echoed in McCarthy's. Carol Brightman's biography of McCarthy, *Writing Dangerously: Mary McCarthy and Her World,* which won the National Book Critics Circle Award, may also appeal to her readers. Gambler Katy Lederer's family memoir, *Poker Face: A Girlhood among Gamblers*, is a similarly humorous, forthright, and well-written story of an offbeat but educational childhood and family life; Jeannette Walls's *Glass Castle: A Memoir* also explores a less than typical family life and childhood.

Selzer, Richard.

Down from Troy: A Doctor Comes of Age. New York: Morrow, 1992 (Boston: Back Bay Books, 1993). 300pp. ISBN 0316780650.

Selzer has a long history of producing readable works of nonfiction about the medical profession, and this more personal memoir is no exception. Starting with his childhood in the 1930s in the small town of Troy, New York, he describes his tightly knit but still independent-minded family, dwelling particularly on his parents' conflicting visions for his future: His mother wanted him to become a writer and his father, a doctor himself, wanted him to become a doctor. In long but lucid chapters he illuminates a childhood whose influences eventually led him to become both.

> **Subjects:** ALA Notable Books • Coming-of-Age • Family Relationships • Medicine • Professions

> **Now try:** Oliver Sacks's memoir of his boyhood love affair with chemistry, which slightly eased the terror of growing up during World War II in England, is titled *Uncle Tungsten: Memories of a Chemical Boyhood.* Loren Eiseley's sensory-rich memoir *The Night Country*, about his coming-of-age as an individual and a scientist, may also appeal to this group. Reporter and NPR *Weekend Edition* host Scott Simon's memoir, *Home and Away: Memoir of a Fan*, combines stories of his youth and career development as a journalist and sports fan.

Stringer, Lee.

Sleepaway School: Stories from a Boy's Life. New York: Seven Stories Press, 2004. 227pp. ISBN 1583224785.

The prequel to Stringer's critically acclaimed first memoir, *Grand Central Winter,* is a surprisingly quiet coming-of-age tale, considering that it details Stringer's childhood in the care of a single mother and then in a boarding school for at-risk kids. The chapters are short, and Stringer's style is unstructured without ever running the risk of becoming sloppy; his voice is stream-of-conscious but never too self-aware. His honest and childlike descriptions of family members and friends also add to the authentic feel of his tale.

> **Subjects:** Coming-of-Age • Education • Family Relationships • Friendships • Poverty • Quick Reads • Urban Life

 8

> **Now try:** Kemp Powers's *The Shooting: A Memoir*, opens with the accidental shooting, by the author, of one of his best friends when he was fourteen; his literary style is brief and punchy (making it similar to Lee's prose) and combines memories of his childhood with his adult experiences. Nathan McCall's *Makes Me Wanna Holler: A Young Black Man in America* is also a memoir that details the experience of growing up in the inner city. Interestingly, Kurt Vonnegut provided the foreword for Stringer's memoir; adventurous readers may also want to track down his memoirs, *Palm Sunday* and *Fates Worse Than Death*, both of which are subtitled "An Autobiographical Collage."

Webber, Thomas L.

Flying Over 96th Street: Memoir of an East Harlem White Boy. New York: Scribner, 2004. 273pp. ISBN 0743247507.

When the author was eight years old, his family moved to a newly built public housing project in East Harlem (the area above 96th Street in New York City), where his father, a minister, managed the East Harlem Protestant Parish. Webber tells an engaging coming-of-age story about both himself and his friends as well as for the civil rights movement; the book is set in the late 1950s and early 1960s.

Subjects: 1950s • Civil Rights • Coming-of-Age • Family Relationships • New York City • Race Relations • Religion • Urban Life

Now try: John Edgar Wideman's memoir of his childhood and his lifelong love affair with playground basketball, *Hoop Roots: Basketball, Race, and Love,* provides a complementary tale of boyhood experiences and racial issues. David Benjamin's *The Life and Times of the Last Kid Picked* is less racially charged but still rich in social class and monetary divides and may also appeal to these readers.

Wolff, Tobias.

This Boy's Life: A Memoir. New York: Atlantic Monthly Press, 1989 (New York: Grove Press, 1999). 288pp. ISBN 0802136680.

A national best seller and eventually a critically acclaimed movie by the same name, Wolff's memoir of life on the road with his divorced mother, separated from his brother and father, is by turns both gentle and frightening. Although he and his mother are close in their own way, Wolff's penchant for getting into trouble, motivated by reasons he can't verbalize, and his mother's marriage to a controlling man who becomes an abusive stepfather, create a childhood that is a less idyllic but still richly nuanced portrait of growing up in the 1950s.

Subjects: 1950s • Abuse • Classics • Coming-of-Age • Dysfunctional Families • Family Relationships—Mothers and Sons • Pacific Northwest

Now try: Richard Rhodes's memoir of his and his brother's abuse at the hands of their stepmother, *A Hole in the World: An American Boyhood,* may also appeal to fans of Wolff's writings, as might Dale Peck's "based on a true story" novel about his father's harsh upbringing, *What We Lost.* Augusten Burrough's coming-of-age memoir, *Running with Scissors* (annotated in the relationships chapter) also details a difficult family situation but is even darker in tone. Wolff himself is also a well-known short story and novel writer; fans of his memoir might want to try *In the Garden of the North American Martyrs,* which includes stories about a teenaged boy who lies compulsively, and *The Barracks Thief,* set at Fort Bragg, North Carolina. He is also the editor of the fabulous American Lives series from the University of Nebraska Press, which includes such titles as Laurie Alberts's exploration of lost love and memory, *Fault Line,* and Lee Martin's *Turning Bones.*

Self-Discovery: Explorations in Identity

Although similar enough in tone and format to coming-of-age memoirs to be listed as a sub-subgenres, "Self-Discovery" memoirs often take a step away from chronological retellings of the author's passage from childhood into adulthood. Instead, the authors of these memoirs examine their growing knowledge and acceptance of representative aspects of their truest selves and identities, such as their sexuality or their gender or racial identities. These memoirs are popular because they serve to make the personal universal; in telling their own stories, these authors also "reflect, in an important way, the lives of other men and women of [their] particular age, race, sexual orientation, or culture" (Hampl 1999, 111). Readers read, and love, these stories, because they help to provide insight into problems and issues that they might previously have believed were theirs to bear alone.

The subjects of the following memoirs vary widely, from sexual self-discovery (*Naked in the Promised Land* and *Becoming a Man*) to racial identification (*Colored People*) to giving up a child for adoption (*Surrendered Child*), but they all share lyrical and reflective writing styles.

Delany, Sarah, and A. Elizabeth (with Amy Hill Hearth).

Having Our Say: The Delany Sisters' First 100 Years. New York: Kodansha International, 1993 (New York: Dell, 1997). 239pp. ISBN 0385312520.

When journalist Amy Hill Hearth first met Sadie and Bessie Delany while on assignment for *The New York Times*, she knew that the recollections and stories of the sisters, ages 102 and 100, respectively, would make a fascinating book, and she was right. Although Hearth periodically interjects informative and historical chapters about the sisters' home state of North Carolina and their other family members, the majority of the story is told directly by the sisters as they describe their childhood and family experiences, their successful studies and careers, and their journey north to Harlem and subsequent lives in New York City. Although the text, like many oral histories, moves at an extremely readable clip, the true appeal here is the title two characters, who, although vastly different personalities, tell honest and complementary tales of hardships endured and joys shared.

> **Subjects:** African Americans • ALA Notable Books • American South • Family Relationships • Gentle Reads • Oral Histories • Quick Reads • Race Relations

> **Now try:** This book was so popular that an inspirational sequel, *The Delany Sisters' Book of Everyday Wisdom* (again coauthored with Amy Hill Hearth), was published in 1996. After her sister Bessie's death in 1995 at the age of 104, Sarah Delany wrote *On My Own at 107: Reflections on Life without Bessie.* Edward Hoagland's collection of essays, *Tigers & Ice: Reflections on Nature and Life,* written when he was in his sixties, also provides an older person's viewpoint (although not quite as old or as feisty as the Delany sisters').

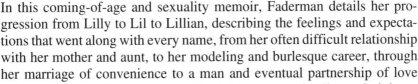

Faderman, Lillian.

Naked in the Promised Land: A Memoir. Boston: Houghton Mifflin, 2003. 356pp. ISBN 0618128751.

In this coming-of-age and sexuality memoir, Faderman details her progression from Lilly to Lil to Lillian, describing the feelings and expectations that went along with every name, from her often difficult relationship with her mother and aunt, to her modeling and burlesque career, through her marriage of convenience to a man and eventual partnership of love with a woman and her career as a feminist author and college administrator. Faderman's writing is clear and honest; interspersed throughout the narrative events of her memoir are italicized interludes providing exposition of her inner thoughts at various times in her life.

Subjects: ALA Notable Books • Dysfunctional Families • Family Relationships— Mothers and Daughters • Homosexuality • Love and Dating • Sexuality

Now try: Although framed by the story of the author's affair with a much older and more experienced man, Esmerelda Santiago's *The Turkish Lover* also explores a woman's coming-of-age, sexually and intellectually. Alison Rose's memoir of her complicated relationships with her family, lovers, and friends, *Better Than Sane: Tales from a Dangling Girl,* takes place in both California and New York City. Jane Juska's bright and brisk sexual coming-of-age memoir (even though the story starts during her sixty-seventh year), *A Round-Heeled Woman: My Late-Life Adventures in Sex and Romance,* may appeal to those readers of Faderman's memoir who wouldn't mind a bit of humor in their reading.

Gates, Henry Louis, Jr.

Colored People: A Memoir. New York: Knopf, 1994 (New York: Vintage Books, 1995). 216pp. ISBN 0679421793.

The title of Gates's memoir announces his intention to speak forthrightly about both his childhood experiences among his African American community in Piedmont, West Virginia, and the many words and attitudes he has spent his life exploring (his personal essay for his Yale application stated that "my grandfather was colored, my father was Negro, and I am black"). At turns humorous, at times poignant, and at others brutally and unsentimentally honest about the many effects, good and bad, of integration, Gates provides an active narrative.

Subjects: African Americans • ALA Notable Books • Essays • Quick Reads • Race Relations • Racism • West Virginia

Now try: Marvin V. Arnett's memoir of her childhood spent in Detroit, *Pieces from Life's Crazy Quilt,* is beautifully written and similarly forthright, about the author's experiences as an African American woman. Cornel West's beautifully written and concise volume of essays, *Race Matters,* was written to engage in what he describes as "a serious discussion of race." bell hooks also offers an examination of the related topics of race and class systems in America in her similarly brief *Where We Stand: Class Matters.* A number of titles, particularly those dealing with civil rights activists, in the "Change-Makers and Activists" subgenre of the biography chapter, might also appeal to Gates's readers.

McElmurray, Karen Salyer.

Surrendered Child: A Birth Mother's Journey. Athens: University of Georgia Press, 2004. 249pp. ISBN 1588180387.

McElmurray relates both straightforward memories of giving birth, getting married, and giving her child up for adoption when she was a young teenager and more reflective interludes dedicated to recapturing the less tangible feelings of loss and loneliness that plagued her for many years after the birth. An assistant professor of creative writing, McElmurray very clearly knows how to use language and has created a powerfully visceral narrative.

Subjects: Adoption • Family Relationships • Marriage • Mental Health • Parenting • Pregnancy

Now try: Many luminaries from the world of fiction provided blurbs for McElmurray's memoir, including Sheri Reynolds (*The Rapture of Canaan*), Lee Smith (*The Last Girls*), and Silas House (*Clay's Quilt*). McElmurray's reflective style is also vaguely reminiscent of that of Terry Tempest Williams; readers may want to try her nonfiction books *Red: Passion and Patience in the Desert* and *Refuge: An Unnatural History of Family and Place*. Readers who want a related read about a single mother's first year of learning how to raise her son might consider Anne Lamott's *Operating Instructions: A Journal of My Son's First Year*.

Monette, Paul.

Becoming a Man: Half a Life Story. New York: Harcourt Brace Jovanovich, 1992 (New York: Perennial Classics, 2004). 278pp. ISBN 0060595647.

Monette details his often angry struggle to accept and be accepted for his homosexuality in a hostile world. Opening with his first sexual encounter and his corresponding first perceived need to hide his sexuality, the author proceeds to describe the effects his sexuality has had on both his childhood and adult relationships, as well as his own gradual progress toward understanding himself. Described appropriately on the back cover as "searingly honest," this multiple award winner is often cited as a classic of coming-out literature.

> **Subjects:** AIDS • ALA Notable Books • Family Relationships • Health Issues • Homosexuality • Love and Dating • National Book Award Winners • Sexuality

> **Now try:** Monette's previous memoir, *Borrowed Time: An AIDS Memoir*, tells the story of the author's years spent caring for Roger Horwitz, his lover, who died from the disease; he also wrote several novels about AIDS, including *Afterlife* and *Halfway Home*. Noel Alumit's debut novel and 2003 winner of the Gay, Lesbian, & Bisexual Book Award, *Letters to Montgomery Clift* also describes a young man's sexual coming-of-age. Randy Shilts's classic investigative work, *And the Band Played On: Politics, People, and the AIDS Epidemic*, might also appeal to Monette's readers.

Wolff, Tobias.

In Pharaoh's Army: Memories of the Lost War. New York: Knopf, 1994 (New York: Vintage Books, 1995). 221pp. ISBN 0679760237.

Wolff's strangely gentle memoir of coming to terms with his approach to interpersonal relationships and difficult situations while serving as an officer during the Vietnam War is nonetheless very personal in its detailing of his inner suspicion that he's not really the type who should be training to be an officer in the military. For those readers who enjoy getting a sense of the inner bleakness that war experiences can cause, but who do not want to be told a lot of gory wartime details, this story of Wolff's training and service will do the job admirably.

> **Subjects:** ALA Notable Books • Friendships • Military • Vietnam War • War Stories • Work Relationships

> **Now try:** Both J. Glenn Gray's *The Warriors: Reflections on Men in Battle* and Colby Buzzell's *My War: Killing Time in Iraq* are unsettling accounts of

wartime service. Robert Graves's wrenching account of his military duty in World War I, *Good-Bye to All That*, is also widely recognized as a classic in the field of war memoirs. Prolific writer and World War II veteran Paul Fussell's memoir of his struggles with military authority and the horrors of war, *Doing Battle: The Making of a Skeptic*, closely resembles Wolff's story in tone, although it is broader in subject matter and includes Fussell's postwar life. Otto Apel Jr. and his son Pat Apel have crafted a memoir of Otto's experiences as a surgeon in the Korean War in *MASH: An Army Surgeon in Korea*. The former worked as a consultant on the popular television series, and his memoir is a concretely detailed account of military hospital work.

Overcoming Adversity

Closely related to the coming-of-age and self-discovery subgenres is "Overcoming Adversity." Also known as "Personal Triumph" books, or "Recovery" stories, these are narratives of horrendous personal hardships and other unfortunate events and problems, including but not limited to drug addiction, illnesses, disabilities, prejudice, and all manners of abuse. In addition to their often harsh stories, they often provide closure in the form of the authors' conquering their problems, living through hardships, or otherwise learning and growing as a person by surviving their tribulations. They are often quite graphic and may be overwhelming in both subject matter and level of detail for some readers. For fans of this subgenre, however, although these stories may be dark in tone and plot, they also often include a sense of the author's triumphing over adversity, making the stories compelling and inspiring (characteristics they they can rarely get enough of).

Many of these stories also feature in-depth examinations of interpersonal relationships, both healthy and not, and may also appeal to fans of the "Relationship Stories" genre. For instance, Mary Karr's best-selling family memoir, *The Liar's Club*, and Alexandra Fuller's *Don't Let's Go to the Dogs Tonight*, can be found there; likewise, readers who enjoy those and other relationship titles might find titles for further reading here.

Beals, Melba Pattillo.

Warriors Don't Cry: A Searing Memoir of the Battle to Integrate Little Rock's Central High. New York: Pocket Books, 1994 (New York: Washington Square Press, 1995). 312pp. ISBN 0671866397.

Beals, one of the original "Little Rock Nine" who sought to integrate Central High in Little Rock, Arkansas, and were able to do so only with the assistance of federal troops sent by President Eisenhower, provides an immediate and riveting account of the 1957 school year. In addition to relating the many difficulties her fellow eight students, as well as her family members, had to endure, Beals uses blunt prose and reminiscences drawn from her 1957 diary to flesh out the story of the terror she felt at the prospect of going to a school where she was often caught between the mob of white citizens protesting integration and the Arkansas National Guard at the school doors, dispatched by the governor to stop her from entering.

Subjects: 1950s • African Americans • ALA Notable Books • American South • Arkansas • Civil Rights • Education • Family Relationships • Integration • Race Relations

Now try: The illustrated book *A Life Is More Than a Moment: The Desegregation of Little Rock's Central High*, featuring the photographs of Will Counts and with essays from different points of view on the issue and events, is a similarly deeply personal and complementary read to Beals's first-person account. Although not a memoir, Kay Mills's fantastic and personal biography of pioneering civil rights activist Fannie Lou Hamer, *This Little Light of Mine: The Life of Fannie Lou Hamer* (annotated in the biography chapter) is also a compelling read.

Bragg, Rick.

All Over But the Shoutin'. New York: Pantheon Books, 1997 (New York: Vintage Books, 1998). 329pp. ISBN 0679774025.

Bragg, a Pulitzer Prize–winning journalist, relates the story of his childhood, paying particular attention to the debt he owes his strong-willed mother, who left his alcoholic father and struggled to raise three sons on welfare and her labor in the cotton fields of Alabama. Bragg also relates the story of his early years as a journalist and winning the Pulitzer Prize. Bragg tells both stories with almost painful honesty and an obviously heartfelt desire to both come to terms with his father's desertion of the family and his own desire to hide both his mother and his unsophisticated past from colleagues.

Subjects: ALA Notable Books • Alcoholism • American South • Classics • Family Relationships—Mothers and Sons • Journalism • Poverty

Now try: Braggs's subsequent book, *Ava's Man*, tells the story of Charlie Bundrum, his mother's father and his grandfather. Mary Karr's popular family memoir, *Liar's Club* (annotated in the relationships chapter), may also appeal to Bragg's fans. Another well-known writer, humorist Tony Hendra, relates the details of his close and transforming friendship with priest Joseph Warrilow in his best seller, *Father Joe: The Man Who Saved My Life*.

Du Bois, W. E. B.

The Souls of Black Folk. New York: Knopf, 1903 (New York: Modern Library, 2003). 268pp. ISBN 0375509119.

Although readers may be reluctant to choose a book first published in 1903 for their recreational reading, Du Bois's seemingly effortless prose should change their minds within a few pages (if they skip all the dryer introductory material that usually accompanies later and "critical" editions of the memoir). Du Bois creates, through his experiences and those of his contemporaries, a picture of African American life in a society not far removed from the Civil War. He leaves very little unspoken, and his first chapter starts immediately with his reaction to the question that he felt was posed all around and to him: "How does it feel to be a problem?"

Subjects: African Americans • American South • Classics • Epic Reads • Race Relations • Racism

Now try: Although Du Bois disagreed with many of his beliefs and recommendations, Booker T. Washington was also a formidable voice in favor of race empowerment, and if you can get readers to try Du Bois, you might offer Washington's *Up From Slavery*, another classic of American autobiography. Although set a hundred years earlier and more of a historical work than an autobiographical one (although it is based on diaries), Laurel Thatcher

Ulrich's *A Midwife's Tale: The Life of Martha Ballard, Based on Her Diary, 1785–1812*, may also appeal to readers who enjoy histories and life stories that are less mainstream.

Flynn, Nick.

Another Bullshit Night in Suck City. New York: Norton, 2004. 347pp. ISBN 0393051390.

Definitely a contender in the most eye-grabbing title category, Flynn's personal story of his work in a homeless shelter that his own father frequented often in the late 1980s definitely matches his title in weary honesty. The narrative can be rather disjointed, skipping around from flashbacks of Flynn's childhood to episodes at the shelter, although the author provides the date of each chapter's action in parentheses. Flynn's struggles with his father are combined with the story of his own personal struggles with alcoholism in this well-written but challenging memoir.

Subjects: Alcoholism • Family Relationships—Fathers and Sons • Mental Health • Poverty • Professions • Urban Life

Now try: Brad Land's melancholy *Goat* and Anna Cypra Oliver's *Assembling My Father: A Daughter's Detective Story* provide similar stories of young people struggling to come to terms with the actions of their family members. Although Antwone Quenton Fisher's father is physically absent from most of *Finding Fish: A Memoir*, Fisher begins his story by detailing his father's family history before explaining the details of his own birth and difficult childhood in foster care. Titles in the relationships chapter, such as Augusten Burroughs's *Running with Scissors*, might also appeal to these readers.

Frey, James.

A Million Little Pieces. New York: Nan A. Talese, 2003 (New York: Random House, 2004). 430pp. ISBN 1400031087.

Frey provides physically explicit recollections of his nearly fatal addiction to both crack and alcohol, as well as of his medical treatment for those addictions. The author has a very distinctive and somewhat disjointed prose style; it's effective enough to make the reader squirm uncomfortably when reading about mental challenges he faces, or the removal of his teeth (which were broken when he fell onto them face-first), during which he could not have painkillers because of the center's policy of allowing its patients no drugs.

Subjects: Alcoholism • Drug Addiction • Friendships • Health Issues • Medicine • Mental Health

Now try: Frey's follow-up to this memoir, *My Friend Leonard*, continues the story of his (and indeed, his friend Leonard's) life after drug addiction; those readers who enjoy Frey's style and dark humor might also enjoy works by Jim Knipfel, such as *Ruining It for Everybody*. Although less about his treatment than his alcoholism, Augusten Burroughs's *Dry: A Memoir* also admirably conveys a sense of the absolute rock bottom to which addiction can take a person.

Ginsberg, Debra.

Raising Blaze: Bringing up an Extraordinary Son in an Ordinary World. New York: HarperCollins, 2002. 292pp. ISBN 0060004320.

The author of two previous and favorably reviewed memoirs, Ginsberg applies both her honest humor and somewhat relentless sincerity to the subject of the diagnosis and management of her son Blaze's numerous and somewhat perplexing learning disabilities. Told chronologically as Blaze ages through elementary school and into seventh grade with varying levels of success at each step, the author is always capable of producing a lively narrative and vibrant character portraits, not only of herself and her son, but also of those involved with his education and her other (many, and close) family members.

> **Subjects:** Education • Family Relationships—Mothers and Sons • Health Issues • Humor • Medicine

> **Now try:** Although much darker in tone and subject matter, Michael Dorris's National Book Critics Circle Award–winning title *The Broken Cord: A Family's Ongoing Struggle with Fetal Alcohol Syndrome* details the many challenges facing children who suffer from the debilitating disease, theirs through no fault of their own, and the pain parents must endure while trying to help them. Paul Raeburn's *Acquainted with the Night: A Parent's Quest to Understand Depression and Bipolar Disorder in His Children* also considers the impact that mental illness can have on an entire family.

Grealy, Lucy.

Autobiography of a Face. Boston: Houghton Mifflin, 1994 (New York: Perennial, 2003). 236pp. ISBN 0060569662.

At the age of nine, Grealy fell prey to a cancer (Ewing's Sarcoma) that eventually claimed a third of her jaw and caused her to spend much of her life undergoing painful (and generally unsuccessful) reconstructive surgeries. In addition to her many physical discomforts, Grealy also suffered the mental anguish to be expected in an adolescent who, in her own words, felt "I was my face, I was ugliness." Grealy eventually found a supportive circle of friends at Sarah Lawrence University and the University of Iowa and achieved fame through her writing, but she also suffered from heroin addiction and continuing feelings of inadequacy; her memoir is hard to put down but can also be hard, with its many bleak moments, to read.

> **Subjects:** Drug Addiction • Cancer • Coming-of-Age • Friendships • Health Issues • Mental Health • Sexuality

> **Now try:** One of Grealy's closest friends, Ann Patchett, also a celebrated novelist, wrote a well-received account of their close but often difficult friendship, *Truth and Beauty: A Friendship*. Those readers interested in the deeper issues of appearance and inner strength might also find C. S. Lewis's mythical tale *Til We Have Faces* a strangely appropriate companion read. Grealy's use of language is also eerily reminiscent of that of fiction author Carol Shields, whose novel *Unless* might also appeal to readers who enjoy Grealy's memoir. Judith Moore also packs a lot of personal history and stories of struggles with her family and her weight into her small volume, *Fat Girl: A True Story.*

Hockenberry, John.

Moving Violations: War Zones, Wheelchairs, and Declarations of Independence. New York: Hyperion, 1995. 371pp. ISBN 0786881623.

At the age of nineteen, Hockenberry and three friends were in a car accident that left him a paraplegic. Refusing to be defined by his disability, Hockenberry went on to become a Peabody and Emmy Award–winning reporter for National Public Radio, covering such events as the first Gulf War and the Palestinian intifada. In addition to relating his thrilling journalistic escapades, the author reflects on the unique situation of his life and mobility, and there's a lot of dark humor in his constant referrals to himself as a "crip," or stories such as the time he found himself trapped under a former lover's bed while she made love with someone else.

> **Subjects:** Accidents • ALA Notable Books • Disabilities • Journalism • World Travel

> **Now try:** Cartoonist John Callahan has written a completely dark and thoroughly engaging autobiography about his life, *Don't Worry, He Won't Get Far on Foot*, including the accident that left him a quadriplegic and his struggle with alcoholism. Although less humorous, Rosellen Brown's powerful novel of a married couple learning to live with the woman's paralysis after her neck is broken in a boating accident, *Tender Mercies*, might also appeal to readers of Hockenberry's first-person narrative. Readers inspired by Hockenberry's positive narrative may also want to try Reynolds Price's inspirational ALA Notable Book, *A Whole New Life: An Illness and a Healing*, about his recovery from spinal cord cancer.

Kaysen, Susanna.

Girl, Interrupted. New York: Turtle Bay Books, 1993 (New York: Vintage Books, 1999). 168pp. ISBN 0679746048.

Kaysen spent nearly two years in McLean Hospital in her late teens, receiving treatment for what was diagnosed as borderline personality disorder. This is an extremely quick read, written in a stream of consciousness style with spare prose and short chapters, but in her descriptions of her experiences with health care professionals, medications, and other patients, Kaysen raises interesting questions about what it really means to be sane and to be treated by others as such.

> **Subjects:** Classics • Coming-of-Age • Friendships • Health Issues • Medicine • Mental Health • Quick Reads

> **Now try:** Although it is much different stylistically, readers interested in Kaysen's experiences in McLean Hospital might also be drawn to Alex Beam's empathetic history of the institution, *Gracefully Insane: The Rise and Fall of America's Premier Mental Hospital*. Kaysen also wrote novels (*Far Afield* and *Asa, As I Knew Him*) and another memoir about her ongoing health problems (*The Camera My Mother Gave Me*). Kaysen has often been compared to Sylvia Plath; readers may want to consider her classic novel about mental illness and feminine identity, *The Bell Jar*.

McBride, James.

The Color of Water: A Black Man's Tribute to His White Mother. New York: Riverhead Books, 1996 (2003). 314pp. ISBN 1573225789.

McBride tells about his upbringing by his white mother and his childhood interactions with eleven siblings, alternating with short chapters set in italics describing the often harsh childhood and family life of his mother, who was born Ruchel Dwajra Zylska in Poland in 1921. The author does a masterful job of blending the two to provide a full tribute to his mother's accomplishment in leaving the home of her Jewish family and abusive father to marry his father, Andrew McBride, while also portraying her feistiness and ability to survive in and love an African American community and neighborhood that was often unwilling to accept her. Although McBride's and his mother's childhood stories contribute to the page-turning nature of the story, the vivid portraits of their family members are what set this book apart.

> **Subjects:** African Americans • ALA Notable Books • Classics • Community Life • Family Relationships • Poverty • Race Relations • Urban Life

> **Now try:** Terry Ryan's simple but powerful (and often humorous) family memoir, *The Prize Winner of Defiance, Ohio: How My Mother Raised 10 Kids on 25 Words or Less*, is a testament to her mother's ability to win jingle-writing and other contests, even in the midst of raising a large family in the 1950s and maintaining peaceful relations with an alcoholic husband. Betty Smith's fiction classic about family relationships, *A Tree Grows in Brooklyn*, set around the turn of the last century, may also appeal to these readers.

Sebold, Alice.

Lucky. New York: Scribner, 1999 (Boston: Back Bay Books, 2002). 246pp. ISBN 0316096199.

The first time I picked up Sebold's memoir I couldn't make it through the first chapter, in which she describes in absolutely brutal and heartbreaking detail being raped in New York City's Central Park while she was a student at Syracuse University, as well as the attitudes of the police officers handling her case, who opined that she was "lucky" because, years before, a woman had been murdered and dismembered in the same spot where the rape took place. Best known for her fiction best seller *The Lovely Bones*, Sebold relates the story of trying to recover from the attack, as well as its effects on her new relationships and those with her family members. If readers can make it through the first chapter, they are guaranteed a memoir that is almost unbelievable in its bravery.

> **Subjects:** Drug Addiction • Family Relationships • Rape • Sexuality • True Crime

8

> **Now try:** Another shocking story of the havoc violence can wreak in one person's life is Jeanine Cummins's *A Rip in Heaven: A Memoir of Murder and Its Aftermath*, which describes the rapes and murders of the author's cousins, as well as the trauma caused when her other cousin was suspected (wrongly) of being their attacker. Lucy Grealy's *Autobiography of a Face* examines a woman's struggle with drug addiction and overcoming a completely unfair twist of fate.

The Immigrant Experience

The subgenre "Immigrant Experience" truly fits memoirs that combine nearly all of the appeal factors in single works or, if they don't, do a spectacular job of offering one or two of them. In a Marie Arana's *American Chica*, the author's description of her family members and their environments in both the United States and Puerto offers vivid character portraits and landscape descriptions, while Joseph Berger's *Displaced Persons* combines wonderfully sensual language and memories of his parents with the compelling story of their escape from Poland during World War II.

We are, for the most part, a nation of immigrants. That fact may also explain the appeal of these titles, which offer universal themes (such as "culture clash") that may already be familiar to many of us from our own family stories and traditions; even if we're not direct immigrants or that experience is far removed from us, the focus of these stories on individuals exploring their identities in foreign surroundings and dealing with their feelings of alienation might still be very familiar to us. Although the phrase "Immigrant Experience" may conjure up images of the nineteenth century and Ellis Island, it is important for the readers' advisor to remember that the vast majority of stories in this subgenre reflect more recent population shifts and trends, including Asian American and Hispanic American narratives.

Arana, Marie.

American Chica: Two Worlds, One Childhood. New York: Dial Press, 2001 (New York: Delta Trade Paperbacks, 2002). 309pp. ISBN 0385319630.

Arana explores her family background and childhood, set against the backdrop of both her father's Peruvian family and her mother's American one. In addition to trying to understand the dynamic of her parents' often turbulent marriage and long periods of separation, Arana tries to understand her own place in the world as a child of two very distinct cultures, through her interactions with relatives and friends in both worlds. The memoir is both reflective (Arana also details her research into the cruel Peruvian rubber baron Julio César Arana and her family's struggle to distance themselves from his name) and as easy to read as any coming-of-age novel.

Subjects: ALA Notable Books • Central America • Coming-of-Age • Culture Clash • Family Relationships • Immigration • Peru

Now try: Esmerelda Santiago's memoir *When I Was Puerto Rican* explores her experiences coming-of-age in two very different cultures and locations, Puerto Rico and New York City. Readers drawn to these memoirs might also enjoy Cristina Garcia's debut novel about three generations of women in a Cuban family, *Dreaming in Cuban*. Family relationships and culture clashes are also explored in Alexandra Fuller's *Don't Let's Go to the Dogs Tonight: An African Childhood.* Julia Alvarez's *How the Garcia Girls Lost Their Accents* or *The House on Mango Street* by Sandra Cisneros might also make good fiction read-alikes to Arana's memoir.

Berger, Joseph.

Displaced Persons: Growing up American after the Holocaust. New York: Scribner, 2001 (New York: Washington Square Press, 2002). 347pp. ISBN 0671027530.

Joseph Berger's personal story of a childhood spent in New York City in the 1940s is a multilayered memoir, examining both his youthful experiences in this country and the traumas endured by his parents, Holocaust survivors and Polish émigrés. Berger, an editor at *The New York Times*, writes in a beautifully lyrical and sensual style that transports the reader to the times and places he describes.

Subjects: 1940s • Culture Clash • Family Relationships • Holocaust • Immigration • Jews and Judaism • New York City • World War II

Now try: Sydney Stahl Weinberg's *The World of Our Mothers: The Lives of Jewish Immigrant Women* might also appeal to Berger's readers, as might Eva Hoffman's more scholarly but still personal *After Such Knowledge: Where Memory of the Holocaust Ends and History Begins.* Early memoirs of the European immigrant experience are harder to find, but tales of nineteenth- and early twentieth-century immigration are widespread in fiction; readers might try Ann Moore's *Leaving Ireland*, Willa Cather's *My Antonia*, or Henry Roth's *Call It Sleep*.

Hoffman, Eva.

Lost in Translation: A Life in a New Language. New York: Dutton, 1989 (New York: Penguin, 1990). 280pp. ISBN 0140127739.

Hoffman relates the details of her family's immigration to Vancouver from Poland in 1959. Focusing particularly on the loss of her native Polish language and her struggle to fit in with both her Canadian elementary classmates and eventually her fellow American students at college in Texas, Hoffman (currently a *New York Times Book Review* editor) provides an ironic but lyrical and beautifully written memoir of displacement.

> **Subjects:** Canada • Culture Clash • Education • Immigration • Jews and Judaism • Poland

> **Now try:** Francine du Plessix Gray's biography of her émigré parents and their triumphs in America, *Them: A Memoir of Parents*, is also a story with the tragic backdrop of Europe's turbulent twentieth-century history. Although less personal, Leila Ahmed's memoir of her Egyptian childhood and emigration to America, *A Border Passage: From Cairo to America—A Woman's Journey*, explores similarly weighty gender and religious identity issues.

Minatoya, Lydia.

Talking to High Monks in the Snow: An Asian American Odyssey. New York: HarperCollins, 1992 (New York: HarperPerennial, 1993). 269pp. ISBN 0060923725.

Minatoya combines reflection on the differences in her family's life in the Japanese and American cultures with more adventurous travel writing detailing her time spent living and working in China, Japan, and Nepal. She does describe her family ancestry but also provides lively anecdotes about many close friends and colleagues, and emerges as an engaging storyteller who successfully conveys her enthusiasm for understanding many different ways of living.

8

> **Subjects:** ALA Notable Books • Culture Clash • Friendships • Immigration • Japan • World Travel

> **Now try:** A combined memoir and scholarly history of Asian American immigration and cultural experiences in the United States is Helen Zia's personal and well-written *Asian American Dreams: The Emergence of an American People.* Although much less linear than Minatoya's narrative, Maxine Hong Kingston's sensually descriptive memoir of her childhood as a Chinese-American daughter of immigrants living in California, *Woman Warrior: Memoirs of a Girlhood Among Ghosts*, is particularly descriptive of the experience of women in both Chinese and immigrant culture. Sven

Birkerts's memoir *My Sky Blue Trades: Growing up Counter in a Contrary Time* reveals his struggles to reconcile the world of his Latvian immigrant parents with his own American one, as well as detailing his coming-of-age as an author.

Multicultural Experiences

As a subgenre of "Immigrant Experience" memoirs, the following "Multicultural Experiences" titles also deal with their authors' issues of identity and how lives are formed and affected by one's surroundings or setting. Some, like those titles found above, reflect "culture clash" issues created by long-term immigration (Ved Mehta describes his inability to understand his own immigrant parents' worldview when they visit his apartment in *The Red Letters*), while others reflect short-term travel or exploration experiences (Peter Hessler describes the volatile reactions of his Chinese students to what he perceives as harmless personal asides in *River Town*).

These titles are similar to the coming-of-age and self-discovery subgenre titles in that they provide a way for their readers to "identify with the subject to recapture heritage and history, to gain a sense of community and belonging, and to share the lives of individuals" (Dawson and Van Fleet 2004, 184–85). With their international and widely varied settings, they may also appeal to readers of travel genre books, particularly those who enjoy the "fish out of water" experiences often described "The Expatriate Life" travel subgenre titles.

Eire, Carlos.

Waiting for Snow in Havana: Confessions of a Cuban Boy. New York: Free Press, 2003 (2004). 390pp. ISBN 0743246411.

Although the back cover copy lauds this as a tale of a young Cuban boy who was exiled to America (one of 14,000 children in total) in 1962, it is much less a tale of two cultures or of forging a new life in a new country than that copy might lead one to believe. Instead, it is a very loosely structured but evocatively written account of Eire's memories of childhood and school in Cuba, as well as the relationships among himself, his parents (whom he often refers to as Louis XVI and Marie Antoinette, in homage to his father's belief in their reincarnation), his biological brother, and his adopted brother, whom their father trusted but who often betrayed that trust by attempting to molest the author and his other brother. There is no strict narrative structure, which some readers might find disconcerting, but all of the chapters, although varying stylistically, stand on their own as perfectly formed glimpses into a childhood spent on a beautiful but volatile and often violent island.

Subjects: Coming-of-Age • Cuba • Culture Clash • Family Relationships • Immigration • National Book Award Winners

Now try: It is set in a very different culture and on a different continent, but Li Cunxin's memoir of growing up during the Cultural Revolution in China, *Mao's Last Dancer*, is similar in its use of the insider's views about a totalitarian regime. Victor Villaseñor's latest memoir, *Burro Genius*, also relates a child's struggle with his racial heritage, as well as the learning disability that made his school experiences unhappy.

Hakakian, Roya.

Journey from the Land of No: A Girlhood Caught in Revolutionary Iran.
New York: Crown Publishers, 2004. 245pp. ISBN 1400046114.

Hakakian was twelve years old in 1979 when the Islamic Revolution
changed everything in her childhood home of Iran, first instilling a sense of
hope but eventually leading to her own disillusionment as her Jewish family felt compelled to emigrate to the United States. In addition to a firsthand view of the revolution, Hakakian also provides a narrative of her
family's history and strives to explain her continuing love for her homeland despite living among an American population that views Iran as either
hopelessly backward or adversely affected by U.S. policy toward it.

Subjects: Culture Clash • Family Relationships • Immigration • Iran • Jews
and Judaism • Religion

Now try: Ana Tortajada's *The Silenced Cry: One Woman's Diary of a Journey to Afghanistan* is less of a childhood memoir but provides an important
firsthand record of experiences in Afghanistan directly after the fall of the
Taliban in 2000. *Persepolis* also centers on the 1979 Revolution and is told
from a woman's point of view, in graphic novel form, while the viewpoint of
a woman who spent her formative years in both America and Iran is found in
Azadeh Moaveni's *Lipstick Jihad: A Memoir of Growing up Iranian in
America and American in Iran.*

Hessler, Peter.

River Town: Two Years on the Yangtze. New York: HarperCollins Publishers,
2001 (New York: Perennial, 2002). 402pp. ISBN 0060953748.

Hessler's memoir about teaching English literature at a college in Fuling,
China, in the early 1990s is a seamless blend of cultural memoir and Yangtze River travelogue. Stories about his students and his teaching experiences, many of which are told with understated humor, aappear in
alternating chapters, offset by his more descriptive chapters about the geography and culture of China in its post–Cultural Revolution restructuring.
The author's tone is offbeat, but the story is often quite touching in its
sincerity.

Subjects: ALA Notable Books • Books and Learning • China • Community
Life • Culture Clash • Education • Humor • Rivers • Travel

◼ 8

Now try: Dana Sachs's tale of her expatriate life in Vietnam, *The House on
Dream Street: Memoir of an American Woman in Vietnam*, also gives the
reader a deeper sense of what it is like to immerse oneself in a different culture and to fall in love with it. Also, much like Azar Nafisi in *Reading Lolita
in Tehran: A Memoir in Books*, Hessler has many opinions about the authors
and the works he assigns to his students, which has the effect of making the
reader of his story want to track down the fiction titles he mentions. *Ms.
Moffett's First Year*, set in America, provides a look into a teacher's often
surprising early-career experiences, and may appeal to those readers who are
most interested in Hessler's experiences as a teacher.

Mehta, Suketu.

Maximum City: Bombay Lost and Found. New York: Knopf, 2004. 542pp. ISBN 0375403728.

This beautifully written story of the author's love affair with his home city Bombay (Mumbai) provides a fully realized character portrait of the huge and complex city in effortless and flowing prose. Mehta frames his story of the city's history and current conditions in the context of a childhood spent in one of its neighborhoods, his family's emigration to America, and his return there as an adult with his wife and child, and his tone is both refreshingly lighthearted and sincere, but the story is truly driven by the author's descriptions of the experiences that are unique to Bombay. From the extreme population density to the bureaucratic nightmares facing every renter and homeowner, the school system to electoral politics, movies to terrorist incidents, Mehta provides a living, breathing evocation of the city.

> **Subjects:** Community Life • Culture Clash • Family Relationships • Immigration • India • Urban Life

> **Now try:** Although much shorter and written in more straightforward prose, George Sarrinikolaou's *Facing Athens: Encounters with the Modern City* also tells the story of a native returning to the city of his youth; Max Rodenbeck's *Cairo: The City Victorious* is also a longtime resident's look at a fascinating historical and cultural city. Readers who willing to try travel narratives might try Pico Iyer's rather sedately surreal collection *Sun after Dark: Flights into the Foreign* or Sarah MacDonald's slightly more irreverent *Holy Cow: An Indian Adventure*.

Mehta, Ved.

The Red Letters: My Father's Enchanted Period. New York: Nation Books, 2004. 190pp. ISBN 1560256281.

The eleventh and final installment in *New Yorker* writer Mehta's <u>Continents of Exile</u> series of memoirs detailing his family's history and relationships, this small and poetic volume focuses on his father's affair with a young woman in India, which was often conducted via "red letters." The love story is heartfelt, but Mehta also explores its hurtful effects on his parents' sixty-one-year marriage and on his mother in particular.

> **Subjects:** Culture Clash • Disabilities • Family Relationships • India • Love Affairs • Marriage • Quick Reads

> **Now try:** Mehta's writing is lyrical, and readers should be encouraged to read more volumes in this series, which hasn't received nearly enough exposure, starting with the memoirs *Daddyji* and *Mamaji*. Travel writing about India, such as Eric Newby's *Slowly Down the Ganges*, with its descriptions of the land and culture, may also appeal to vans of Mehta's short but evocative memoirs.

Nafisi, Azar.

Reading Lolita in Tehran: A Memoir in Books. New York: Random House, 2003 (2004). 356pp. ISBN 081297106X.

Nafisi recounts her experiences leading a literature class for women at her home in Tehran in the face of increasing vigilance regarding women and education at the hands of Iran's theocratic government. Over the course of several years, she and her students read and discussed a variety of classics such as Nabokov's *Lolita*, Fitzgerald's *The Great Gatsby*, James's *Daisy Miller*, and Austen's *Pride and Prejudice*, pondering their significance as works of art and as influences in their own lives. Although Nafisi and her husband eventually left Iran, this memoir explores her love for her homeland and her complex relationships with her individual students.

> **Subjects:** Book Sense Award Winners • Books and Learning • Education • Friendships • Iran • Women's Contributions

> **Now try:** Nafisi's book includes a plethora of related reading suggestions within its text; readers should be encouraged to follow up her book by reading Nabokov, Austen, Fitzgerald, and James. Eudora Welty's literary coming-of-age memoir, *One Writer's Beginnings* might also appeal to fans of Nafisi's story, as might Åsne Seierstad's investigative book about the power of books and learning in all cultures, *The Bookseller of Kabul*.

Working Life Memoirs

Ever go to a cocktail party or some other event where you didn't know many people? How many times were you asked, "So, what do you do?" This phenomenon provides a handy way to understand the popularity and staying power of memoirs focused on work and career.

Work memoirs address a huge part of our lives. Depending on what your patrons do, many will understand the frustration of often having to spend more time with their work colleagues than they do with their family members or friends, or spending more of their lives engaged in unpleasant or challenging work tasks than in recreational or leisure activities. Luckily, in addition to offering unique author voices and interesting, "behind the scenes" looks at a variety of professions, many of these stories include elements of humor. They also offer a range of language and subject matters; from Bourdain's and Ginsberg's (*Waiting*) honest and often quite earthy descriptions of the food and beverage industry to Edward Conlon's (*Blue Blood*) and Atul Gawande's (*Complications*) more subtle and reflective stories about their careers in law enforcement and medicine, respectively, librarians should be able to find titles here and in their collections that would address the professional lives of most of their patrons.

Although the style of the memoirs annotated in this section is often reminiscent of the that used by investigative and immersion journalists, particularly those works relating to work (Ehrenreich's *Nickel and Dimed*, Conover's *Newjack: Guarding Sing Sing*), they differ in that they are deeply personal stories, told by practitioners who are professionals in their described careers first, writers second.

Basbanes, Nicholas.

> ***Patience and Fortitude: A Roving Chronicle of Book People, Book Places, and Book Culture.*** New York: HarperCollins, 2001 (New York: Perennial, 2003). 636pp. ISBN 0060514469.

> The author's thoroughly engaging exploration of what it means to own, pursue, and love books, for both their intangible charms and their physical presence, is named for the lions that stand guard outside New York City's

Public Library. From the history of libraries to his encounters with "book people" (including readers, writers, booksellers, librarians, and editorial types), Basbanes provides a broad picture of the consumers and purveyors of all things literary.

Subjects: Books and Learning • Investigative Stories • Libraries • Travel

Now try: Basbanes gave us the word "bibliomania," as well as the defining work on the subject: *A Gentle Madness: Bibliophiles, Bibliomanes, and the Eternal Passion for Books* (1999), which is a must-read for all those who work with books, as is Paul Collins's *Sixpence House: Lost in a Town of Books*. Anyone who loves books will also enjoy the collection of book-related essays in *The Romance of the Book*, edited by Marshall Brooks, which covers such book world notables as Colette, Henry Miller, and Edgar Allan Poe, to name just a few. John Dunning's series of Cliff Janeway mysteries, which feature a main character who is a used and rare book dealer, might also appeal to the reader who loves books: *Booked to Die, The Bookman's Wake, The Bookman's Promise,* and *The Sign of the Book*.

Bourdain, Anthony.

Kitchen Confidential: Adventures in the Culinary Underbelly. New York: Bloomsbury, 2000 (New York: Ecco Press, 2000). 302pp. ISBN 0060934913.

Named after various courses of a meal, the sections in Bourdain's work memoir are a roughly chronological tale of his development as a chef (in "Appetizer" and "First Course" he details his early experiences with food, as well as his training at the Culinary Institute of America). Although the book is truly an enjoyable romp through a work life filled with many professional triumphs as well as many personal digressions (drug and alcohol use, numerous relationships), it is not for those who are at all squeamish about what and where they eat; Bourdain's use of the word "underbelly" is truly astute, considering his descriptions of what really goes on in busy restaurant kitchens.

Subjects: Food • Humor • Professions • Quick Reads • Work Relationships

Now try: Any of the titles listed in this chapter's "Foodie Memoirs" subgenre might appeal to Bourdain's readers, but advisors are reminded that most are comparatively gentle compared with Bourdain's no-holds-barred honesty in storytelling. Readers interested in kitchen tales of all kinds might enjoy *Girl Cook*, a fast-reading novel about a young female chef trying to make her way into New York's most prestigious kitchens, or Toby Cecchini's closely related bartending memoir, *Cosmopolitan: A Bartender's Life*.

Conlon, Edward.

Blue Blood. New York: Riverhead Books, 2004. 562pp. ISBN 1573222666.

Conlon opens his work memoir with a lengthy chapter describing his first shifts as a cop in the Bronx projects, effectively re-creatingfor the reader how overwhelming patrol officers' early careers can be. In further chapters Conlon backtracks and explains the shared history between his family and the New York City police department (his grandfather was a cop whom Conlon frankly admits was on the take), as well his own progression through the ranks of the department. Honest and lively, Conlon has provided a personal history rich with colorful characters and quick-reading action.

Subjects: Community Life • Epic Reads • Family Relationships • Law Enforcement • New York City • Professions

Now try: Miles Corwin's examinations of the inner workings of the L.A. Police Department, *Homicide Special: A Year with the LAPD's Elite Detective Unit* (annotated in the "Police Procedurals" subgenre of the true crime chapter) and *The Killing Season: A Summer Inside and LAPD Homicide Division*, are similar to Conlon's story of life as a law enforcement officer. Bernard Kerik's professional memoir, *The Lost Son: A Life in Pursuit of Justice*, is also a story of the appeal of working as part of a police department (Kerik became the Commissioner of the NYPD); Zac Unger offers a similarly themed memoir of his "accidental" career as a firefighter in *Working Fire: The Making of an Accidental Fireman*.

Craig, Emily.

Teasing Secrets from the Dead. New York: Crown Publishers, 2004. 286pp. ISBN 1400049229.

Forensic anthropologist Emily Craig wastes no time exposing the details of her work to the reader; speaking in the first person, she opens her narrative with a case in which she is trying to create an accurate model of a victim's head and face. Although this book is as quickly paced as its counterpart on television, *CSI*, Craig focuses primarily on the process of investigating crimes, and it is sometimes disconcerting to come to the end of a chapter without hearing the outcome of the cases she describes.

> **Subjects:** Anthropology • Forensic Science • Law Enforcement • Professions • Quick Reads • True Crime

> **Now try:** The foreword for this book is by Kathy Reichs, whose very popular thriller series focuses on the work of forensic anthropologist Tempe Brennan (the series began with *Deja Dead* in 1997and *Death du Jour* in 1999). Karin Slaughter writes thrillers about a female coroner (*Blindsided*, *Kisscut*, *A Faint Cold Fear*, and *Indelible*), and Patricia Cornwell's recurring character Kay Scarpetta is also a medical examiner (and appears in Cornwell's first novels, *Postmortem* and *Body of Evidence*, as well as in many subsequent ones).

Gass, Thomas Edward.

Nobody's Home: Candid Reflections of a Nursing Home Aide. Ithaca, N.Y.: Cornell University Press, 2004. 189pp. ISBN 0801442435.

This completely candid narrative of a typical year in the life of a nursing home aide is noteworthy on two accounts: It is not typical in this genre, in which authors primarily write about lifelong professions or careers; and it is not typical of academic press books, which are not known for their accessibility to popular audiences. Thomas Gass is first and foremost a health care worker who is only secondarily (and this is the amazing part) a superior writer. In short and unflinching (read: often graphic) chapters he lays bare the typical heavy duties and low salaries of aide workers, the anguish of trying to help disabled and disoriented elderly patients, and the numerous afflictions and indignities suffered by those people. Although he could have caricatured his colleagues and his patients, his character descriptions are nuanced and his voice unique.

Subjects: Elderly • Health Issues • Medicine • Professions • Quick Reads • Work Relationships

Now try: Frank Huyler's short and punchy stories from the medical front lines, *The Blood of Strangers: Stories from Emergency Medicine*, is another compelling book from an author who is emphatically a professional first and an illuminating writer second. Stephen Seager's *Psychward: A Year Behind Locked Doors* details a new psychology professional's challenging year spent treating the mentally ill in the Los Angeles County General Hospital.

Gawande, Atul.

Complications: A Surgeon's Notes on an Imperfect Science. New York: Metropolitan Books, 2002 (New York: Picador Books, 2002). 269pp. ISBN 0312421702.

Gawande provides a well-rounded treatise on his experiences as a surgical resident; he wrote the book after completing his eighth year as a doctor, but says that his viewpoint was further informed by his being a parent of a child with special medical needs, as well as his personal interactions with both superlative and burnt-out colleagues. Although he writes cool prose that is itself almost surgical in its efficiency, he relates many patients' stories with care and hope, and even if this is not a book you'd want to have along to read in the hospital, it does offer a calm and empathetic glance into the medical establishment.

Subjects: ALA Notable Books • Family Relationships • Medicine • Professions

Now try: Richard Selzer's classic *Confessions of a Knife*, as well as his coming-of-age memoir *Down from Troy: A Doctor Comes of Age*, also provide personal access to the medical world. Readers interested in this sort of narrative but looking for a surgeon with a few more years of experience might also try Richard Karl's *Across the Red Line: Stories from the Surgical Life*, which is also well-written but provides even more shocking interludes, such as Karl's own experiences with hepatitis and a spinal injury, both incurred through his work as a surgeon.

Ginsberg, Debra.

Waiting: The True Confessions of a Waitress. New York: HarperCollins, 2000 (New York: Perennial, 2001). 298pp. ISBN 0060932813.

Ginsberg illuminates the world of waitressing, describing her co-workers and customers with unflinching and often hilarious honesty, and relates many of her personal experiences, including single parenthood, while considering what it means to wait both on tables and for something better to come along.

Subjects: Family Relationships • Humor • Love and Dating • Professions • Quick Reads • Work Relationships

Now try: Readers who enjoy Ginsberg's honesty might also enjoy her two subsequent memoirs, both focusing on family relationships. In *Raising Blaze*, she describes her interactions with the educational system in her struggle to help her son overcome his learning disabilities; in *About My Sisters*, she describes her complicated but always close relationship with her three sisters, as well as with her brother and parents. Those readers who enjoy the insider's view and the restaurant setting might also like Ty Wenzel's bartending memoir, *Behind Bars: The Straight-Up Tales of a Big-City Bartender*, although it is less personally affecting than Ginsberg's memoir and adopts more of a "Sex in the City" young urban professional tone.

Marcus, James.

Amazonia: Five Years at the Epicenter of the Dot.com Juggernaut. New York: New Press, 2004. 261pp. ISBN 1565848705.

Marcus's behind-the-scenes narrative of his editorial job "providing content" at Amazon.com is another literary/work memoir that should be required reading for all librarians, not to mention all other readers interested in the meteoric rise and current market dominance of Amazon.com. As employee number 55 with the company, Marcus was originally tapped as one of the site's editors who would provide reviews and other articles but was eventually displaced by the "culture of metrics" and the relational databases for which the site has become famous.

> **Subjects:** Books and Learning • Business • Pop Culture • Work Relationships

> **Now try:** Douglas Coupland's novel *Microserfs* is a thoroughly enjoyable and quickly paced story about a group of twenty-somethings going about their social and personal lives, but only in the rare moments when they're not devoting their lives to their work at Microsoft. Although it's more of an investigative work than a memoir, Adam Cohen's *The Perfect Store: Inside eBay* is based on numerous interviews with the Internet site's founders, managers, and participants, and might also appeal to fans of Marcus's Amazon.com story. Readers interested in personal business histories might also consider Doris Christopher's upbeat *The Pampered Chef: The Story Behind the Creation of One of Today's Most Beloved Companies*, or even Christopher Byron's decidedly less upbeat *Martha Inc.: The Incredible Story of Martha Stewart Living Omnimedia*.

Shea, Suzanne Strempek.

Shelf Life: Romance, Mystery, Drama, and Other Page-Turning Adventures from a Year in a Bookstore. Boston: Beacon Press, 2004. 223pp. ISBN 0807072583.

Another narrative that should be required reading for all those interested in books and reading, Shea provides a closer look into the inner workings of a bookstore, including thoughts on advertising, marketing, and customer relationships and service. While recovering from debilitating cancer treatments, Shea was offered a temporary job by her friend, a bookstore owner in Springfield, Massachusetts, and found it was exactly the boost her spirit and health needed (so much so that three years after she started, she's still working there). Shea offers compelling character portraits of both her colleagues and the books they sell, including delightful asides such as a closing routine that requires telling the darkened bookstore that she loves it.

![8]

> **Subjects:** Books and Learning • Business • Cancer • Friendships • Retail • Work Relationships

> **Now try:** Nancy Pearl's fantastic titles listing her subject- and mood-oriented book picks, *Book Lust* and *More Book Lust*, display a similar love for and close attention to the connections between books and readers. Any of Nicholas Basbanes's investigative stories about book people and places, such as *A Gentle Madness: Bibliophiles, Bibliomanes, and the Eternal Passion for Books* or *Among the Gently Mad: Strategies and Perspectives for the Book-Hunter in the 21st Century* might appeal to fans of Shea's story. John

Baxter's memoir of book collecting, *A Pound of Paper: Confessions of a Book Addict*, displays a similar attention to the love of books and book people. Shea also devotes a fair amount of time to describing her experiences hand-selling a local author's book (it just happens to be Hampton Sides's hugely popular *Ghost Soldiers: The Epic Account of World War II's Greatest Rescue Mission*), and her description may whet readers' appetite for that particular work. Sara Nelson's *So Many Books, So Little Time: A Year of Passionate Reading* may also appeal to the booklovers who like Shea's story.

Swope, Sam.

I Am a Pencil: A Teacher, His Kids, and Their World of Stories. New York: Henry Holt, 2004. 297pp. ISBN 0805073345.

Swope's author blurb describing him as a somewhat cranky children's author sets the tone for his personal, affecting, and extremely well-written memoir of his experience teaching a writing workshop to a class of third-graders in Queens, New York. He found the original experience so interesting that he continued to visit and teach the class for two more years, until they graduated from the fifth grade. He shares many of their stories and poems, which cover the full spectrum from poignant to hilarious, as well as his friendships with the students and their families, many of whom are immigrants struggling for their daily existence. There is no unadulterated pap here; Swope does not seek to draw larger life lessons from the kids' writings but shares them with an appealing honesty and knowledge that he is really only a part-time teacher who can, at the most, simply hope for the best for his students.

Subjects: Books and Learning • Education • Gentle Reads • Humor • New York City • Urban Life

Now try: Abby Goodnough's year-in-the-life of an inexperienced but enthusiastic teacher in New York City, *Ms. Moffett's First Year*, might also appeal to the audience of this book. There's no shortage of heavy hitters providing blurbs on Swope's book jacket; the names there include Dave Eggers, Alex Kotlowitz, and Linda Perlstein. Kotlowitz's *There Are No Children Here*, although describing more violence, may also appeal to these readers due to its focus on nine- and eleven-year-old protagonists.

Transue, Emily R.

On Call: A Doctor's Days and Nights in Residency. New York: St. Martin's Press, 2004. 242pp. ISBN 0312324839.

Told by a practicing medical professional, this tale of a doctor's somewhat surreal first year as a resident (as opposed to her multiple years as a medical student) is action-oriented in tone but provides valuable and interesting insight into what goes on in the minds of doctors. At times humorous and at times deeply sad, Transue's short chapters provide immediately affecting stories and character portraits, as well as honesty about doctors' thought processes (for example, her first thought upon hearing that a patient died was not sympathy for the patient's family but a panicked denial of any wrongdoing in the case).

Subjects: Humor • Medicine • Professions • Work Relationships

Now try: Atul Gawande's *Complications: A Surgeon's Notes on an Incomplete Science*, also written by a medical professional rather new to his field, may appeal to readers looking for the inside story on medicine. Scott Turow's *One L: The Turbulent*

True Story of a First Year at Harvard Law School covers a completely different profession but also conveys a sense of the shock of a first year in a new and tough career (or even obtaining the training for one).

Yancey, Richard.

Confessions of a Tax Collector: One Man's Tour of Duty Inside the IRS. New York: HarperCollins, 2004 (New York: Perennial, 2005). 364pp. ISBN 0060555610.

Yancey details his "tour of duty" as a revenue officer for the IRS in the 1980s, with brutally frank depictions of the varied personalities of his co-workers and the often desperate people whose assets he was charged with seizing for nonpayment of taxes. Readers should note that although Yancey tells a page-turning tale, he admits in the introduction to changing all of the names of people involved and rearranging some events to aid in narrative flow. He is still able to turn a nice phrase, especially when describing truisms such as how fast neighbors will rat each other out when they see IRS credentials.

Subjects: Government • Humor • Professions • Work Relationships

Now try: John Perkins's *Confessions of an Economic Hit Man*, a memoir of his years spent working as an economist with intelligence agencies to support the policies of the World Bank in "LDCs" (Less Developed Countries), may also appeal to Yancey's readers, although librarians should be aware that it's fairly politically charged. A veritable sequel to Yancey's IRS story is Charles Rossotti's *Many Unhappy Returns: One Man's Quest to Turn Around the Most Unpopular Organization in America*, which describes his tenure as commissioner of the IRS starting in 1997. Those readers more interested in Yancey's distinctive, at-the-edge-of-bad-boy voice may also enjoy his debut novel, *A Burning in Homeland*, about a murder and memory in 1960s Florida.

Foodie Memoirs

For a nation that now spends a lot of time going out to eat and less time than ever actually preparing meals, the recent explosion in popular works that outline people's experiences with food seems hard to explain. It shouldn't be; these books, often written by food critics or cookbook authors, are delightfully evocative and attempt to describe the many ways in which food and the act of eating are indelibly etched into the memories of our childhoods and the fabric of our everyday lives. We may not cook at home as much as we used to, but it appears that we're more than happy to devote time to reading about food and its preparation and presentation.

"Foodie Memoirs" have a proud history. One of the pioneers of the genre, M. F. K. Fisher, began publishing in the 1940s, while Calvin Trillin produced the first volume in his "Tummy Trilogy," *American Fried*, back in 1974.

Colwin, Laurie.

Home Cooking: A Writer in the Kitchen. New York: Knopf, 1988 (New York: Harper Perennial, 2000). 193pp. ISBN 0060955309.

Novelist and *Gourmet* magazine columnist Colwin celebrates all aspects of cooking and eating, even dwelling lovingly on "repulsive dinners" (meals she prepared that didn't go at all well), in this collection of short and quickly readable essays. Her style is conversational and homey without being folksy, and it is a tragedy for the subgenre that Colwin died unexpectedly at the too-young age of forty-eight.

> **Subjects:** Classics • Essays • Food • Humor • Quick Reads

> **Now try:** A second collection of Colwin's essays, titled *More Home Cooking: A Writer Returns to the Kitchen*, is fully as enjoyable as the first; her novels, in particular *Happy All the Time,* and the story collection *The Lone Pilgrim* might also appeal to her foodie fans. Readers looking for another personable and accessible (albeit much more Southern) writer might also try Michael Lee West's *Consuming Passions: A Food-Obsessed Life.*

Fisher, M. F. K.

The Art of Eating. Cleveland, Ohio: World Publishing Company, 1954 (Hoboken, N.J.: Wiley, 2004). 749pp. ISBN 0764542613.

Fisher traveled extensively and lived a life rich in both interpersonal experiences and culinary discoveries and joys, and this collection of essays provides ample amounts of personal reminiscences and musings, as well as groundbreaking food writing and journalism.

> **Subjects:** Classics • Essays • Food • Journalism • Literary Lives • Women's Contributions • World Travel

> **Now try:** Fisher was a prolific epicurean and writer; readers may want to check out her other collections, such as *The Gastronomical Me,* or her expatriate travel narrative, *Long Ago in France: The Years in Dijon.* Another collection of essays that might appeal to Fisher's readers is Calvin Trillin's *Feeding a Yen* (annotated in the travel chapter).

Hesser, Amanda.

Cooking for Mr. Latte: A Food Lover's Courtship, with Recipes. New York: Norton, 2003 (2004). 336pp. ISBN 0393325598.

Food critic and cookbook author Hesser combines the story of her courtship of fellow writer and future husband Ted Friend with stories of cooking mishaps, triumphs, and a fine collection of recipes. Her voice is informal, and her obvious love for food and the aspects of what she considers to be the good life are passionately described.

> **Subjects:** Food • Humor • Love and Dating • Quick Reads

> **Now try:** Fans of this memoir might want to peruse Hesser's favorably reviewed cookbook/essay collection *The Cook and the Gardener: A Year of Recipes and Writings for the French Countryside.* She also describes a meal she ate with famous food writer Jeffrey Steingarten, author of *The Man Who Ate Everything. Pass the Polenta: And Other Writings from the Kitchen* by Teresa Lust is another essay collection, complete with recipes.

Reichl, Ruth.

Tender at the Bone: Growing up at the Table. New York: Random House, 1998 (New York: Broadway Books, 1999). 282pp. ISBN 0767903382.

Best known as the editor of *Gourmet* magazine, Reichl employs her foodie writing skills in a childhood memoir that primarily centers on her relationship with her mother, who, in addition to being a unique character, didn't have much in the way of cooking skills. Reichl also tells about her own school days and development into adulthood, as well as her greater understanding of her manic depressive mother and emotionally distant father. Her sympathetically drawn but never pitiable characters are the appeal of this narrative, which also features humor, clean prose, and a sampling of some of her favorite recipes.

Subjects: Classics • Coming-of-Age • Family Relationships • Food • Quick Reads

Now try: Reichl is also the author of the memoirs *Comfort Me with Apples: More Adventures at the Table* and *Garlic and Sapphires: The Secret Life of a Critic in Disguise.* Patricia Volk's *Stuffed: Adventures of a Restaurant Family* is an extremely humorous and tender portrait of her upbringing in a restaurant family. Louise DeSalvo's memoir of her family's relationships with food and each other in *Crazy in the Kitchen: Food, Feuds, and Forgiveness in an Italian American Family* is less humorous than Reichl's and Volk's but also examines the links between family ethnicity, history, and love. From the male point of view, British food journalist Nigel Slater also offers a witty and personal story of youth and food in his memoir *Toast: The Story of a Boy's Hunger.*

Humorous Memoir

The genius in the work of the authors of humorous memoir is their universal ability to take an everyday or mundane experience and use language and imagery, not to mention tone, to make those situations funny. Any other person, when forced to work as an elf in Santa's Village at Macy's department store, might just have done the job, collected a paycheck, and never looked at a candy cane without shuddering again; David Sedaris, however, took the experience and used it to ruminate, hilariously, on all manner of children's quirks and the multiple indignities of the retail or service profession (*Barrel Fever*). Dave Barry has been writing humorous newspaper columns for years on the not-new subject of love relationships and child-raising. Hollis Gillespie and Jim Knipfel both explore the darker and more cynical sides of humor, while David Foster Wallace gives his humorous essays a cultural studies spin.

8

The subjects may be varied, but the end result is always the same: funny, popular, and quickly paced books that people love to read.

Barry, Dave.

Dave Barry Is from Mars and Venus. New York: Crown Publishers, 1997 (New York: Ballantine Books, 1998). 269pp. ISBN 0345425782.

A Pulitzer Prize–winning humor columnist for *The Miami Herald*, in this collection Barry examines both the commonplace (colliding with his son during a round of laser tag and their trip to the emergency room) and the more fantastic experiences attendant on being a famous columnist (his appearance on the game show *Wheel of Fortune* for charity, or swimming with the U.S. Synchronized Swimming National Team).

Subjects: Essays • Gentle Reads • Humor • Love and Dating • Marriage • Pop Culture • Quick Reads

Now try: Dave Barry's collections of his syndicated column are always best sellers, and many readers will want to read everything he has published; a few of his more recent collections, which cover a wide variety of subjects, are *Boogers Are My Beat: More Lies, But Some Actual Journalism, Dave Barry Hits Below the Beltline: A Vicious and Unprovoked Attack on Our Most Cherished Political Institutions*, and *Dave Barry Is Not Taking This Sitting Down!*; he is also starting to make forays into comic crime novels with his *Big Trouble* and *Tricky Business*. Readers who enjoy Barry might also find a lot to like in P. J. O'Rourke's caustic collections (although be forewarned, they're darker and very cynical), which also cover a variety of subjects; his most recent titles are *Peace Kills: America's Fun New Imperialism, The CEO of the Sofa*, and *Eat the Rich*.

Gillespie, Hollis.

Bleachy-Haired Honky Bitch: Tales from a Bad Neighborhood. New York: Regan Books, 2004. 279pp. ISBN 006056198X.

Gillespie is a frequent contributor to NPR programs, and her memoir of growing up with a missile scientist mother and a salesman dad, as well as her continuing search for a home she can afford in any neighborhood, is written in short chapters that read as easily as though she were speaking right to the reader. Although her vignettes are gentle in a distinctly postmodern way, readers should be aware that she's an enjoyably earthy author who doesn't avoid profanity or dark topics.

Subjects: Community Life • Culture Clash • Family Relationships • Friendships • Homes • Humor • Quick Reads

Now try: Laurie Notaro's provocatively titled and humorous collections of essays, *The Idiot Girls' Action-Adventure Club* and *Autobiography of a Fat Bride: True Tales of a Pretend Adulthood*, match Gillespie's story in style and wit. Although it appears as a read-alike to other family and relationship memoirs, Jeannette Walls's *The Glass Castle: A Memoir* also features a pair of independent-minded parents. Gillespie cites as influences such humor writers as Dave Barry and Carl Hiassen; readers may want to track down some of their works for fun and light related reads.

Knipfel, Jim.

Ruining It for Everybody. New York: Penguin Books, 2004. 235pp. ISBN 1585423378.

Knipfel's dust jacket quote says that when he hears the word spiritual, he reaches for his revolver. With that sentiment gracing the bright yellow cover, it may be hard for the reader to believe that this is actually a "spiritual biography" (of sorts). Beset by many physical problems, including a rare genetic eye disease and a brain lesion,

Knipfel turns his thoughts to his lifetime spent combining various acts of self and overt destruction with his growing adherence to a belief system centered around not being "a shit." Darkly humorous, he would most likely hate hearing his story described here as strangely sincere self-help for cynics.

Subjects: Disabilities • Health Issues • Humor • Literary Lives • Quick Reads • Spirituality

Now try: This is the third in a series of memoirs by Knipfel; the first, *Slackjaw*, opens with his uncle warning him about the possibility of going blind while at his grandma's funeral and continues on to detail his many other physical disabilities; in the second, *Quitting the Nairobi Trio*, he describes spending six months in a psych ward and undertakes his own analysis of his mental issues. Knipfel's humor is darker than dark and not for everyone, but those readers who love him will want to read everything he has written.

Murphy, Austin.

How Tough Could It Be: The Trials and Errors of a Sportswriter Turned Stay-at-Home Dad. New York: Henry Holt, 2004. 239pp. ISBN 0805074805

In his career as a sportswriter for *Sports Illustrated*, Murphy became aware that his heavy traveling schedule was making him miss a lot of time with his kids. Determined to rectify that, he proposed that his wife Lauren return to work so he could be a stay-at-home dad to their eight- and six-year-olds, Willa and Devin. Over the course of his time "off" Murphy realized that between cooking, cleaning, scheduling playdates, and battling constant kid's colds and various events such as school head lice inspections, staying at home is anything but the easier option.

Subjects: Family Relationships • Gentle Reads • Humor • Parenting • Professions

Now try: Faulkner Fox's similar book from the female point of view, *Dispatches from a Not-So-Perfect Life, Or How I Learned to Love the House, the Man, the Child*, was originally a column at Salon.com and shares the same journalistic style. Lisa Belkin's memoir *Life's Work: Confessions of an Unbalanced Mom* might appeal to these readers, as might Allison Pearson's novel about working moms, *I Don't Know How She Does It*.

O'Rourke, P. J.

Eat the Rich. New York: Atlantic Monthly Press, 1998 (1999). 246pp. ISBN 0871137607.

O'Rourke has long been a reliable source of biting cultural and political commentary, and this title, one of the most familiar to readers, is no exception. O'Rourke spins a narrative out of using his journalist's frequent flyer miles to travel about to different countries and point out the foibles (as he perceives them, and readers are warned that O'Rourke is not shy about divulging his own political and social opinions) of their economic systems.

Subjects: Humor • Economics • Journalism • Politics

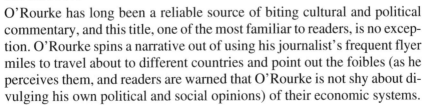

Now try: O'Rourke's latest, *Peace Kills: America's Fun New Imperialism* is as cynical as ever, but many reviewers despaired at its less humorous tone;

readers seeking more obviously humorous works from O'Rourke might want to try *The CEO of the Sofa* or *Parliament of Whores*. O'Rourke also turns up on a lot of read-alike lists for Hunter Thompson, whose darkly humorous *Fear and Loathing in Las Vegas* and *Hey Rube: Blood Sport, the Bush Doctrine, and the Downward Spiral of Dumbness* might be enjoyable reads for O'Rourke fans.

Sedaris, David.

Dress Your Family in Corduroy and Denim. Boston: Little, Brown, 2004 (New York: Back Bay Books, 2005). 257pp. ISBN 0316010790.

Sedaris tells stories that really aren't that much different from anyone else's: He discusses his childhood (including the neighbors down the street who "didn't believe in television"), his family, attending his cousin's wedding, and his interactions with his friends (which sometimes resemble verbal Keystone Kops routines when he doesn't catch on to what they're saying). It's just that he makes those stories funnier than most other writers can.

Subjects: Essays • Family Relationships • Friendships • Humor • Pop Culture

Now try: Sedaris's earlier collections, *Barrel Fever* and *Me Talk Pretty One Day*, are also both extremely funny collections of his thoughts on life, his family, and most famously, his experiences as a Christmas elf at Macy's department store (*Barrel Fever*). David Rakoff, in addition to sharing Sedaris's first name, has also published two hilarious essay collections, *Fraud* and *Don't Get Too Comfortable*. Sarah Vowell's *The Partly Cloudy Patriot* includes more political commentary but is very similar to Sedaris's work in her descriptions of her interactions with her family and friends. Sedaris and Augusten Burroughs are also often compared to each other for their use of humor, but readers are advised that much of Burroughs's nonfiction is darker in tone and subject matter than is Sedaris's.

Wallace, David Foster.

A Supposedly Fun Thing I'll Never Do Again. Boston: Little, Brown, 1997 (1998). 353pp. ISBN 0316925284.

In this collection of essays Wallace ruminates on, among other things, his mediocre talent as a high school tennis player who was good at figuring out how to hit into the omnipresent Illinois plains wind, as well as on the effects of television on modern fiction (and vice versa) and his experience covering the Illinois State Fair for *Harper's* magazine, where numerous women mistook him for a *Harper's Bazaar* reporter and immediately assured him they loved his magazine's recipes. Always beautifully written, usually somewhat surreal, absolutely never dull, the entire collection is worth reading.

Subjects: Essays • Humor • Mass Media • Pop Culture

Now try: In his use of subtle humor and pop culture references, Wallace's essays are similar to those of David Sedaris, a hugely popular essayist whose collections include *Me Talk Pretty One Day* and *Dress Your Family in Corduroy and Denim*; for my money, it just doesn't get any funnier than his *Holidays on Ice: Stories* volume, in which he details his trials and tribulations as a department store Santa. Readers who enjoy Wallace and Sedaris and/or the essay and short story format might also want to try the new *The Best American Nonrequired Reading* collections, which were inaugurated in 2002 with an issue edited by Dave Eggers (who is still the series editor).

AUTOBIOGRAPHY

Although the appeal of autobiographies is still their main characters, the very act of those characters telling their own stories often leads to a much different reading experience for the fans of more stereotypical memoirs (and their relatives in the life stories grouping, biographies). Because many literary theorists and publishers agree that autobiography can seem much more similar, in form and appeal, to memoir writing than to biography, they have been included here as a separate category that parallels the format and appeal of memoirs. There are, however, several major differences between the two: memoirs often tell stories about very specific periods in their authors' lives (*Amazonia: Five Years at the Epicenter of the Dot.com Juggernaut*, *In Pharaoh's Army: Memories of the Lost War*), while autobiography authors often tell the entire story of their "life and times," usually in chronological order. Memoirs are often distinguished by what their authors do or experience, while autobiographies are more often noteworthy for whom their authors are. Although autobiographies can provide life stories of people who are not typically famous (*Nobody Nowhere*, *I Will Bear Witness*), they are most often penned by individuals who are not authors, but rather famous in for other achievements or experiences (*My Life* by Bill Clinton and *Personal History* by Katharine Graham are good examples). Accordingly, they are usually requested by readers by the name of the author ("Do you have the new book by Jane Fonda?") rather than by their genre classification. At least once a day I am asked where we keep the biographies in the library where I work; I have yet to encounter a reader asking for our "autobiography" section.

Last but not least, the tones of memoirs and autobiographies can vary widely. Memoirs tend to be more reflective and introspective, and often include the authors' explorations of their own subjective reactions to their surroundings and experiences. Although it might seem at first glance that autobiographies, defined by *Webster's* as "a biography of a person narrated by himself," would be even more subjective in tone than memoirs, autobiographers tend to focus less on their subjective experiences and more on the chronological and factual happenings of their lives.

What follows is a brief sampling of well-known and time-tested autobiographies. Because they have been grouped according to format, they have not been subdivided according to subject, and advisors should refer to the annotations to determine their topics and mood.

Angelou, Maya.

I Know Why the Caged Bird Sings. New York: Random House 1969 (2002). 281pp. ISBN 0375507892.

Angelou provides the quintessential account of a young African American woman's challenging childhood and the struggles she faced as, in her own words, a "Southern Black girl." Raised by her grandmother in a rural Arkansas community, Angelou saw firsthand the hard labor in the cotton fields; when her mother retrieved her and her brother and moved them to St. Louis, she also became a victim of sexual abuse at the hands of her mother's live-in boyfriend. On the *New York Times* best-seller list for more than three years, the book also includes character portraits of individuals

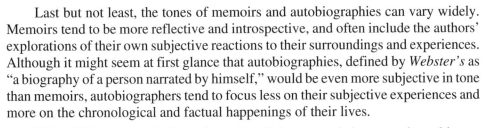

(including her brother Bailey and her grandmother "Momma") and culminates with the birth of the author's son.

Subjects: Abuse • African Americans • American South • Angelou, Maya • Autobiographies • Classics • Family Relationships • Literary Lives • Racism • Sexuality

Now try: This is the first installment in Angelou's six-volume autobiography; readers who enjoy her unique voice and skill with language might be interested in any or all of the following volumes: *Gather Together in My Name, Singin' and Swingin' and Gettin' Merry Like Christmas, The Heart of a Woman, All God's Children Need Traveling Shoes,* and *A Song Flung up to Heaven.* Angelou is also a prolific writer of poetry; many of her titles are available and performed impeccably by their author in audio format (including *Phenomenal Woman* and *The Maya Angelou Poetry Collection*). Zora Neale Hurston's autobiography, *Dust Tracks on a Road*, is also a compelling read, as are Alice Walker's works of nonfiction, including *In Search of Our Mother's Gardens: Womanist Prose*, and her best-selling novel *The Color Purple*, which was also a Pulitzer Prize winner.

Black, Lewis.

Nothing's Sacred. New York: Simon Spotlight Entertainment, 2005. 217pp. ISBN 0689876475.

Not all autobiographies are weighty tomes that relate their authors' entire lives with an eye to recording their momentous achievements for posterity or deeply lyrical reflections of self-discovery and growth. Some are out-and-out enjoyable reads, and Black offers just such a one in the story of his youth in Washington D.C., relationships with members of his family, education, and career as a playwright (not so successful) and comedian and mainstay on Comedy Central's *The Daily Show* (much more successful). The language is frank, the stories hilarious, the chapters short, and the overall reading experience fast and fun.

Subjects: Autobiographies • Coming-of-Age • Family Relationships • Humor • Politics • Pop Culture

Now try: Readers who enjoy Black's cynical humor might also find much to enjoy in the mock-text *America: The Book*, edited by the writers of *The Daily Show*, or George Carlin's humor collections, such as *Napalm and Silly Putty* and *When Will Jesus Bring the Pork Chops?* Another "guilty pleasure" autobiography is Bruce Campbell's extremely fun *If Chins Could Kill: Confessions of a B Movie Actor.*

Clinton, Bill.

My Life. New York: Knopf, 2004. 957pp. ISBN 0375414576.

Former U.S. president and still controversial political figure Bill Clinton leaves no childhood stone unturned or incidental name uncovered in this controversial and meaty autobiography. Although it was derided by many critics for being dull and too packed with litanies of names, it is still a highly personal story from an individual who very few readers could accuse of being dull.

Subjects: Autobiographies • Clinton, Bill • Epic Reads • Government • Politics • Presidents

Now try: Readers interested enough to make it to the end of Clinton's massive book might not have the energy to immediately face Hillary Clinton's autobiography, *Living History*, but should be reassured to find that it is only half as long. Clinton's respect and admiration for John F. Kennedy as a political role model is widely acknowledged; readers of his autobiography might also want to try Kennedy's classic *Profiles in Courage*.

Graham, Katharine.

Personal History. New York: Knopf, 1997 (2001). 642pp. ISBN 0394585852.

Both critically acclaimed and a huge best seller, Graham's well-told autobiography is informative about the changing roles and expectations of professional women in the twentieth century. From her childhood to her marriage to Phil Graham, through their marriage and struggle with her husband's depression and eventual suicide, to her immersion in the boys' club of the *Washington Post*, this story is both personal and the product of a woman with a journalist's eye for detail and context.

Subjects: Autobiographies • Epic Reads • Family Relationships • Journalism • Marriage • Professions • Pulitzer Prize Winners • Work Relationships

Now try: Readers interested in Katharine Graham's personal story may also be interested in one of the biggest stories ever to come from her newspaper: Carl Bernstein's and Bob Woodward's *All the President's Men* (annotated in the "Investigative Writing" chapter) or another famous journalist's personal story, Ben Bradlee's *A Good Life: Newspapering and Other Adventures*.

Haley, Alex.

Roots: The Saga of an American Family. Garden City, N.Y.: Doubleday, 1976 (New York: Gramercy Books, 2000). 688pp. ISBN 0517208601.

Haley recounts the story of his family back from its roots in Africa in 1750 and the birth of the patriarch, Kunta Kinte, whose story occupies most of the book. Brought to America as a slave, Kinte started a family here that, six generations later, included the author. Saga is the correct word for Haley's epic work; it is not a standard work of history in that it has no footnotes and consists primarily of created episodes and dialogue, which makes it read as quickly and compellingly as a novel. The book was a huge best seller (and was also made into a popular miniseries), but throughout the years controversy has arisen over Haley's methods of scholarship, plagiarism issues, and historical re-creation. Although librarians and readers should be aware of those issues, the fact remains that very few works of biography or history that encompass 150 years and 688 pages are so readable.

Subjects: Africa • African Americans • American South • Autobiographies • Classics • Epic Reads • Family Relationships • Race Relations • Slavery

Now try: Readers of Alex Haley's opus might also consider *The Autobiography of Malcolm X: As Told to Alex Haley* (annotated in the biography chapter). Richard Wright's "novelistic autobiography" *Black Boy* is less of a historical saga than Haley's work, but it is also a powerful account of the author's childhood struggle to overcome the twin hurdles of racism and poverty. Edward Ball's family histories are less novelistic than Haley's but are still engaging reads: *Slaves in the Family* was published in 1998 and won the

National Book Award; *The Sweet Hell Inside: The Rise of an Elite Black Family in the Segregated South* followed in 2002.

Klemperer, Victor.

I Will Bear Witness, 1933–1941: A Diary of the Nazi Years. New York: Random House, 1998 (New York: Modern Library, 1999). 519pp. ISBN 0375753788.

A Jewish person married to a Protestant, Klemperer barely survived both the Holocaust and the Allied fire-bombing of the German city Dresden, where he lived and kept his diary. A university professor, his diary entries are highly descriptive and all the more terrifying due to the combination of curiously banal recitations of the author's awareness of the horror going on around him and the mundane details of daily life.

Subjects: ALA Notable Books • Autobiographies • Diaries • Epic Reads • Family Relationships • Germany • Holocaust • Jews and Judaism • World War II

Now try: The second volume of Klemperer's diary is a must-read for those who have read his first; it is titled simply *I Will Bear Witness, 1942–1945* and is more frightening than the first because of it heightened scenes of intimidation. His third volume, *The Lesser Evil: The Diaries of Victor Klemperer, 1945–1959*, has received less positive critical attention but may be necessary for some readers who want to obtain some closure on the saga of his life. Any reader who finds these volumes illuminating may also want to try Anne Frank's *Anne Frank: The Diary of a Young Girl* (if they haven't already read it); the definitive edition from Doubleday includes many diary entries that were previously unpublished due to their author's frankness about her other family members and growing attraction to a boy with whom her family hid from the Nazis. Alexandra Zapruda, an employee of the U.S. Holocaust Memorial Museum, has compiled a collection of similarly intimate Holocaust diaries in *Salvaged Pages: Young Writers' Diaries of the Holocaust*.

Mead, Margaret.

Blackberry Winter: My Earlier Years. New York: Morrow, 1972 (New York: Kodansha International, 1995). 305pp. ISBN 156836069X.

Mead's autobiography is remarkably forthright in her discussion of her childhood, professional life and travels, and relationships with her three husbands, two of whom collaborated with her on her anthropological work, and with her friends and mentors, including Ruth Benedict. Her writing is personal but never overblown, and the scientific crispness of her prose is exemplified by her assertion halfway through her narrative that, "I was seventeen. I was engaged to be married. But above all else I was eager to enter the academic world for which all my life had prepared me" (p. 87).

Subjects: Anthropology • Autobiographies • Classics • Family Relationships • Friendships • Love and Dating • Marriage • Professions • Women's Contributions

Now try: Lois W. Banner's double biography of Mead and her mentor and lover Ruth Benedict, *Intertwined Lives: Margaret Mead, Ruth Benedict, and Their Circle*, is more scholarly in tone than Mead's own writing, but also provides more personal details about the pair, gleaned from her access to both women's private and previously unavailable archives.

Stein, Gertrude.

The Autobiography of Alice B. Toklas. New York: Harcourt Brace, 1933 (New York: Modern Library, 1993). 342pp. ISBN 0679600817.

Perhaps one of the most stylistically unique entries in this chapter, author Gertrude Stein's tongue-in-cheek autobiography of her friend Alice B. Toklas's life is actually a thinly disguised autobiography. Full of humor and egotism masterfully masked by self-deprecation and set in Paris between World Wars I and II, this is a sometimes difficult, circular read, but it is also widely recognized as a classic of American literature.

Subjects: Autobiographies • Classics • France • Friendships • Humor • Literary Lives • Women's Contributions

Now try: Although not a light read often requested by today's pleasure readers, *The Education of Henry Adams: An Autobiography* is also a "classic" in the field and, first mass published in 1918, provides a complementary look at the era right before the one Stein describes. Ernest Hemingway's *A Moveable Feast* also tells about Parisian life in the 1920s.

Williams, Donna.

Nobody Nowhere: The Extraordinary Autobiography of an Autistic. New York: Times Books, 1992 (New York: Perennial, 2002). 219pp. ISBN 0380722178.

Williams reports the experience of being autistic in this stream-of-consciousness, honest autobiography. From family members at a loss for how to really interact with her, to the multiple doctors who diagnosed her condition, Williams portrays her struggle to reach a vast array of characters in this inside look at a still largely misunderstood condition.

Subjects: Abuse • Autism • Autobiographies • Coming-of-Age • Disabilities • Family Relationships • Health Issues

Now try: Williams also wrote a sequel to this well-received autobiography, *Somebody Somewhere*, which continues her story of seeking belonging and supportive relationships; another personal view of autism (Asperger's Syndrome) is Dawn Prince-Hughes's short but compelling *Songs of the Gorilla Nation: My Journey Through Autism*. Both Lucy Grealy's *Autobiography of a Face* and Julia DePree's *Body Story*, although they deal with vastly different issues (jaw cancer and anorexia, respectively) offer intimate memoirs regarding body and self-image issues. The recent *Dante's Cure: A Journey out of Madness* by Daniel Dorman, is about one woman's recovery from schizophrenia from the points of view of both the patient and the doctor. Mark Haddon's novel *The Curious Incident of the Dog in the Nighttime* might also work as a related read.

Consider Starting With . . .

The following list offers tried and true memoirs likely to appeal to a broad range of readers.

Arana, Marie. *American Chica: Two Worlds, One Childhood.*

Beals, Melba Pattillo. *Warriors Don't Cry: A Searing Memoir of the Battle to Integrate Little Rock's Central High.*

Frank, Anne. *Anne Frank: The Diary of a Young Girl.*

Ginsberg, Debra. *Waiting: The True Confessions of a Waitress.*

Hickam, Homer H., Jr. *Rocket Boys: A Memoir.*

McBride, James. *The Color of Water: A Black Man's Tribute to His White Mother.*

Mehta, Suketu. *Maximum City: Bombay Lost and Found.*

Reichl, Ruth. *Tender at the Bone: Growing up at the Table.*

Sedaris, David. *Dress Your Family in Corduroy and Denim.*

Fiction Read-Alikes

- **Alexie, Sherman.** Alexie has been widely lauded for writing short stories and novels that accurately portray the coming-of-age and cultural struggles of Native Americans. Although many of his stories focus on dark subjects and seemingly hopeless situations, they are also character-driven and may therefore appeal to memoir readers. *Tonto and the Lone Ranger Fistfight in Heaven* and *The Toughest Indian in the World* are story collections, while *Reservation Blues* and *Indian Killer* are novels.

- **Alvarez, Julia.** Readers who enjoy nonfiction memoirs that deal particularly with the issues of cultural identity and its effect on relationships will find much to like in Alvarez's novels *How the García Girls Lost Their Accents* (a collection of interrelated stories) and *In the Time of the Butterflies.*

- **Amis, Kingsley, and Martin Amis.** In addition to being father and son, both authors write darkly comic novels that focus with almost memoir-like detail on their main characters. Kingsley is best known for his novel *Lucky Jim*, a life-and-times type story about Jim Dixon and his experience as a lecturer at an English university in the 1950s (the book was published in 1954), and his Booker Prize–winning novel *The Old Devils*, about friends, drinking, and marital infidelity. Martin's debut novel, *The Rachel Papers*, is a thoroughly circular work of fiction, focusing on the main character's focusing on his sexual exploits (and his journaling of them), while later novels like *The Information* and *Night Train* also delve deep into character foibles and motivation.

- **Berg, Elizabeth.** Many of Berg's novels relate the experiences of women coming to terms with their lives, relationships, and surroundings, in the tradition of memoir writing about transforming experiences. Her most recent novels are *The Year of Pleasures*, *The Art of Mending*, and *Say When.*

- **Bourdain, Anthony.** In addition to being a popular chef and memoirist, Bourdain has produced two novels that are also firmly grounded in the world of the culinary arts: *Bone in the Throat: A Novel of Death and Digestion* and *The Bobby Gold Stories.*

- **Danticat, Edwidge.** The majority of Danticat's unflinching novels reflect both the experiences of Haitian immigrants and the challenges facing families still living in Haiti. Her first novel, *Breath, Eyes, Memory*, which became an Oprah Book Club choice and best seller, is loosely autobiographical; other novels such as *Krik? Krak!* and *Behind the Mountains* mimic the character-driven appeal of many relationship and coming-of-age memoirs.

- **Hijuelos, Oscar.** Hijuelos firmly grounds his novels in his Cuban American background, and his novels, such as *The Mambo Kings Play Songs of Love* and *Empress of the Splendid Season,* showcase characters seeking to come to terms with their cultural heritage and its effects on their personal characteristics and relationships.

- **Morrison, Toni.** Morrison has already been mentioned as a read-alike for bell hooks's memoir *Bone Black*, but she is such a huge literary figure and cultural icon that she warrants mention again here. Many readers who enjoy nonfiction memoirs of the African American experience in America might also become fans of her novels; in addition to the titles listed above, consider suggesting her Pulitzer Prize–winning *Beloved*, about former slave Sethe and her family in the years after the Civil War, or her most recent novel, *Love*, about a community and the histories and lives of its members.

- **Smith, Zadie.** British novelist Smith has so far only produced three novels, but then she is only nearing her thirties. Her first novel, *White Teeth*, which focused on the friendship and lives of two friends in modern-day London, one a native Brit and the other a Muslim from Bangladesh, received rave critical reviews. In *The Autograph Man*, she further explores issues of identity and relationships through her autograph dealer protagonist's lack of direction in his own life, combined with a fanatical love for a former movie star.

- **Woolf, Virginia.** Many of Woolf's novels, including *The Voyage Out* (a coming-of-age story), *Mrs. Dalloway* (which explores the thoughts and feelings of an older woman), and *To the Lighthouse*, employ a stream-of-consciousness style that is often displayed in memoirs.

8

Further Reading

Hampl, Patricia.

I Could Tell You Stories: Sojourns in the Land of Memory. New York: Norton, 1999 (2000). 229pp. ISBN 0393320316.

Hampl is the author of two other memoirs, *A Romantic Education* and *Virgin Time*, and provides here a thought-provoking and highly descriptive treatise on the style and appeal of memoirs, as well as a consideration of how they are crafted out of an author's (often imperfect) memories.

Kappel, Lawrence, ed.

Autobiography. (The Greenhaven Press Companion to Literary Movements and Genres series). San Diego: Greenhaven Press, 2001. 224pp. ISBN 0737706724.

Although this volume contains more literary criticism than history of the development of the autobiographical form, it does have some interesting essays on classics in the field, particularly in the subject areas of women's and culturally diverse writings. Although many of the works cited are too historical to be of much use to the public librarian, either for research or title advisory purposes, the memoir chapter by Annie Dillard and those referring to Norman Mailer, Alex Haley, and Maya Angelou are all studies pertinent to the public library. The book also contains a bibliography of subject-appropriate scholarly resources (more so than representative autobiographies) that the interested librarian may wish to pursue.

Lopate, Phillip, ed.

The Art of the Personal Essay: An Anthology from the Classical Era to the Present. New York: Anchor Books, 1994 (1995). 777pp. ISBN 038542339X.

Lopate provides a comprehensive introduction to characteristics of personal essay writing, which is closely related to the longer form of memoir writing, as well as a history of the form and its earliest practitioners. Many of the authors and works included in the latter half of the anthology (M. F. K. Fisher, Edward Hoagland, Annie Dillard, and Richard Rodriguez among them) are also well-known memoir authors.

Murdock, Maureen.

Unreliable Truth: On Memoir and Memory. New York: Seal Press, 2003. 180pp. ISBN 1580050832.

Murdock combines her own memoir of her mother's struggle with Alzheimer's disease with thoughts on the crafting of memories into memoirs, providing many references to other seminal memoirs and memoirists. The author has also compiled an excellent bibliography of suggested memoirs and memoir-writing books.

Parini, Jay, ed.

The Norton Book of American Autobiography. New York: Norton, 1999. 711pp. ISBN 039304677X.

Parini introduces this collection of autobiographical pieces with a short essay discussing the history of autobiography, and portions from many seminal works have been included (on people such as Malcolm X, Maxine Kingston, Annie Dillard, Terry Tempest Williams, and Sherman Alexie).

References

Baxter, Charles, ed. 1999. *The Business of Memory: The Art of Remembering in an Age of Forgetting.* (Graywolf Forum Three). Saint Paul, Minn.: Graywolf Press.

Dawson, Alma, and Connie Van Fleet. 2004. "Books That Inspire: Nonfiction for a Multicultural Society." In *Nonfiction Readers' Advisory,* ed. Robert Burgin, 175–98. Westport, Conn.: Libraries Unlimited.

Fitzgerald, Mark. 2002. "When Does Creative Nonfiction Get Too Creative?" *Writer* 115, no. 11 (November): 15–17.

Hampl, Patricia. 1999. *I Could Tell You Stories: Sojourns in the Land of Memory.* New York: Norton.

Lopate, Phillip. 1995. *The Art of the Personal Essay: An Anthology from the Classical Era to the Present.* New York: Anchor Books.

Chapter 9

Relationships

Definition of the Relationships Genre

When Augusten Burroughs tells the story of his horrific childhood in *Running with Scissors*, complete with his mother's decision to relinquish him to the care and household of her psychiatrist, he provides for the reader vividly drawn characters and the story of his new life and family, but he also provides the impetus for the reader to continue by posing the unspoken questions: What kind of mother gives her son to her psychiatrist? What kind of doctor accepts a child from a patient? What on earth do the psychiatrist's other family members think of their new son/brother/stepbrother? Does a child to whom this happens still love his mother, and his former family? In short, Burroughs tells a story about relationships.

Anybody who has ever made the statement "I just don't know what she sees in him" (or any variation thereof) knows that the fascination with stories about relationships to both their participants and observers can often be hard to explain, much less define. Many of the titles selected for this chapter are memoirs (Mary Karr's *Liar's Club* and Dave Eggers's *A Heartbreaking Work of Staggering Genius*, to name but two), leading me to believe that, as is case in that genre, character development must be a large part of the appeal. However, in addition to these authors examining their inners thoughts and feelings and describing their development as individuals through their life experiences, they add the component of examining their interactions and seeking to discover the truth and motives behind the actions of those people (or sometimes even animals) to whom they are related, by ties of blood, love, friendship, or community. James Carroll writes about his experience as a Vietnam War protestor solely through the lens of trying to imagine how his father, a Lieutenant General, perceives his activities (*An American Requiem*), while Lawrence LaRose's realization that marriage means having to account for two opinions colors the entire story of remodeling his and his new wife's fixer-upper (*Gutted*). These are the stories of people's lives, told in the context of their relationships.

As prevalent as they are, memoirs are not the only literary form to make an appearance here. Biographies such as Gillian Gill's *The Nightingales* and Benita Eisler's *Chopin's Funeral* frame their entire narrative in terms of how the more famous characters in each story related to each other; in Gill's story Florence Nightingale is depicted first and foremost as a daughter and a sister, and only secondarily as a nurse, while in Eisler's narrative the tempestuous love story of George Sand and Frédéric Chopin is told in much more detail than tales of either of their prodigious professional lives.

Appeal of the Genre

Romance fiction, in addition to appealing to readers because of its vividly portrayed and individualistic characters, also undeniably devotes a large part of its narrative space to exploring the development, maintenance, and primarily the triumph of relationships. Romance also, as Diana Tixier Herald has said, "appeals to the heart and celebrates the power of love" (Herald 2000, 202). Although statistics for nonfiction romance or relationships titles are not available, the Romance Writers of America's (2005) finding that 33.8 percent of all popular fiction sold is romance fiction is indicative of that fiction genre's popularity. That association's further finding that 93 percent of all romance readers in 2002 were female is also illuminating. The fiction read-alike titles listed at the end of the chapter, although drawn from all genres of fiction, also reflect this lean toward romance and love relationships, primarily because this nonfiction genre is one of the most appealing to female readers. Romances are not the only works of fiction that might appeal to readers of relationship nonfiction (and vice versa); much literary fiction is often referred to as "women's fiction," which is defined by authors such as Susan Elizabeth Phillips and Jane Heller (two practitioners of the form) as "about women's empowerment," and "novels written with any relationship at the core of the plot" (Writingworld.com 2000) respectively.

You will not find the genre heading "Relationships" in any library catalog or nonfiction stack location. It is one of the categories we were most interested in pursuing for this collection, however, largely because of that fact. Readers and librarians are advised that, unlike bookstore "relationship" sections, which typically include self-help and inspirational titles for those looking to start, improve, or fix their relationships with family members, lovers, and friends; this chapter largely offers narratives that highlight the authors' personal experiences in groupings of many kinds.

Readers who enjoy these relationships titles might also enjoy the "people stories" found in the biography and memoir chapters. In particular, the "Coming-of-Age" and "Overcoming Adversity" subgenres of the "Memoirs and Autobiography" chapter might be rich sources of complementary reading choices for fans of the books annotated in this chapter.

Organization of the Chapter

The titles are divided into subgenres that explore various types of relationships—family relationships ("All in the Family," further divided into challenging and gentle reads), love stories in "All You Need Is Love" (although the phenomenon of love also appears in many family relationship stories, the use of the term here denotes relationships between lovers and spouses), friendships, and "Community Life." They have been placed in this order to roughly correspond with a "from the inside out" philosophy; most of us experience our first relationships within the context of our families, and then broaden our horizons to include our love interests, friends, and communities.

All in the Family

Some of the most complex relationships in our lives are those we share with family members and other relatives. The maxim "you can choose your friends but not your relatives" comes close to defining the sometimes claustrophobic atmosphere of family relationships; we all came from somewhere, and some of the most compelling nonfiction published in recent years has been that written by authors seeking to explore their relationships with their parents and siblings.

Family stories, as noted in the introduction to the chapter, tend to be delivered in memoir format, but they are unique in their authors' focus on the interpersonal and group dynamic, as opposed to the more introspective and personal "Coming-of-Age" or "Self-Discovery" memoirs.

Challenging Family Stories

Readers seeking to define both the fascination and the universality of not-so-sugarcoated stories about families need look no further than Leo Tolstoy's enduring novel *Anna Karenina*, in which he famously opined that "Happy families are all alike; every unhappy family is unhappy in its own way." The narratives in this section highlight families that face unhappy situations, such as unexpected illness or death (Allende's *Paula*, Eggers's *A Heartbreaking Work of Staggering Genius*), or individual weaknesses or conflicts (pretty much every other title). Most of these books, regardless of length, contain compelling stories in addition to character portraits, and as a result, many of them read quite quickly, even though they can be quite graphic in describing dysfunction, abuse, or other hardships.

Allende, Isabel.

Paula. New York: HarperCollins, 1995 (New York: HarperPerennial, 1996). 330pp. ISBN 0060927216.

When famous author Isabel Allende's twenty-eight-year-old daughter Paula became ill and fell into a coma, Allende began to write her complicated family history as a way to pass the time spent waiting with Paula in hospitals and at home, and in the hope that when Paula recovered, she could tell her all the family details she had missed. Told in Allende's distinctive voice, more that of a storyteller than a straightforward memoirist, the story details the relationships between Allende's grandparents, her parents and siblings, and her husbands and other children, and is heartbreaking in its acceptance of Paula's eventual death and passage into the spirit world.

Subjects: ALA Notable Books • Family Relationships—Mothers and Daughters • Health Issues • Memoirs

Now try: Allende's works of fiction often center on issues of family dynamics; readers who find this memoir compelling reading may also want to try some of her popular works, such as *The House of the Spirits* or *Daughter of Fortune*. She is also the author of a reflective travel memoir about her native country, *My Invented Country: A Nostalgic Journey through Chile*.

Burroughs, Augusten.

Running with Scissors: A Memoir. New York: St. Martin's Press, 2002 (New York: Picador, 2003). 315pp. ISBN 031242227X.

Definitely belonging to the "you have to read it to believe it" category, Burroughs's childhood memoir details his relationships with not one, but two challenging families: his dysfunctional biological family, including fighting parents and a distant brother, and his adoptive family, headed by Dr. Finch, his mother's psychiatrist, to whom his mother simply relinquished his care. In addition to having to become accustomed to several new adoptive siblings at the age of twelve, Burroughs also became illicitly involved with another of their much-older adopted sons. Those recommending this title to readers should remember that Burroughs is quite frank about all of his relationships throughout.

Subjects: Alcoholism • Drug Addiction • Dysfunctional Families • Family Relationships —Mothers and Sons • Memoirs • Psychiatry • Sexual Abuse

Now try: Marr Karr's memoir of her family, *Liar's Club: A Memoir*, may also appeal to fans of Augusten's writing. Burroughs's second memoir, *Dry: A Memoir*, relates his struggle with alcoholism, while *Magical Thinking: True Stories* is a less traumatic collection of essays, but all three of his works exhibit the author's extremely dark humor. Readers drawn to narratives describing less-than-healthy family relationships might consider Julie Gregory's powerful *Sickened: The Memoir of a Munchausen by Proxy Childhood*.

Carroll, James.

An American Requiem: God, My Father, and the War That Came Between Us. Boston: Houghton Mifflin, 1996. 279pp. ISBN 039585993X.

Carroll, author and former Roman Catholic priest, provides a memoir that explores both his childhood and his early adulthood experiences as a Vietnam War protestor, above all a story of the overriding influence on his life of his relationship with his father, Lieutenant General Joseph Carroll, who was the director of the Defense Intelligence Agency that chose Vietnamese targets. By turns a history of the war, a memoir of Catholic life, and a personal coming-of-age story when Carroll leaves the priesthood in favor of marriage and family life, the narrative is at all times an investigation of how the author's relationships with his parents and siblings affected his belief system and actions.

Subjects: Family Relationships—Fathers and Sons • Memoirs • National Book Award Winners • Religion • Vietnam War

Now try: James Tollefson's moving collection *The Strength Not to Fight: Conscientious Objectors of the Vietnam War—In Their Own Words* might appeal to readers who are intrigued by Carroll's story. Although it veers more toward the theological than does Carroll's personal memoir, John Yoder's *The Politics of Jesus* also examines the role of pacifism in religion. Readers most interested in the dynamics of father-and-son relationships might be drawn to memoirs such as *Native Son: A Memoir* by Tony Cohan, or Mikal Gilmore's superlative *Shot in the Heart*.

Eggers, Dave.

A Heartbreaking Work of Staggering Genius. New York: Simon & Schuster, 2000 (New York: Vintage Books, 2001). 437pp. ISBN 0375725784.

When Dave Eggers's parents both died of cancer within thirty-four days of each other, he undertook the guardianship of his then eight-year-old brother Toph, and they moved from their native Chicago to live nearer their sister Beth in California. In a style that was lauded critically and somehow manages to be self-effacing even while calling attention to itself, Eggers uses often breathless paragraphs and massive amounts of dialogue to relate the story of his relationships with his parents (particularly during their illnesses), his siblings, and the many other twenty-somethings who populate the narrative.

Subjects: ALA Notable Books • California • Cancer • Classics • Family Relationships—Siblings • Memoirs

Now try: Eggers's writing is as effortless to read as really good prose fiction, so readers might consider some fiction titles as read-alikes. Daniel Wallace's offbeat *Big Fish: A Novel of Mythic Proportions* (the film version appeared just a short while ago) examines a father's and son's relationship during the father's last illness; the main character in Kazuo Ishiguro's haunting *When We Were Orphans* also loses his parents at a young age; and Nathaniel Bellows's first novel, *On This Day: A Novel,* also follows the lives of two twenty-something siblings whose parents died from cancer and suicide. His book was hailed as a new (and sometimes raw) and self-aware form of memoir; another loudly honest book, for which he provided a blurb, is Donnell Alexander's *Ghetto Celebrity: Searching for My Father in Me.* The book is fascinating, a young black man's memoir of growing up in the ghetto in Sandusky, Ohio, but librarians may want to preview the book for language and tone before recommending it. Sean Wilsey, an editor-at-large for Eggers's Web site (www.mcsweeneys.net), has also written a memoir of his family's complicated life, *Oh the Glory of It All.*

Fuller, Alexandra.

Don't Let's Go to the Dogs Tonight: An African Childhood. New York: Random House, 2001 (2002). 315pp. ISBN 0375758992.

Fuller's memoir of her childhood in Rhodesia (now Zimbabwe) in the 1970s and early 1980s focuses primarily on her close but complex relationship with her mother Nicola and the rest of her family. Fuller tells a novelistic story of the family's many moves and tragedies, and places them adroitly against the background of the African continent she deeply loves.

Subjects: Africa • Book Sense Award Winners • Family Relationships • Landscape • Memoirs • World Travel

9

Now try: A surprisingly wide variety of memoirs in which the authors explore their intertwined experiences of place and family relationships have been published recently; *West of Then* (mother and daughter relationship, Hawaii) and *The Noise of Infinite Longing* (mother and daughter, Puerto Rico) are two of the most compelling. Fiction readers might also find George Hagen's superlative *The Laments,* a literary novel about one family's close and complicated relationships and constant moves, a good fiction reading companion.

Harpaz, Beth J.

Finding Annie Farrell: A Family Memoir. New York: St. Martin's Press, 2004. 271pp. ISBN 0312301510.

Although Harpaz's mother eventually became too depressed to leave the house or overcome her alcohol addition, her early life was a story of triumph over adversity, eventually making it to New York City after her mother died and she and her six siblings were abandoned by their father. This is a true family story, and Harpaz uses her journalistic skills to re-create her mother's childhood and family life, as well as her storytelling skills to weave a powerful story of her own attachments to her parents, her much older sister, and their four aunts.

Subjects: Alcoholism • Dysfunctional Families • Family Relationships • Investigative Stories • Memoirs

Now try: Francine du Plessix Gray also writes about her struggle to understand her parents' relationship to each other and herself, in *Them: A Memoir of Parents*; Helene Stapinski's forthright family memoir, *Five-Finger Discount: A Crooked Family History*, might also appeal to fans of Harpaz's book (Stapinski provided a blurb used on Harpaz's cover). Anna Cypra Oliver's *Assembling My Father: A Daughter's Detective Story* also follows much the same pattern, but with the opposite parent. Calvin Trillin's simple but moving biography of his father, *Messages from My Father*, is somewhat gentler than these memoirs of more dysfunctional families but still an illuminating look into family dynamics from the male point of view.

Karr, Mary.

The Liar's Club: A Memoir. New York: Viking, 1995 (New York: Penguin Books, 1996). 320pp. ISBN 0140179836.

Karr's relentlessly honest and sometimes unnerving series of childhood memories includes a "nervous" mother who reads Camus and Sartre and abandoned her previous family and children, a father who spends enough time at the bar to be part of the local male bullshitting "Liar's Club," her grandmother's painful death from cancer, an incident of sexual abuse by a neighborhood boy, and the author's complicated love for her sister and family. Karr's writing is straightforward, but it is her compelling story that will propel readers through the pages.

Subjects: ALA Notable Books • Alcoholism • Classics • Dysfunctional Families • Family Relationships • Memoirs

Now try: The subgenre of challenging family memoirs is a popular one, if one believes the best-selling lists: Augusten Burroughs's *Running with Scissors* is the story of a dysfunctional family from the male point of view; Jeannette Walls's *The Glass Castle: A Memoir* is similar to Karr's in its tone and the theme of still loving a family through difficulty and dysfunction. Adeline Yen Mah's *Falling Leaves: The Memoir of an Unwanted Chinese Daughter* explores the unhappy connections between siblings, as well as between children and their parents. Pulitzer Prize finalist Kim Barnes also tells a story of family heartbreak, as well as her coming-of-age in Idaho in her memoir *In the Wilderness: Coming of Age in Unknown Country*.

Kendall, Elizabeth.

American Daughter: Discovering My Mother. New York: Random House, 2000. 225pp. ISBN 0679452923.

Kendall explores both her extremely close relationship with her mother and the history of her parents' marriage, as well as her relationships with her aunts and siblings, in this lucidly written memoir that is highly evocative of both her parents' 1940s era and her 1960s childhood. Kendall also doesn't hide the fact that tragedy intruded upon her life and the lives of her siblings at a young age; her preface tells the story of the car accident in 1969 that took her mother's life and saddled Kendall (who was driving) with guilt for many years.

> **Subjects:** Accidents • Family Relationships • Marriage • Memoirs

> **Now try:** Alison Smith's memoir *Name All the Animals* is a similarly heartbreaking work that begins with a family tragedy. Smith is a frequent contributor to *McSweeney's,* and her prose is all the more stunning for its simplicity. Jamaica Kincaid's memoir of her brother's death from AIDS, *My Brother*, is also a story of struggling to understand her brother's lifestyle and their relationship as brother and sister. Although the death in Anne Tyler's novel is that of a child, rather than of a parent, her *The Tin Can Tree* also dwells on the difficulty of trying to resume a normal family life after a tragedy.

McCourt, Frank.

Angela's Ashes: A Memoir. New York: Scribner, 1996 (2003). 363pp. ISBN 068484267X.

Darkly humorous as only a story about a truly terrible childhood can be, McCourt's memoir relates the details of his parents' meeting and his birth in New York City, their return to County Donegal in Ireland and life of poverty there, the deaths of his twin brothers and sister, his Catholic education, and his father's ceaseless struggle with alcoholism and his mother's anguish when her children start returning to America. As relentlessly dreary as the wet weather McCourt describes, the memoir does retain a tone of boyish honesty and, thankfully, a sense of hardships endured and overcome, and it provides a lyrically nuanced account of family life in poverty-ridden Limerick.

> **Subjects:** ALA Notable Books • Alcoholism • Classics • Dysfunctional Families • Family Relationships • Immigration • Ireland • National Book Critics Circle Award Winners • Poverty • Pulitzer Prize Winners

> **Now try:** Frank McCourt also wrote a memoir about his early years in New York City, *'Tis*, and his brother Malachy has written a memoir entitled *A Monk Swimming*. Dan Barry's memoir of the Irish immigrant experience, *Pull Me Up: A Memoir*, is set in the 1960s, and details some gritty realities but a bit less adversity to face overall. McCourt also provides a blurb on the jacket of historian Thomas Fleming's dark father-and-son memoir, *Mysteries of My Father: An Irish-American Memoir.*

Roth, Philip.

Patrimony: A True Story. New York: Simon & Schuster, 1991 (New York: Vintage Books, 1996). 238pp. ISBN 0679752935.

Roth recounts his father's diagnosis of brain tumor and explores the experiences and consequences of Roth's necessary decision making about his father's treatment and eventual death. Personal but never sentimental, simple in prose style but never dull, Roth's accounts of his father's relationships with his peers are often as frustrating and humorous as that of his relationship with his sons.

Subjects: Death and Dying • Family Relationships—Fathers and Sons • Health Issues • National Book Critics Circle Award Winners • Memoirs

Now try: Terry Pluto's baseball memoir, which relies more on the story of his dad inspiring his appreciation for the Cleveland Indians, is titled *Our Tribe: A Baseball Memoir*. The somewhat contentious relationship between Art Spiegelman and his father is chronicled in his two-volume graphic novel about his parents' survival of the Holocaust, *Maus: My Father Bleeds History* and *Maus: And Here My Troubles Began*. Roth is of course much more recognized for his fiction writing; his family-relationship–centered novels that might appeal to these readers are *American Pastoral* and *I Married a Communist*.

Gentle Family Reads

Not all readers looking for a good story about family relationships will be in the mood for the more challenging works listed above. These "Gentle Family Reads" not only tell stories of families that (by and large) get along and draw strength and companionship from one another, but are told in a correspondingly more positive fashion and with fewer unsettling details and plot twists. They are feel-good reads, told by their authors with either a sense of wonder at the rareness and gift of family harmony (Debra Ginsberg's *About My Sisters*) or a healthy dose of humor (Ann Leary's *An Innocent, a Broad*).

Briggs, Raymond.

Ethel and Ernest: A True Story. New York: Knopf, 1998 (New York: Pantheon Books, 2001). 103pp. ISBN 0375714472.

Thoroughly enjoyable and a lightning-quick read, Briggs's story of his parents' meeting and marriage in England during World War II is gently and sympathetically told. Briggs, best known as the author of the perennial children's favorite picture book *The Snowman*, provides both an interesting period piece, as well as a surprisingly subtle consideration of his cockney father's relationship with his mother, who often aspired to be more "proper."

Subjects: England • Family Relationships • Gentle Reads • Graphic Novels • Love and Dating • Marriage • Quick Reads

Now try: Roddy Doyle transcribes the oral stories of his parents in *Rory and Ita*, in which they relate the details of their lives together in Dublin. Elizabeth Jane Howard's series, the <u>Cazalet Chronicle</u>, tells the story of an English family, their servants, and their relationships among themselves in the same time period (it begins in 1937). The books in the series (in order) are *The Light Years, Marking Time, Confusion,* and *Casting Off;* they cover three generations of Cazalet family life.

Gill, Gillian.

The Nightingales: The Extraordinary Upbringing and Curious Life of Miss Florence Nightingale. New York: Ballantine Books, 2004. 535pp. ISBN 0345451872.

Although ostensibly a group biography of the entire fascinating Nightingale family, Gill's narrative focuses primarily on the relationships among the various members, rather than outlining the chronological details of each family member or even that of their most famous daughter, nurse Florence Nightingale. Although the first few chapters explaining who married who read rather slowly, the reader who can make it past them will be rewarded with the fascinating and rich-in-character-detail story of the rich (but sometimes conflicted) friendship between Florence and her sister Parthenope, as well between the siblings and their parents. The book is long and convincingly researched, and the writing often sparkles in its honesty and intimacy.

> **Subjects:** Biographies • Epic Reads • Family Relationships • Health Issues • Nineteenth Century • Women's Contributions

> **Now try:** Judith Flanders's *Inside the Victorian Home: A Portrait of Domestic Life in Victorian England* provides even more detail on domestic and family life during that era. Another famous family of sisters is described in Flora Fraser's *Princesses: The Six Daughters of George III*, whose lives, along with those of their five brothers and their mother, were complicated by the madness of their royal father. Readers who enjoy the early nineteenth-century time period and familial details of the Nightingale story might also enjoy fiction classics by Jane Austen, who was writing slightly before that period, but who devoted a lot of attention to exploring the minutiae of family life.

Ginsberg, Debra.

About My Sisters. New York: HarperCollins, 2004 (New York: Perennial, 2005). 299pp. ISBN 0060522038.

Although Ginsberg's three very individual sisters feature most prominently in this memoir, she also considers her and their relationships with her brother, her parents, and her son. The book is organized chronologically and details both her specific interactions with her family members as individuals and their group dynamic, in extremely honest and accessible prose that never delves into sentimentality but rather evokes the complicated nature of close families, simultaneously summed up in the phrases "if you can't beat them, join them," and "can't live with them, can't live without them."

> **Subjects:** Family Relationships—Siblings • Gentle Reads • Humor • Memoirs

> **Now try:** Amy Wilensky's *The Weight of It: A Story of Two Sisters* is also a first-person look at the close but sometimes contentious relationship between two sisters. Patricia Volk's memoir, *Stuffed: Adventures of a Restaurant Family*, in addition to being a broadly based family story, also includes a wonderful description of the close relationship between the author and her sister.

Leary, Ann.

An Innocent, a Broad. New York: William Morrow, 2004. 244pp. ISBN 0060527234.

Ann Leary, wife of comedian Denis Leary and mother of two, relates the details of the birth of their first son Jack, who was born three months premature and in a London hospital (the couple was in England so Denis could perform in a comedy showcase). Heartily humorous despite the seriousness of the premature birth, Leary tells a story rich in family detail and gratitude for the English medical staff, whom she got to know quite well during her extended stay there.

Subjects: Family Relationships • Health Issues • Humor • Marriage • Pregnancy • Quick Reads

Now try: Judith Newman's narrative about her pregnancy, *You Make Me Feel Like an Unnatural Woman: Diary of a New (Older) Mother* may also appeal to fans of Leary's book, as might Lisa Belkin's *Life's Work: Confessions of an Unbalanced Mom* (those readers looking for the male point of view might enjoy Austin Murphy's *How Tough Could It Be: The Trials and Errors of a Sportswriter Turned Stay-at-Home Dad*). Dan Savage tells a funny but brutally honest tale of getting a baby with his boyfriend Terry (not for the delicate, due to language) and the travails of adoption, birth mothers with drug and alcohol problems, etc., in *The Kid: What Happened After My Boyfriend and I Decided to Get Pregnant*. Fiction readers might want to consider Allison Pearson's *I Don't Know How She Does It*.

Lennertz, Carl.

Cursed by a Happy Childhood: Tales of Growing Up, Then and Now. New York: Harmony Books, 2004. 199pp. ISBN 1400050456.

In the form of short and extremely quick-reading letters to his daughter, Lennertz describes the many happy moments of his own childhood so that she may someday better understand how parents bring their own experiences and memories to their parenting styles. The book is extremely light in tone and covers a variety of universal topics, such as the music tastes of different generations, cliques and teachers, and the ever-present dangers posed by such teen temptations as alcohol and drugs.

Subjects: Family Relationships • Gentle Reads • Parenting • Quick Reads

Now try: Peter Smith's memoir of his connection to his son through the music of the Beatles is titled *Two of Us: The Story of a Father, a Son, and the Beatles;* it showcases the relationship between a father and his children. Although about two friends rather than a father and son, Mitch Albom's *Tuesdays with Morrie* might also appeal to these readers, with its gentle tone and words of advice.

Sparks, Nicholas.

Three Weeks with My Brother. New York: Warner Books, 2004. 356pp. ISBN 0446532444.

When best-selling novelist Sparks got a flyer in the mail advertising a round-the-world tour, he almost threw it away—until he hit upon the plan of asking his brother Micah if he wanted to take the trip with him. Leaving their families behind and rediscovering their friendship with each other, the brothers worked through a seemingly endless list of family health tragedies and deaths in the course of their travels. Surprisingly positive in both tone and ending for a book with so many sorrows in it, the portrait of the Sparks brothers' love for each other and the rest of their family is the heartiest aspect of this narrative.

Subjects: Family Relationships—Siblings • Gentle Reads • Health Issues • Memoirs • World Travel

Now try: Jonathan Weiner's medical science book *His Brother's Keeper*, which follows the story of one brother diagnosed with a debilitating disease and another brother working in genetics looking for a way to help him, also illustrates the lengths to which brothers can and will go to help each other. Although readers may find his non-*Catcher in the Rye* texts a bit dated, J. D. Salinger's series of novellas about the Glass family also provide a strong portrait of sibling relationships; *Franny and Zooey, Raise High the Roof Beam, Carpenters,* and *Seymour: An Introduction* are short novels that pack a lot of family dynamics into a little space.

Steiker, Valerie.

The Leopard Hat: A Daughter's Story. New York: Pantheon Books, 2002 (New York: Vintage Books, 2003). 326pp. ISBN 0375726209.

The daughter of a Belgian-Jewish mother who came to America after having been hidden from the Nazis, Steiker tells the story of her and her sister's childhood in New York City and their experiences being raised by an urbane and fascinating mother with whom they were exceptionally close. Steiker's prose is exceptionally and sensually descriptive, particularly when describing her mother, and episodes such as her teenage rebellion against her mother's European sensibilities and her mother's death when she was only a junior in college are all detailed with honesty, providing a rich portrait of the relationships between a mother and her daughters.

Subjects: Culture Clash • Family Relationships—Mothers and Daughters • Immigration • Jews and Judaism • Memoirs • New York City • Urban Life

Now try: Rick Bragg's proud and loving memoirs of his mother and grandparents, *All Over But the Shoutin'* and *Ava's Man*, respectively, might also appeal to fans of Steiker's tribute to her mother. Paul Rudnick's great comic novel, *I'll Take It*, is the story of three urbane New York City sisters, one of their sons, and their autumn drive to see the leaves change (and maybe do a little shopping along the way).

Tucker, Neely.

Love in the Driest Season: A Family Memoir. New York: Crown Publishers, 2004. 242pp. ISBN 0609609769.

A staff reporter for the *Washington Post*, Neely details his and his wife Vita's journey to Zimbabwe to report on the civil war there in 1997 and volunteering in an orphanage where many of the children were afflicted with AIDS and other diseases. It was there that they found Chipo, a tiny baby girl who had been abandoned in the countryside and hovered on the brink of death for many months after her admittance into the orphanage hospital. Although Neely interjects journalistic details of his and Vita's experiences in the middle of a war-torn country, the main story here is his relationship with his wife (the "girl next door" he met in Detroit) and their becoming a family when they adopted Chipo as their own daughter, as well as their place in the world community.

Subjects: Adoptions • Africa • Family Relationships • Health Issues • Love and Dating • Marriage • World Travel

Now try: Janis Cooke Newman's memoir of her and her husband's experience adopting a Russian child is detailed in *The Russian Word for Snow: A True Story of Adoption*, and is particularly similar to Tucker's memoir in its detailing of the economy of bribes and cash payments. Joanna Catherine Scott's novel about three Korean girls adopted by an American mother, *The Lucky Gourd Shop*, might also appeal to those readers interested in the subject.

All You Need Is Love

Sometimes there's just no accounting for the experience of love. In addition to providing the fodder for all kinds of folk wisdom, such as "opposites attract" or "absence makes the heart grow fonder," romantic love relationships provide an air of intangibility that makes these books seem vaguely like mystery stories without the blood and gore (although sometimes there are plenty of guilty parties, for a variety of reasons). In recognition of the fact that many romance readers have made their preference for happy endings known, many of the titles below feature happy endings and heartfelt affirmations (Harwood's *The Oldest Gay Couple in America*, Schlossberg's *The Curse of the Singles Table*); while some feature fascinating but somewhat tragic or doomed relationships that readers may have a hard time looking away from (Eisler's *Chopin's Funeral*, Santiago's *The Turkish Lover*).

Eisler, Benita.

Chopin's Funeral. New York: Knopf, 2003 (New York: Vintage Books, 2004). 230pp. ISBN 0375708685.

Eisler details a lovers' relationship fully as complicated as any found in our current century in her dual biography of the composer and pianist Frédéric Chopin and French novelist and prototype feminist George Sand. Although Eisler bows to biographical convention long enough to share the particulars of their childhoods and early lives, she primarily elaborates on their often difficult but also strangely mutually dependent affair, which Sand ended when Chopin criticized her treatment of her daughter. Although by all accounts their affair (and Sand's many others) was deeply passionate, the author's style is somewhat Victorian in her lack of description on that point, and this story will appeal to the many readers who don't need their biographies to be too explicit.

Subjects: Biographies • Literary Lives • Love Affairs • Music and Musicians • Nineteenth Century

Now try: Eisler is also the author of another dual biography exploring the love between two of the twentieth century's most iconic artists, *O'Keeffe and Stieglitz: An American Romance*. A more modern European couple who might interest readers are Princess Grace and Prince Rainier of Monaco; the story of their lives after the fairytale wedding is told in the double biography *Once Upon a Time: Behind the Fairy Tale of Princess Grace and Prince Rainier*.

Harwood, Gean.

The Oldest Gay Couple in America: A 70-Year Journey Through Same-Sex America. Secaucus, N.J.: Carol Publishing, 1997. 304pp. ISBN 1559724269.

Although Harwood's narrative serves as a double autobiography and history of same-sex relationships in America, his sincere recollection of his relationship with Bruhs Mero, which spanned more than sixty years, is the focus of his story. His prose is personal and simply styled; his assertion that his love for Bruhs "is the only thing of any permanence in my life" stark testimony to the strength of their relationship. The book is organized chronologically and relates the details of twentieth-century life, from the New York City theatrical scene of the 1920s and 1930s, to the McCarthyism of the 1950s, to the sexual revolution of the 1970s.

> **Subjects:** Art and Artists • Biographies • Homosexuality • Love and Dating • Memoirs • Sexuality

> **Now try:** Although the author notes that her narrative is "creative nonfiction," in that she mingles the details of personal memoir with poetic license, Barrie Jean Borich's tale of her twelve-year relationship with Linnea Stenson, *My Lesbian Husband: Landscapes of a Marriage,* recounts a similarly long-term relationship story, albeit with less history and more sensual details than Harwood's book.

Johnson, Jonathan.

Hannah and the Mountain: Notes Toward a Wilderness Fatherhood. Lincoln: University of Nebraska Press, 2005. 224pp. ISBN 0803226012.

No sooner had twenty-nine-year-old Johnson and his new wife Amy moved to his family's cabin in Idaho than they learned Amy was pregnant. Although they thought their greatest challenge would be getting the cabin in shape for their new arrival, the couple faced a series of greater challenges over the early years of their marriage as Amy's first pregnancy, with a daughter they called Hannah, ended in failure to bring the baby to term, and a second pregnancy resulted in a traumatic miscarriage. The couple's odyssey to both "return to the land" and have a child is intertwined to powerful effect in this short but substantive narrative.

> **Subjects:** Idaho • Landscape • Love and Dating • Marriage • Memoirs • Pregnancy • Rural Life

> **Now try:** Other titles in the <u>American Lives</u> series, edited by Tobias Wolff, that may appeal to Johnson's readers are *Fault Lines* by Laurie Alberts, *Pieces from Life's Crazy Quilt* by Marvin Arnett, and *Thoughts from a Queen-Sized Bed* by Mimi Schwartz.

9

LaRose, Lawrence.

Gutted: Down to the Studs in My House, My Marriage, My Entire Life. New York: Bloomsbury, 2004. 278pp. ISBN 1582343926.

In this book LaRose, the author of the dating manual *The Code: How to Get What You Want from Women Without Marrying Them,* finds himself newly married and in a "fixer-upper" home, the fixing up of which is starting to consume his life. Readers of both sexes should find this an enjoyable read between the multiple Home Depot moments and the all-too-familiar early marital squabbles and compromises. Quickly paced and humorous, LaRose's tale provides a healthy dose of what he describes as "home porn" (stories about remodeling) and realizations about marriage, including the "near-debilitating realization that marriage means *two* sets of opinions."

Subjects: Homes • Humor • Marriage • Memoirs • Quick Reads

Now try: David Owen's *Life Under a Leaky Roof: Reflections on Home, Tools, and Life Outside the Big City* is also an enjoyable "fixer-upper" read. Kate Whouley's *Cottage for Sale: Must Be Moved* does not include a marriage, but she also tells an enjoyable story of home maintenance and her close circle of friends. Spalding Gray's short marriage and family memoir, *Morning, Noon and Night,* although missing the home improvement dimension, is remarkably similar in its dryly sardonic tone and humorous insights.

Santiago, Esmerelda.

The Turkish Lover. Cambridge, Mass.: Da Capo Press, 2004. 341pp. ISBN 0738208205.

One week after her twenty-first birthday, Santiago left the home where she lived with her extended family and controlling mother to join her much older lover Ulvi, with whom she shared a relationship based more on passion than companionship. Although that relationship overshadows the rest in the book, she also tells the story of her family's migration from Puerto Rico to the United States and back again.

Subjects: Culture Clash • Family Relationships • Love Affairs • Memoirs • Sexuality

Now try: *The Turkish Lover* is actually the third installment in Santiago's series of memoirs; both *When I Was Puerto Rican* and *Almost a Woman* were also favorably reviewed and detail many relationships between friends and family members.

Schlossberg, Suzanne.

The Curse of the Singles Table: A True Story of 1,001 Nights without Sex. New York: Warner Books, 2004. 257pp. ISBN 0446690546.

Although Schlossberg presents her "Celibacy Era" with tragic overtones, she in fact tells a very enjoyable and admirably self-effacing and lighthearted tale of the trials and tribulations of dating, her chapters/essays dwelling on such various horrors as the "Singles Table" at weddings and speed dating. She is a likable narrator, and by beginning her book with her trip to arctic Russia to celebrate her dubious title achievement, she adds a little adventure to her standard romantic laments.

Subjects: Essays • Humor • Love and Dating • Memoirs • World Travel

Now try: Jennifer Cox's extremely humorous dating travelogue, *Around the World in 80 Dates,* might appeal to Schlossberg's readers. Brett Leveridge mined his mother's story of her dating exploits in his hilarious essay collection, *Men My Mother Dated.* A few of my favorite fiction read-alikes to this book are Rita Ciresi's *Pink Slip, Dating without Novocaine* by Lisa Cach, and *See Jane Date* by Melissa Senate (all from Red Dress Ink); they might provide a similar cynically hopeful laugh and read.

Tarte, Bob.

    Enslaved by Ducks: How One Man Went from Head of the Household to Bottom of the Pecking Order. Chapel Hill, N.C.: Algonquin Books of Chapel Hill, 2003 (2004). 308pp. ISBN 1565124502.

    Freelance writer and music columnist Tarte provides a lighthearted look at his and his wife Linda's life surrounded by the members of their animal menagerie. Starting with their antisocial bunny Binky and including vignettes about all of their pets, from parrots to cats to ducks, Tarte details the complex but loving relationships they have with each other and their pets that are the mainstay of their rural life.

        Subjects: Animals • Gentle Reads • Humor • Marriage • Memoirs • Rural Life

        Now try: *The Wild Parrots of Telegraph Hill: A Love Story . . . with Wings*, by Mark Bittner, also explores a man's becoming at home as a member of his community, among birds he befriends, and with the woman he loves. Jeanne Marie Laskas provides a feminine version of the same story of love among animals and humans in her amusingly titled *Fifty Acres and a Poodle: A Story of Love, Livestock, and Finding Myself on a Farm*. Bernd Heinrich's story of seasons spent observing the family lives of geese, *The Geese of Beaver Bog*, might also appeal to animal lovers.

With a Little Help from My Friends

    Sometimes, after all, that's all we need to get by. Friendship stories explore the dynamics of our relationships with those people whom we choose to befriend but sometimes neglect as a result of more demanding family and love relationships and expectations. Because they are usually freely chosen, however, they represent an important facet of our emotional lives; friends often fulfill for us needs that aren't met by any other companions in our lives. Friendships are often uplifting, as reflected by titles such as Albom's *Tuesdays with Morrie*, but can also be challenging due to human nature and habits that can change and follow paths either closer to those of our friends or more divergent from them, as illustrated in Ann Patchett's heartrending *Truth and Beauty*, about her relationship with fellow author Lucy Grealy. In addition to being compelling stories, many titles listed here are also quite short and can be considered good "light" or "beach" reads.

    One title that may seem out of place is Sterling North's childhood memoir about his pet raccoon, Rascal. It is here because it is primarily the story of the relationship between a boy and his closest companion and friend for the summer, in which the friend just happens to be an animal. Readers particularly fond of North's book may consider branching out from this chapter and into the "Animals" section of the environmental chapter for related reads about the special friendships that often exist between humans and animals.

9

Albom, Mitch.

Tuesdays with Morrie: An Old Man, a Young Man, and Life's Greatest Lesson. New York: Doubleday, 1997 (New York: Broadway Books, 2002). 192pp. ISBN 076790592X.

When journalist Albom learned that his college professor and mentor Morrie Schwartz was dying from ALS (Lou Gehrig's Disease), he asked to visit him, and eventually turned the visits into regular weekly events. Although Albom ostensibly sought simply to let Schwartz know how much he had already learned from him, over the course of the visits he learned even more about the truly important things in life.

Subjects: Classics • Education • Friendships • Gentle Reads • Health Issues • Quick Reads • Spirituality

Now try: Albom's small volume was on best-seller lists for years and continues to circulate well; fans of his work might also enjoy his most recent and similarly spiritual novel, *The Five People You Meet in Heaven*. Tim Russert's *Big Russ and Me: Father and Son—Lessons of Life* delivers exactly what its subtitle promises in his similar tribute to his father. Female readers might enjoy Marie Brennan's book of interviews with prominent women whom she was inspired by; her use of the first person voice in *Great Dames: What I Learned from Older Women* is also similar to Albom's style. Although the friendship described in *The World According to Mister Rogers: Important Things to Remember* is between a television personality and his legions of fans rather than between two individuals, readers might enjoy the volume's gentle reflections on love and courage.

Anderson, Joan.

A Walk on the Beach: Tales of Wisdom from an Unconventional Woman. New York: Broadway Books, 2004. 223pp. ISBN 0767914740.

When she retreated to a small cottage near a Cape Cod beach, Anderson originally set out to spend some time by herself in meditation and solitude, but during one of her many walks on the beach, she met Joan Erikson, widow of the famous psychoanalyst Erik Erikson. Struggling through her own midlife crisis, Anderson good-naturedly examines the irony present in her growing friendship with the wife of the man who coined the term "identity crisis," and comes to appreciate the quiet wisdom offered to her by the older woman.

Subjects: Atlantic Coast • Friendships • Gentle Reads • Landscape

Now try: This is Anderson's most recent title; it is actually the third in her series of books ruminating on relationships, marriage, and spirituality (the first two are *A Year by the Sea: Tales of Wisdom from an Unconventional Woman* and *An Unfinished Marriage*). Readers who enjoy Anderson's description of her process of discovering what it means to be an individual and a friend and a partner might also enjoy Anne Tyler's novel *Ladder of Years*, in which the protagonist one day simply walks away from her not unhappy marriage and forms a new and independent life for herself.

Berry, Carmen Renee, and Tamara Traeder.

Girlfriends: Invisible Bonds, Enduring Ties. Berkeley, Calif.: Wildcat Canyon Press, 1995. 230pp. ISBN 1885171080.

Less a series of stories about female friendships than a collection of essays considering the formation and importance of friendships among women, this small volume offers numerous quotes and literary allusions on the subject, and the authors use them to paint a synthesized portrait of feminine relationships. From the phenomenon of feeling instant rapport with a new friend to the heartbreak caused when losing one to death or distance, the authors create a solid picture of the ephemeral nature of being "girlfriends."

> **Subjects:** Essays • Friendships • Gentle Reads • Sociology

> **Now try:** Berry's follow-up title, *Girlfriends for Life: Friendships Worth Keeping Forever*, also delves into examples and the meanings of female friendships; multiple fiction books cover this title as well (the subject heading "Female Friendship-Fiction" retrieved 513 hits in my library catalog search; the heading for nonfiction titles retrieved 25); searches on novelists and "women's fiction" authors such as Elizabeth Berg, Jane Heller, Cassandra King, Lorna Landvik, Nancy Thayer, or Rebecca Wells might also yield some suitable related reads.

Duriez, Colin.

Tolkien and C. S. Lewis: The Gift of Friendship. Mahwah, N.J.: Hidden Spring Books, 2003. 244pp. ISBN 1587680262.

Duriez bows to biographical convention enough to open his narrative with short overviews of the childhoods of Tolkien and Lewis, but the majority of the text focuses on the strong friendship between the two authors while they were both teaching at Oxford, as well as the influence of each other's ideas and opinions on their literary works. There are few salacious or overly personal details here, and it is a well-reasoned examination of the often complicated friendship between two famous British authors.

> **Subjects:** Biographies • Friendships • Literary Lives

> **Now try:** Harmon Smith's *My Friend, My Friend: The Story of Thoreau's Relationship with Emerson* also describes a literary friendship. Lynn Schooler's quietly poignant *The Blue Bear: A True Story of Friendship, Tragedy, and Survival in the Alaskan Wilderness* describes the author's friendship with wildlife photographer Michio Hoshino.

Hirsch, James S.

Two Souls Indivisible: The Friendship That Saved Two POWs in Vietnam. Boston: Houghton Mifflin, 2004. 274pp. ISBN 0618273484.

A friendship strong enough to save the lives of its participants is the core story of this examination of the POW experiences of two Vietnam veterans. Although much of the narrative relates the individual details of Fred Cherry's and Porter Halyburton's lives, military careers, and separate experiences in a North Vietnamese prison, their experience as cell roommates for seven months, during which Halyburton cared for a severely injured Cherry and Cherry's mental toughness inspired a despairing Halyburton, is the author's focus. Although the North Vietnamese may have hoped that racial differences (Halyburton was a white naval lieutenant from North Carolina, Cherry an African American Air Force pilot) would provide further anguish for the prisoners, each man eventually credited the other with saving his life. Although details of torture and medical

9

horrors are not lingeringly described, readers should be aware that portions of the story do pertain to physical ailments and torture.

> **Subjects:** Friendships • Health Issues • Prisons • Racism • Vietnam War

> **Now try:** Although Mark Bowden's *Black Hawk Down: A Story of Modern War* depends more on its action for its appeal, it also provides a glimpse of the camaraderie among soldiers in wartime. Lewis Carlson's oral histories from Korean War veterans and their families are collected in *Remembered Prisoners of a Forgotten War: An Oral History of Korean War POWs*, and also provide a character-rich narrative of survival.

Konik, Michael.

In Search of Burningbush: A Story of Golf, Friendship, and the Meaning of Irons.
New York: McGraw-Hill, 2004. 279pp. ISBN 0071435212.

Author Konik and his friend Don Naifeh met while Konik was playing in Binion's World Series of Poker and Naifeh was a dealer; during the course of their conversation they discovered that each loved the game of golf to distraction. In addition to their tale of friendship and transcendental golf outings, Konik's description of Naifeh's struggling to rise to the level of his own best game while suffering from osteogenesis imperfecta (brittle-bone disease) is both understated and inspiring; the book culminates in the pair's playing on the legendary Scottish course named in the title.

> **Subjects:** Friendships • Gentle Reads • Golf • Health Issues • Quick Reads

> **Now try:** Stephen Ambrose's short collection of essays celebrating male friendships between brothers, peers, friends, and veterans, *Comrades: Brothers, Heroes, Sons, Pals*, includes stories about relationships among his own family and peer groups, as well as those between such luminaries as Dwight Eisenhower and his brothers and between Lewis and Clark. Brian De Vido's *Every Time I Talk to Liston: A Novel* describes a friendship that developed through sports.

North, Sterling.

Rascal: A Memoir of a Better Era.
New York: Dutton, 1963 (New York: Puffin Books, 2004). 189pp. ISBN 0142402524.

Although this older book most often shows up in juvenile nonfiction, there's absolutely nothing about it that won't also appeal to adult readers, particularly older readers who might remember a time closer to the book's era of 1918. Primarily the autobiographical story of North's friendship with a wild raccoon that he adopted and named Rascal, it also includes reminiscences about his kindly family members (particularly his sister, who tried in the absence of their deceased mother to comfort the young North) and community life in the early twentieth century. Both lyrical and spare, this is a book that asks to be read in one sitting.

> **Subjects:** Animals • Classics • Family Relationships • Friendships • Gentle Reads • Memoirs • Rural Life • Wisconsin

> **Now try:** Ben Logan's similarly autobiographical *The Land Remembers* also includes animal stories, but most resemblesi this book through the memories about his family members and a childhood spent on a farm. Readers who enjoy gentler works about better times gone by might also enjoy Wendell Berry's novels, many of which are set in the fictional community Port Williams, Kentucky: *Jayber Crow, A Place on Earth*, and *Hannah Coulter*.

Patchett, Ann.

Truth and Beauty: A Friendship. New York: HarperCollins, 2004. 257pp. ISBN 0060572140.

The main character in novelist Patchett's account of her friendship with author Lucy Grealy is the friendship itself. Patchett doesn't shirk from detailing the many trials of their lives together as friends and roommates, honestly describing Grealy's often unhealthily dependent relationships and financial, medical, and drug addictions until her premature death at age thirty-nine; she does a creditable job of illuminating the intangible qualities that all friendships, and theirs in particular, offer.

> **Subjects:** Alcoholism • Drug Addiction • Friendships • Health Issues • Literary Lives • Memoirs

> **Now try:** Lucy Grealy is well-known for her memoir detailing her struggle with jaw cancer, reconstructive surgery, drug addiction, and personal demons, *Autobiography of a Face*; that book should definitely be read as a companion to this one. Patchett is also a novelist, and readers may want to try her best seller *Bel Canto: A Novel*, or *The Magician's Assistant*, in both of which she develops her stories with a masterful use of language, but at a slightly slower pace than many modern novels use.

Community Life

Anyone looking for a place to live could tell you that, although it might be nice to choose your residence based on your neighbors and community attributes, most often issues of economics and other relationships dictate your living situation, and you very rarely get to choose your neighbors. In addition to being driven by a number of entertaining and individual characters, the following books derive much of their charm and appeal from both their settings and their descriptions of the relationships between people who can have vastly different personalities and attributes while occupying the same geographical piece of earth. Readers who enjoy these titles might also enjoy those listed in the "Back to the Land" subgenre of the environmental chapter, as those titles also rely heavily on the appeal of setting and its physical and psychological effects on the inhabitants of certain locales.

Herriot, James.

All Creatures Great and Small. New York: St. Martin's Press, 1972 (2004). 442pp. ISBN 0312084986.

Herriot's first novelistic memoir of life as a rural vet in England packs two relationship whammies in one book; not only does he describe the practical but often loving bonds between farmers and village residents and their animals, but he also devotes a considerable amount of space to relating the details of his relationships with his colleagues (the Farnon brothers, Siegfried and Tristan), his wife and family, and his adopted Yorkshire community. Although Herriot's use of language is wonderful in its understated simplicity, he also tells a rollicking good story.

Subjects: Agriculture • Animals • Classics • Community Life • England • Family Relationships • Gentle Reads • Landscape • Rural Life

Now try: Herriot wrote numerous memoirs about his veterinary practice (the volumes after this one are *All Things Bright and Beautiful, All Things Wise and Wonderful*, and *The Lord God Made Them All*) as well as story collections such as *James Herriot's Dog Stories* and *James Herriot's Cat Stories*. Douglas Whynott's *A Country Practice: Scenes from the Veterinary Life* follows the experiences of a group of vets in practice in America. Anglophile fans of Herriot's works might also include Agatha Christie's mysteries featuring Miss Jane Marple, who lives in the small English village St. Mary Mead and extrapolates crime solutions from the personalities of small-town characters she knows. Jan Karon's popular <u>Mitford</u> series, set in a small town in the Blue Ridge Mountains, are also gentle reads, about a minister and his community (the series starts with *At Home in Mitford, A Light in the Window*, and *These High, Green Hills*).

Lende, Heather.

If You Lived Here, I'd Know Your Name: News from Small-Town Alaska. Chapel Hill, N.C.: Algonquin Books of Chapel Hill, 2005. 281pp. ISBN 1565123166.

Set in the small town of Haines, Alaska, 800 from Anchorage, Lende's smooth narrative of small-town life is interrupted only by periodic articles published in the town newspaper's "Duly Noted" column, which she writes. A frequent contributor to NPR, Lende's descriptions of her neighbors and frontier life are always honest but nevertheless commendably gentle.

Subjects: Alaska • Community Life • Family Relationships • Friendships • Humor • Journalism • Memoirs

Now try: Robert McG. Thomas was an obituary writer for *The New York Times*. His personal and beautifully written life stories appear in *52 McGs.: The Best Obituaries from Legendary* New York Times *Reporter Robert McG. Thomas*. There is also a blurb on the back of Lende's book by Stewart O'Nan, whose many novels, including *Wish You Were Here*, also explore the ties that bind (in good and bad ways) in families and in communities.

Perry, Michael.

Population 485: Meeting Your Neighbors One Siren at a Time. New York: HarperCollins, 2002 (2003). 234pp. ISBN 0060958073.

In chapters that tell poignant but never sentimentalized stories about his neighbors, family members, and friends, Perry explores his move back to his rural hometown, New Auburn, Wisconsin, and his experiences as a volunteer EMT for the local fire department. Perry makes a number of literary and philosophical allusions, combining them convincingly with modest and enjoyable humor.

Subjects: Community Life • Family Relationships • Friendships • Humor • Memoirs • Professions • Rural Life • Wisconsin

Now try: Suzanne Strempek Shea also gets to know her colleagues and her Massachusetts community while working at her local bookstore; she describes the experience in her memoir *Shelf Life: Romance, Mystery, Drama, and Other Page-Turning Adventures from a Year in a Bookstore*. Those readers who wouldn't mind a sports book might also want to consider *Hoosiers: The Fabulous Basketball Life of Indiana*, which examines the importance of the sport to communities throughout the state, at both the high school and college levels.

Consider Starting With . . .

The titles below represent the tried and true, likely to be popular with readers who enjoy relationship stories.

Albom, Mitch. *Tuesdays with Morrie*.

Briggs, Raymond. *Ethel and Ernest: A True Story*.

Karr, Mary. *The Liar's Club: A Memoir*.

LaRose, Lawrence. *Gutted: Down to the Studs in My House, My Marriage, My Entire Life*.

Perry, Michael. *Population 485: Meeting Your Neighbors One Siren at a Time*.

Fiction Read-Alikes

- **Baxter, Charles.** Baxter's novels are definitely character-driven, and many quietly explore the dynamics of relationships, particularly those within families. *First Light*, published in 1987, is a novel told backwards; it begins with the strain between brother and sister Hugh and Dorsey and progresses back through their lives, ending with Dorsey first being introduced to her older brother. Likewise, *Shadow Play* and *The Feast of Love* both focus on family and community relations, as well as friendships.

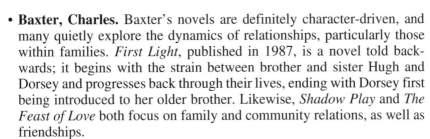

- **Binchy, Maeve.** The great majority of Binchy's novels explore family relationships and community friendships in their rural Irish settings. She is hugely popular, particularly among female readers, and her novels *Silver Wedding* and *Tara Road,* as well as her collection of intertwined stories in *The Lilac Bus* might be good starting points for readers looking to try her.

- **Desai, Anita.** Desai brings an international awareness to her critically praised stories about cultural and familial expectations and constraints; many of them are set in both India and America. *Fasting, Feasting* tells the story of an Indian family and their two daughters and one son; *Journey to Ithaca* explores the dynamics of a married couple's relationship as they travel to India.

- **Dickey, Eric Jerome.** Dickey is skilled at portraying complex relationships of all types; in his first novel, *Sister, Sister*, he tells the story of a close-knit but still widely different extended family, while *Milk in My Coffee* is often hailed as a humorous and romantic story of the love relationship between a white woman and a black man.

9

- **Hamilton, Jane.** Hamilton packs a lot of relationship punch into her novels. In *The Book of Ruth*, her main protagonist goes from a challenging and stunted childhood family life to an unhealthy marriage; in *A Map of the World* she considers both her main characters' married relationship and their status as outsiders in the rural community they seek to join as dairy farmers.

- **Minot, Susan.** Minot's debut novel *Monkeys* follows the rather rambunctious family life of the Vincent family, complete with two parents and seven children; her collection of stories, *Lust and Other Stories*, is a series of vignettes of modern love relationships that are all, to varying degrees, unsuccessful.

- **Shields, Carol.** Pulitzer Prize–winning author Shields has an extraordinary ability to portray the lives and relationships of "ordinary" people in such a way that their stories take on a quiet, universal beauty. *The Stone Diaries*, for which she won the Pulitzer, is a novel in diary form, written by Daisy Goodwill Flett, who writes about her connections to her parents, children, husband, and friends; in *The Box Garden* she explores a woman's failed marriage and her single-handed raising of her son; in her last novel, *Unless*, she tells the story of a family whose daughter chooses to live on the streets of Toronto after a traumatizing event, and their struggle to come to terms with each other's different ways of dealing with the situation.

- **Sparks, Nicholas.** Many of Sparks's best-selling novels, which are heavy on the romance, have also been made into successful movies (*Message in a Bottle* and *The Notebook* among them). His latest titles are *True Believer*, *The Guardian*, and *The Wedding*.

- **Tan, Amy.** Tan's first novel, *The Joy Luck Club*, relates the intertwined stories of a group of Chinese American mothers and their daughters. Many of her subsequent novels, such as *The Kitchen God's Wife* and *The Bonesetter's Daughter*, have also received favorable critical attention for their detailing of relationships between the (primarily) female characters.

- **Tyler, Anne.** Tyler, like Carol Shields, is often lauded for her ability to weave dramatic and sympathetic stories around rather ordinary characters. She won the Pulitzer Prize for *Breathing Lessons*, the story of Maggie and Ira Moran's marriage and their relationships with their children; she also describes several generations of families in *The Clock Winder*, *Dinner at the Homesick Restaurant*, *Saint Maybe*, and *The Accidental Tourist*.

- **Wells, Rebecca.** All of Wells's best-selling novels—*Little Altars Everywhere*, *Divine Secrets of the Ya-Ya Sisterhood*, and *Ya-Yas in Bloom*—examine the ties of friendship and love among Southern women and their families.

- **Wodehouse, P. G.** Sure, they're supposed to be employer and employee, rather than friends, but the relationship between Wodehouse's enduring comic creation, Bertie Wooster, and his long-suffering valet, Jeeves, is a masterpiece of humor and a testament to the enduring strength of male camaraderie. It's a challenge to create a purely chronological list of Jeeves titles, but *How Right You Are, Jeeves*, *Jeeves and the Tie That Binds*, *Life with Jeeves*, and *Thank You, Jeeves* are all highly recommended.

- **Wolitzer, Meg.** Wolitzer's thoroughly unsentimental portraits of husbands and wives, as well as of families, in her recent novels *The Wife* and *The Position,* offer literary and enjoyable stories about the nitty-gritty details of relating to other people.

Further Reading

Aron, Paul.

>*Count the Ways: The Greatest Love Stories of All Time.* Chicago: Contemporary Books, 2002. 288pp. ISBN 0071381740.

>Aron has compiled a number of the most famous love stories, Paul Newman and Joanne Woodward to Spencer Tracy and Katharine Hepburn, from Johnny Cash and June Carter Cash to Amelia Earhart and G. P. Putnam. Although this is not a scholarly volume about relationships in literature, it might provide inspiration for related biographical readings relating to love stories.

References

Herald, Diana Tixier. 2000. *Genreflecting: A Guide to Reading Interests in Genre Fiction.* 5th ed. Englewood, Colo.: Libraries Unlimited.

Romance Writers of America. 2005. www.rwanational.org/statistics/industry_stats.htm (accessed April 21, 2005).

Writingworld.com. 2000. www.writing-world.com/romance/craig.shtml (accessed August 20, 2005).

Part 4

Stylistic Genres

Investigative Writing

Making Sense . . .

Chapter 10

Investigative Writing

Definition of Investigative Writing

The roots of investigative writing can be found, to a large degree, in the long tradition of American journalism. In the 1860s, numerous reporters produced the first "frontline" reports from Civil War battlefields, by 1871 muckraking reporters had broken the story of the Boss Tweed ring in *The New York Times*, and by 1888 Nellie Bly was taking a trip around the world just so she could describe her experiences to her readers.

The first book-length work of exposé journalism, Ida Tarbell's *The History of the Standard Oil Company* (published in 1904) first appeared as a serial in *McClure's Magazine*, and was not so much a history of the company as an examination of its operating procedures and the methods of its chairman, John D. Rockefeller (Weinberg 2005, 25). Eventually the popularity of such muckraking pieces, written by Tarbell and her contemporaries (including Upton Sinclair) faded, and newspapers turned to new methods to sell papers, but the methods of the writers continued to be used: comprehensive research, combined with extensive interviews, and dramatic and skillful (and still sometimes quite sensationalistic) prose writing.

In addition to providing annotations about more stereotypical works of journalism and reporting, this chapter includes many titles that fall into the category of "new journalism," or "literary journalism." Pioneered by such authors as Tom Wolfe (*The Right Stuff*), Gay Talese, and Truman Capote (whose *In Cold Blood* is annotated in the true crime chapter), who mastered the format and increased the popularity of the personality profile, the new journalism has been defined in many ways but can most easily be thought of as that school of reporting that seeks to employ four basic narrative techniques—scene-by-scene construction, use of recorded dialogue, a third-person point of view allowing readers to feel that they are inside the character's mind, and the recording of "everyday" gestures and manners—to report on actual persons and events, and which started to be discussed in the mid-1960s (Wolfe and Johnson 1973, 31–32).

As if keeping track of the new journalism movement weren't hard enough, there is currently a consensus that a "new new journalism" has also made a strong showing in the nonfiction book realm. In the introduction to *The New New Journalism*, author Robert S. Boynton refers to the work of these authors as "reportorially based, narrative-driven long-form nonfiction," and asserts that "the New New Journalism may well be the most popular and influential development in the history of American literary nonfiction" (Boynton 2005, xi). Examples of such authors are Eric Schlosser (*Fast Food Nation*), Calvin Trillin (*Feeding a Yen*), Ted Conover (*Newjack: Guarding SingSing*), and Alex Kotlowitz (*There Are No Children Here*).

Investigative titles can often be found in bookstores in the reader interest category "Current Affairs," which is wonderfully descriptive in one sense but otherwise fraught with problems of classification. When does an affair stop being current? When does a seminal investigative work, such as Carl Bernstein's and Bob Woodward's *All the President's Men*, about the Watergate scandal, get placed among books on politics or history instead? Is a book about one new teacher's first year in a New York City program designed to entice professionals into teaching without an educational background really a book about "current affairs" (*Ms. Moffet's First Year*)? The appeal of the "latest" titles based on news stories, business breakthroughs, or the discovery of skeletons in politicians' closets cannot be overstated, but in addition to those books, many of which lose their impact mere months after publication, there are many enduring works of characterization and compelling storytelling.

Although its titles' frequent appearance in such categories as "Current Affairs" or "Current Interest" lend a true genre-like air to this category, they vary too widely in subject matter and in voice to constitute a true and reliable genre grouping. If you recommend a travel or true crime book to a patron or customer, you can be reasonably sure that those labels provide readers with some kind of idea about the type of book they're getting; in offering investigative works, you have no such assurance. They range from scathing exposés (*Fast Food Nation*) to poignant character-driven narratives (*The Ticket Out: Darryl Strawberry and the Boys of Crenshaw*), from first-person experiences (*Newjack: Guarding Sing Sing*) to coolly rational third-person reporting (*The Outlaw Sea*). For the most part, the one attribute that they all share is their authors' dedicated and sometimes relentless drive to provide a bit more information on a subject, to get "the story behind the story," to provide a new perspective, or to make personal experiences universal enough to be understood by their readers.

Appeal of the Genre

The consensus seems to be that at least part of the appeal of investigative books for their readers is their focus on facts, or evidence, or that they tell the "inside" stories of real people and real events. The titles in this chapter have a heavy dose of those characteristics, but also tend to promote specific points of view and to provide new perspectives and insights into previously unexplored or underexplored subject matter. They are primarily compelling stories that their authors researched at great length, both in libraries and through news accounts, but also by going to the source and interviewing the people involved. Because, as Steve Weinberg pointed out in his introduction to the genre in *Bookmarks* magazine, "no library shelving classification or bookstore section exists for 'investigative journalism,' the titles fall into different categories" (2005, 25). They have been collected as one genre here, based on the framework of their authors' journalistic techniques.

In addition to appealing to readers who want to know a little something about a lot of things, many of these titles are interesting stories that are told well and depend heavily on the skill of their authors in using language and style to create nonfiction books that "read like fiction." Because they are stories about people, as well as about places, events, and things, they also often appeal to readers on the basis of the characters who inhabit their pages.

As well as being able to recommend enjoyable nonfiction reads to their patrons, there is some evidence that all readers' advisory and reference librarians should be reading them anyway, in addition to magazine and newspaper news stories, in order to better serve their patrons. In their excellent article in *Public Libraries*, Juris Dilevko and Moya Mason not only explore the proud tradition of library schools exhorting their graduates to stay abreast of current events (back through at least the 1920s) but also recommend that, since reference staff with high levels of cultural literacy and familiarity of current news were better at answering patron questions than referring them elsewhere, "library administrators may wish to consider providing each member of the reference team with paid time in order to peruse relevant material such as newspapers or magazines" (2000, 85–97). The authors also realistically stated that theirs was a controversial proposal, but their point is relevant to the job of the readers' advisor as well. Many of the authors annotated in this chapter write for large newspapers, as well as for magazines such as *Atlantic Monthly*, *Harper's*, and the *National Review*. Even if you do not have time to read entire books by these authors, make time to sneak a quick peek at their magazine writing, to familiarize yourself with different authors and styles. Although in this era of incessant budget cuts the timing may not be good to ask for paid time to read papers and magazines, reference staff should to point out to administrators that doing so will actually increase their productivity as both reference librarians and readers' advisors, particularly where investigative writing titles are concerned.

Like memoirs, to which they are related, investigative works are often the targets of criticism by reviewers and readers, who periodically claim they are more fiction than nonfiction. As stated elsewhere in this guide, an author's choice to use narrative techniques to tell a true story does not mean that he or she is allowed to dispense with all the usual rules of journalism requiring writers to cite their sources and accurately quote their subjects, nor does it mean he or she is free to arrange the sequence of events to create a more compelling narrative, or to eschew fact-checking. Although readers are not often overly concerned about these issues, in this era of Jayson Blairs and broadcast commentators receiving payments to favorably review politicians' policies, it behooves librarians and other book industry professionals to be aware of author statements, often made in prefaces or introductions, that "composite characters" or "re-created dialogue" were used to aid the "narrative flow" of their stories. Whenever possible, such disclaimers have been added to the annotations below to aid in that understanding. For the most part, however, many of the practitioners of investigative writing seem more than happy to abide by Lee Gutkind's (the editor of the literary journal *Creative Nonfiction*) admonition never to make stuff up, as well as by University of Chicago professor Dina Elenbogen's statement that "creative nonfiction doesn't believe in invention" (Fitzgerald 2002, 16).

In addition to the cross-genre appeal between investigative writing and memoir (many of the titles in the "Immersion Journalism" section in particular often reveal as much about people's inner lives as do most memoirs), fans of investigative works might also be referred effectively to many titles annotated in the history chapter. Readers who enjoy Don Bortolotti's investigative history of the international organization Doctors Without Borders (*Hope in Hell: Inside the World of Doctors Without Borders*) might also be interested in Philip Gourevitch's historical investigation of the international community's reaction to the Rwandan genocide, *We Wish to Inform You That Tomorrow We Will Be Killed with Our Families*; John Hersey's story of the effects of the nuclear bomb in *Hiroshima* might also lead a reader to become interested in books about the history of World War II, such as John Dower's *Embracing Defeat: Japan in the Wake of World War II*.

Organization of the Chapter

The first subgenre listed, "In-Depth Reporting," is the one that readers most typically envision when they think about works of investigative storytelling. Including such familiar titles as Anne Fadiman's *The Spirit Catches You and You Fall Down* and Studs Terkel's *Working*, these are stories told with great detail, but in which the authors or reporters rarely, or unobtrusively, insert themselves and their thoughts into the narrative. Many of the titles in the next subgenre, "Immersion Journalism" are even more recognizable (Barbara Ehrenreich's *Nickel and Dimed*, George Plimpton's *Paper Lion*), but the authors of those works rarely hesitate to insert themselves into their stories, and often their immersion experiences are the stories. "Exposés" round out the triumvirate of the most often used forms of investigative writing; their appeal lies primarily in their authors' ability to bring a hidden or shocking truth to light and to support it with the fruits of their research and interviews (Eric Schlosser's *Fast Food Nation* has been one of the most commercially successful titles of this type in recent years, while John Perkins's *Confessions of an Economic Hit Man* has become a sleeper hit). A section of "Character Profiles" also depends on the character-driven style of reporting used by current practitioners of the "new new" journalism, and these are some of the most compelling stories around (it took Adrian LeBlanc a decade to feel she had achieved the personal story she wanted to in her Brooklyn tale *Random Family*).

The final categories, "Political" and "Business" reporting, are two subject areas in which readers of investigative writing are often interested. The titles annotated there include some that can be found in bookstore "Current Affairs" sections, as well as classics in the field such as Woodward and Bernstein's *All the President's Men*. Readers and advisors are cautioned that works by political pundits or commentators are not annotated here; see appendix C for a list of popular (and often party-affiliated) writers.

In-Depth Reporting

Aspiring journalists learn that before they write anything else, they must first address the key aspects of their stories; in other words, they must provide for their readers the who, what, why, when, and where of the people or the events they're covering. This opening section pays tribute to titles exhibiting the best of old school journalistic techniques; these authors do not hide their identities as writers from their sources, live their stories, or, for the most part, editorialize about them. Instead, they research the history of their story. They observe and write about the details of their surroundings, and they interview the people involved. They then combine their research, observations, and interview responses into (primarily) third-person narratives that are often crisply and evocatively written. They may not be perfectly objective about their topics or interview subjects, but they very rarely interject their own personal opinions and reactions into their stories in any observable fashion.

In the best tradition of journalistic writing, which is designed to impart a lot of information in a little space (the most important newspaper stories are designed to appear almost exclusively "above the fold," so that readers can get a feel for the day's news just by looking at the front of a folded paper), these tales are often story-driven and heavily dependent on factual and anecdotal evidence. They may take as their subjects emotionally charged issues or controversial topics, but they differ from speculative and incendiary "Exposé" titles in that they very rarely offer details of how they found or reported the stories, and they do not offer suggestions for change or their own personal biases and viewpoints.

Baker, Nicholson.

Double Fold: Libraries and the Assault on Paper. New York: Random House, 2001 (New York: Vintage Books, 2002. 370pp. ISBN 0375726217.

Novelist Baker has written a rather cantankerous story of his quest to save hardbound copies of newspapers from destruction by creating a nonprofit organization, the American Newspaper Repository. In addition to indicting the Library of Congress, the British Library, and multiple librarians for their decisions to copy historic runs of the papers onto microfilm and then dispose of the originals, Baker provides a succinctly written account of the "double fold" test (folding a paper corner back and forth once to determine condition), the history of paper-making technology, microfilming and scanning technology, and current debates regarding library space and collection policies. This may be a challenging sell to general readers, but it should be required reading for all librarians and library students.

Subjects: Books and Learning • Libraries • National Book Critics Circle Award Winners • Professions

Now try: Aaron Lansky's more personal ALA Notable Book *Outwitting History: The Amazing Adventures of a Man Who Saved a Million Yiddish Books* follows the same story line; Lansky, shocked at the numbers of Yiddish books that were being thrown out when their owners died or moved to smaller homes, set out to create a foundation to save the books himself. John Baxter's *A Pound of Paper: Confessions of a Book Addict* provides an insider's view of the book collecting world, while Andre Schiffrin's *The Business of Books: How the International Conglomerates Took Over Publishing and Changed the Way We Read* describes the genesis of the New Press and how the book publishing business is changing.

Bogira, Steve.

Courtroom 302: A Year Behind the Scenes in an American Criminal Courthouse.
New York: Knopf, 2005. 404pp. ISBN 0679432523.

Chicago Reader journalist Bogira faithfully chronicles a year in the life of a criminal court in Chicago's Cook County. In addition to describing the jail attached to the courthouse and the legal proceedings within, he tells many more personal stories of both those being charged with crimes (from daily drug offenses to more high profile murder cases) and those dispensing justice.

> **Subjects:** Chicago • Law and Lawyers • Prisons • Professions • True Crime

> **Now try:** Pulitzer Prize winner Edward Humes provides an even more evocative report on the juvenile prison and court system in *No Matter How Loud I Shout: A Year in the Life of Juvenile Court.* Another "insider's look" at a related part of the criminal justice system is Edward Conlon's memoir about his life as a New York City police officer, *Blue Blood.*

Bortolotti, Dan.

Hope in Hell: Inside the World of Doctors Without Borders. Buffalo, N.Y.: Firefly Books, 2004. 303pp. ISBN 1552978656.

This beautifully produced and photographed book provides a biography of the Médicins Sans Frontières (Doctors Without Borders), from its genesis in 1968, to its official founding in Paris in 1971, to its current struggle to remain a completely neutral human organization as opposed to a political human rights organization. The group's history is not devoid of controversy, and many of its members are compellingly described here in the context of both their humanitarian work and their differing viewpoints about the organization's mission to provide aid without judging the rightness of any one group's claims or conflicts.

> **Subjects:** Africa • France • Health Issues • Human Rights • Medicine • Organizations • Work Relationships

> **Now try:** Tracy Kidder's story of Dr. Paul Farmer and his struggle to make the best possible health care available to all Haitians, *Mountains Beyond Mountains: The Quest of Dr. Paul Farmer, a Man Who Would Cure the World*, is also a compelling and quickly paced history. The extremely personal collection of stories in *Another Day in Paradise: International Humanitarian Workers Tell Their Stories*, edited by Carol Bergman, also provides an evocative picture of the struggles and triumphs of medical and other humanitarian aid workers worldwide.

Fadiman, Anne.

The Spirit Catches You and You Fall Down: A Hmong Child, Her American Doctors, and the Collision of Two Cultures. New York: Farrar, Straus & Giroux, 1997 (1998). 341pp. ISBN 0374525641.

Fadiman recounts the tale of Hmong couple Foua Yang and Nao Kao, whose youngest daughter (the only one born in the United States) Lia Lee suffered from epilepsy, and their struggle to understand and comply with their American doctors' recommendations and treatments. Fadiman explores the cultural gap between the Hmong family's more spiritual approach to bodily health (Lia's parents ascribed her illness to a "spirit entering her" and causing her seizures) and the doctors' physical approach, which the family did not understand due to both poor explanations and language difficulties. Based on Fadiman's interviews with individuals on both sides, the story is told with admirable objectivity and skillful pacing.

> **Subjects:** Classics • Culture Clash • Family Relationships • Health Issues • Medicine • National Book Critics Circle Award Winners

> **Now try:** Barron Lerner's ALA Notable Book *The Breast Cancer Wars: Hope, Fear & the Pursuit of a Cure in Twentieth-Century America* is also a compellingly quick medical read, and presents the different opinions of men (mainly cast as the doctors, particularly in the 1950s) and women (primarily the patients) regarding such different radical treatments as complete mastectomies and chemotherapies, as well as the controversy surrounding the need for yearly mammograms. Abraham Verghese relates his experiences treating victims of AIDS in a small community in Tennessee in the 1980s, in his quiet and even-handed *My Own Country: A Doctor's Story*. Another story of the history of controversial medical issues is Cynthia Gorney's ALA Notable Book *Articles of Faith: A Frontline History of the Abortion Wars*.

Goldberger, Paul.

Up from Zero: Politics, Architecture, and the Rebuilding of New York. New York: Random House, 2004. 273pp. ISBN 1400060176.

Architecture critic and *New Yorker* writer Goldberg provides a fascinating and refreshingly objective tale about the process of rebuilding at the World Trade Center ground zero site and relates the intimate details of the machinations among many of the key players with a stake in the new structure: businesspeople, politicians, architects, government agencies, and victims' families and community groups.

> **Subjects:** Architecture • Business • Community Life • Government • New York City • Organizations • September 11, 2001

> **Now try:** Readers interested in the engineering and architectural challenges of the World Trade Center site might backtrack and read William Langewiesche's quietly elegiac *American Ground: Unbuilding the World Trade Center*. Neal Bascomb's *Higher: A Historic Race to the Sky and the Making of a City* tells an earlier tale of the characters and methods involved in building New York's Chrysler and Empire State buildings, and James Traub's comprehensive (although not as compelling) discussion of another New York City institution, *The Devil's Playground: A Century of Pleasure and Profit in Times Square,* might appeal to readers who are particularly interested in recent developments (such as "Disneyfication") in urban renewal and planning.

Goodnough, Abby.

Ms. Moffett's First Year: Becoming a Teacher in America. New York: Public Affairs, 2004. 258pp. ISBN 1586482599.

When the New York State education department implemented a program called "New York City Teaching Fellows," seeking "talented professionals" with little or no previous teaching experience to swell the ranks of entry-level teachers, no one was expecting it to draw the 2,300 applicants that it did. One of the 350 professionals accepted was Donna Moffett, a middle-aged legal secretary who had long had an interest in switching careers.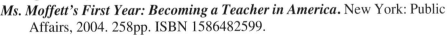

The author's evenhanded treatment of all individuals affected by the program, from Ms. Moffett to her school administrators to her first grade pupils and their parents, provides a journalistically objective portrait of an unprecedented educational experiment, and also places it in the greater current milieu of the state of education, especially after passage of the No Child Left Behind Act.

Subjects: Community Life • Education • Government • New York City • Organizations • Professions • Quick Reads • Work Relationships

Now try: Also set in New York City, Anemona Hartocollis's story of a young Finnish music teacher who sought to bond with her students through gospel music, *Seven Days of Possibilities: One Teacher, 24 Kids, and the Music That Changed Their Lives Forever*, examines one specific teacher's experiences within the social and political structure of a public school over the course of one year. Sam Swope's curmudgeonly but still subtly humorous *I Am a Pencil: A Teacher, His Kids, and Their Worlds of Stories*, also follows a volunteer writing teacher's unforgettable experiences in the world of the classroom.

Hart, Matthew.

Diamond: A Journey to the Heart of an Obsession. New York: Walker & Company, 2001 (New York: Plume, 2002). 276pp. ISBN 0452283701.

Journalist (and former editor of the industry magazine *Rapaport Diamond Report*) Matthew Hart leaves no stone unturned (literally) in his investigative quest to discover how these most precious of jewels are found, mined, advertised, sold to finance revolutions, and moved around the world as both the centerpieces of jewelry and highly useful industrial tools. His writing is crisp and detailed, and he interviewed many of the people involved in different aspects of diamond discovery and marketing.

Subjects: Business • Diamonds • Geology • Quick Reads • World Travel

Now try: Matthew Hart is one of those great nonfiction authors who just hasn't written enough books yet. His most recent title, *The Irish Game: A True Story of Crime and Art*, is a quick introduction to some of the most recent and spectacular international art heists. Hart's writing style, journalistic but elegant, personal but not sentimental, seems vaguely reminiscent of *Atlantic Monthly* correspondent William Langewiesche's, and fans of this book may also want to check out some of his titles, including *The Outlaw Sea: A World of Freedom, Chaos, and Crime*, or *American Ground: Unbuilding the World Trade Center*.

Kennedy, Randy.

Subwayland: Adventures in the World Beneath New York. New York: St. Martin's Griffin, 2004. 226pp. ISBN 0312324340.

A compilation of *New York Times* reporter Kennedy's "Tunnel Vision" columns, this rider's view of the city's subway system is both dryly sardonic and warmly descriptive. Written in the true reporter's style (in which the reporter is invisible), each short column provides a perfect thumbnail sketch of both the system's mechanical workings and its more memorable employees, fans, and customers.

Subjects: Essays • Humor • New York City • Quick Reads • Transportation

Now try: Phillip Lopate chose to document a different part of New York City's unique geography and transportation system in *Waterfront: A Journey around Manhattan*. Charlie LeDuff's book of *New York Times* columns, *Work and Other*

Sins: Life in New York City and Thereabouts, sometimes wanders farther afield than the city for its subjects, but it is much the same in its honest and absentee narrator form.

Langewiesche, William.

The Outlaw Sea: A World of Freedom, Chaos, and Crime. New York: North Point Press, 2004. 239pp. ISBN 0865475814.

Atlantic Monthly correspondent Langewiesche investigated the largest yet least examined part of the globe: the ocean, those who live and work on it, and those individuals and governments who try to regulate it. The 1994 sinking of the ferry ship *Estonia* in the Baltic Sea, at the cost of 852 lives, anchors the book's examination of the wild and fundamentally uncontrollable nature of the sea. Langewiesche's writing is often described as "lyrical," and he tells these compelling stories with a reporter's attention to detail and characterization.

> **Subjects:** Business • Government • Maritime Disasters • Oceans • Professions • Quick Reads

> **Now try:** Richard Pollak spent five weeks aboard the container ship the *Colombo Bay*, and he combines stories of his experiences there with other tales of adventure and piracy in the present world of worldwide shipping and ocean navigation in *The Colombo Bay*, which is less quietly lyrical than Langewiesche's book but is similarly disquieting and even more suspenseful. Those readers who wouldn't mind a dose of history with their sea adventure might also find Laurence Bergreen's *Over the Edge of the World: Magellan's Terrifying Circumnavigation of the Globe* a compelling nautical read.

Roach, Mary.

Stiff: The Curious Lives of Human Cadavers. New York: Norton, 2003 (2004). 303pp. ISBN 0393050939.

Roach offers unstinting research, interviews, and dark humor in her attempt to study the life of our bodies after death. Organized thematically, the book describes her visits to morgues, crematoriums, research farms where bodies are left to decay in the elements to aid forensic science, and laboratories and classrooms with equal aplomb, and introduces a wide array of professionals employed in those situations. Not for the squeamish. Roach's quick prose and often self-effacingly humorous asides and use of dialogue make this an ironically lively read.

> **Subjects:** Death and Dying • Forensic Science • Humor • Professions

> **Now try:** Jessica Mitford's tell-all about the funeral industry, *The American Way of Death*, is extremely similar to this title in both subject matter and darkly humorous tone, although her conclusion that the funeral industry is one that's on the make is refuted by Gary Laderman in his more scholarly *Rest in Peace: A Cultural History of Death and the Funeral Home in Twentieth-Century America*. Those readers more interested in the science surrounding bodily remains and/or their preservation might also like the slightly drier (no pun intended) *The Mummy Congress: Science, Obsession, and the Everlasting Dead* by Heather Pringle. Fiction readers of the unsqueamish variety might also be drawn to Jim Crace's fascinating novel

Being Dead, in which the life story of a murdered couple is told against the backdrop of the decay of their bodies, or even Sean Doolittle's crime novel *Dirt*, which is set in a funeral home.

Terkel, Studs.

Working. New York: Pantheon Books, 1974 (New York: New Press, 2004). 589pp. ISBN 1565843428.

Although it was first published in 1972, there is something timeless about Terkel's unobtrusive interviews with members of the working classes, including professions from "hooker" to "executive" to "janitor" to "department store salesman." Although the majority of the narrative is told by the interviewees in their own distinctive voices, Terkel introduces each of his subjects with an evocative introductory description; his questions, sprinkled throughout the interviews, are informal but always advance the stories in unexpected and fascinating ways.

Subjects: Classic • Epic Reads • Oral Histories • Professions • Work Relationships

Now try: Although it is not as poignant as Terkel's volume, readers looking for a more current view of the work world might enjoy *Gig: Americans Talk about Their Jobs at the Turn of the Millennium*, edited by John Bowe, Marissa Bowe, and Sabin Streeter. Terkel, of course, is a master in the production of oral histories; his other volumes include *Hard Times: An Oral History of the Great Depression, American Dreams: Lost and Found*, and *Race*.

Whynott, Douglas.

A Country Practice: Scenes from the Veterinary Life. New York: North Point Press, 2004. 289pp. ISBN 0865476470.

Although Whynott leaves himself out of the narrative, this extremely readable and personal account of many days in the lives of veterinary practitioners in rural New Hampshire is anything but hands-off. The character-driven narrative revolves around Chuck Shaw, the owner of the practice; his associate Roger Osinchuk, who specializes in horse treatment; and the newly graduated Erika Bruner, their latest addition to the firm. All are portrayed honestly but with sympathy for the many challenges facing modern-day vets: long hours, industrialized farming techniques that focus on animal productivity rather than animal husbandry, and the difficulty of recruiting and keeping well-educated and young staff members in rural settings.

Subjects: Animals • Community Life • Professions • Rural Life • Work Relationships

Now try: Susan Nusser's in-depth study of racehorses and the grooms who care for them, *In Service to the Horse: Chronicles of a Labor of Love*, is set against the backdrop of their owners, stables, and competitive world, and is similar to Whynott's work in its unapologetic examination of a very unique world. Likewise, any of James Herriot's books about his veterinary practice, which are set in post–World War II England, will provide complementary (but even gentler) reads to Whynott's story; Herriot's series includes *All Creatures Great and Small, All Things Bright and Beautiful, All Things Wise and Wonderful*, and *The Lord God Made Them All*.

Winerip, Michael.

9 Highland Road: Sane Living for the Mentally Ill. New York: Pantheon Books, 1994 (New York: Vintage Books, 1995). 451pp. ISBN 09679761608.

Winerip details a large chunk of the history behind the "group home" concept of supervised but independent living for individuals suffering from mental illnesses, but the majority of his narrative rests on his own experiences, over the course of two years, of visiting and observing the multiple residents of 9 Highland Road in Glen Cove, New York. In addition to providing a journalistically sound account of the opening of the house and the community's protests about it, Winerip also provides a number of complex and sympathetic character portraits of several of the home's more troubled occupants, including a woman whose multiple personality disorder wasn't diagnosed until some time after she moved in, and a schizophrenic man, both struggling to prove that they could function in society.

Subjects: ALA Notable Books • Community Life • Health Issues • Mental Health • New York

Now try: Alex Beam's history of a famous mental health institution, McLean Hospital, *Gracefully Insane: The Rise and Fall of America's Premier Mental Hospital*, provides another perspective on the treatment of mental diseases in America. Matt Ruff's novel *Set This House in Order* revolves around the multiple personalities of its main characters, and may appeal to readers who are fascinated by the story of 9 Highland Road's residents.

Immersion Journalism

Immersion journalism is what writers engage in when they go beyond the bounds of objectively researching a story and interviewing its principal participants and step into their own story, living whatever experience they're writing about, in addition to periodically interjecting their own inner thoughts and reactions into their surroundings. Reporters and writers producing works of immersion journalism today are taking more time than ever to fully report a story (Adrian Le Blanc spent nearly a decade researching *Random Family*) and are producing what Boynton refers to as the literature of the everyday; they are "drilling down into the bedrock of ordinary experience" and "reporting on the minutiae of the ordinary" (Boynton 2005, xv). The approach is not new; Tom Wolfe referred to it in his 1973 anthology of "New Journalism" pieces and provided a glimpse into the secret of its appeal: "The idea was to give the full objective description, plus something that readers always had to go to novels and short stories for: namely, the subjective or emotional life of the characters" (Wolfe 1973, 21). In an article for the *Atlanta Journal Constitution*, Teresa K. Weaver provided an admirable explanation of why readers find these books so alluring: "The best are the result of months or years spent trailing someone in trouble, someone dangerous or someone in danger of falling through society's cracks altogether" (Weaver 2004).

These are firsthand accounts, often told in the first person, allowing readers to vicariously experience the story. Thus, the voice of the author, or language, is a strong appeal. These titles have a more intimate feel and often offer more in the way of character and reflective writing appeal than do the titles in the "In-Depth Reporting" subgenre; Ted Conover's *Newjack: Guarding Sing Sing*, about his experiences working as a prison guard, includes numerous personal asides, as does Dennis Covington's story within a story, *Salvation on Sand Mountain*, which begins as an investigative story about a snake handler charged with attempted murder but includes details about Covington's own religious experiences in the Appalachian communities he visits.

A very small subgenre of immersion journalism, known as "Gonzo Journalism," is defined at Wikipedia as "a journalistic style, most famously used by Hunter S. Thompson . . . central to gonzo journalism is the notion that journalism can be more truthful without strict observance of traditional rules of factual reportage. The reporter and the quest for information are central, with other considerations taking a back seat" (*Gonzo Journalism* 2005). Although Thompson was this sub-subgenre's most famous practitioner, other journalists who are considered to share his writing style and fictional/dialogue techniques include George Plimpton, Gay Talese, Norman Mailer, and P. J. O'Rourke.

Bamberger, Michael.

Wonderland: A Year in the Life of an American High School. New York: Atlantic Monthly Press, 2004. 207pp. ISBN 0871139170.

Sports Illustrated journalist Bamberger spent a year mingling with a variety of high school students at Pennsbury High School, a large Pennsylvania school known for its always-elaborate spring prom. Over the course of the narrative, organized chronologically over the school year, Bamberger introduces the reader to a representative group of students: the class presidents, the couple who conceive and keep their baby but don't let it stop them from going to the prom, the star athlete, the overextended but feisty female field hockey player, and the less-popular students who dream of escorting the most beautiful girl in school to the dance. The majority of the story takes place before the prom, which makes the rather brief description of it somewhat anticlimactic, but the author provides as much closure as possible for most of the interrelated dramas he followed throughout the year.

> **Subjects:** Community Life • Education • Friendships • Love and Dating • Pennsylvania

> **Now try:** Education reporter Linda Perlstein also spent a year going back to school and getting to know students personally, and she used those experiences to produce a very similar book about slightly younger kids, *Not Much Just Chillin': The Hidden Lives of Middle Schoolers*. Slightly older (college) kids are the focus of Alexandra Robbins's *Pledged: The Secret Life of Sororities*; Curtis Sittenfeld's novel *Prep*, about a boarding school student on scholarship, may also appeal to readers enthralled by Bamberger's insider's look at the high school experience.

Conover, Ted.

Newjack: Guarding Sing Sing. New York: Random House, 2000 (New York: Vintage Books, 2001). 331pp. ISBN 0375726624.

When the New York State Department of Correctional Services wouldn't allow Ted Conover into its training academy or prisons to write a story about corrections officers, he got in the only way he could think of: as a new recruit. Conover shares the often bleak details of his life and work as a corrections officer (one of the first things he noted is that none of them liked to be called "prison guards") for a year in the maximum security Sing Sing prison in Ossining. From the training academy to his regular work detail, interacting with his colleagues and the inmates, Conover provides the reader with a clearer understanding of both prison myths and truths.

> **Subjects:** Classics • National Book Critics Circle Award Winners • Prisons • Professions • True Crime • Work Relationships

> **Now try:** Conover is an institution in the world of investigative journalism; he also wrote *Rolling Nowhere: Riding the Rails with America's Hoboes*, *Coyotes: A Journey Through the Secret World of America's Illegal Aliens*, and *Whiteout: Lost in Aspen*. Although he is alluded to only briefly, Lewis Lawes was the warden of Sing Sing for twenty years and eventually became an outspoken critic of capital punishment; readers who enjoy Conover's account of prison life might also be interested in Lawes's work, described in *Miracle at Sing Sing: How One Man Transformed the Lives of America's Most Dangerous Prisoners.*

Covington, Dennis.

Salvation on Sand Mountain: Snake Handling and Redemption in Southern Appalachia. Reading, Mass.: Addison-Wesley, 1995 (New York: Penguin, 1996). 240pp. ISBN 0140254587.

In the course of researching the story of snake handling preacher Glenn Summerford, who was convicted of attempted murder for holding a gun to his wife's head and forcing her to stick her arm into a rattlesnake's cage, Covington's travels and interviews in Appalachia affected him much more personally and spiritually than he had imagined. Over the course of the narrative he describes his own experiences attending snake handling worship services, his own snake handling and preaching experiments, and his discovery that the quintessentially Southern practice has a long history in his own family.

> **Subjects:** ALA Notable Books • American South • Family Relationships • Religion • Spirituality

> **Now try:** *Spirit and Flesh: Life in a Fundamentalist Baptist Church* by James M. Ault Jr. also provides an "inside look" at the religious experience. Kim Barnes's memoir *In the Wilderness: Coming of Age in Unknown Country* examines her family's turn to fundamentalist religiosity as a way to deal with economic and social turmoil. Barbara Kingsolver's novel *The Poisonwood Bible* features a family driven by their evangelical Baptist father to become missionaries to the Belgian Congo.

Ehrenreich, Barbara.

Nickel and Dimed: On (Not) Getting by in America. New York: Metropolitan Books, 2001 (New York: Henry Holt, 2002). 230pp. ISBN 0805063897.

The Nation and *The Progressive* magazine contributor Ehrenreich decided that if she was going to understand the world of trying to support oneself on minimum wage, she was probably going to have to live it. She spent a year working in various jobs (including housecleaner, waitress, and Wal-Mart associate) in different locations, and found that all the jobs she held were not only physically and mentally demanding, but were also so poorly compensated that making a living from them wasn't really feasible.

Ehrenreich provides a lot of disturbing financial and economic statistics but also uses her strident voice and first-person storytelling to make her case that these demoralizing jobs aren't good for the employees or our society.

> **Subjects:** Business • Classics • Labor History • Quick Reads • Retail • Work Relationships

> **Now try:** Ehrenreich has long been an outspoken and liberal writer on many sociological topics, from *Fear of Falling: The Inner Life of the Middle Class* to her more feminist texts such as *For Her Own Good: Two Centuries of the Experts' Advice to Women* (coauthored with Deirdre English). Readers interested in her "insider's look" at minimum wage jobs might also consider David Shipler's recent *The Working Poor: Invisible in America*, while another, more personal story of poverty is related by Michelle Kennedy in her memoir *Without a Net: Middle Class and Homeless (with Kids) in America*. Readers more intrigued by Ehrenreich's personal reactions to working service industry jobs may also enjoy Louise Rafkin's straightforward and amusing memoir of her life as a housecleaner, *Other People's Dirt: A Housecleaner's Curious Adventures*.

Kirk, Donald.

Tell It to the Dead: Stories of a War. Chicago: Nelson-Hall, 1975 (Armonk, New York: M.E. Sharpe, 1996). 280pp. ISBN 1563247186.

The collected dispatches of Vietnam War correspondent Donald Kirk, these honest and bitterly descriptive articles on the war's battles, soldiers, and victims (on both sides) are beautifully written but hard to read due to their personal pathos, attributable to Kirk's predilection for speaking directly with the grunt soldiers in the field and ability to weave their quotes into his factual accounts. Kirk did not actually enlist as a combatant, but his familiarity and rapport with military personnel are an early example of today's "embedded reporting" methods.

> **Subjects:** American History • Journalism • Military • Vietnam War • War Stories

> **Now try:** Michael Herr has published *Dispatches*, a volume of soldiers' firsthand Vietnam War experiences, gathered while he was there as a war correspondent for *Esquire* magazine. Although World War II was a vastly different conflict and is viewed quite differently in American history, Ernie Pyle's ability to connect with the common soldier, as evidenced in the collection *Ernie's War: The Best of Ernie Pyle's World War II Dispatches*, edited by David Nichols, may appeal to readers who like the shorter form of journalistic sketches. Otto Apel Jr.'s account of his experiences in a military hospital, *MASH: An Army Surgeon in Korea,* also provides an insider's view of the consequences of war.

Plimpton, George.

Paper Lion: Confessions of a Last-String Quarterback. New York: Harper & Row, 1966 (Guilford, Conn.: Lyons Press, 2003). 362pp. ISBN 1592280153.

Intrepid reporter and founder of the *Paris Review*, Plimpton stopped at nothing to get his insider's view of football in this classic of sports and narrative journalism. Although the majority of the story focuses on his learning the quarterback position and observing the interactions between the 1963 Detroit Lions team members and their coaching staff in both training camp and real games, Plimpton also weaves into the story the details of his persistent quest to get some football team to add him to the roster, to great effect. Thirty-six-year-old Plimpton did eventually get to take the field for five plays in an exhibition game, an experience he relates with self-deprecating honesty and humor.

> **Subjects:** Classics • Football • Humor • Sports • Work Relationships

> **Now try:** This is Plimpton's most famous insider's sports story, but he went on to produce a number of works in the same vein, including *Out of My League: The Classic Hilarious Account of an Amateur's Ordeal in Professional Baseball* (which was actually published, without the overblown subtitle, before *Paper Lion*, in 1961), *The Bogey Man: A Month on the PGA Tour*, *Shadow Box: An Amateur in the Ring*, and *Open Net*. Readers who enjoy this mixture of sports and humor might also enjoy Tim Moore's anecdotal *French Revolutions: Cycling the Tour de France*.

Reed, Cheryl L.

> ***Unveiled: The Hidden Lives of Nuns.*** New York: Berkley Books, 2004. 331pp. ISBN 0425195112.

> The author cites her childhood fear of nuns as the impetus for investigating just exactly what it is that nuns in various religious orders do. Over the course of four years, she traveled to multiple religious communities and met more than 300 nuns from 50 orders; she offers here her observations and discoveries about their many different vocations (spiritually and literally) and includes quotes from tape-recorded interviews. From cloistered orders to inner city communities, Reed found that many nuns are more than willing to tackle controversial subjects such as sex, the habit, and their position within their respective religions.

> **Subjects:** Friendships • Nuns • Professions • Religion • Spirituality • Women's Contributions • Work Relationships

> **Now try:** Less journalistic and more spiritual in tone, Kathleen Norris's *New York Times* Notable Book *The Cloister Walk* describes her personal search for inner peace by exploring various monastic orders. Kristin Ohlson's *Stalking the Divine: Contemplating Faith with the Poor Clares* illuminates life inside the Poor Clares cloistered community, whose mission is to pray nonstop for the sorrows of the world, as well as Ohlson's own spiritual journey.

Seierstad, Åsne.

> ***The Bookseller of Kabul.*** Translated by Ingrid Christopherson. Boston: Little, Brown, 2003 (Boston: Back Bay Books, 2004). 287pp. ISBN 0316159417.

> Journalist Seierstad relates the day-to-day details of the year she spent living with the Khan family in Kabul in the spring after the fall of the Taliban, providing an intimate look at Afghan culture and family life through her interactions with Sultan Khan, the family patriarch and bookseller, and the rest of his family members. Although most of the family relationships are observed and described firsthand, Seierstad does make use of some more creative nonfiction techniques in ascribing inner thoughts and feelings to several of the family members.

> **Subjects:** Afghanistan • Books and Learning • Culture Clash • Family Relationships • Religion

Now try: Geraldine Brooks's ALA Notable Book *Nine Parts of Desire: The Hidden World of Islamic Women* also closely examines the daily lives of women living in Islamic countries and contrasts them with the rule of law as described in the Koran and as lived historically by other Islamic women, including the prophet Muhammad's wives and daughters. Judith Miller's ALA Notable Book *God Has Ninety-Nine Names: Reporting from a Militant Middle East* may also appeal to readers hoping to learn more about Middle Eastern culture and society. The love of books and learning exhibited throughout this title are also reflected in Azar Nafisi's extremely popular memoir *Reading Lolita in Tehran: A Memoir in Books*. Jason Elliot's travel title *An Unexpected Light: Travels in Afghanistan* might also appeal to these readers, as might several other titles in the "Armchair Travel: Adventures" section of the travel chapter.

Thompson, Hunter S.

Fear and Loathing in Las Vegas: A Savage Journey to the Heart of the American Dream. New York: Random House, 1971 (New York: Vintage Books, 1998). 204pp. ISBN 0679785892.

"Gonzo" journalist Thompson (often referred to as the "creator of the aggressively subjective approach to reporting") pulled out all the stops to immerse himself in the story of his reporter's lifestyle and coverage of a Las Vegas sporting event and a law enforcement conference on drug use, complete with ingesting (and describing the effects of) massive amounts of drugs. With his road trip companion, described throughout as his attorney, Thompson tells a breathless story of drug use, random encounters with other travelers, and, only incidentally, the Mint 400 motorcycle race and the National District Attorney's Convention.

Subjects: Alcoholism • Classics • Drug Addiction • Las Vegas • Law Enforcement • Sports • Travel

Now try: *Fear and Loathing* was chosen for annotation because many readers recognize its title if not its subject matter, but Thompson's earlier work, *Hell's Angels: A Strange and Terrible Saga*, originally written for *The Nation* magazine, is a more powerful and less drug-heavy work of reportage. Although not often referred to as gonzo journalists, writers who share Thompson's immersion style include Tom Wolfe, Gay Talese, Norman Mailer, and rock reporter Lester Bangs.

Exposés

Exposés are defined in the eleventh edition of *Merriam-Webster's Collegiate Dictionary* as, first, "a formal statement of facts," but the second half of the definition provides a glimpse into the reason for their popularity: "an exposure of something discreditable." The only thing more interesting than a well-written news story is a story that takes as its subject matter a nefarious subject, such as government cover-ups, appalling incidents caused by incompetence or evil design, or widespread and pervasive conspiracies. The authors listed in this subgenre do not shy away from subjects that are deeply disturbing (John Hersey's classic and descriptive *Hiroshima*, which details the effects of atomic weapons on human flesh, or Jonathan Harr's *A Civil Action*, about a town's tainted water supply that caused cancer in many of its youngest residents), but rather use their narrative prowess and skillful exposition of detail to tell the most compelling story possible. Like the titles listed in the "Immersion Journalism" subgenre, those listed here often display their authors' strident and less objective voices in their interpretations of various facts and events. As (primarily) subjective works, they seek to appeal to their readers' sense of fair play and compassion and often make use of some of the most basic plot conflicts from both mythology and fiction: "Us vs. Them," "David vs. Goliath," "Right vs. Wrong."

Although the characters portrayed in these stories are often vividly drawn and highly sympathetic, it is still the story that takes precedence. For that reason, fans of this subgenre may also enjoy titles from the true crime genre, many of which, although they tell stories about crimes, are reported with a similar tone of outrage and depend on their authors' stringent research and personal observations. Fans of these titles might also enjoy selections from the "New Perspectives" and "Secret Histories" subgenres of the history chapter, which often re-examine stories that have developed over a longer period of time than those listed here.

Campbell, Greg.

Blood Diamonds: Tracing the Deadly Path of the World's Most Precious Stones. Boulder, Colo.: Westview Press, 2002 (2004). 251pp. ISBN 0813342201.

Investigative journalist Campbell traces the paths taken in the illegal diamond trade. From Sierra Leone, where revolutionaries on all sides mine diamonds to fund their civil wars, to Lebanese diamond markets where all the complex politics of setting diamond prices and the trade intersect, Campbell interviewed key players at all levels in the illicit industry, from impoverished miners to De Beers company executives. The diamonds are used to fund violence, and readers should be aware that there are graphic descriptions in this book.

> **Subjects:** ALA Notable Books • Business • Diamonds • Micro-Histories • Sierra Leone • True Crime

> **Now try:** Matthew Hart's *Diamond: A Journey to the Heart of an Obsession* details more of the geological origins of diamonds but also reflects on their often violent milieu. Michael Klare's *Resource Wars: The New Landscape of Global Conflict* examines a variety of scarce resources (diamonds, water, oil, etc.) and their role in global warfare.

Didion, Joan.

Salvador. New York: Simon & Schuster, 1982 (New York: Vintage International, 1994). 108pp. ISBN 0679751831.

Didion's journalistic account of the tumultuous political and social atmosphere of El Salvador in the 1980s is a lean but thoroughly visceral and frightening report. From her own travels and experiences in the country to her meeting with the U.S. ambassador in San Salvador, Deane Hinton, Didion examines not only the country but also the larger forces that were at work within it as the Cold War reached its peak.

> **Subjects:** Central America • El Salvador • Government • Society • Travel

> **Now try:** Those readers interested in the complex and often horrific situation in 1980s El Salvador might also want to try Mark Danner's *The Massacre at El Mozote*, an account of a tragedy in 1982 that was uncovered ten years later. Readers more interested in the strange overlaps between politics

and geography might also find William Langewiesche's *Cutting for Sign*, about the border between the United States and Mexico, an informative read. "Armchair Travel: Adventures" titles might also appeal to readers who feel that Didion's choice of setting constitutes a large part of the appeal of this slim volume.

Drakulíc, Slavenka.

They Would Never Hurt a Fly: War Criminals on Trial in the Hague. New York: Viking, 2004. 209pp. ISBN 0670033324.

For the most part, once war criminals are captured, their stories tend to fade from public view and media headlines. Drakulíc provides the story after the story, often finding herself the only journalist (or witness, period) present at the international trials of both Croatians and Serbs who committed terrible crimes during the struggle for independence in Yugoslavia from 1991 to 1995. The author's writing is investigative, but her tone is reflective; she cynically notes that even the most hard-core of idealistic enemies imprisoned together in the Hague typically forget their differences long enough to work together to receive the best possible treatment. Quietly chilling, this book reads quickly but is hard to forget.

> **Subjects:** Europe • Government • Homicides • Human Rights • Prisons • World Leaders • Yugoslavia

> **Now try:** Drakulíc's ALA Notable Book *The Balkan Express: Fragments from the Other Side of War* is a fascinating and evocative account of living in Yugoslavia during the ethnic violence of the early 1990s; she has also written a novel, *S: A Novel about the Balkans*. Courtney Angela Brkic's *The Stone Fields: An Epitaph for the Living* is a poignant memoir about her family's history, intertwined with her experiences interviewing victims of ethnic violence in the area. Tom Gjeltsen's ALA Notable Book *Sarajevo Daily: A City and Its Newspaper under Siege* examines the surreal nature of continuing life and professional duties under the shadow of war. Readers enthralled with this courtroom and justice system narrative might also consider titles from the "Courtroom Dramas" true crime subgenre.

Hallinan, Joseph T.

Going Up the River: Travels in a Prison Nation. New York: Random House, 2001 (2003). 268pp. ISBN 0812968441.

Hallinan investigates what he terms the "prison-industrial complex" by researching the current trends of rising incarceration rates and the boom in prison construction. Hallinan, who visited several prisons, describes their sometimes psychosis-inducing environment, considers the desire of communities to build prisons to create jobs, and describes the dangerous living conditions for both staff and inmates. The tone of the work is definitely no-nonsense journalistic reporting.

> **Subjects:** ALA Notable Books • Community Life • Economics • Prisons • Professions

> **Now try:** Readers more interested in personal prison narratives might try Jennifer Wynn's collection of interviews with inmates, *Inside Rikers: Stories from the World's Largest Penal Colony* (or any title from the "Street and Prison Life" true crime subgenre), Jennifer Gonnerman's exploration of life after prison in *Life on the Outside: The Prison Odyssey of Elaine Bartlett*, or even Adrian Nicole LeBlanc's *Random Family: Love, Drugs, Trouble, and Coming of Age in the Bronx*, in which many of the principal characters spend much of their time going into and being released from prison.

Harr, Jonathan.

A Civil Action. New York: Random House, 1995 (New York: Vintage Books, 1996). 502pp. ISBN 0679772677.

Harr's book comes as close to novelistic writing as any work of nonfiction can be said to; using foreshadowing and building both strong characterizations and a suspenseful story, he relates the struggle of a number of residents of Woburn, Massachusetts, to prove that their children's diseases were attributable to heavy metal pollution in their water. Part environmental history and part courtroom drama, the book focuses primarily on Anne Anderson, whose son died from leukemia, and Jan Schlichtmann, the lawyer who represented her and her neighbors and bankrupted himself in the process of proving corporate negligence in toxic waste disposal. There is no real happy ending here, but the book, once started, is extremely hard to put down.

Subjects: Business • Cancer • Classics • Community Life • Health Issues • Law and Lawyers • National Book Critics Circle Award Winners • Pollution

Now try: Gillian Clucas's *Leadville: The Struggle to Revive an American Town* tells the story of the battle to clean up toxic mining by-products in the town of Leadville, Colorado, and the town residents' complicated relationship with the EPA and the mining companies. Randy Shilts's classic of investigative journalism, *And the Band Played On: Politics, People, and the AIDS Epidemic*, tracks the AIDS epidemic in America chronologically and delivers the story on how and why it spread.

Hersey, John.

Hiroshima. New York: Knopf, 1946 (2002). 196pp. ISBN 0394548442.

This small but horrific book-length article first appeared in *The New Yorker*. It follows Hersey's experience interviewing the survivors of the atomic bomb in Hiroshima just days after it happened. As a journalist, Hersey is completely absent in his own text, which leaves him able to describe the horrific aftermath and unbelievable medical and emotional fallout of the weapon without egotistical distractions or pat interpretations.

Subjects: Atomic Bomb • Atrocities • Classics • Health Issues • Japan • Quick Reads • Radiation • Weapons • World War II

Now try: For those readers who can stand to learn any more about the effects of the atomic bomb on human bodies, as well as on landscapes, the illustrated *Rain of Ruin: A Photographic History of Hiroshima and Nagasaki*, by Donald Goldstein, J. Michael Wenger, and Katherine V. Dillon, might also be a powerful complementary and visual read. Hersey was also a Pulitzer Prize–winning author of fiction; his novel *A Bell for Adano* is set in World War II Italy, and *The Wall* is a story of life inside the Jewish ghetto of Warsaw during the same time period. Another atrocity of war is described in well-known journalist Seymour Hersh's *My Lai 4: A Report on the Massacre and Its Aftermath*.

Kluger, Richard.

Ashes to Ashes: America's Hundred-Year Cigarette War, the Public Health, and the Unabashed Triumph of Philip Morris. New York: Knopf, 1996 (New York: Vintage Books, 1997). 811pp. ISBN 0375700366.

This vast history of an institution examines the public's love affair with cigarettes and smoking in the context of the tobacco industry, from cultivation to production to marketing, and all points in between. *Wall Street Journal* reporter Kluger's densely factual text is a vast and tirelessly researched work of investigative journalism that exposes all sides of the smoking debate and provides particular insight into the company histories of both R. J. Reynolds and Philip Morris, offering predictions regarding the future of the industry and possible paths that might be followed by tobacco companies, government regulators, and individual smokers.

> **Subjects:** Business • Epic Reads • Health Issues • Pulitzer Prize Winners • Secret Histories • Smoking

> **Now try:** Bryan Burrough's and John Helyar's *Barbarians at the Gate: The Fall of RJR Nabisco*, often referred to as one of the seminal works of business history, features the story of the leveraged buyout of RJR Nabisco (a company that also produces cigarettes) and the massive egos and amounts of money involved. Kluger also recently published a massive and favorably reviewed account of civil rights and legal battles, *Simple Justice: The History of Brown v. Board of Education and Black America's Struggle for Equality.*

Kozol, Jonathan.

Savage Inequalities: Children in America's Schools. New York: Crown Publishers, 1991 (New York: HarperPerennial, 1992). 262pp. ISBN 0060974990.

I first had to read this book for a college course on the history of education, and it's one of the few books that I can remember from my college career. Kozol, a former teacher himself, visited public schools in East St. Louis, North Lawndale (Illinois), New York City, Camden (New Jersey), Washington, D.C., and San Antonio. He describes not only the children and their school experiences but also the economics of their surroundings, which are characterized almost solely by extreme poverty. Although he provides a host of relevant and shocking statistics, Kozol's true skill lies in describing the students, whose many talents and needs stand in sharp contrast to the bleakness of their surroundings.

> **Subjects:** ALA Notable Books • Classics • Community Life • Education • Poverty • Urban Life

> **Now try:** Kozol's first book, *Death at an Early Age*, won the National Book Award and consists of his experiences teaching poor children in Boston's public schools. Lee Stringer's memoir of his two years in a school for at-risk children, *Sleepaway School,* is both a compellingly quick read and a personal story of childhood in an atmosphere of poverty and racial discrimination.

Martinez, Ruben.

Crossing Over: A Mexican Family on the Migrant Trail. New York: Metropolitan Books, 2001 (New York: Picador, 2002). 330pp. ISBN 0312421230.

In April 1996, eight illegal Mexican migrant workers were killed while being smuggled into the United States; pursued by Border Patrol officers, their driver lost control of their truck and crashed. Journalist Martinez spent two years following migrant families on their journeys back and forth between their homes in Mexico and their jobs in the United States, and in particular tells the story of María Elena Chávez, who lost three sons in the 1996 accident, and her Mexican village, Cherán. Quietly factual in tone, the book presents a comprehensive picture of the current state of border policy as well as the personal story of the migrants whose lives it most directly affects.

> **Subjects:** ALA Notable Books • Culture Clash • Family Relationships • Immigration • Law Enforcement • Mexico

> **Now try:** William Langewiesche's journalistic but still lyrical *Cutting for Sign* also describes life on both sides of the border, as well as the mechanics of crossing it. There are also blurbs on the back of the book from fiction authors Sandra Cisneros and Julia Alvarez; this seems fitting, as a large part of the narrative focuses less on the politics of border crossing and more on its effects on family relationships. Cisneros's *The House on Mango Street* (set in one of Chicago's Hispanic neighborhoods) or Alvarez's *In the Time of the Butterflies* (set in the Dominican Republic but still applicable) might be good places for interested readers to start. Another investigative work that explores issues of race, economics, and family is J. Anthony Lukas's Pulitzer Prize–winning *Common Ground: A Turbulent Decade in the Lives of Three American Families.*

Ortega, Bob.

In Sam We Trust: The Untold Story of Sam Walton and How Wal-Mart Is Devouring America. New York: Times Business, 1998 (New York: Three Rivers Press, 2000). 417pp. ISBN 0812932978.

Although fans of Wal-Mart may fault this book for its strong allegations, Ortega is an award-winning journalist with *The Wall Street Journal* and has a reputation that can withstand criticism. Wal-Mart is currently the largest private-sector employer in North America, and Ortega examines all aspects of its being, from its founding by Sam Walton as a discount store to rival the Ben Franklin chain to its current status as retail behemoth. Although the author also provides biographical details about Walton and his family, the main focus of this narrative is the company history and a consideration of its current business practices.

> **Subjects:** Biographies • Business • Organizations • Retail • Wal-Mart

> **Now try:** Constance Hays's enlightening look at the Coca-Cola company's contentious history with its own bottlers and within its managing hierarchy, *The Real Thing: Truth and Power at the Coca-Cola Company*, is much more interesting than its dry subject heading of "business" might lead the reader to believe; Hays has proven her mettle as a longtime food and beverage industry reporter for *The New York Times*. Those readers who are particularly fascinated by Wal-Mart might also find Robert Slater's *The Wal-Mart Decade: How a New Generation of Leaders Turned Sam Walton's Legacy into the World's #1 Company* an illuminating read (it definitely offers a different viewpoint; Amazon.com reviewers point out that the author gave up "critical journalism" for unprecedented access); conversely, Liza Featherstone questions the company's treatment of women in her recent work, *Selling Women Short: The Landmark Battle for Workers' Rights at Wal-Mart.*

Perkins, John.

Confessions of an Economic Hit Man. San Francisco: Berrett-Koehler Publishers, 2004. 250pp. ISBN 1576753018.

Perkins's confessional, a *New York Times* best seller, takes the reader behind the scenes of World Bank and international economics schemes. A longtime corporate consultant, originally recruited by the National Security Agency, Perkins spent nearly thirty years traveling the globe creating economics forecasts for developing countries that were intended to help them secure large loans that they would never be able to repay. In short, riveting chapters, Perkins describes how he was re-cruited, how he performed his job, and how he now feels about his former role as an "EHM" (Economic Hit Man).

Subjects: Business • Central America • Economics • Government • Memoirs • Profes-sions • Saudi Arabia • Secret Histories • World Travel

Now try: Perkins's diverse chapters on the histories and economies of such countries as Panama, Saudi Arabia, and Iran might whet readers' appetites for related works of history; John Lindsay-Poland's *Emperors in the Jungle: The Hidden History of the U.S. in Panama*, although a university press book, is informative and surprisingly readable; Gerald Posner's *Secrets of the Kingdom: The Inside Story of the Secret Saudi-U.S. Connection* might also appeal.

Schlosser, Eric.

Fast Food Nation: The Dark Side of the All-American Meal. Boston: Houghton Mifflin, 2001 (New York: Perennial, 2002). 383pp. ISBN 0060938455.

Arguably the most immediately recognizable book in this chapter, Schlosser's in-vestigative account of the state of fast food preparation and consumption in Amer-ica was a huge best seller and immediately sent shock waves through many consumers who had happily been devouring McDonald's hamburgers without giv-ing their origins any thought whatsoever. Schlosser's tone, while alarmist at times, is justified by much of his comprehensive research, but the amount of information and rather dense prose in the narrative means that it, unlike the meals offered by the establishment he's questioning, cannot be devoured quickly.

Subjects: ALA Notable Books • Business • Classics • Food • Health Issues • Retail

Now try: Schlosser's groundbreaking work has spawned a host of related texts; two of the most readable are Peter Pringle's examination of genetically modified foods, *Food, Inc.: Mendel to Monsanto—The Promises and Perils of the Biotech Harvest*, and Ken Midkiff's shorter *The Meat You Eat: How Corporate Farming Has Endan-gered America's Food Supply*, which also offers more concrete suggestions for ob-taining food that is produced in accordance with more organic and environmentally friendly methods. Readers seeking a more character-driven and less dense narrative on a similar subject might be better served by Peter Lovenheim's *Portrait of a Burger As a Young Calf: The Story of One Man, Two Calves, and the Feeding of a Nation*, in which the author follows his food from birth to consumption and observes current farming techniques up close while doing so. Of course, those readers who are not averse to classics may find Upton Sinclair's famous work of muckraking fiction about stockyard conditions at the beginning of the twentieth century, *The Jungle*, an appro-priate if depressing companion read to Schlosser's nonfiction work.

Character Profiles: The People Are the Story

Although she was really writing about immersion journalism, Teresa K. Weaver's comments also apply to character-driven news stories: "Journalists know that writing about any heavy, serious topic—imprisonment, drug abuse, poverty—requires a human face, a personal prism through which to tell what an overwhelming 'issue' really means to people's lives. Finding the right face to fill that role is crucial" (2004). The stories listed in this subgenre are investigative ones heavy on the who, what, when, where, and why details, but they add the dimension of detailed (and often empathetic) character development.

Because these are personal and often very compelling stories, populated by compelling and sympathetic characters, they provide some of the quickest reads in this genre. Readers who begin the books about Steven Sharp's horrific injury and extreme personal will to survive it (*A Measure of Endurance*), or the struggle of inner city youths to achieve the world of their dreams through baseball (*The Ticket Out*), are hereby warned that they may not be able to stop reading them until they reach the very last page. Many are similar to the majority of titles in the "Personal Triumph" subgenre of memoirs, and readers' advisors may want to consider recommending those titles to fans of these books, and vice versa.

Belkin, Lisa.

Show Me a Hero: A Tale of Murder, Suicide, Race, and Redemption. Boston: Little, Brown, 1999 (2000). 331pp. ISBN 0316088641.

Journalist Belkin investigates the ten-year period from 1988 to 1998 when, by court order, public housing units were built in a majority white neighborhood in Yonkers, New York. In interviewing and telling the stories of the key players in the controversy, Belkin narrates a compelling and character-driven story. From Judge Leonard Sand, who first handed down the 1985 decision that segregation in Yonkers was deliberately planned by city leaders, to Nicholas Wasicsko, the twenty-eight-year-old mayor who was in office when the order was enforced, to neighborhood individuals Mary Dorman and Alma Febles, who found themselves on opposite sides of the debate, Belkin illustrates through personalities the challenges of economic and racial divides in urban communities.

Subjects: ALA Notable Books • Community Life • Government • New York City • Politics • Race Relations • True Crime • Urban Life

Now try: Jonathan Harr's legal classic *A Civil Action* is similar to Belkin's title in its character-driven narrative and tale of community-wide activism. Belkin is also the author of *First, Do No Harm*, which follows the medical cases of several patients in a Houston hospital.

LeBlanc, Adrian Nicole.

Random Family: Love, Drugs, Trouble, and Coming of Age in the Bronx. New York: Scribner, 2003 (2004). 409pp. ISBN 0743254430.

Journalist LeBlanc spent ten years getting to know several families in the Bronx, and her subtitle admirably sums up the many challenges facing the borough's children and families. Although character-driven and as forcefully written as a physical jab to the stomach, this is a dense and nuanced narrative, and it does take some time to read (which is only fitting; it took a decade to write). Although many of the stories, particularly those involving drug use, prison life, and the many hardships faced by most of the book's extremely young mothers, have an almost unreal quality and unrelenting pace, the author manages to present an incredibly well-written account that is gritty without being bleak.

Subjects: ALA Notable Books • Drug Addiction • Family Relationships • Love and Dating • Prisons • Poverty • Urban Life

Now try: Ron Suskind's similarly journalistic but sympathetic *A Hope in the Unseen: An American Odyssey from the Inner City to the Ivy League* details the remarkable strength of character and family relationships of its subject, Cedric Jennings. Although written by a professor of anthropology, *Sugar's Life in the Hood: The Story of a Former Welfare Mother* (written by Tracy Bachrach Ehlers through interviews with Sugar Turner) is also a personal and evocative inside look at Turner's experiences in her neighborhood and relationships. Jason DeParle's *American Dream: Three Women, Ten Kids, and a Nation's Drive to End Welfare* focuses more on the history and efficacy of welfare programs, but also tells the extremely personal stories of his main characters.

Mishler, William.

A Measure of Endurance: The Unlikely Triumph of Steven Sharp. New York: Knopf, 2003. 306pp. ISBN 037541133X.

In this quiet and compelling book Mishler tells the story of Steven Sharp, who lost both his arms in a farm accident in the summer of 1992. Paired with the narrative detailing his remarkable force of personality and drive to rehabilitate himself, the author details the story of the lengthy trial at which Sharp and his attorney, Bill Manning (a fascinating character in his own right) alleged that the Case Corporation, which manufactured the engaging mechanism on the farm equipment in which Steven was injured, should be held liable for the defective machinery, and makes personal the often dry details of personal injury litigation and corporate responsibility. Although labeled "current events" on its jacket, this narrative is appealing both for the momentum of its story as well as the indomitable spirit of the individuals involved.

Subjects: Accidents • Agriculture • Business • Family Relationships • Law and Lawyers • Organizations • Rural Life • Underdogs

Now try: William Mishler died in 2002, which is a tremendous loss to readers. Fans of this community and legal story may also try Paul VanDevelder's *Coyote Warrior: One Man, Three Tribes, and the Trial That Forged a Nation*, which illuminates the legal process by telling the compelling story of three Native American tribes' battles to win compensation for the 1953 Garrison Dam flooding of their homelands. The much older (publication date 1976) but still compelling page-turner *The Buffalo Creek Disaster: The Story of the Survivors' Unprecedented Lawsuit*, might also appeal to readers of character-driven, legal underdog stories.

Orlean, Susan.

The Orchid Thief: A True Story of Beauty and Obsession. New York: Random House, 1998 (New York: Ballantine, 2000). 284pp. ISBN 044900371X.

Part extended character profile of eccentric orchid hunter and all-around collecting enthusiast John Laroche, part adventure story of orchid hunting and traversing the competitive world of orchid conferences and shows, and part travelogue of Florida, Orlean's story of her two-year odyssey following the exploits of Laroche truly adds up to even more than the sum of all those parts. The narrative is told in the first person, and Orlean offers both commendable scientific orchid details and a highly personable account of her journalistic relationship with Laroche.

> **Subjects:** ALA Notable Books • Classics • Florida • Friendships • Horticulture • Travel

> **Now try:** Susan Orlean is a highly respected travel writer, and her *The Bullfighter Checks Her Makeup: My Encounters with Ordinary People* and *My Kind of Place: Travel Stories from a Woman Who's Been Everywhere* may also appeal to readers who enjoy her mix of character development and descriptive journalism. Readers who enjoy a bit more adventure in their horticultural stories might also try Tom Hart Dyke's and Paul Winder's *The Cloud Garden: A True Story of Adventure, Survival, and Extreme Horticulture*, in which an orchid hunter and his friend are captured and held for ransom while backpacking through Central America.

Sacco, Joe.

The Fixer: A Story from Sarajevo. Montreal: Drawn & Quarterly Publications, 2003. 105pp. ISBN 1896597602.

Joe Sacco relates his reporting experiences in post-Balkan conflict Sarajevo by telling the story of Neven, a former soldier in the Yugoslav People's Army and current "fixer," who finds stories and prostitutes for Western journalists with equal ease and comparable expense. Stark in black-and-white, and subtly horrifying, Sacco's book relates his first meeting with Neven, Neven's war experiences, and his current life in a city still suffering the aftermath of war.

> **Subjects:** Friendships • Graphic Novels • Journalism • Quick Reads • War Stories • Yugoslavia

> **Now try:** Often referred to as the first "comic book journalist," Sacco is also the author of the graphic novels *Palestine* (based on his travels to the West Bank and the Gaza Strip during the 1990s) and *Safe Area Gorazde: The War in Eastern Bosnia, 1992-1995*. Readers who enjoy this brand of history through visuals might also enjoy memoirs such as Marjane Satrapi's *Persepolis: The Story of a Childhood* and Art Spiegelman's decidedly surreal *In the Shadow of No Towers* (about the events of September 11, 2001 as he and his family experienced them).

Sokolove, Michael.

The Ticket Out: Darryl Strawberry and the Boys of Crenshaw. New York: Simon & Schuster, 2004. 291pp. ISBN 0743226739.

A character portrait of an entire high school baseball team, Sokolove's narrative following the school and playing careers of the 1979 Crenshaw High team begins with their heartbreaking loss of the LA City Championship to a team from a more affluent area high school. Heartbreaking is the operative word for this story, as Sokolove interviewed many of the players and was thus granted full access to their world of childhood poverty and hardships, personality conflicts among team members, their struggles with drugs and other temptations (a full chapter is devoted to Darryl Strawberry and his volatile career), and above all, the failure to fulfill the hopes spawned by their aggregate amount of raw talent.

> **Subjects:** ALA Notable Books • Athletes • Baseball • Biographies • Friendships • Sports • Urban Life

> **Now try:** Darcy Frey's ALA Notable Book *The Last Shot: City Streets, Basketball Dreams* is set on a different coast and focuses on a different sport, but provides a similarly simultaneously heartbreaking and hopeful story about the dreams of young athletes. Don Wallace's *One Great Game: Two Teams, Two Dreams, in the First Ever National Championship High School Football Game* does the same. Set even farther afield, sportswriter S. L. Price's travel/sports title *Pitching Around Fidel: A Journey into the Heart of Cuban Sports* portrays the slow demise of the island's fabled athletics program. H. G. Bissinger's *Friday Night Lights: A Town, a Team, and a Dream* might also appeal to readers who enjoy character-rich sports stories, although its tone is more one of "yay team" nostalgia.

Suskind, Ron.

A Hope in the Unseen: An American Odyssey from the Inner City to the Ivy League. New York: Broadway Books, 1998 (1999). 373pp. ISBN 0767901266.

Suskind details the struggle of inner city student Cedric Jennings, whom he first encountered as a junior in crime-ridden Ballou Senior High in Washington, D.C., and his quest to gain both admittance to an Ivy League college and comfort in surroundings that are decidedly not familiar to minorities or members of lower economic classes. Driven only by his hard work and dreams, Jennings is a complex subject for Suskind's journalistic study, and the story of his triumph and experiences at Brown University is a compelling and page-turning account.

> **Subjects:** ALA Notable Books • Education • Poverty • Race Relations • Racism • Urban Life

> **Now try:** Jonathan Kozol's *Savage Inequalities: Children in America's Schools* and Alex Kotlowitz's *There Are No Children Here: The Story of Two Boys Growing Up in the Other America* might provide complementary reading to fans of Suskind's character-driven narrative, as might Tracy Kidder's superlative story of a fifth-grade classroom, *Among Schoolchildren*.

Political Reporting

A great many of the "Current Affairs" titles you'll see in bookstores revolve around what some people consider the real American pastime: politics. Although many readers seeking "politics" books will already have preferred authors and subjects in mind (see appendix C), another category of political books exist. Although they are often produced in response to issues of the day (Bernstein's and Woodward's *All the President's Men*) they often hold up better to the test of time than do many other current affairs and political op-ed books that are produced in response to presidential elections (think Swiftboat veterans and John Kerry) or to reiterate party affiliations and positions.

Like the titles in the rest of the chapter, these investigative writing titles depend heavily on the exposition of referenced facts and research, as well as personal interviews. They are similar in tone and style to those books listed in the "In-Depth Reporting" subgenre at the start of the chapter but differ in their authors' dedicated focus on the subject of political issues and events.

Bernstein, Carl, and Bob Woodward.

All the President's Men. New York: Simon & Schuster, 1974 (1999). 349pp. ISBN 0684863553.

The authors of this book, the nation's two most famous investigative reporters, tell the blow-by-blow history of one of the biggest news stories of the twentieth century. From the very first phone call relating that a burglary had been reported at the Watergate Hotel in Washington, D.C., on June 17, 1972, right through to the resignation of President Nixon, Bernstein and Woodward provide an action-filled narrative complete with secret sources ("Deep Throat"), threats to their safety, and a powerful president surrounded by loyal supporters.

Subjects: American History • Classics • Epic Reads • Government • Journalism • Politics • Professions • Work Relationships

Now try: The identity of Deep Throat has been revealed, and Bob Woodward got to write the sequel to his own classic, *The Secret Man: The Story of Watergate's Deep Throat.* A related autobiography to this story of investigative journalism is Katharine Graham's Pulitzer Prize–winning *Personal History,* in which her years spent working at *The Washington Post* and with Bernstein and Woodward occupy a large place. Bernstein and Woodward, of course, have authored many books since this one was published; Bernstein produced a fantastic historical and literary biography of Pope John Paul II, *His Holiness: John Paul II and the Hidden History of Our Time,* while Woodward also received critical acclaim for *Plan of Attack* and *Bush at War,* both about the inner workings of George W. Bush's administration and foreign policy.

Ferguson, Niall.

Colossus: The Price of America's Empire. New York: Penguin Press, 2004 (2005). 386pp. ISBN 0143034790.

Debates regarding the imperial nature of the foreign policies of the United States have become particularly heated since the events of September 11, 2001, and author Ferguson weighs in with his opinion on the topic by exploring the history of America's foreign policies and the American peoples' opinions of them. The crux of Ferguson's treatise is that American ambivalence about being perceived as an empire hampers the ability of the nation's political leaders to effectively intervene in or direct international affairs. Dense and scholarly but still accessible, Ferguson's book makes assertions readers may not agree with but will not be able to dismiss easily, which he supports using both historical examples and more journalistic stories and statistics.

> **Subjects:** American History • Business • Economics • Europe • Government • September 11, 2001

> **Now try:** Ferguson, a British historian, is known for making provocative statements. Readers intrigued by his stance might also consider Chalmers Johnson's *The Sorrows of Empire* (which presents the opposing viewpoint), Jeremy Rifkin's *The European Dream: How Europe's Vision of the Future Is Quietly Eclipsing the American Dream*, or Timothy Garton Ash's *Free World: America, Europe, and the Surprising Future of the West* .

Friedman, Thomas.

The Lexus and the Olive Tree: Understanding Globalization. New York: Farrar, Straus & Giroux, 1999 (2000) 469pp. ISBN 0374185522.

Friedman is a Pulitzer Prize–winning journalist whose investigative stories are often informed by historical events and cultural precedents. This particular collection explores his realization (and subsequent investigation) that most conflict in world politics and social systems stems from half the world's inhabitants desire to own Lexuses and other luxury goods, while the other half is equally focused on more traditional values and needs, as represented by the olive tree.

> **Subjects:** Classics • Consumerism • Economics • Government • Politics • Sociology

> **Now try:** Friedman is a prolific and popular author; his other well-received and best-selling titles include *Longitudes and Attitudes*, a collection of his columns about globalization and terrorism, and his most recent best seller, *The World Is Flat: A Brief History of the Twenty-First Century*, in which he describes the current "flatness" of our world, in which billions of people can, thanks to technology and other advances, simultaneously do business with each other. Fans of Friedman's intellectual writing, mixed with definite theories about event causes and events, may also enjoy titles by authors such as Jared Diamond or Jacques Barzun.

Halberstam, David.

War in a Time of Peace: Bush, Clinton, and the Generals. New York: Scribner, 2001 (New York: Simon & Schuster, 2002). 557pp. ISBN 0743223233.

Halberstam is a Pulitzer Prize–winning journalist and prolific investigative author, and this book is similar to the rest of his works in its well-written but demanding prose and its in-depth descriptions of the complicated interplay between politics, foreign relations, and the use of military force. He also devotes a lot of space to describing the personality quirks and characteristics of the main players in his book, including Bill Clinton, Colin Powell, and George H. W. Bush, and examining how those personal traits affect politics and governmental processes.

> **Subjects:** ALA Notable Books • American History • Bush, George H. W. • Clinton, Bill • Epic Reads • Government • Military • Politics • Presidents

> **Now try:** Fans of this book won't have to wander far to find similar ones; Halberstam is a popular author with political junkies, and his previous titles include *The Best and the Brightest*, about the Vietnam War, and *The Powers That Be*, about the American media and their relationship to politics. He is also the author of investigative works on sports topics, including *Playing for Keeps: Michael Jordan and the World He Made*, as well as his classic about baseball, *Summer of '49*.

Business Reporting

As was the case with the titles listed in the "Political Reporting" subgenre, many business and investing books can be quite ephemeral in nature and are likely to be requested by their titles or authors (popular self-help/investment writers include such best-selling and omnipresent authors as Suze Orman, Robert T. Kiyosake, and Sharon L. Lechter, the authors of the <u>Rich Dad, Poor Dad</u> series). However, there are a great many business and economics books that can and have stood the test of time, and they are chosen by readers not for immediate investing assistance or business know-how, but rather for their broader scope and skillful writing.

Evans, Philip, and Thomas S. Wurster.

Blown to Bits: How the New Economics of Information Transforms Strategy.
Boston, Mass.: Harvard Business School Press, 2000. 261pp. ISBN 087584877X.

Business consultants Evans and Wurster weigh in on what they feel are the main issues shaping and affecting the "information economy" today. Using numerous business case studies ranging from the general (newspapers, retail banking) to the specific (Dell, Microsoft), question-and-answer sections to help readers understand new information economy strategies, and end-of-chapter recaps, the authors provide a readable, thought-provoking, and ultimately practical treatise on both new business opportunities and technologies.

> **Subjects:** Business • Computers • Economics • Technology

> **Now try:** Lawrence Lessig's *Free Culture: How Big Media Uses Technology and the Law to Lock Down Culture and Control Creativity* might also appeal to readers interested in the interplay between technology and business. Another best-selling business book that uses case studies of companies and chapter summaries and key findings at the end of every chapter is Jim Collins's *Good to Great: Why Some Companies Make the Leap . . . and Others Don't*. Although less business-oriented, Steven Levitt's and Stephen Dubner's *Freakonomics: A Rogue Economist Explores the Hidden Side of Everything* also makes some interesting connections between economic principles and societal phenomena.

Fishman, Ted C.

China, Inc.: How the Rise of the Next Superpower Challenges America and the World. New York: Scribner, 2005. 342pp. ISBN 0743257529.

China is currently the largest maker of toys, clothing, and consumer electronics in the world, and Fishman argues that the nation's productive dominance and abundant labor pool will make the twenty-first century the "Chinese Century." Using both quantitative data and anecdotes, Fishman illuminates China's business history over the past three decades speculates about the nation's (and, by extension, the world's) business future.

Subjects: Business • China • Economics • Politics • Technology

Now try: Richard Florida's *The Rise of the Creative Class: And How It's Transforming Work, Leisure, Community, and Everyday Life* provides another viewpoint on the ever-changing world of workplace and societal demographics and how those changes affect both our business and personal lives.

Lewis, Michael.

Liar's Poker: Rising Through the Wreckage on Wall Street. New York: Norton, 1989 (New York: Penguin Books, 1990). 249pp. ISBN 0140143459.

Although closer in writing style and tone to immersion journalism (Lewis himself was a Wall Street bond trader) and memoir, Lewis's story is nonetheless an important investigation into the world of high finance. The events described took place in the heady mid-1980s and culminated with the market crash of October 1987; this book will appeal to readers who enjoy a dash of the personal "insider's look" perspective about the world of investment banking.

Subjects: 1980s • Classics • Finance • Memoirs • Professions

Now try: Nomi Prins's less personal but rigorously reported *Other People's Money: The Corporate Mugging of America* might also appeal to Lewis's readers, as might Kurt Eichenwald's best-selling *Conspiracy of Fools*, about Enron's financial implosion.

Underhill, Paco.

Why We Buy: The Science of Shopping. New York: Simon & Schuster, 1999 (2000). 255pp. ISBN 0684849143.

Ostensibly a manual for those retail and sales professionals who are in charge of organizing their merchandise and stores to entice shoppers to spend money, Underhill's extensive insights into shopping behavior, gleaned from years of research in the field he calls retail anthropology (of which he and his firm Envirosell were the first practitioners) is fascinating reading for both sellers and shoppers. Underhill's information is delivered in rapid-fire business style and is enjoyable in its brisk clarity, although the main focus here is the statistical and quantitative findings from his research. References to this work and to Underhill in general abound in a surprising amount of other, even nonbusiness works, as well as newspaper and magazine articles.

Subjects: Business • Classics • Consumerism • Professions • Quick Reads • Retail

Now try: Underhill's follow-up title, *The Call of the Mall*, is also interesting but not as broadly based or applicable. On the other hand, Douglas Atkin's *The Culting of*

Brands: When Customers Become True Believers is a similarly crisp and well-researched exposition of the phenomenon of brand loyalty and how it has been used by various companies (as is Juliet Schor's *Born to Buy: The Commercialized Child and the New Consumer Culture*). Readers more interested in the shopping end of Underhill's work, rather than the business applications, might also appreciate Pamela Klaffke's enjoyable whirlwind tour through the history of consumption, *Spree: A Cultural History of Shopping.*

Consider Starting With . . .

The tried and true titles listed below are likely to appeal to fans of investigative writing.

Conover, Ted. *Newjack: Guarding Sing Sing.*

Fadiman, Anne. *The Spirit Catches You and You Fall Down.*

Hersey, John. *Hiroshima.*

Langewiesche, William. *The Outlaw Sea: A World of Freedom, Chaos, and Crime.*

Mishler, William. *A Measure of Endurance: The Unlikely Triumph of Steven Sharp.*

Roach, Mary. *Stiff: The Curious Lives of Human Cadavers.*

Underhill, Paco. *Why We Buy: The Science of Shopping.*

Fiction Read-Alikes

- **Banks, Russell.** Banks credits his ability to effectively write about the trials of New England working class families to having grown up in one. In his novels, such as *Affliction* and *The Sweet Hereafter*, he illuminates the increasingly desperate world of working-class men and the many secrets in a small community, respectively.

- **Byatt, A. S.** Although Byatt's fans may say that her novels are driven more by her characters than by her stories, her best-known books, including *Possession*, *The Biographer's Tale*, and *The Matisse Stories,* provide an insider's eye for detail about scholarly and artistic studies and pursuits.

- **Cook, Robin.** Cook is a practicing doctor and includes snippets of actual news stories about horrific medical experiments and discoveries in most of his medical thrillers. Although rather dated, his first book, *Coma*, is still a chilling read, and more recent books like *Seizure* and *Shock* continue to provide medical horror stories that are just a little too real.

10

- **Grisham, John.** Grisham's complementary blurbs show up on numerous nonfiction legal narratives, such as Jonathan Harr's *A Civil Action*, so it seems only logical that readers who enjoy an inside look at the legal world might also enjoy his fictional legal thrillers. Some of his earliest works, such as *The Firm*, *The Pelican Brief*, and *The Rainmaker*, are also his most accessible. A hugely popular writer, Grisham brings credibility and detail to his legal thrillers due to his earlier career as a criminal, and later a civil law, attorney.

- **Martini, Steve.** Martini, a former journalist and attorney, is the author of multiple courtroom dramas, including *Compelling Evidence*, *Prime Witness*, and his latest title, *Double Tap* (2005).

- **Reichs, Kathy.** Reichs is a practicing forensic anthropologist and brings all of the knowledge she has gained from investigating up to eighty criminal cases a year to her thrillers, which feature recurring character Temperance Brennan. Her first novel was published in 1997 (*Deja Dead*), and her most recent titles featuring Brennan are *Grave Secrets*, *Bare Bones*, and *Monday Mourning*.

Further Reading

Boynton, Robert S.

The New New Journalism: Conversations with America's Best Nonfiction Writers on Their Craft. New York: Vintage, 2005. 456pp. ISBN 140003356X.

Boynton provides an explanatory introduction to the "New New Journalists" and a description of their works; the rest of the book comprises interviews with the practitioners of the style, including Ted Conover, Jonathan Harr, William Langewiesche, Michael Lewis, Susan Orlean, Eric Schlosser, and Gay Talese.

Flippin, Royce, ed.

<u>The Best American Political Writing</u> **(series).** New York: Thunder's Mouth Press, 2002–present.

Those advisors wishing to become more familiar with current political events and investigative and political authors should peruse these collections, which include topical articles written by prominent journalists, many of whom also write politically themed books.

Wolfe, Tom, and E. W. Johnson.

The New Journalism: With an Anthology Edited by Tom Wolfe and E. W. Johnson. New York: Harper & Row, 1973. 394pp. ISBN 0060471832.

Those readers seeking to understand the "New Journalism" movement need look no further than this credo, penned by acknowledged leaders in the field. In addition to the valuable and explanatory introductory essays, Wolfe and Johnson provide a wide-ranging selection of new journalism writings and authors.

References

Boynton, Robert S. 2005. *The New New Journalism*. New York: Vintage.

Dilevko, Juris, and Moya Mason. 2000. "Why You Should Read the Papers: Improving Reference Service in Public Libraries." *Public Libraries* 39, no. 2 (March/April): 85–97.

Fitzgerald, Mark. 2002. "When Does Creative Nonfiction Get Too Creative?" *Writer* 115, no. 11 (November): 15–17.

Gonzo Journalism. 2005. http://en.wikipedia.org/wiki/Gonzo_journalism (accessed July 6, 2005).

Weaver, Teresa K. 2004. "Books: An Ex-con's Daily Struggle and the Long Arm of the Law." *Atlanta Journal-Constitution* (August 22). www.lifeontheoutside.com/atlanta_journal.html (accessed April 22, 2005).

Weinberg, Steve. 2005. "Speaking Truth to Power: Contemporary Classics in Investigative Journalism." *Bookmarks* (May/June): 25–30.

Wolfe, Tom, and E. W. Johnson. 1973. *The New Journalism: With an Anthology Edited by Tom Wolfe and E.W. Johnson.* New York: Harper & Row.

Chapter 11

Making Sense . . .

Definition of Making Sense . . . Books

This chapter is a radical departure from the majority of the others in this book, which have been delineated primarily along subject and genre lines and secondarily by the characteristics of their appeal. Much as in the relationships chapter, however, the subgenres of this chapter do not reflect any sort of subject classification that librarians or their patrons will be able to find in the catalog (although those headings can still be found in their assigned "Subjects," and have been indexed by them as well), nor does it represent any of the "reader interest" categories currently being used by many bookstores and some libraries. I cannot open this chapter with a history of the genre or describe it using representative authors, because it has never really been organized or described as such. What I can do is try to intrigue you by suggesting that the books listed in the following subgenres are fascinating reads in their own rights, are typically titles that garner a lot of media and reader attention, and are also among the easiest for which to provide further reader recommendations.

The title "Making Sense . . . ," complete with the ellipsis, is meant to be inserted before each of the titles of the four subgenres discussed (e.g., "Making Sense . . . of Ourselves and Each Other" or "Making Sense . . . of Culture and Society"). In my defense against the charge that the label is trite, I would like to assure doubters that it was derived directly from the introductions of many titles annotated herein; for example, Kathryn Jay's *More Than Just a Game: Sports in American Life Since 1945*, a book on the connection of Americans' self-images with their role as sports fans, states that she wants to "make sense of why that is." The phrase is more tied to the stylistic conventions of the following titles rather than to their subject matter; Malcolm Gladwell's best seller *The Tipping Point* and Alain de Botton's *Status Anxiety* are about "causality" and "social status," respectively, but both share a tone of reflection based on the authors' synthesizing of numerous facts, theories, and other literary and artistic works. I hesitate to refer to these books as "scholarly," although they derive a large part of their appeal from their informative nature. They are anything but dull and are usually written in a more popular style that relies more on its ability to weave strands of narrative and factual findings together than on documentation.

345

In addition to their authors' dependence on their unique and skillful nonfiction prose styles, "Making Sense . . ." books are characterized by their authors' neologisms, theorizing, and subject synthesis. Malcolm Gladwell helped an entire generation of readers understand (and perhaps try to utilize for their own benefit) the "tipping point" phenomenon, in *The Tipping Point*. Steven Johnson posits that popular culture is actually making us smarter and describes the "Sleeper Curve" (his term) as a continuum that shows the products of all media forms, such as computer games, film, and television, as becoming more nuanced and complex, in *Everything Bad Is Good for You*. Alain de Botton explains how status anxiety is driving us all slightly crazy (*Status Anxiety*), and Gregg Easterbrook tries to illuminate why more people are depressed even though our quality of life is the highest it has ever been in human history (*The Progress Paradox*). Organizing these books along subject lines alone would fail to do them justice; calling all of the above "Sociology" titles is about as exciting and inspiring to readers as letting each book languish in its assigned and lonely spot on the Dewey Decimal or Library of Congress shelves.

That said, a few rough subject area guidelines for each "Making Sense . . ." subgenre do apply. "Of Ourselves and Each Other" contains works typically classified as psychology and sociology; "Of Our Culture and Society" contains works that include thoughts on cultural anthropology, pop culture descriptions and critiques, and essay collections that reflect our current societal norms (and often poke a little fun at them); "Of Our Surroundings" touches on geography and environmental issues; and "Of Our History" contains titles that further ideas first touched upon in the history chapter, in addition to cultural studies. All of the titles contain a touch of philosophy as well, but few would be classified exclusively as such, and the vast majority offer new and subjective perspectives on their subjects. They were written to make readers think and to interest them in reading other benchmark, classic, or controversial works on the subject.

The upshot is, of course, that these books are goldmines of potential related reads and read-alikes. Even if the reader doesn't want to tackle the entire *Encyclopaedia Britannica*, like A. J. Jacobs did before writing his book, there are plenty of other options here: David Denby, in *Great Books*, suggests many titles from the Western canon; Naomi Klein, in *No Logo*, suggests the reader try any number of works on globalization; Pete Hamill even goes so far in his *Downtown: My Manhattan* as to provide a suggested bibliography of works about New York City at the end of his memoir. So how can librarians identify books that seek to make sense of our lives? Usually a quick flip through the text is all that's necessary; if you can see at a glance that the author is referring to other thinkers, writers, and theorists and citing their works (and inadvertently doing your recommending work for you), chances are good that you're looking at a "Making Sense . . ." title.

Appeal of the Genre

Much like the corresponding fiction authors listed in the read-alikes section at the end of the chapter, many of these authors use their command of language and their ability to combine numerous references and various sources into a cohesive whole to add to the appeal of their stories. Just as Don DeLillo and Italo Calvino have very distinct literary styles, so too do Alberto Manguel and Naomi Klein. This language appeal strongly parallels that of many literary fiction titles and corresponds closely with the definition of language-driven literature provided by Nancy Pearl: "the author's use of language is evocative, unusual, thought provoking, or poetic. . . . Novels with Language as an appeal characteristic make us look at the world in a different way" (Pearl 1999, xiii). Substitute the word "nonfiction" for "novel" and you're in business.

Perhaps more than any other genre in this book, the titles listed here depart from the typically story-driven, narrative nonfiction format that has come to dominate the world of publishing. Very few of these titles show up on "Nonfiction That Reads Like Fiction" lists, and even fewer of them show up on the mass market or trade paperback best-seller lists (Gladwell's *The Tipping Point* being one of the exceptions to that rule), but that doesn't mean they're not worth reading or knowing about. The popularity of many of them is analogous to "cult hit" movies; traveling under the radar, books like Robert Putnam's *Bowling Alone* show up in numerous other magazine and online articles, and Naomi Klein's *No Logo* is a classic work of economic and cultural synthesis that is often referred to by other business, economic, and sociological authors.

In general, readers who enjoy "Making Sense . . ." titles might truly be your most generalist readers, interested in a little bit of everything and even more interested in reading about the many connections that skillful authors can make between seemingly unrelated facts and topics, regardless of subject matter. They may be your most challenging readers to identify (readers who like *The Tipping Point* or *Opening Skinner's Box* will probably not be announcing to you that they enjoy works on causality, "Making Sense . . ." books, or "synthesizing" books), but once you find and interact with them, you might find that they are among the easiest of your customers to advise due to their wide-ranging interests and propensity to track down authors and titles simply because they were mentioned in other titles they enjoyed. Titles in this chapter reflect a broad variety of subjects, so keep in mind that readers of books about how espionage fiction and nonfiction accounts developed (*The Great Game*) might also be interested in "Espionage True Adventure" titles; fans of Hopper's investigation of prominent historians' plagiarism (*Past Imperfect*) might be curious to read at least some of the works of the authors he discusses; those fascinated by Russell Martin's account of his nephew's autism (*Out of Silence*) might also be open to trying some works of science writing or medical histories.

Organization of the Chapter

The most important thing to note about the annotations in this chapter is that they tend to be longer, and include more "Now try" suggestions, than the annotations found in other chapters. This has been done by design, not only because many of these books are fairly nuanced and complex and just take a bit longer to describe, but also because within their own texts they offer so many references and recommendations for other works that it would have been counterproductive not to take advantage of that information. The annotations and their suggestions for further reading have been designed to help you understand the book and make use of its references without having to read every single one cover to cover.

Much as in the relationships chapter, which was organized with a "from the inside out" philosophy, the subgenres in this chapter have been placed in the order of their broad applicability. "Of Ourselves and Each Other" titles, which roughly correspond to the subject areas of psychology and sociology, open the chapter, followed by the "Of Our Culture and Society" titles, which also correspond to sociology but with more focus on broad cultural (pop and otherwise) trends than on interpersonal relationships. The final two subgenres, "Of Our Surroundings" and "Of Our Histories," are more subject-driven categories that include titles in which the authors try to explore our relationships (as both individuals and members of society) with our surroundings (whether they're natural, or societal constructs such as the workplace), and our sense of collective history. These are titles that, at first glance, seem like they would be better placed elsewhere (e.g., in the environmental and history chapters), but which, due to their simultaneously meditative and more scholarly qualities, differ too much in mood and style to be placed alongside their more stereotypical cousins in those chapters.

Of Ourselves and Each Other

Although the titles in this subgenre depend heavily on their authors' voices, they are also completely fascinating little stories in their own right, and if you're interested in the foibles of people's personalities and social interactions, they can yield innumerable fun facts that can be used in small talk, comfortable or otherwise. As noted in the chapter introduction, their subject matter is primarily psychology and sociology, the science of mind and behavior, and the science of social relationships, respectively. Readers who enjoy these titles may also be tempted by some of those in the biography and memoir chapters, which often place their main characters firmly in the cultural milieu of their times, as well as in the relationships chapter, which also examines people's interactions with one another.

Gladwell, Malcolm.

The Tipping Point. Boston: Little, Brown, 2000 (2002). 301pp. ISBN 0316346624.

Gladwell's hugely popular and often-cited book investigates the relationships among what he claims are the main forces behind events that pass the "tipping point" and become epidemics: types of people who create and further trends (he calls them "Connectors," "Mavens," and "Salesmen"), "stickiness," and the power of context. Want to know more about what those terms mean, and how they can be understood through examples as wide-ranging as crime in the New York City subway and Hush Puppy shoe fashion trends? You'll just have to read the book and contribute to its passing its own tipping point to become a landmark sociological work of the early twenty-first century.

Subjects: Classics • Quick Reads • Society • Sociology

Now try: Gladwell's most recent book, *Blink: The Power of Thinking Without Thinking,* is another masterful look at the science and theory inherent in the efficacy of our decision-making processes, and also utilizes many case studies to illustrate his point that making decisions based on snap judgments isn't always a bad thing. James Surowiecki's *The Wisdom of Crowds: Why the Many Are Smarter Than the Few and How Collective Wisdom Shapes Business, Economies, and Nations* is a slightly tougher read than Gladwell's effortlessly readable narrative, it speaks to the same sociological constructs and phenomena. Frans Johansson's *The Medici Effect: Breakthrough Insights at the Intersection of Ideas, Concepts, & Cultures* also explores the explosions in thought and innovation that result from the intersections be-tween cultures, professions, and personalities. Although its subject matter veers closer to technology than sociology, Christian Crumlish's *The Power of Many: How the Living Web Is Transforming Politics, Business, and Everyday Life* is also an illuminating and synthesizing look at how interpersonal and business connections are made in today's technology-driven society and, much like Gladwell's text, examines specific case studies, such as Howard Dean's successful Internet fundraising during the 2004 campaign, to emphasize its points.

Jacobs, A. J.

The Know-It-All: One Man's Humble Quest to Become the Smartest Person in the World. New York: Simon & Schuster, 2004. 386pp. ISBN 0743250605.

Inspired by a father who undertook the same task but only got to "Borneo," Jacobs set out to read all thirty-two volumes of the *Encyclopaedia Britannica* (2002 version) from cover to cover. The book is organized alphabetically, and Jacobs does a masterful and enjoyable job of interspersing trivial facts from his reading with more personal stories, such as his and his wife's struggle to conceive a child, his appearance on *Who Wants to Be a Millionaire?*, and his experience meeting and interviewing Alex Trebek.

> **Subjects:** Books and Learning • Family Relationships • Gentle Reads • Humor • Memoirs

> **Now try:** Lynn Truss's surprise best seller on both sides of the Atlantic, *Eats, Shoots, and Leaves*, is organized topically and is an extremely quick romp through the enjoyable vagaries of the English language and those people who (inexcusably, according to Truss) abuse it, and might appeal to readers who find one man's quest to read the encyclopedia informative. You may also try to tempt readers of this humorous work with Paul Collins's *Sixpence House*, in which he describes he and his wife moving to Hay-on-Wye in Wales, a town with 1,500 residents and 40 antiquarian bookstores. Readers looking for a slightly more serious perspective on learning and formal education may want to consider Neil Postman's ALA Notable Book *The End of Education: Redefining the Value of School*.

Jamison, Kay Redfield.

Exuberance: The Passion for Life. New York: Knopf, 2004. 405pp. ISBN 037540144X.

Jamison introduces her book-length study of human exuberance (most often defined as an effervescent mix of joy and enthusiasm) by lamenting that, in their desire to focus on more darkly interesting psychoses or mental problems, psychologists have almost completely ignored it, as both a topic and a subject for study. She cites numerous personal examples of what she considers to be prime examples of exuberance: Theodore Roosevelt's indomitable spirit of exploration, Wilson "Snowflake" Bentley's unending fascination with snowflakes, and James Watson's passionate pursuit of the structure of DNA (to name just a few). Well documented and written with clarity, Jamison's story is not a page-turner but does manage to quietly entrance.

Subjects: Biographies • Mental Health • Psychology

Now try: Just as there are "micro-history" and "micro-science" books most often ear-marked by their one-word titles, one might say that there are also "micro-synthesizing" titles dealing with more intangible things, like exuberance. Aaron Lazare's *On Apology* is another of these titles in which the author considers a psychological or so-ciological characteristic and its effect within our human society, as is Joseph Epstein's *Snobbery: The American Version*. Readers more taken with Jamison's readable style might also consider her groundbreaking memoir about manic depression, *An Unquiet Mind*. For those readers who enjoy just a touch of science along with their historical and literary allusions, evolutionary psychologist David Livingstone Smith's short treatise on lying, *Why We Lie: The Evolutionary Roots of Deception and the Uncon-scious Mind,* is also an interesting look at a defiantly human characteristic. Last but definitely not least, the New York Public Library's fantastic The Seven Deadly Sins series, including volumes by Joseph Epstein, Francine Prose, and Simon Blackburn, among others, explore human frailties using numerous historical and literary allu-sions, and each comes in at around an extremely readable 100 pages.

Martin, Russell.

Out of Silence: A Journey into Language. New York: Henry Holt, 1994 (New York: Penguin Books, 1995). 300pp. ISBN 0140247017.

In turns both investigative and scientific, Russell follows his nephew Ian's struggle with autism, immerses himself in the lives of his sister's family to understand the disease's effects on family members, and undertakes a detailed and physiological consideration of how humans form and produce language. His overall goal of de-scribing how language formation defines us as human beings, based on both first-hand observations and multiple citations of experts' thoughts on the subject, is much more synthesizing as he tries to understand both the specifics of Ian's symp-toms and difficulties and the universality of his very human need to be understood.

Subjects: ALA Notable Books • Autism • Family Relationships • Mental Health • Technology

Now try: Steven Pinker's informative *The Language Instinct* might provide an enjoy-able related read to Martin's work, if the patron isn't averse to a bit more scientific language. Leah Hager Cohen's ALA Notable Book *Train Go Sorry: Inside a Deaf World* is a highly personal investigation of the formation of language and learning of American Sign Language at the Lexington School for the Deaf (where her parents taught), where the author and her siblings, who are all able to hear, grew up and inter-acted with the deaf community. Barry Neil Kaufman published one of the earliest books on autism in 1976; *Son-Rise* detailed his and his wife's struggle to reach their son Raun, whom it was thought suffered from autism. Although Kaufman and his Op-tion Institute have been the targets of varied criticism regarding their methodology and Kaufman's original diagnosis of Raun, there's no doubt it was an influential book in the field; the more recent *Son-Rise: The Story Continues* is still cited as a valuable resource for families with children suffering from autism.

Slater, Lauren.

Opening Skinner's Box: Great Psychological Experiments of the Twentieth Century. New York: Norton, 2004. 276pp. ISBN 0393050955.

Although Slater's voice often seems more journalistic than synthesizing (she inter-viewed many people who knew the psychologists considered, and even reenacted

one of the famous experiments herself), her subject matter, famous twentieth-century psychologists and their often controversial experiments, emphatically takes a broad view of their research findings and their influence
on all manner of psychological studies, and is also rich in suggestions for
further reading about them. Most readers will pick up this book to learn
more about behaviorist B. F. Skinner raising his daughter Deborah in a
box, or about Stanley Milgram's assertion that many ordinary people, in
the right situation, will obey authority and agree to hurt other people (even
when they're not really hurting them), and Slater offers those stories as her
first two chapters, but the diligent readers who continue will also find a
variety of interesting results and various interpretations.

> **Subjects:** Biographies • Experiments • Psychology • Sociology

> **Now try:** Many readers drawn to Slater's book will be picking it up for its
> references to Skinner and Milgram; therefore, biographies on the famous re-
> searchers, such as Daniel W. Bjork's *B. F. Skinner: A Life* or Thomas Blass's
> *The Man Who Shocked the World: The Life and Legacy of Stanley Milgram*,
> may interest them. Deborah Blum's *Love at Goon Park: Harry Harlow and
> the Science of Affection* details a groundbreaking set of psychological exper-
> iments about affection conducted in the mid-twentieth century.

Of Our Culture and Society

Whenever I visit the "Cultural and Popular Studies" section of my local bookstore, I can never be sure what kinds of titles I'll find there, but I do know that, even if
they're widely disparate in subject matter, length, and writing style, they're also
pretty much guaranteed to be universally interesting. They also correlate with another of Catherine Ross's findings about nonfiction readers: "Readers read nonfiction to follow up on their interests in and engagement with the world" (2004, 113). In
addition to providing information about our culture, these titles also frequently offer
a fairly vivid character portrait of the author; the personalities and opinions of David
Denby and Chris Turner, for example, are so much on display in their narratives as to
give their books a definite feel of memoir. These books also tend to be the most investigative in tone of the "Making Sense . . . " titles and as such may also appeal to
readers of investigative stories, in which the writers, typically journalists, provide
historical and cultural contextual details in their narratives.

De Botton, Alain.

> *Status Anxiety*. New York: Pantheon Books, 2004. 306pp. ISBN 0375420835.

> Quietly fascinating author De Botton spends half of his book describing
> the causes of "status anxiety," caused when we place undue importance on
> what others think of us, and the other half describing various methods indi-
> viduals have found to lessen such anxiety. His chapters are not short but
> are conveniently divided into neatly numbered paragraphs that make this
> an easy book to dip into periodically. The sources of our anxieties are
> many—fear of not being loved, high expectations that can never be met,
> instances of snobbery, and the fear of unemployment—but readers should

take heart; the consolations of society are also many: philosophy, art, engaging in political discourse, or indulging in a bohemian lifestyle. De Botton cites many sources to support his statements; Adam Smith, Machiavelli, Tolstoy, Dante, and Walden are just a very few of the thinkers alluded to here.

Subjects: Community Life • Illustrated Books • Philosophy • Society • Sociology

Now try: De Botton rarely tackles the same subject twice, but he always ends up with something that can make a reader pause and think. In *How Proust Can Change Your Life: Not a Novel*, he combines literary biography and humorous self-help; *The Consolations of Philosophy* does much the same but using the framework of philosophers and their theories; and in *The Art of Travel* he masterfully combines the stories of famous travelers with descriptions of their destinations and theories regarding their travel motivations to make a truly light and reflective travel narrative of his own. Robert Sullivan's enjoyably tongue-in-cheek *How Not to Get Rich: Or Why Being Bad Off Isn't So Bad* might also appeal to De Botton fans. Those readers looking for another thought-provoking author may want to consider reading Gregg Easterbrook; his recent *The Progress Paradox: How Life Gets Better While People Feel Worse* covers similar territory of the phenomenon of people paying more attention to what other people have than to their own needs.

Denby, David.

Great Books: My Adventures with Homer, Rousseau, Woolf, and Other Indestructible Writers of the Western World. New York: Simon & Schuster, 1996 (1997). 492pp. ISBN 0684835339.

Denby, *New York* magazine's film critic, decided to go back to college in his middle years (thirty years after his first college career) and re-read classics of the "Western canon," as taught in the courses "Literature Humanities" and "Contemporary Civilization." In the book he offers new thoughts about the many classics he reads and is taught, as well as observations on the reactions of the much younger students around him to the authors and their works. The writing is dense and the story reflective, which means the book is not a quick read, but it will appeal to anyone who loves literature and wants to examine further what it means to read and be affected by reading, as well as those people who like to ponder the state of higher education and the choices made by those setting the curriculum and the tone of the classroom discussions.

Subjects: ALA Notable Books • Books and Learning • Education • Epic Reads • Memoirs

Now try: Denby addresses some of the controversy surrounding the naming of certain works as "Great Books"; consequently, any works by the many authors he list might be fun related reads. The authors he mentions include (but are not limited to) Plato, Hobbes, Machiavelli, Jane Austen, Joseph Conrad, and Virginia Woolf. Those readers who find themselves most enjoying Denby's very apparent personality and style might also consider reading his newest book (published in 2005), *American Sucker*, which is an account of how his marriage ended in 2000 and he sought to become instantly wealthy in the stock market (a task he undertook partially to fund his purchase of their apartment from his former wife); alternatively, readers more interested in the confluence of culture and literature might consider lit theorist extraordinaire Harold Bloom's *The Western Canon: The Books and School of the Ages* or his much shorter *How to Read and Why*. Aaron Lansky's memoir of his quest to save physical copies of Yiddish books, *Outwitting History: The Amazing Adventures of a Man Who Rescued a Million Yiddish Books,* is also an impressive testimonial to the power of bibliomania (and is an ALA Notable Book, to boot).

Hitz, Frederick P.

The Great Game: The Myth and Reality of Espionage. New York: Knopf, 2004. 211pp. ISBN 0375412107.

A masterful literature review of both fiction and nonfiction stories of espionage masquerading as a work of history, Hitz's compact volume is not only a fascinating study of the contrasts between truth and fiction but an ode to the theory that truth is often stranger than fiction. In reviewing the real lives and exploits of many prominent spies and engagers in espionage, Hitz also provides a succinct overview of the spy game and what it means to its sometimes willing, sometimes unwilling, participants.

Subjects: Biographies • Books and Learning • Espionage • Government

Now try: Hitz refers to many works by espionage writer extraordinaire John Le Carré, whose most famous works include *The Spy Who Came in from the Cold*; *Tinker, Tailor, Soldier, Spy*; and *The Tailor of Panama*; readers looking for even more exciting reading might try any of Ian Fleming's James Bond novels. A number of espionage and spy histories are annotated in the adventure chapter; two of the most applicable to this section are Verne Newton's *The Cambridge Spies: The Untold Story of Maclean, Philby, and Burgess in America* and Patrick K. O'Donnell's *Operatives, Spies, and Saboteurs: The Unknown Story of the Men and Women of WWII's OSS.* Those readers interested in works that more closely resemble literary criticism and thoughts on narrative forms might consider Maureen Murdock's *Unreliable Truth: On Memoir and Memory*, in which the author combines the story of her mother's struggle with Alzheimer's disease with thoughts on the exercise of memory and the writing of memoirs (and in which she makes many recommendations about other seminal memoirs and memoirists).

Jay, Kathryn.

More Than Just a Game: Sports in American Life Since 1945. New York: Columbia University Press, 2004. 287pp. ISBN 0231125348.

Jay has written a surprisingly readable scholarly examination of the post–World War II era of sports competition in America, and she covers a variety of sports from professional baseball and football to golf, stock car racing, and Olympic competitions. The author also relates developments in sports to cultural shifts (for example, racial integration in baseball) and draws on numerous statistical and historical sources to illustrate her point that Americans in particular view their sports as displaying their greatest personal qualities.

Subjects: Baseball • Community Life • Football • Sports

Now try: Michael Mandelbaum, who is by profession a foreign policy analyst, is also a sports fan who likes to give a lot of thought to why he's a sports fan, and he has compiled his research and thoughts into *The Meaning of Sports: Why Americans Watch Baseball, Football, and Basketball, and What They See When They Do*. Franklin Foer has also recently published

How Soccer Explains the World: An Unlikely Theory of Globalization, which seeks to place the importance of sports and fandom in its proper global focus; while Nick Hornby's autobiographical and journalistic account of soccer fandom, *Fever Pitch,* was the basis for two movies.

Johnson, Steven.

Everything Bad Is Good for You: How Today's Popular Culture Is Actually Making Us Smarter. New York: Riverhead Books, 2005. 238pp. ISBN 1573223077.

Author and *Wired* magazine contributor Johnson takes as his central thesis the belief that the products of today's media and popular culture (video and computer games, television, film, etc.) are actually much more nuanced and complex than those previously offered, and may in fact be making us smarter and more able to take in ever-increasing amounts of stimuli and information with increasing effectiveness. He offers numerous examples of games, television shows, and movies, as well as referring to others' writings on the subject and offering his own "Sleeper Curve" theory, in which he posits that our media are slowly raising our IQ levels and developing new cognitive abilities. The lack of an index means this is a book scholars won't be able to use after their first reading, but general interest readers might find it thought-provoking.

> **Subjects:** Education • Mass Media • Pop Culture • Society

> **Now try:** Fans of Johnson's work might want to try titles by David Foster Wallace, who makes many and varied cultural references in both his works of fiction (*Infinite Jest*) and essay collections (*A Supposedly Fun Thing I'll Never Do Again*). Johnson provides a list of selected subject- and tone-similar read-alikes at the end of his book, including books on the gaming industry and classics such as Malcolm Gladwell's *The Tipping Point* and *The Selfish Gene* by Richard Dawkins.

Klein, Naomi.

No Logo. New York: Picador, 1999 (2002). 502pp. ISBN 0312421435.

Subtitled "No Space, No Choice, No Jobs, No Logo," in this book Klein persuasively argues that the fascination with logos and brands often leads to a self-fulfilling prophecy of ubiquitous marketing (no space without ads), brand popularity leading to less variety (no choice), and the propensity of manufacturers to seek the cheapest possible worldwide labor (no jobs). This is by no means a fast read; Klein quotes a variety of source material that fans of this work might enjoy reading and often uses an admirably light tone in spite of her heavy subject matter (including her own personal history of spending a lot of her time in fourth grade checking out the logos on the butts of her female classmates).

> **Subjects:** Business • Consumerism • Economics • Investigative Stories • Retail

> **Now try:** Alissa Quart's journalistic *Branded: The Buying and Selling of Teenagers*, speaks directly to the phenomenon of branding as discussed in Klein's work. The deceptively light and illustrated *Affluenza: The All-Consuming Epidemic*, by John De Graaf, also explores the causes and effects of consumerism; those readers who wouldn't be scared by denser reading might also find helpful Juliet B. Schor's often-cited *Born to Buy: The Commercialized Child and the New Consumer Culture* or her earlier *The Overspent American: Upscaling, Downshifting, and the New Consumer*; she also wrote the brief *Do Americans Shop Too Much?*, a title in Beacon Press's New Democracy Forum series (others in that series, all of which are under

100 pages long, might also appeal to readers who enjoyed Klein's sensibilities but are looking for a shorter read). Readers who enjoy the economic ideas found in Klein and Schor might also be drawn to many of Christopher Lasch's titles, which add philosophy and cultural ideals to the mix; one of his more widely read titles is *Culture of Narcissism: American Life in an Age of Diminishing Expectations.*

Lessig, Lawrence.

Free Culture: How Big Media Uses Technology and the Law to Lock Down Culture and Control Creativity. New York: Penguin Press, 2004 (2005). 345pp. ISBN 0143034650.

Lessig, a professor at Stanford Law School, discusses the ways in which culture, technology, and law (particularly copyright law) intersect to affect our lives, and how intellectual property rights affect us even when we think they don't. In five sections designed to introduce the reader to both property rights and the piracy of those rights, Lessig examines a variety of case studies from multiple industries (film, music, cable, etc.) and discusses their impact on the formation of our culture and innovations. It's not a particularly easy work to understand, but it does cover many cultural phenomena that librarians in particular should be familiar with and even provides a number of strategies with which to face the brave new world of privacy and intellectual property issues.

Subjects: Business • Economics • Law and Lawyers • Mass Media • Sociology • Technology

Now try: *The Anarchist in the Library: How the Clash Between Freedom Is Hacking the Real World and Crashing the System*, by Siva Vaidhyanathan, also explores the interplay between the struggle to control information and the desire to obtain or disseminate it freely.

Manguel, Alberto.

A History of Reading. New York: Viking, 1996 (New York: Penguin Books, 1997). 372pp. ISBN 0140166548.

Manguel's sensual memoir of his lifelong love affair with reading is deceptively titled, but we'll forgive him since it's an impressive work of scholarship and a highly personal admission of the importance of literature and words in his life (although few details of his personal life proper intrude upon the story). This is not a chronological history of the act of reading, but rather a thematically organized description of the physical process of reading (for example: readers always used to read out loud; now we all read to ourselves) and a philosophical consideration of how those processes affect our relationship with words, knowledge, and learning.

Subjects: Books and Learning • Classics • Epic Reads • Memoirs • Philosophy

Now try: Manguel's introduction alone contains numerous references to books that deeply affected him, including Vladimir Nabokov's *Lolita;* the novels of Jules Verne; Anton Chekhov's *The Hunt;* and the stories of Rudyard Kipling, Charles Dickens, and Evelyn Waugh. Readers may wish to check out Manguel's similar title *A Reading Diary: A Passionate Reader's Reflections on a Year of Books.* Readers interested in reading "books about books" that aren't quite as heavy philosophically might enjoy any number of texts on the subject, including but not limited to Sara Nelson's (Nelson is also the current publisher of trade journal *Publishers Weekly*) *So Many Books, So Little Time: A Year of Passionate Reading*, Lynne Sharon Schwartz's *Ruined by Reading: A Life in Books*, or John Baxter's *A Pound of Paper: Confessions of a Book Addict*. For a recommendation that wanders a bit from the subject of books, musically inclined patrons might wish to try *The Piano Shop on the Left Bank: Discovering a Forgotten Passion in a Paris Atelier*, in which author Thad Carhart does for pianos what Manguel does for books (Carhart even thanks Manguel for his support in his acknowledgments, an added connection).

Putnam, Robert D.

Bowling Alone: The Collapse and Revival of American Community. New York: Simon & Schuster, 2000 (2001). 541pp. ISBN 0743203046.

Putnam's fascinating (although debatable) premise in this dense sociological treatise is that, as Americans join fewer community-based organizations (those numbers aren't debatable; Putnam cites numerous statistical sources to prove that point), their interest in their communities and the welfare of others also declines. Based on two major lifestyle studies and surveys and divided into five sections describing the phenomenon and its possible effects, the author, while not the first to coin the term "social capital," helps to define it as the web of social connections among individuals and addresses its importance to the health of society.

Subjects: Classics • Community Life • Epic Reads • Organizations • Society • Sociology

Now try: Putnam followed this book in 2003 with his more proscriptive *Better Together: Restoring the American Community.* Readers who feel Putnam may be overstating the problem of our currently disjointed society might enjoy the slightly more cynical *The Way We Never Were: American Families and the Nostalgia Trap*, in which Stephanie Coontz posits that the "good old days" weren't really that good. In the course of reading any amount of nonfiction that veers toward the sociological or cultural, one almost inevitably comes across the name Robert Putnam. I sometimes play the game "Find Putnam"; whenever I pick up a new work that deals in any way with sociology or American community life I check the index for Putnam. I found him again just the other day in the index for Christian Crumlish's *The Power of Many: How the Living Web Is Transforming Politics, Business, and Everyday Life.*

Rothbart, Davy.

Found: The Best Lost, Tossed, and Forgotten Items from Around the World. New York: Simon & Schuster, 2004. 252pp. ISBN 0743251148.

All right, if you can think of a better way to classify this book, I challenge you to do so! An entirely sweet, always unpredictable collection of letters, notes, e-mails, drawings, photographs, and other detritus of life, collected and commented on by Rothbart, the founder of the extremely popular magazine of the same name, this book can be read with equal ease in small bursts or in one sitting. Although most of the items are extremely gentle, librarians and readers are advised that some of the items use explicit language, and some of the notes, just like the ones you wrote in high school that you wouldn't have wanted your parents to read, are a bit racy.

Subjects: Humor • Illustrated Books • Quick Reads

Now try: Ian Phillips's short book *Lost: Lost and Found Pet Posters from around the World* is not as surreal as *Found* but is a touching read nonetheless. Paul Auster's collection of true stories submitted by NPR listeners, *I Thought My Father Was God: And Other True Tales from NPR's National Story Project*, might also appeal to Rothbart's fans (he's a regular contributor to NPR's *This American Life*). Rothbart has also published a collection of short stories, *The Lone Surfer of Montana, Kansas.*

Steele, Shelby.

The Content of Our Character: A New Vision of Race in America. New York: St. Martin's Press, 1990 (New York: HarperPerennial, 1998). 175pp. ISBN 006097415X.

From his opening essay, which describes the uncomfortable silences that follow the raising of race relations topics at cocktail parties, through successive chapters that describe his experiences in predominantly white neighborhoods and academic institutions, Steele attempts to define and explore what he calls "race fatigue" and "integration shock," among other phenomena, and their effects on society. In synthesizing his current experiences with historical incidents and precedent through the use of his lucid writing, he provides a valid viewpoint for the reader to consider.

Subjects: Community Life • Essays • National Book Critics Circle Award Winners • Race Relations • Racism

Now try: Steele is also the author of *A Dream Deferred: The Second Betrayal of Black Freedom in America*, which continues his theory that the "stigmatization of whiteness" and government programs such as affirmative action have only led to worsened race relations. Clarence Page's ALA Notable Book *Showing My Color: Impolite Essays on Race in America* is similar in tone and format to Steele's, while James Baldwin's collection of essays detailing his youth and life in Harlem, *Notes of a Native Son,* is a powerful first-person narrative about issues of racism faced by the author.

Taleb, Nassim Nicholas.

Fooled by Randomness: The Hidden Role of Chance in the Markets and in Life. New York: Texere, 2001 (2004). 277pp. ISBN 158799190X.

Drawing on myths and folklore, derivatives trader Taleb examines the role of randomness in both the financial markets and our broader lives. Although he dispenses with a scholarly style and offers no citations that didn't flow naturally from his own memory or experiences, this is a well-reasoned and intellectual treatise on the human tendency to ascribe our successes to skill rather than to luck, and the courses of our lives to our own determinism rather than randomness. By combining his mathematical and financial experience with stories from ancient Greek mythology, as well as other works of literature, Taleb has created a truly thoughtful work that is less about finance than it is about our perception of fate and ambition.

Subjects: Business • Economics • Mathematics • Philosophy

Now try: Among others, Taleb references George Soros (author of *The Alchemy of Finance*) and Karl Popper (Bryan Magee's *Philosophy and the*

Real World: An Introduction to Karl Popper might be a good related read), two widely disparate individuals who practice trading and philosophy, respectively. Readers who like to combine financial reading with their more philosophical sides might enjoy Peter Bernstein's *Against the Gods: The Remarkable Story of Risk* or Steven Levitt's and Stephen Dubner's *Freakonomics: A Rogue Economist Explores the Hidden Side of Everything*. Deborah Bennett's *Randomness* provides a more factual but never dull consideration of the history and applications of statistics.

Theriault, Reg.

How to Tell When You're Tired: A Brief Examination of Work. New York: Norton, 1995 (1997). 188pp. ISBN 0393315576.

Actually an extended essay written by a former San Francisco longshoreman, this short but meaty treatise not only describes a great many physically demanding jobs but also ruminates on the non–labor-related forces that conspire to make workers tired, such as questionable management techniques and interpersonal work relationships. Although it is a largely autobiographical story detailing Theriault's experiences, the author touches on labor history issues, racial discrimination, the gender gap in compensation, and numerous other social and cultural phenomena that affect our work culture.

Subjects: Labor History • Memoirs • Philosophy • Professions • Quick Reads

Now try: A blurb by Studs Terkel on the back of the book attests to the quality of this short work; readers who enjoy it might also try Terkel's seminal oral history, *Working*. Several other work memoirs might also appeal to fans of Theriault; Debra Ginsberg's *Waiting: The True Confessions of a Waitress* and Thomas Gass's *Nobody's Home: Candid Reflections of a Nursing Home Aide* are particularly poignant stories about challenging jobs. Barbara Ehrenreich's more politically charged *Nickel and Dimed: On (Not) Getting by in America* might also be a suitable read-alike to Theriault's inside look at labor.

Turner, Chris.

Planet Simpson: How a Cartoon Masterpiece Defined a Generation. Cambridge, Mass.: Da Capo Press, 2004. 450pp. ISBN 0306813416.

Love it or hate it, there's no denying that the animated television show *The Simpsons*, currently in its seventeenth season on Fox, is an entertainment powerhouse. Turner offers an extended and thoroughly enjoyable love letter to the show, examining how its main characters and themes both comment on and are influenced by cultural and social norms. The book is emphatically not an episode guide or a fan's gushing recap, but is instead a lighthearted look at the philosophy of the show's creators, writers, and fans, and although viewers of *The Simpsons* will probably get the most out of it, anyone who enjoys reading about pop culture will find a lot to interest here.

Subjects: Epic Read • Humor • Mass Media • Philosophy • Pop Culture

Now try: Readers who aren't tired of the Simpsons after reading this book might also be drawn to a work including them in a discussion of philosophy: William Irwin's *The Simpsons and Philosophy: The D'oh! of Homer* (Irwin is also the editor of the earlier pop culture titles *Seinfeld and Philosophy: A Book about Everything and Nothing* and *The Matrix and Philosophy: Welcome to the Desert of the Real*). Chuck Klosterman's very amusing book of essays, *Sex, Drugs, and Cocoa*

Puffs: A Low Culture Manifesto, is less scholarly than Turner's study of *The Simpsons* but manages to touch on many pop culture icons beloved by the same generation, from John Cusack to MTV's *The Real World*. Franklin Foer's *How Soccer Explains the World* offers soccer as a metaphor for globalization in politics and economics.

Vidal, Gore.

United States: Essays, 1952–1992. New York: Random House, 1993 (New York: Broadway Books, 2001). 1,295pp. ISBN 0767908066.

I can't imagine that many readers checking this massive tome out of the library will actually read the whole thing, but if they do, they'll get a surprisingly well-rounded exposition of the cultural, political, and historical milieu of the United States in the latter half of the twentieth century, making this book's title more apt than I had believed it could be. Vidal's essays cover the gamut from literature and the arts to political profiles and opinions to personal reflections on his own recreational reading and work in television and the movies. Vidal's writing is well-informed but surprisingly accessible, and all librarians should read his wonderfully cantankerous thoughts regarding the fiction best sellers of 1973 for historical context.

Subjects: ALA Notable Books • American History • Essays • Mass Media • National Book Award Winners • Sociology

Now try: Love him or hate him, very few critics can accuse Vidal of being anything other than forthright in his writings; in his subsequent collection of essays, *The Last Empire: Essays, 1992–2000*, he pulls very few punches in his literary criticism (particularly that regarding John Updike) or political opinions. In addition to his numerous collections of essays, Vidal is also a prodigious writer of historical fiction; a listing of some of his titles can be found in the history chapter.

Of Our Surroundings and the Natural World

Although elements of history and culture are also included in the following titles, they primarily seek to examine what it means to be physically located in one particular place. As such, they clearly offer the secondary appeal of setting, and readers who enjoy these titles might also be enticed by similar titles from the environmental chapter that do the same, such as Gretel Ehrlich's *The Solace of Open Spaces* or Henry David Thoreau's famous *Walden*. These titles also correspond to those travel titles that offer detailed descriptions of discrete locations, such as Frank Conroy's *Time and Tide: A Walk through Nantucket* and Joan Didion's *Salvador*. This section is not limited to describing our surrounding landscapes but also considers, in the form of Reg Theriault's *How to Tell When You're Tired*, our less natural surroundings such as our work environments and in the form of Davy Rothbart's *Found*, examines the bits of detritus with which we share our environment.

Gillis, John R.

Islands of the Mind: How the Human Imagination Created the Atlantic World. New York: Palgrave Macmillan, 2004. 217pp. ISBN 1403965064.

Gillis explores the place of the island world in the human psyche and imagination, exploring ancient Greek epics, religious stories, myths, maps, and materials from the modern tourism industry. He concludes that our human conception of our existence on a great "sea of islands" colors our political, economic, and ecological patterns of thought.

> **Subjects:** Geography • Islands • Landscape • Mythologies • World Travel

> **Now try:** Travel writer Lawrence Durrell's "landscape series"—*Prospero's Cell, Reflections on a Marine Venus*, and *Bitter Lemons*—vividly evokes that author's love affair with the Greek islands of Corfu and Cyprus; his self-proclaimed "islomania" might appeal to readers who enjoy Gillis's work. Gretel Ehrlich's more generally reflective *Islands, the Universe, Home* offers thoughts on islands and on such far-reaching subjects as architecture, astronomy, and time.

Hamill, Pete.

Downtown: My Manhattan. New York: Little, Brown, 2004. 289pp. ISBN 0316734519.

Novelist Hamill's short and beautifully written consideration of "his" Manhattan is as personal and heartfelt as its title. Elegantly organized by geography (moving from the tip of Manhattan and continuing upward into Harlem) and effortlessly intertwining the history of his family's immigrant roots and the history of the city, Hamill uses present-day observations and many literary allusions to describe his home city. Librarians in particular should note Hamill's bibliography of his favorite books about New York City.

> **Subjects:** Geography • Memoirs • New York City • Quick Reads • Urban Life

> **Now try:** Hamill's novels also make beautiful use of language and are also almost exclusively set in New York City; two such examples are *Snow in August* and *Forever*, both of tackle such weighty topics as religious discrimination and the immigrant experience. Other similar "city books" are Suketu Mehta's *Maximum City: Bombay Lost and Found* and George Sarrinikolaou's *Facing Athens: Encounters with the Modern City*.

Horgan, John.

The End of Science: Facing the Limits of Knowledge and the Twilight of the Scientific Age. Reading, Mass.: Addison-Wesley, 1996 (New York: Broadway Books, 1997). 322pp. ISBN 0553061747.

Who better than a senior writer at *Scientific American* to provide one of the best works of science/philosophy/history/biography available? In extremely accessible prose, Horgan details the largest discoveries and names in the history of science, including chapters on physics, cosmology, evolutionary biology, and the social sciences, all in pursuit of an answer to the question: Is the great era of scientific discovery about ourselves and our world over?

> **Subjects:** Cosmology • Neuroscience • Philosophy • Physics • Religion

> **Now try:** Each chapter in Horgan's book is a veritable bibliography of science writers (many of whose works are annotated in the science chapter), including, but not limited to, Richard Feynman, Roger Penrose, Stephen Jay Gould, E. O. Wilson, and Francis

Crick (and of course, Horgan provides a more formal bibliography, another gold mine, at the end of the book). Those seeking another science book with the same approach might consider Michael Ruse's *The Evolution Wars: A Guide to the Debates*, which provides a similarly broad history of the theory of evolution and is noteworthy for its inclusion of mini-bibliographies in each chapter.

Rybczynski, Witold.

City Life: Urban Expectations in a New World. New York: Scribner, 1995. 256pp. ISBN 0684813025.

Proving that all environmental writing does not have to be about rural or wide open spaces, Rybczynski's small book, filled with large ideas about what it means to live in cities, as well as understanding and appreciating their different origins and characteristics, is firmly rooted in its urban landscape. Whether describing Paris or Chicago, the author, an architect by training, provides the historical and structural explanation necessary to provide a fully grounded description of his natural urban environment.

> **Subjects:** Essays • Homes • Philosophy • Urban Life
>
> **Now try:** Robert Sullivan's *Rats: Observations on the History and Habitat of the City's Most Unwanted Inhabitants* might contain a little too much historical detail for readers of this genre, but the author's firm belief in exploring his urban environment and its animal residents results in a spectacular work of urban description. Alison Isenberg's scholarly *Downtown America: A History of the Place and the People Who Made It* also provides an urban perspective on a residential environment, as does Mitchell Duneier's *Sidewalk*.

Vollmann, William T.

The Atlas. New York: Viking, 1996 (New York: Penguin Books, 1997). 459pp. ISBN 0140254498.

Although it's rather hard to make sense of Vollmann's self-described "palindromic" (the first chapter corresponds thematically to the last, and so on), episodic chapters describing worldwide locations and experiences, it is unique. Vollmann is known for his distinct prose poetry style, and although readers in search of a narrative will most definitely want to look elsewhere, other readers seeking to immerse themselves in words meant to evoke sensations rather than construct plot will be at home in Vollmann's world.

> **Subjects:** Epic Reads • Geography • Memoirs • Philosophy • World Travel
>
> **Now try:** Reviewers have compared Vollmann's sometimes disturbing, always self-aware, sometimes fictional nonfiction works to those of authors such as Thomas Pynchon (on the avant-garde fiction side) and Robert Kaplan (author of such travel works as *Mediterranean Winter: The Pleasures of History and Landscape in Tunisia, Sicily, Dalmatia, and Greece*). Those readers who enjoy this book as a travelogue might also enjoy David Yeadon's *The Back of Beyond: Travels to the Wild Places of the Earth*; those who enjoy this book more as a rumination on our current world might also be up for his seven-volume *Rising Up and Rising Down: Some Thoughts on Violence, Freedom, and Urgent Means*, which in 2004 was mercifully released in a condensed version by Ecco.

Of Our Histories

Not all history books tell strictly chronological and detailed stories. Some, such as those annotated here, touch briefly on their titular historical events and then get on with the business of examining what those events have meant to the development of our societies and lifestyles. These titles relate strongly to many of those listed in the history chapter (many of them, in fact, displayed their publisher-assigned interest category "History" on their book jackets) but often dispense with footnotes and historical re-creation or storytelling in favor of lively and broad speculations and discussions about historical happenings. They also roam freely among diverse subject matter and include works on business, political, philosophical, and literary history.

Connell, Evan S.

The Aztec Treasure House: New and Selected Essays. Washington, D.C.: Counterpoint, 2001 (2002). 470pp. ISBN 1582432538.

A generalist's dream, this book provides a series of seemingly unrelated essays on topics from the true history of the Etruscans and the nature of archaeological discoveries regarding them, to an examination of the development of astronomy, all somewhat related by their emphasis on original thinkers and visionaries. Other than that theme, there is absolutely no inter-chapter narrative thread; instead, each essay provides a vivid snapshot of history and science combined, and all cite a truly mind-boggling array of literary, historical, and scientific sources, making the book a unique reading experience.

Subjects: ALA Notable Books • Ancient History • Archaeology • Essays • History of Science

Now try: Connell is fascinated by characters on the edge of their professions and relationships, and references both Thomas Huxley's defense of Darwin's theories of evolution and the confrontation between Galileo and the Roman Catholic Church; therefore, titles on those subjects, such as Janet Browne's *Charles Darwin: The Power of Place* or William R. Shea's and Mariano Artigas's *Galileo in Rome: The Rise and Fall of a Troublesome Genius* may appeal to readers of Connell's book. Connell is also a favorably reviewed and best-selling author of both fiction (*Mrs. Bridge* and *The Alchymist's Journal*) and nonfiction (*The White Lantern*, about astronomy, and *Son of the Morning Star*, about the Battle of the Little Bighorn).

Diamond, Jared.

Collapse: How Societies Choose to Fail or Succeed. New York: Viking, 2005. 575pp. ISBN 0670033375.

Diamond, by education and profession a physiologist and ecologist, has made a name for himself tackling sweeping topics such as the past 13,000 years of human history (in *Guns, Germs, and Steel*) or the collapse of influential ancient societies such as those of the Maya and Viking empires (in this title) and offering geographical and sociological reasons for why human history developed as it did. Diamond uses a broad array of sources and numerous examples to make his points, which makes the comprehensive and synthesizing feel of his books possible. That feel places his works in the "Making Sense . . ." category as well as in history; as Amazon.com reviewer Jennifer Buckendorff noted, "While it might seem a stretch to use medieval Greenland and the Maya to convince a skeptic about the seriousness of global warming, it's exactly this type of cross-referencing that makes *Collapse* so compelling."

> **Subjects:** Anthropology • Epic Reads • Geography • Society • Sociology
>
> **Now try:** Diamond became a cultural touchstone when his earlier book, *Guns, Germs, and Steel: The Fates of Human Societies* (annotated in the history chapter), won the Pulitzer Prize. Other titles that may appeal to his readers are Thomas Friedman's investigative history, *The World Is Flat: A Brief History of the Twenty-first Century*; Marvin Harris's *Cows, Pigs, Wars, and Witches: The Riddles of Culture*; Alvin Toffler's *The Third Wave* or *Future Shock*; and Marvin Cetron's and Owen Davies's *Probable Tomorrows*.

Edmonds, David, and John Eidinow.

> *Wittgenstein's Poker: The Story of a Ten-Minute Argument Between Two Great Philosophers.* New York: Ecco, 2001 (2002). 340pp. ISBN 0060936649.

Although ostensibly telling only the story of a brief argument between two moral philosophers at Cambridge University's Moral Science Club in 1941, Edmonds and Eidinow actually provide a history of twentieth-century philosophy, based on the attributes and thoughts of the two philosophers in question, as well as the memories of other prominent philosophers who were witnesses to the argument. Whether or not Ludwig Wittgenstein actually meant to threaten Karl Popper with a poker is never definitively settled, but the passion of that era of philosophical discussion is never in doubt; by placing the argument in the greater context of both academic and social and political events the authors provide a complete snapshot of the time.

> **Subjects:** Classics • Friendships • Philosophy
>
> **Now try:** The <u>Very Short Introductions</u> series from the Oxford University Press may come in handy here; advisors could offer readers A. C. Grayling's *Wittgenstein: A Very Short Introduction*. Unfortunately, there is no corresponding title for Popper, but readers might also consider Bryan Magee's *Philosophy and the Real World: An Introduction to Karl Popper*. The authors tackle the Cold War in their most recent joint publication, *Bobby Fischer Goes to War: How the Soviets Lost the Most Extraordinary Chess Match of All Time*, a story that brilliantly contrasts the personalities of American Bobby Fischer and Russian Boris Spassky to tell the larger story of tension between their two nations and politics and national sensibilities in 1972.

Greider, William.

> *Who Will Tell the People: The Betrayal of American Democracy.* New York: Simon & Schuster, 1992 (1993). 464pp. ISBN 0671867407.

More than a decade old but frighteningly applicable to today's cultural milieu of disillusionment with politics and low voter turnout, Greider's book presents his belief that our current dissatisfaction with democracy is not caused by the politics of election but rather by the inherent processes of the government itself. What does that mean? It means that Greider, by use of examples such as the savings and loan disaster in the late 1980s and the

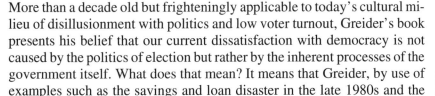

predilection of special interest groups to contribute money in exchange for lenient tax regulations, presents a nuanced but easily understandable snapshot of how our elected government really functions on a daily basis. He also chastises uninvolved citizens, the media, and both the Democratic and Republican political parties for their roles in the degeneration of our democracy.

> **Subjects:** ALA Notable Books • American History • Epic Reads • Government • Investigative Stories • Politics

> **Now try:** William Greider also wrote *Secrets of the Temple: How the Federal Reserve Runs the Country,* which provides the same sort of inside look at the Federal Reserve's operations that the above title provides for government. Readers interested in the interplay of economics, government, and culture might also want to try Greg Palast's never-subtle (but also never dull) *The Best Democracy Money Can Buy: The Truth about Corporate Cons, Globalization, and High-Finance Fraudsters* or Chalmers Johnson's *Blowback: The Cost and Consequences of American Empire.*

Hoffer, Peter Charles.

Past Imperfect: Facts, Fictions, Fraud—American History from Bancroft and Parkman to Ambrose, Bellesiles, Ellis, and Goodwin. New York: Public Affairs, 2004. 287pp. ISBN 1586482440.

A surprisingly fascinating "history of history," Hoffer's book outlining the different ages of American historical writing (from consensus history to the "New History") provides a framework for readers to classify works of history they've read in the past. The second half of the book focuses on the recent research falsification charges against Michael Bellesiles (author of the controversial *Arming America*); plagiarism charges against both Stephen Ambrose and Doris Kearns Goodwin (the former denied all charges, while the latter admitted fault); and accusations that Joseph Ellis, award-winning author of such works as *American Sphinx* and *Founding Brothers*, exaggerated stories regarding his Vietnam War service and civil rights activities; this should be required reading for all librarians and other editorial professionals in the business of evaluating and promoting historical works.

> **Subjects:** Books and Learning • Education • History • Literary Lives

> **Now try:** Ron Robins covers similar territory and more specific cases in *Scandals and Scoundrels: Seven Cases That Shook the Academy.* Readers who enjoy this sort of thing might also want to peruse the works that Hoffer describes; any titles by Stephen Ambrose, Joseph Ellis, or Doris Kearns Goodwin might be enjoyable and education-related reads. It's a bit of a reach, but Christopher Mason's *The Art of the Steal: Inside the Sotheby's-Christie's Auction House Scandal,* with its emphasis on collusion and price-fixing in the art world, might also appeal to readers who like to read about academic and cultural scandals.

Hoffman, Eva.

After Such Knowledge: Memory, History, and the Legacy of the Holocaust. New York: Public Affairs, 2004. 301pp. ISBN 1586480464.

Hoffman explores the effects of the Holocaust on the generations born after the event, as well as on the survivors and their descendants. Using both personal stories (the narrative is written in the first person; Hoffman is the daughter of Polish Jews who survived by being hidden by their neighbors) and numerous literary allusions, she offers a scholarly but readable consideration of the impact of traumatic historical events not only on their victims but also on victims' descendants and society as a whole.

> **Subjects:** Atrocities • Holocaust • Immigration • Jews and Judaism • Memoirs

> **Now try:** Hoffman references many other references and scholarly works in her text, among them Helen Epstein's *Children of the Holocaust: Conversations with Sons and Daughters of Survivors*, Barbara Ehrenreich's *Blood Rites: Origins and History of the Passions of War*, Helen Fremont's *After Long Silence*, and Peter Novick's *The Holocaust in American Life*. The legacy of violence is also the subject of Theodore Nadelson's *Trained To Kill: Soldiers at War*, in which he describes his experiences counseling military victims of post-traumatic stress disorder (PTSD).

Kanigel, Robert.

The One Best Way: Frederick Winslow Taylor and the Enigma of Efficiency.
New York: Viking, 1997 (New York: Penguin Books, 1999). 675pp. ISBN 0140260803.

Any doubts a librarian might have about this being a synthesizing work, rather than a work of history or biography (both of which it resembles) should be dispelled after the prologue; drawing on such varied sources as Neil Postman's *Technopoly* and George Orwell's *1984*, Kanigel sets the tone for his thesis that Taylor's theories of scientific management and timed efficiency studies set the stage for an America dominated by the need for productivity and efficiency. The author also contrasts Taylor's widespread fame and success with his detractors' contentions that his theories were cruelly used to exploit workers and discusses the results of that conflict in our current business and cultural norms.

> **Subjects:** Biographies • Business • Economics • Epic Reads • Professions • Technology

> **Now try:** Eli Zaretsky tracks a similarly influential twentieth-century phenomenon in *Secrets of the Soul: A Social and Cultural History of Psychoanalysis*, which also provides a mix of biographical and historical details. A similar study of more recent downsizing and organizational reshuffling trends is Charles Heckscher's *White-Collar Blues: Management Loyalties in an Age of Corporate Restructuring*; likewise, Jeremy Rifkin's *The End of Work: The Decline of the Global Labor Force and the Dawn of the Post-Market Era* considers the impact of automation and global economies on the sensibilities of laborers and employees. Those readers interested in this subject matter but looking for a much lighter and rather tongue-in-cheek labor history might want to consider Iain Levison's descriptively titled *A Working Stiff's Manifesto: A Memoir of Thirty Jobs I Quit, Nine That Fired Me, and Three I Can't Remember*.

Menand, Louis.

The Metaphysical Club: A Story of Ideas in America. New York: Farrar, Straus & Giroux, 2001 (2002). 546pp. ISBN 0374528497.

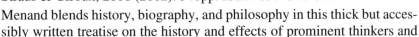

Menand blends history, biography, and philosophy in this thick but accessibly written treatise on the history and effects of prominent thinkers and their ideas on American society and culture. He takes as his time period the years after the Civil War, and although he does provide historical context about the time and a few biographical details about his characters, he devotes most of the book to discussing their philosophical ideas, as well as how they were formed and how they influenced other American thinkers and events. A very few of the many familiar individuals he describes are Oliver Wendell Holmes Jr., William James (philosopher and psychologist, brother of author Henry James), Charles Sanders Peirce, and John Dewey; he also briefly describes less well-known individuals such as Louis Agassiz, a prominent Harvard science professor, and Chauncey Wright, a mathematician and untiring conversationalist. Using personal character details and a well-constructed narrative that covers a lot of time and territory, Menand binds his principal characters together and creates a portrait of thinkers coming together (often literally, in meetings of their "Metaphysical Club") to try to understand their world and the future.

> **Subjects:** American History • Biographies • Epic Reads • Friendships • Nineteenth Century • Philosophy • Pulitzer Prize Winners

> **Now try:** Biographies or writing collections of any of the many famous people who were members of the "Metaphysical Club" might also be of interest to readers who enjoy Menand's work. A few places to start are *The Essential Holmes: Selections from the Letters, Speeches, Judicial Opinions, and Other Writings of Oliver Wendell Holmes, Jr.*; R. W. B. Lewis's *The Jameses: A Family Narrative* or Jacques Barzun's *A Stroll with William James*; Joseph Brent's *Charles Sanders Peirce: A Life;* and Jay Martin's *The Education of John Dewey: A Biography*. The Pulitzer Prize winner for 1973, Daniel Boorstin's *The Americans: The Democratic Experience* covers roughly the same period as Menand's work and may prove more interesting to readers of history than Menand's rather philosophical text.

Stille, Alexander.

The Future of the Past. New York: Farrar, Straus & Giroux, 2002 (2003). 339pp. ISBN 0312420943.

Traveling among such varied archaeological and conservation sites as Egypt's Great Pyramids, China's terra cotta warriors at Xi'an, and Madagascar's woodlands, the author seeks to understand the process by which technology and preservation both save and destroy the physical remains of our collective past. He traveled extensively and interviewed many of the scientists, archaeologists, and ecologists involved, and also provides synthesizing chapters on the effects of losing our physical access to our past, as well as thoughts on libraries and knowledge preservation of the past and the future.

> **Subjects:** ALA Notable Books • Ancient History • Archaeology • Essays • Libraries • Technology

> **Now try:** Although Neil Postman considers our current culture more than our historical monuments in his ALA Notable Book *Technopoly: The Surrender of Culture to Technology,* it might also appeal to readers who are looking for ways to balance the advantages of technology with its relentless requirements. Sven Birkerts's *The Gutenberg Elegies: The Fate of Reading in an Electronic Age* might also appeal to readers who seek to understand the role of technology in our cultural and everyday lives.

Consider Starting With . . .

The following titles are some of the most accessible and popular of the "Making Sense . . ." genre.

De Botton, Alain. *Status Anxiety.*

Gladwell, Malcolm. *The Tipping Point.*

Klein, Naomi. *No Logo.*

Rybczynski, Witold. *City Life: Urban Expectations in a New World.*

Stille, Alexander. *The Future of the Past.*

Fiction Read-Alikes

- **Calvino, Italo.** Calvino is famous for layering his works of fiction with deeper levels of meaning, most particularly his penchant for including and reworking fables in many of his works, such as *Invisible Cities*, in which Marco Polo and Kublai Khan have a conversation; in *If On a Winter's Night a Traveler*, he uses a "novel within a novel" to poke a bit of fun at modern literary fiction styles and criticism.

- **Chabon, Michael.** Chabon's critically lauded and popular novels often make numerous pop culture references and combine elements of genre fiction with a literary fiction writer's attention to prose styling. In *Wonder Boys* he tells the story of a washed-up novelist struggling to finish his first new work in years; in *The Amazing Adventures of Kavalier and Clay* he delves into the world of 1930s pulp fiction and superheroes, concurrently exploring themes of guilt and the historical impact of the Holocaust; and in *The Final Solution: A Story of Detection,* he resurrects the character of Sherlock Holmes in a new (and short, at 130 pages) suspense novel.

- **Coupland, Douglas.** Coupland is also known for his use of pop culture references. He used annotations in his first novel, *Generation X: Tales for an Accelerated Culture,* and helped coin such words as "McJobs." His latest novels, *Hey Nostradamus!* and *Eleanor Rigby,* have been hailed as more mature than his earlier works but are still wildly unique and synthesizing stories.

- **DeLillo, Don.** DeLillo's second novel, *End Zone*, used football as a metaphor for nuclear war, and his subsequent novels have been similarly ambitious. *Libra* is based on the events surrounding the assassination of JFK, and *The Body Artists* drops the reader into a married couple's breakfast conversation, only later revealing that the husband commits suicide on the same day.

- **Eco, Umberto.** Eco's most popular novel, *The Name of the Rose*, is an epic historical mystery set in a religious community in 1327; it examines the nature of knowledge and its dissemination through its librarian monk characters. *Foucault's Pendulum* and *The Island of the Day Before* also seek, in the words of critic Patrick Rengger, to "excavate truths by sifting language and meaning."

- **Eugenides, Jeffrey.** He's not prolific, but his two works of fiction have already had a huge effect on the literary world. *The Virgin Suicides* examines the possible reasons why a family of five sisters living in suburbia would all have committed suicide, while *Middlesex* is a novel about a hermaphrodite whose parents seek to "correct" her sexual identity through surgical means; it examines questions of gender and personal identity.

- **Maguire, Gregory.** Maguire makes a good living updating and reimagining our most dearly held fairy tales and mythologies (as well as from his numerous and popular children's books), as well he should; they're enjoyable and creative reads that are based in familiar stories but provide no shortage of new perspectives. His first such story was *Wicked: The Life and Times of the Wicked Witch of the West*; his subsequent titles are *Confessions of an Ugly Stepsister*, *Lost: A Novel*, and *Mirror, Mirror*.

- **Murakami, Haruki.** Murakami has often been referred to as the "Japanese Jay McInerney" for his use of Western pop culture references. Critics have also pointed out that his novels focus on seemingly surface and materialistic issues but contain intimations that there is something much deeper behind them; some of his most popular novels have been *Sputnik Sweetheart* and *South of the Border, West of the Sun*.

- **Oates, Joyce Carol.** Amazingly prolific and extremely popular, Oates has carved her own niche in the world of letters, producing fiction, poetry, and nonfiction with equal aplomb. She has referred to herself as a "chronicler of the American experience," and her books cover such a wide array of styles and genres that there should be something of hers to appeal to everyone. *Blonde*, one of her most successful books, is a fictional account of the life of Marilyn Monroe; *I'll Take You There* is a semiautobiographical coming of age narrative; *Zombie* is a horror story that drops the reader into the mind of a serial killer; and *We Were the Mulvaneys* is a look at the role a community plays in one family's life and vice versa.

- **Palahniuk, Chuck.** Although many reviewers note that Palahniuk's main talent is making his readers uncomfortable, he has often cited numerous philosophers (Kierkegaard, Sarte, Foucault) and other thinkers as influences on his stories, most of which are indeed labyrinthine character studies that explore some of the darkest impulses in humans. *Fight Club,* his first novel, was made into a successful movie; his two most recent titles, *Lullaby* and *Diary*, are the first two volumes in a horror series that combines poetry and other written works with the occurrence of unsettling events.

- **Wallace, David Foster.** Although it's a solid brick of a book that may require some investment of time from the reader, Wallace's novel *Infinite Jest* is a perfect example of a "making sense" fiction book; it even has the footnotes and the multiple cultural references to prove it. Set in the not-too-distant future, when even the years are sponsored by advertisers, Wallace's novel follows the exploits of two brothers.

References

Pearl, Nancy. 1999. *Now Read This: A Guide to Mainstream Fiction, 1978–1998.* Englewood, Colo.: Libraries Unlimited.

Ross, Catherine. 2004. "Reading Nonfiction for Pleasure: What Motivates Readers?" In *Nonfiction Readers' Advisory,* ed. Robert Burgin, 105–20. Westport, Conn.: Libraries Unlimited.

Political Pundits Overview

Books on political figures and events are a popular and lucrative segment of the publishing industry, but they differ slightly from the many other narrative and expository nonfiction books annotated in this book due to the dedication and loyalty of their (often political party-affiliated) readers. For the most part, readers seeking books by these authors know exactly what they want and when it will be published and will not be shy about asking you to provide them. Future editions of this guide may include a more in-depth consideration of these titles, but it is our hope that the following list of popular political writers and some of their benchmark titles will assist booksellers and readers' advisors who don't normally read them, or who only read titles within their own personal political affiliations and interests.

Authors on the "Right"

David Brooks.

Brooks is a senior editor at *The Weekly Standard* and a contributing editor at *Newsweek* and *Atlantic Monthly* magazines. His best-known books are *Bobos in Paradise* and *On Paradise Drive: How We Live Now (and Always Have) in the Future Tense.*

Patrick Buchanan.

Buchanan is best known for his work as a media commentator, advisor to Presidents Nixon and Ford, and frequent presidential candidate. His works include *The Conscience of a Conservative* (1990), *The Great Betrayal: How American Sovereignty and Social Justice Are Being Sacrificed to the Gods of the Global Economy* (1998), and *Where the Right Went Wrong: How Neoconservatives Subverted the Reagan Revolution and Hijacked the Bush Presidency* (2004), as well as his autobiography, *Right from the Beginning* (1988).

William F. Buckley Jr.

Buckley has produced copious amounts of fiction and nonfiction, but he is famous for his works of political commentary and being the founder of conservative magazine *National Review*. He started his career with a bang by publishing *God and Man at Yale: The Superstitions of "Academic Freedom,"* in 1951, in which he accused his alma mater of encouraging atheism and collectivism, which he felt went against the spirit of the college's founders. A collection of his ideas and journalistic pieces was published in 1993 as *Happy Days Were Here Again*, and he has also produced works of spiritual and literary biography, *Nearer, My God: An Autobiography of Faith* (1997) and *Miles Gone By: A Literary Autobiography* (2004).

Mona Charen.

Charen is the author of a syndicated news column and has appeared on CNN's discussion program *The Capital Gang*. Her most recent titles are *Useful Idiots: How Liberals Got It Wrong in the Cold War and Still Blame America First* (2003) and *Do-gooders: How Liberals Hurt Those They Claim to Help—and the Rest of Us* (2004).

Ann Coulter.

Ann Coulter is currently perhaps the most popular author in this list; her works include *Treason: Liberal Treachery from the Cold War to the War on Terrorism* (2003) and *How to Talk to a Liberal (If You Must)* (2004).

Newt Gingrich.

Time magazine's Man of the Year in 1995 was also the highly influential Speaker of the House of Representatives, a position he held until resigning it in 1999 after admitting to a tax violation. His manifesto, also published in 1995, was *To Renew America*. Gingrich has also written Civil War novels and a memoir, *Lessons Learned the Hard Way: A Personal Report* (1998), founded a communications and consulting firm, and reappeared on the publishing map in 2005 with *Winning the Future: A 21st Century Contract with America*.

Bernard Goldberg.

Goldberg is a journalist and best-selling author whose most popular works to date have been *Bias: A CBS Insider Exposes How the Media Distort the News* (2002) and *100 People Who Are Screwing Up America (and Al Franken is #37)* (2005).

Sean Hannity.

His name is often bandied about as the successor to Rush Limbaugh, and Hannity has made inroads in both television and radio, particularly with his Fox show *Hannity & Colmes*. He is the author of *Let Freedom Ring: Winning the War of Ideas in Politics, Media, and Life* (2002) and *Deliver Us from Evil: Defeating Terrorism, Despotism, and Liberalism* (2004).

Bill O'Reilly.

O'Reilly is also a hugely popular radio commentary show host. His books are always best sellers, and his previous titles are *The O'Reilly Factor: The Good, Bad, and Completely Ridiculous in American Life* (2000), *No-Spin Zone: Confrontation Within the Powerful and Famous in America* (2001), and *Who's Looking Out for You?* (2003).

Bill Sammon.

Sammon is a White House correspondent for the *Washington Times* and a political analyst for the Fox News Channel. His most recent book is *Misunderestimated: The President Battles Terrorism, John Kerry, and the Bush Haters* (2004); his previous books, *At Any Cost* (2001) and *Fighting Back* (2004), were also *New York Times* best sellers.

Authors on the "Left"

Maureen Dowd.

Maureen Dowd is a political columnist for *The New York Times* and the author of the recent best seller *Bushworld: Enter at Your Own Risk* (2004).

Thomas Frank.

Frank is a cultural critic who cofounded the newsletter *Baffler* (a collection of pieces in the magazine was published in 1997 as *Commodify Your Dissent: Salvos from the* Baffler). He is also the author of *The Conquest of Cool: Business Culture, Counterculture, and the Rise of Hip Consumerism* (1997) and *What's the Matter with Kansas?: How Conservatives Won the Heart of America* (2004).

Al Franken.

Franken started his career as an actor and writer for *Saturday Night Live* (1975–1980 and 1988–1995), but currently he is the host of a syndicated radio program for Air America. He fired his first political shot across the bow in 1996 with *Rush Limbaugh Is a Big Fat Idiot and Other Observations* and also scored a huge best seller in 2003 with *Lies and the Lying Liars Who Tell Them: A Fair and Balanced Look at the Right*. The sequel to that book, *The Truth (with Jokes),* was published in 2005.

Seymour Hersh.

Hersh is by trade an investigative reporter, and most of his works reflect his journalistic style. His first major book, *My Lai Four: A Report on the Massacre and Its Aftermath*, was initially rejected by numerous publishers but was eventually released in 1970. He has also produced two popular and in-depth works about previous presidents and their indiscretions, *The Price of Power: Kissinger in the Nixon White House* in 1983 and *The Dark Side of Camelot* in 1997, as well as a recent best seller about the Abu Ghraib prison scandal in 2004, *Chain of Command: The Road from 9/11 to Abu Ghraib.*

Christopher Hitchens.

Hitchens, a British journalist based in Washington, D.C., is a columnist and writer. His essays have been collected into two volumes: *Prepared for the Worst: Selected Essays and Minority Reports* (1988) and *For the Sake of Argument: Essays and Minority Reports* (1993). Hitchens was personally involved in President Clinton's impeachment proceedings and wrote *No One Left to Lie To: The Triangulations of William Jefferson Clinton* about the experience in 1999.

Molly Ivins.

Texas native and newspaper columnist Ivins is known for her earthy plain talk about politics and politicians. Her most popular titles are *You Got to Dance with Them What Brung You: Politics in the Clinton Years* (1998), *Shrub: The Short But Happy Political Life of George W. Bush* (2000), and *Bushwhacked: Life in George's W. Bush's America* (2003).

Michael Lind.

Lind began his political writing career as editor of the conservative journal *National Interest* but eventually changed his political affiliation and became a senior editor at *Harper's* magazine. Recent titles of his include *Up from Conservatism: Why the Right Is Wrong for America* (1996), *The Radical Center: The Future of American Politics* (2001), and *Made in Texas: George W. Bush and the Southern Takeover of American Politics* (2003).

Michael Moore.

Filmmaker, television documentary maker, and author Moore is one of the best known names on the political left. His first documentary, produced in 1989, followed his journey to meet with Roger Smith, the CEO of GM, and ask about downsizing and layoffs in his hometown of Flint, Michigan (*Roger & Me*). Since then he has become a best-selling author, famous for such titles as *Stupid White Men: And Other Sorry Excuses for the State of the Nation!* (2002), *Dude, Where's My Country?* (2003), and *Will They Ever Trust Us Again?* (2004).

Authors "Less Obviously Aligned"

Ronald Kessler.

Kessler has been a reporter for both the *Washington Post* and the *Wall Street Journal* and has written many political exposés, including *Inside the White House: The Hidden Lives of the Modern Presidents and the Secrets of the World's Most Powerful Institution* (1995), *Inside Congress: The Shocking Scandals, Corruption, and Abuse of Power Behind the Scenes on Capitol Hill* (1997), and *A Matter of Character: Inside the White House of George W. Bush* (2004).

Paul Krugman.

Krugman writes op-ed columns for the *New York Times* and is a professor of political science. His most recent books include *The Great Unraveling: Losing Our Way in the New Century* (2003) and *The Accidental Theorist and Other Dispatches from the Dismal Science* (1998).

Ron Suskind.

Suskind, a freelance journalist and Pulitzer Prize winner for feature writing, is also the author of *A Hope in the Unseen* (1998) and the recent best seller *The Price of Loyalty: George W. Bush, the White House and the Education of Paul O'Neill* (2004).

Bob Woodward.

Woodward, of Woodward and Bernstein and Watergate fame, is the author of many groundbreaking and popular works of investigative journalism, including *All the President's Men* (1974), *Plan of Attack* (2004), and *Bush at War* (2002), and the book in which he reveals his infamous source, *The Secret Man: The Story of Watergate's Deep Throat* (2005).

Spirituality Writers Overview

Books on religious and spiritual topics are extremely popular, both in bookstores and in libraries. Like political and Current Affairs books, many of the authors and works listed below have very dedicated and knowledgeable audiences who will not hesitate to ask for certain works by name, or by religious affiliation. Future editions of this guide may include a more in-depth consideration of this subject area, but it is our hope that the following list of popular political writers and some of their benchmark titles might assist those who don't normally read them, or who only read titles within their own personal spiritual beliefs and denominations.

Karen Armstrong.

Former Roman Catholic nun and Oxford-educated historian and author Armstrong is a prolific producer of intellectual texts about both religion and spirituality. Her memoirs (*Through the Narrow Gate* [1981] and *The Spiral Staircase* [2004]) have been as well-received as her more scholarly works have been, including *A History of God: The 4,000-Year Quest of Judaism, Christianity, and Islam* (1993) and *In the Beginning: A New Interpretation of Genesis* (1996).

Sylvia Browne.

Psychic Browne is less a spirituality than a self-help and "Body, Mind, and Spirit" writer, but many of her most popular titles offer what she refers to as "joy, fulfillment, and renewed spirituality." Her recent titles include *Sylvia Browne's Life Lessons* (2004), *Mother God: The Feminine Principle to Our Creator* (2004), and *The Other Side and Back: A Psychic's Guide to Our World and Beyond* (1999).

Dalai Lama.

His Holiness the Fourteenth Dalai Lama, the spiritual leader of the Tibetan people, has written a number of popular inspirational titles, including *The Art of Happiness: A Handbook for Living* (1998), *How to Practice: The Way to a Meaningful Life* (2002), and *An Open Heart: Practicing Compassion in Everyday Life* (2001).

Deepak Chopra.

Chopra began his career as a traditional physician but eventually developed an interest in alternative health treatments and care and has written many popular health titles such as *Creating Health* (1991) and *Quantum Healing* (1989). He has lately turned his hand to spiritual writing and produced *How to Know God: The Soul's Journey into the Mystery of Mysteries* (2000) and *The Deeper Wound: Preserving Your Soul in the Face of Fear and Tragedy* (2001).

Wayne Dyer.

Wayne Dyer has gone from selling his own self-published books out of the trunk of his car to having his own regular television specials and spiritual publishing niche. Many of his most popular titles are written for those seeking "inner peace"; they include *Manifest Your Destiny: The Nine Spiritual Principles for Getting Everything You Want* (1997), *There's a Spiritual Solution to Every Problem* (2001), and *The Power of Intention: Learning to Co-Create Your World Your Way* (2004).

Anne Lamott.

Lamott is a critically acclaimed novelist and memoirist. Her memoirs veer closest to topics of spirituality, particularly her two most recent titles, *Traveling Mercies: Some Thoughts on Faith* (1999) and *Plan B: Further Thoughts on Faith* (2005).

Thomas Merton.

Merton was a prolific author and Catholic monk who is often acknowledged as having combined Eastern mysticism with Western religious beliefs, to great effect. His most well-known works are his inspirational autobiographies, including *The Seven Storey Mountain* (1948) and his seven-volume *Journals of Thomas Merton* (1996–1999).

Thomas Moore.

Moore is a therapist and former monk who writes books about ways to revive spirituality in our own lives. His first best seller, *Care of the Soul: A Guide for Cultivating Depth and Sacredness in Everyday Life*, was published in 1992; he has since published *The Soul of Sex: Cultivating Life as an Act of Love* (1998) and *The Soul's Religion: Cultivating a Profoundly Spiritual Way of Life* (2002).

Caroline Myss.

Myss blends diverse religious and spiritual beliefs in her extremely popular "Mind, Body, and Spirit" titles, such as *Anatomy of the Spirit: The Seven Stages of Power and Healing* (1996), *Sacred Contracts: Awakening Your Divine Potential* (2001), and *Invisible Acts of Power: The Divine Energy of a Giving Heart* (2004).

Kathleen Norris.

The memoir form is popular among spirituality writers, and Norris is one of the virtuosos of the subject and form. Her memoirs, *Dakota: A Spiritual Geography* (1993; annotated in the environmental chapter), *The Cloister Walk* (1996), and *Amazing Grace: A Vocabulary of Faith* (1998) have all been popular and critically well-received works.

Parker Palmer.

Although best known for his famous book that has served as a manifesto to many teachers, *The Courage to Teach: Exploring the Inner Landscape of a Teacher's Life* (1998), Palmer is also a writer of numerous works on spirituality. Some of his most recent titles are *Let Your Life Speak: Listening for the Voice of Vocation* (2000), *The Active Life: A Spirituality of Work, Creativity, and Caring* (1990), and *A Hidden Wholeness: The Journey Toward an Undivided Life* (2004).

Cheryl Richardson.

Richardson is a best-selling author who writes about her belief that the benevolent energy of the universe can be harnessed for our own spiritual needs. Her most popular titles include *That Unmistakable Touch of Grace* (2005), *Take Time for Your Life* (1998), and *Stand Up for Your Life* (2002), in which she suggests that a healthy relationship with yourself can lead to spiritual peace.

Eckhart Tolle.

Tolle's runaway best sellers, *The Power of Now* (1999) and *Stillness Speaks* (2003), both advocate developing inner peace by "living in the now" and practicing the art of "inner stillness."

Rick Warren.

According to my latest *Publishers Weekly*, Warren's *The Purpose-Driven Life: What on Earth Am I Here For?* (2002) has been on the nonfiction best-sellers list for 127 weeks straight. Even more amazing than the sales record of Warren's inspirational book is its sales method: Warren, a pastor at the Saddleback Church in Lake Forest, California, asked church groups everywhere to devote their book clubs to his title for forty days (Warren's biblically based text asks readers to develop their spirituality over "forty days of purpose") and to promote the title through word-of-mouth.

Bruce Wilkinson.

Wilkinson's *The Prayer of Jabez: Breaking through to the Blessed Life* (2000), based on an obscure prayer in the biblical book of Chronicles, was a huge best seller when it first appeared and still has quite a high rank as a seller on Amazon.com. President of Walk Thru the Bible Ministries, he is also the author of *The Prayer of Jabez for Women* (1992) and *Secrets of the Vine: Breaking through to Abundance* (1999).

Marianne Williamson.

Williamson has been referred to as both a "pop guru" and the "Prophet of Love" (the latter by *The New York Times*). In her books she writes about her own transformation from having a life that was a "mess" to spiritual happiness. Her most popular titles include *A Return to Love: Reflections on the Principles of "A Course in Miracles"* (1992) and *Enchanted Love: The Mystical Power of Intimate Relationships* (1999).

Nonfiction Book Awards

This compilation of nonfiction book award Web sites is highly selective and focuses primarily on the most widely recognized and popular awards. The emphasis of this list is also on awards given in North America.

American Library Association Black Caucus Nonfiction Awards
Background: www.bcala.org/awards/literary.htm
Awards List: www.bcala.org/awards/past_winners.htm

The BCALA Nonfiction Literary Award (BCALA also honors fiction works) was established to "honor cultural, historical, political, or social criticism or academic and/or professional research which significantly advances the body of knowledge currently associated with the people and the legacy of the Black Diaspora." The awards have been given annually since 1994.

American Library Association Notable Nonfiction Books
History: www.ala.org/ala/rusa/rusaprotools/rusanotable/notablebooks.htm
Lists of Notable Books: www.ala.org/ala/rusa/rusaprotools/rusanotable/thelists/notablebooks.htm

Each year a twelve-member committee from the CODES (Collection Development and Evaluation Section) of the association selects twenty-five titles each in fiction, poetry, and nonfiction that are "very good, very readable, and at times very important." The Notable Books listings have existed, in various forms, since 1944.

The Book Sense Book of the Year Award
Awards List: www.booksense.com/readup/awards/index.jsp
Book Sense Weekly Best Sellers: www.bookweb.org/booksense/bestsellers/
Books Sense Best Sellers by Category: www.bookweb.org/booksense/listmarketing/5677.html

Although this is a fairly new award (it was first given in 2000), it is awarded by the nation's independent booksellers, who vote annually to reward those books that have been their favorites to sell and their readers' favorites to read. Awards are given in the categories of adult fiction and nonfiction; children's literature and illustrated books; and paperback and rediscovery books (old favorites that continue to sell).

Edgar Awards for Fact Crime
About the Awards: www.mysterywriters.org/pages/awards/index.htm
Searchable Awards Archive: www.mysterywriters.org/pages/awards/search.htm

Sponsored by the Mystery Writers of America organization, the Edgar Awards are given to authors of distinguished works in the mystery genre. The Best Fact Crime category awards nonfiction and true crime books, and was first presented in 1948.

Edna Staebler Award for Creative Non-Fiction
History: http://info.wlu.ca/~wwwlib/internet/prizes/staebler.html
Awards List: http://info.wlu.ca/~wwwlib/internet/prizes/winners.html

The Edna Staebler Award has been given annually since 1991 to award and recognize Canadian authors of creative nonfiction, which they define as literary rather than journalistic. Each winner not only must be written by a Canadian author but must also include a "Canadian locale or a particular Canadian significance."

J. Anthony Lukas Book Prize
History: www.jrn.columbia.edu/events/lukas/
Awards List: www.jrn.columbia.edu/events/lukas/winners/

The Lukas Prize was established in 1998 with the simple charge of honoring the best American nonfiction. It is administered jointly by the Columbia University Graduate School of Journalism and the Nieman Foundation at Harvard University.

James Beard Awards
About the Awards: www.jamesbeard.org/awards/policies.shtml
Awards Archive: www.jamesbeard.org/awards/2004/html/index.shtml

The James Beard Foundation exists to support the appreciation of the culinary arts in America. Each year it recognizes numerous cookbooks and other nonfiction works, and the awards were established in 1990. Interestingly enough, many of the broad category headings under which awards are given are determined anew after each year's entries are received, to reflect publishing trends.

The John Burroughs Medal
About the John Burroughs Association: www.johnburroughs.org/jb_assoc/assoc.htm
List of Winners: http://naturewriting.com/johnBaw.htm

The John Burroughs Medal is awarded to works that display outstanding natural history writing, and has been awarded annually since 1926 by the John Burroughs Association.

The LAMBDA Literary Awards
About the Awards: www.lambdalit.org/lammy.html
Awards Archives: www.lambdalit.org/Lammy/lammy_archives.html

Lambda Literary Awards are given annually (and have been since 1988) in twenty categories, to recognize the best works of lesbian, gay, bisexual, and transgender literature.

The *Los Angeles Times* Book Awards
About the Awards: www.latimes.com/extras/bookprizes/prizes2003.html
Winners Lists: www.latimes.com/extras/bookprizes/winners.html

The *Los Angeles Times* has distributed a variety of both fiction and nonfiction awards (including biography, current interests, and science and technology) annually since 1980.

National Academies Communications Awards

About the Awards and Winners: www7.nationalacademies.org/keck/Awards.html

The National Academies annually present awards in three areas of publishing: books; magazine, newspaper, or online journalism; and television and radio broadcasting. These awards reflect the educational missions of the National Academies of Science, Engineering, the Institute of Medicine, and the National Research Council. The National Academy first presented these three awards in 2003.

The National Book Award

About the National Book Foundation: www.nationalbook.org/history.html
Awards Archives: www.nationalbook.org/nbawinners.html

The National Book Award has been given since 1950, but the National Book Foundation, which helps to support its choices, was established in 1989 to "raise the cultural appreciation of great writing in America." Each year it names one award winner each, based on literary merit, in the categories of fiction, nonfiction, and poetry.

The National Book Critics Circle Award

Awards Archives: www.bookcritics.org/page2.html

The National Book Critics Circle was founded in 1974 and currently consists of more than 700 active book reviewers. Its board of directors nominates and selects the winners of its annual award in the categories of fiction, general nonfiction, biography/autobiography, poetry, and criticism.

National Outdoor Book Awards

About the Awards: www.isu.edu/departments/outdoor/bookpol.htm#General
Awards Lists: www.isu.edu/departments/outdoor/bookpol.htm

The National Outdoor Book awards are given annually (and have been awarded since 1997) in nine categories, including History, Literature, Nature, Adventure Guidebook, and Outdoor Classic.

The Pulitzer Prizes

History of the Pulitzer Prizes: www.pulitzer.org/
Awards Archives: www.pulitzer.org/

Pulitzer Prizes are awarded to "distinguished" works in three major areas of nonfiction: biography or autobiography, history, and general nonfiction. The awards for the first two categories have been given since 1917, and the award for the latter was instituted in 1962.

Samuel Johnson Prize for Nonfiction

www.bbc.co.uk/bbcfour/books/features/samueljohnson/

Authors of all nonfiction books published in the United Kingdom are eligible to receive the BBC Four Samuel Johnson Prize, which has been awarded annually since 1999.

The Thomas Cook Travel Book Award

About the Award: www.thomascookpublishing.com/travelbookawards.htm
Awards List: www.thomascookpublishing.com/ba_prev_winners.htm

The Thomas Cook Group, a travel book publisher, founded this award in 1980 to recognize authors of quality literary travel narratives.

William Saroyan Award

http://library.stanford.edu/saroyan/index.html

The William Saroyan International Prize for Writing was established in 2002 to "encourage new and emerging writers" of both nonfiction and fiction. It is administered jointly by the Stanford University Libraries and the William Saroyan Foundation.

Appendix D

Internet Resources

Ann Arbor Public Library Books Blog (blog)

www.aadl.org/catalog/books

> The Ann Arbor (Michigan) Books Blog is a surprisingly universal and interesting blog recounting book news and linking to numerous award sites and other book and reading-related news. It is frequently updated.

BiblioTravel

www.bibliotravel.com

> The BiblioTravel site promises "books that take you away," and delivers on that promise by allowing readers to locate books set in particular locales and destinations. The site was founded and is run by two librarians, Fiona Scannell and James Schellenberg.

Bookbitch

www.bookbitch.com/nonfiction.htm

> Bookbitch is primarily a fiction review site, but nonfiction reviews are available as well. It is run by Stacy Alesi, who contributed a chapter on "Reader's Advisory in the Real World" to Libraries Unlimited's *Nonfiction Readers' Advisory*, edited by Robert Burgin.

BookBrowse

www.bookbrowse.com

> The BookBrowse site allows readers to browse multiple reviews of current and popular books, and can be navigated by genre (including history, biography, travel, and true crime titles) and publication date.

Booklist Center

http://home.comcast.net/~dwtaylor1

> The Booklist Center site boasts that it offers the "Web's Largest Collection of Book Lists," and currently at 346 lists in 82 categories, it may deserve that distinction. Readers may browse lists by categories such as Crime and Essays, Letters, and Literary Criticism, or by date added to the database; many lists provide links to award sites as well as to compiled lists.

Bookreporter.com

www.bookreporter.com

> Bookreporter.com is jam-packed with information about books, from award lists to reviews to reading group guides, not to mention a very helpful "Books to Movies" page that discusses the latest movie adaptation news.

Books 'n' Bytes

www.booksnbytes.com/reviews_list.html

> Although it focuses primarily on mysteries and science fiction and fantasy titles, the Books 'n' Bytes site also includes nonfiction book reviews. The reviews are short and personal and can provide a real flavor for a variety of nonfiction works.

Book Sense

www.booksense.com

> The Book Sense site lists recent best sellers and fiction and nonfiction favorites in independent bookstores (making for some lists that can vary greatly from more mainstream and chain bookstores) across the country.

Bookslut

www.bookslut.com

> Bookslut features reviews of both fiction and nonfiction books, updated monthly. The site also has numerous columns about books and interviews with authors, as well as a fantastic and frequently updated blog at www.bookslut.com/blog/.

Boston Public Library Booklists for Adults

www.bpl.org/research/adultbooklists/booklists.htm

> The Boston Public Library offers beautifully comprehensive nonfiction booklists on biography, general nonfiction, and science topics.

Bruce Dobler's Creative Nonfiction Compendium

www.pitt.edu/~bdobler/readingnf.html

> This is one of the best sites I've found listing creative nonfiction definitions, as well as a list of suggested titles to start with, that is currently available. It is written by Bruce Dobler, an associate professor of English at the University of Pittsburgh.

Burlington Public Library (Ontario)

www.bpl.on.ca/reading/nonfic/travel.htm

> The Burlington Public Library offers a nice variety of nonfiction booklists, particularly their "Armchair Travel" list.

Civil War Bookshelf

www.cw-book-news.com

> This site is a great place to find new and classic Civil War books.

Court TV's Crime Library

www.crimelibrary.com

> The comprehensive and detailed Crime Library site contains nutshell descriptions of numerous true crime cases (in short articles that include bibliographies listing

book titles), in case you're looking for the details before recommending true crime books.

Creative Nonfiction (journal)
www.creativenonfiction.org

Founded by author and academic Lee Gutkind in 1993, *Creative Nonfiction* is a journal devoted exclusively to the creative nonfiction genre. The site offers descriptions of creative nonfiction works and suggestions about popular authors in the genre.

Curled Up with a Good Book
www.curledup.com

The Curled Up with a Good Book site offers both fiction and nonfiction reviews and comprehensive author interviews. It is also an attractive site that features graphics of each book cover and a 1 to 5 star rating system, and many of the nonfiction books included are more specific and scholarly ones that aren't often reviewed at other sites.

Dear Reader
www.dearreader.com

Dear Reader is a great and personable site at which you can sign up to receive daily excerpts of nonfiction (and other) titles via e-mail.

Elegant Variation (blog)
http://marksarvas.blogs.com/elegvar/

A "Literary Weblog," Elegant Variation offers all manner of book and entertainment news and links. It also is a great resource for thumbnail reviews of new books.

Elmhurst Public Library (Illinois) booklists
www.elmhurst.lib.il.us/booklist

Many of the Elmhurst Public Library lists are fiction only, but a great many also include nonfiction titles.

Fiction_L
www.webrary.org/rs/Flmenu.html

Fiction_L is a listserv devoted to readers' advisory and fiction (although the collective brain is great at answering nonfiction questions as well). The Morton Grove Public Library site (where Fiction_L is archived) also provides booklists periodically culled from the listserv.

Fimoculous (blog)
www.fimoculous.com

A blog that offers multiple thoughts on books (and compiles very helpful "Best of . . ." literary lists at the end of the year) but is even more interesting for its other entertainment news and media links.

Genreflecting

www.genreflecting.com

> Genreflecting.com remains a great site at which to view overviews of fiction genres, which may help readers draw comparisons between nonfiction titles and related fiction genre titles and resources (particularly valuable are the "must read authors" sections).

Gnooks

http://gnooks.com

> Enter an author you like, and Gnooks will provide a visual map of similar authors. It doesn't include a lot of nonfiction authors yet, but more are appearing all the time.

Harford County Public Library (Md.) Readers Place

www.hcplonline.info/readers/recommendedbooks.html

> A nice service that provides new fiction and nonfiction reviews, as well as a collection of links to Web sites for book lovers.

Metacritic

www.metacritic.com

> The Metacritic site compiles reviews of films, music, and books from numerous publications and lists them in order from positive to negative. In addition to listing media reviews it also allows site viewers to vote on each book.

Morton Grove Public Library Webrary

www.webrary.org/rs/bibmenu.html

> As noted in the Fiction_L annotation, this site also features nonfiction booklists as created by Morton Grove librarians and Fiction_L contributors.

National Public Radio Books Page

www.npr.org/books/

> The National Public Radio site offers book recommendations, book reviews, and author information.

New York Times Best-Seller Lists

www.nytimes.com/pages/books/bestseller/index.html

> This site offers current best-seller lists, broken down not only by fiction and nonfiction but also by paperback nonfiction, advice, business, and many other categories.

Overbooked

www.overbooked.org

> Overbooked provides lists of books that have received starred reviews in any or all of the higher profile review publications, including *Library Journal, Booklist, Publishers Weekly,* and *Kirkus.* Although its focus is primarily fiction titles, it also includes nonfiction booklists.

Other Side of the Wall

www.prisonwall.org/books.htm

This site offers a comprehensive list of prison narratives.

Reader's Club Non-Fiction Book Reviews

www.readersclub.org/category.asp?cat=2

The Reader's Club Web site offers to be "your guide to enjoyable books" and seeks to fulfill that promise by offering one-paragraph reviews of fiction and nonfiction titles. The site is maintained by a group of librarians in North Carolina.

Reading Group Choices

www.readinggroupchoices.com

Reading Group Guides

www.readinggroupguides.com

Both these reading group sites provide numerous and thoughtful questions for book discussions of fiction and nonfiction titles.

Waterboro Public Library (Maine)

www.waterborolibrary.org/bklistnonf.htm

The Waterboro Public Library site offers a collection of booklists from various libraries, all offering "nonfiction that reads like fiction."

Author/Title Index

The page numbers where main entries appear are boldface.

Subject Index

About the Author and Editor

SARAH STATZ CORDS is a librarian who works at the reference and circulation desks at Madison Public Library, Alicia Ashman Branch, Wisconsin, and teaches "Reading Interests of Adults" at the School of Library and Information Studies, University of Wisconsin, Madison. Previously she worked as a reference and instruction academic librarian at the University of Wisconsin, Madison. She is also a book reviewer for *Library Journal* and Bookslut.com, and the author of *Public Speaking Handbook for Librarians and Information Professionals* (2003).

Photo by Rich Gassen

ROBERT BURGIN is a professor at North Carolina Central University's School of Library and Information Sciences. He has published numerous articles, is editor of *Nonfiction Readers' Advisory* (Libraries Unlimited, 2004) and is co-editor of *The Readers' Advisor's Companion* (Libraries Unlimited, 2002). He is currently Vice-President/President-Elect of the North Carolina Library Association.